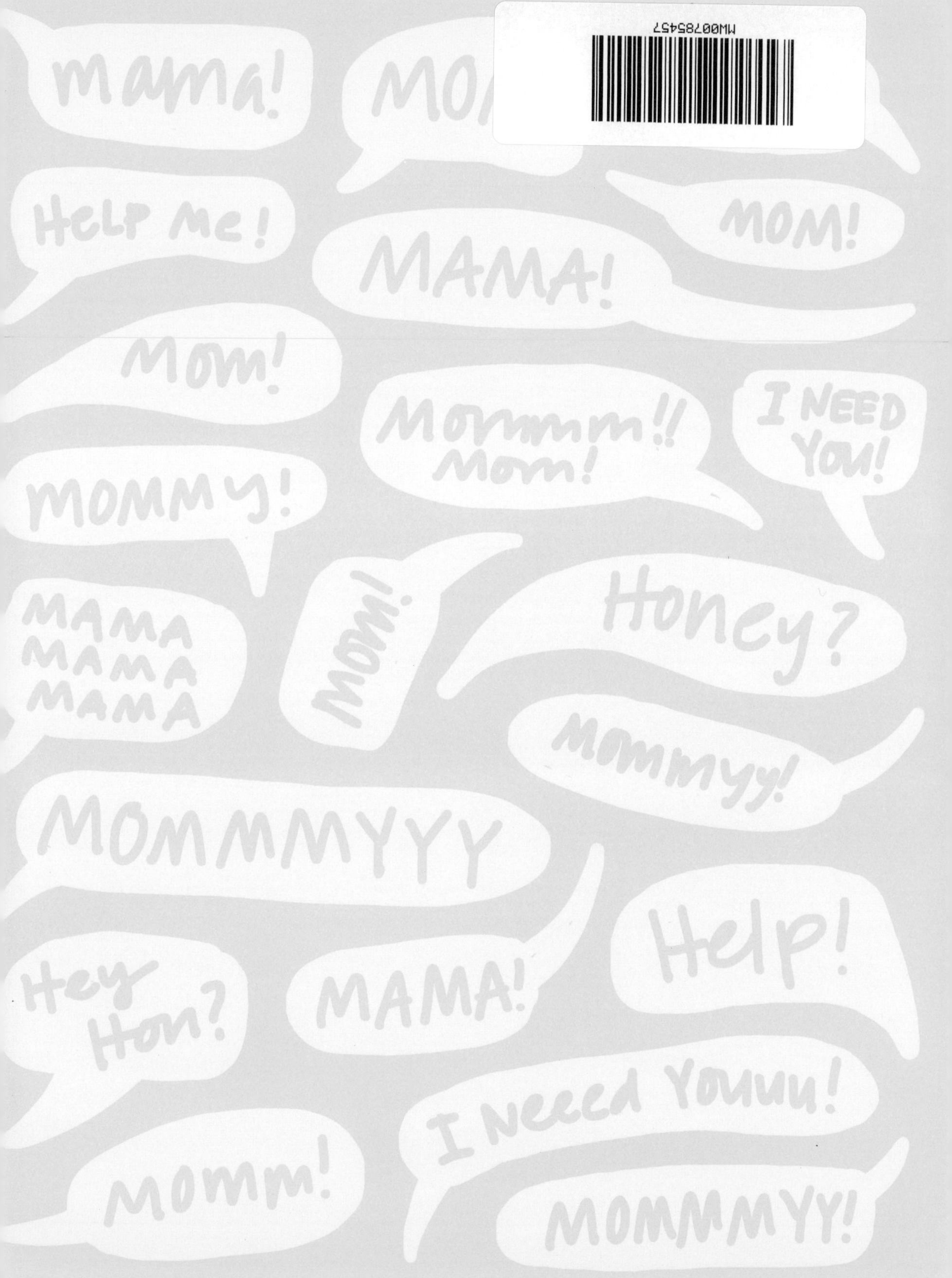
Mama!
MOM
Help Me!
MOM!
MAMA!
Mom!
Mommm!!
Mom!
I NEED YOU!
MOMMY!
MAMA
MAMA
MAMA
MOM!
Honey?
MOMMYY!
MOMMMYYY
Hey Hon?
MAMA!
Help!
I Neeed Youuu!
Momm!
MOMMMYY!

Mama Needs
a Minute!

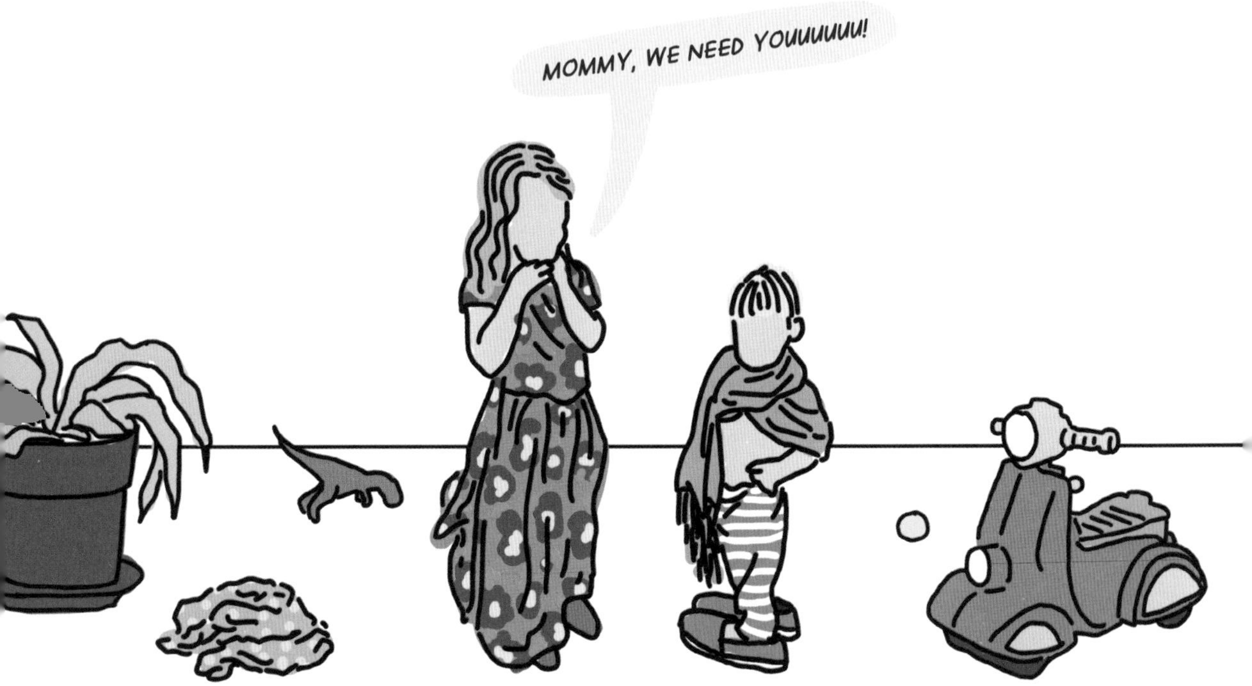
MOMMY, WE NEED YOUUUUUU!

# Mama Needs a Minute!

A Candid, Funny, All-Too-Relatable Comic Memoir about Surviving Motherhood

MARY CATHERINE STARR

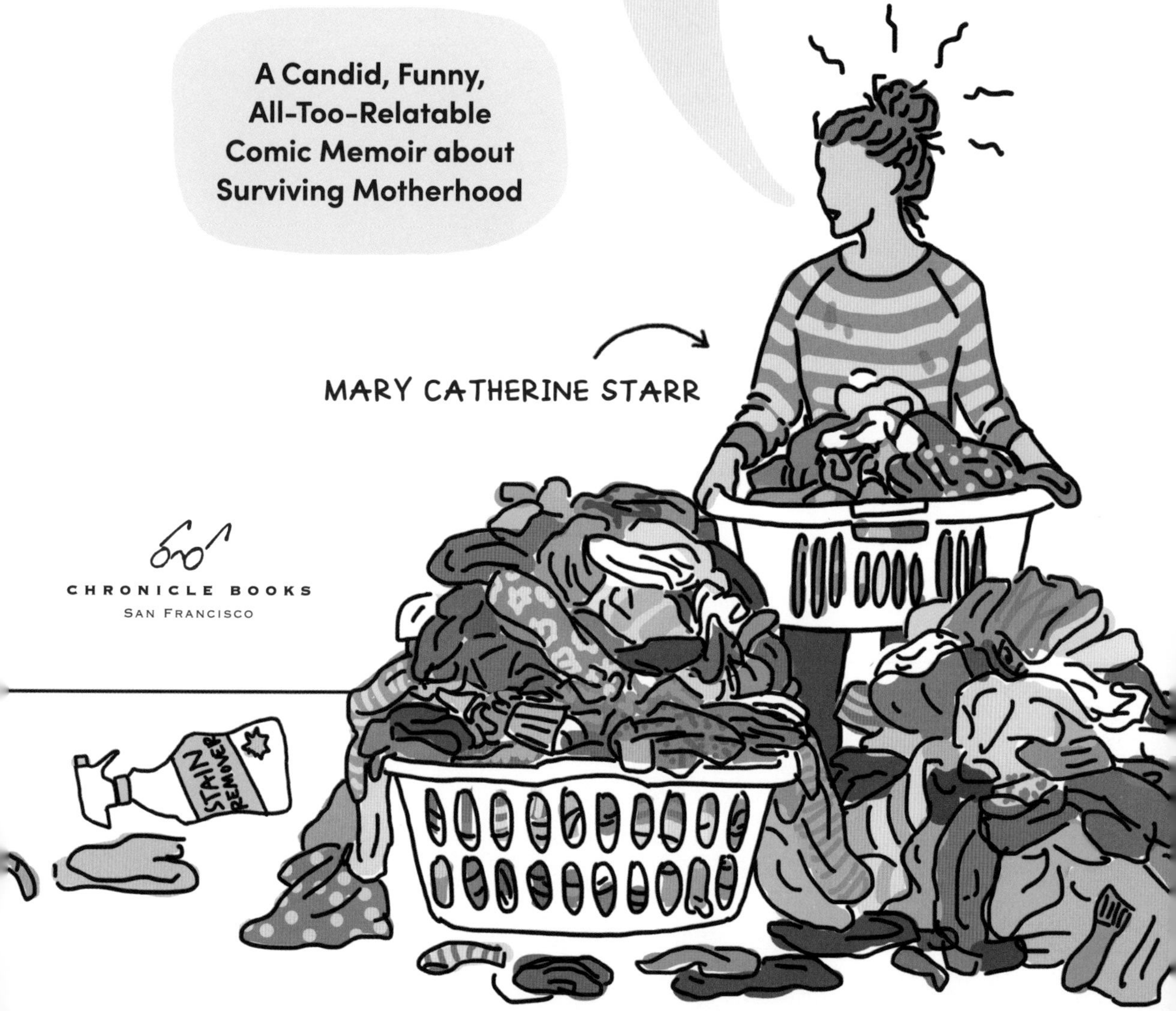
STAIN REMOVER

CHRONICLE BOOKS
San Francisco

Library of Congress Cataloging-in-Publication Data available.

ISBN 978-1-7972-2686-6

Manufactured in China.

MIX
Paper | Supporting responsible forestry
FSC™ C008047

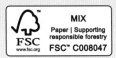

Design by Mary Catherine Starr and Wynne Au-Yeung.

10 9 8 7 6 5 4 3 2 1

Chronicle books and gifts are available at special quantity discounts to corporations, professional associations, literacy programs, and other organizations. For details and discount information, please contact our premiums department at corporatesales@chroniclebooks.com or at 1-800-759-0190.

Chronicle Books LLC
680 Second Street
San Francisco, California 94107
www.chroniclebooks.com

## FOR BEN

MY PARTNER IN LIFE, PARENTING, AND
LAUNDRY. THANK YOU FOR SUPPORTING
ME IN TELLING THIS VERY PERSONAL
STORY (WHICH IS REALLY OUR STORY).

# Contents

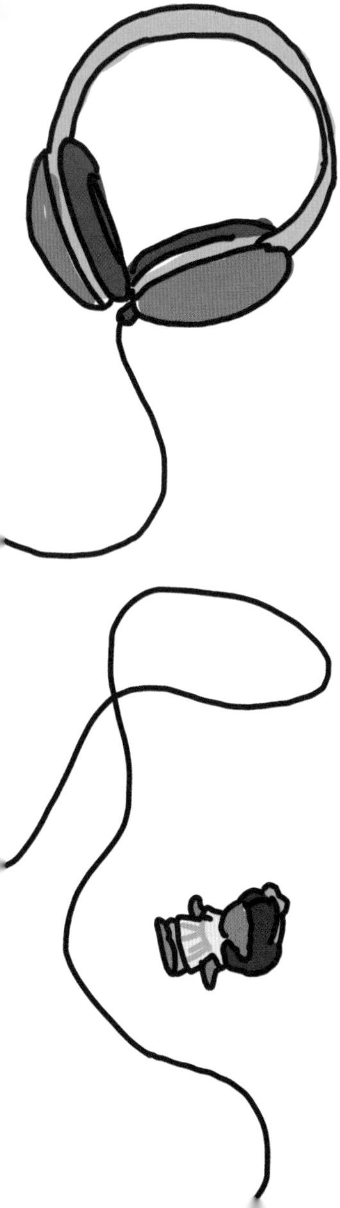

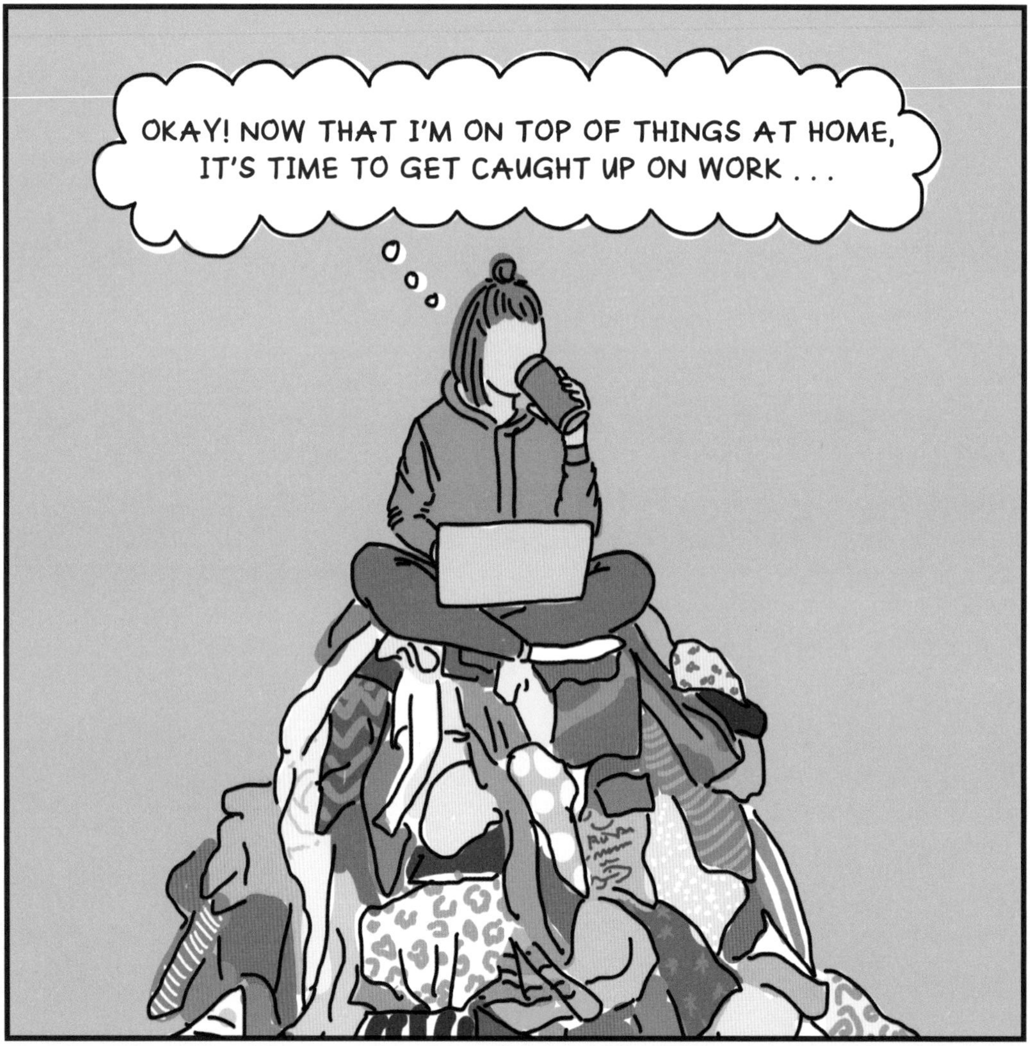
OKAY! NOW THAT I'M ON TOP OF THINGS AT HOME, IT'S TIME TO GET CAUGHT UP ON WORK . . .

PREFACE

# A Tale as Old as Time

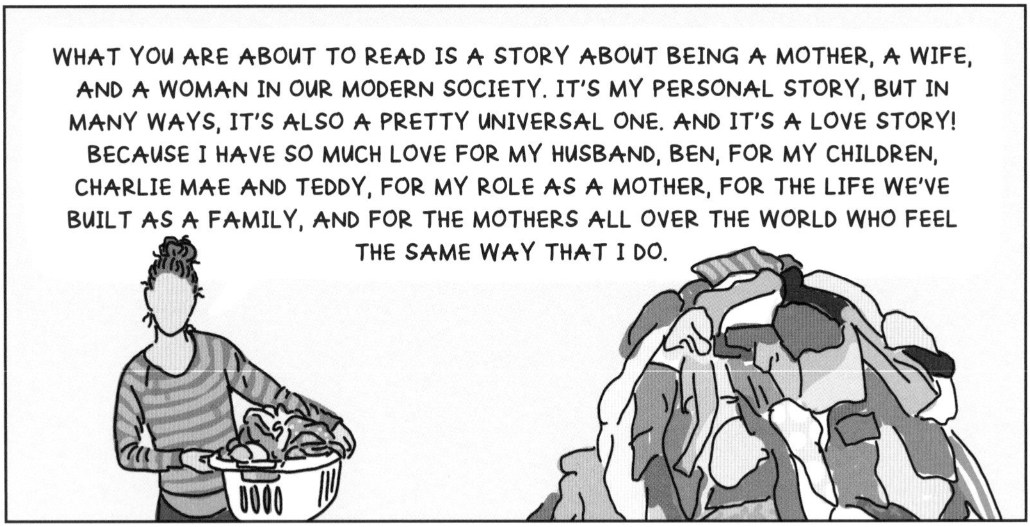
WHAT YOU ARE ABOUT TO READ IS A STORY ABOUT BEING A MOTHER, A WIFE, AND A WOMAN IN OUR MODERN SOCIETY. IT'S MY PERSONAL STORY, BUT IN MANY WAYS, IT'S ALSO A PRETTY UNIVERSAL ONE. AND IT'S A LOVE STORY! BECAUSE I HAVE SO MUCH LOVE FOR MY HUSBAND, BEN, FOR MY CHILDREN, CHARLIE MAE AND TEDDY, FOR MY ROLE AS A MOTHER, FOR THE LIFE WE'VE BUILT AS A FAMILY, AND FOR THE MOTHERS ALL OVER THE WORLD WHO FEEL THE SAME WAY THAT I DO.

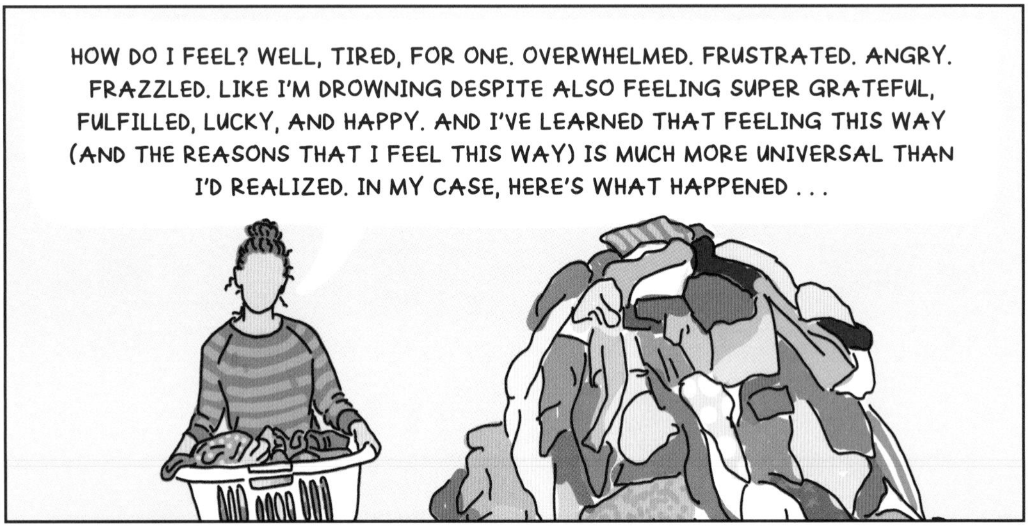
HOW DO I FEEL? WELL, TIRED, FOR ONE. OVERWHELMED. FRUSTRATED. ANGRY. FRAZZLED. LIKE I'M DROWNING DESPITE ALSO FEELING SUPER GRATEFUL, FULFILLED, LUCKY, AND HAPPY. AND I'VE LEARNED THAT FEELING THIS WAY (AND THE REASONS THAT I FEEL THIS WAY) IS MUCH MORE UNIVERSAL THAN I'D REALIZED. IN MY CASE, HERE'S WHAT HAPPENED . . .

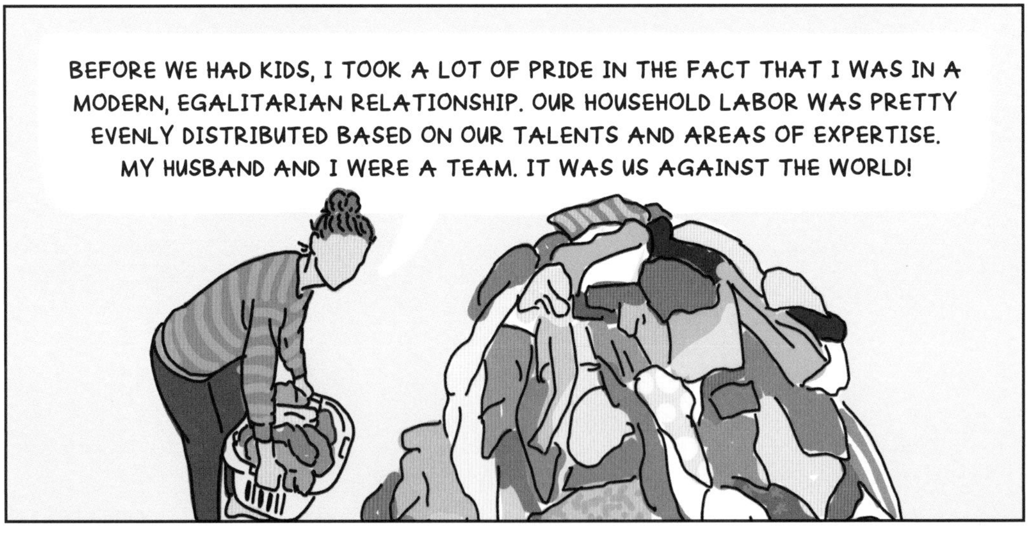
BEFORE WE HAD KIDS, I TOOK A LOT OF PRIDE IN THE FACT THAT I WAS IN A MODERN, EGALITARIAN RELATIONSHIP. OUR HOUSEHOLD LABOR WAS PRETTY EVENLY DISTRIBUTED BASED ON OUR TALENTS AND AREAS OF EXPERTISE. MY HUSBAND AND I WERE A TEAM. IT WAS US AGAINST THE WORLD!

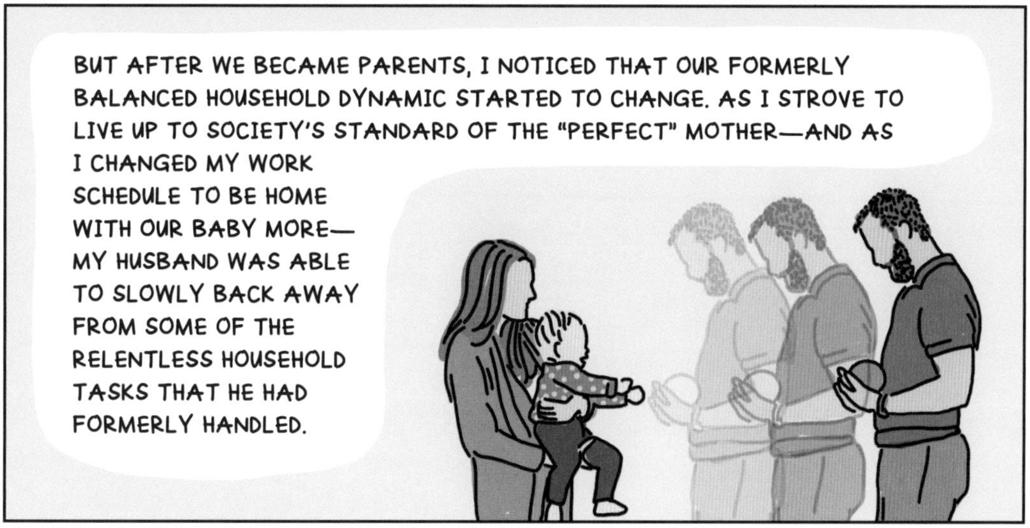
BUT AFTER WE BECAME PARENTS, I NOTICED THAT OUR FORMERLY BALANCED HOUSEHOLD DYNAMIC STARTED TO CHANGE. AS I STROVE TO LIVE UP TO SOCIETY'S STANDARD OF THE "PERFECT" MOTHER—AND AS I CHANGED MY WORK SCHEDULE TO BE HOME WITH OUR BABY MORE—MY HUSBAND WAS ABLE TO SLOWLY BACK AWAY FROM SOME OF THE RELENTLESS HOUSEHOLD TASKS THAT HE HAD FORMERLY HANDLED.

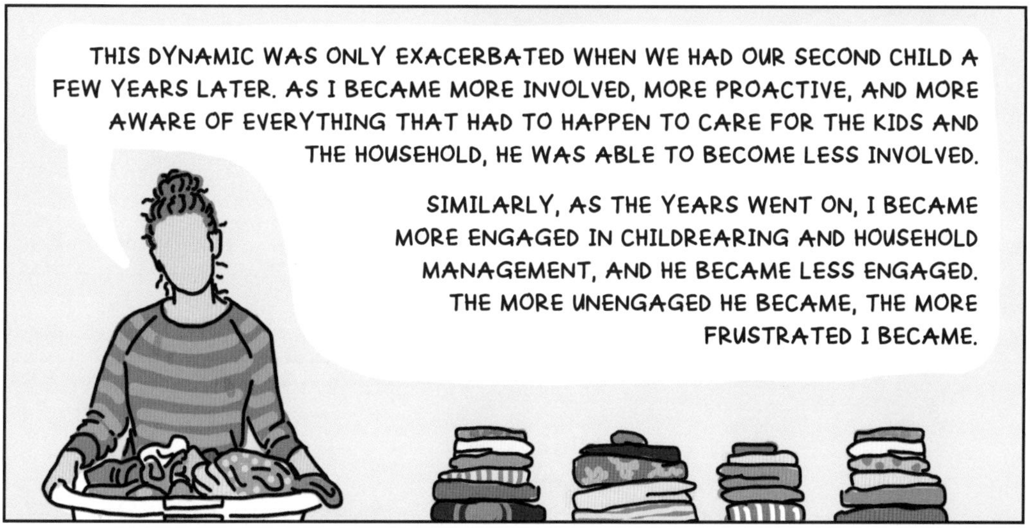
THIS DYNAMIC WAS ONLY EXACERBATED WHEN WE HAD OUR SECOND CHILD A FEW YEARS LATER. AS I BECAME MORE INVOLVED, MORE PROACTIVE, AND MORE AWARE OF EVERYTHING THAT HAD TO HAPPEN TO CARE FOR THE KIDS AND THE HOUSEHOLD, HE WAS ABLE TO BECOME LESS INVOLVED.
SIMILARLY, AS THE YEARS WENT ON, I BECAME MORE ENGAGED IN CHILDREARING AND HOUSEHOLD MANAGEMENT, AND HE BECAME LESS ENGAGED. THE MORE UNENGAGED HE BECAME, THE MORE FRUSTRATED I BECAME.

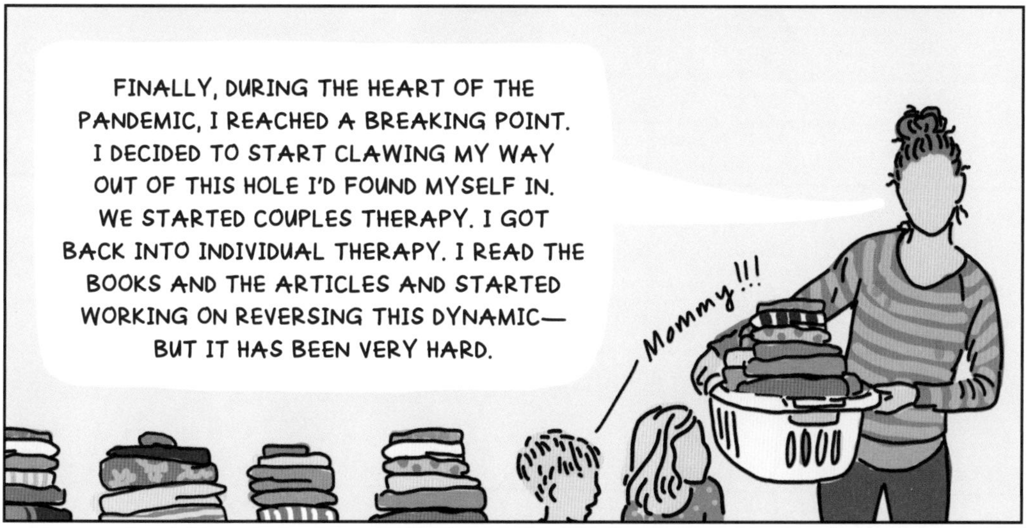
FINALLY, DURING THE HEART OF THE PANDEMIC, I REACHED A BREAKING POINT. I DECIDED TO START CLAWING MY WAY OUT OF THIS HOLE I'D FOUND MYSELF IN. WE STARTED COUPLES THERAPY. I GOT BACK INTO INDIVIDUAL THERAPY. I READ THE BOOKS AND THE ARTICLES AND STARTED WORKING ON REVERSING THIS DYNAMIC—BUT IT HAS BEEN VERY HARD.
Mommy!!!

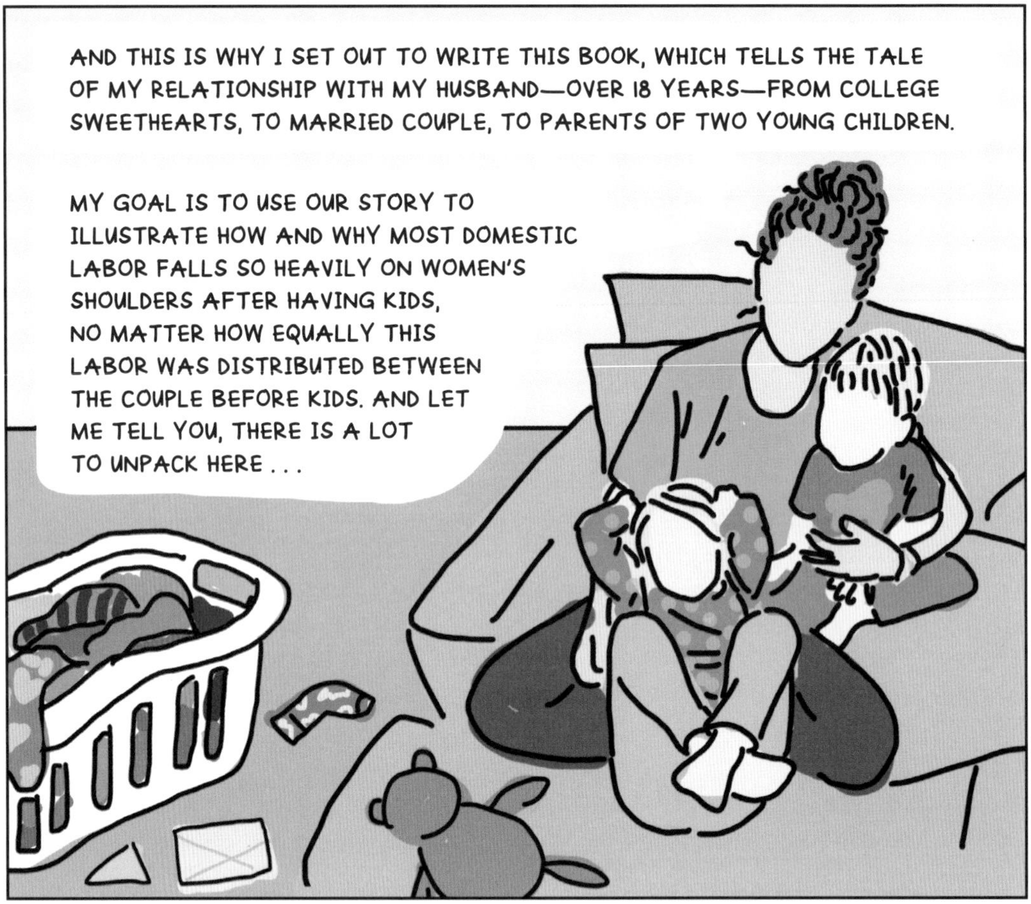
AND THIS IS WHY I SET OUT TO WRITE THIS BOOK, WHICH TELLS THE TALE OF MY RELATIONSHIP WITH MY HUSBAND—OVER 18 YEARS—FROM COLLEGE SWEETHEARTS, TO MARRIED COUPLE, TO PARENTS OF TWO YOUNG CHILDREN.
MY GOAL IS TO USE OUR STORY TO ILLUSTRATE HOW AND WHY MOST DOMESTIC LABOR FALLS SO HEAVILY ON WOMEN'S SHOULDERS AFTER HAVING KIDS, NO MATTER HOW EQUALLY THIS LABOR WAS DISTRIBUTED BETWEEN THE COUPLE BEFORE KIDS. AND LET ME TELL YOU, THERE IS A LOT TO UNPACK HERE . . .

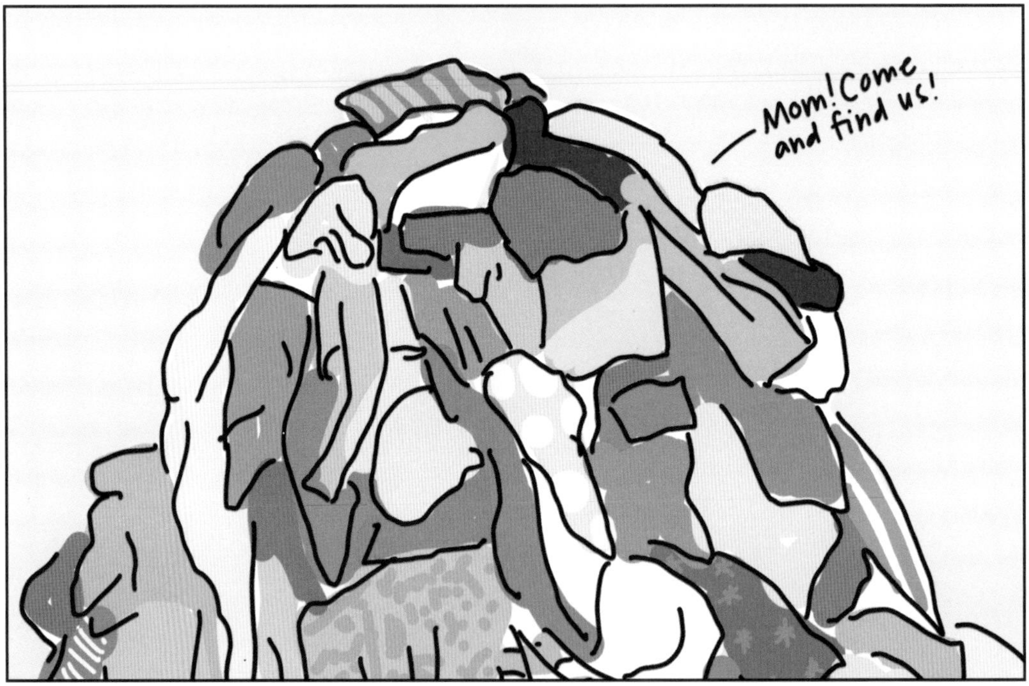
Mom! Come and find us!

I began talking about the mental load of motherhood in webcomic form in January 2020. Then, as the pandemic took hold and staying at home became our reality, making little comics became therapeutic—they became my way to vent about how hard life had become and to connect with like-minded moms while trapped inside my house with my family.

Fast-forward to January 2022: I'd decided to start an Instagram account solely dedicated to my comics, and one of my posts about "The Double Standards of Parenting" (see pages 14–15) went viral. All of a sudden I had way more eyes on my work than ever before.

While I had no idea what "going viral" would end up meaning for my life, what I quickly learned was this: Moms ALL OVER THE WORLD are drowning and feel completely alone in the challenges of modern motherhood. I knew it was an issue here in the United States, but I had no idea that this feeling was so universal.

Since then, I've become a sounding board for moms who are experiencing inequality in their households, families, work, and relationships (primarily heterosexual relationships, but I have heard from some in same-sex relationships who say they experience similar dynamics).

Even though women write to me from all over the globe, their stories all sound extremely similar. Many of these moms are women who, just like me, "thought I was the only one who felt this way" (despite tons of information out there that proves the contrary).

Obviously, countless books have been written about the mental load of motherhood, invisible labor, and household inequality. I've read many of these books myself and found them quite helpful.

But something that I've always felt was missing when reading these kinds of books is the deep, emotional, insider's perspective on this topic— the memoir-esque version of this story that doesn't end in a clear-cut solution, rainbows and butterflies, or a breakup or divorce. I want to read about the love story (and the journey that follows) that results in a mother feeling like she's drowning and all alone despite having a loving, present partner with whom she wants to remain in a relationship (even though she's angry and overwhelmed a lot of the time).

How does this happen? How does it feel when you're in it? Why is this situation so common despite women being more connected, empowered, and informed than ever before?

That's what I set out to explore in this book. And while not necessarily inspiring or uplifting, my hope is that, when told through comics and illustrations, this story becomes both funny and relatable while touching on some tough truths about the state of motherhood in our modern world.

# The Comic That Helped Me Find My People (And Helped My People Find Me!)

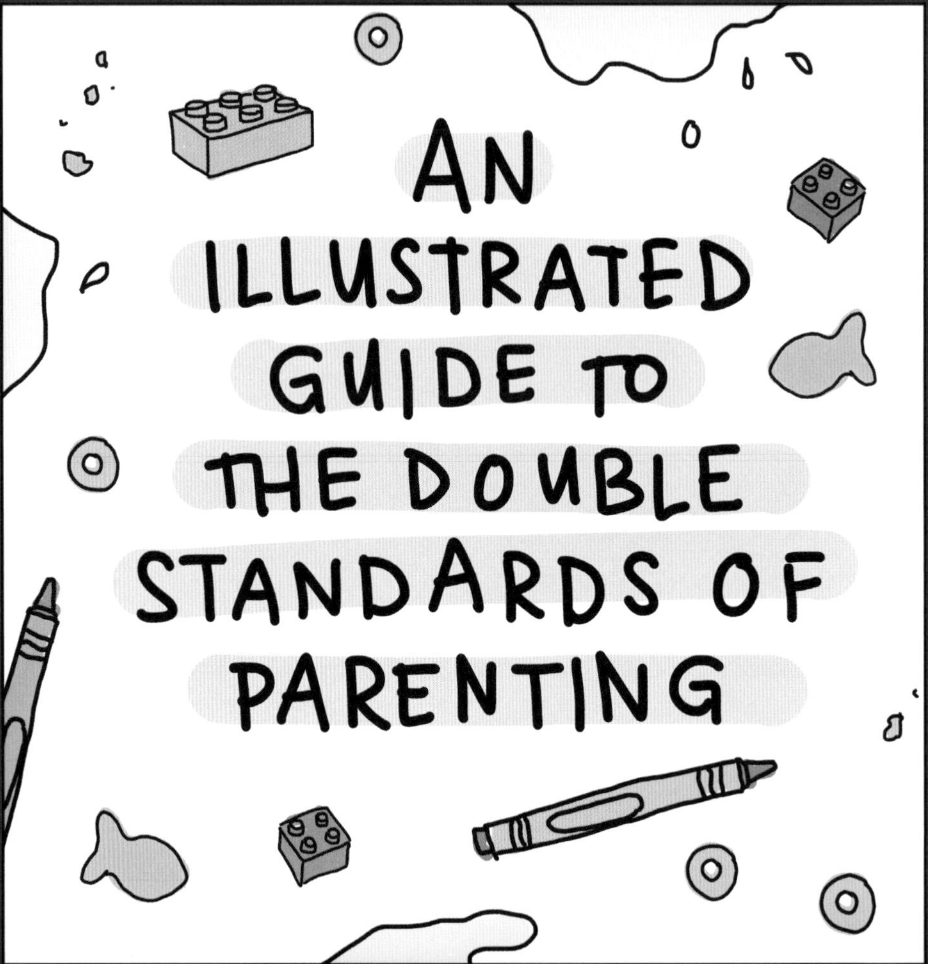
AN ILLUSTRATED GUIDE TO THE DOUBLE STANDARDS OF PARENTING

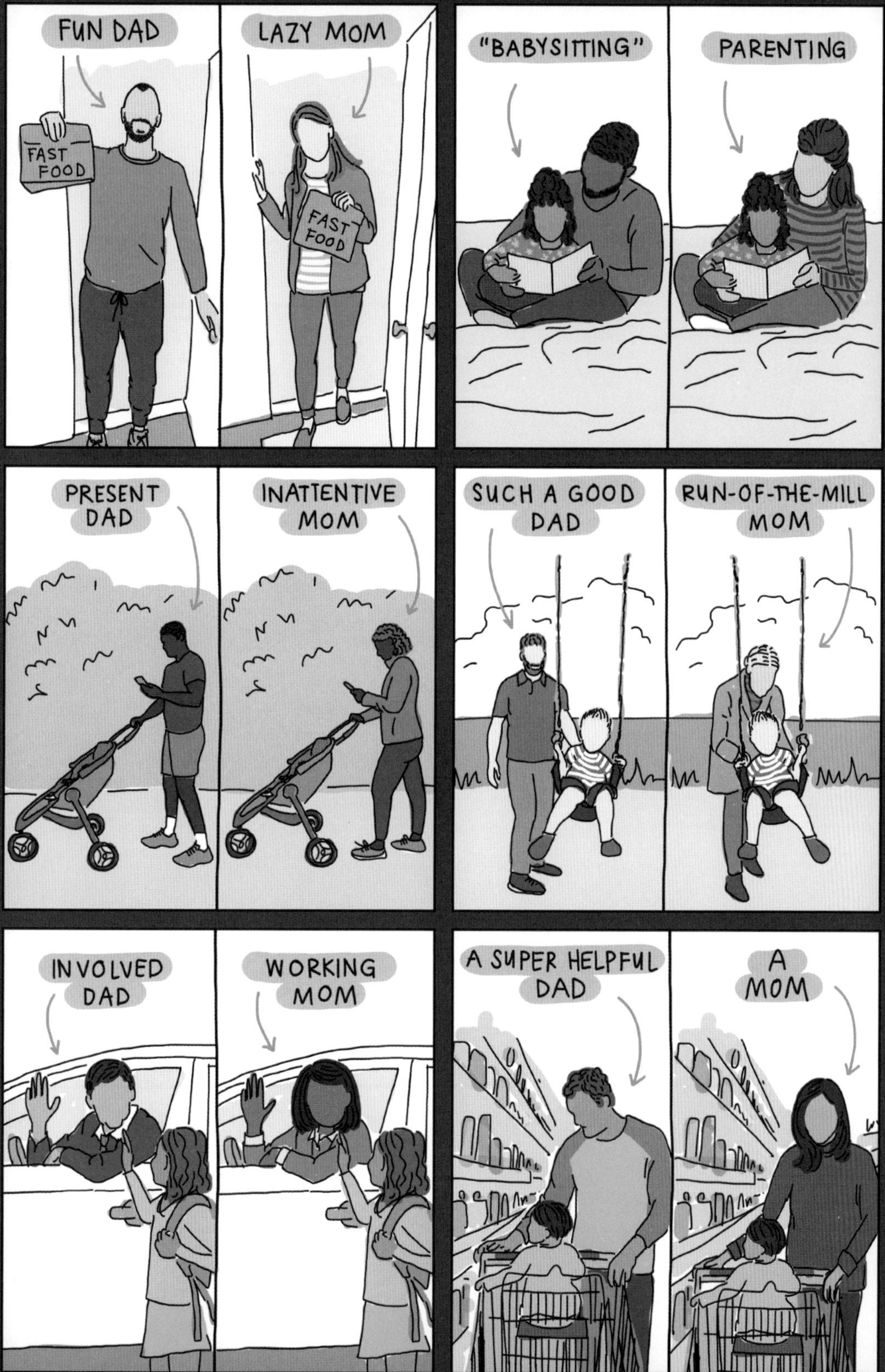
FUN DAD
FAST FOOD
LAZY MOM
FAST FOOD
"BABYSITTING"
PARENTING
PRESENT DAD
INATTENTIVE MOM
SUCH A GOOD DAD
RUN-OF-THE-MILL MOM
INVOLVED DAD
WORKING MOM
A SUPER HELPFUL DAD
A MOM

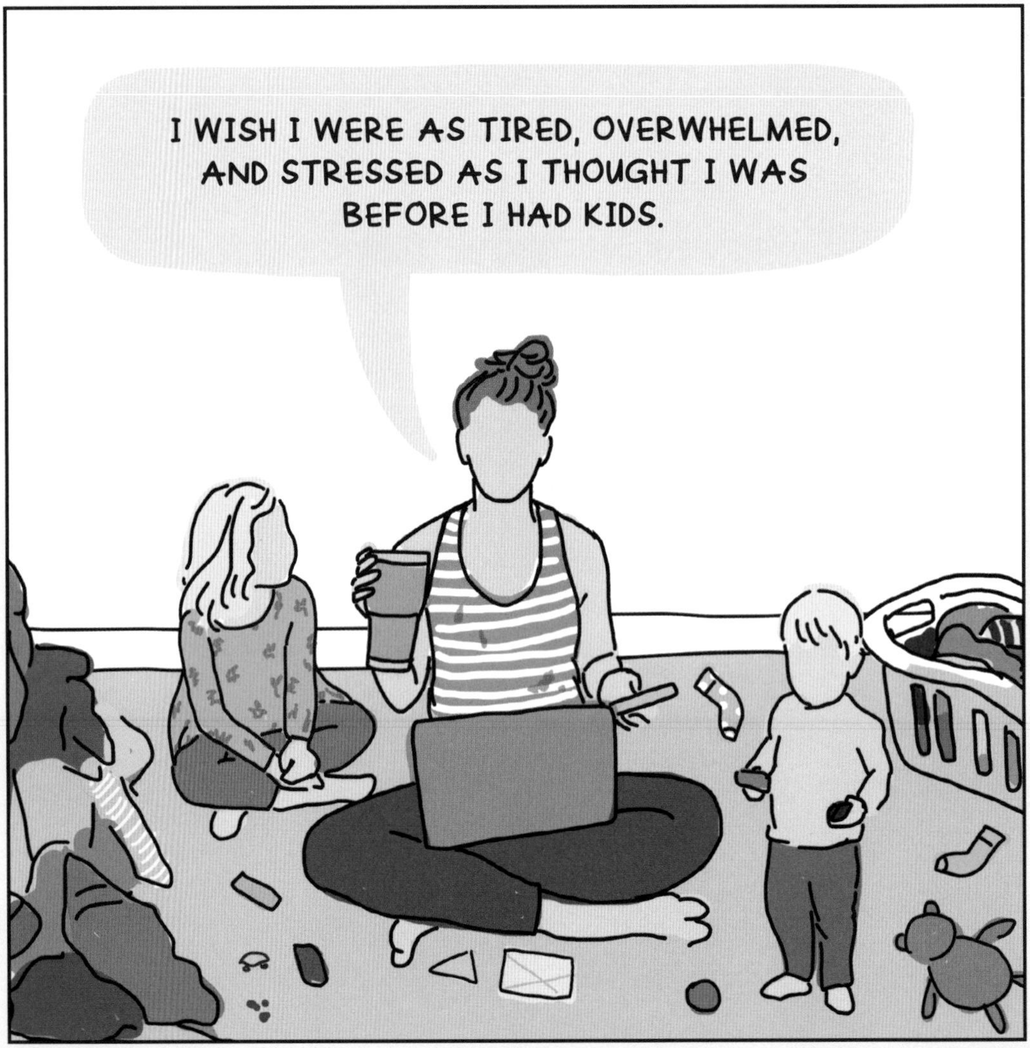
I WISH I WERE AS TIRED, OVERWHELMED, AND STRESSED AS I THOUGHT I WAS BEFORE I HAD KIDS.

# CHAPTER 1

# Ah, the Easy Years: Life before Kids

# First Comes Love

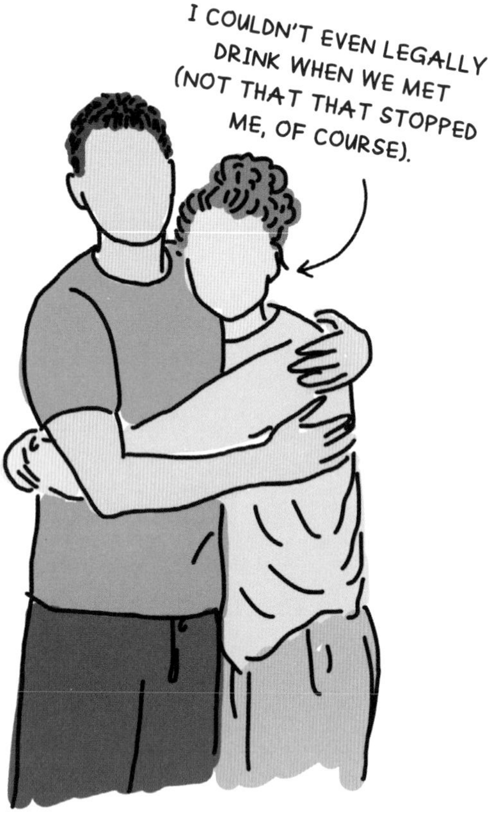
I COULDN'T EVEN LEGALLY DRINK WHEN WE MET (NOT THAT THAT STOPPED ME, OF COURSE).

My now-husband, Ben, and I met in college, as many couples do. Our love story began at a small school in a small town in Kentucky called Centre College, where we both chose to go despite hailing from Cape Cod (Ben) and Atlanta (me).

He dated a friend of mine for a few weeks during my freshman year and his junior year, but both that relationship and that friendship were short-lived; the relationship ended badly, and my friend moved on to a different crowd. Ben and I had no real reason to interact for a few months after that.

One of our first "real" interactions took place on AOL Instant Messenger later that year. It went something like this:

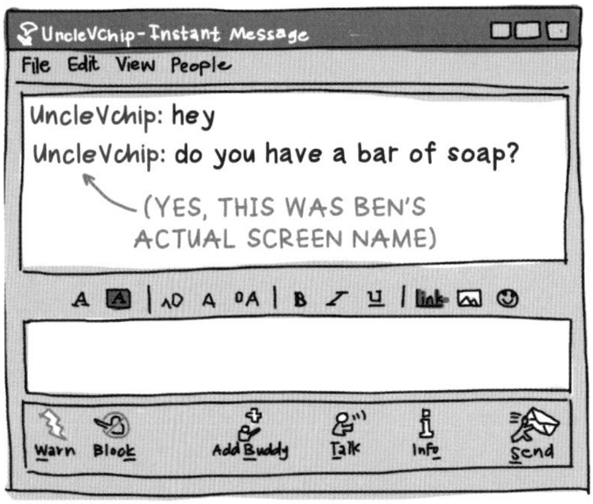
UncleVChip - Instant Message
File Edit View People
UncleVchip: hey
UncleVchip: do you have a bar of soap?
(YES, THIS WAS BEN'S ACTUAL SCREEN NAME)
Warn Block Add Buddy Talk Info Send

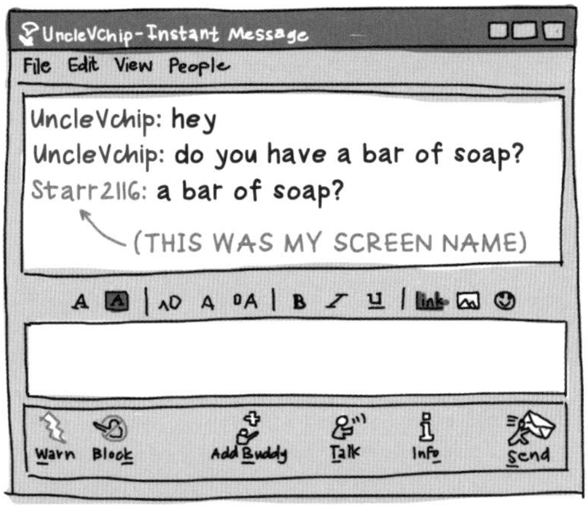
UncleVChip - Instant Message
File Edit View People
UncleVchip: hey
UncleVchip: do you have a bar of soap?
Starr2116: a bar of soap?
(THIS WAS MY SCREEN NAME)
Warn Block Add Buddy Talk Info Send

UncleVchip - Instant Message
UncleVchip: hey
UncleVchip: do you have a bar of soap?
Starr2116: a bar of soap?
UncleVchip: yeah, no one in our apartment has one
UncleVchip - Instant Message
Starr2116: a bar of soap?
UncleVchip: yeah, no one in our apartment has one
Starr2116: no one? No one in your apartment of 5 junior guys has any soap?
UncleVchip - Instant Message
UncleVchip: yeah, no one in our apartment has one
Starr2116: no one? No one in your apartment of 5 junior guys has any soap?
UncleVchip: nope. so do you have any?
UncleVchip - Instant Message
Starr2116: no one? No one in your apartment of 5 junior guys has any soap?
UncleVchip: nope. so do you have any?
Starr2116: Um, yes, I have some extra soap
UncleVchip - Instant Message
Starr2116: Um, yes, I have some extra soap
UncleVchip: can you throw it out of your window for me?*
Starr2116: okay . . .
Here you go . . .
Thanks!

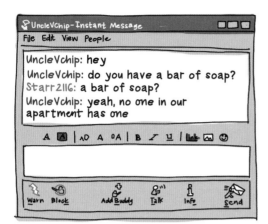

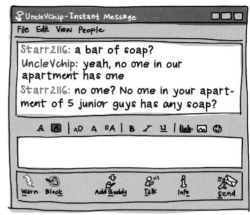

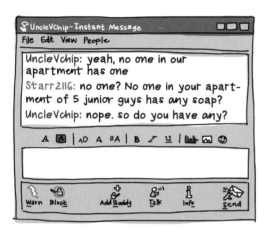

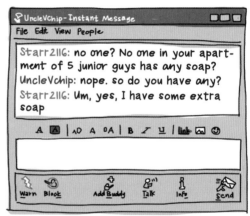

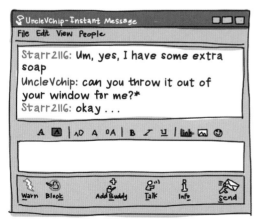

*Guys weren't allowed in our dorms after a certain time at night . . . seems crazy to think about now, but that was the rule!

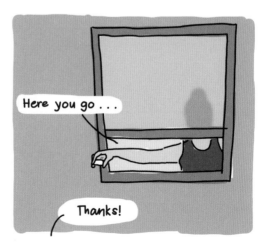

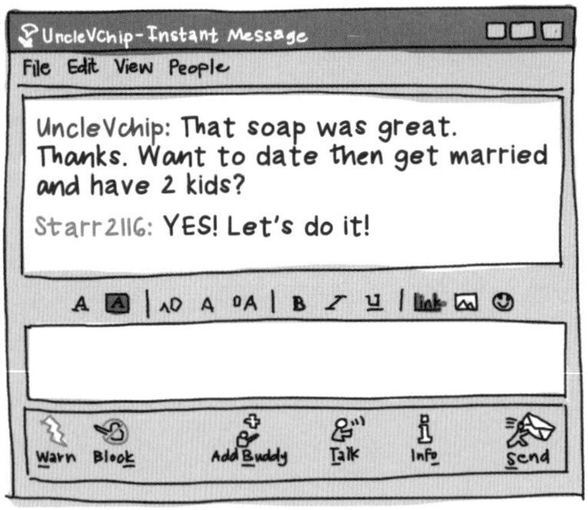
UncleVChip-Instant Message
File Edit View People
UncleVchip: That soap was great. Thanks. Want to date then get married and have 2 kids?
Starr2116: YES! Let's do it!
Warn Block Add Buddy Talk Info Send

And just like that, we were madly in love.

NOT!

In actuality, this weird exchange was just a blip on my freshman year radar. We didn't actually start dating for another year or so. However, the fact that our relationship started with him needing my help with a basic life need is not lost on me now.

But long before we had kids, I liked taking care of him. From the time that we first started dating (almost a year after this AIM/soap interaction), it felt good to be able to help him—to have a positive impact on his life and his understanding of the world.

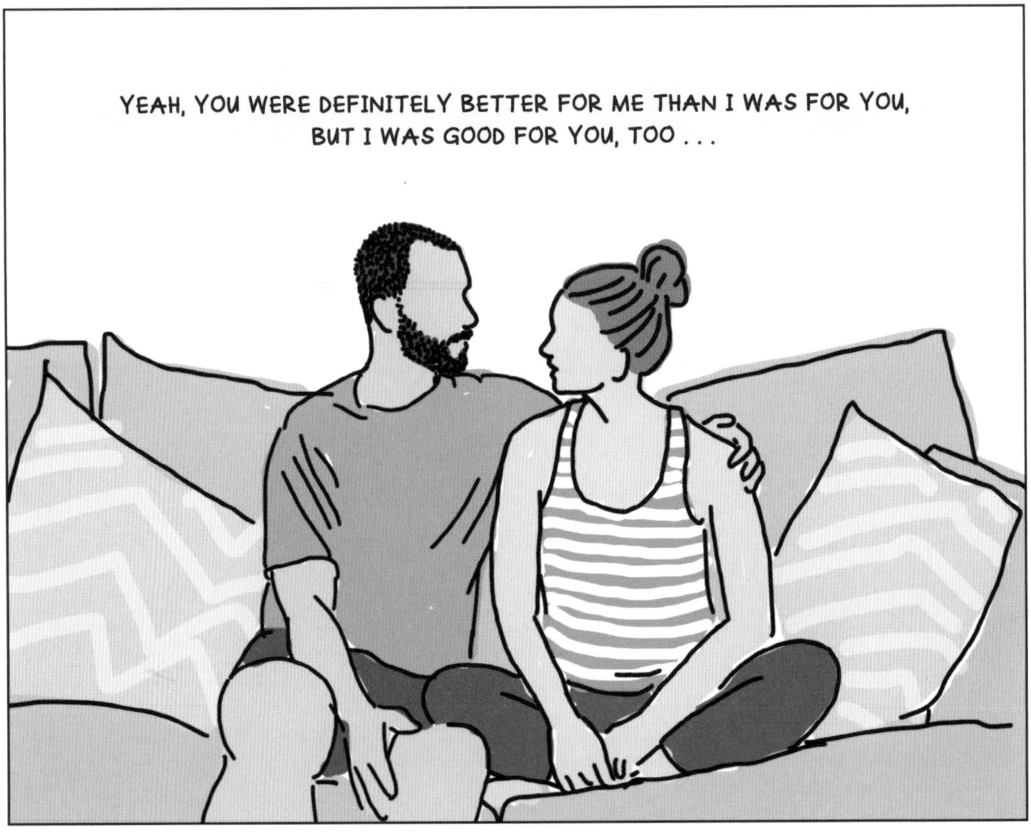
YEAH, YOU WERE DEFINITELY BETTER FOR ME THAN I WAS FOR YOU, BUT I WAS GOOD FOR YOU, TOO . . .

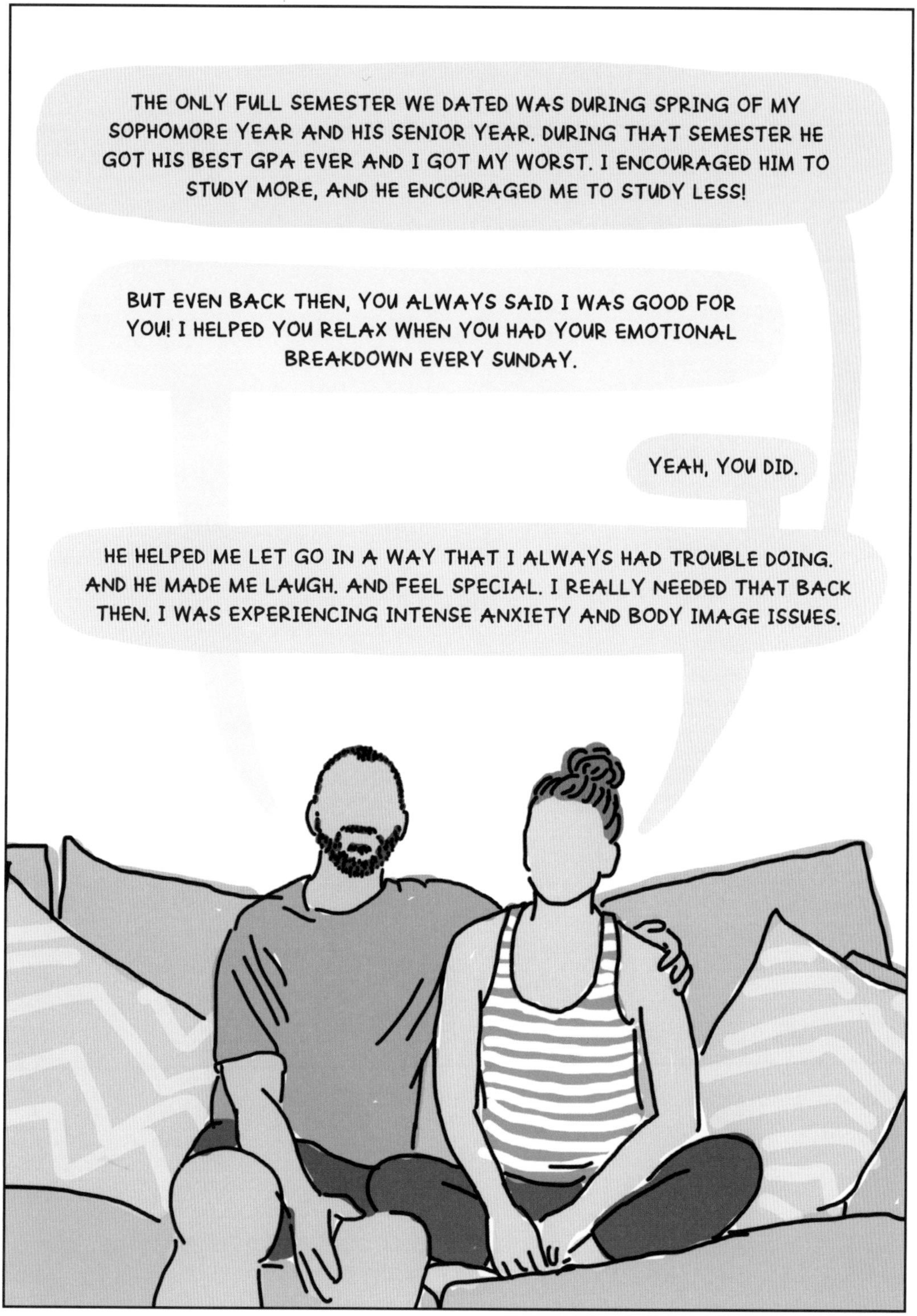
THE ONLY FULL SEMESTER WE DATED WAS DURING SPRING OF MY SOPHOMORE YEAR AND HIS SENIOR YEAR. DURING THAT SEMESTER HE GOT HIS BEST GPA EVER AND I GOT MY WORST. I ENCOURAGED HIM TO STUDY MORE, AND HE ENCOURAGED ME TO STUDY LESS!
BUT EVEN BACK THEN, YOU ALWAYS SAID I WAS GOOD FOR YOU! I HELPED YOU RELAX WHEN YOU HAD YOUR EMOTIONAL BREAKDOWN EVERY SUNDAY.
YEAH, YOU DID.
HE HELPED ME LET GO IN A WAY THAT I ALWAYS HAD TROUBLE DOING. AND HE MADE ME LAUGH. AND FEEL SPECIAL. I REALLY NEEDED THAT BACK THEN. I WAS EXPERIENCING INTENSE ANXIETY AND BODY IMAGE ISSUES.

So we started dating just a few months before he graduated, which was a bummer. But even though he was leaving and I had two more years of college, we decided to stay together. And we did! We were long distance for four years. Here's how that went down:

## Map of Our Long-Distance Relationship

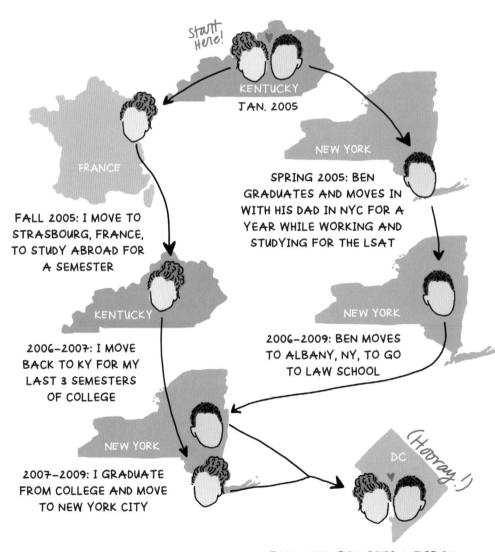

start here!

KENTUCKY
JAN. 2005

NEW YORK

FRANCE

FALL 2005: I MOVE TO
STRASBOURG, FRANCE,
TO STUDY ABROAD FOR
A SEMESTER

SPRING 2005: BEN
GRADUATES AND MOVES IN
WITH HIS DAD IN NYC FOR A
YEAR WHILE WORKING AND
STUDYING FOR THE LSAT

KENTUCKY

NEW YORK

2006-2007: I MOVE
BACK TO KY FOR MY
LAST 3 SEMESTERS
OF COLLEGE

2006-2009: BEN MOVES
TO ALBANY, NY, TO GO
TO LAW SCHOOL

NEW YORK

DC

(Hooray!)

2007-2009: I GRADUATE
FROM COLLEGE AND MOVE
TO NEW YORK CITY

FALL 2009: BEN GETS A JOB IN
WASHINGTON, DC, AND WE FINALLY
MOVE IN TOGETHER

Before we moved in together, while he was in law school, Ben lived in a duplex with a roommate. I'll never forget that place because it told me so much about how he would function in his natural state:

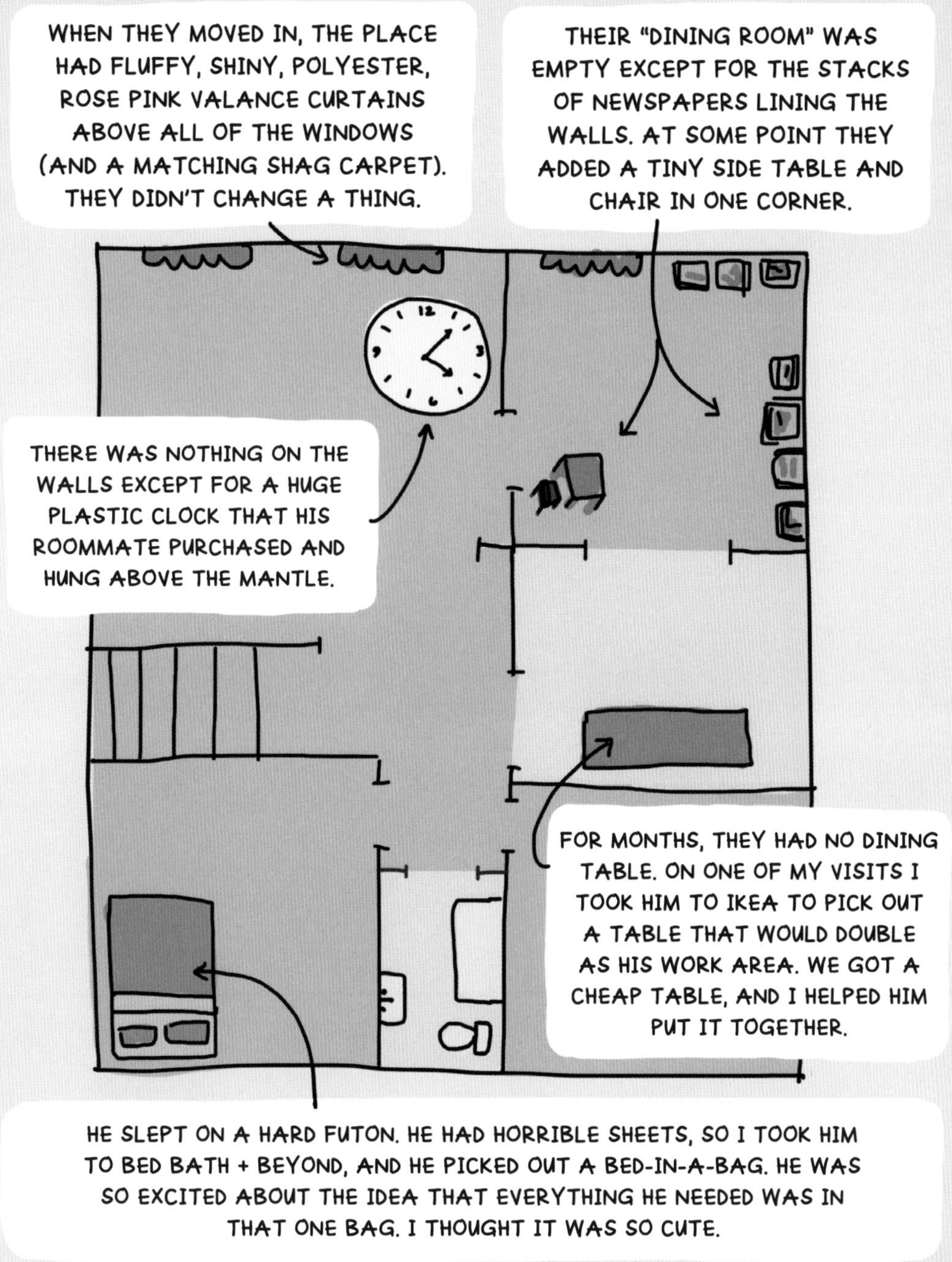
WHEN THEY MOVED IN, THE PLACE HAD FLUFFY, SHINY, POLYESTER, ROSE PINK VALANCE CURTAINS ABOVE ALL OF THE WINDOWS (AND A MATCHING SHAG CARPET). THEY DIDN'T CHANGE A THING.
THEIR "DINING ROOM" WAS EMPTY EXCEPT FOR THE STACKS OF NEWSPAPERS LINING THE WALLS. AT SOME POINT THEY ADDED A TINY SIDE TABLE AND CHAIR IN ONE CORNER.
THERE WAS NOTHING ON THE WALLS EXCEPT FOR A HUGE PLASTIC CLOCK THAT HIS ROOMMATE PURCHASED AND HUNG ABOVE THE MANTLE.
FOR MONTHS, THEY HAD NO DINING TABLE. ON ONE OF MY VISITS I TOOK HIM TO IKEA TO PICK OUT A TABLE THAT WOULD DOUBLE AS HIS WORK AREA. WE GOT A CHEAP TABLE, AND I HELPED HIM PUT IT TOGETHER.
HE SLEPT ON A HARD FUTON. HE HAD HORRIBLE SHEETS, SO I TOOK HIM TO BED BATH + BEYOND, AND HE PICKED OUT A BED-IN-A-BAG. HE WAS SO EXCITED ABOUT THE IDEA THAT EVERYTHING HE NEEDED WAS IN THAT ONE BAG. I THOUGHT IT WAS SO CUTE.

At times, dating Ben felt like helping a young child figure out the ways of the world. There were so many basic life skills he seemed to be lacking, despite being a bright and competent young adult. But he was so excited and grateful when I taught him something new, and it felt good to help him! I liked being a caretaker.

I'd never been loved in the way Ben loved me (and still loves me!). He was my rock; he knew me at my worst and still wanted to be with me, and that meant so much. I'd struggled with an eating disorder and major anxiety (and a little depression) for years, and he was always there to listen and hold me while I cried.

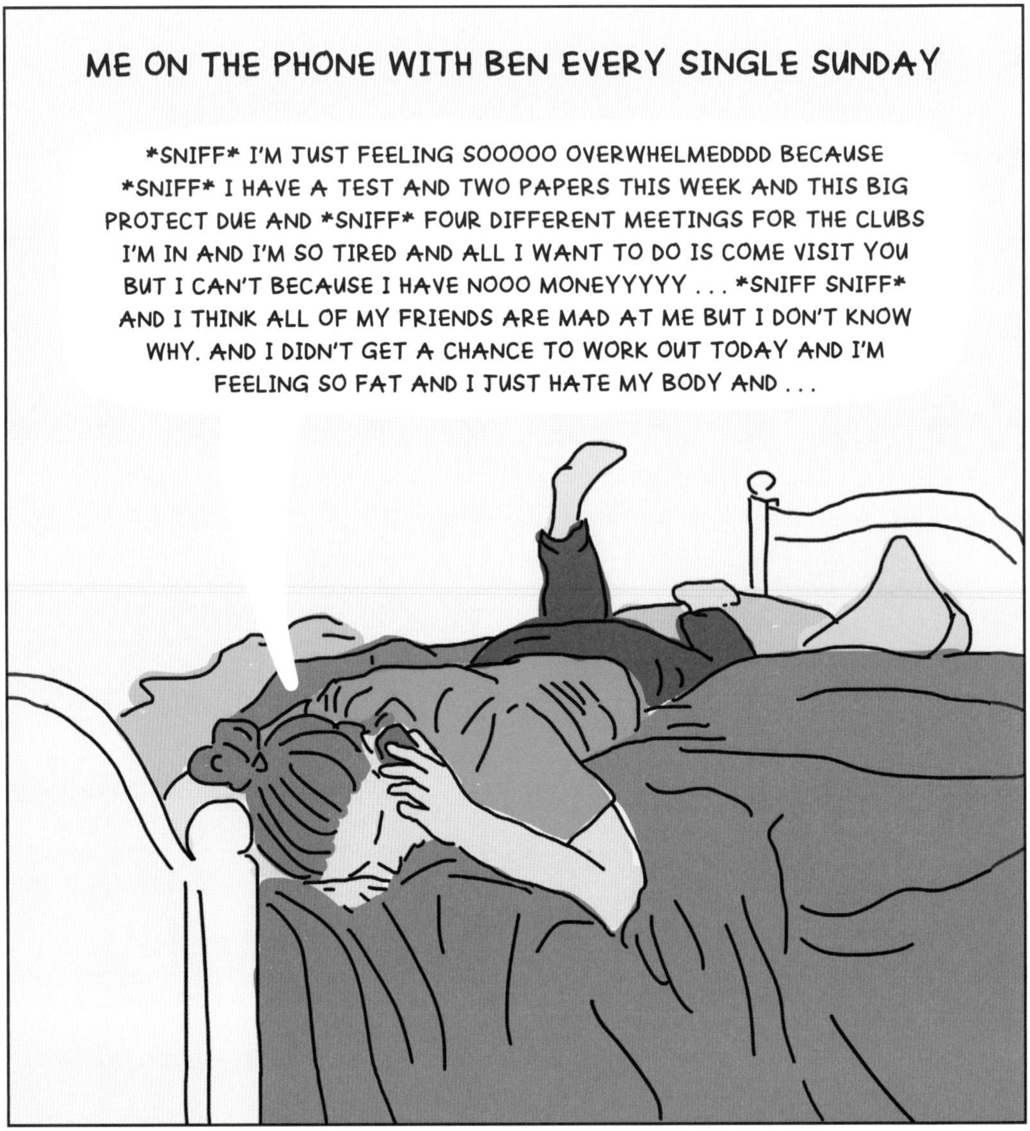
ME ON THE PHONE WITH BEN EVERY SINGLE SUNDAY
*SNIFF* I'M JUST FEELING SOOOOO OVERWHELMEDDDD BECAUSE *SNIFF* I HAVE A TEST AND TWO PAPERS THIS WEEK AND THIS BIG PROJECT DUE AND *SNIFF* FOUR DIFFERENT MEETINGS FOR THE CLUBS I'M IN AND I'M SO TIRED AND ALL I WANT TO DO IS COME VISIT YOU BUT I CAN'T BECAUSE I HAVE NOOO MONEYYYYY . . . *SNIFF SNIFF* AND I THINK ALL OF MY FRIENDS ARE MAD AT ME BUT I DON'T KNOW WHY. AND I DIDN'T GET A CHANCE TO WORK OUT TODAY AND I'M FEELING SO FAT AND I JUST HATE MY BODY AND . . .

I was much more organized and on top of things than he was. I helped him get his shit together, and he helped me be less uptight. But I was also a feminist, and I helped him see the many ways that his Southern, football-player-filled fraternity was sexist and horrible. He helped me see that needing help wasn't a bad thing and that my sorority also had its issues.

When it came to our families, Ben and I had a lot in common. We're both children of divorced families. And not just one divorce—MANY! We're like the Kardashians of divorce!

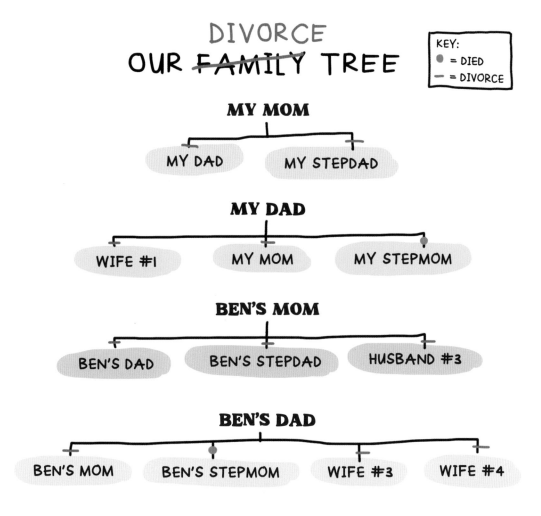

OUR ~~FAMILY~~ DIVORCE TREE

KEY:
● = DIED
— = DIVORCE

**MY MOM**
MY DAD          MY STEPDAD

**MY DAD**
WIFE #1          MY MOM          MY STEPMOM

**BEN'S MOM**
BEN'S DAD          BEN'S STEPDAD          HUSBAND #3

**BEN'S DAD**
BEN'S MOM          BEN'S STEPMOM          WIFE #3          WIFE #4

Oh, and get this: All of our biological parents are currently unmarried. So we've got twelve marriages between our four parents, and at this point, they're all unmarried.

Because we both had these histories, we talked openly about marriage fairly early in our relationship and learned that we felt very differently about it:

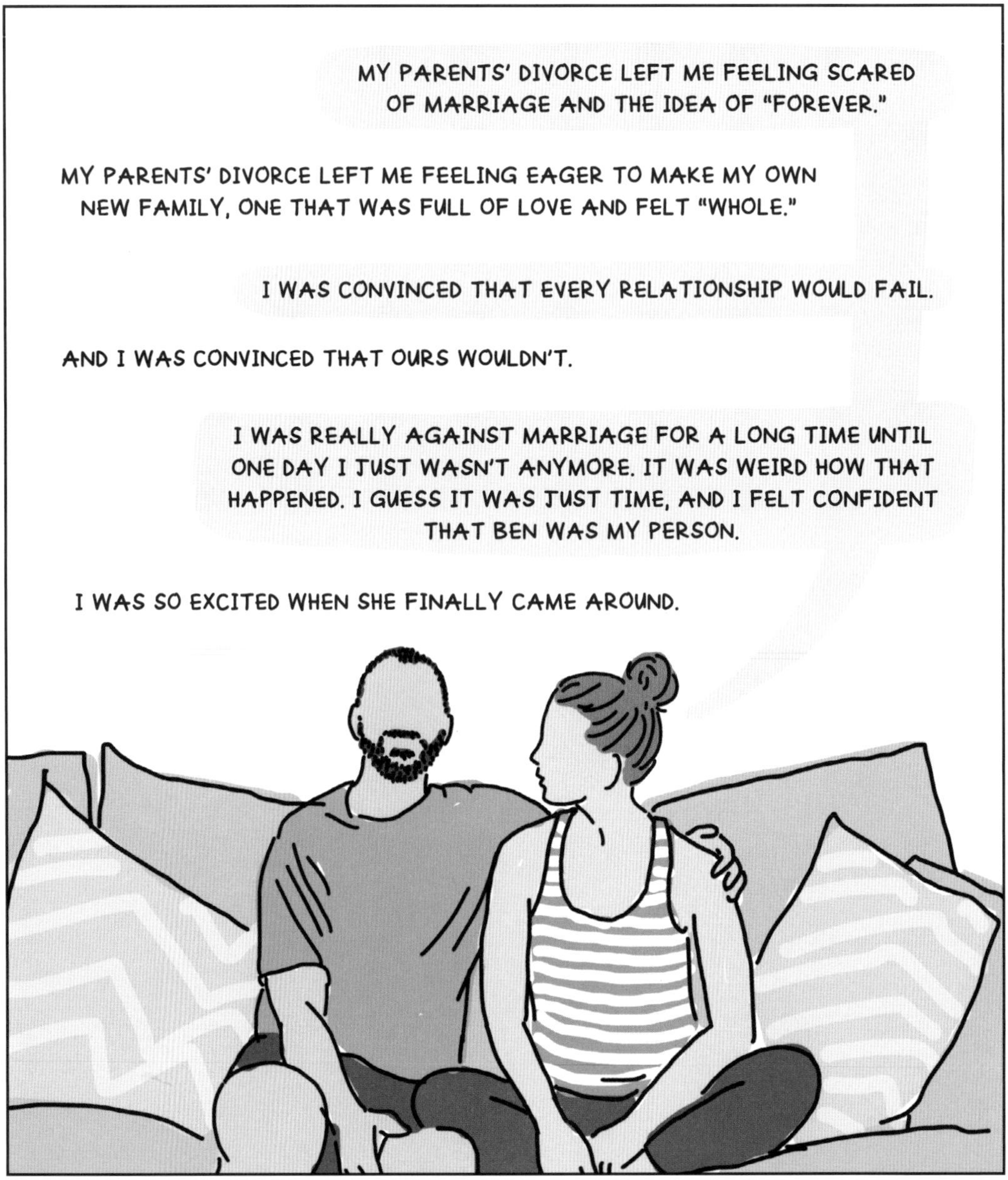
MY PARENTS' DIVORCE LEFT ME FEELING SCARED OF MARRIAGE AND THE IDEA OF "FOREVER."
MY PARENTS' DIVORCE LEFT ME FEELING EAGER TO MAKE MY OWN NEW FAMILY, ONE THAT WAS FULL OF LOVE AND FELT "WHOLE."
I WAS CONVINCED THAT EVERY RELATIONSHIP WOULD FAIL.
AND I WAS CONVINCED THAT OURS WOULDN'T.
I WAS REALLY AGAINST MARRIAGE FOR A LONG TIME UNTIL ONE DAY I JUST WASN'T ANYMORE. IT WAS WEIRD HOW THAT HAPPENED. I GUESS IT WAS JUST TIME, AND I FELT CONFIDENT THAT BEN WAS MY PERSON.
I WAS SO EXCITED WHEN SHE FINALLY CAME AROUND.

We entered into our relationship with all of this divorce baggage and no marriage role models on either side of our families. Neither of us had any idea what a successful marriage looked or felt like.

So, we dated long distance for four years. And every couple of months, I resisted one of Ben's drunken, late-night marriage proposals, telling him we were too young and I needed some time to be independent.

After college, I spent the summer living with Ben (and his dad) in NYC, and when fall rolled around and Ben went back to law school, I moved into a 400-square-foot studio apartment in the East Village. I worked in marketing and was broke as a joke, but I loved it there.

I painted on the weekends, discovered yoga, drank too much on nights out with friends, stepped over human excrement and puke on my doorstep as I headed out to work in the mornings, and continued to deal with the fallout of the eating disorder I'd suffered from since I was in my early teens.

*Ah, the many ups and downs of being in your early twenties!*

Ben studied hard and applied himself like he never had before. We spent the weekends together whenever we could and continued to make our way in the world, separate but together.

We were super in love. And so, so young.

THAT'S ME! LOOK HOW INDEPENDENT I WAS! SUCH A COOL NEW YORK WOMAN.

HERE'S AN ACTUAL EMAIL EXCHANGE
BETWEEN US THAT I DUG UP:

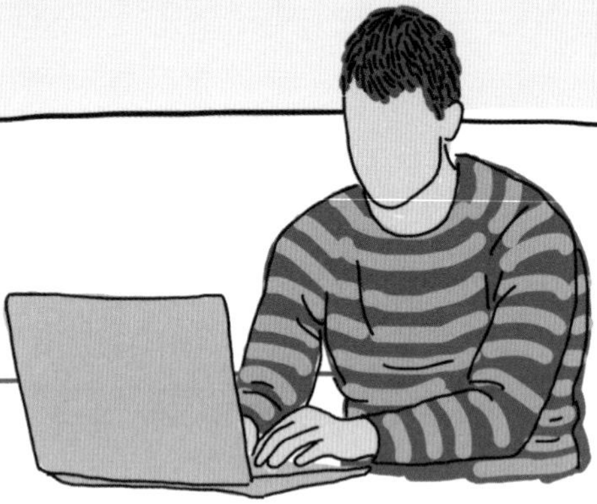

Ben <[redacted]@gmail.com>
to me
Sat, Oct 13, 2007, 3:43 PM

hey momma clam,

i know you are busy at work, but i just wanted to say hello before i left for the grocery store.

i am going to pick up all the stuff we need to make chicken burritos so that we can make them together when you come this week. and, if you are unable to come this week, i will attempt to make them myself. you must be pretty excited about your party tonight too. sounds like it is going to be fun. that is so crazy that two girls from college are coming. i hope someone doesn't have to stand in the bathroom because your apartment is so small, haha. anyways, i love you so much and can't wait to talk to you after you get off work. i miss you like the desert misses the rain.

Sparky

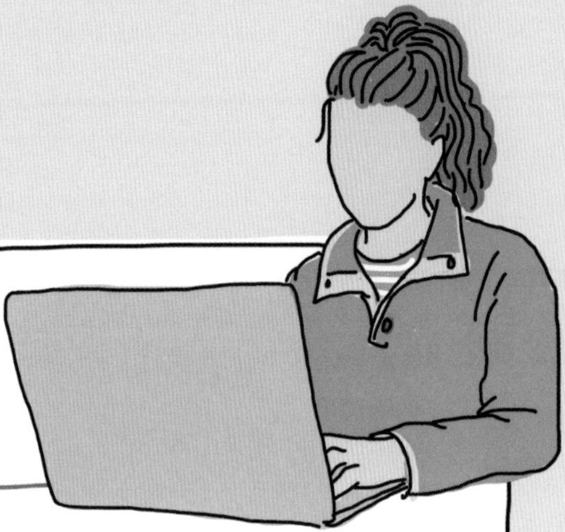

**Mary Catherine <[redacted]@gmail.com>**
**to Ben**
**Sun, Oct 14, 2007, 11:36 AM**

---

hey sparky,

thank you so much for that SWEET email. it was really nice to open it up and read it this morning. i really miss you! and for your information, the apartment WAS big enough to have a lot of people there, and no one had to stand in the bathroom.

but anyways, its gonna be busy today so i need to go—and im SOOOOO hungover its absolutely horrible. it really sucks. oh well . . .

okay well i love you so much—even more than i love apples. i cant wait to see you this week (hopefully!!!!)

love, love, love love love,
mamma clam

We exchanged hundreds of emails just like this. Our emails were just casual, meandering, mushy thoughts that didn't really mean anything but made us feel more connected.

They're actually really embarrassing now, but I like looking back at them because they remind me of how crazy we were for each other. Look at these!

Mary Catherine <●●@gmail.com>
to Ben
Mon, Oct 22, 2007, 10:26 AM

hey honey . . . i didnt hear from you this morning and i was just wondering what youre doing? i miss you SOOOOOOOOOOOOOOOOOOOOOOOOOOOOOOOOOO OOOOOOOOOOOOOOOOOOOOOOOOOOOOOOOOOO OOOOOOOOOOOOOOOOOOOOOOOOOOOO much and cant wait to see you.

also, im in a sucky mood today and DONT want to be at work. im exhausted.

okay well i hope youre in a better mood than i am . . .

i love you more than wine and chocolate,
mc

Mary Catherine <🌸@gmail.com>
to Ben
Thu, Jan 3, 2008, 10:21 AM

hi baby. just wanted to say that i love you SOOOO much. thanks for your wonderful email yesterday. youre the most wonderful man in the world, even if you do smell weird.

haha jk!

anyways, call me when you get up, sleepy head! you little mongoose, you.

i wish i was seeing you this weekend! kiss kiss!

lovelove,lovelovelove,
mc

When I read emails like this, I can hardly believe that I'm the person who wrote them. I don't talk to Ben like this anymore . . . but you know who I *do* talk to like this? My kids!

But I'm getting ahead of myself.

After dating for four years, we moved in together. Ben had graduated from law school and gotten a job in the DC area so we moved there. He loaded a U-Haul with the most random collection of items and then drove to New York City to pick me up.

He arrived with very little room in the back of the truck for my *entire* apartment's worth of belongings—and lots of items that were just loose in the back of the truck. Here are some very important items he didn't think we could live without in DC:

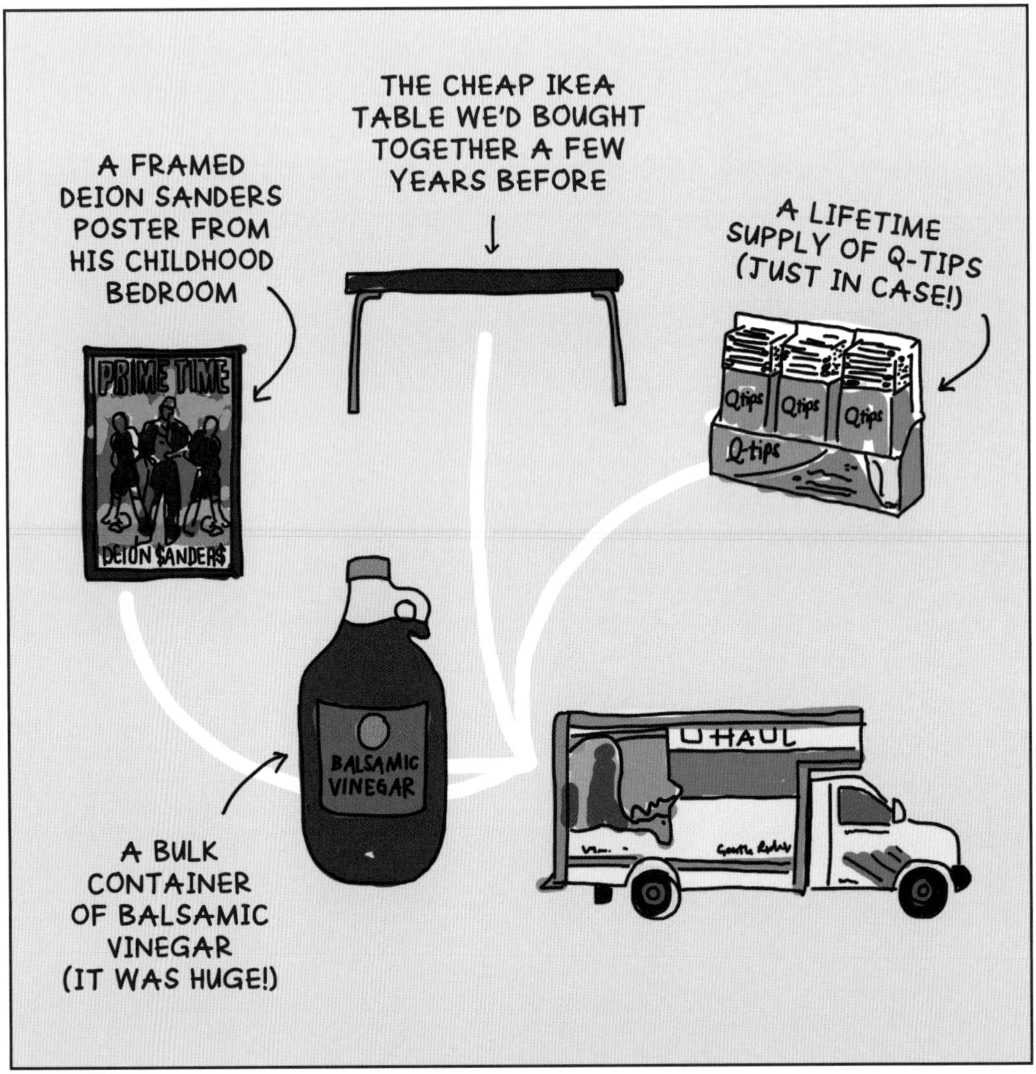

A FRAMED DEION SANDERS POSTER FROM HIS CHILDHOOD BEDROOM
PRIME TIME
DEION SANDERS
THE CHEAP IKEA TABLE WE'D BOUGHT TOGETHER A FEW YEARS BEFORE
A LIFETIME SUPPLY OF Q-TIPS (JUST IN CASE!)
Qtips
Qtips
Qtips
Q-tips
BALSAMIC VINEGAR
A BULK CONTAINER OF BALSAMIC VINEGAR (IT WAS HUGE!)
UHAUL

WHEN WE ARRIVED AT OUR HOTEL ON THE FIRST NIGHT OF OUR TRAVELS, I NOTICED THAT SOMETHING WAS DRIPPING OUT OF THE BACK OF OUR U-HAUL. IT LOOKED LIKE BLOOD.

WE OPENED UP THE BACK TO INVESTIGATE, AND GUESS WHAT WE FOUND? THE INDUSTRIAL-SIZED JUG OF BALSAMIC VINEGAR THAT BEN HAD "PACKED" (I USE THAT TERM LOOSELY) HAD BROKEN. THE LIQUID HAD SPILLED AND SLOWLY SEEPED INTO ALL OUR BELONGINGS THAT WERE TOUCHING THE FLOOR OF THE TRUCK.

NEEDLESS TO SAY, OUR NEW APARTMENT SMELLED LIKE BALSAMIC FOR WEEKS (WEEKS!). ALSO, OUR MATTRESS LOOKED LIKE IT HAD BEEN TAKEN FROM A CRIME SCENE.

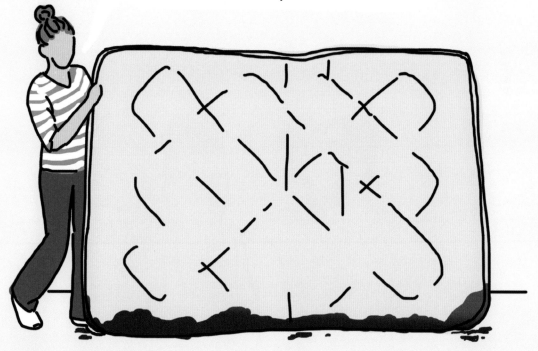

HI, NEW NEIGHBORS! IT'S NOT WHAT IT LOOKS LIKE, I PROMISE!

# Then Comes . . . the Biggest Fight We've Ever Had

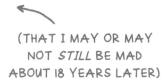

(THAT I MAY OR MAY NOT *STILL* BE MAD ABOUT 18 YEARS LATER)

LET'S BACK UP A MINUTE—I HAVE ANOTHER STORY FROM OUR COLLEGE YEARS THAT I WANT TO TELL. HERE'S THE BACKGROUND:

DURING FALL OF MY JUNIOR YEAR, I HEADED TO FRANCE TO STUDY ABROAD FOR A SEMESTER. BEN, WHO HAD GRADUATED THE PREVIOUS YEAR, STAYED PUT ON CAPE COD, LIVING AT HIS GRANDPARENTS' HOUSE WHILE WORKING AT A LOCAL HOTEL AND STUDYING TO GET INTO LAW SCHOOL.

IT WAS DURING THIS TIME—DURING MY SEMESTER ABROAD—THAT WE HAD OUR WORST FIGHT EVER . . . ONE THAT I STILL BRING UP TO THIS DAY, ALMOST 18 YEARS LATER.

I CANNOT BELIEVE YOU'RE STILL MAD ABOUT THIS. IT'S SO RIDICULOUS.

NO, IT'S NOT! AND I THINK THE READERS NEED TO KNOW THIS. I WANT TO TELL THIS STORY BECAUSE IT FEELS IMPORTANT FROM A THEMATIC STANDPOINT . . .

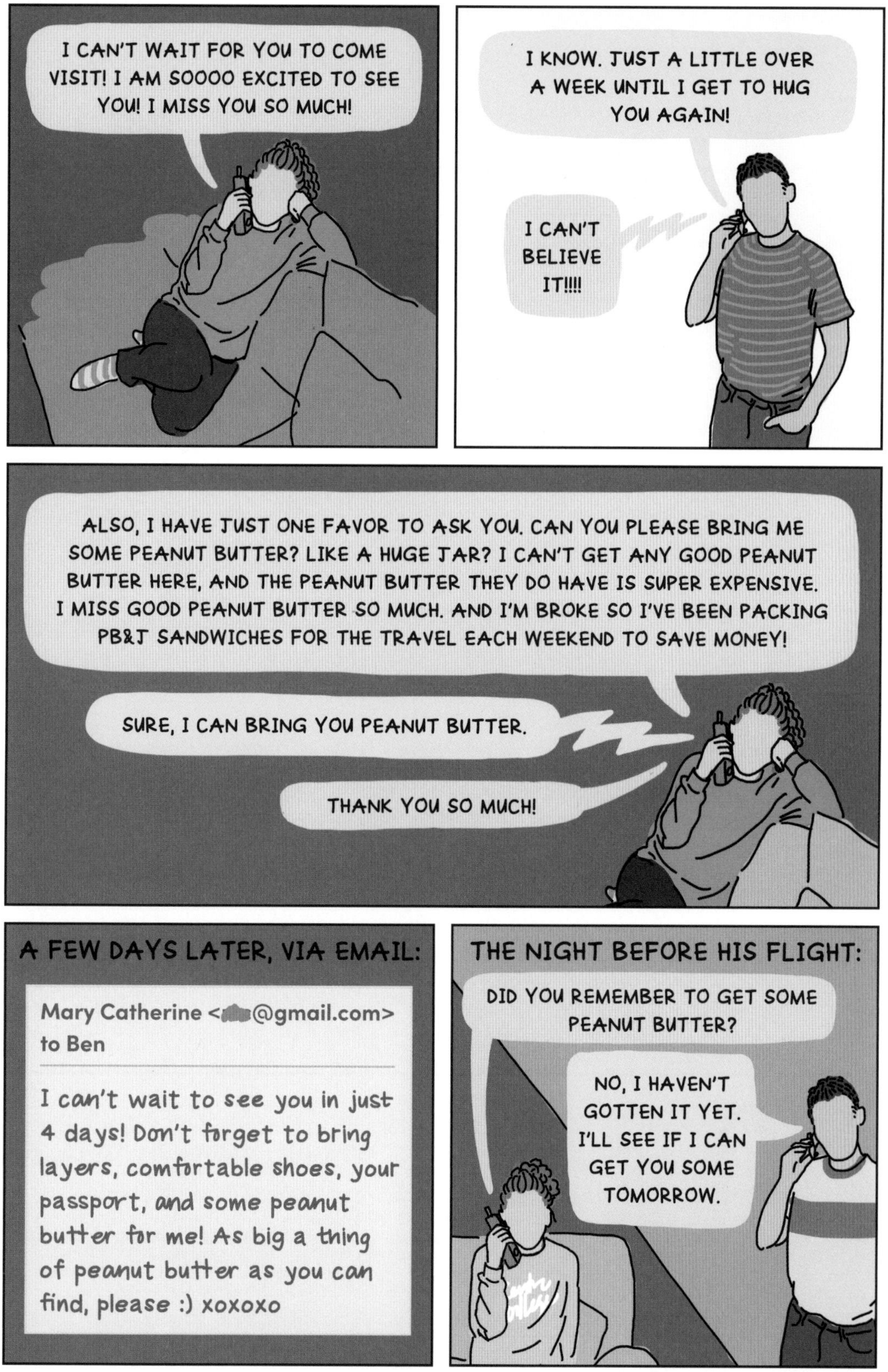
I CAN'T WAIT FOR YOU TO COME VISIT! I AM SOOOO EXCITED TO SEE YOU! I MISS YOU SO MUCH!
I KNOW. JUST A LITTLE OVER A WEEK UNTIL I GET TO HUG YOU AGAIN!
I CAN'T BELIEVE IT!!!!
ALSO, I HAVE JUST ONE FAVOR TO ASK YOU. CAN YOU PLEASE BRING ME SOME PEANUT BUTTER? LIKE A HUGE JAR? I CAN'T GET ANY GOOD PEANUT BUTTER HERE, AND THE PEANUT BUTTER THEY DO HAVE IS SUPER EXPENSIVE. I MISS GOOD PEANUT BUTTER SO MUCH. AND I'M BROKE SO I'VE BEEN PACKING PB&J SANDWICHES FOR THE TRAVEL EACH WEEKEND TO SAVE MONEY!
SURE, I CAN BRING YOU PEANUT BUTTER.
THANK YOU SO MUCH!
A FEW DAYS LATER, VIA EMAIL:
Mary Catherine <[redacted]@gmail.com>
to Ben
I can't wait to see you in just 4 days! Don't forget to bring layers, comfortable shoes, your passport, and some peanut butter for me! As big a thing of peanut butter as you can find, please :) xoxoxo
THE NIGHT BEFORE HIS FLIGHT:
DID YOU REMEMBER TO GET SOME PEANUT BUTTER?
NO, I HAVEN'T GOTTEN IT YET. I'LL SEE IF I CAN GET YOU SOME TOMORROW.

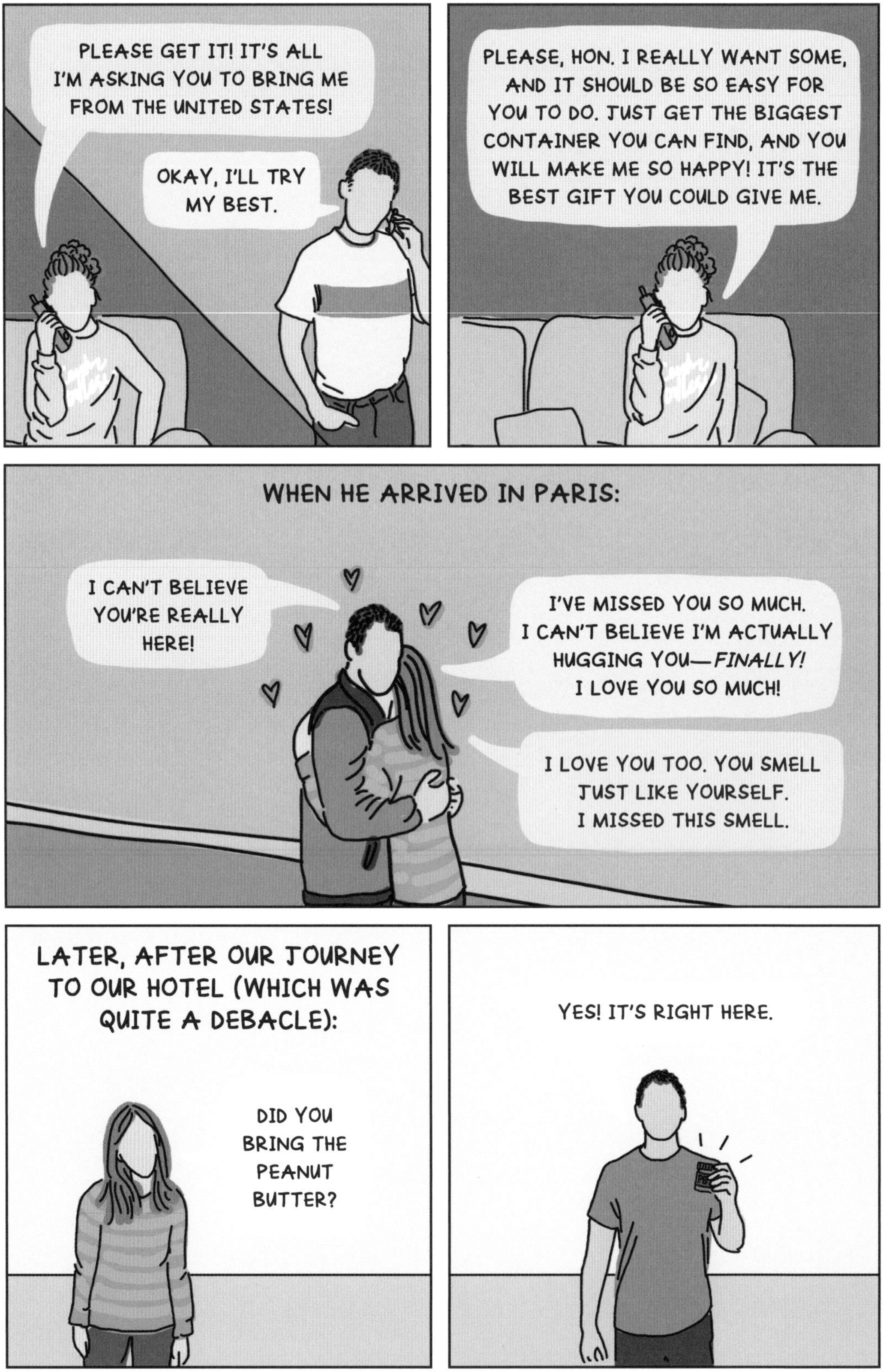
PLEASE GET IT! IT'S ALL I'M ASKING YOU TO BRING ME FROM THE UNITED STATES!
OKAY, I'LL TRY MY BEST.
PLEASE, HON. I REALLY WANT SOME, AND IT SHOULD BE SO EASY FOR YOU TO DO. JUST GET THE BIGGEST CONTAINER YOU CAN FIND, AND YOU WILL MAKE ME SO HAPPY! IT'S THE BEST GIFT YOU COULD GIVE ME.
WHEN HE ARRIVED IN PARIS:
I CAN'T BELIEVE YOU'RE REALLY HERE!
I'VE MISSED YOU SO MUCH. I CAN'T BELIEVE I'M ACTUALLY HUGGING YOU—*FINALLY!* I LOVE YOU SO MUCH!
I LOVE YOU TOO. YOU SMELL JUST LIKE YOURSELF. I MISSED THIS SMELL.
LATER, AFTER OUR JOURNEY TO OUR HOTEL (WHICH WAS QUITE A DEBACLE):
DID YOU BRING THE PEANUT BUTTER?
YES! IT'S RIGHT HERE.

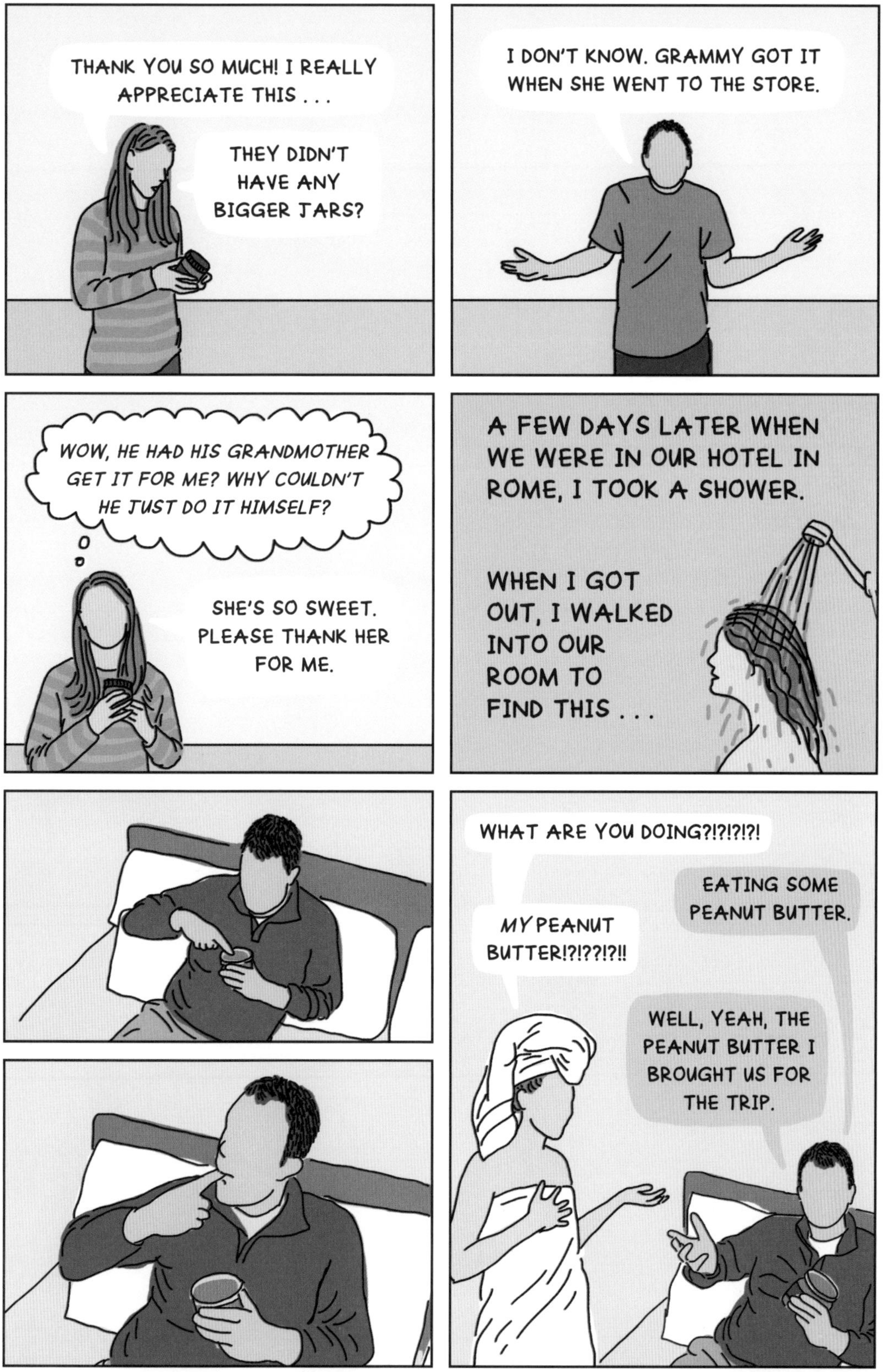
THANK YOU SO MUCH! I REALLY APPRECIATE THIS . . .
THEY DIDN'T HAVE ANY BIGGER JARS?
I DON'T KNOW. GRAMMY GOT IT WHEN SHE WENT TO THE STORE.
WOW, HE HAD HIS GRANDMOTHER GET IT FOR ME? WHY COULDN'T HE JUST DO IT HIMSELF?
SHE'S SO SWEET. PLEASE THANK HER FOR ME.
A FEW DAYS LATER WHEN WE WERE IN OUR HOTEL IN ROME, I TOOK A SHOWER.
WHEN I GOT OUT, I WALKED INTO OUR ROOM TO FIND THIS . . .
WHAT ARE YOU DOING?!?!?!?!
EATING SOME PEANUT BUTTER.
MY PEANUT BUTTER!?!??!?!!
WELL, YEAH, THE PEANUT BUTTER I BROUGHT US FOR THE TRIP.

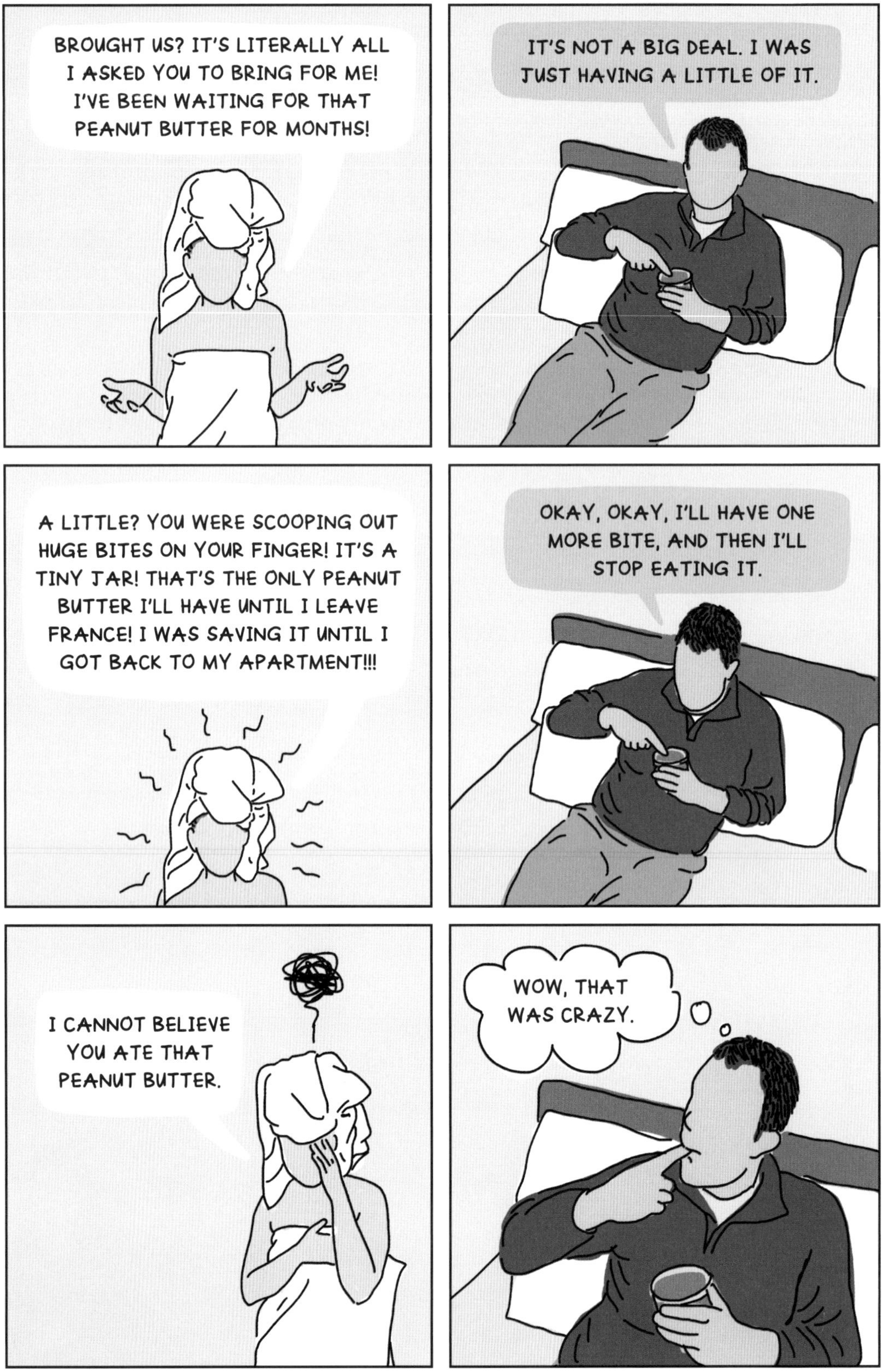
BROUGHT US? IT'S LITERALLY ALL I ASKED YOU TO BRING FOR ME! I'VE BEEN WAITING FOR THAT PEANUT BUTTER FOR MONTHS!
IT'S NOT A BIG DEAL. I WAS JUST HAVING A LITTLE OF IT.
A LITTLE? YOU WERE SCOOPING OUT HUGE BITES ON YOUR FINGER! IT'S A TINY JAR! THAT'S THE ONLY PEANUT BUTTER I'LL HAVE UNTIL I LEAVE FRANCE! I WAS SAVING IT UNTIL I GOT BACK TO MY APARTMENT!!!
OKAY, OKAY, I'LL HAVE ONE MORE BITE, AND THEN I'LL STOP EATING IT.
I CANNOT BELIEVE YOU ATE THAT PEANUT BUTTER.
WOW, THAT WAS CRAZY.

A few hours later, we took a bus tour of Rome. We started bickering about something silly—I don't remember what started it, but I know that what began as a squabble quickly escalated. And then came one of the most dramatic moments of our relationship: our biggest fight ever, in Vatican City, right in the middle of St. Peter's Square. And of course in the middle of this fight, it started raining . . .

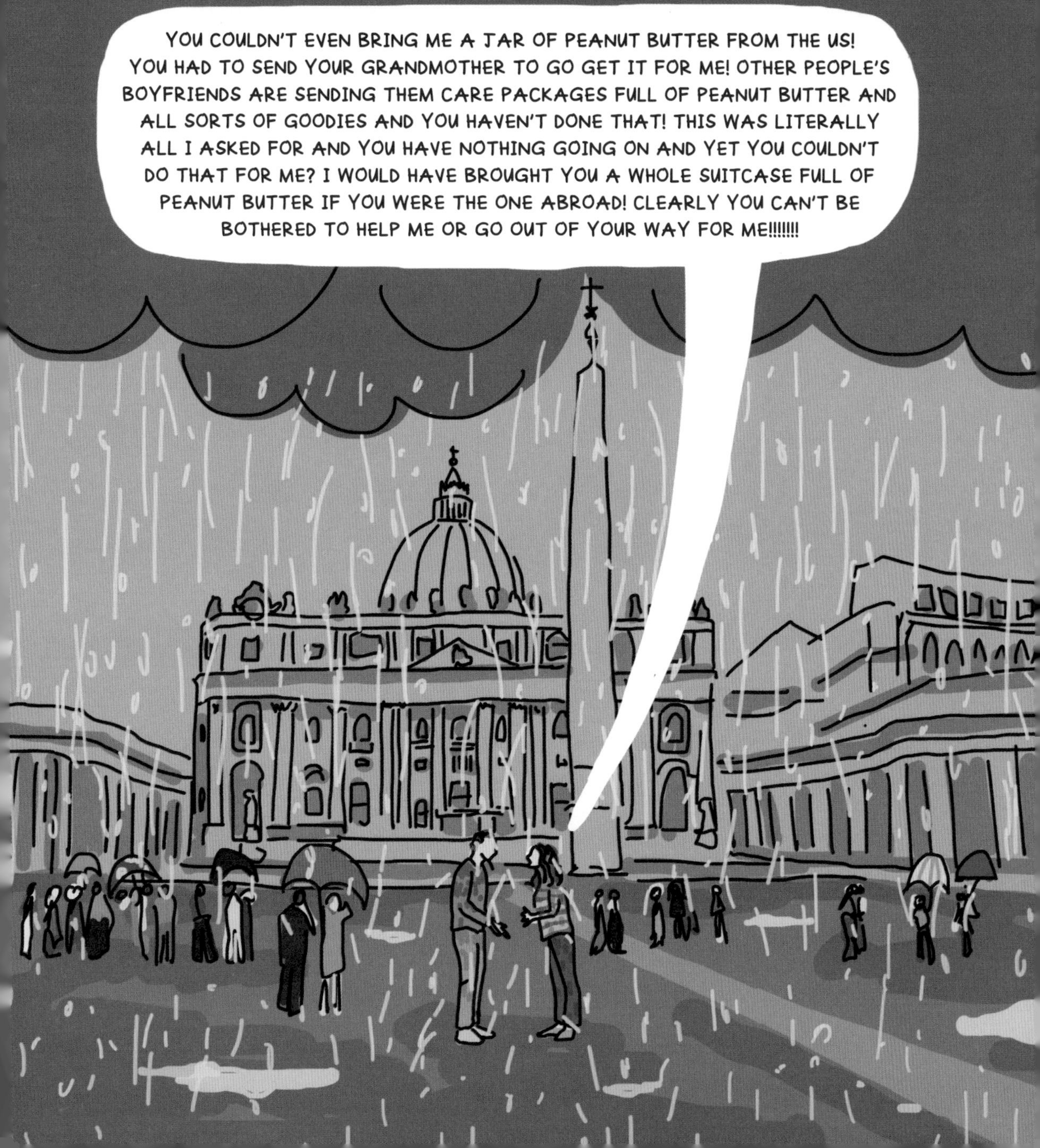
YOU COULDN'T EVEN BRING ME A JAR OF PEANUT BUTTER FROM THE US! YOU HAD TO SEND YOUR GRANDMOTHER TO GO GET IT FOR ME! OTHER PEOPLE'S BOYFRIENDS ARE SENDING THEM CARE PACKAGES FULL OF PEANUT BUTTER AND ALL SORTS OF GOODIES AND YOU HAVEN'T DONE THAT! THIS WAS LITERALLY ALL I ASKED FOR AND YOU HAVE NOTHING GOING ON AND YET YOU COULDN'T DO THAT FOR ME? I WOULD HAVE BROUGHT YOU A WHOLE SUITCASE FULL OF PEANUT BUTTER IF YOU WERE THE ONE ABROAD! CLEARLY YOU CAN'T BE BOTHERED TO HELP ME OR GO OUT OF YOUR WAY FOR ME!!!!!!!

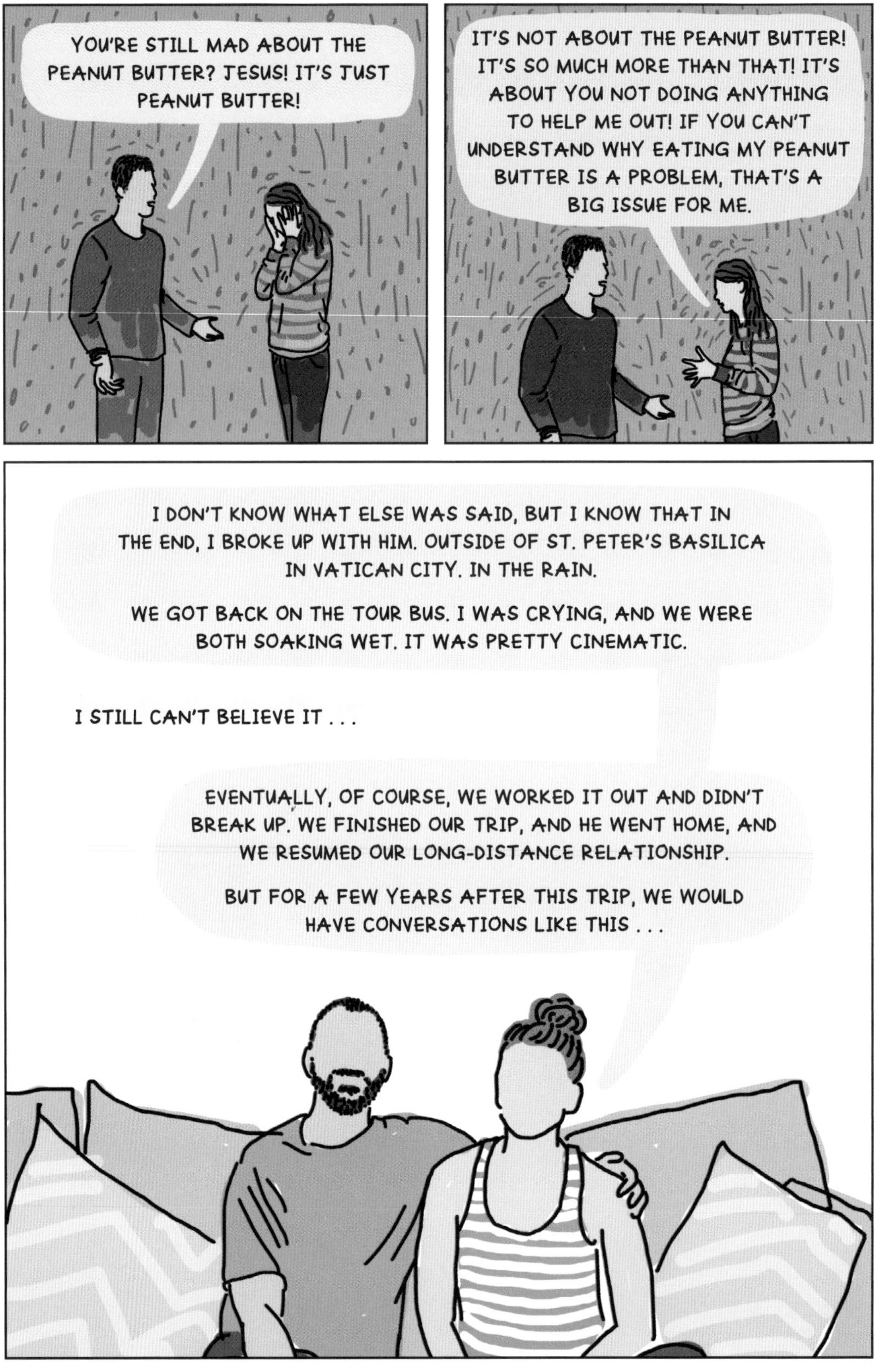
YOU'RE STILL MAD ABOUT THE PEANUT BUTTER? JESUS! IT'S JUST PEANUT BUTTER!
IT'S NOT ABOUT THE PEANUT BUTTER! IT'S SO MUCH MORE THAN THAT! IT'S ABOUT YOU NOT DOING ANYTHING TO HELP ME OUT! IF YOU CAN'T UNDERSTAND WHY EATING MY PEANUT BUTTER IS A PROBLEM, THAT'S A BIG ISSUE FOR ME.
I DON'T KNOW WHAT ELSE WAS SAID, BUT I KNOW THAT IN THE END, I BROKE UP WITH HIM. OUTSIDE OF ST. PETER'S BASILICA IN VATICAN CITY. IN THE RAIN.
WE GOT BACK ON THE TOUR BUS. I WAS CRYING, AND WE WERE BOTH SOAKING WET. IT WAS PRETTY CINEMATIC.
I STILL CAN'T BELIEVE IT . . .
EVENTUALLY, OF COURSE, WE WORKED IT OUT AND DIDN'T BREAK UP. WE FINISHED OUR TRIP, AND HE WENT HOME, AND WE RESUMED OUR LONG-DISTANCE RELATIONSHIP.
BUT FOR A FEW YEARS AFTER THIS TRIP, WE WOULD HAVE CONVERSATIONS LIKE THIS . . .

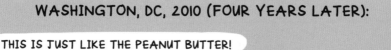

WASHINGTON, DC, 2010 (FOUR YEARS LATER):

THIS IS JUST LIKE THE PEANUT BUTTER!

OH COME ON, IT'S NOTHING LIKE THAT . . . AND I CAME ALL THE WAY TO EUROPE TO VISIT YOU AND YOU BROKE UP WITH ME OVER A JAR OF PEANUT BUTTER! WHO DOES THAT?!?

IT WAS NOT ABOUT THE PEANUT BUTTER! I'VE EXPLAINED THIS TO YOU SO MANY TIMES!!! THE PEANUT BUTTER WAS SYMBOLIC OF YOU THINKING MORE ABOUT YOURSELF THAN YOU DID ABOUT ME!!!

I JUST DIDN'T THINK IT WAS THAT BIG OF A DEAL. EATING THE PEANUT BUTTER HAS NOTHING TO DO WITH HOW MUCH I LOVE YOU.

Over the years, this refrain has become one I use in many instances to make a point: "It's not about the peanut butter."

And it isn't. It's about feeling like my partner wants to help me and wants to make my life better, easier, and more enjoyable. It's about knowing he's thinking of me. It's the small stuff that makes a big impact! Like when he goes out to grab a coffee for himself and brings home a chai tea or a bagel for me.

And now that we have kids, it's about him thinking about them, too. For instance, if we're all home for lunch on a Saturday, I want to know that he's going to make lunch for the kids before making it for himself, instead of making his own lunch and then sitting down to eat while I make lunch for the kids and myself.

Or hey, why don't you throw in a load of the kids' laundry or add some of their clothes into your own load when you're doing *JUST your laundry?*

It really isn't about the peanut butter at all. It's about putting your loved ones' needs and desires before your own. Not all the time, but sometimes . . .

OKAY, SURE, BUT IN ITALY, IT ACTUALLY WAS ABOUT THE PEANUT BUTTER.

WELL, YEAH, OF COURSE IT WAS ABOUT THE PEANUT BUTTER, TOO! I STILL CAN'T BELIEVE YOU DID THAT! AND WITH YOUR FINGER, NONETHELESS! IT'S ALMOST UNFORGIVABLE . . .

ALMOST, BUT NOT QUITE.

MAYBE I SHOULD HAVE CUT MY LOSSES THEN AND THERE?

HA! NO, I THINK YOU MADE THE RIGHT CHOICE.

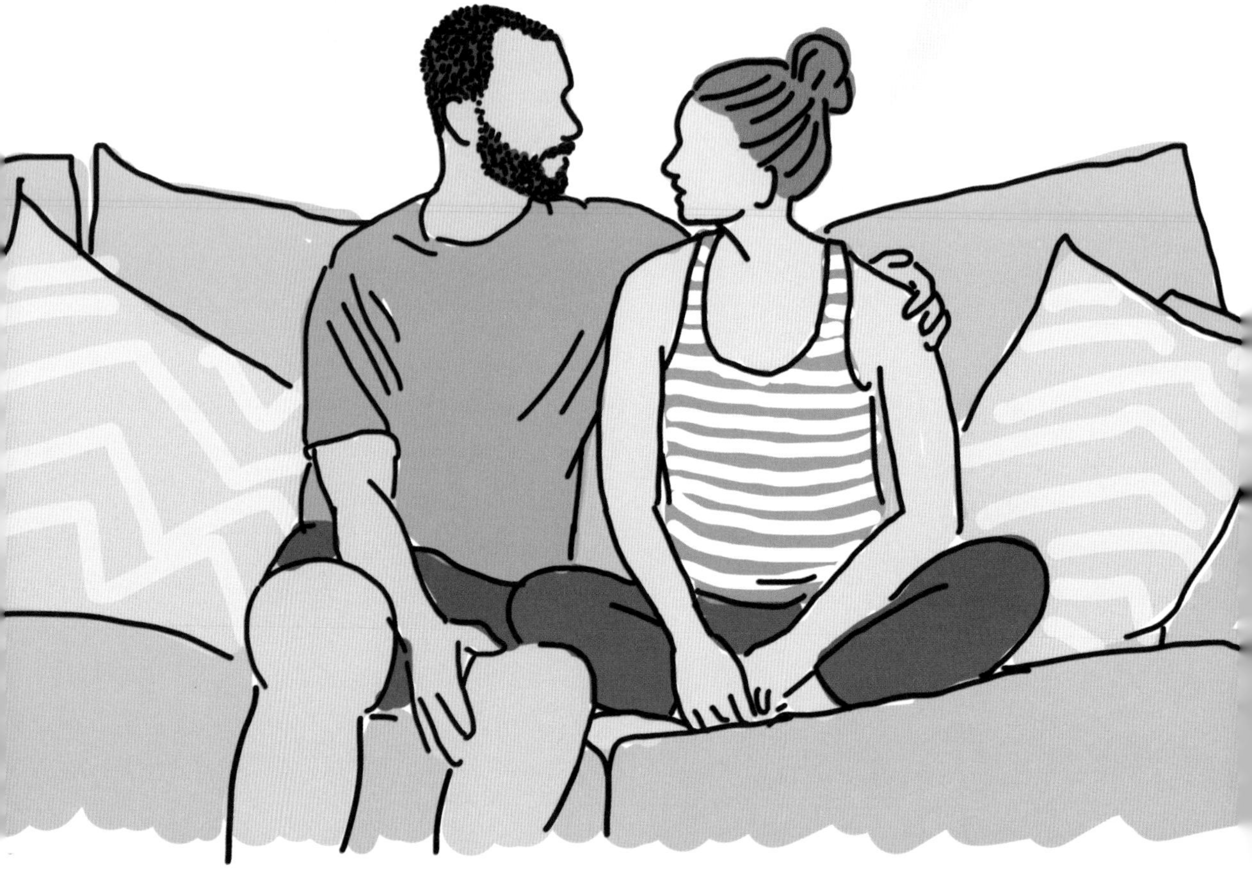

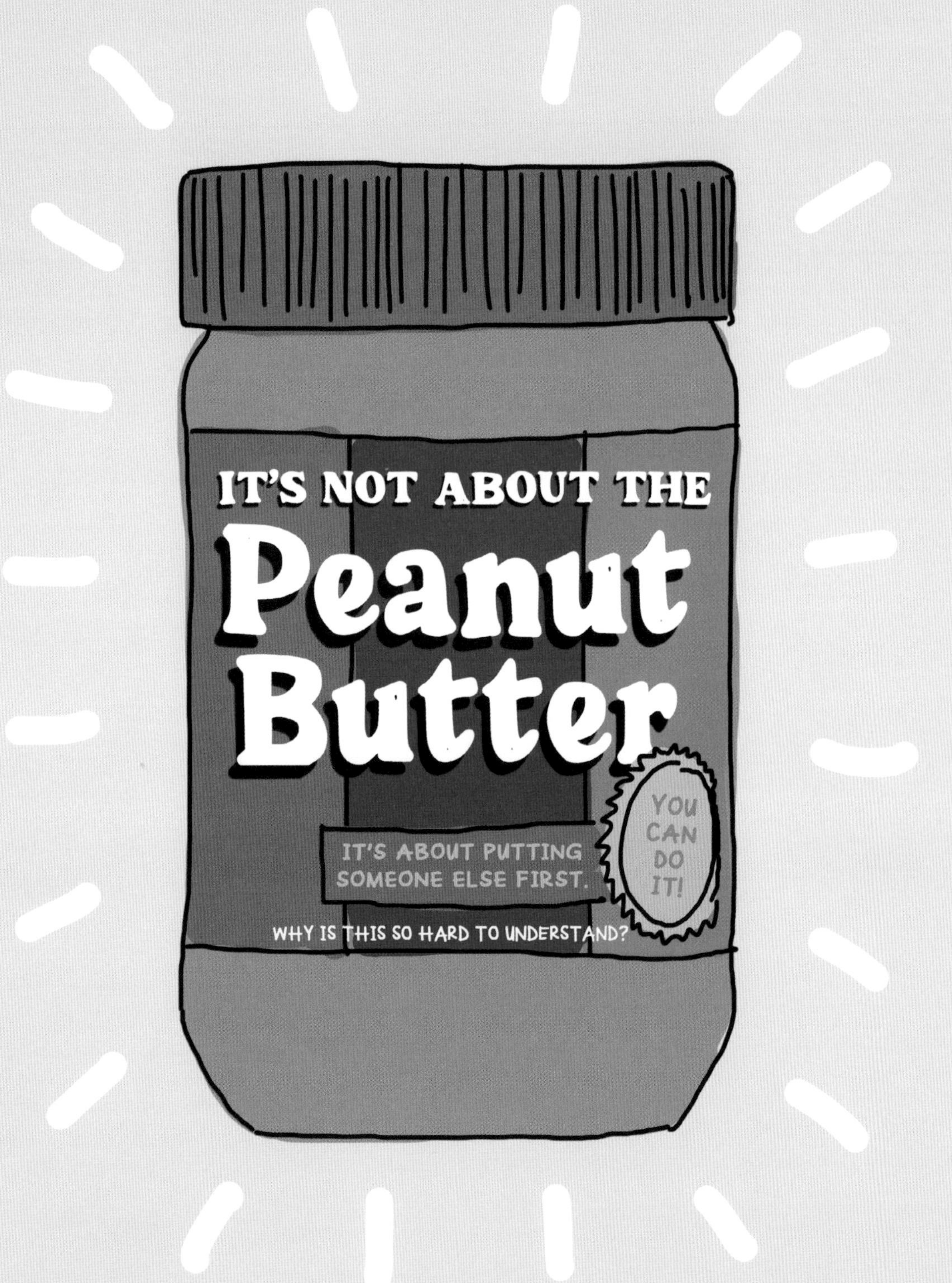
IT'S NOT ABOUT THE
Peanut Butter
IT'S ABOUT PUTTING SOMEONE ELSE FIRST.
YOU CAN DO IT!
WHY IS THIS SO HARD TO UNDERSTAND?

# *THEN* Comes Marriage!

After we'd lived together for a year, we started talking about marriage. I'd been so scared of it for so long, but after we'd been living together, I started to feel ready.

My life had felt really uncertain for so long, but Ben had been by my side for many years at this point, and things felt stable. He made me feel safe and at home. We were such great partners; I wanted to do this life thing with him!

We got married in 2012. I shouldered all of the wedding planning (truly, almost all of it!) but had no idea that this imbalance was a harbinger of things to come. I was into every aesthetic detail of the wedding, and all he cared about was "the food and the music," so I understood it that way. I DIY-ed the hell out of our special day, and it was just as I'd imagined.

At our wedding, we had Ben's grandmother read a poem that perfectly captures how we both feel about marriage. We still reference it all the time (*"I need you to come hold up the ceiling!"*):

A MARRIAGE by Michael Blumenthal

YOU ARE HOLDING UP A CEILING
WITH BOTH ARMS. IT IS VERY HEAVY,
BUT YOU MUST HOLD IT UP, OR ELSE
IT WILL FALL DOWN ON YOU. YOUR ARMS
ARE TIRED, TERRIBLY TIRED,
AND, AS THE DAY GOES ON, IT FEELS
AS IF EITHER YOUR ARMS OR THE CEILING
WILL SOON COLLAPSE.

BUT THEN,
UNEXPECTEDLY,
SOMETHING WONDERFUL HAPPENS:
SOMEONE,
A MAN OR A WOMAN,
WALKS INTO THE ROOM
AND HOLDS THEIR ARMS UP
TO THE CEILING BESIDE YOU.

SO YOU FINALLY GET
TO TAKE DOWN YOUR ARMS.
YOU FEEL THE RELIEF OF RESPITE,
THE BLOOD FLOWING BACK
TO YOUR FINGERS AND ARMS.
AND WHEN YOUR PARTNER'S ARMS TIRE,
YOU HOLD UP YOUR OWN
TO RELIEVE HIM AGAIN.

AND IT CAN GO ON LIKE THIS
FOR MANY YEARS
WITHOUT THE HOUSE FALLING.

From *Against Romance* (Viking-Penguin, 1987), reprinted with permission from the author.

During the seven years we lived together before we became parents, we took turns relieving each other and keeping the house from falling down. Throughout that time period, here's how our division of household labor went:

| BEN | ME | BOTH |
|---|---|---|
| -FOOD PREP | -HOUSEHOLD MANAGEMENT (DECORATING, ORGANIZING, PURCHASING, ETC.) | -GROCERY SHOPPING |
| -COOKING | | -CLEANING |
| -BILLS | -SCHEDULING + PLANNING | -DISHES |
| -INVESTING | | -LAUNDRY |

LOOK HOW EQUAL WE WERE! WE DID EVERYTHING TOGETHER! AND WE HAD FUN WHILE DOING IT, TOO! WE HAD A DISHES SONG WE MADE UP AND WOULD SING WHILE WE DID THE DISHES TOGETHER EVERY NIGHT AFTER DINNER!

After living in DC together for almost four years, we moved to Cape Cod (Ben's hometown). We were married, we'd been together for eight years, and we were ready to settle down.

Childless married life was really good. We got a rescue dog who we treated like a child (she had lots of issues, but man, did we love her). We bought a house. We DIY-ed before moving in. I was the general contractor and designer, and he was the laborer, but we were A TEAM.

Did I do most of the packing, unpacking, and decorating in our new house? Sure. But I enjoyed decorating and wanted it done my way—the right away (of course!). He handled the yard and decking-out our garage workout area. WE WERE A TEAM, GOSHDARNIT!

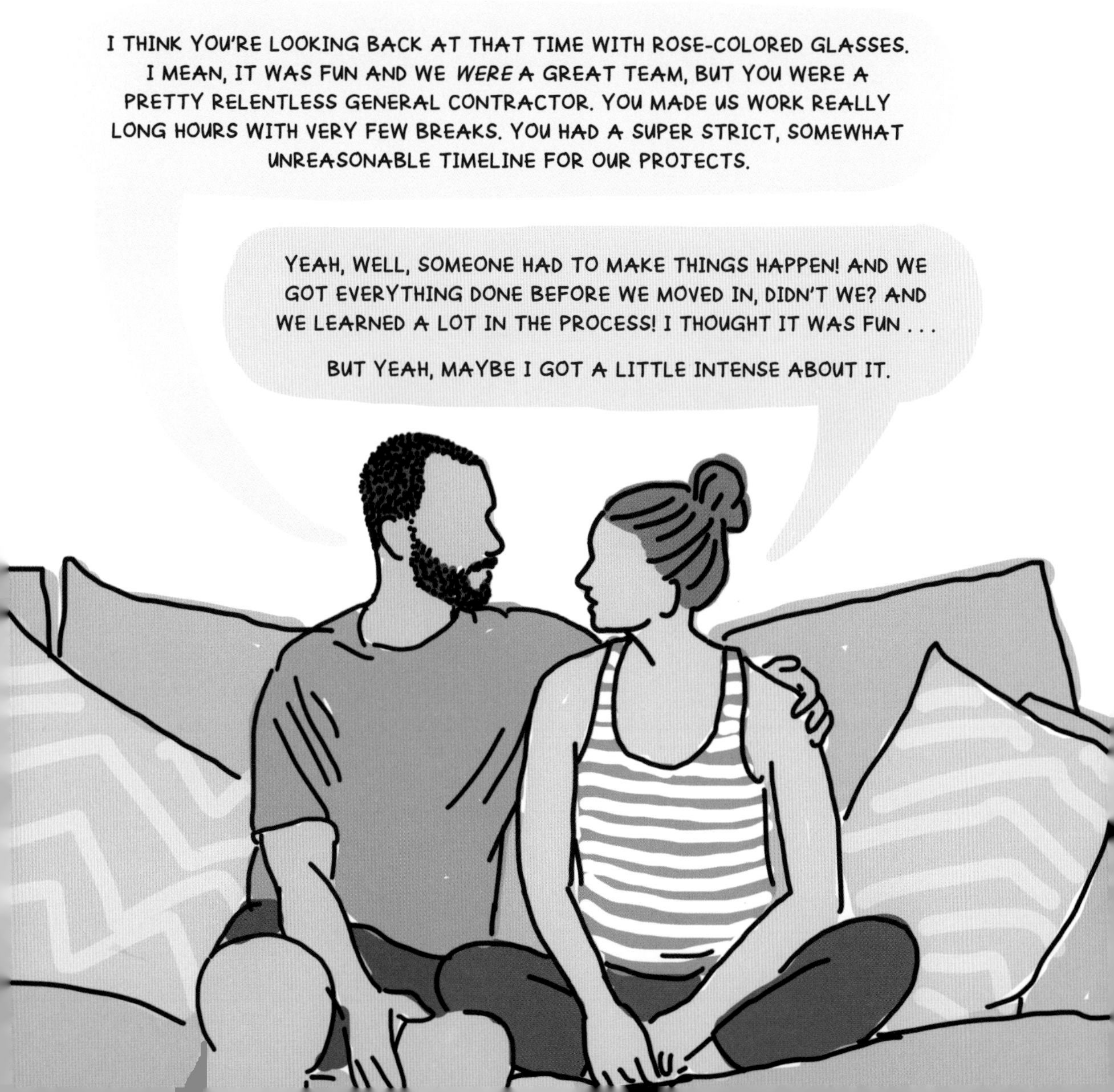
I THINK YOU'RE LOOKING BACK AT THAT TIME WITH ROSE-COLORED GLASSES. I MEAN, IT WAS FUN AND WE *WERE* A GREAT TEAM, BUT YOU WERE A PRETTY RELENTLESS GENERAL CONTRACTOR. YOU MADE US WORK REALLY LONG HOURS WITH VERY FEW BREAKS. YOU HAD A SUPER STRICT, SOMEWHAT UNREASONABLE TIMELINE FOR OUR PROJECTS.
YEAH, WELL, SOMEONE HAD TO MAKE THINGS HAPPEN! AND WE GOT EVERYTHING DONE BEFORE WE MOVED IN, DIDN'T WE? AND WE LEARNED A LOT IN THE PROCESS! I THOUGHT IT WAS FUN . . .
BUT YEAH, MAYBE I GOT A LITTLE INTENSE ABOUT IT.

# Marriage Role Models

As Ben and I settled into our marriage and our new home together, we also began to settle into our household roles. Speaking of roles, there's something else that I want to address before we go any further. It might sound obvious, but it's pretty important.

I grew up as a woman in this world, and Ben grew up as a man. We learned how to be woman and man, wife and husband, and mom and dad from what we saw around us: our own families, our friends' families, popular culture, and society.

Ben's primary role model for a good marriage was his grandparents' relationship, which was as traditional as they come *despite* his grandmother being a feminist (for her time). My grandparents' relationship was similar, and I grew up watching my mom and her sister fuss over and serve my grandfather, too.

MY GRANDFATHER WAS SUCH A PATRIARCH. HE WAS THE ONLY MAN IN THEIR FAMILY OF FOUR, AND HE RULED THE ROOST. LOOKING BACK, IT FEELS SO OLD-FASHIONED!

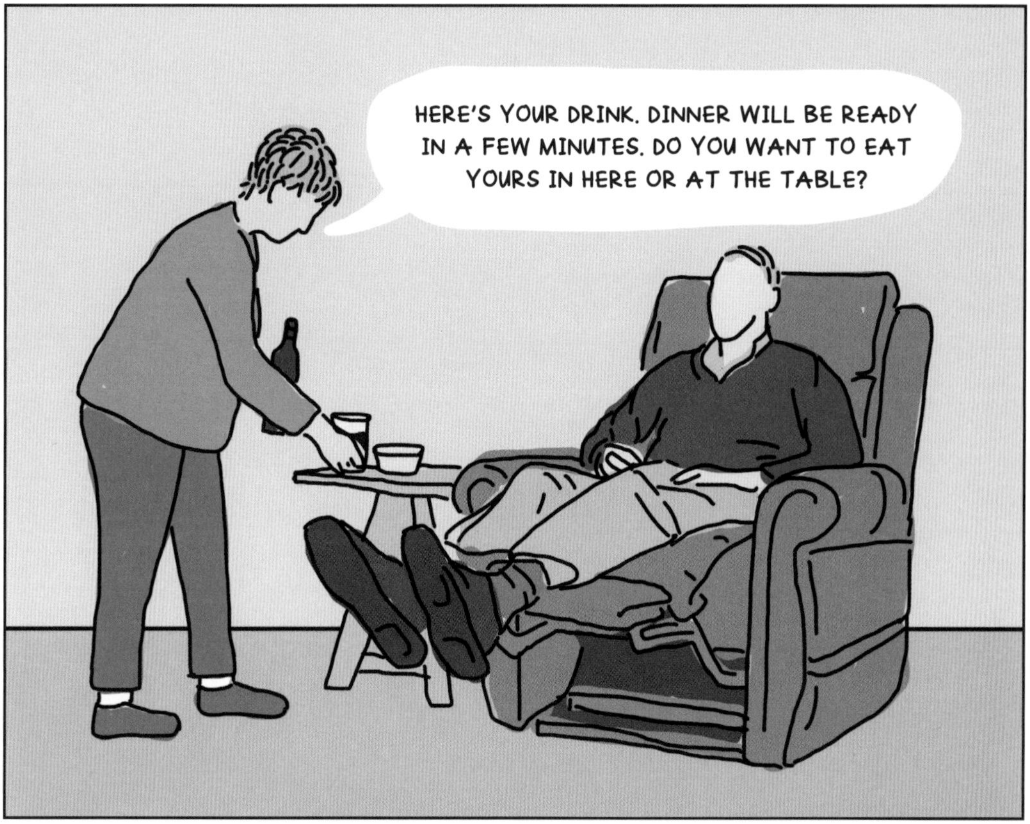
HERE'S YOUR DRINK. DINNER WILL BE READY IN A FEW MINUTES. DO YOU WANT TO EAT YOURS IN HERE OR AT THE TABLE?

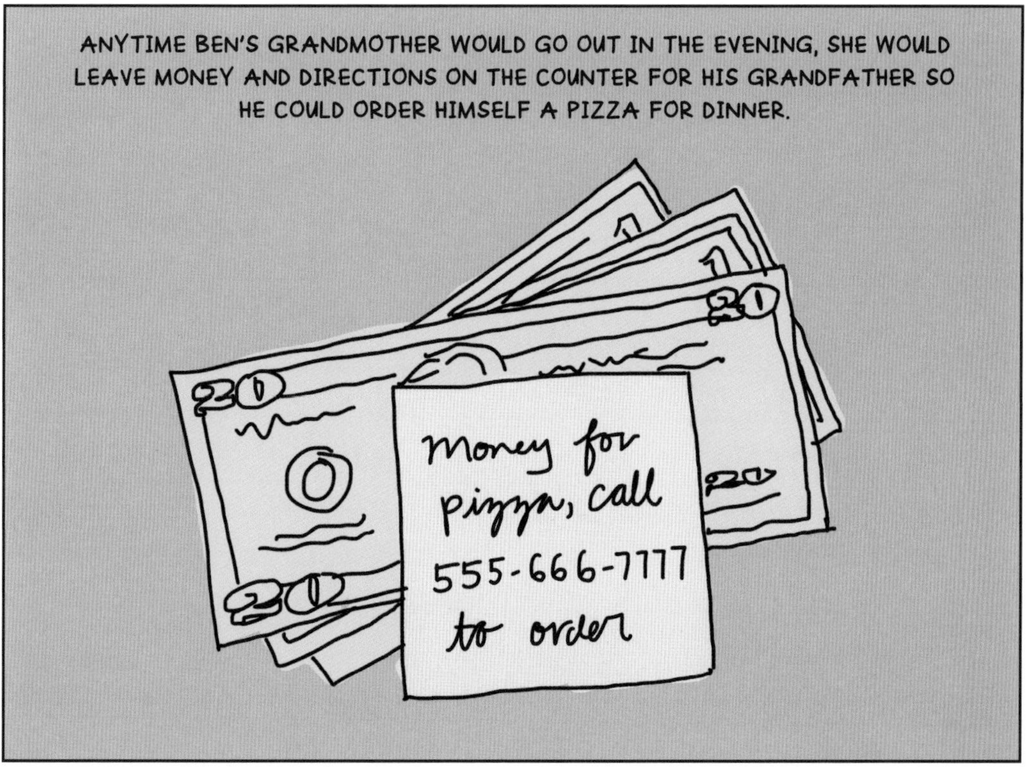
ANYTIME BEN'S GRANDMOTHER WOULD GO OUT IN THE EVENING, SHE WOULD LEAVE MONEY AND DIRECTIONS ON THE COUNTER FOR HIS GRANDFATHER SO HE COULD ORDER HIMSELF A PIZZA FOR DINNER.
money for pizza, call 555-666-7777 to order

My primary role model of what it means to be a woman, mother, and wife in this world was my mom—a stay-at-home mom who carried the heavy mental load of our (always clean) household mostly on her own. Although she never said anything like this aloud, her actions inadvertently taught me that as a woman and a mother, a big part of your value lies in how much you can get done, how hard you work, how clean your house is, and how much of yourself you give up to care for your family. (I know she learned this from her mother, who probably learned it from hers . . . )

My mom did everything for everyone.

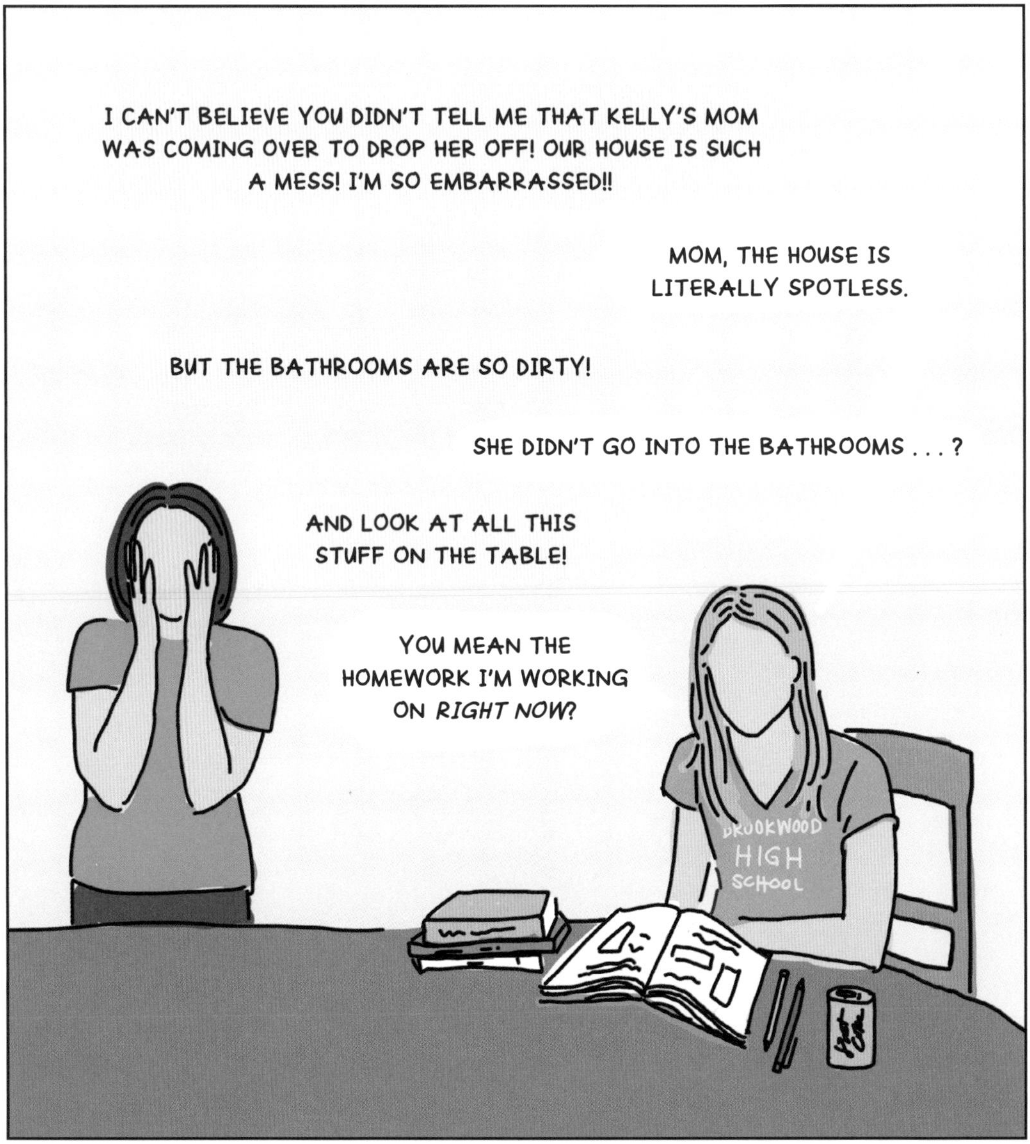
I CAN'T BELIEVE YOU DIDN'T TELL ME THAT KELLY'S MOM WAS COMING OVER TO DROP HER OFF! OUR HOUSE IS SUCH A MESS! I'M SO EMBARRASSED!!
MOM, THE HOUSE IS LITERALLY SPOTLESS.
BUT THE BATHROOMS ARE SO DIRTY!
SHE DIDN'T GO INTO THE BATHROOMS . . . ?
AND LOOK AT ALL THIS STUFF ON THE TABLE!
YOU MEAN THE HOMEWORK I'M WORKING ON *RIGHT NOW*?
BROOKWOOD HIGH SCHOOL

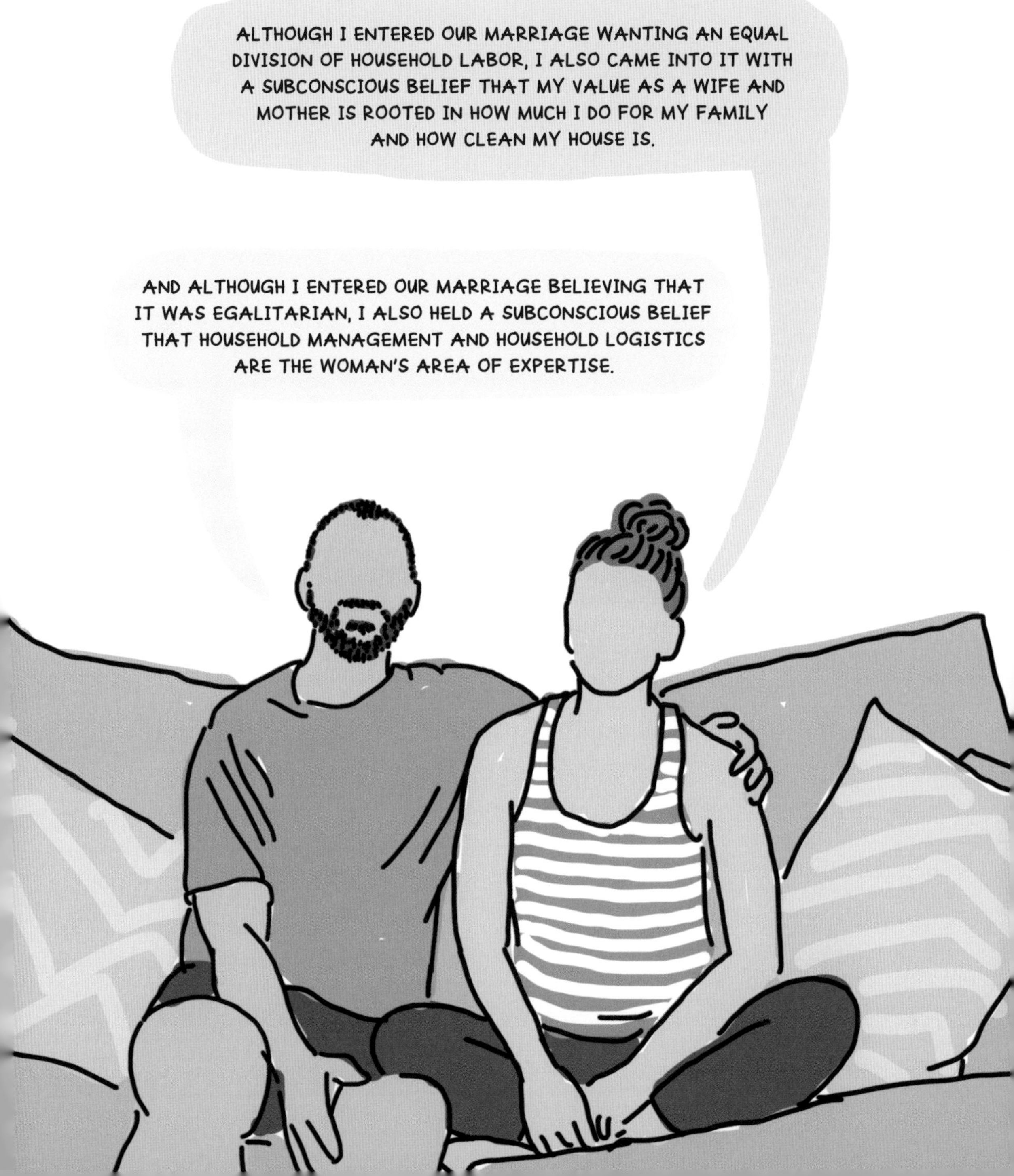
ALTHOUGH I ENTERED OUR MARRIAGE WANTING AN EQUAL DIVISION OF HOUSEHOLD LABOR, I ALSO CAME INTO IT WITH A SUBCONSCIOUS BELIEF THAT MY VALUE AS A WIFE AND MOTHER IS ROOTED IN HOW MUCH I DO FOR MY FAMILY AND HOW CLEAN MY HOUSE IS.
AND ALTHOUGH I ENTERED OUR MARRIAGE BELIEVING THAT IT WAS EGALITARIAN, I ALSO HELD A SUBCONSCIOUS BELIEF THAT HOUSEHOLD MANAGEMENT AND HOUSEHOLD LOGISTICS ARE THE WOMAN'S AREA OF EXPERTISE.

# Societal Expectations

Oh, and there's one more super obvious point I want to make here: Ben is a middle-class white male.

He was born and raised in a system that rolled out the red carpet for him. He hasn't had a lot of societal adversity. He hasn't ever felt like a second-class citizen, and for much of his life, people (women) have done things for him. This doesn't mean that his life has been easy (he's had lots of challenges thrown his way), but the challenges he's encountered haven't been cultural or societal.

I am a middle-class white woman. Although I, too, am very privileged, I have grown up in a society that was not built for women. The world has taught me that I have to work way harder than the average man in order to succeed and that I should be able to do everything all at once while feeling guilty about everything I'm not doing—and if I can't, I am a failure. Oh, and don't forget to be thin and look pretty while you're doing everything for everyone (perfectly).

OH! And don't be bossy, and don't forget to smile, and don't you dare talk about inequality or you're a whiny, narcissistic, ungrateful feminist bitch. So there's that.

In 2015, we decided to try to start a family. We'd been together for more than ten years and felt as ready as we were ever going to be: Ben was working as a prosecutor for the local district attorney's office. I was teaching yoga, leading workshops and retreats, and running my graphic design/consulting/illustration/custom art business. We were both working hard and spending our downtime together or working on our house.

As a couple, we'd been through a lot; we'd gone through big losses, big disappointments, tough family issues, lots of changes and moves, and big fights . . . and for all of these reasons, I truly thought we were prepared for any challenges that becoming parents would throw our way.

We knew it was supposed to be really hard. We knew we were supposed to "sleep while you can!" But knowing these things and experiencing them firsthand are two very different things.

Looking back, we were COMPLETELY CLUELESS about what parenthood had in store for us.

LIKE SO MANY CHILD-FREE COUPLES WHO CAME BEFORE US, WE KIND OF THOUGHT THAT TAKING CARE OF OUR NEEDY RESCUE DOG WAS SIMILAR TO WHAT HAVING A BABY WOULD BE LIKE. HAHAHAHAHAHAHAHAHA!

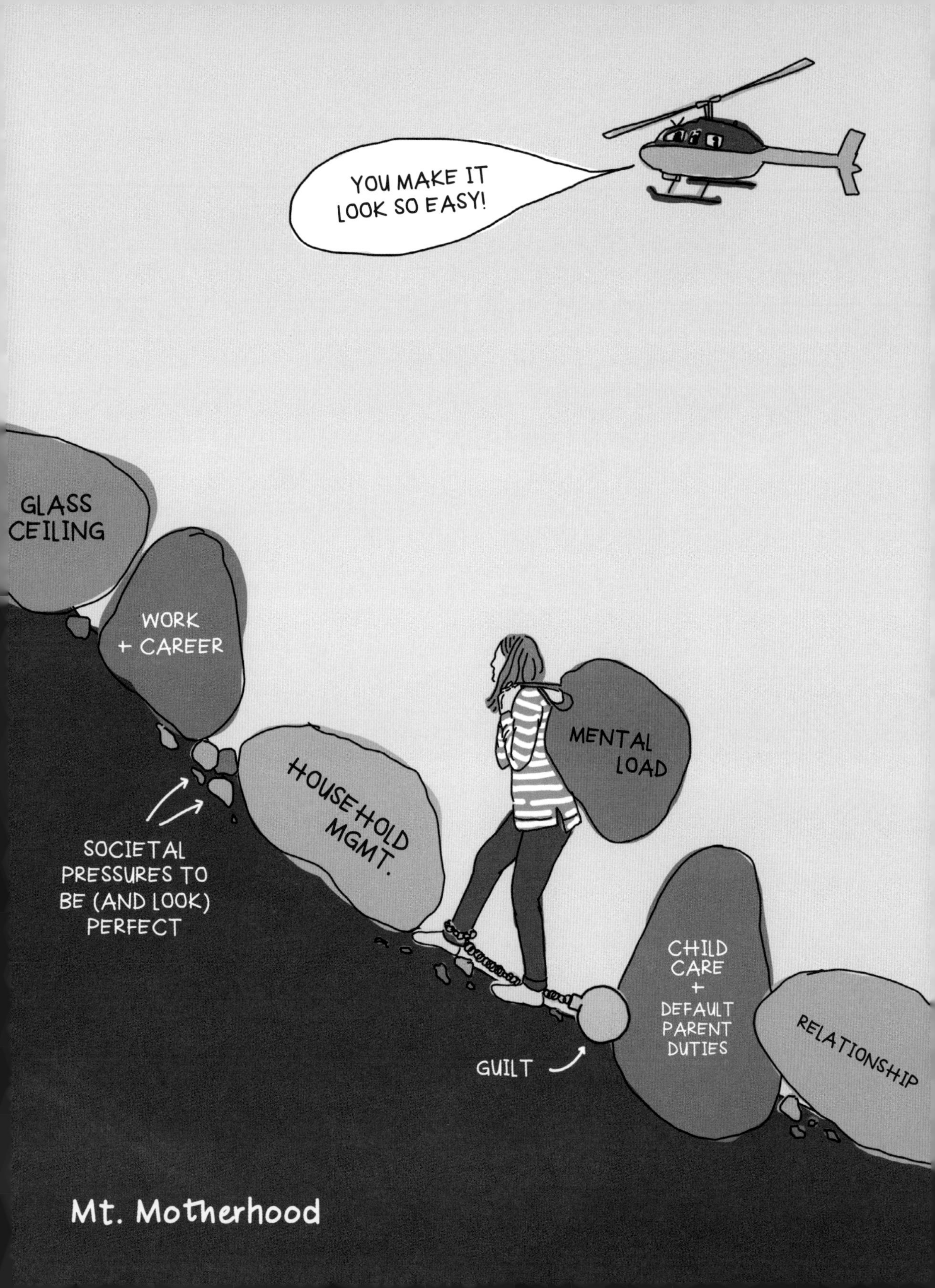
YOU MAKE IT LOOK SO EASY!
GLASS CEILING
WORK + CAREER
HOUSEHOLD MGMT.
MENTAL LOAD
SOCIETAL PRESSURES TO BE (AND LOOK) PERFECT
CHILD CARE + DEFAULT PARENT DUTIES
RELATIONSHIP
GUILT
Mt. Motherhood

# We're in the Area. Can We Stop By and Say Hi?

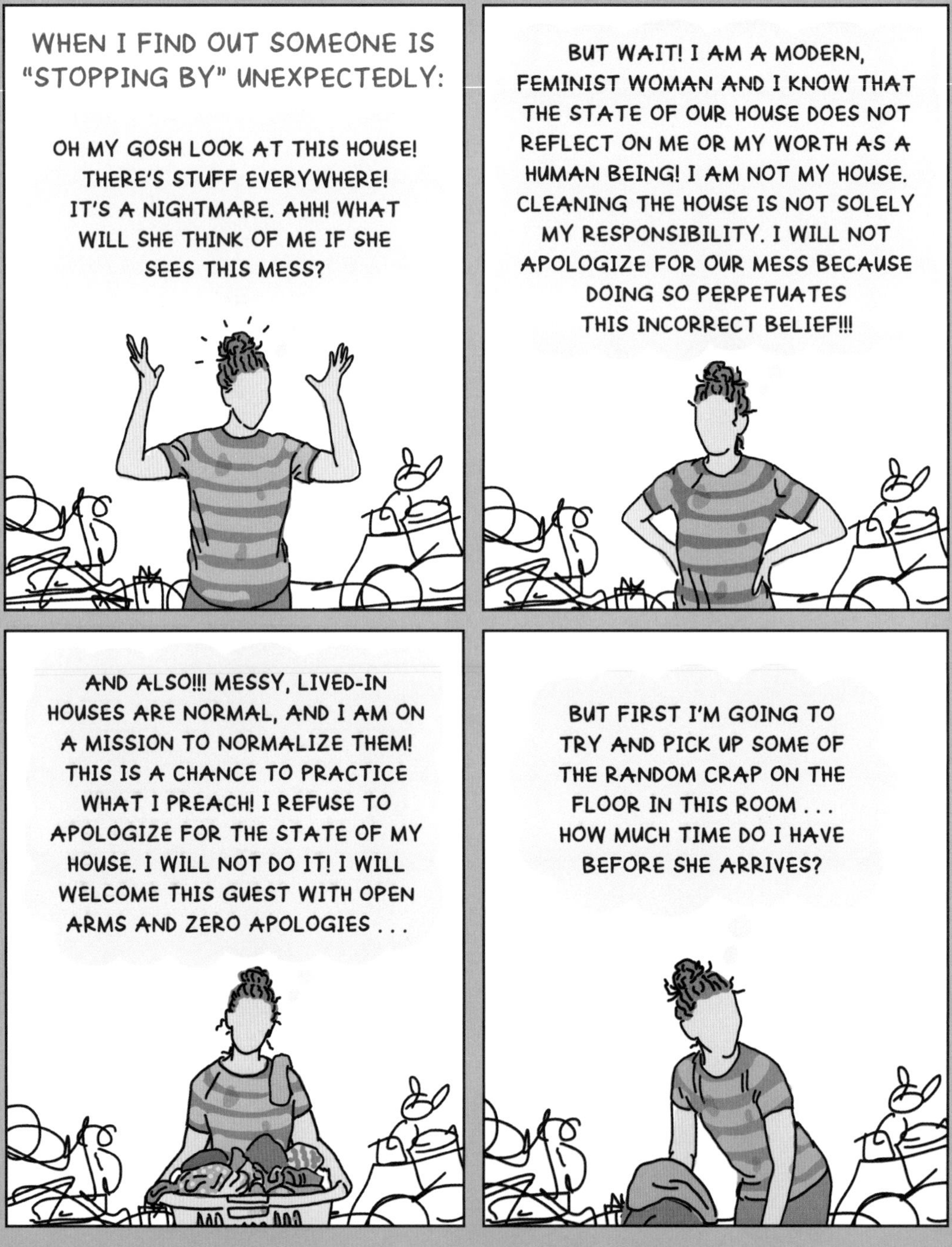
WHEN I FIND OUT SOMEONE IS "STOPPING BY" UNEXPECTEDLY:
OH MY GOSH LOOK AT THIS HOUSE! THERE'S STUFF EVERYWHERE! IT'S A NIGHTMARE. AHH! WHAT WILL SHE THINK OF ME IF SHE SEES THIS MESS?
BUT WAIT! I AM A MODERN, FEMINIST WOMAN AND I KNOW THAT THE STATE OF OUR HOUSE DOES NOT REFLECT ON ME OR MY WORTH AS A HUMAN BEING! I AM NOT MY HOUSE. CLEANING THE HOUSE IS NOT SOLELY MY RESPONSIBILITY. I WILL NOT APOLOGIZE FOR OUR MESS BECAUSE DOING SO PERPETUATES THIS INCORRECT BELIEF!!!
AND ALSO!!! MESSY, LIVED-IN HOUSES ARE NORMAL, AND I AM ON A MISSION TO NORMALIZE THEM! THIS IS A CHANCE TO PRACTICE WHAT I PREACH! I REFUSE TO APOLOGIZE FOR THE STATE OF MY HOUSE. I WILL NOT DO IT! I WILL WELCOME THIS GUEST WITH OPEN ARMS AND ZERO APOLOGIES . . .
BUT FIRST I'M GOING TO TRY AND PICK UP SOME OF THE RANDOM CRAP ON THE FLOOR IN THIS ROOM . . . HOW MUCH TIME DO I HAVE BEFORE SHE ARRIVES?

<KNOCK! KNOCK!>
OH NO!
HELLO? I'M HERE!
AGHH! I'M SO SORRY THE HOUSE IS SUCH A MESS! WE'RE SUCH A MESS! I'M HORRIFIED! I SUCK! I'M THE WORST MOM EVER!

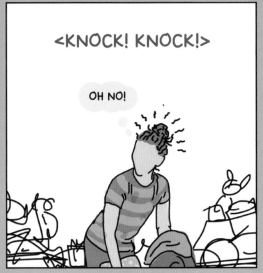

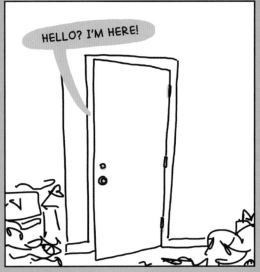

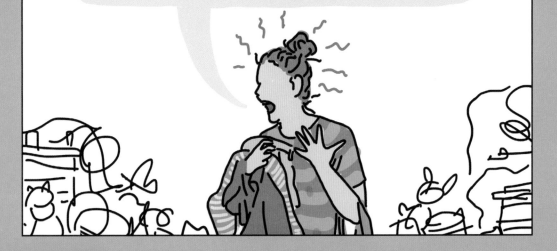

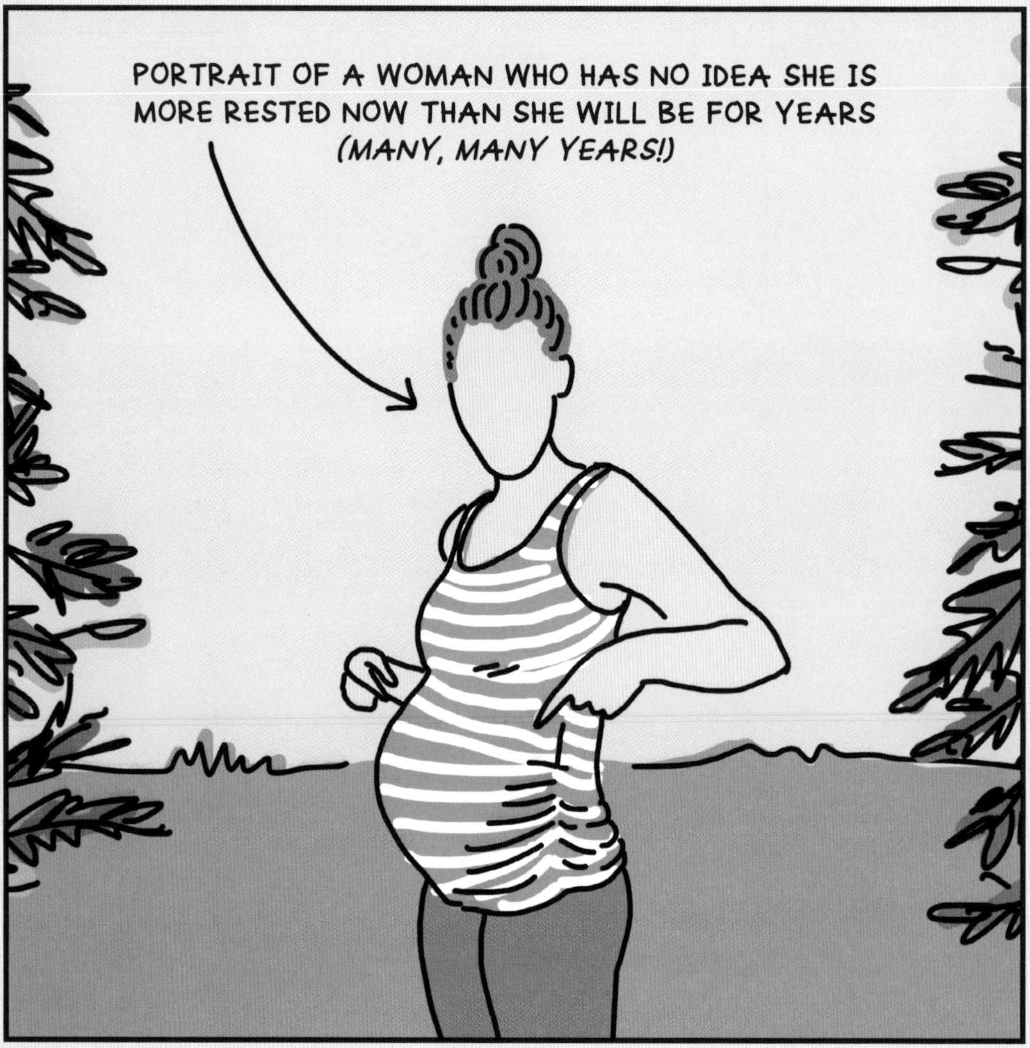
PORTRAIT OF A WOMAN WHO HAS NO IDEA SHE IS MORE RESTED NOW THAN SHE WILL BE FOR YEARS
(MANY, MANY YEARS!)

# CHAPTER 2

# We're Having a Baby! (And So It Begins . . . )

# That Pregnancy Glow

Don't hate me, but I loved being pregnant. Both times.

IT WAS ONE OF MY FEW MOTHERHOOD-RELATED WINS IN THE EARLY YEARS, SO JUST LET ME HAVE IT, OKAY?!

Sure, I had the usual aches and pains and complaints (and tons of anxiety, OBVIOUSLY), but overall, pregnancy was great for me.

But you know what wasn't so great? Being in charge of ALL of the pre-baby planning. In fact, looking back, it's become clear to me that our household imbalance started when I was pregnant.

Throughout my pregnancy, I had a never-ending "household" to-do list of items that needed to be done "before baby"; Ben didn't. To be fair, he did have to deal with some of the logistics of bringing a new baby into the world, but just as is the case now, they were the one-and-done kinds of tasks . . .

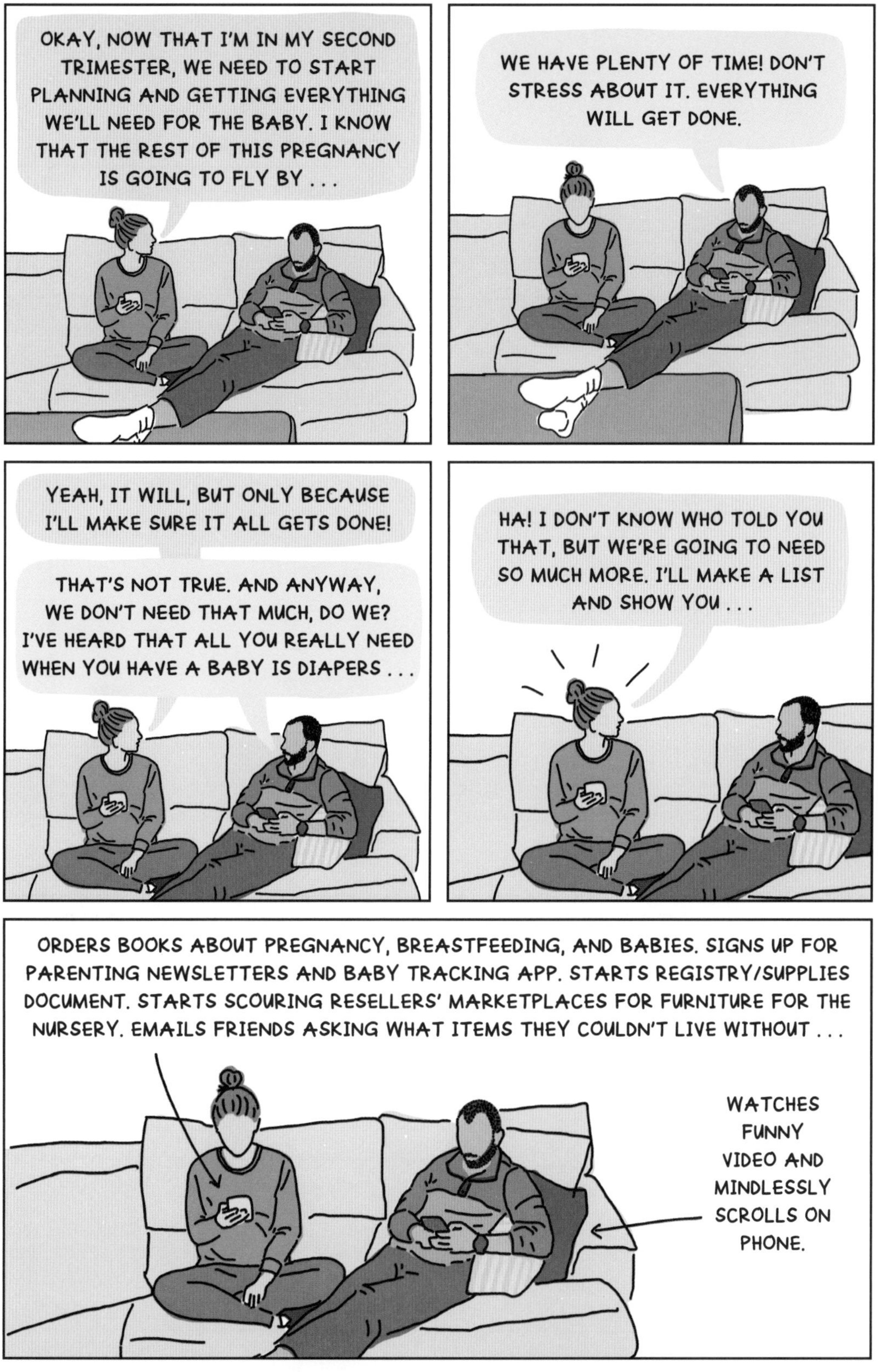
OKAY, NOW THAT I'M IN MY SECOND TRIMESTER, WE NEED TO START PLANNING AND GETTING EVERYTHING WE'LL NEED FOR THE BABY. I KNOW THAT THE REST OF THIS PREGNANCY IS GOING TO FLY BY . . .
WE HAVE PLENTY OF TIME! DON'T STRESS ABOUT IT. EVERYTHING WILL GET DONE.
YEAH, IT WILL, BUT ONLY BECAUSE I'LL MAKE SURE IT ALL GETS DONE!
THAT'S NOT TRUE. AND ANYWAY, WE DON'T NEED THAT MUCH, DO WE? I'VE HEARD THAT ALL YOU REALLY NEED WHEN YOU HAVE A BABY IS DIAPERS . . .
HA! I DON'T KNOW WHO TOLD YOU THAT, BUT WE'RE GOING TO NEED SO MUCH MORE. I'LL MAKE A LIST AND SHOW YOU . . .
ORDERS BOOKS ABOUT PREGNANCY, BREASTFEEDING, AND BABIES. SIGNS UP FOR PARENTING NEWSLETTERS AND BABY TRACKING APP. STARTS REGISTRY/SUPPLIES DOCUMENT. STARTS SCOURING RESELLERS' MARKETPLACES FOR FURNITURE FOR THE NURSERY. EMAILS FRIENDS ASKING WHAT ITEMS THEY COULDN'T LIVE WITHOUT . . .
WATCHES FUNNY VIDEO AND MINDLESSLY SCROLLS ON PHONE.

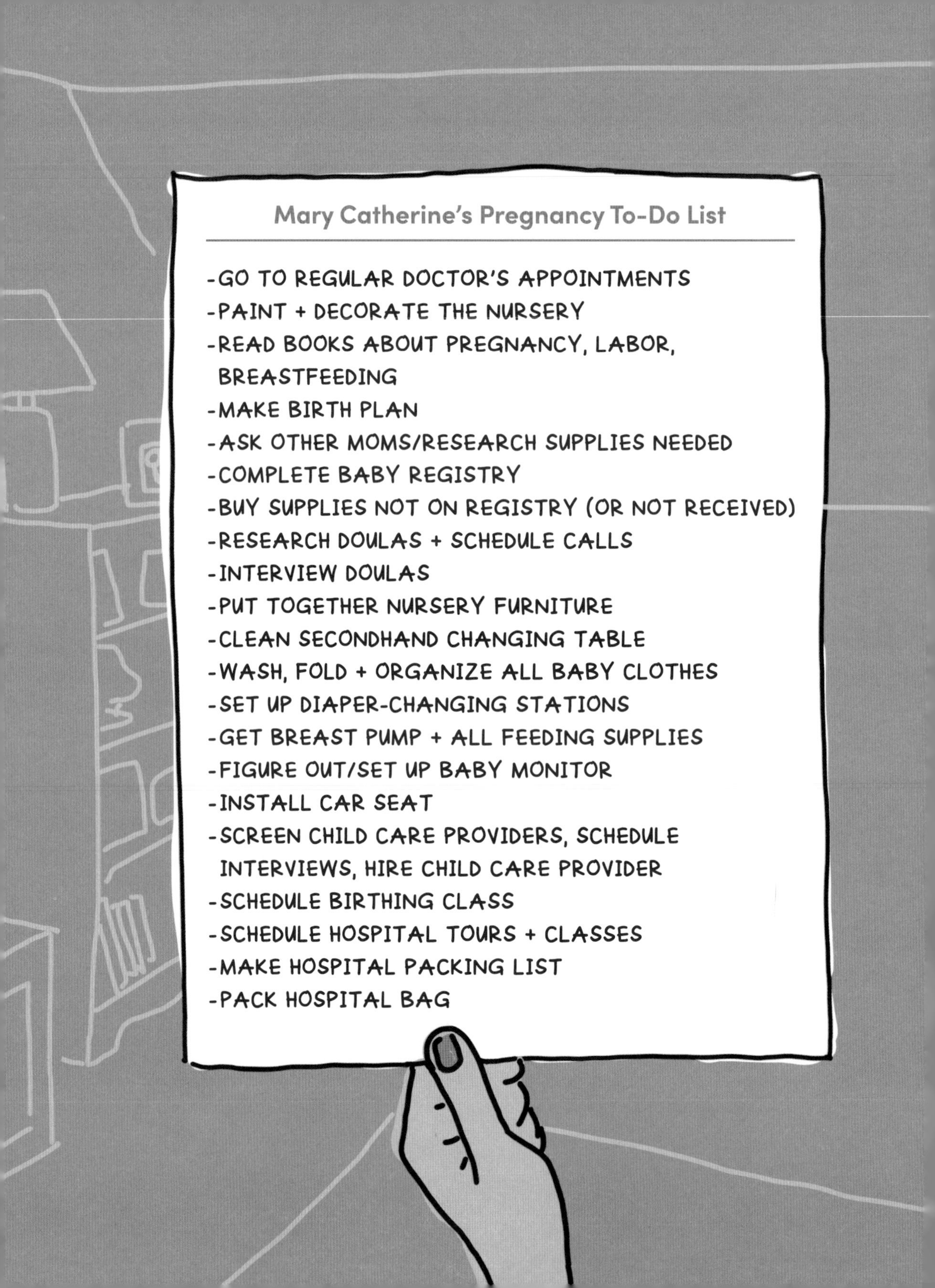

# Mary Catherine's Pregnancy To-Do List

- GO TO REGULAR DOCTOR'S APPOINTMENTS
- PAINT + DECORATE THE NURSERY
- READ BOOKS ABOUT PREGNANCY, LABOR, BREASTFEEDING
- MAKE BIRTH PLAN
- ASK OTHER MOMS/RESEARCH SUPPLIES NEEDED
- COMPLETE BABY REGISTRY
- BUY SUPPLIES NOT ON REGISTRY (OR NOT RECEIVED)
- RESEARCH DOULAS + SCHEDULE CALLS
- INTERVIEW DOULAS
- PUT TOGETHER NURSERY FURNITURE
- CLEAN SECONDHAND CHANGING TABLE
- WASH, FOLD + ORGANIZE ALL BABY CLOTHES
- SET UP DIAPER-CHANGING STATIONS
- GET BREAST PUMP + ALL FEEDING SUPPLIES
- FIGURE OUT/SET UP BABY MONITOR
- INSTALL CAR SEAT
- SCREEN CHILD CARE PROVIDERS, SCHEDULE INTERVIEWS, HIRE CHILD CARE PROVIDER
- SCHEDULE BIRTHING CLASS
- SCHEDULE HOSPITAL TOURS + CLASSES
- MAKE HOSPITAL PACKING LIST
- PACK HOSPITAL BAG

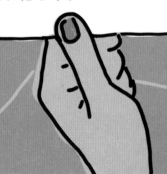

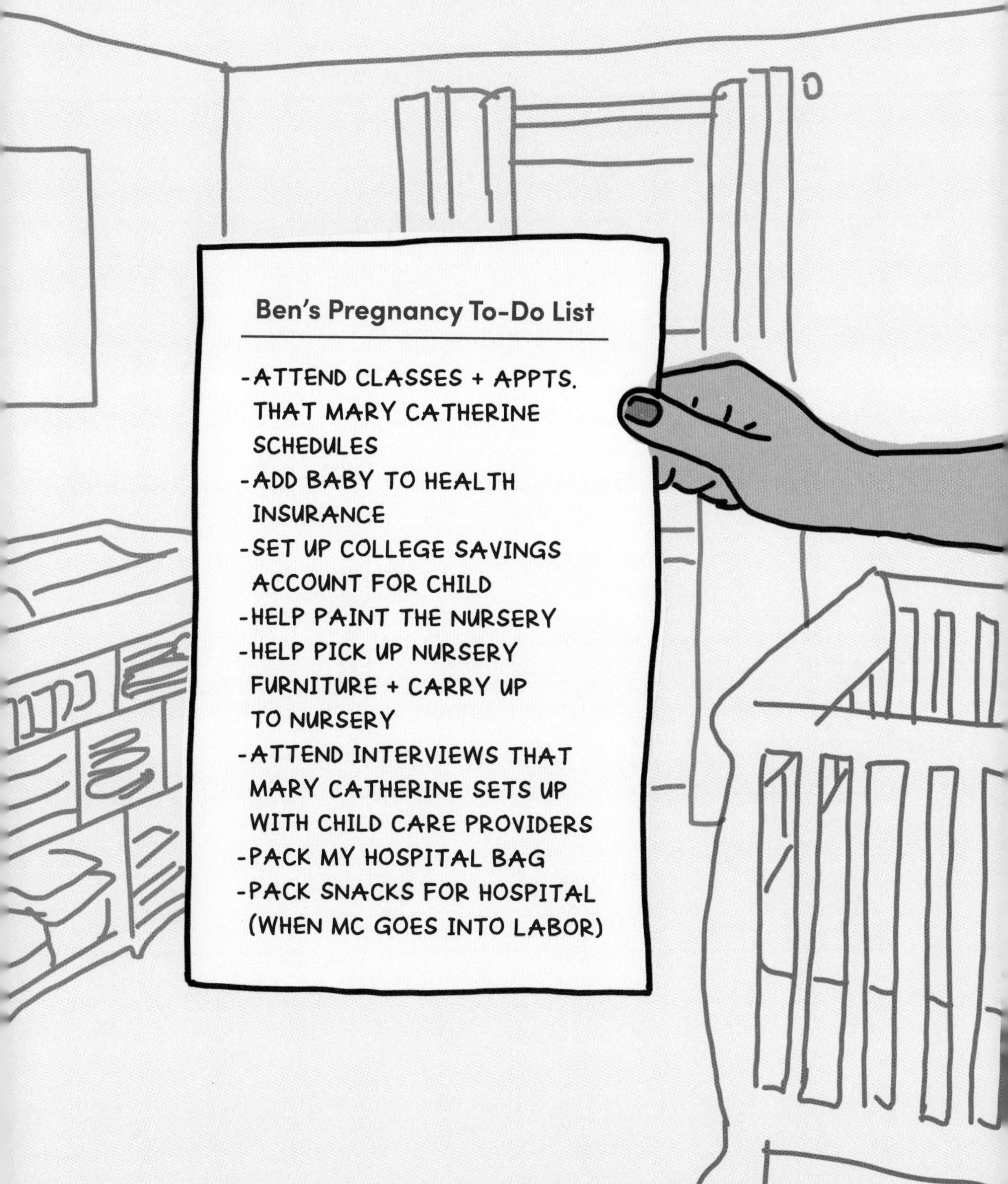
Ben's Pregnancy To-Do List
-ATTEND CLASSES + APPTS. THAT MARY CATHERINE SCHEDULES
-ADD BABY TO HEALTH INSURANCE
-SET UP COLLEGE SAVINGS ACCOUNT FOR CHILD
-HELP PAINT THE NURSERY
-HELP PICK UP NURSERY FURNITURE + CARRY UP TO NURSERY
-ATTEND INTERVIEWS THAT MARY CATHERINE SETS UP WITH CHILD CARE PROVIDERS
-PACK MY HOSPITAL BAG
-PACK SNACKS FOR HOSPITAL (WHEN MC GOES INTO LABOR)

Ben didn't read a single book about parenthood or babies. He didn't take a very active role in planning the birth or decorating the nursery or making our registry or buying ANYTHING we would need to care for our baby.

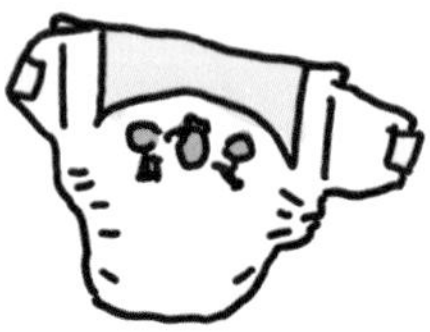

I'm the one who handled, washed, and put away every single item of clothing that we got for our new baby. I purchased her diapers. I read the books. I asked my friends for advice.

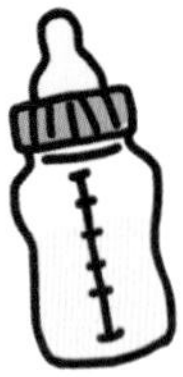

I know that Ben was thinking a lot about what life would look like once we were parents and that he was going through his own pre-baby-related stress and anxiety (because of course we talked about this!), but that ruminating didn't translate into action steps or practical learning that would help him care for our new baby and navigate the baby-related supplies when the time came to use them.

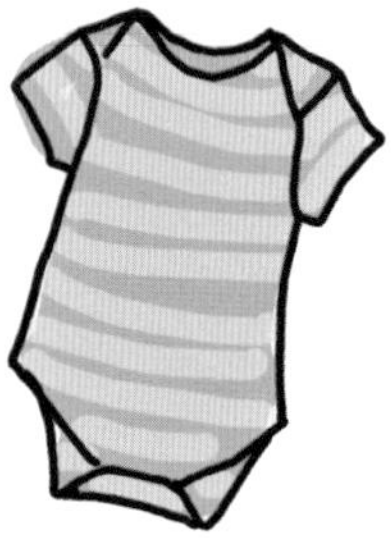

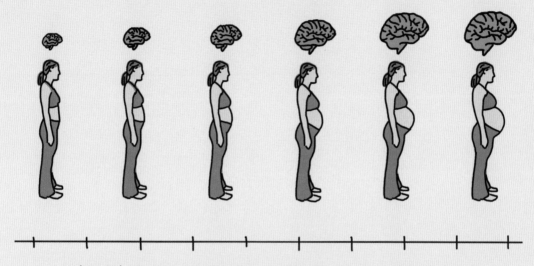

MY BABY-RELATED GROWTH OVER THE COURSE OF MY PREGNANCY

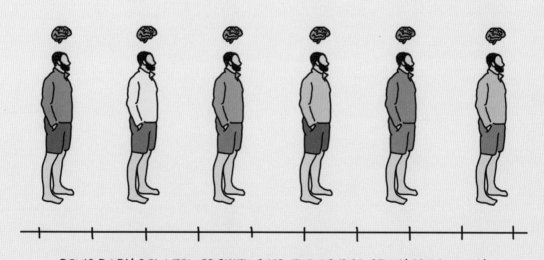

BEN'S BABY-RELATED GROWTH OVER THE COURSE OF MY PREGNANCY

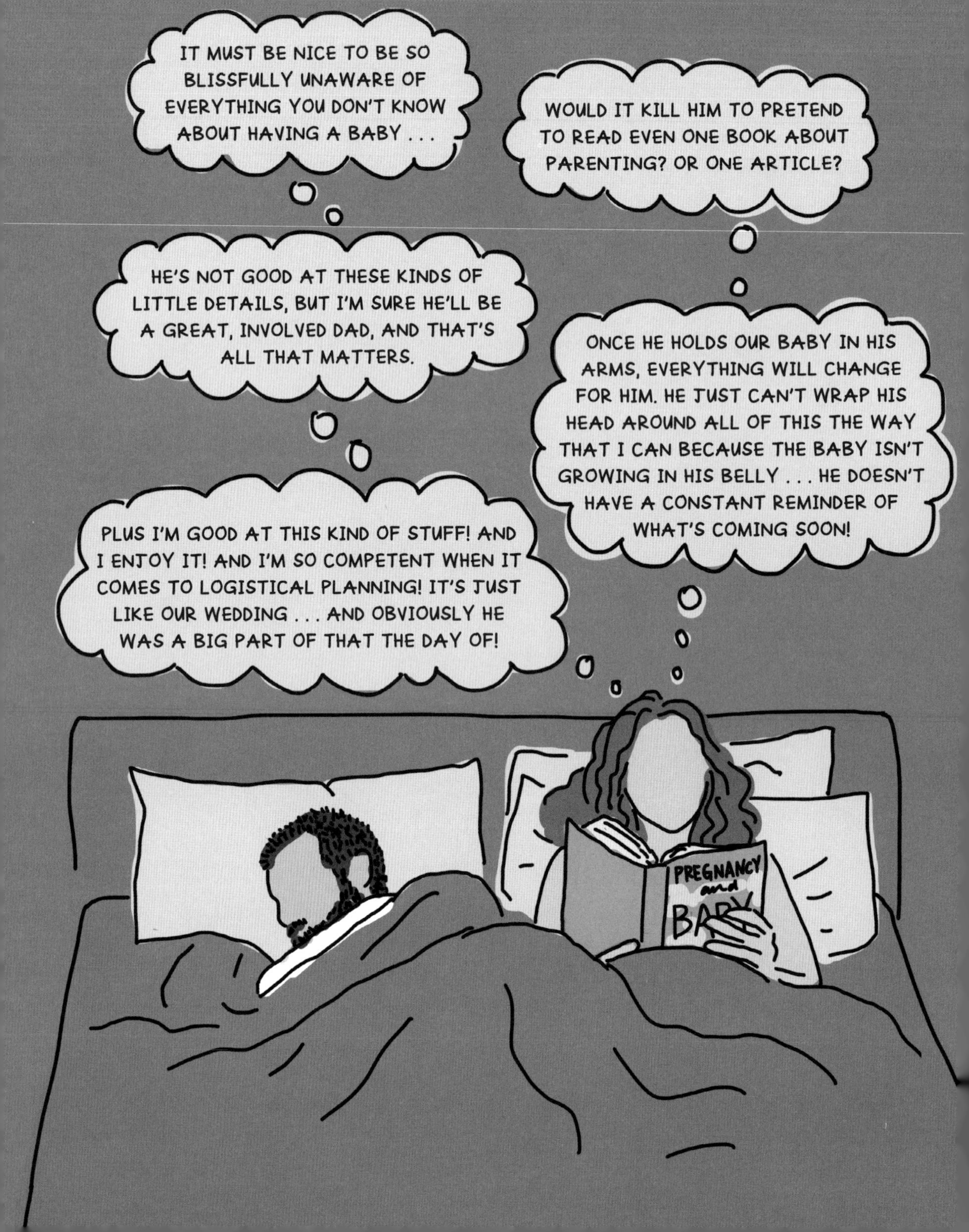
IT MUST BE NICE TO BE SO BLISSFULLY UNAWARE OF EVERYTHING YOU DON'T KNOW ABOUT HAVING A BABY . . .
WOULD IT KILL HIM TO PRETEND TO READ EVEN ONE BOOK ABOUT PARENTING? OR ONE ARTICLE?
HE'S NOT GOOD AT THESE KINDS OF LITTLE DETAILS, BUT I'M SURE HE'LL BE A GREAT, INVOLVED DAD, AND THAT'S ALL THAT MATTERS.
ONCE HE HOLDS OUR BABY IN HIS ARMS, EVERYTHING WILL CHANGE FOR HIM. HE JUST CAN'T WRAP HIS HEAD AROUND ALL OF THIS THE WAY THAT I CAN BECAUSE THE BABY ISN'T GROWING IN HIS BELLY . . . HE DOESN'T HAVE A CONSTANT REMINDER OF WHAT'S COMING SOON!
PLUS I'M GOOD AT THIS KIND OF STUFF! AND I ENJOY IT! AND I'M SO COMPETENT WHEN IT COMES TO LOGISTICAL PLANNING! IT'S JUST LIKE OUR WEDDING . . . AND OBVIOUSLY HE WAS A BIG PART OF THAT THE DAY OF!
PREGNANCY and BABY

What I didn't understand at the time was that with every new baby supply I set up, with every page I read, with every clothing item I bought for when the baby was 6 or 12 or 18 months old, I was taking on more and more of the future mental load of parenting.

When I purchased her diapers, I learned about the diaper-sizing charts. When I purchased the changing table sheets and pads, I gained the knowledge that we had extras—and how many extras and where they were located—for when one would inevitably get dirty and need to be replaced in the future.

As I laundered and handled her clothing, I made a mental catalog of the kinds of clothes we had for her, what they were worn for, what detergent we used for her clothing, and what size she wore.

Without realizing it, by doing all of this prepping (some would say overprepping?), I was involuntarily volunteering to be the person who handled these tasks for our kid(s) forever and ever, amen.

By the time our parenting journey actually started, I was leaps and bounds ahead of Ben when it came to the household as it related to our baby; he was clueless about what we had and where everything was.

This is when the invisible imbalance started for us.

HINDSIGHT IS 20/20, AND IT PISSES ME OFF. BUT MAYBE IT'S NOT TOO LATE FOR YOU? SAVE YOURSELLLLFFFF!!!

I HAD NO IDEA THAT THIS (3 WEEKS INTO PARENTOOD):

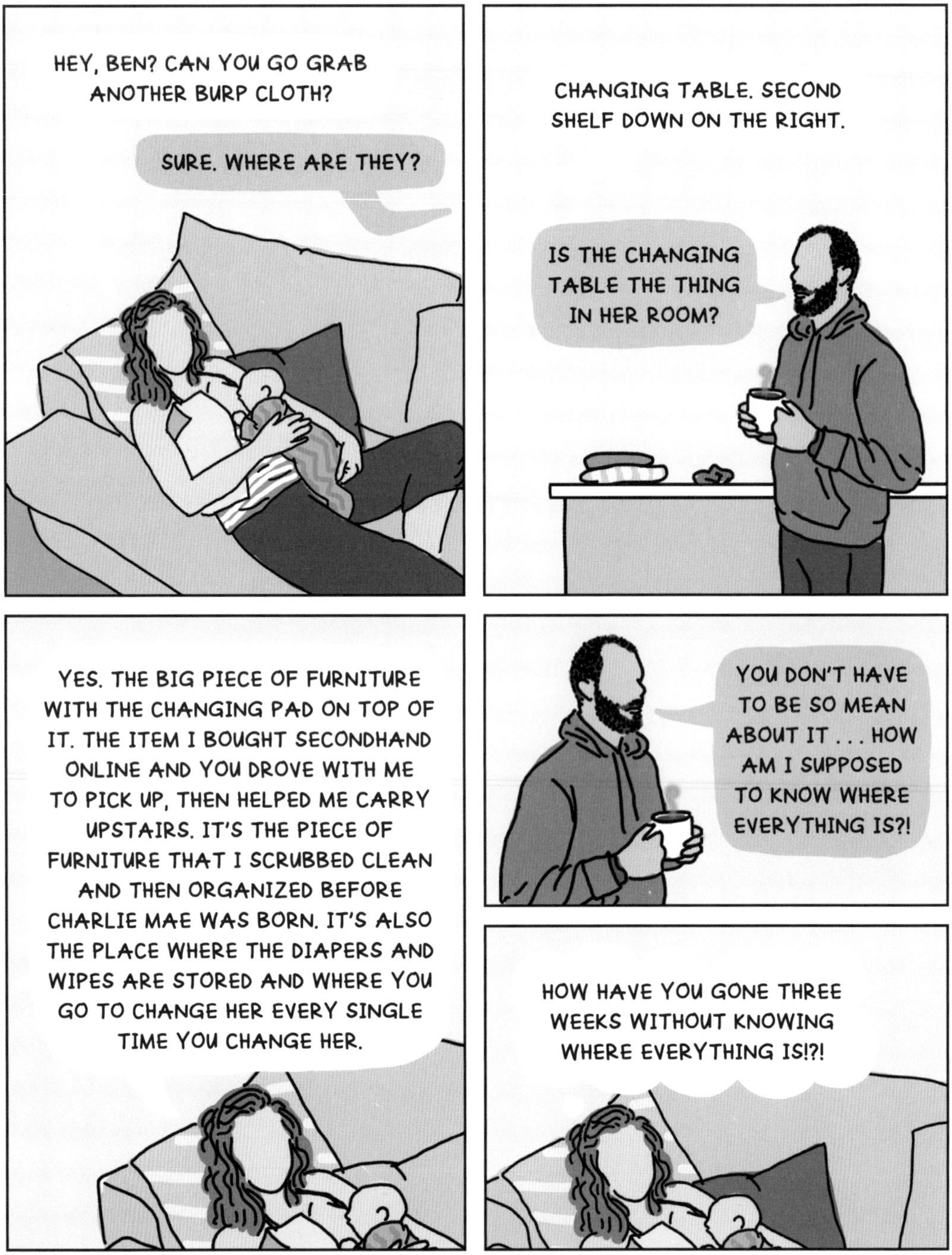
HEY, BEN? CAN YOU GO GRAB ANOTHER BURP CLOTH?
SURE. WHERE ARE THEY?
CHANGING TABLE. SECOND SHELF DOWN ON THE RIGHT.
IS THE CHANGING TABLE THE THING IN HER ROOM?
YES. THE BIG PIECE OF FURNITURE WITH THE CHANGING PAD ON TOP OF IT. THE ITEM I BOUGHT SECONDHAND ONLINE AND YOU DROVE WITH ME TO PICK UP, THEN HELPED ME CARRY UPSTAIRS. IT'S THE PIECE OF FURNITURE THAT I SCRUBBED CLEAN AND THEN ORGANIZED BEFORE CHARLIE MAE WAS BORN. IT'S ALSO THE PLACE WHERE THE DIAPERS AND WIPES ARE STORED AND WHERE YOU GO TO CHANGE HER EVERY SINGLE TIME YOU CHANGE HER.
YOU DON'T HAVE TO BE SO MEAN ABOUT IT . . . HOW AM I SUPPOSED TO KNOW WHERE EVERYTHING IS?!
HOW HAVE YOU GONE THREE WEEKS WITHOUT KNOWING WHERE EVERYTHING IS!?!

WOULD TURN INTO THIS (5 YEARS AND 2 KIDS LATER):

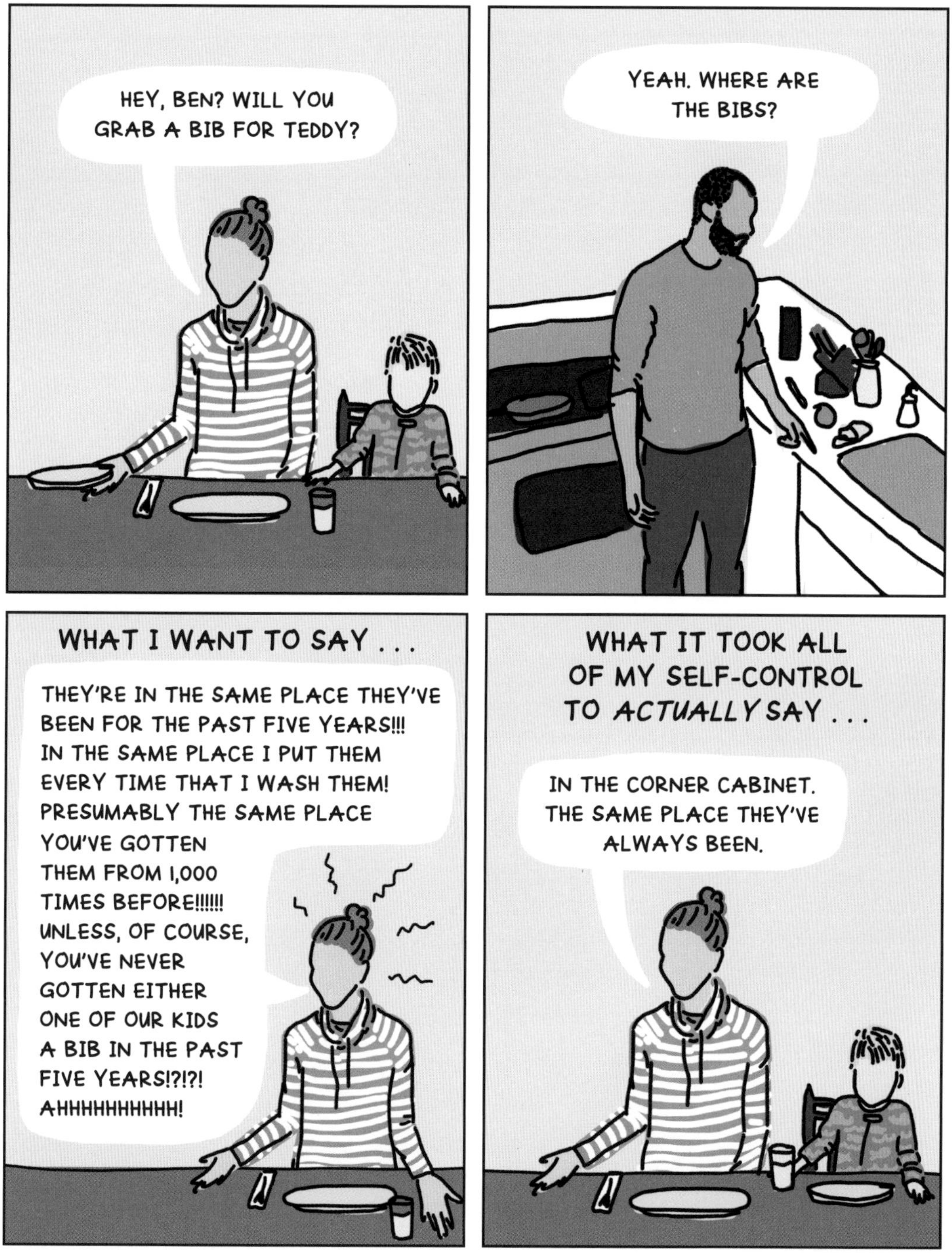
HEY, BEN? WILL YOU GRAB A BIB FOR TEDDY?
YEAH. WHERE ARE THE BIBS?
WHAT I WANT TO SAY . . .
THEY'RE IN THE SAME PLACE THEY'VE BEEN FOR THE PAST FIVE YEARS!!! IN THE SAME PLACE I PUT THEM EVERY TIME THAT I WASH THEM! PRESUMABLY THE SAME PLACE YOU'VE GOTTEN THEM FROM 1,000 TIMES BEFORE!!!!!! UNLESS, OF COURSE, YOU'VE NEVER GOTTEN EITHER ONE OF OUR KIDS A BIB IN THE PAST FIVE YEARS!?!?! AHHHHHHHHHH!
WHAT IT TOOK ALL OF MY SELF-CONTROL TO *ACTUALLY* SAY . . .
IN THE CORNER CABINET. THE SAME PLACE THEY'VE ALWAYS BEEN.

What do I wish we'd done differently? It's so much clearer in retrospect, but I wish I'd done the necessary work to get Ben more involved in everything from the get-go. I wish I'd found a way to communicate to him that I needed him to take on half of the baby preparation duties from the moment we learned we were going to become parents—and then again and again every step along the way.

## IF I COULD DO IT OVER . . .

OKAY, NOW THAT I'M IN MY SECOND TRIMESTER, WE NEED TO START PLANNING AND GETTING EVERYTHING WE'LL NEED FOR THE BABY. I KNOW THAT THE REST OF THIS PREGNANCY IS GOING TO FLY BY . . .

WE HAVE PLENTY OF TIME! DON'T STRESS ABOUT IT. EVERYTHING WILL GET DONE.

THE ONLY WAY EVERYTHING WILL GET DONE IS IF *WE* DO IT. THE BUCK STOPS AT US, HON! LET'S SCHEDULE A TIME TO SIT DOWN TOGETHER AND MAKE A LIST OF EVERYTHING WE NEED TO DO, THEN DIVVY IT UP SO I DON'T GET STUCK DOING EVERYTHING.

OKAY, IF YOU WANT TO DO THAT, WE CAN DO IT.

I DO WANT TO. I THINK WE NEED TO.

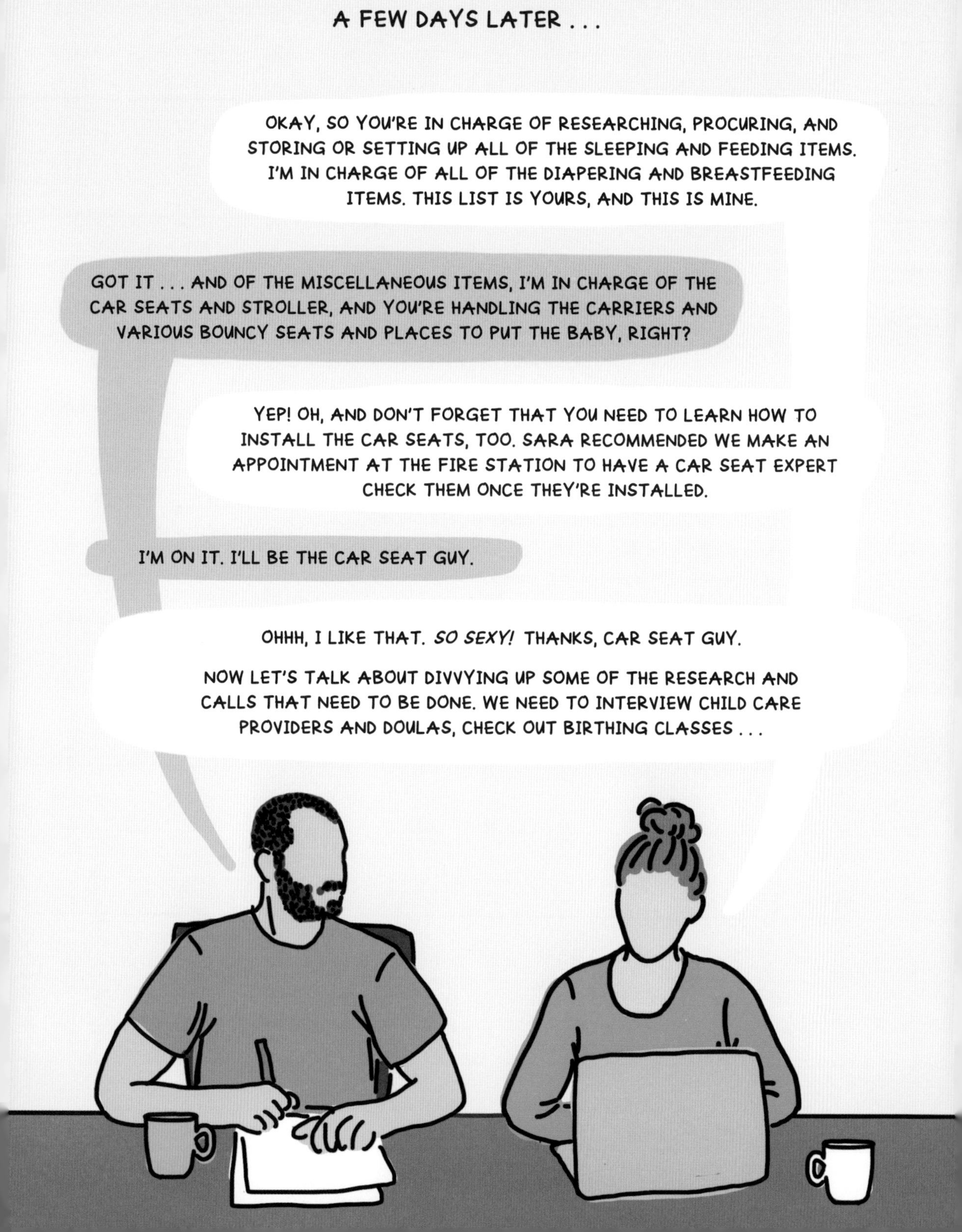
A FEW DAYS LATER . . .
OKAY, SO YOU'RE IN CHARGE OF RESEARCHING, PROCURING, AND STORING OR SETTING UP ALL OF THE SLEEPING AND FEEDING ITEMS. I'M IN CHARGE OF ALL OF THE DIAPERING AND BREASTFEEDING ITEMS. THIS LIST IS YOURS, AND THIS IS MINE.
GOT IT . . . AND OF THE MISCELLANEOUS ITEMS, I'M IN CHARGE OF THE CAR SEATS AND STROLLER, AND YOU'RE HANDLING THE CARRIERS AND VARIOUS BOUNCY SEATS AND PLACES TO PUT THE BABY, RIGHT?
YEP! OH, AND DON'T FORGET THAT YOU NEED TO LEARN HOW TO INSTALL THE CAR SEATS, TOO. SARA RECOMMENDED WE MAKE AN APPOINTMENT AT THE FIRE STATION TO HAVE A CAR SEAT EXPERT CHECK THEM ONCE THEY'RE INSTALLED.
I'M ON IT. I'LL BE THE CAR SEAT GUY.
OHHH, I LIKE THAT. *SO SEXY!* THANKS, CAR SEAT GUY.
NOW LET'S TALK ABOUT DIVVYING UP SOME OF THE RESEARCH AND CALLS THAT NEED TO BE DONE. WE NEED TO INTERVIEW CHILD CARE PROVIDERS AND DOULAS, CHECK OUT BIRTHING CLASSES . . .

When I imagine what could have been if we'd approached parenting differently, if we'd had a plan and been more thoughtful about who was going to do what, I can't help but feel a little sad about what came to be. I like to think that if Ben knew, back then, that his actions were planting the seeds of parental imbalance and parental preference way down the line, he would have done things differently, too.

MY NEXT BOOK: JUST A SHORT LIL' LIST OF ALL OF THE THINGS I WISH WE'D DONE DIFFERENTLY FROM THE VERY BEGINNING . . .

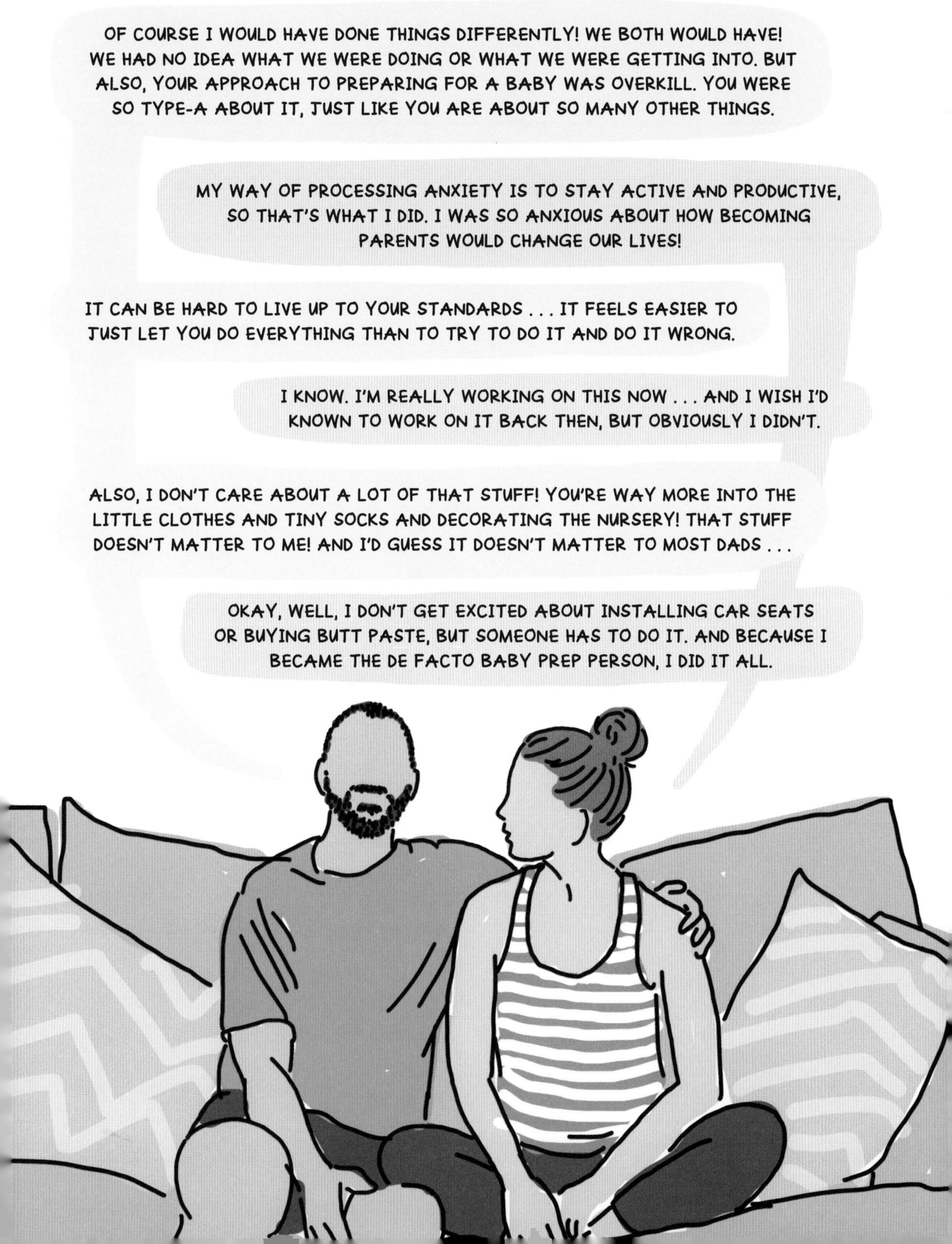
OF COURSE I WOULD HAVE DONE THINGS DIFFERENTLY! WE BOTH WOULD HAVE! WE HAD NO IDEA WHAT WE WERE DOING OR WHAT WE WERE GETTING INTO. BUT ALSO, YOUR APPROACH TO PREPARING FOR A BABY WAS OVERKILL. YOU WERE SO TYPE-A ABOUT IT, JUST LIKE YOU ARE ABOUT SO MANY OTHER THINGS.
MY WAY OF PROCESSING ANXIETY IS TO STAY ACTIVE AND PRODUCTIVE, SO THAT'S WHAT I DID. I WAS SO ANXIOUS ABOUT HOW BECOMING PARENTS WOULD CHANGE OUR LIVES!
IT CAN BE HARD TO LIVE UP TO YOUR STANDARDS . . . IT FEELS EASIER TO JUST LET YOU DO EVERYTHING THAN TO TRY TO DO IT AND DO IT WRONG.
I KNOW. I'M REALLY WORKING ON THIS NOW . . . AND I WISH I'D KNOWN TO WORK ON IT BACK THEN, BUT OBVIOUSLY I DIDN'T.
ALSO, I DON'T CARE ABOUT A LOT OF THAT STUFF! YOU'RE WAY MORE INTO THE LITTLE CLOTHES AND TINY SOCKS AND DECORATING THE NURSERY! THAT STUFF DOESN'T MATTER TO ME! AND I'D GUESS IT DOESN'T MATTER TO MOST DADS . . .
OKAY, WELL, I DON'T GET EXCITED ABOUT INSTALLING CAR SEATS OR BUYING BUTT PASTE, BUT SOMEONE HAS TO DO IT. AND BECAUSE I BECAME THE DE FACTO BABY PREP PERSON, I DID IT ALL.

# You Can Do It All!

Another dynamic that contributed to our eventual, post-kids household imbalance is the difference in our professional situations. By the time I was pregnant, I'd been self-employed for five years as a graphic designer, yoga teacher, artist, and business consultant. I made my own schedule. I was super ambitious and had big dreams for my businesses—and was determined that having a baby wouldn't change these ambitions. *I could do it all, dammit! Isn't that what I'd been told since I was a young girl?*

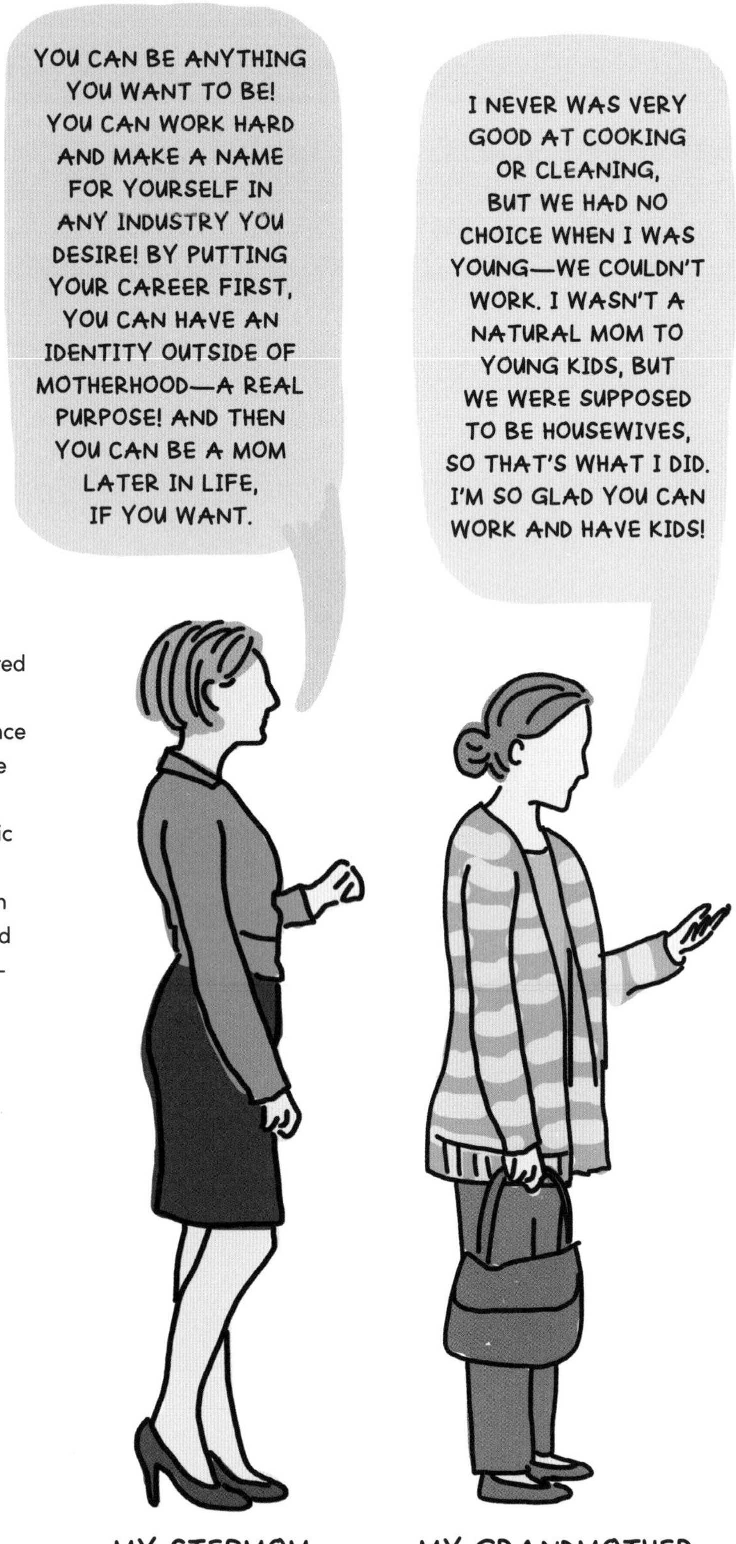
YOU CAN BE ANYTHING YOU WANT TO BE! YOU CAN WORK HARD AND MAKE A NAME FOR YOURSELF IN ANY INDUSTRY YOU DESIRE! BY PUTTING YOUR CAREER FIRST, YOU CAN HAVE AN IDENTITY OUTSIDE OF MOTHERHOOD—A REAL PURPOSE! AND THEN YOU CAN BE A MOM LATER IN LIFE, IF YOU WANT.
I NEVER WAS VERY GOOD AT COOKING OR CLEANING, BUT WE HAD NO CHOICE WHEN I WAS YOUNG—WE COULDN'T WORK. I WASN'T A NATURAL MOM TO YOUNG KIDS, BUT WE WERE SUPPOSED TO BE HOUSEWIVES, SO THAT'S WHAT I DID. I'M SO GLAD YOU CAN WORK AND HAVE KIDS!

MY STEPMOM

MY GRANDMOTHER

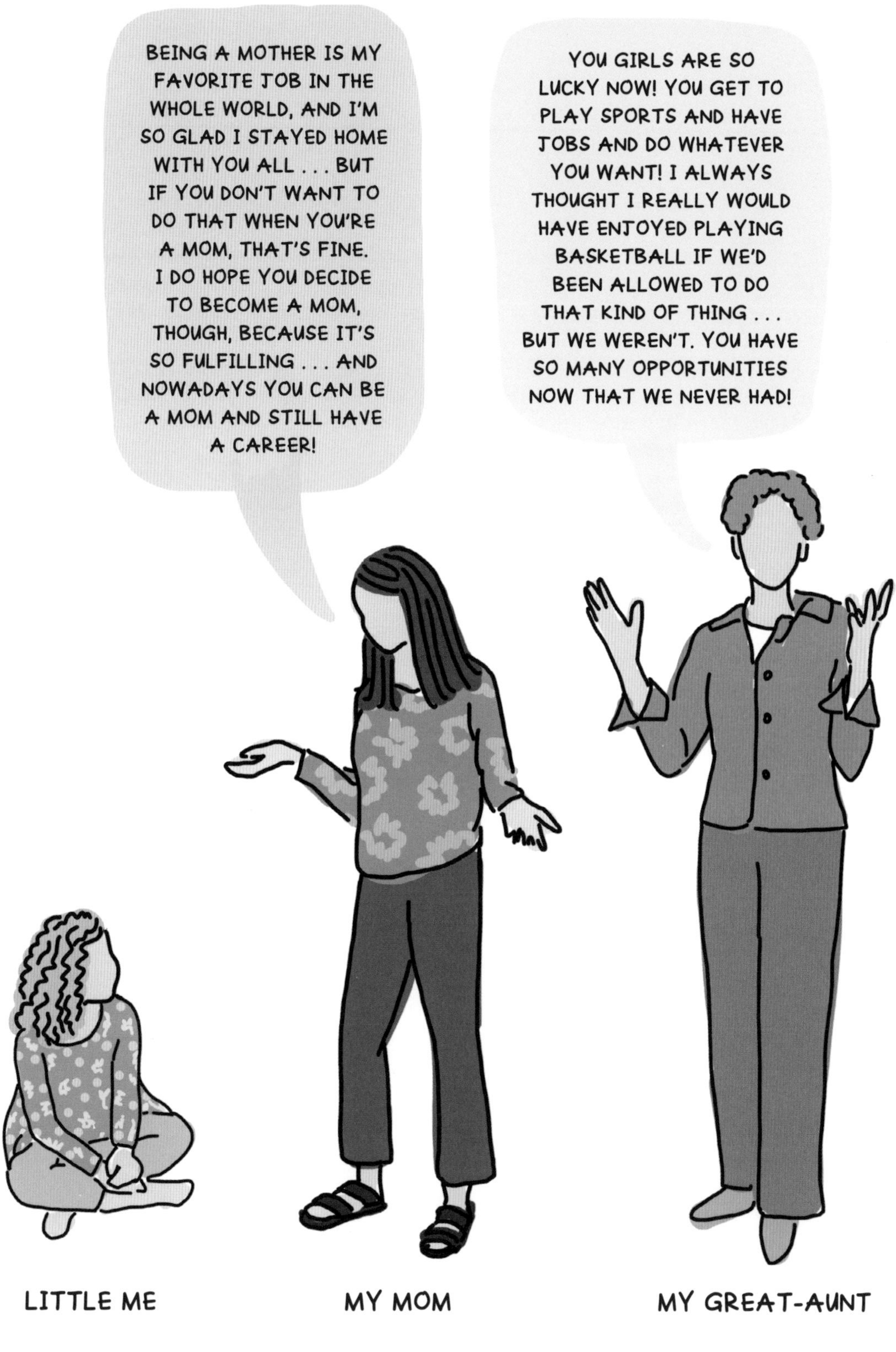
BEING A MOTHER IS MY FAVORITE JOB IN THE WHOLE WORLD, AND I'M SO GLAD I STAYED HOME WITH YOU ALL . . . BUT IF YOU DON'T WANT TO DO THAT WHEN YOU'RE A MOM, THAT'S FINE. I DO HOPE YOU DECIDE TO BECOME A MOM, THOUGH, BECAUSE IT'S SO FULFILLING . . . AND NOWADAYS YOU CAN BE A MOM AND STILL HAVE A CAREER!
YOU GIRLS ARE SO LUCKY NOW! YOU GET TO PLAY SPORTS AND HAVE JOBS AND DO WHATEVER YOU WANT! I ALWAYS THOUGHT I REALLY WOULD HAVE ENJOYED PLAYING BASKETBALL IF WE'D BEEN ALLOWED TO DO THAT KIND OF THING . . . BUT WE WEREN'T. YOU HAVE SO MANY OPPORTUNITIES NOW THAT WE NEVER HAD!
LITTLE ME
MY MOM
MY GREAT-AUNT

On the other hand, Ben was a lawyer working for the local DA's office. He had a very set schedule and very little day-to-day flexibility because he had to be in court almost all day, every day. He also had a basketball training side-hustle that filled his evenings and weekends.

My schedule was much more flexible than his—I had more wiggle room in what my daily life could look like. And I was grateful for this! I thought it was the perfect schedule for a new mom.

What I didn't anticipate was that my drive, my yearning to create, wasn't going to change after becoming a mother. Yes, I could stay home more if needed, but when it came down to it, I didn't want to scale back! I wanted to get back to work as soon as possible! But I also wanted to be a present mom! And I wanted to spend as much time as possible with my baby!

I really thought I could do both and didn't realize that in order to actually do my job to the standard I was used to, I was going to need A LOT more help than a few days per week of child care. But because I didn't *have* to have that help and was my own boss, getting more help made me feel like a bad mom.

Meanwhile, Ben didn't struggle with ANY of these kinds of internal battles. Because he didn't have any ingrained expectations for himself about how he would show up as a dad on a daily basis, he just kept working full-time as always because "that's what dads do" and that's what was expected of him. Why would he feel guilty about it or need to change his schedule at all after becoming a dad? He wouldn't.

I'M SO LUCKY BECAUSE I MAKE MY OWN SCHEDULE, SO I CAN PICK WHICH DAYS I WORK AND WHICH DAYS I'LL BE HOME WITH THE BABY. AND I CAN SCALE UP OR DOWN AS NEEDED AND WORK FROM HOME WHENEVER I HAVE TIME. I THINK IT WILL BE A GREAT SCHEDULE AS A NEW MOM!

OH, THAT DOES SOUND GREAT!

SO CLUELESS, HOPEFUL, AND IN DENIAL ABOUT WHO SHE IS AND HER ABILITY TO JUST "GO WITH THE FLOW" AND GET HER WORK DONE "WHENEVER"!

## WHAT THE "YOU CAN DO IT ALL" MESSAGING FORGOT TO MENTION:

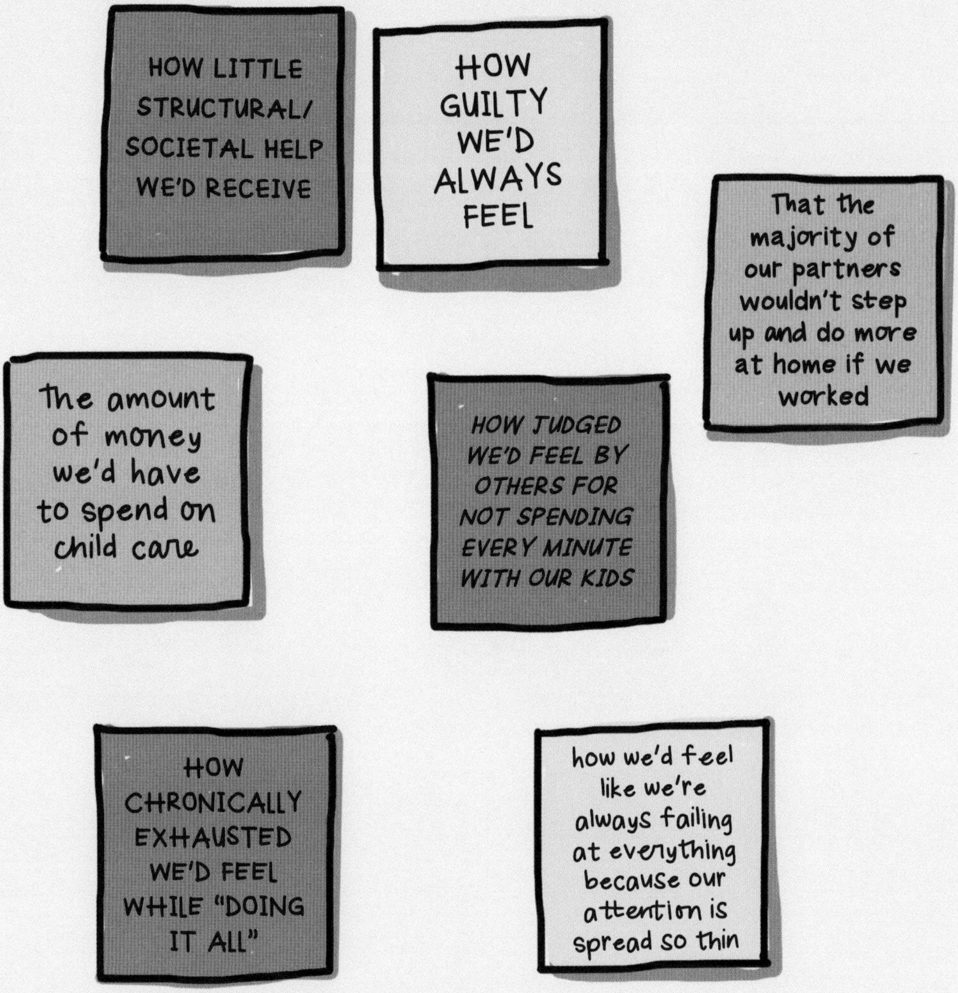
HOW LITTLE STRUCTURAL/ SOCIETAL HELP WE'D RECEIVE
HOW GUILTY WE'D ALWAYS FEEL
That the majority of our partners wouldn't step up and do more at home if we worked
The amount of money we'd have to spend on child care
HOW JUDGED WE'D FEEL BY OTHERS FOR NOT SPENDING EVERY MINUTE WITH OUR KIDS
HOW CHRONICALLY EXHAUSTED WE'D FEEL WHILE "DOING IT ALL"
how we'd feel like we're always failing at everything because our attention is spread so thin

So yeah, while I was pregnant—and nesting and reorganizing and painting dressers and buying everything and reading and going to appointments and taking hypnobirthing classes—I had no idea how my actions in the present moment would ultimately set us down a path toward household and parental inequality and thus resentment, rage, and complete overwhelm.

By the way, this "you can do it all" messaging is *REALLY* ingrained In me—so much so that within a few weeks of writing this chapter, the following conversation happened in my household:

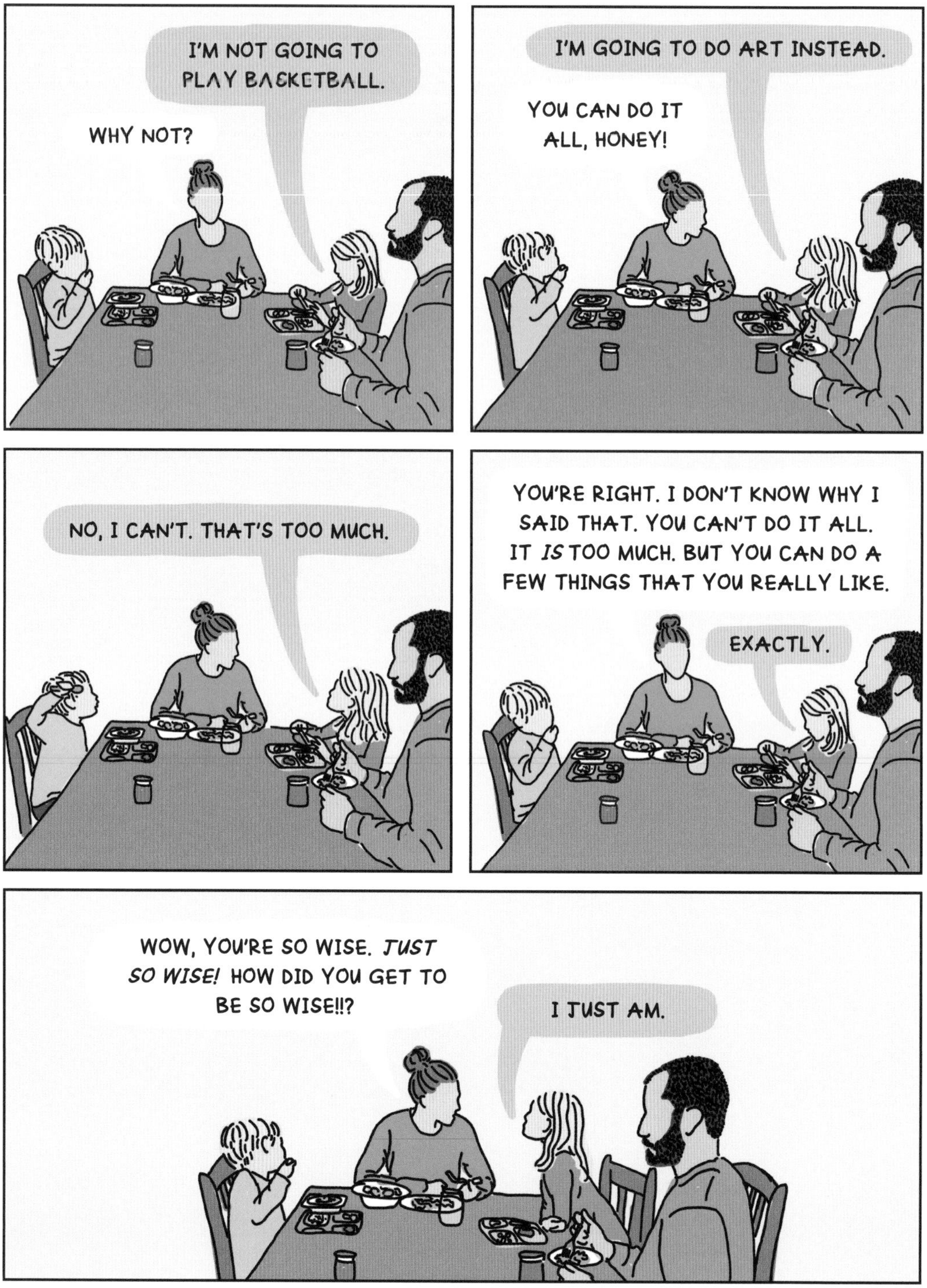

I'M NOT GOING TO PLAY BASKETBALL.
WHY NOT?
I'M GOING TO DO ART INSTEAD.
YOU CAN DO IT ALL, HONEY!
NO, I CAN'T. THAT'S TOO MUCH.
YOU'RE RIGHT. I DON'T KNOW WHY I SAID THAT. YOU CAN'T DO IT ALL. IT *IS* TOO MUCH. BUT YOU CAN DO A FEW THINGS THAT YOU REALLY LIKE.
EXACTLY.
WOW, YOU'RE SO WISE. *JUST SO WISE!* HOW DID YOU GET TO BE SO WISE!!?
I JUST AM.

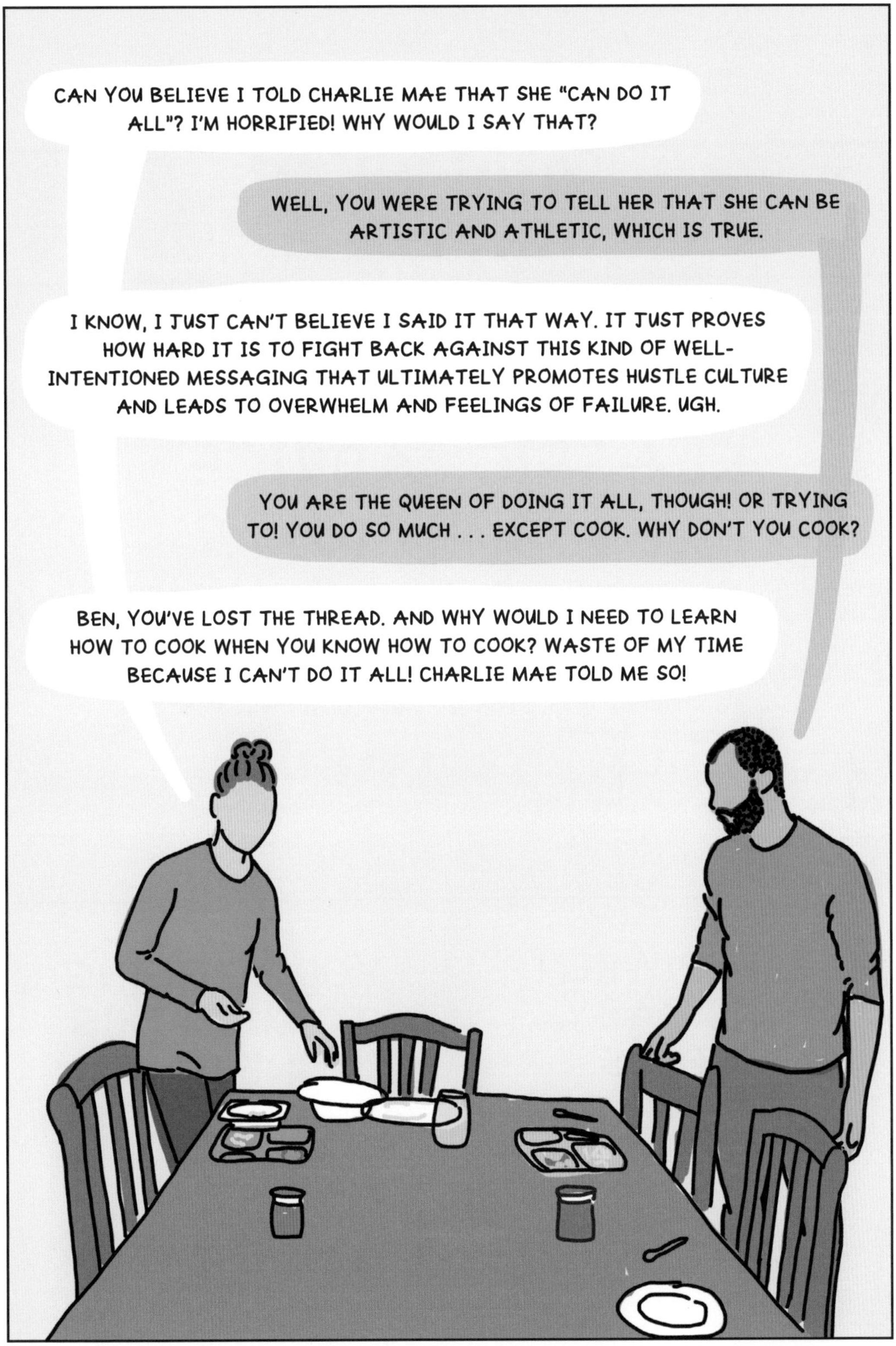
CAN YOU BELIEVE I TOLD CHARLIE MAE THAT SHE "CAN DO IT ALL"? I'M HORRIFIED! WHY WOULD I SAY THAT?
WELL, YOU WERE TRYING TO TELL HER THAT SHE CAN BE ARTISTIC AND ATHLETIC, WHICH IS TRUE.
I KNOW, I JUST CAN'T BELIEVE I SAID IT THAT WAY. IT JUST PROVES HOW HARD IT IS TO FIGHT BACK AGAINST THIS KIND OF WELL-INTENTIONED MESSAGING THAT ULTIMATELY PROMOTES HUSTLE CULTURE AND LEADS TO OVERWHELM AND FEELINGS OF FAILURE. UGH.
YOU ARE THE QUEEN OF DOING IT ALL, THOUGH! OR TRYING TO! YOU DO SO MUCH . . . EXCEPT COOK. WHY DON'T YOU COOK?
BEN, YOU'VE LOST THE THREAD. AND WHY WOULD I NEED TO LEARN HOW TO COOK WHEN YOU KNOW HOW TO COOK? WASTE OF MY TIME BECAUSE I CAN'T DO IT ALL! CHARLIE MAE TOLD ME SO!

# Oh Yeah, **I'd Love Your Unsolicited Feedback,** Thanks!

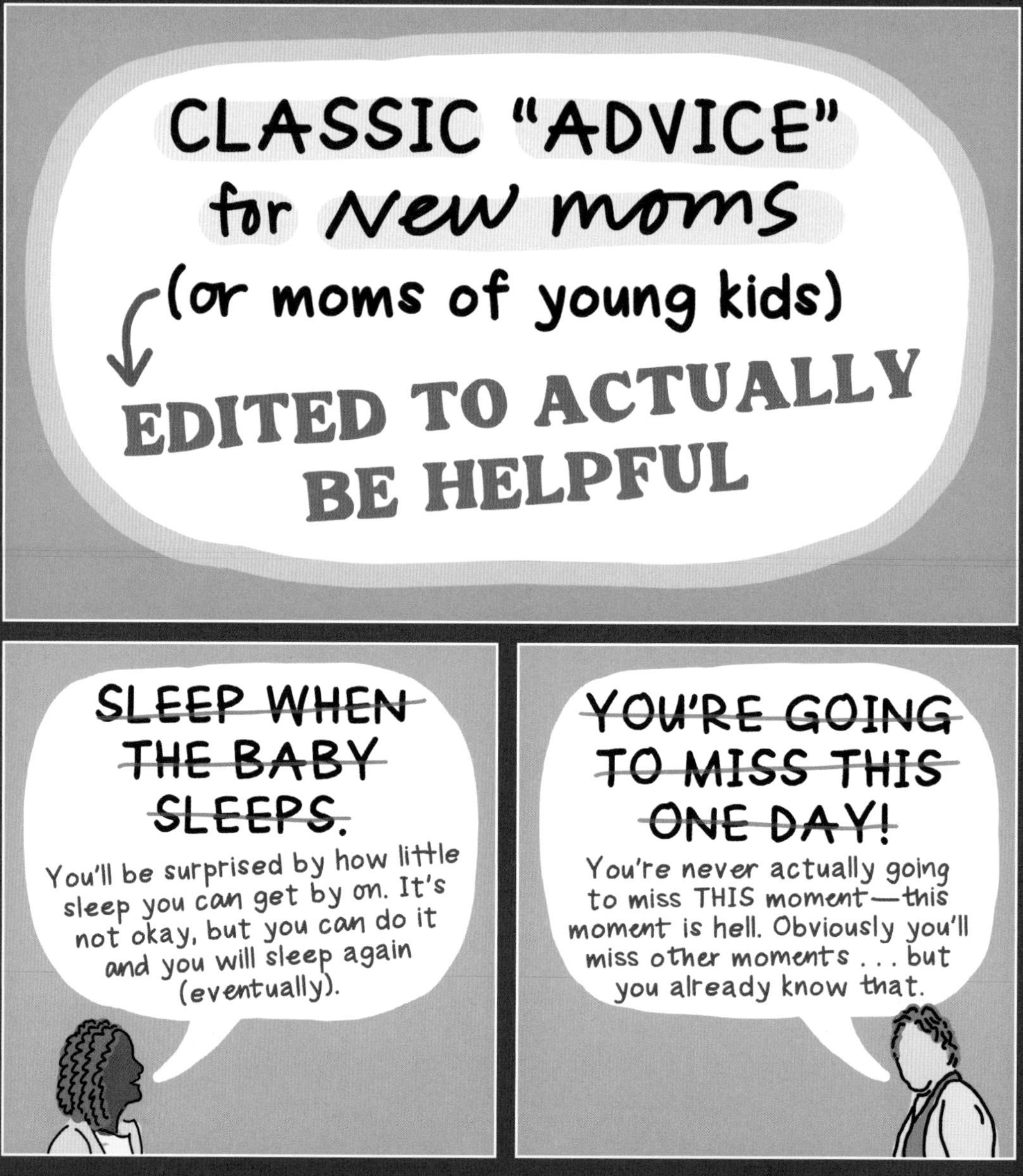
CLASSIC "ADVICE" for New moms
(or moms of young kids)
EDITED TO ACTUALLY BE HELPFUL
~~SLEEP WHEN THE BABY SLEEPS.~~
You'll be surprised by how little sleep you can get by on. It's not okay, but you can do it and you will sleep again (eventually).
~~YOU'RE GOING TO MISS THIS ONE DAY!~~
You're never actually going to miss THIS moment—this moment is hell. Obviously you'll miss other moments . . . but you already know that.

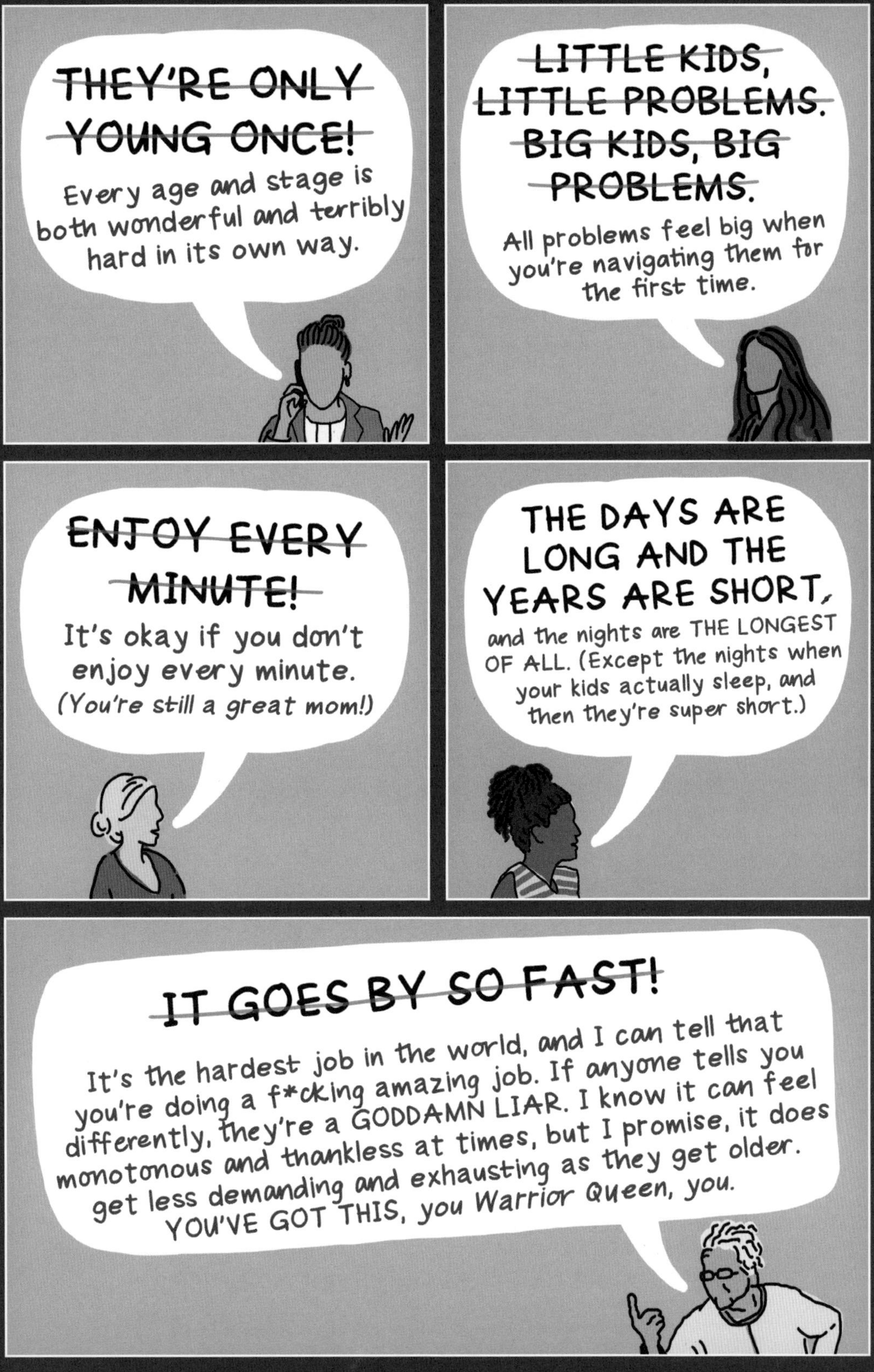
THEY'RE ONLY YOUNG ONCE!
Every age and stage is both wonderful and terribly hard in its own way.
LITTLE KIDS, LITTLE PROBLEMS. BIG KIDS, BIG PROBLEMS.
All problems feel big when you're navigating them for the first time.
ENJOY EVERY MINUTE!
It's okay if you don't enjoy every minute. (You're still a great mom!)
THE DAYS ARE LONG AND THE YEARS ARE SHORT,
and the nights are THE LONGEST OF ALL. (Except the nights when your kids actually sleep, and then they're super short.)
IT GOES BY SO FAST!
It's the hardest job in the world, and I can tell that you're doing a f*cking amazing job. If anyone tells you differently, they're a GODDAMN LIAR. I know it can feel monotonous and thankless at times, but I promise, it does get less demanding and exhausting as they get older. YOU'VE GOT THIS, you Warrior Queen, you.

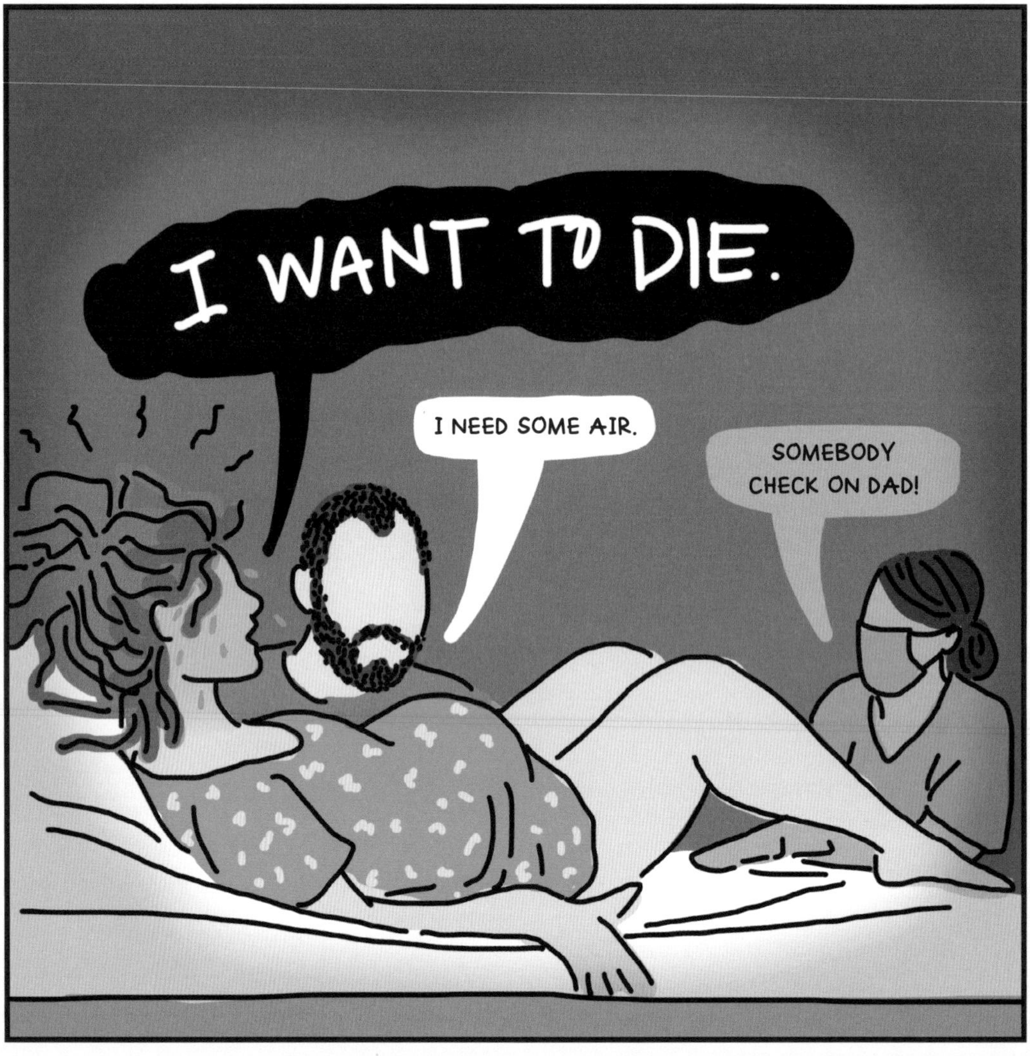
I WANT TO DIE.
I NEED SOME AIR.
SOMEBODY CHECK ON DAD!

# CHAPTER 3

# The (Long-Ass) Birth of a Mother

WHAT I HOPED LABOR AND BIRTH WOULD BE LIKE:

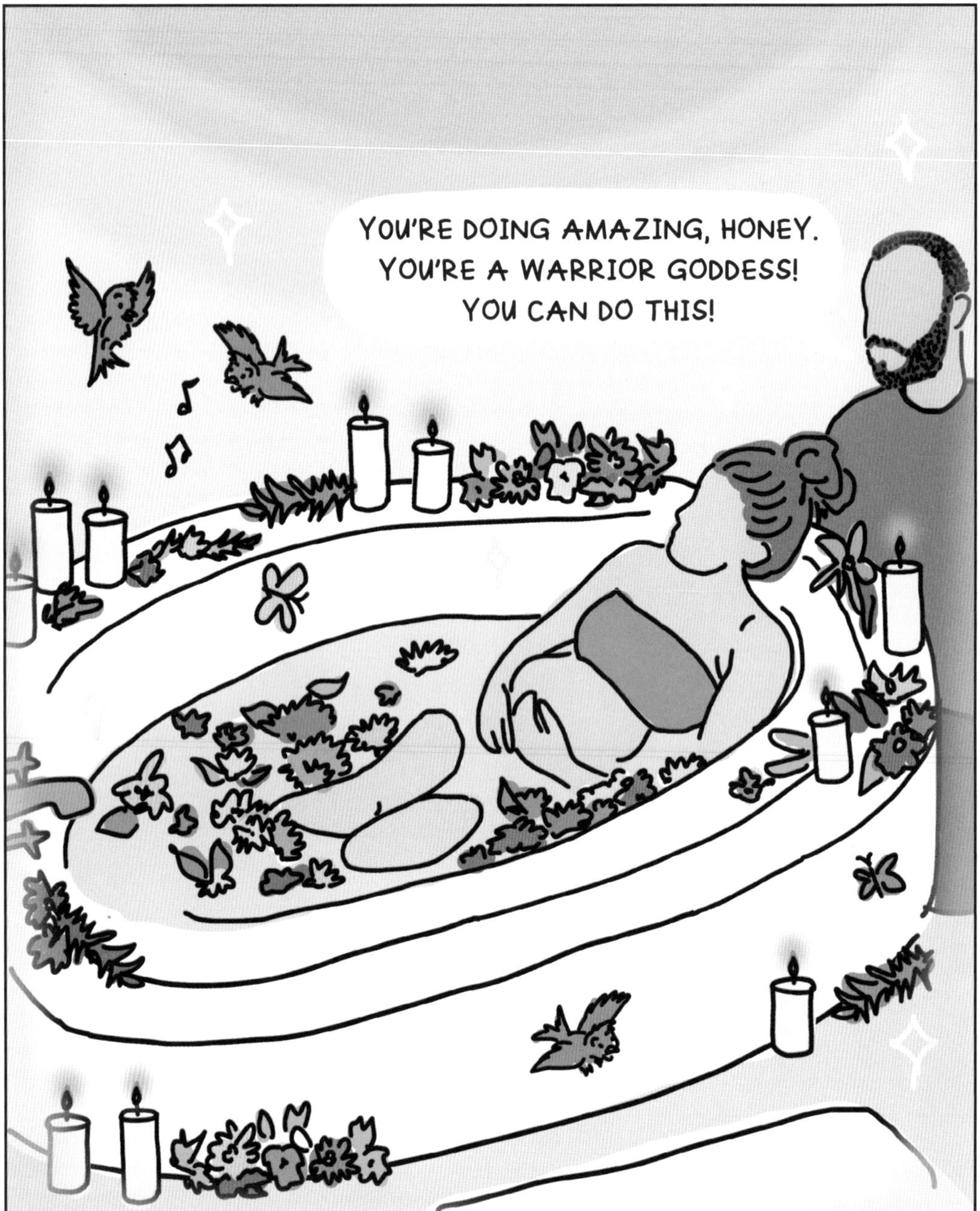
YOU'RE DOING AMAZING, HONEY. YOU'RE A WARRIOR GODDESS! YOU CAN DO THIS!

WHAT LABOR AND BIRTH WERE ACTUALLY LIKE:

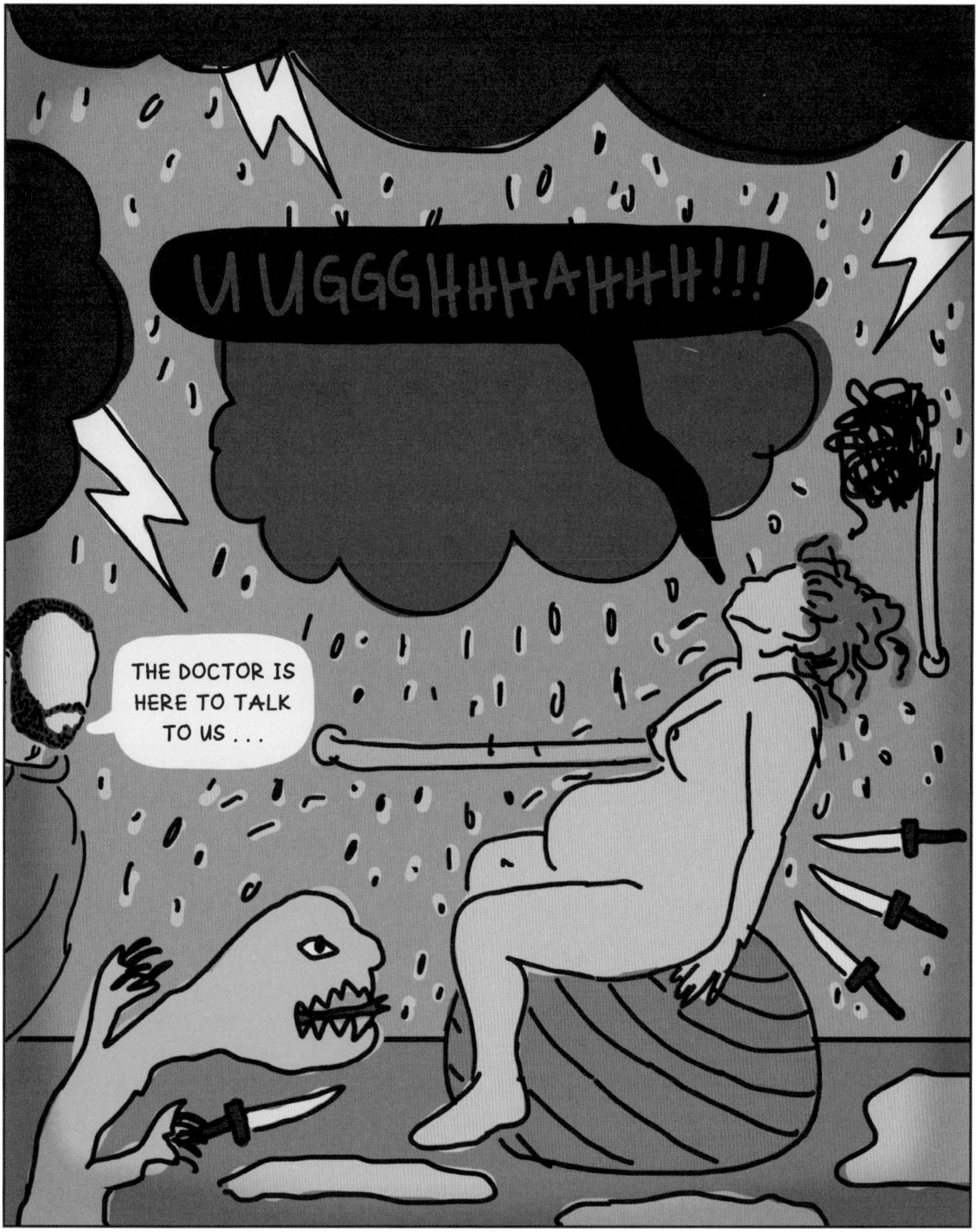
UUGGGHHHAHHHH!!!
THE DOCTOR IS HERE TO TALK TO US . . .

# The Birth Story

Sharing a challenging birth story is, well, a challenge. There are many reasons for this, but just a few are as follows:

- I don't want to scare anyone who hasn't given birth yet and is pregnant or plans to be someday.

- I don't want to be judged for my decisions during my labor and delivery.

- I don't want to come across as judgmental toward anyone who wants a different kind of birth.

- I don't want to make anyone feel bad about their birth process, no matter what the outcome.

- I don't want to sound ungrateful for a process that, in the end, provided me with a completely healthy baby.

BECAUSE I AM SO, SO, SO GRATEFUL! ALWAYS GRATEFUL. IN THE WORDS OF GLENNON DOYLE, "IT'S NOT EITHER/OR, IT'S AND/BOTH."

But to me, my daughter's birth was completely symbolic of motherhood. Everything about it was not what I expected: It was traumatic, it was hard, it was scary, and it was overwhelming. There were a lot of bodily fluids and lots of anxiety and lots of unknowns. I felt totally unprepared. Ben left the room multiple times to "get some fresh air" and was gone longer than I'd have liked him to be.

However, at the end of the day, it was full of love, wonder, and endurance, as so many birth stories are. I know I don't need to say this to you, but I'm going to, anyway: It was worth it, and I'd do it over and over again if it meant being a mom . . . but it was still the hardest thing I've ever done. Just like basically every part of motherhood, huh?

Here's how my daughter's birth went . . .

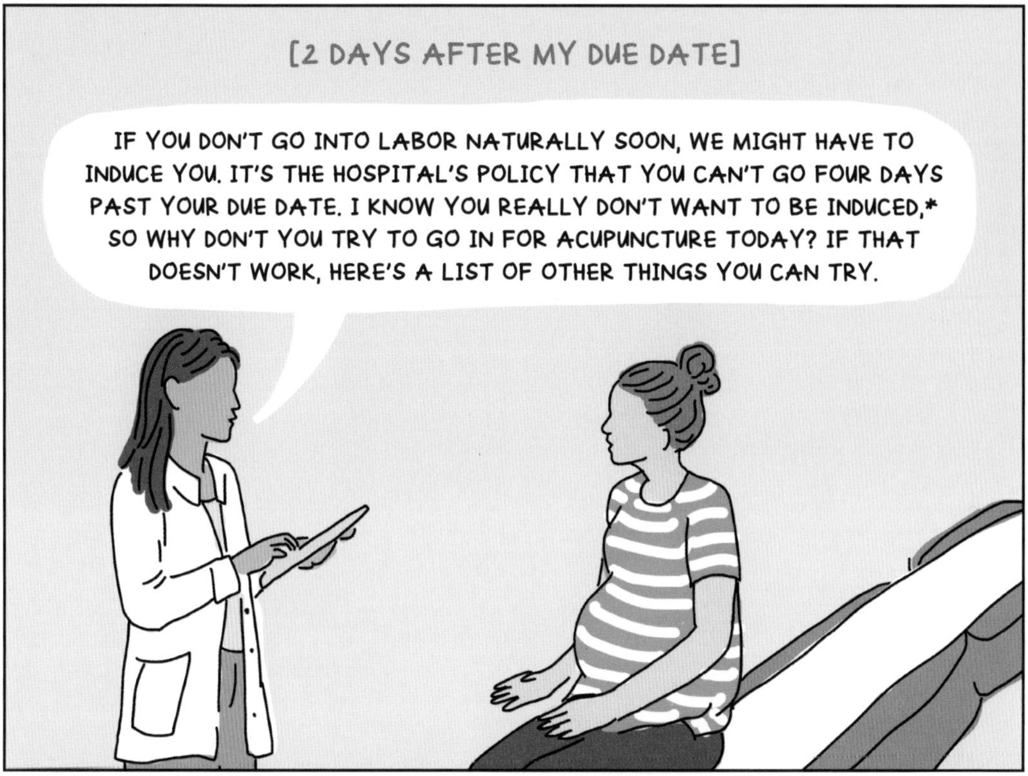
[2 DAYS AFTER MY DUE DATE]
IF YOU DON'T GO INTO LABOR NATURALLY SOON, WE MIGHT HAVE TO INDUCE YOU. IT'S THE HOSPITAL'S POLICY THAT YOU CAN'T GO FOUR DAYS PAST YOUR DUE DATE. I KNOW YOU REALLY DON'T WANT TO BE INDUCED,* SO WHY DON'T YOU TRY TO GO IN FOR ACUPUNCTURE TODAY? IF THAT DOESN'T WORK, HERE'S A LIST OF OTHER THINGS YOU CAN TRY.

*I REALLY WANTED AN INTERVENTION-FREE BIRTH EXPERIENCE, AND I HAD DONE A LOT TO PREPARE FOR THIS KIND OF BIRTH. MY MIDWIFE WAS FULLY SUPPORTIVE OF THE KIND OF BIRTH I WANTED BUT PRACTICED AT A HOSPITAL THAT HAD RULES.

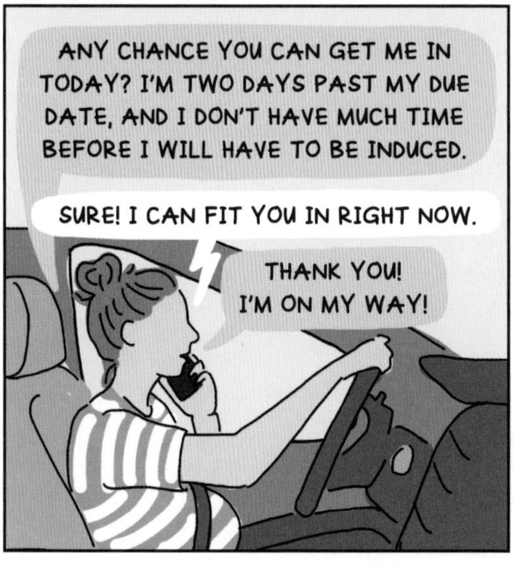
ANY CHANCE YOU CAN GET ME IN TODAY? I'M TWO DAYS PAST MY DUE DATE, AND I DON'T HAVE MUCH TIME BEFORE I WILL HAVE TO BE INDUCED.
SURE! I CAN FIT YOU IN RIGHT NOW.
THANK YOU! I'M ON MY WAY!

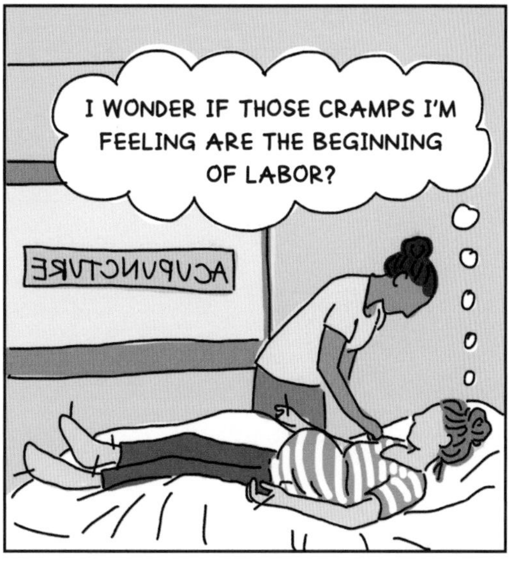
I WONDER IF THOSE CRAMPS I'M FEELING ARE THE BEGINNING OF LABOR?
ACUPUNCTURE

[A FEW HOURS LATER]

HEY, HON . . . I'VE BEEN HAVING CRAMPS AT FAIRLY REGULAR INTERVALS FOR A FEW HOURS NOW. I THINK THIS MIGHT BE THE BEGINNING OF LABOR . . .

ARE YOU SERIOUS!?!? DO YOU NEED ME TO COME HOME RIGHT NOW? HOW MUCH TIME DO YOU THINK WE HAVE?

[9:00 P.M. THAT NIGHT]

WHY DON'T YOU GO TO BED? I WANT TO LABOR AT HOME AS LONG AS POSSIBLE SO YOU SHOULD GET SOME SLEEP WHILE WE'RE STILL AT HOME.

OKAY, WAKE ME UP WHEN YOU NEED ME.

OKAY, I WILL.

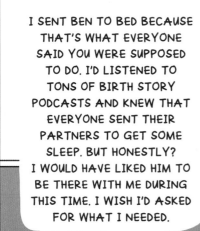

[9:30 P.M.]

I SENT BEN TO BED BECAUSE THAT'S WHAT EVERYONE SAID YOU WERE SUPPOSED TO DO. I'D LISTENED TO TONS OF BIRTH STORY PODCASTS AND KNEW THAT EVERYONE SENT THEIR PARTNERS TO GET SOME SLEEP. BUT HONESTLY? I WOULD HAVE LIKED HIM TO BE THERE WITH ME DURING THIS TIME. I WISH I'D ASKED FOR WHAT I NEEDED.

Mmmm...

[10:00 P.M.]

THIS IS JUST LIKE I IMAGINED. I CAN DO THIS!

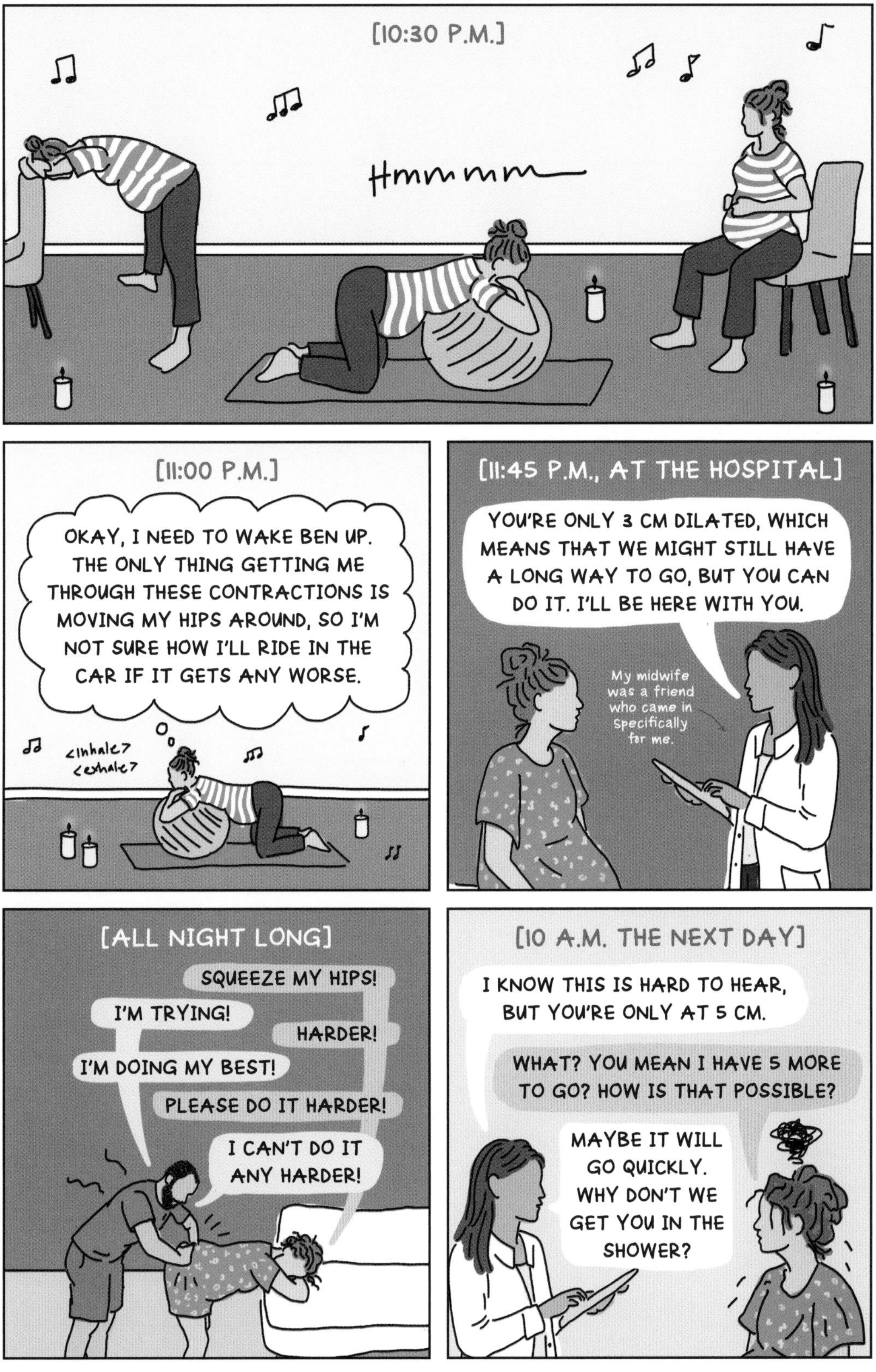
[10:30 P.M.]
Hmmmmm
[11:00 P.M.]
OKAY, I NEED TO WAKE BEN UP. THE ONLY THING GETTING ME THROUGH THESE CONTRACTIONS IS MOVING MY HIPS AROUND, SO I'M NOT SURE HOW I'LL RIDE IN THE CAR IF IT GETS ANY WORSE.
<inhale>
<exhale>
[11:45 P.M., AT THE HOSPITAL]
YOU'RE ONLY 3 CM DILATED, WHICH MEANS THAT WE MIGHT STILL HAVE A LONG WAY TO GO, BUT YOU CAN DO IT. I'LL BE HERE WITH YOU.
My midwife was a friend who came in specifically for me.
[ALL NIGHT LONG]
SQUEEZE MY HIPS!
I'M TRYING!
HARDER!
I'M DOING MY BEST!
PLEASE DO IT HARDER!
I CAN'T DO IT ANY HARDER!
[10 A.M. THE NEXT DAY]
I KNOW THIS IS HARD TO HEAR, BUT YOU'RE ONLY AT 5 CM.
WHAT? YOU MEAN I HAVE 5 MORE TO GO? HOW IS THAT POSSIBLE?
MAYBE IT WILL GO QUICKLY. WHY DON'T WE GET YOU IN THE SHOWER?

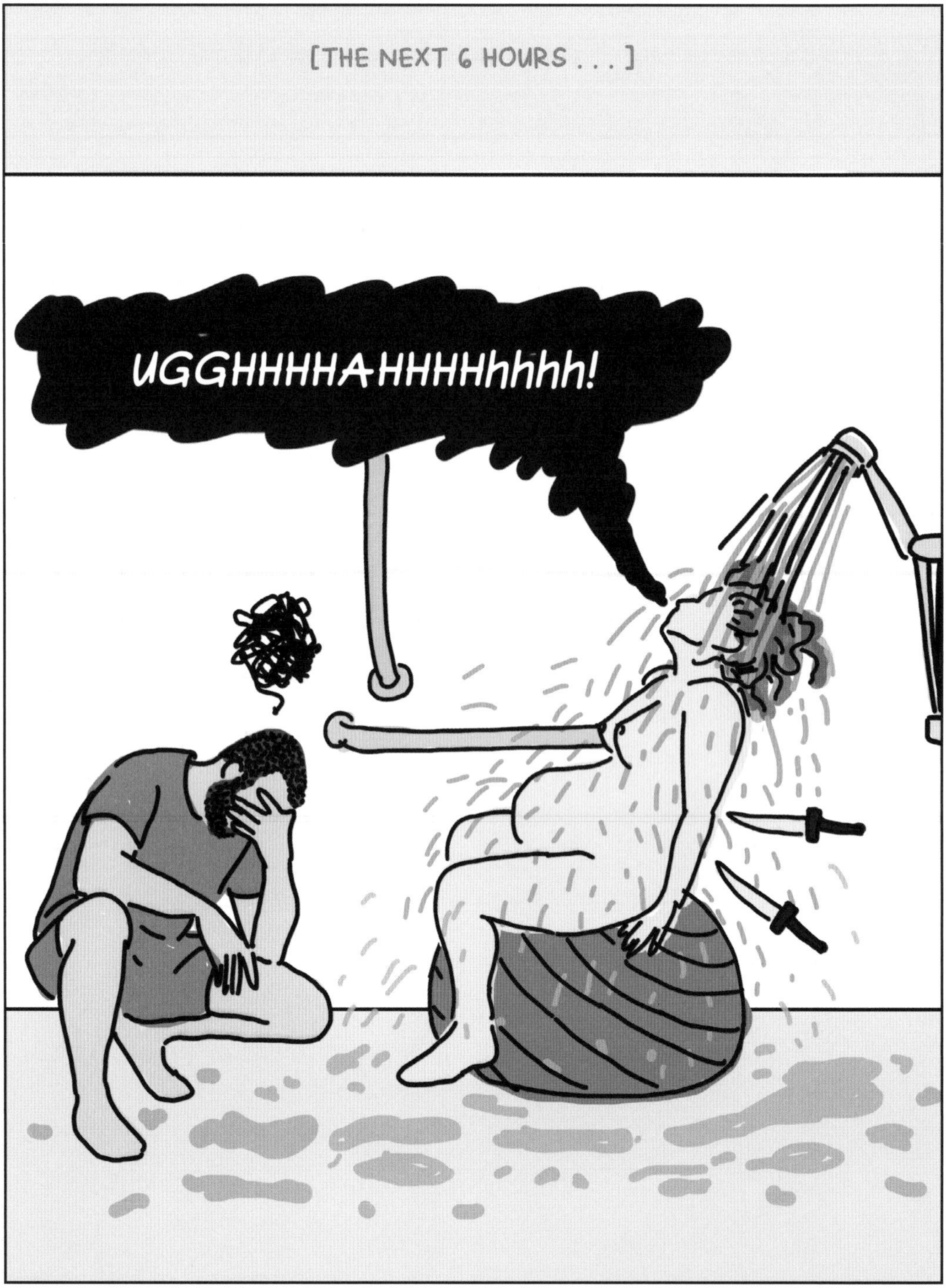
[THE NEXT 6 HOURS . . .]
UGGHHHHAHHHHhhhh!

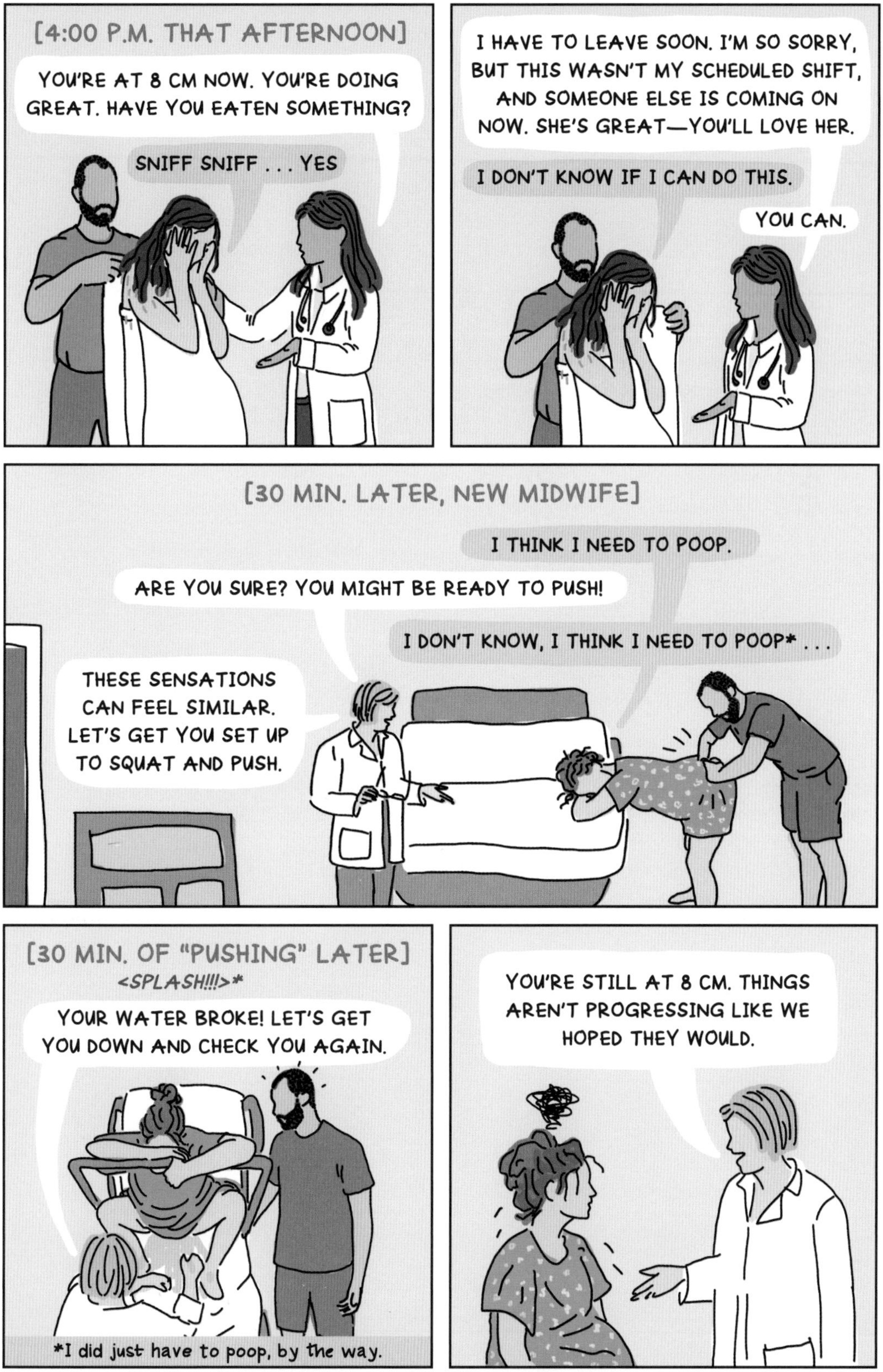
[4:00 P.M. THAT AFTERNOON]
YOU'RE AT 8 CM NOW. YOU'RE DOING GREAT. HAVE YOU EATEN SOMETHING?
SNIFF SNIFF . . . YES
I HAVE TO LEAVE SOON. I'M SO SORRY, BUT THIS WASN'T MY SCHEDULED SHIFT, AND SOMEONE ELSE IS COMING ON NOW. SHE'S GREAT—YOU'LL LOVE HER.
I DON'T KNOW IF I CAN DO THIS.
YOU CAN.
[30 MIN. LATER, NEW MIDWIFE]
I THINK I NEED TO POOP.
ARE YOU SURE? YOU MIGHT BE READY TO PUSH!
I DON'T KNOW, I THINK I NEED TO POOP* . . .
THESE SENSATIONS CAN FEEL SIMILAR. LET'S GET YOU SET UP TO SQUAT AND PUSH.
[30 MIN. OF "PUSHING" LATER]
<SPLASH!!!>*
YOUR WATER BROKE! LET'S GET YOU DOWN AND CHECK YOU AGAIN.
*I did just have to poop, by the way.
YOU'RE STILL AT 8 CM. THINGS AREN'T PROGRESSING LIKE WE HOPED THEY WOULD.

What I didn't realize in the first half of my labor but found out later on was that the crazy intense contractions I was having were called back labor.

Back labor contractions are WAY stronger than regular contractions. Each time you have a contraction, it feels like someone is sawing your back open with a jagged knife. The only thing that helped me was moving my hips, bending over, having someone press on my hips as I contracted, and/or being in the shower, moving on a birth ball, with the hot water on my lower back. It was crazy intense and exhausting.

IS THIS DESCRIPTION GRUESOME ENOUGH? NO? HOW ABOUT THIS: IT FEELS LIKE YOU'RE BEING STABBED IN THE BACK OVER AND OVER AGAIN WHILE SIMULTANEOUSLY BEING PRIED OPEN WITH A RUSTY CROWBAR. YEP, THAT FEELS ACCURATE.

So here I was, over twenty-four hours into labor, and I wasn't dilating all of the way. My energy was starting to dip, and in the meantime, the back labor contractions had continued to get stronger and stronger. I also still felt very strongly that I didn't want any interventions or drugs.

This next part of the story is where things start to get pretty hazy for me because I was delirious from the pain and exhaustion.

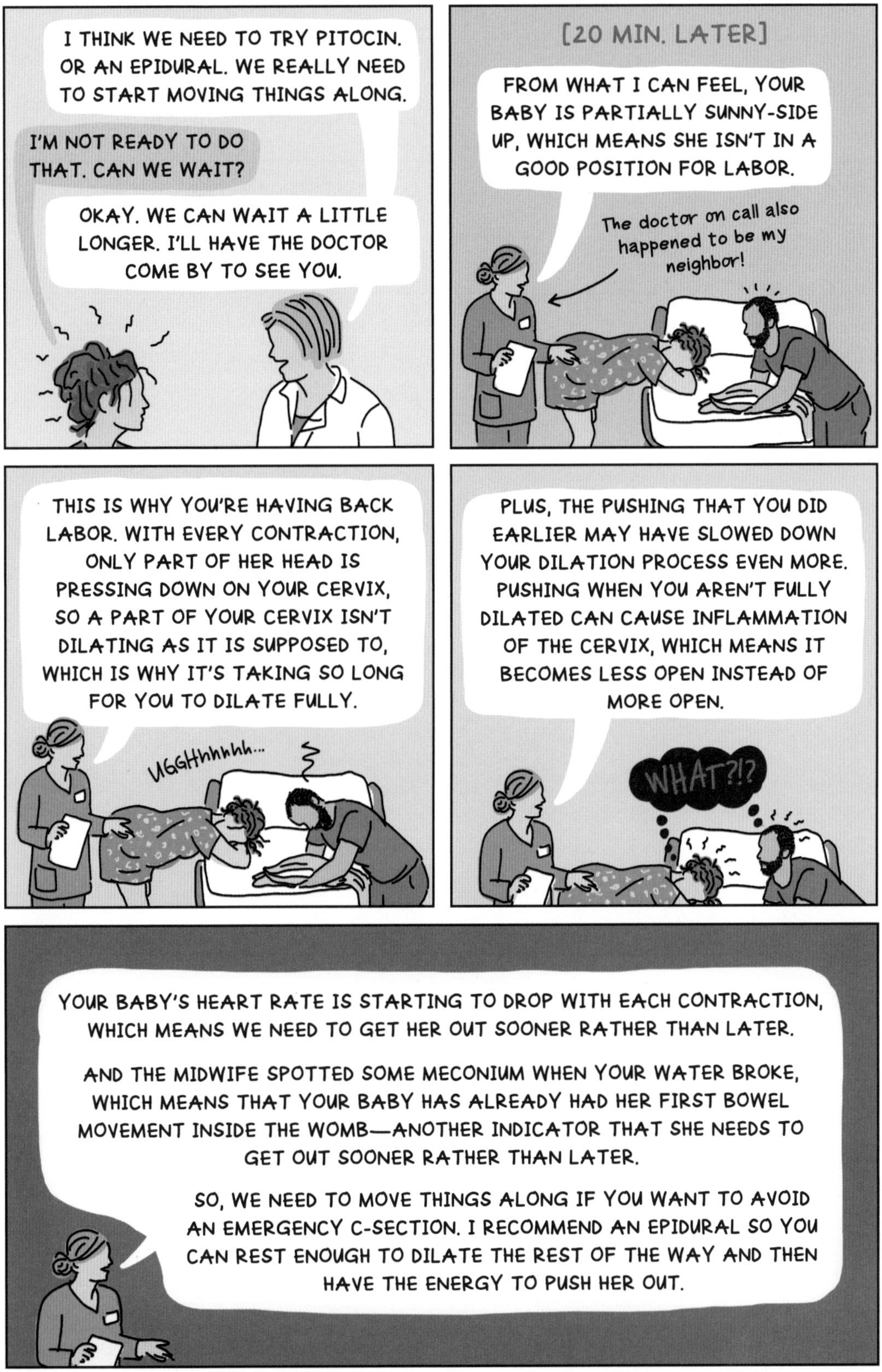
I THINK WE NEED TO TRY PITOCIN. OR AN EPIDURAL. WE REALLY NEED TO START MOVING THINGS ALONG.
I'M NOT READY TO DO THAT. CAN WE WAIT?
OKAY. WE CAN WAIT A LITTLE LONGER. I'LL HAVE THE DOCTOR COME BY TO SEE YOU.
[20 MIN. LATER]
FROM WHAT I CAN FEEL, YOUR BABY IS PARTIALLY SUNNY-SIDE UP, WHICH MEANS SHE ISN'T IN A GOOD POSITION FOR LABOR.
The doctor on call also happened to be my neighbor!
THIS IS WHY YOU'RE HAVING BACK LABOR. WITH EVERY CONTRACTION, ONLY PART OF HER HEAD IS PRESSING DOWN ON YOUR CERVIX, SO A PART OF YOUR CERVIX ISN'T DILATING AS IT IS SUPPOSED TO, WHICH IS WHY IT'S TAKING SO LONG FOR YOU TO DILATE FULLY.
UGGHhhhhh...
PLUS, THE PUSHING THAT YOU DID EARLIER MAY HAVE SLOWED DOWN YOUR DILATION PROCESS EVEN MORE. PUSHING WHEN YOU AREN'T FULLY DILATED CAN CAUSE INFLAMMATION OF THE CERVIX, WHICH MEANS IT BECOMES LESS OPEN INSTEAD OF MORE OPEN.
WHAT?!?
YOUR BABY'S HEART RATE IS STARTING TO DROP WITH EACH CONTRACTION, WHICH MEANS WE NEED TO GET HER OUT SOONER RATHER THAN LATER.
AND THE MIDWIFE SPOTTED SOME MECONIUM WHEN YOUR WATER BROKE, WHICH MEANS THAT YOUR BABY HAS ALREADY HAD HER FIRST BOWEL MOVEMENT INSIDE THE WOMB—ANOTHER INDICATOR THAT SHE NEEDS TO GET OUT SOONER RATHER THAN LATER.
SO, WE NEED TO MOVE THINGS ALONG IF YOU WANT TO AVOID AN EMERGENCY C-SECTION. I RECOMMEND AN EPIDURAL SO YOU CAN REST ENOUGH TO DILATE THE REST OF THE WAY AND THEN HAVE THE ENERGY TO PUSH HER OUT.

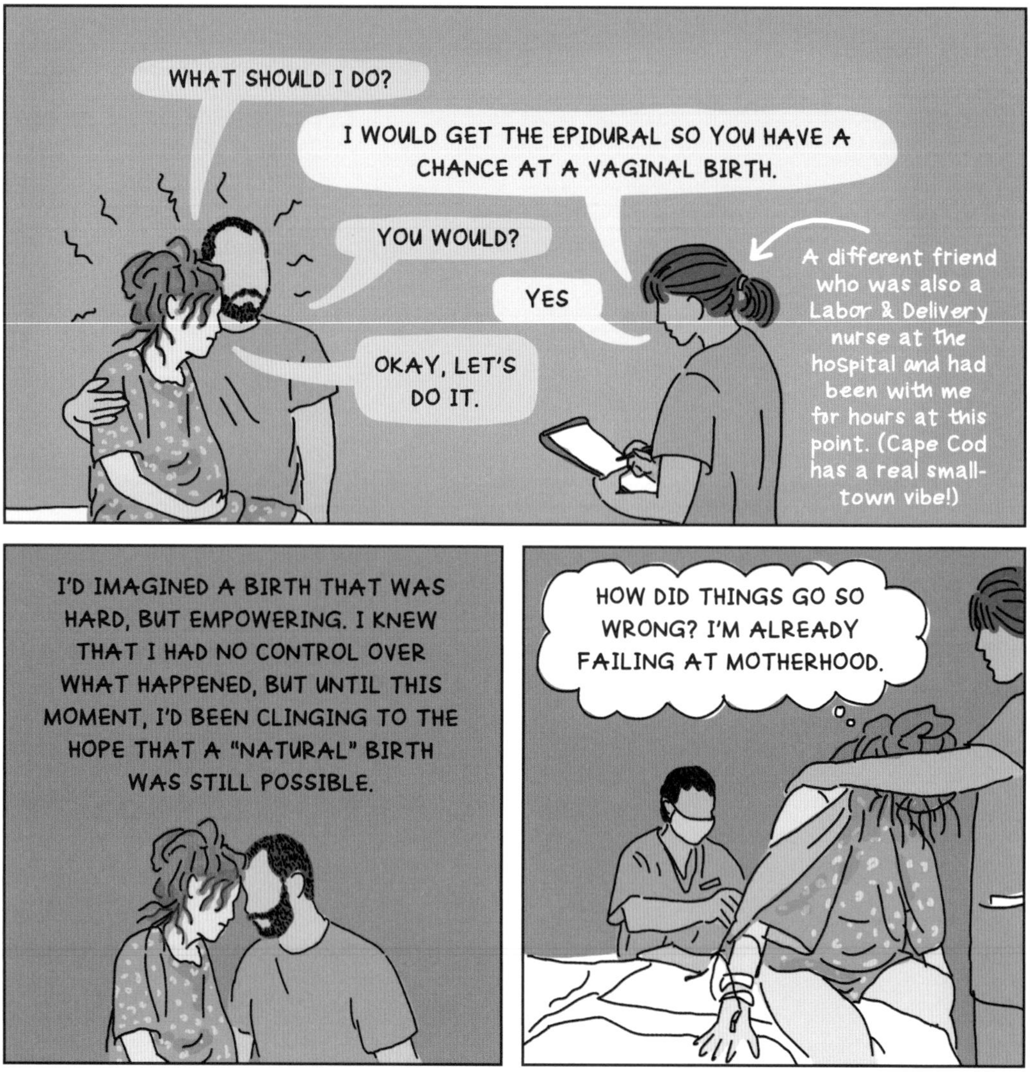
WHAT SHOULD I DO?
I WOULD GET THE EPIDURAL SO YOU HAVE A CHANCE AT A VAGINAL BIRTH.
YOU WOULD?
YES
OKAY, LET'S DO IT.
A different friend who was also a Labor & Delivery nurse at the hospital and had been with me for hours at this point. (Cape Cod has a real small-town vibe!)
I'D IMAGINED A BIRTH THAT WAS HARD, BUT EMPOWERING. I KNEW THAT I HAD NO CONTROL OVER WHAT HAPPENED, BUT UNTIL THIS MOMENT, I'D BEEN CLINGING TO THE HOPE THAT A "NATURAL" BIRTH WAS STILL POSSIBLE.
HOW DID THINGS GO SO WRONG? I'M ALREADY FAILING AT MOTHERHOOD.

The good news: The epidural did eventually give me a chance to rest enough to dilate the rest of the way.

The bad news: The epidural only worked on half of my body and didn't work on my back labor, so once I was all set up and told I could no longer move (the only thing that relieved the pain of back labor), I still felt the pain of the contractions in my back. It was pure hell having to lie still and let each contraction move over me without being able to move myself.

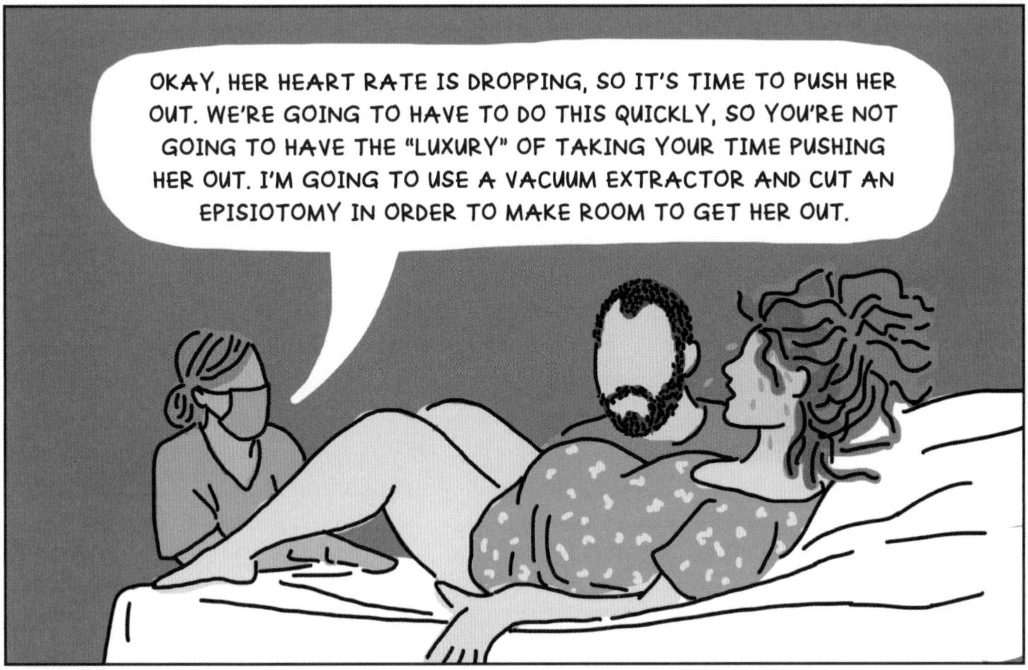
OKAY, HER HEART RATE IS DROPPING, SO IT'S TIME TO PUSH HER OUT. WE'RE GOING TO HAVE TO DO THIS QUICKLY, SO YOU'RE NOT GOING TO HAVE THE "LUXURY" OF TAKING YOUR TIME PUSHING HER OUT. I'M GOING TO USE A VACUUM EXTRACTOR AND CUT AN EPISIOTOMY IN ORDER TO MAKE ROOM TO GET HER OUT.

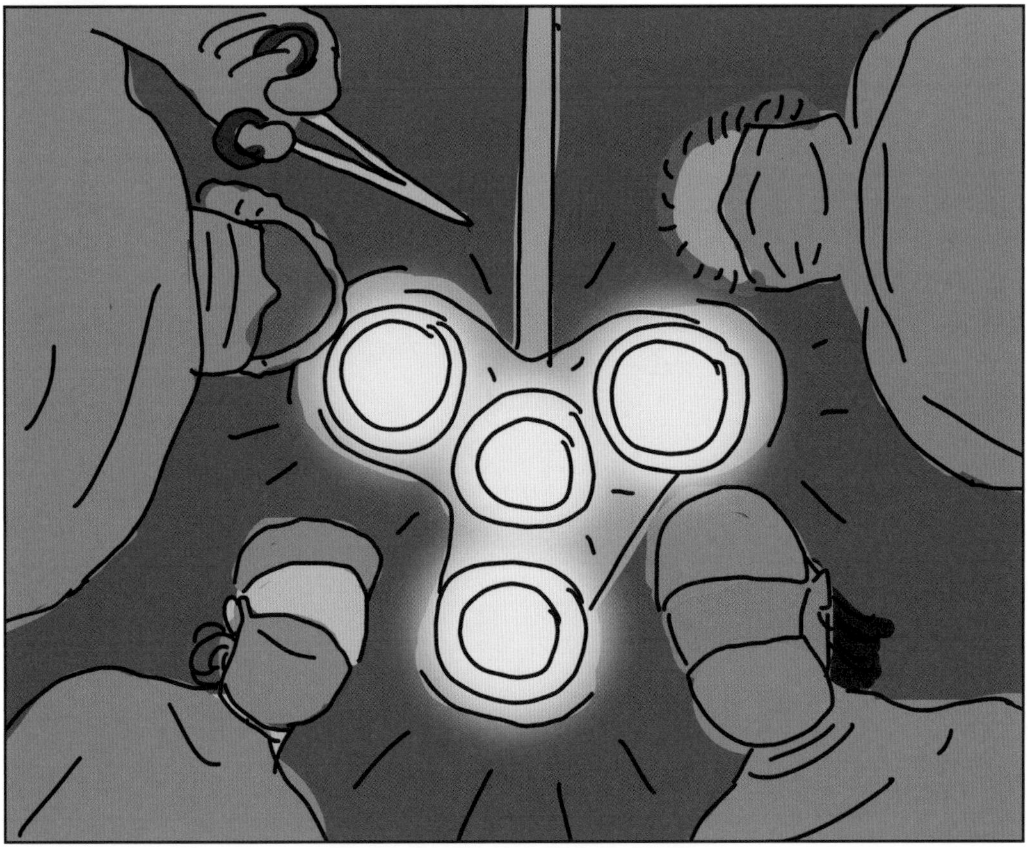

Here's what I remember about delivery: There was a lot of blood, and it was pretty scary—spotlights all around me, a bunch of faces looking down at me, Ben's voice somewhere in the dark. I felt like I was in an *ER* episode, and it was nothing like the peaceful, yoga-filled birth that I had hoped for and experienced for the first twenty-four hours of my labor.

At one point before the pushing started I even heard Ben say:

I AM SO SCARED. THIS IS THE WORST DAY OF MY LIFE.

Which is not something you want your partner to be feeling when you're about to have your baby. He was worried he was going to lose me or our daughter. He hated seeing me in so much pain when there was nothing he could do. I hated hearing him sound so upset.

This experience was traumatic for Ben, too. I know that. But this moment was horrible for me—I remember it so vividly because I felt scared and alone and hearing him say this from across the room made me even more scared that something was wrong. I had wanted this experience to be magical for all of us, and it wasn't.

But then . . .

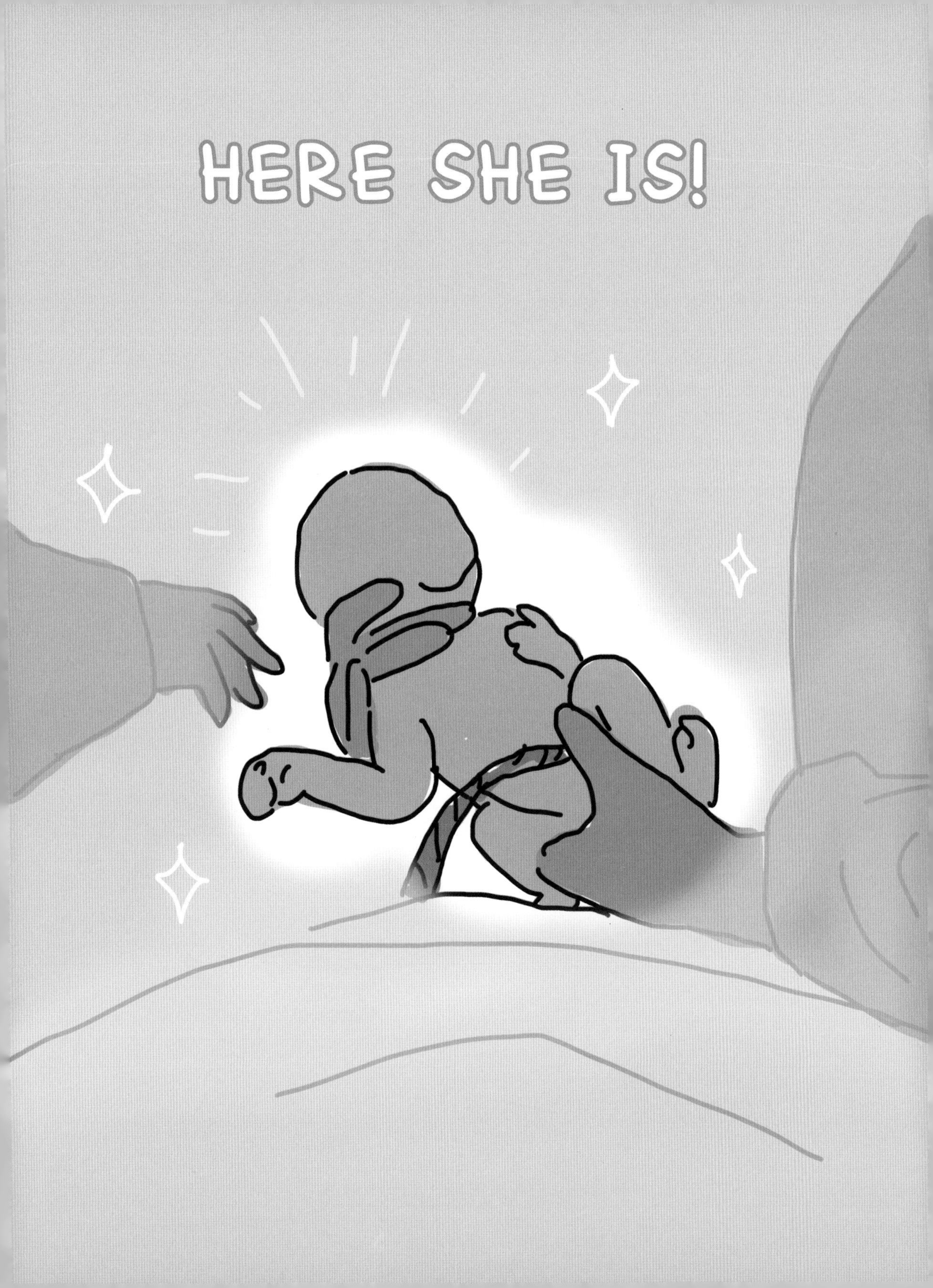
HERE SHE IS!

The morning after Charlie Mae was born, I was feeling all of the emotions at once. One by one, everyone who had worked with me throughout my labor came by to help me process what had happened. I remember telling my midwife, through tears, that I didn't think I could ever have another child because I could never go through that again. I was thoroughly traumatized by the experience, despite being completely in love with our daughter.

My labor experience left me raw, open, vulnerable. My entry into motherhood started with the scariest experience of my life. I had had fourth-degree "tearing" (from the episiotomy) and was injured. I was exhausted. I was emotionally wrecked. I had said—multiple times—during labor:

I WANT TO DIE.

And at the time, I'd meant it. But now that was all over and I had a baby to care for . . .

This is not a great way to start the most important role of your life. And I know I'm not alone in this experience.

Similarly, Ben was also left feeling traumatized by Charlie Mae's birth. He saw me go through hell. He felt helpless. He was tired and emotionally spent, too. I knew that, but I wanted more from him—and he couldn't give it because he was going through his own processing, which for him meant needing space, fresh air, and time to himself. This made me feel so angry and alone.

Although Ben was there for the entire birth in the best way that he could be, at the end of the day, this experience happened INSIDE my body—I spent almost thirty-six hours feeling like I was being ripped in two in order to bring our baby into the world. And I think I spent the first year of her life trying to make up for the fact that I "failed" at birthing her in the calm, peaceful way I'd wanted to.

Looking back now, I see that Ben never had a chance at being an "equal" because I was too busy proving myself and holding him to the highest, unattainable standards I'd set for myself.

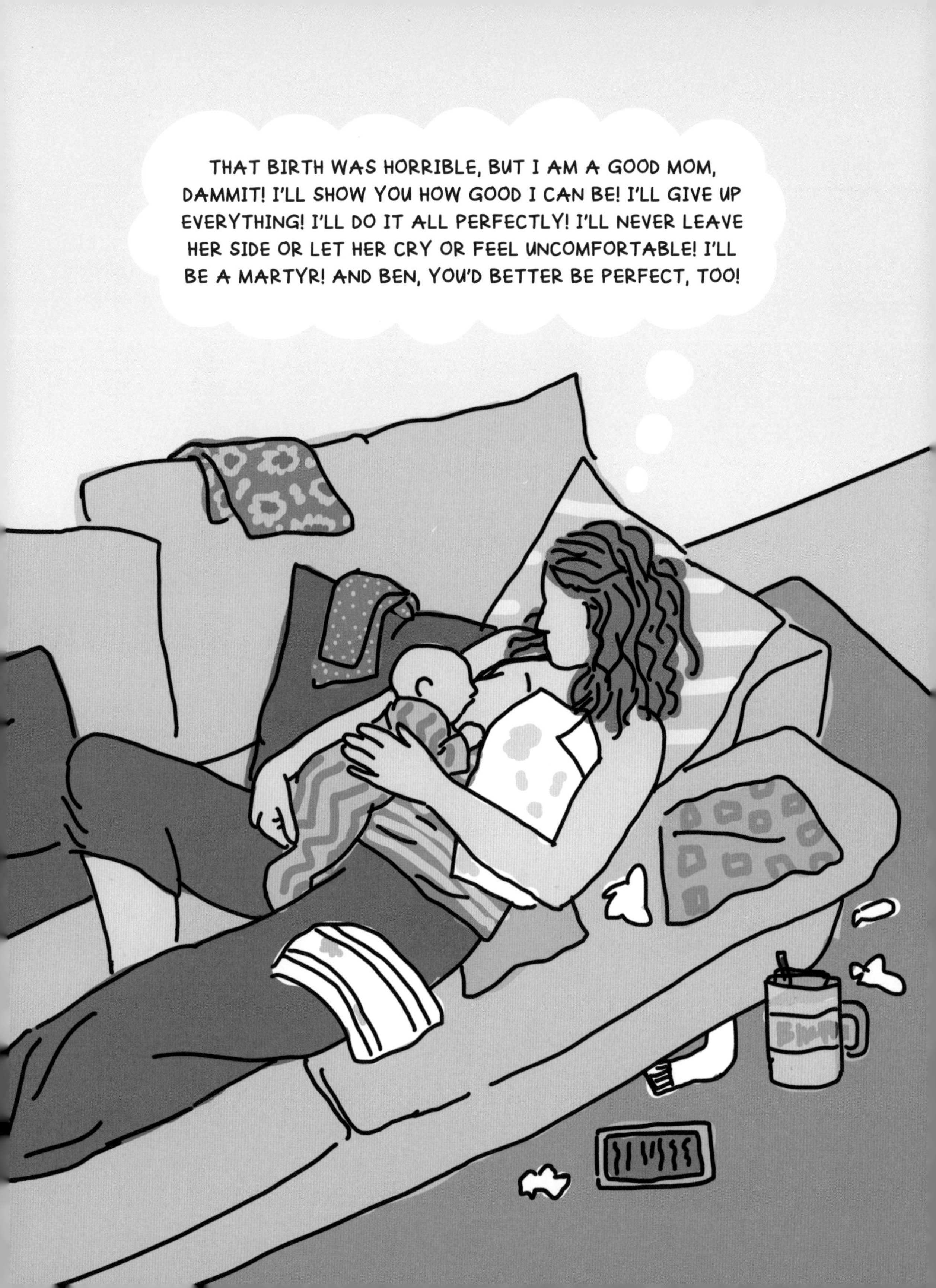
THAT BIRTH WAS HORRIBLE, BUT I AM A GOOD MOM, DAMMIT! I'LL SHOW YOU HOW GOOD I CAN BE! I'LL GIVE UP EVERYTHING! I'LL DO IT ALL PERFECTLY! I'LL NEVER LEAVE HER SIDE OR LET HER CRY OR FEEL UNCOMFORTABLE! I'LL BE A MARTYR! AND BEN, YOU'D BETTER BE PERFECT, TOO!

# Such a Great Butthole.

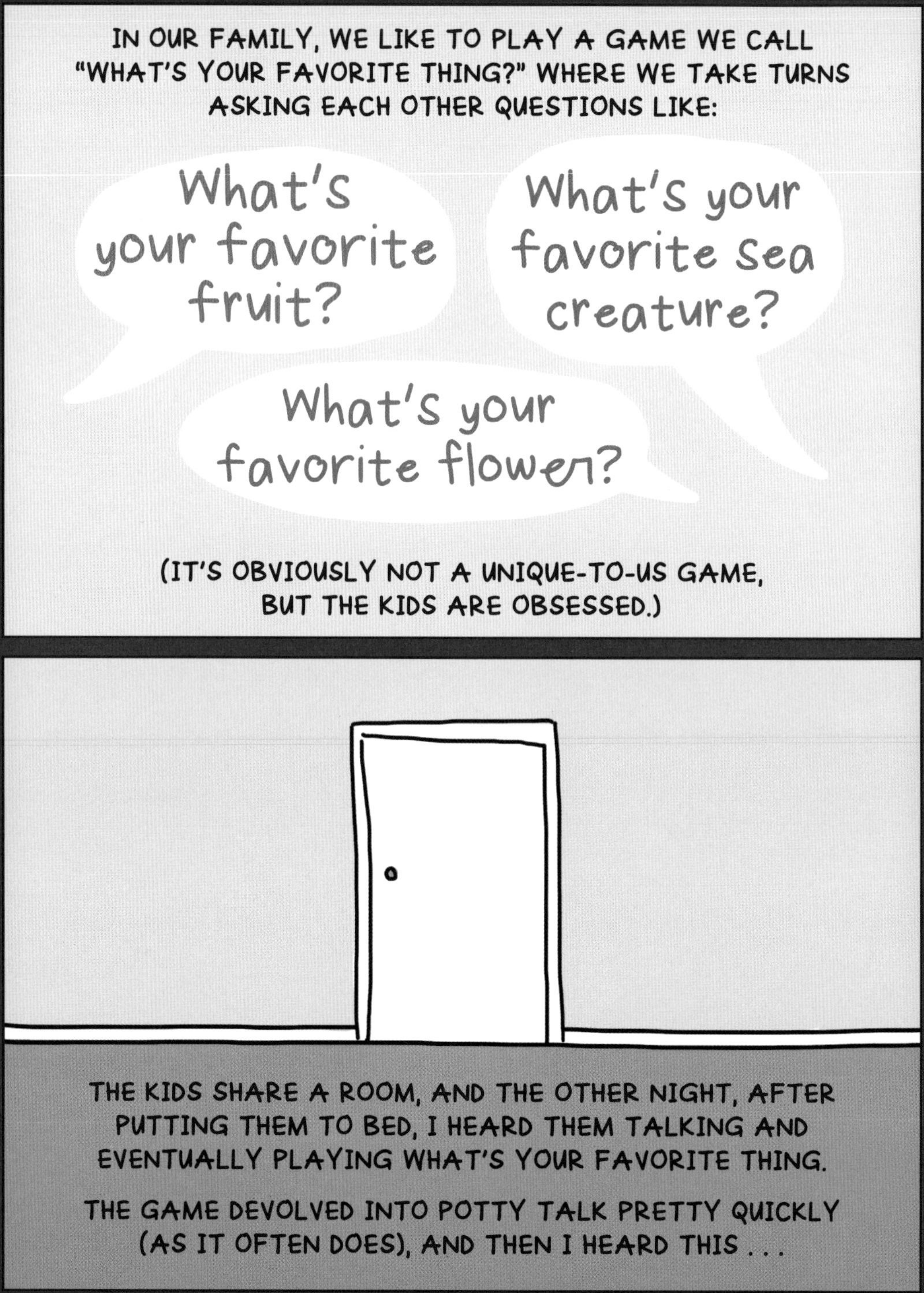
IN OUR FAMILY, WE LIKE TO PLAY A GAME WE CALL "WHAT'S YOUR FAVORITE THING?" WHERE WE TAKE TURNS ASKING EACH OTHER QUESTIONS LIKE:
What's your favorite fruit?
What's your favorite sea creature?
What's your favorite flower?
(IT'S OBVIOUSLY NOT A UNIQUE-TO-US GAME, BUT THE KIDS ARE OBSESSED.)
THE KIDS SHARE A ROOM, AND THE OTHER NIGHT, AFTER PUTTING THEM TO BED, I HEARD THEM TALKING AND EVENTUALLY PLAYING WHAT'S YOUR FAVORITE THING.
THE GAME DEVOLVED INTO POTTY TALK PRETTY QUICKLY (AS IT OFTEN DOES), AND THEN I HEARD THIS . . .

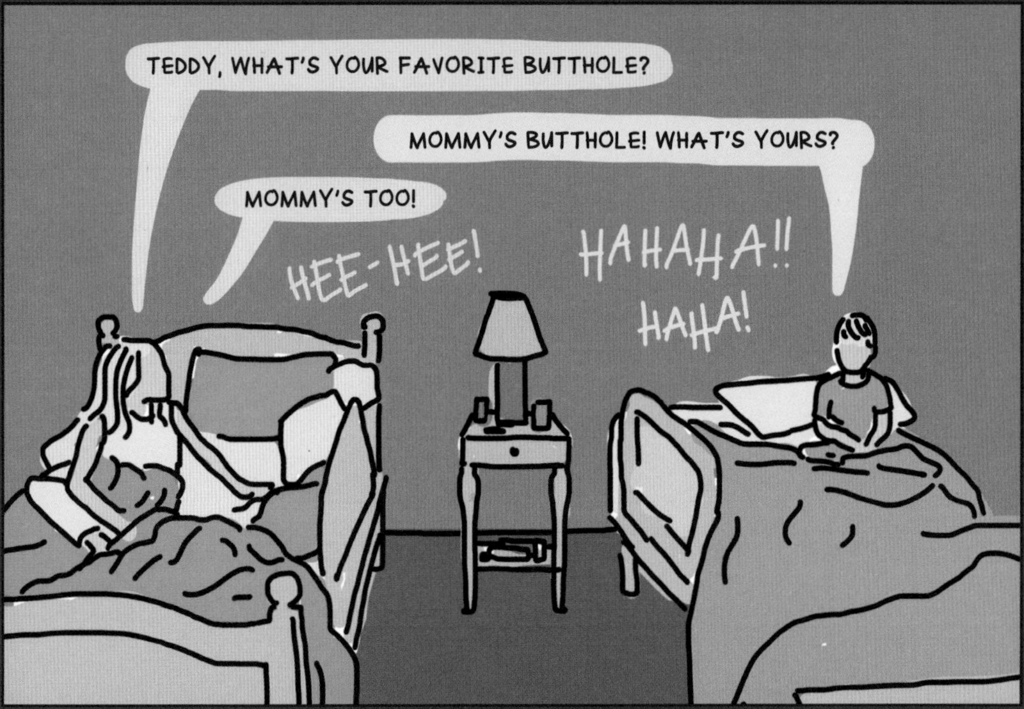
TEDDY, WHAT'S YOUR FAVORITE BUTTHOLE?
MOMMY'S BUTTHOLE! WHAT'S YOURS?
MOMMY'S TOO!
HEE-HEE!
HAHAHA!!
HAHA!

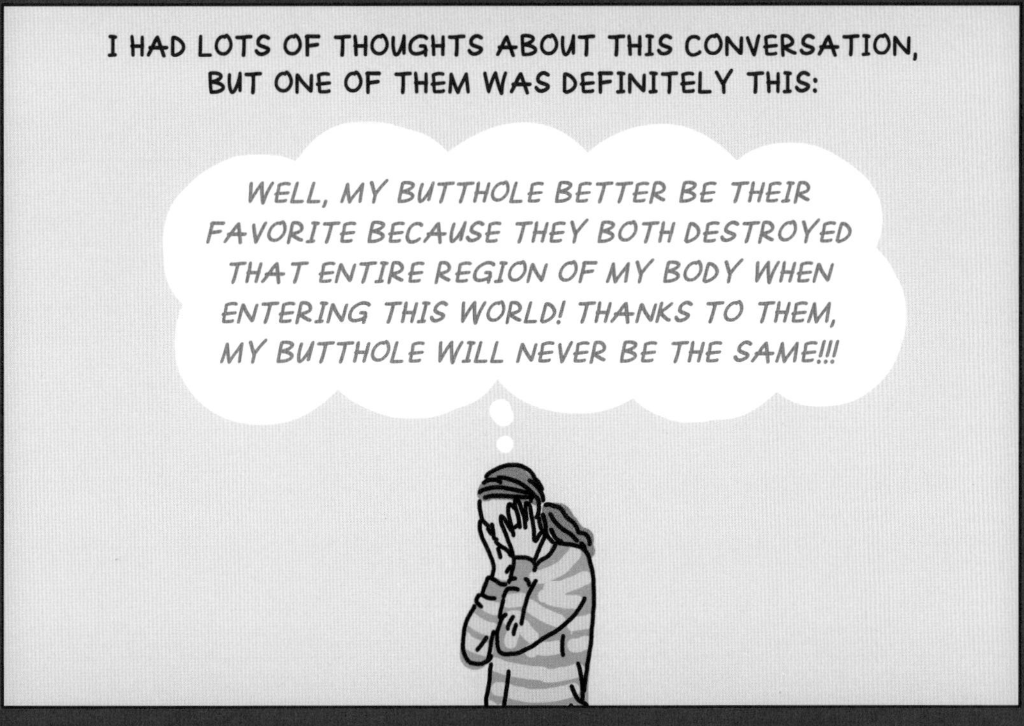
I HAD LOTS OF THOUGHTS ABOUT THIS CONVERSATION, BUT ONE OF THEM WAS DEFINITELY THIS:
WELL, MY BUTTHOLE BETTER BE THEIR FAVORITE BECAUSE THEY BOTH DESTROYED THAT ENTIRE REGION OF MY BODY WHEN ENTERING THIS WORLD! THANKS TO THEM, MY BUTTHOLE WILL NEVER BE THE SAME!!!

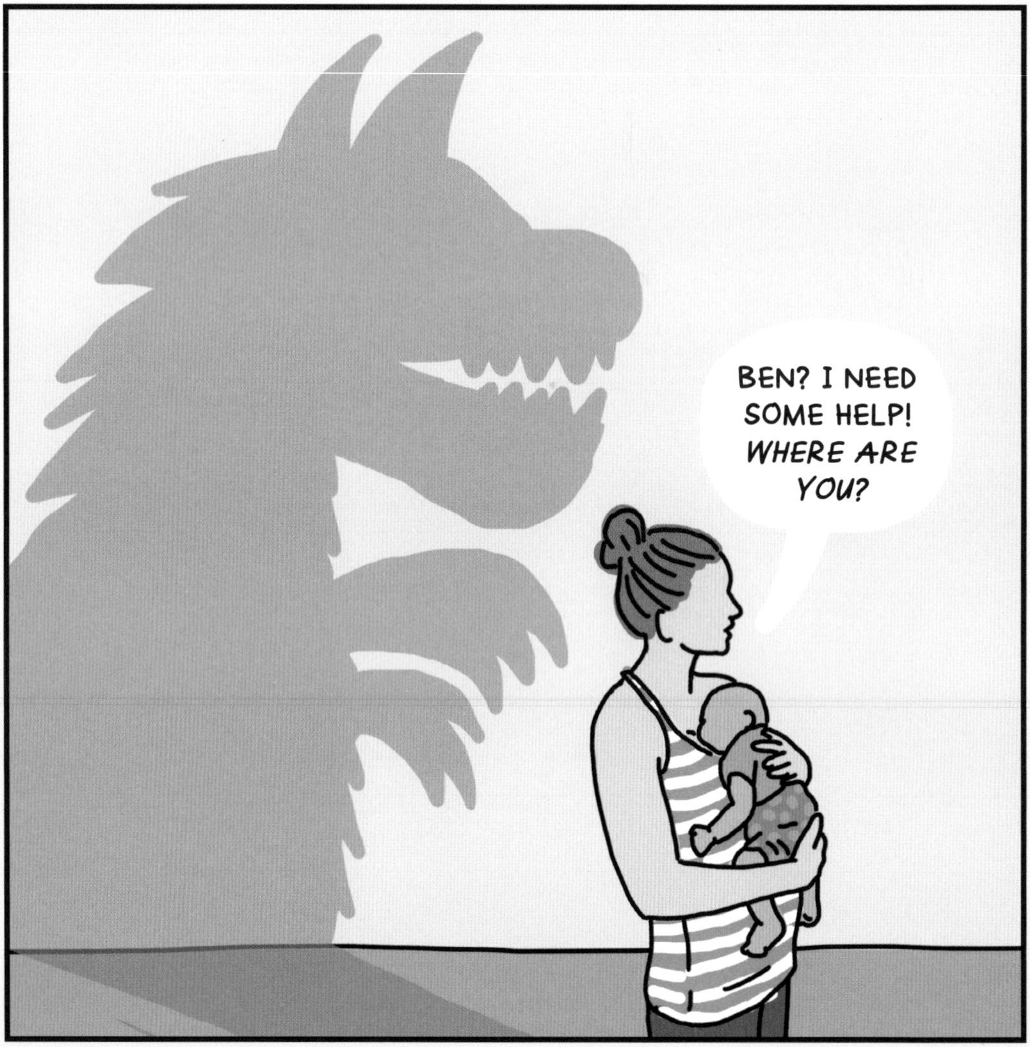
BEN? I NEED SOME HELP! *WHERE ARE YOU?*

# CHAPTER 4

# Postpartum Period No. 1:

# I'm Fine, Everything's Fine

# Why the First Year Was So Hard

When I think back on my daughter's first year of life, I feel so many mixed emotions. But what stands out the most—second to how much I loved becoming her mother, of course (OF COURSE! I'm not going to waste your time with disclaimers about how much I love my kids because you know that!!!)—is how anxious, tired, and miserable I was that year. And how utterly alone I felt despite having a loving partner by my side. Looking back, the reasons this year was so hard are very clear to me:

Charlie Mae really STRUGGLED with sleeping, and therefore I didn't sleep much. She woke up multiple times per night—most nights—until she was around 14 months.

Charlie Mae never took a bottle (or Binky), so I was her sole source of nutrition and soothing. This meant that I couldn't be away from her for more than two hours.

Charlie Mae was a very sensitive baby and would often cry for hours at a time if I wasn't the one holding her (and sometimes, even when I was!).

Because she wouldn't take a bottle and cried whenever she wasn't with me, it was hard to find child care for Charlie Mae. But I had a business to run, so reliable child care or not, I was back at work twelve weeks postpartum despite not having any sort of regular help . . .

Once I finally found child care that was a good fit for Charlie Mae, she wouldn't nap there. In order to get her the nap that she desperately needed, I only sent her to daycare for a half day so that I could bring her home to nap. I did this for months.

I had postpartum anxiety and postpartum rage . . . both of which are extra hard to navigate when you're as sleep-deprived as I was.

For many reasons, I became the preferred parent, the default parent, and the sole nighttime parent . . . which means that for the most part, I was the only person who could handle the bulk of Charlie Mae's care.

Like so many mothers during the postpartum period, I didn't have the perspective to deal with—or understand—any of this at the time because I was just in survival mode. I couldn't get mad at my precious little baby because none of this was her fault, so the only person I could turn my anger toward was Ben.

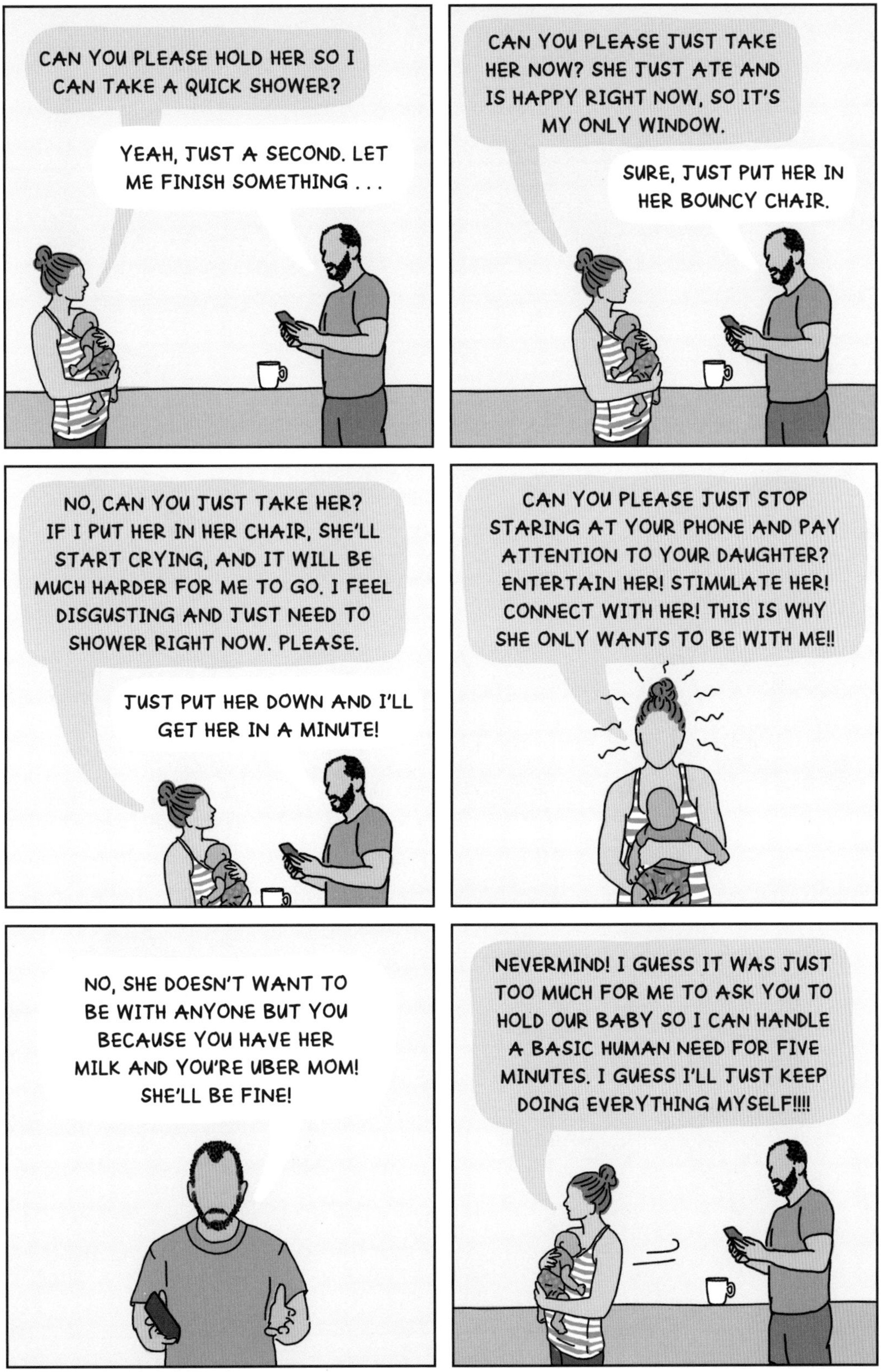
CAN YOU PLEASE HOLD HER SO I CAN TAKE A QUICK SHOWER?
YEAH, JUST A SECOND. LET ME FINISH SOMETHING . . .
CAN YOU PLEASE JUST TAKE HER NOW? SHE JUST ATE AND IS HAPPY RIGHT NOW, SO IT'S MY ONLY WINDOW.
SURE, JUST PUT HER IN HER BOUNCY CHAIR.
NO, CAN YOU JUST TAKE HER? IF I PUT HER IN HER CHAIR, SHE'LL START CRYING, AND IT WILL BE MUCH HARDER FOR ME TO GO. I FEEL DISGUSTING AND JUST NEED TO SHOWER RIGHT NOW. PLEASE.
JUST PUT HER DOWN AND I'LL GET HER IN A MINUTE!
CAN YOU PLEASE JUST STOP STARING AT YOUR PHONE AND PAY ATTENTION TO YOUR DAUGHTER? ENTERTAIN HER! STIMULATE HER! CONNECT WITH HER! THIS IS WHY SHE ONLY WANTS TO BE WITH ME!!
NO, SHE DOESN'T WANT TO BE WITH ANYONE BUT YOU BECAUSE YOU HAVE HER MILK AND YOU'RE UBER MOM! SHE'LL BE FINE!
NEVERMIND! I GUESS IT WAS JUST TOO MUCH FOR ME TO ASK YOU TO HOLD OUR BABY SO I CAN HANDLE A BASIC HUMAN NEED FOR FIVE MINUTES. I GUESS I'LL JUST KEEP DOING EVERYTHING MYSELF!!!!

## WHAT I WAS TOLD WHEN I WAS PREGNANT:

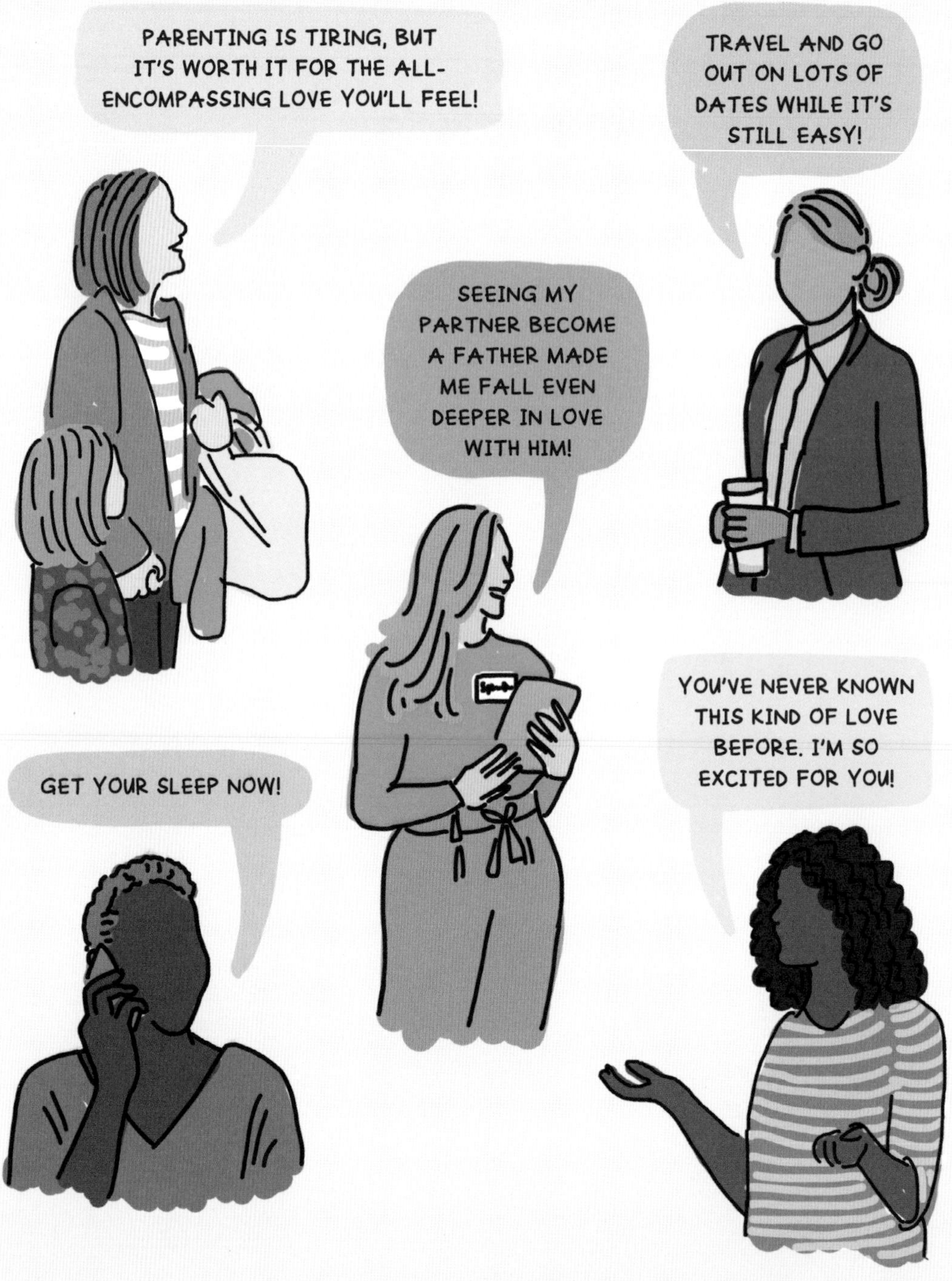
PARENTING IS TIRING, BUT IT'S WORTH IT FOR THE ALL-ENCOMPASSING LOVE YOU'LL FEEL!
TRAVEL AND GO OUT ON LOTS OF DATES WHILE IT'S STILL EASY!
SEEING MY PARTNER BECOME A FATHER MADE ME FALL EVEN DEEPER IN LOVE WITH HIM!
GET YOUR SLEEP NOW!
YOU'VE NEVER KNOWN THIS KIND OF LOVE BEFORE. I'M SO EXCITED FOR YOU!

WHAT I WISH I'D BEEN TOLD WHEN I WAS PREGNANT:

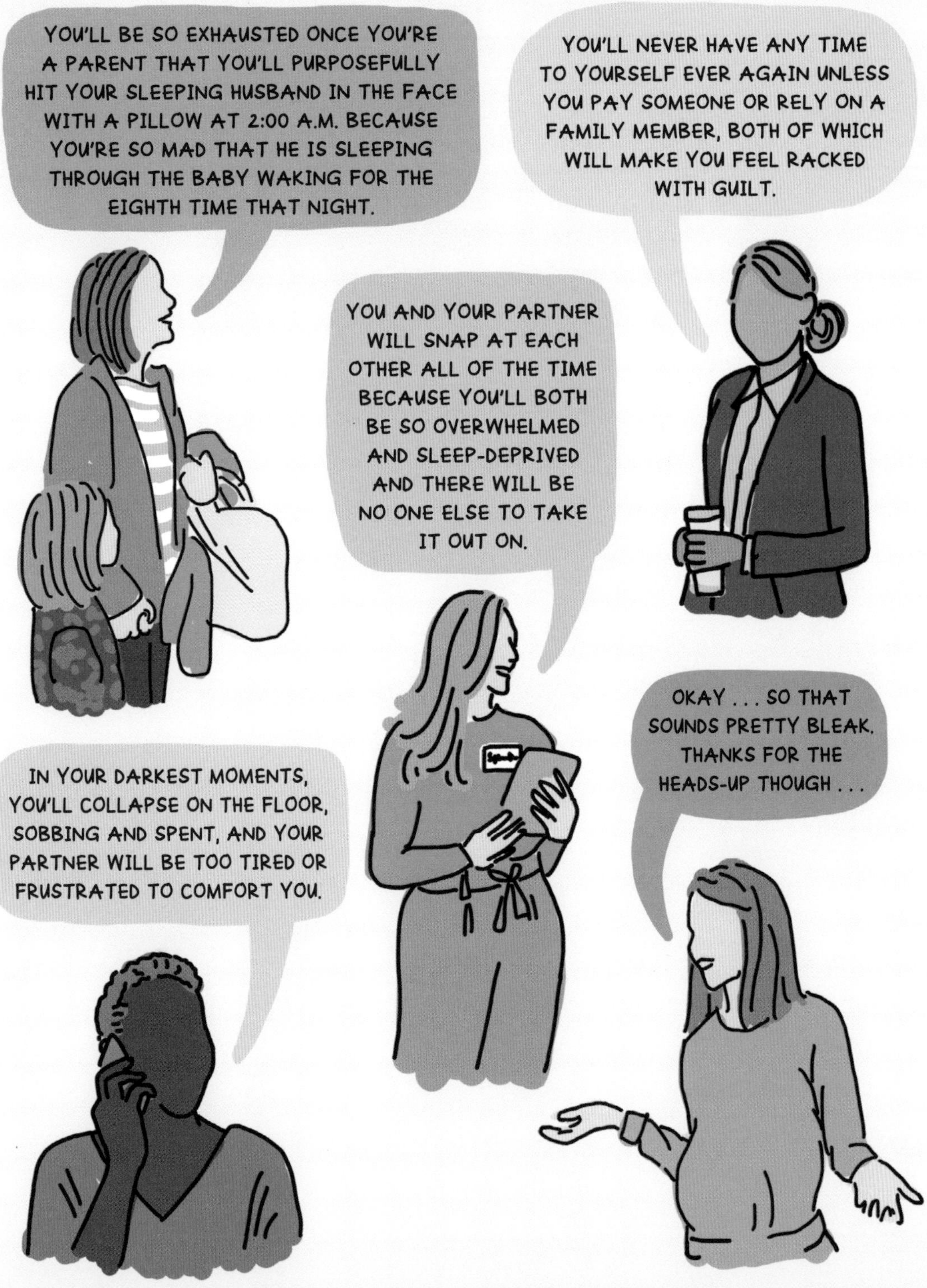
YOU'LL BE SO EXHAUSTED ONCE YOU'RE A PARENT THAT YOU'LL PURPOSEFULLY HIT YOUR SLEEPING HUSBAND IN THE FACE WITH A PILLOW AT 2:00 A.M. BECAUSE YOU'RE SO MAD THAT HE IS SLEEPING THROUGH THE BABY WAKING FOR THE EIGHTH TIME THAT NIGHT.
YOU'LL NEVER HAVE ANY TIME TO YOURSELF EVER AGAIN UNLESS YOU PAY SOMEONE OR RELY ON A FAMILY MEMBER, BOTH OF WHICH WILL MAKE YOU FEEL RACKED WITH GUILT.
YOU AND YOUR PARTNER WILL SNAP AT EACH OTHER ALL OF THE TIME BECAUSE YOU'LL BOTH BE SO OVERWHELMED AND SLEEP-DEPRIVED AND THERE WILL BE NO ONE ELSE TO TAKE IT OUT ON.
IN YOUR DARKEST MOMENTS, YOU'LL COLLAPSE ON THE FLOOR, SOBBING AND SPENT, AND YOUR PARTNER WILL BE TOO TIRED OR FRUSTRATED TO COMFORT YOU.
OKAY . . . SO THAT SOUNDS PRETTY BLEAK. THANKS FOR THE HEADS-UP THOUGH . . .

There's a reason people don't often tell the whole truth when you're pregnant: It brings down the mood. It takes away from the joy of pregnancy and the excitement about what could be. There's a fine line between being honest and being a total Debbie Downer (or worse, a miserable wife and mother).

Every couple experiences challenges during their first year of parenting, but some weather more challenges than others do. In our case, we weathered a lot of challenges in Charlie Mae's first sixteen months of life. The coping mechanisms that we used in that first year— coping mechanisms that were often deployed out of sheer desperation in order to just survive the day—created some really unfortunate, long-term imbalances and patterns within our family that we're still working through six years later.

Obviously, we had no idea that this was the case at the time (and we would have done things differently if we'd understood the ramifications!), but man, have the dynamics from the early years caused us a lot of conflict, frustration, and inequality. And because of this, I'm sure these dynamics will affect our children as they grow up, too.

A.K.A., SCREW THEM UP IN THE WAY THAT ALL PARENTS SCREW UP THEIR KIDS *EVEN AS THEY TRY THEIR VERY BEST TO NOT SCREW THEM UP.*

Here are some of the situations, challenges, and dynamics that led us down the path we're still on now but are trying our hardest to get the hell off of (please, someone tell me how to get off of this stupid, ass-backward path!) . . .

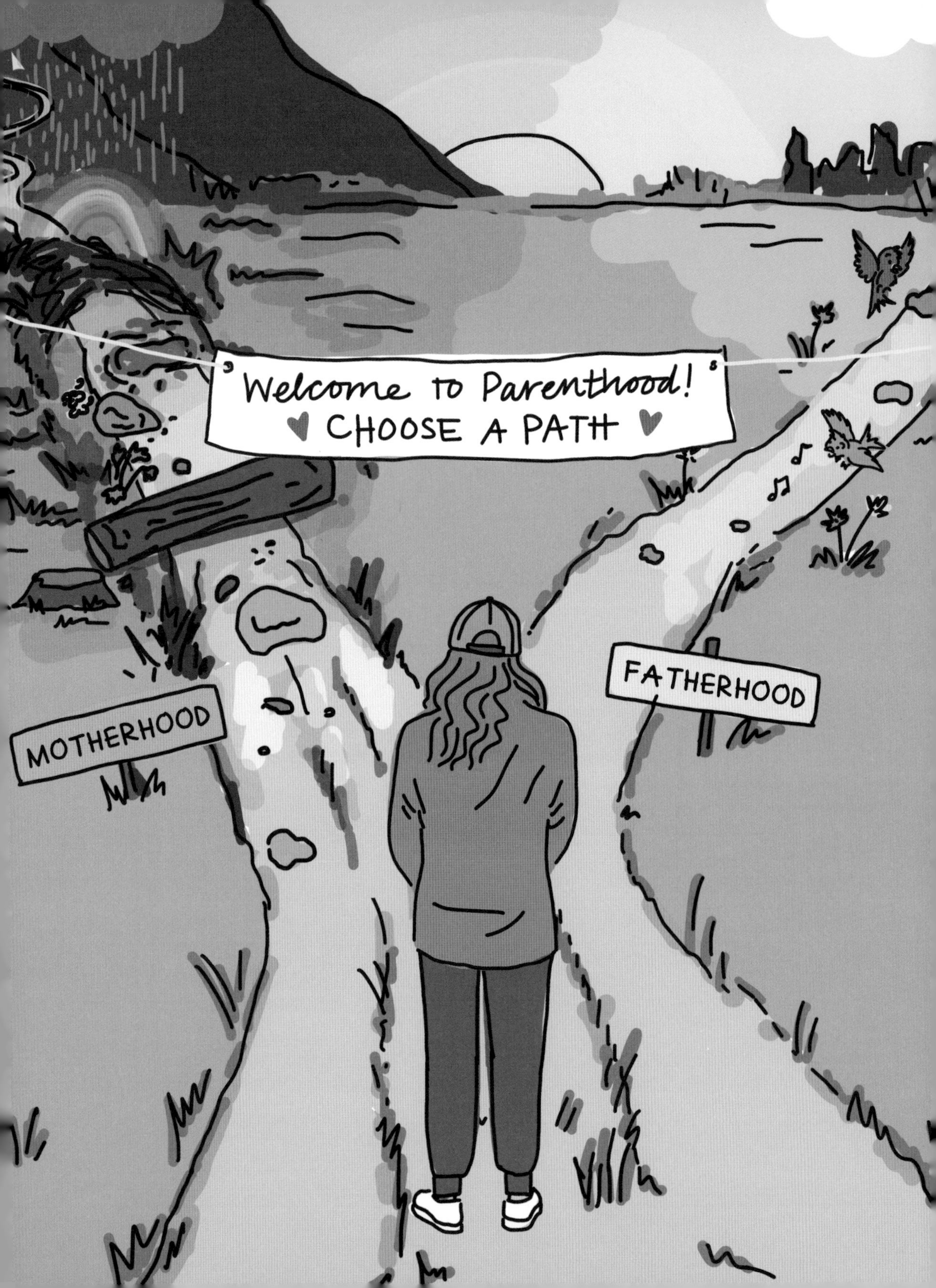
Welcome to Parenthood!
CHOOSE A PATH
MOTHERHOOD
FATHERHOOD

# Nighttime Parenting and Sleep Deprivation

Sleep deprivation is used as a form of torture because it is torture. It's TOTAL TORTURE. I say that as someone who has been steeped in sleep deprivation for many, many years now. Going without sleep does crazy things to your mind and body. Exhaustion transforms you from someone who has the bandwidth to deal with minor frustrations into someone who can't handle ANYTHING without major anxiety, rage, and/or depression.

I trace all of my issues in my first year of motherhood back to sleep—or lack thereof. People who have babies who are/were "good sleepers" or who had partners who split the nighttime parenting load evenly won't understand this, but those who unwittingly became the solo nighttime parent to a "bad sleeper" (as I did) will understand.

I KNOW, I KNOW, BABIES AREN'T "GOOD" OR "BAD" SLEEPERS. THEY'RE JUST BABIES TRYING TO SLEEP. BUT SERIOUSLY: AS A BABY, MY DAUGHTER WAS THE BADDEST OF BAD SLEEPERS.

There are many reasons that one parent [*cough* the mom *cough*] becomes the default nighttime parent, and we've dealt with almost all of these reasons in our household . . .

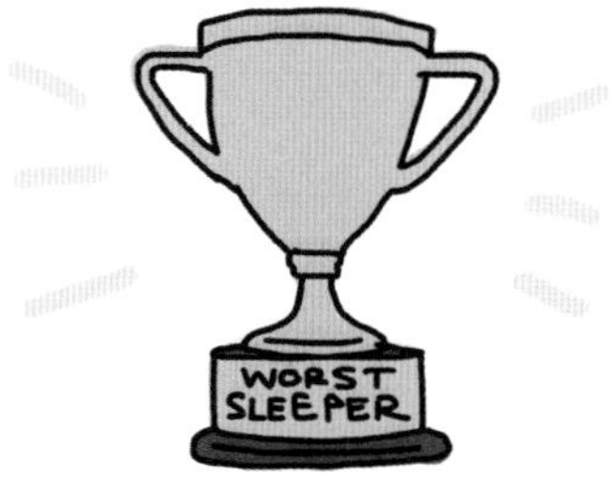
WORST SLEEPER

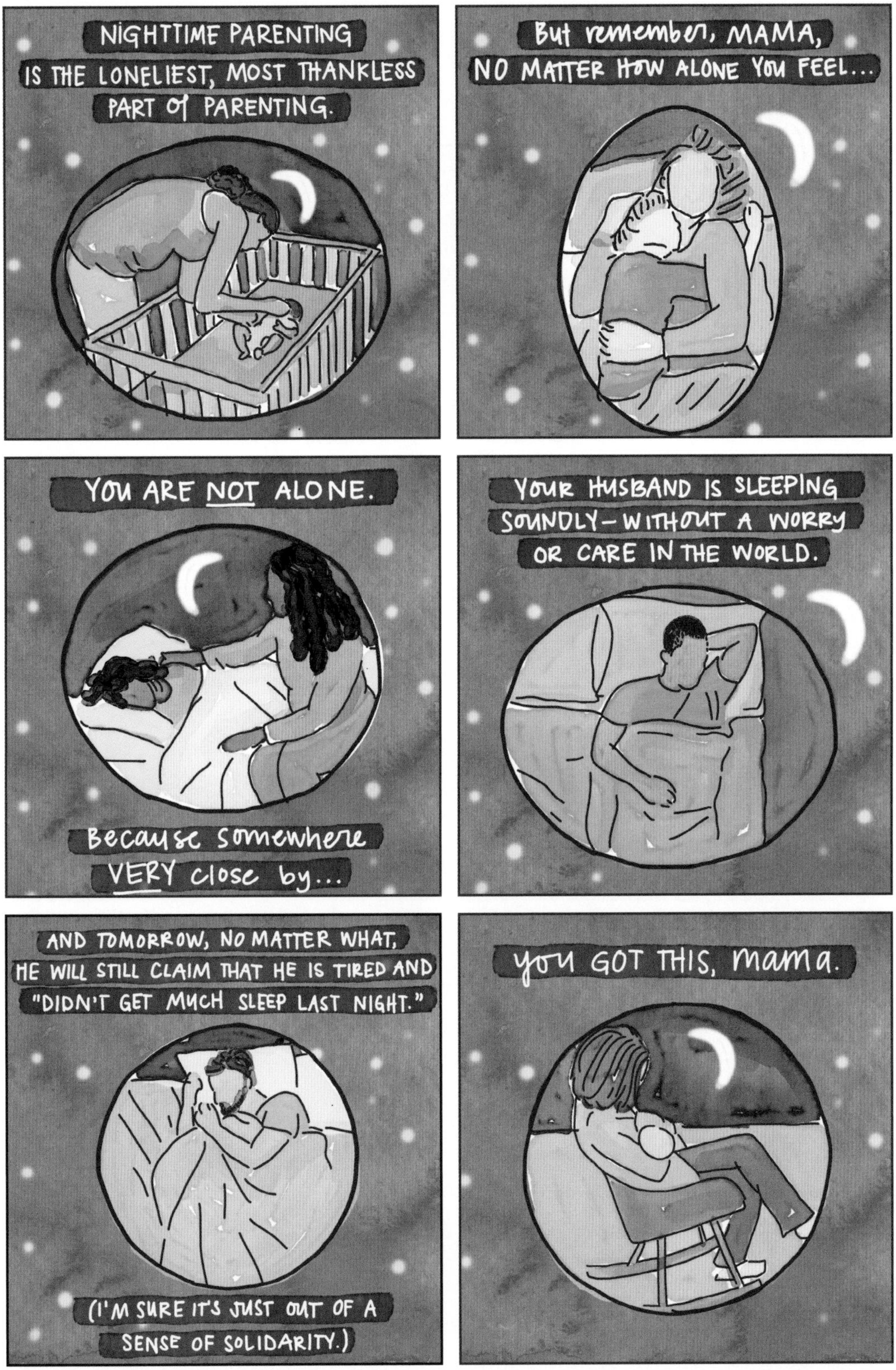
NIGHTTIME PARENTING IS THE LONELIEST, MOST THANKLESS PART OF PARENTING.
But remember, MAMA, NO MATTER HOW ALONE YOU FEEL...
YOU ARE NOT ALONE.
Because somewhere VERY close by...
YOUR HUSBAND IS SLEEPING SOUNDLY—WITHOUT A WORRY OR CARE IN THE WORLD.
AND TOMORROW, NO MATTER WHAT, HE WILL STILL CLAIM THAT HE IS TIRED AND "DIDN'T GET MUCH SLEEP LAST NIGHT."
(I'M SURE IT'S JUST OUT OF A SENSE OF SOLIDARITY.)
YOU GOT THIS, mama.

# Why So Many Moms Become the Default Nighttime Parents

HINT: IT'S NOT
BECAUSE HER
PARTNER SUCKS!

STARTING AT BIRTH/FIRST FEW WEEKS:

## Mom Is Up All Night Breastfeeding

If mom breastfeeds, she immediately gets in the habit of waking
with the baby every few hours during the night (it's just easier
if she does it*). Because her body physically responds to the
baby's cry, she is often on high alert all night and becomes very
attuned to baby's noises—even while sleeping.

*Yes, she could pump and her husband could offer a bottle, but
plenty of babies don't take bottles, and pumping is also a huge
pain for mom.

10:00 P.M.          12:00 A.M.          3:00 A.M.

5:00 A.M.          6:30 A.M.

THE FIRST FEW MONTHS:

## Mom Starts to Develop Nighttime Parenting Routines

If mom gets parental leave and dad doesn't (or gets a much shorter leave), there is an assumption that "he has to get sleep because he's working the next day," so mom handles all night wakings while she's on leave. Mom is also baby's primary caregiver while dad is at work, so she adapts to baby's sleeping and eating schedule.

For all of these reasons (and more), mom usually handles most of the night wakings for the first few months of baby's life. This means that by the time the baby is 3 to 4 months old, dad hasn't had much of a chance to practice soothing the baby at night.

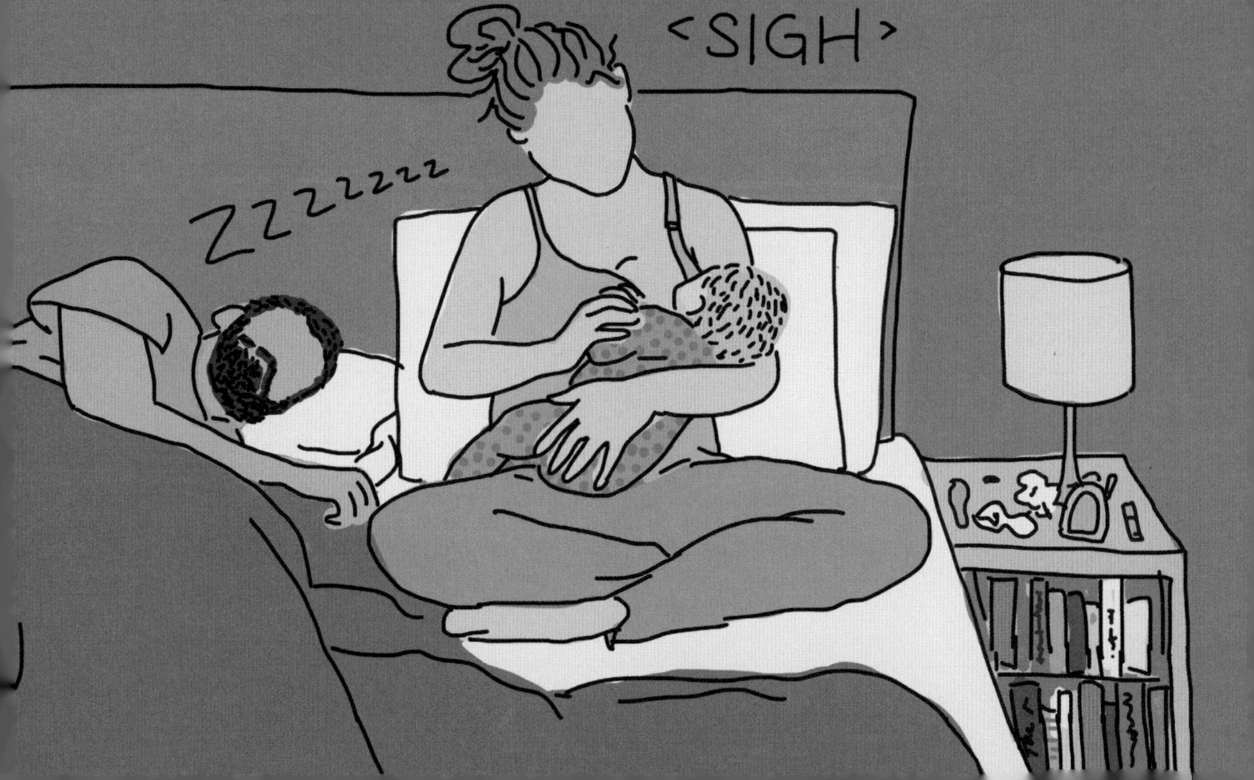
<SIGH>
ZZZZZZZ

## Four-Month Sleep Regression

Mom is up every forty-five minutes—all night long—almost every night.

She tries EVERYTHING to teach her baby how to sleep. She becomes an expert on this regression and all things baby sleep; she knows so much that she should probably become a sleep consultant for other families. But she still can't get her own child to sleep.

6 MONTHS:

## Baby Is Still Regressed/Mom Is Still Not Getting Any Sleep

Mom hasn't been sleeping for at least six months, and she's past the point of desperation. She's an anxious, exhausted mess, and she's full of resentment for her well-rested partner. She might seek expert help at this point, she might have a breakdown, or she might do both. The situation has gotten dire.

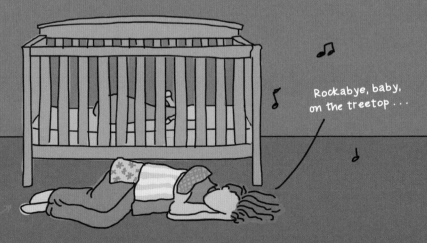

Rockabye, baby, on the treetop . . .

WILL TIPTOE OUT OF BABY'S ROOM AND PROBABLY WAKE THE BABY DESPITE MAKING ABSOLUTELY NO NOISE.

THROUGHOUT THE REST OF THE FIRST YEAR:

## Mom Continues to Be the Primary Nighttime Parent While Baby Continues to NOT Sleep

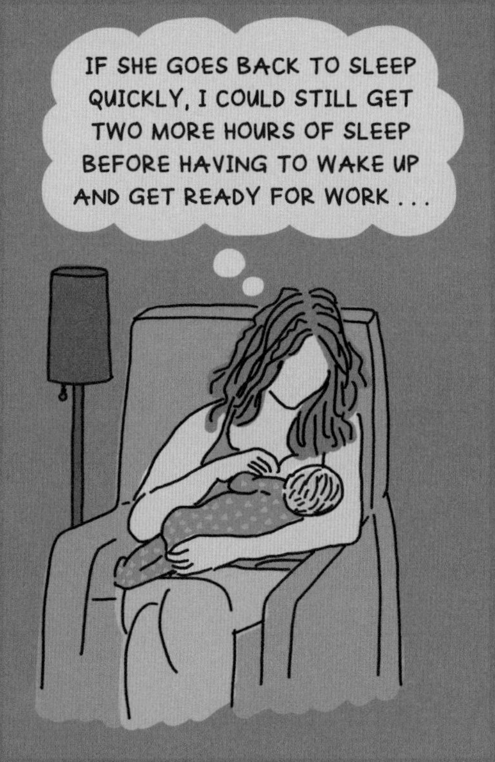
IF SHE GOES BACK TO SLEEP QUICKLY, I COULD STILL GET TWO MORE HOURS OF SLEEP BEFORE HAVING TO WAKE UP AND GET READY FOR WORK . . .

If mom works outside the home, by the time she goes back to work the routine and expectation have already been set: She's the one who handles nighttime parenting. She is now the most attuned and efficient nighttime parent. (And dad has learned to sleep through nighttime wake-ups.)

If mom doesn't work outside the home, the idea that dad "has to work the next day" (even though mom works, too, just not outside the home) means that mom usually gets stuck with all nighttime wake-up duties.

Similarly, many babies continue to wake up multiple times per night throughout their first year of life (ours sure did!), so even if mom has gone back to work, she's still getting up with the baby at night and trying desperately to get her baby to *just freaking sleep* so she can return to feeling human.

12 MONTHS AND BEYOND:

## Yep, Mom Is STILL Up 2–3x/Night

Mom continues to get very little sleep. Every once in a while, she tells dad that she can't keep doing all of the nighttime wake-ups and needs his help. He says he'll try.

But because dad isn't well-versed in handling nighttime wake-ups, when he does try to handle one, he either doesn't know how OR the baby cries harder, asks for mom, or completely rejects dad. Eventually, dad gets so frustrated that he asks mom to take over.

She stops asking for help.

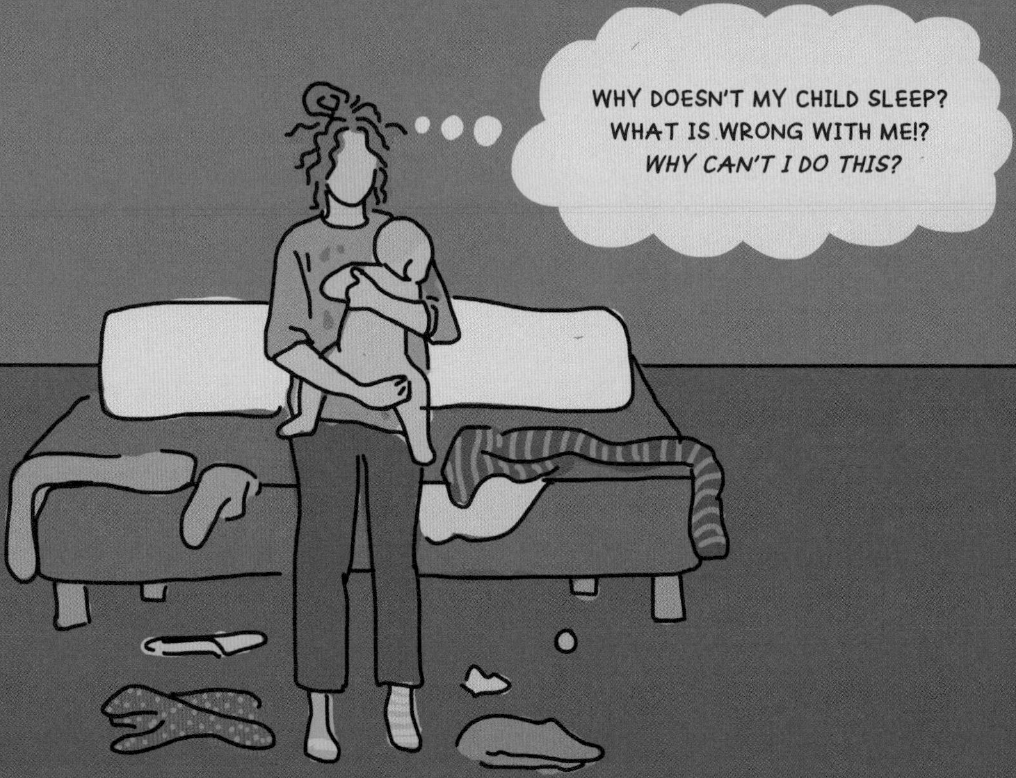
WHY DOESN'T MY CHILD SLEEP?
WHAT IS WRONG WITH ME!?
*WHY CAN'T I DO THIS?*

14–16 MONTHS:

## Baby Is FINALLY Sleeping, buuuuuut Mom Is Not

Since mom hasn't gotten real, good sleep for over a year now, she's an anxious mess at night. Whether or not the baby is awake, she worries. She worries when the baby is sleeping because a sleeping baby is so abnormal in their house. She opens her eyes at every sound on the monitor, worried that even the smallest noise is the baby waking. She wakes up early and can't go back to sleep because she's sure the baby will be up any minute, so what's the point?

Mom now has major nighttime/sleep-related trauma and has forgotten how to sleep deeply; she's always waiting for the other shoe to drop.

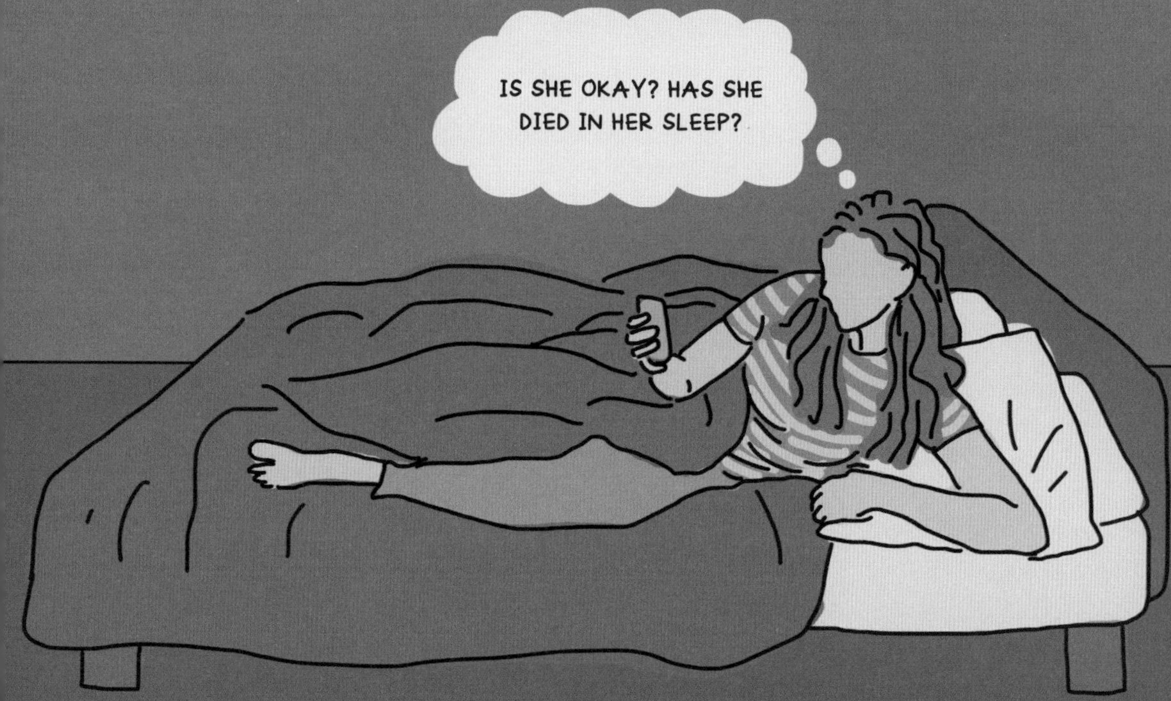
IS SHE OKAY? HAS SHE DIED IN HER SLEEP?

16-ISH MONTHS AND BEYOND:

## Mom Has Now Earned Herself the Title of Default Nighttime Parent FOREVER

Mom is often angry at/frustrated with dad because he sleeps through all nighttime wake-ups and isn't helpful at night. She walks around feeling like a shadow of her former self because she hasn't slept well in months or, more likely, in YEARS (I'm looking at you, Pregnancy).

Dad feels angry at/frustrated with mom because he's not trying to be unhelpful on purpose; he simply doesn't have the necessary tools to handle nighttime wake-ups and therefore feels useless (so there's no point in him getting up).

He may also be tired because his sleep is often interrupted—but he has NO CLUE what it's like to be mom-tired (which also makes mom mad).

And here's where we arrive at our issue:
No one is exactly "at fault," but things are very imbalanced, and mom is at the end of her rope.

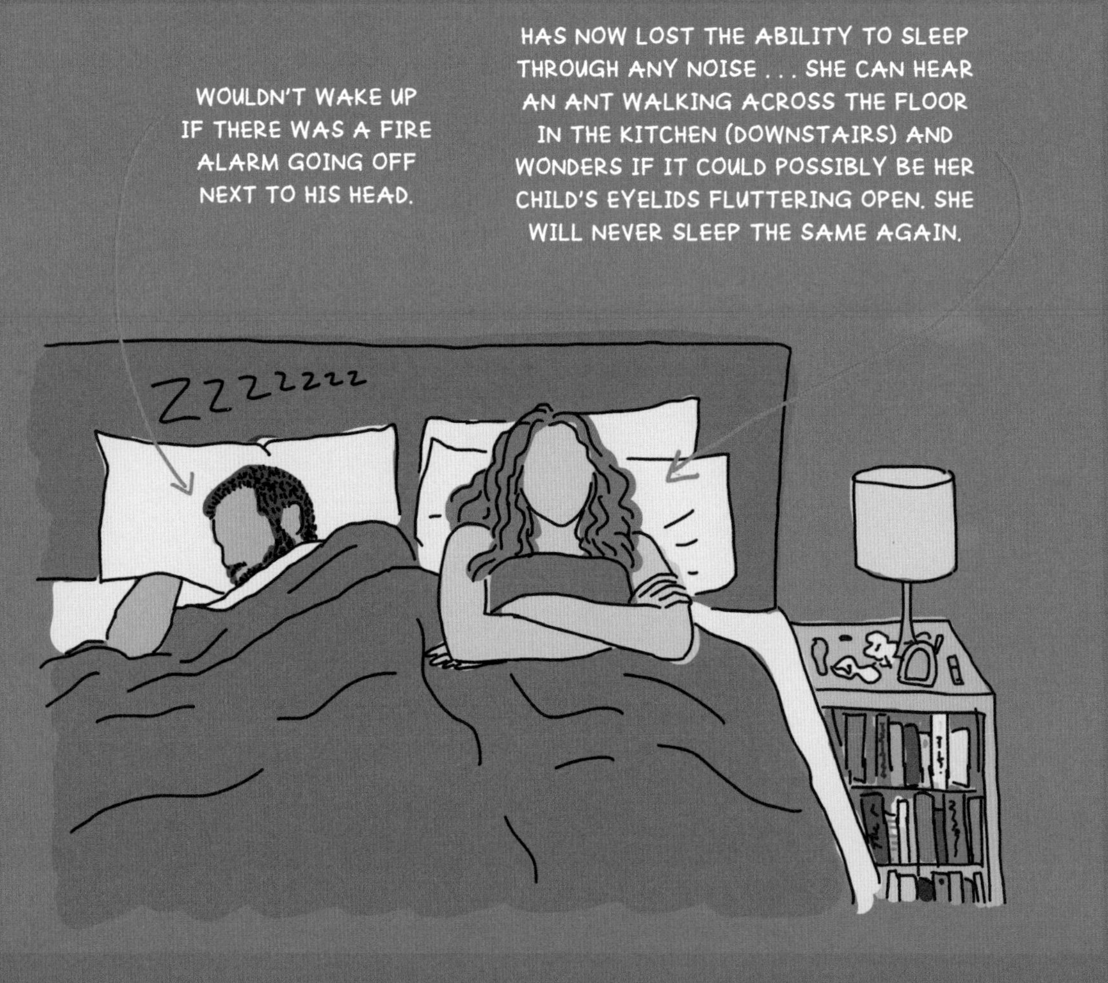
WOULDN'T WAKE UP IF THERE WAS A FIRE ALARM GOING OFF NEXT TO HIS HEAD.
HAS NOW LOST THE ABILITY TO SLEEP THROUGH ANY NOISE . . . SHE CAN HEAR AN ANT WALKING ACROSS THE FLOOR IN THE KITCHEN (DOWNSTAIRS) AND WONDERS IF IT COULD POSSIBLY BE HER CHILD'S EYELIDS FLUTTERING OPEN. SHE WILL NEVER SLEEP THE SAME AGAIN.
ZZZZZZZ

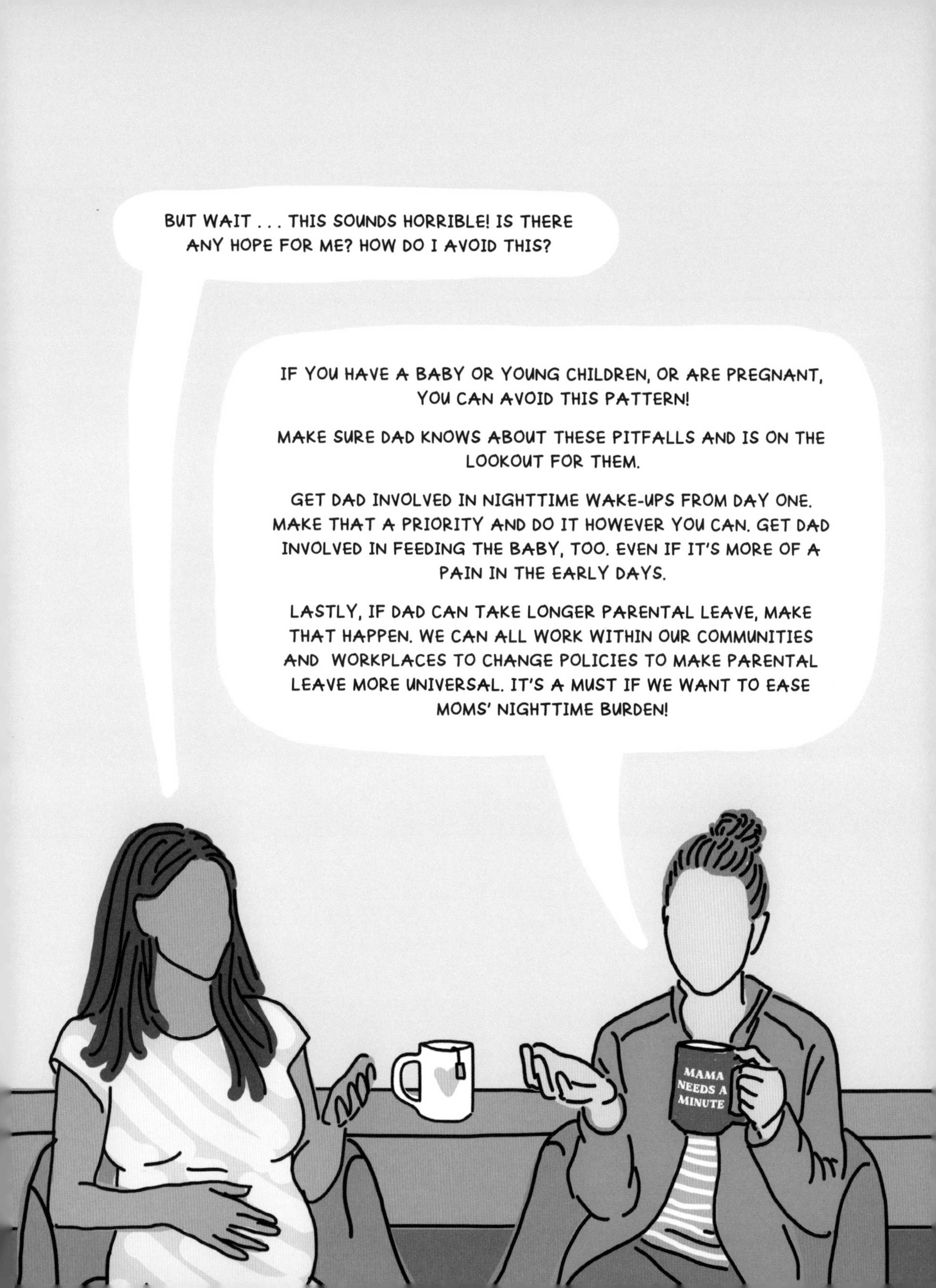
BUT WAIT . . . THIS SOUNDS HORRIBLE! IS THERE ANY HOPE FOR ME? HOW DO I AVOID THIS?
IF YOU HAVE A BABY OR YOUNG CHILDREN, OR ARE PREGNANT, YOU CAN AVOID THIS PATTERN!
MAKE SURE DAD KNOWS ABOUT THESE PITFALLS AND IS ON THE LOOKOUT FOR THEM.
GET DAD INVOLVED IN NIGHTTIME WAKE-UPS FROM DAY ONE. MAKE THAT A PRIORITY AND DO IT HOWEVER YOU CAN. GET DAD INVOLVED IN FEEDING THE BABY, TOO. EVEN IF IT'S MORE OF A PAIN IN THE EARLY DAYS.
LASTLY, IF DAD CAN TAKE LONGER PARENTAL LEAVE, MAKE THAT HAPPEN. WE CAN ALL WORK WITHIN OUR COMMUNITIES AND WORKPLACES TO CHANGE POLICIES TO MAKE PARENTAL LEAVE MORE UNIVERSAL. IT'S A MUST IF WE WANT TO EASE MOMS' NIGHTTIME BURDEN!
MAMA NEEDS A MINUTE

We were a textbook example for all of these issues. As the months went by and Charlie Mae continued to struggle with sleep, I cemented my role as the more competent, aware, capable nighttime parent in our household.

Because of this, I felt like Charlie Mae's refusal to sleep was my fault. I was the nighttime parent, after all! I was the one who had created these "horrible" patterns of breastfeeding at night! I was the one doing all the research and reading and sleep courses and who, despite all of this, couldn't get the job done. I was failing at something so basic.

The more sleep-deprived I became, the more lost, hopeless, and alone I felt. I spent so many nights rocking or breastfeeding her in the dark, crying about her inability to sleep. I spent so much energy being angry at Ben because he "couldn't" help. And while I was dealing with all of this, my anxiety skyrocketed.

Obviously, now I know that Charlie Mae's inability to sleep wasn't my fault, but even six years later, I still feel traumatized by this year without sleep.

Now we have two kids, and at least one of them is up in the night a couple of nights per week . . . and guess who is still the

default nighttime parent for both kids? Yep, you guessed it.

Every time I'm up in the night—even now—I feel that familiar panic from Charlie Mae's first year of life.

WHAT IS HAPPENING? WHY IS MY CHILD AWAKE RIGHT NOW? WILL I EVER SLEEP AGAIN? WHAT CAN I DO TO GET MY CHILD TO SLEEP?

It's a very helpless feeling that has been burned into my memory forever.

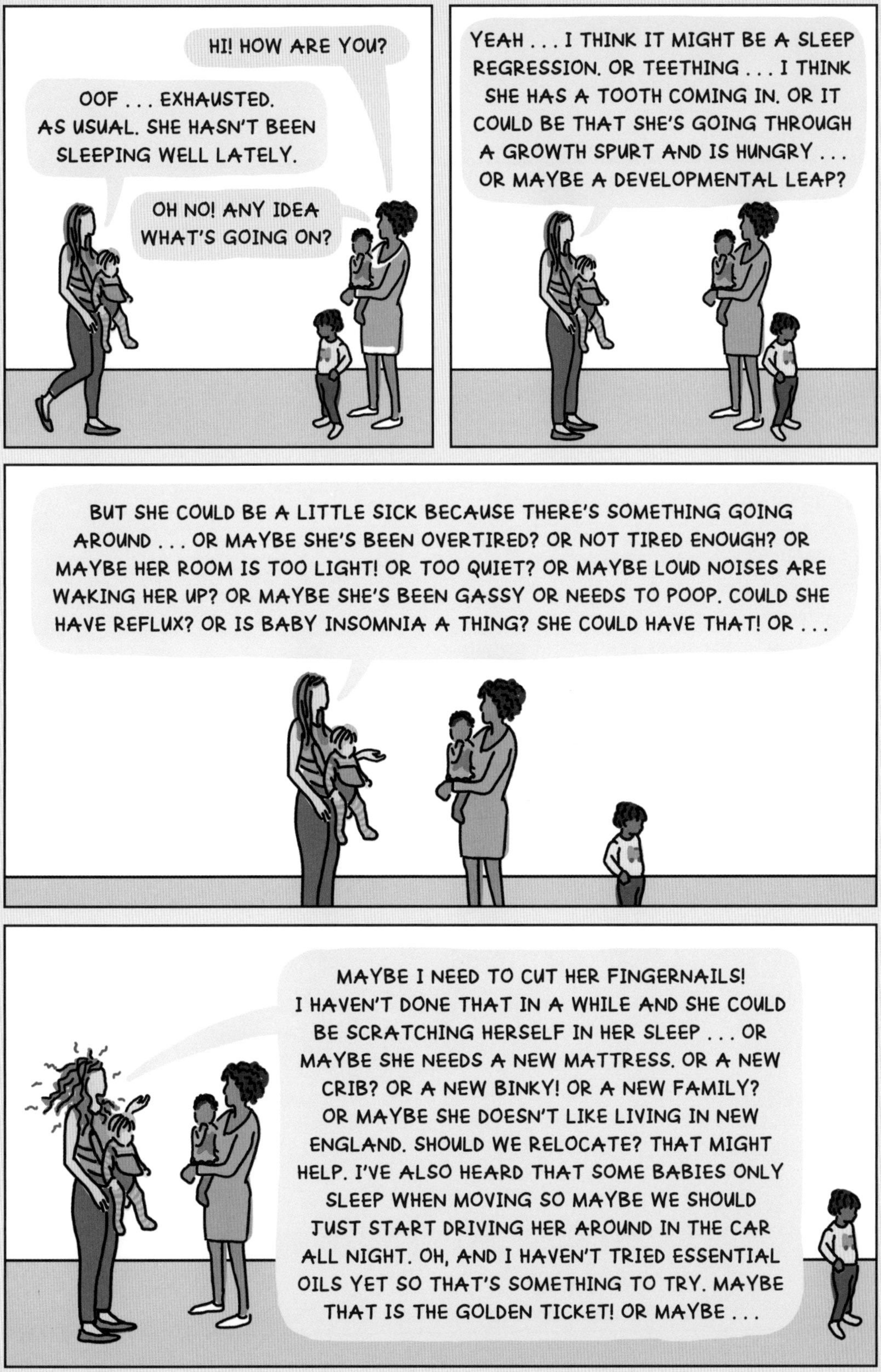
HI! HOW ARE YOU?
OOF . . . EXHAUSTED. AS USUAL. SHE HASN'T BEEN SLEEPING WELL LATELY.
OH NO! ANY IDEA WHAT'S GOING ON?
YEAH . . . I THINK IT MIGHT BE A SLEEP REGRESSION. OR TEETHING . . . I THINK SHE HAS A TOOTH COMING IN. OR IT COULD BE THAT SHE'S GOING THROUGH A GROWTH SPURT AND IS HUNGRY . . . OR MAYBE A DEVELOPMENTAL LEAP?
BUT SHE COULD BE A LITTLE SICK BECAUSE THERE'S SOMETHING GOING AROUND . . . OR MAYBE SHE'S BEEN OVERTIRED? OR NOT TIRED ENOUGH? OR MAYBE HER ROOM IS TOO LIGHT! OR TOO QUIET? OR MAYBE LOUD NOISES ARE WAKING HER UP? OR MAYBE SHE'S BEEN GASSY OR NEEDS TO POOP. COULD SHE HAVE REFLUX? OR IS BABY INSOMNIA A THING? SHE COULD HAVE THAT! OR . . .
MAYBE I NEED TO CUT HER FINGERNAILS! I HAVEN'T DONE THAT IN A WHILE AND SHE COULD BE SCRATCHING HERSELF IN HER SLEEP . . . OR MAYBE SHE NEEDS A NEW MATTRESS. OR A NEW CRIB? OR A NEW BINKY! OR A NEW FAMILY? OR MAYBE SHE DOESN'T LIKE LIVING IN NEW ENGLAND. SHOULD WE RELOCATE? THAT MIGHT HELP. I'VE ALSO HEARD THAT SOME BABIES ONLY SLEEP WHEN MOVING SO MAYBE WE SHOULD JUST START DRIVING HER AROUND IN THE CAR ALL NIGHT. OH, AND I HAVEN'T TRIED ESSENTIAL OILS YET SO THAT'S SOMETHING TO TRY. MAYBE THAT IS THE GOLDEN TICKET! OR MAYBE . . .

# Postpartum Anxiety

If you're already an anxious person, when you become a mother, you unlock an entire new world of anxieties. Each day you discover something new you can (and definitely should!) worry about.

Among moms with postpartum anxiety (PPA), everyone's anxiety looks different, but mine, for the most part, was focused on sleep (no surprise there). And specifically, Charlie Mae's sleep schedule. Because she didn't sleep, I did all of the research on all of the sites and read all of the articles by all of the sleep experts in an effort to learn how to get her to sleep.

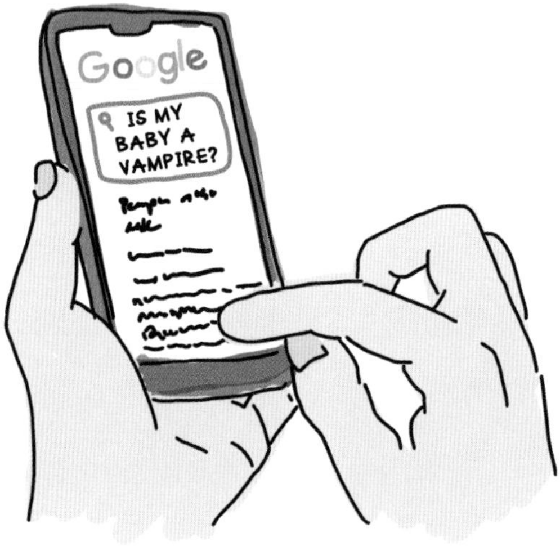
Google
IS MY BABY A VAMPIRE?

## MY GENERALIZED BRAND OF PPA

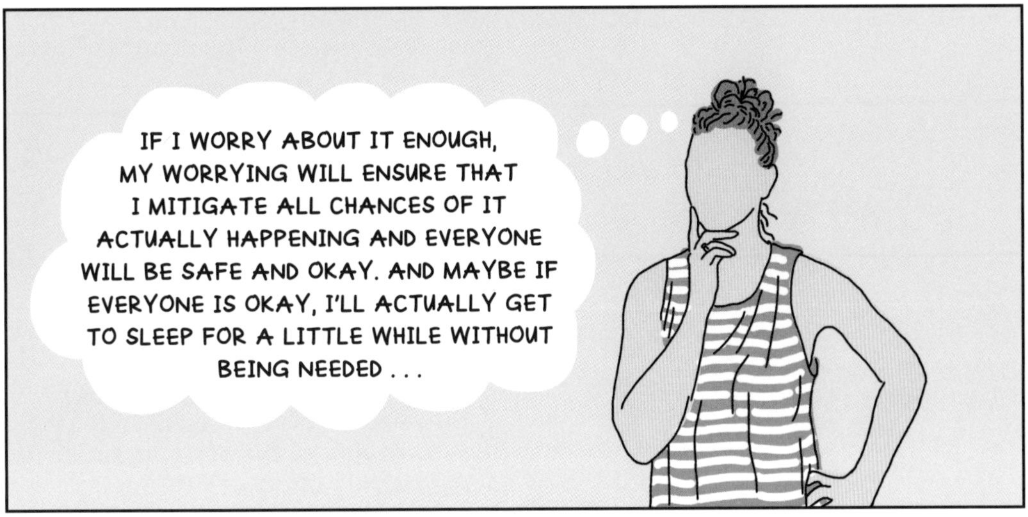
IF I WORRY ABOUT IT ENOUGH, MY WORRYING WILL ENSURE THAT I MITIGATE ALL CHANCES OF IT ACTUALLY HAPPENING AND EVERYONE WILL BE SAFE AND OKAY. AND MAYBE IF EVERYONE IS OKAY, I'LL ACTUALLY GET TO SLEEP FOR A LITTLE WHILE WITHOUT BEING NEEDED . . .

## MY SPECIFIC BRAND OF PPA

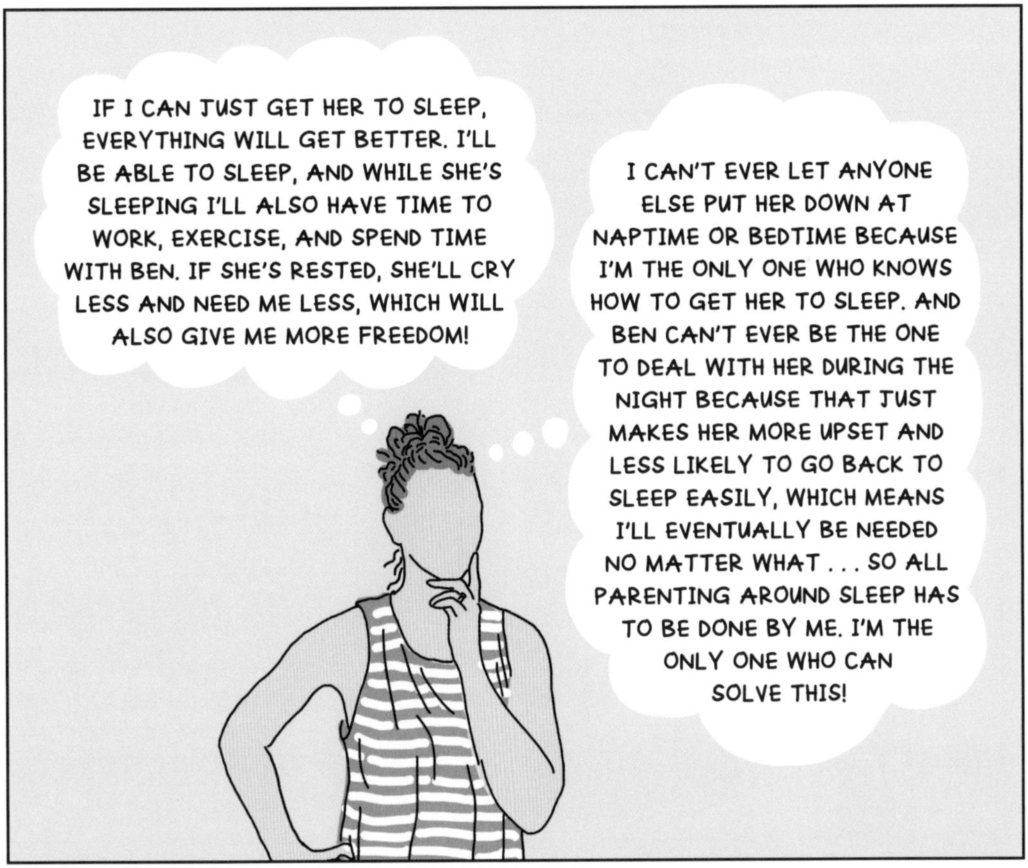
IF I CAN JUST GET HER TO SLEEP, EVERYTHING WILL GET BETTER. I'LL BE ABLE TO SLEEP, AND WHILE SHE'S SLEEPING I'LL ALSO HAVE TIME TO WORK, EXERCISE, AND SPEND TIME WITH BEN. IF SHE'S RESTED, SHE'LL CRY LESS AND NEED ME LESS, WHICH WILL ALSO GIVE ME MORE FREEDOM!
I CAN'T EVER LET ANYONE ELSE PUT HER DOWN AT NAPTIME OR BEDTIME BECAUSE I'M THE ONLY ONE WHO KNOWS HOW TO GET HER TO SLEEP. AND BEN CAN'T EVER BE THE ONE TO DEAL WITH HER DURING THE NIGHT BECAUSE THAT JUST MAKES HER MORE UPSET AND LESS LIKELY TO GO BACK TO SLEEP EASILY, WHICH MEANS I'LL EVENTUALLY BE NEEDED NO MATTER WHAT . . . SO ALL PARENTING AROUND SLEEP HAS TO BE DONE BY ME. I'M THE ONLY ONE WHO CAN SOLVE THIS!

And while my anxiety was most triggered by sleep issues, I also felt the intense biological anxieties that everyone talks about, as well . . .

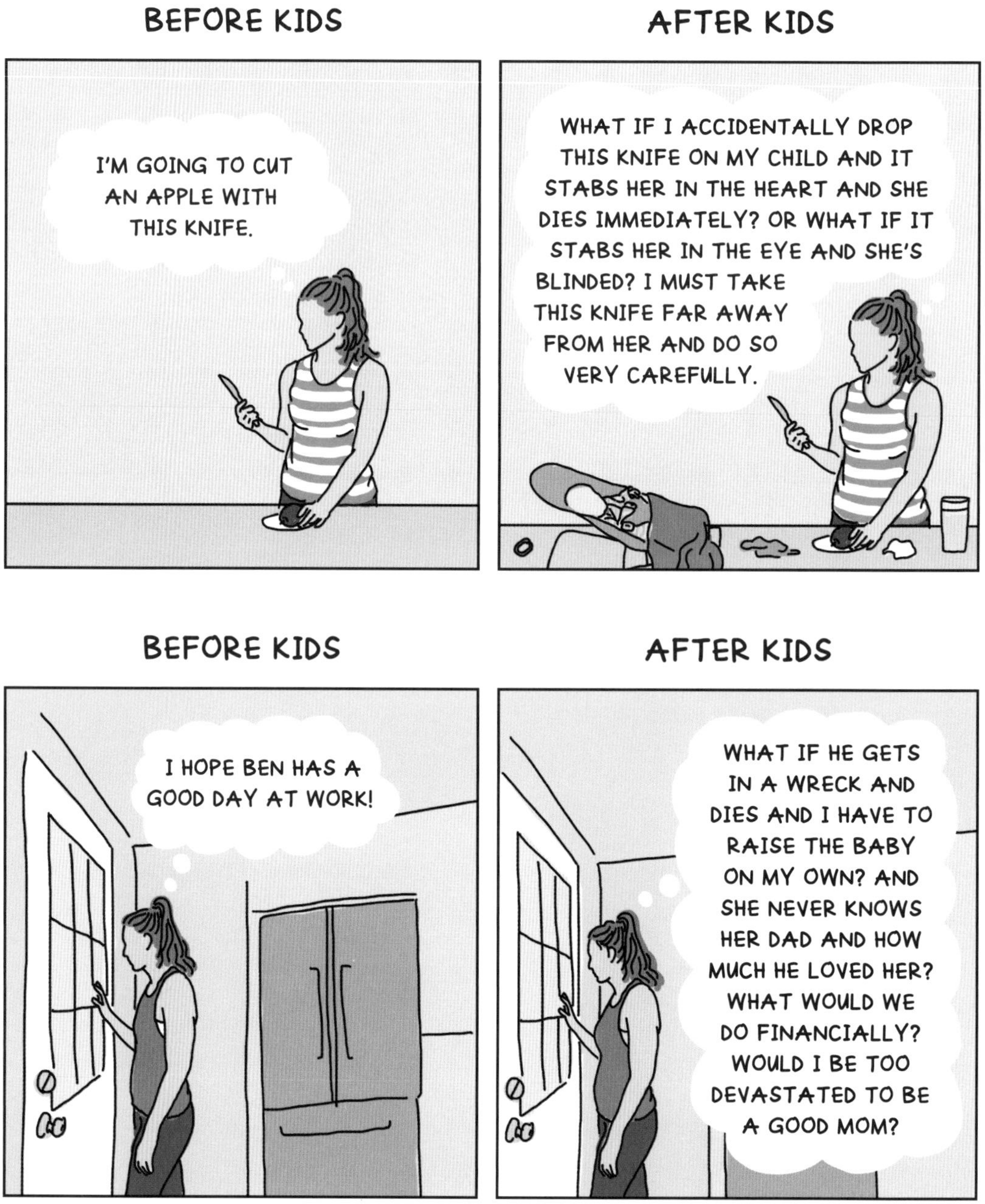
BEFORE KIDS
I'M GOING TO CUT AN APPLE WITH THIS KNIFE.
AFTER KIDS
WHAT IF I ACCIDENTALLY DROP THIS KNIFE ON MY CHILD AND IT STABS HER IN THE HEART AND SHE DIES IMMEDIATELY? OR WHAT IF IT STABS HER IN THE EYE AND SHE'S BLINDED? I MUST TAKE THIS KNIFE FAR AWAY FROM HER AND DO SO VERY CAREFULLY.
BEFORE KIDS
I HOPE BEN HAS A GOOD DAY AT WORK!
AFTER KIDS
WHAT IF HE GETS IN A WRECK AND DIES AND I HAVE TO RAISE THE BABY ON MY OWN? AND SHE NEVER KNOWS HER DAD AND HOW MUCH HE LOVED HER? WHAT WOULD WE DO FINANCIALLY? WOULD I BE TOO DEVASTATED TO BE A GOOD MOM?

It's like the time that someone came to my yoga class and mentioned that she was worried because she accidentally started the dryer before she came to class and was afraid that her house was going to burn down while she was gone. I'd never heard this before, so I'd never worried about it! But as soon as I knew it was a thing to stress about, I started worrying about it. To this day, every time that I start the dryer, I think about it.

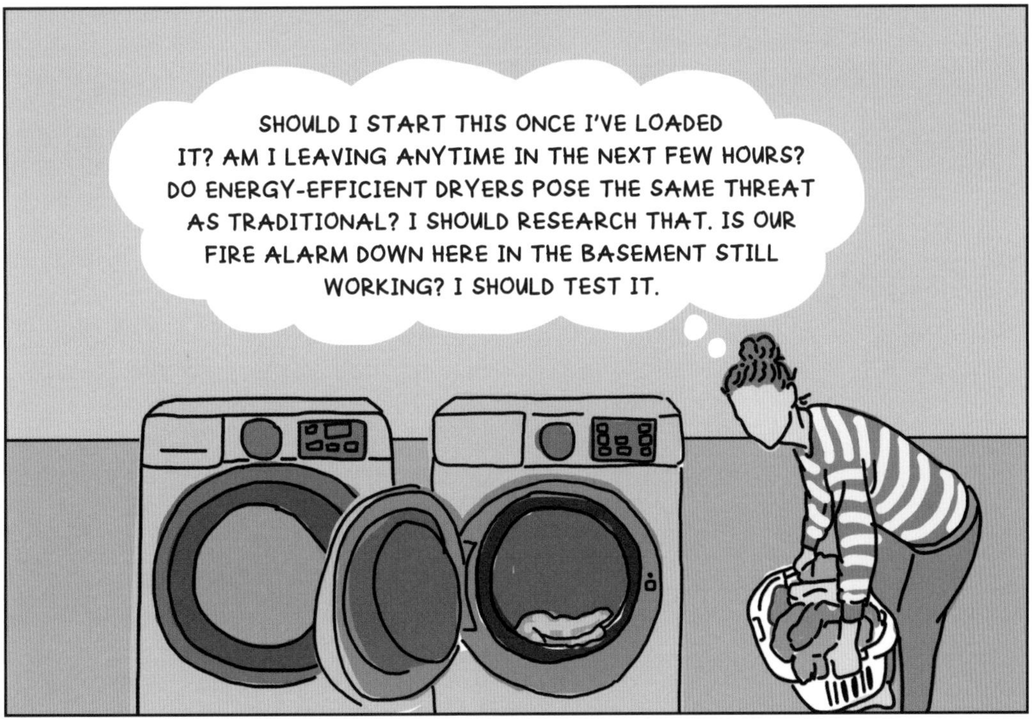
SHOULD I START THIS ONCE I'VE LOADED IT? AM I LEAVING ANYTIME IN THE NEXT FEW HOURS? DO ENERGY-EFFICIENT DRYERS POSE THE SAME THREAT AS TRADITIONAL? I SHOULD RESEARCH THAT. IS OUR FIRE ALARM DOWN HERE IN THE BASEMENT STILL WORKING? I SHOULD TEST IT.

For me, motherhood is worrying about dryer fires—something you didn't ever worry about until you knew that it was a possible threat—all day every day. If you're the primary parent or primary caregiver (which, in our culture, is still typically the mom even if both parents work "outside the home"), you spend all day anticipating disasters and trying to keep your baby alive, healthy, and happy.

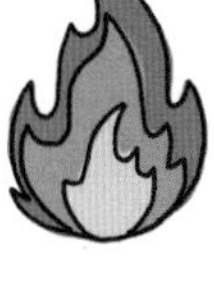

If you also have raging hormones coursing through your postpartum body—and you've been putting out possible dryer fires all day long—you're going to approach parenting very differently than your partner who was at work all day, with the only threat being a disgruntled coworker or a paper cut on their finger.

"RELAXING" ONCE THE BABY IS FINALLY ASLEEP . . .

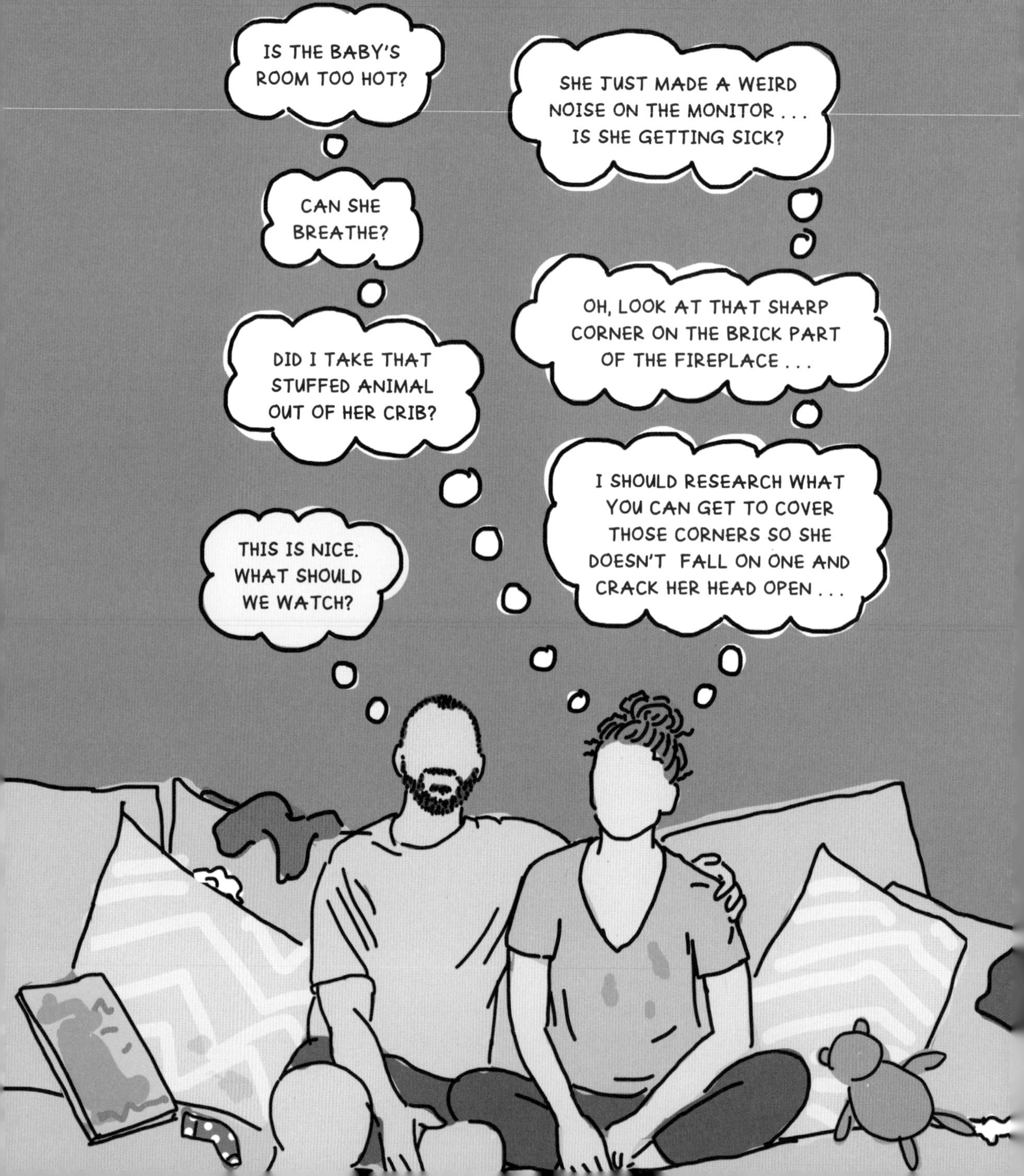
IS THE BABY'S ROOM TOO HOT?
SHE JUST MADE A WEIRD NOISE ON THE MONITOR . . . IS SHE GETTING SICK?
CAN SHE BREATHE?
OH, LOOK AT THAT SHARP CORNER ON THE BRICK PART OF THE FIREPLACE . . .
DID I TAKE THAT STUFFED ANIMAL OUT OF HER CRIB?
I SHOULD RESEARCH WHAT YOU CAN GET TO COVER THOSE CORNERS SO SHE DOESN'T FALL ON ONE AND CRACK HER HEAD OPEN . . .
THIS IS NICE. WHAT SHOULD WE WATCH?

So, during the first year of parenthood, because of my personality and my postpartum anxiety, I quickly became the de facto Family Worrier™. This is a very important job in every family because if you're worried about something, you're going to do whatever needs to be done so that you can, theoretically, stop worrying about it ("theoretically" being a keyword here).

When one parent is the Family Worrier™, the other parent realizes that they don't have to do as much worrying because the Family Worrier™ is going to handle all of the worry-worthy issues. And therein lies another dynamic that started in our first year of parenting and is still at play in our family—I worry* and therefore I handle all of the things that need to be handled. Ben then tells me to "calm down because it will all work itself out," which makes me rage because I am the reason things work out, and the cycle continues.

*Let me be clear: Ben worries, too! He has anxiety, too! But his anxiety is focused on other areas of life and manifests in a very different way than mine does. Lucky us!

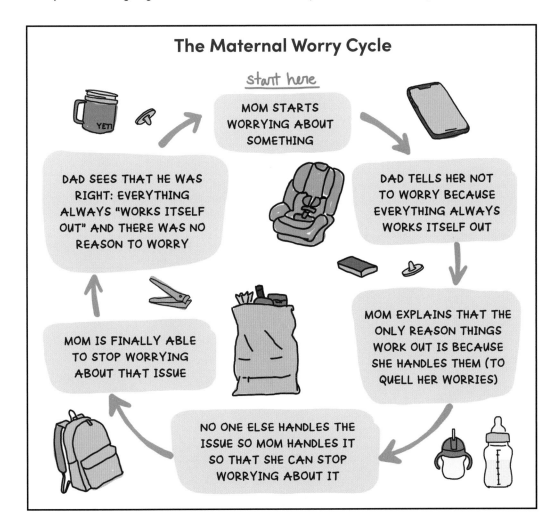

# The Maternal Worry Cycle

start here

MOM STARTS WORRYING ABOUT SOMETHING

DAD TELLS HER NOT TO WORRY BECAUSE EVERYTHING ALWAYS WORKS ITSELF OUT

MOM EXPLAINS THAT THE ONLY REASON THINGS WORK OUT IS BECAUSE SHE HANDLES THEM (TO QUELL HER WORRIES)

NO ONE ELSE HANDLES THE ISSUE SO MOM HANDLES IT SO THAT SHE CAN STOP WORRYING ABOUT IT

MOM IS FINALLY ABLE TO STOP WORRYING ABOUT THAT ISSUE

DAD SEES THAT HE WAS RIGHT: EVERYTHING ALWAYS "WORKS ITSELF OUT" AND THERE WAS NO REASON TO WORRY

# Postpartum Rage

When I was pregnant and preparing for my postpartum period, I was on high alert for postpartum depression and postpartum anxiety. As someone who has suffered from depression and anxiety in the past, I knew I was a likely candidate for both. But you know what I wasn't on the lookout for? Postpartum rage. I didn't even know it was a thing. So when I was postpartum and started feeling blinding rage toward Ben when he did something seemingly small, I just thought I was a crazy, horrible person.

But I've learned that postpartum rage is much more common than I realized. In my case, I took all of that rage out on Ben because I felt that he was the only "safe" place to put it. I couldn't direct it at my precious baby who was helpless and wonderful and had no idea that her inability to sleep or be held by ANYONE BUT ME was causing me to feel like a fire-breathing dragon!

Although my "postpartum" brand of rage is long gone now, I still have a lot of rage directed toward Ben—who, as you know by now, I love very much.

This rage isn't helpful for so many reasons, but lucky for me, Ben has proved to be a "safe" place for my rage in that he is wonderfully devoted to me and committed to our relationship and is always there for me no matter how horrible I am toward him (ugh).

Also, he definitely does (and says) some boneheaded things, so I feel justified in some of the rage I feel these days—or if not justified, confident that my rage is at least understandable to a fellow mom.

Here's how I like to explain both my postpartum rage and my current brand of what I like to call "spousal rage" . . .

## The Pot of Soup:
### An Attempt to Explain Seemingly Unprovoked Spousal Rage

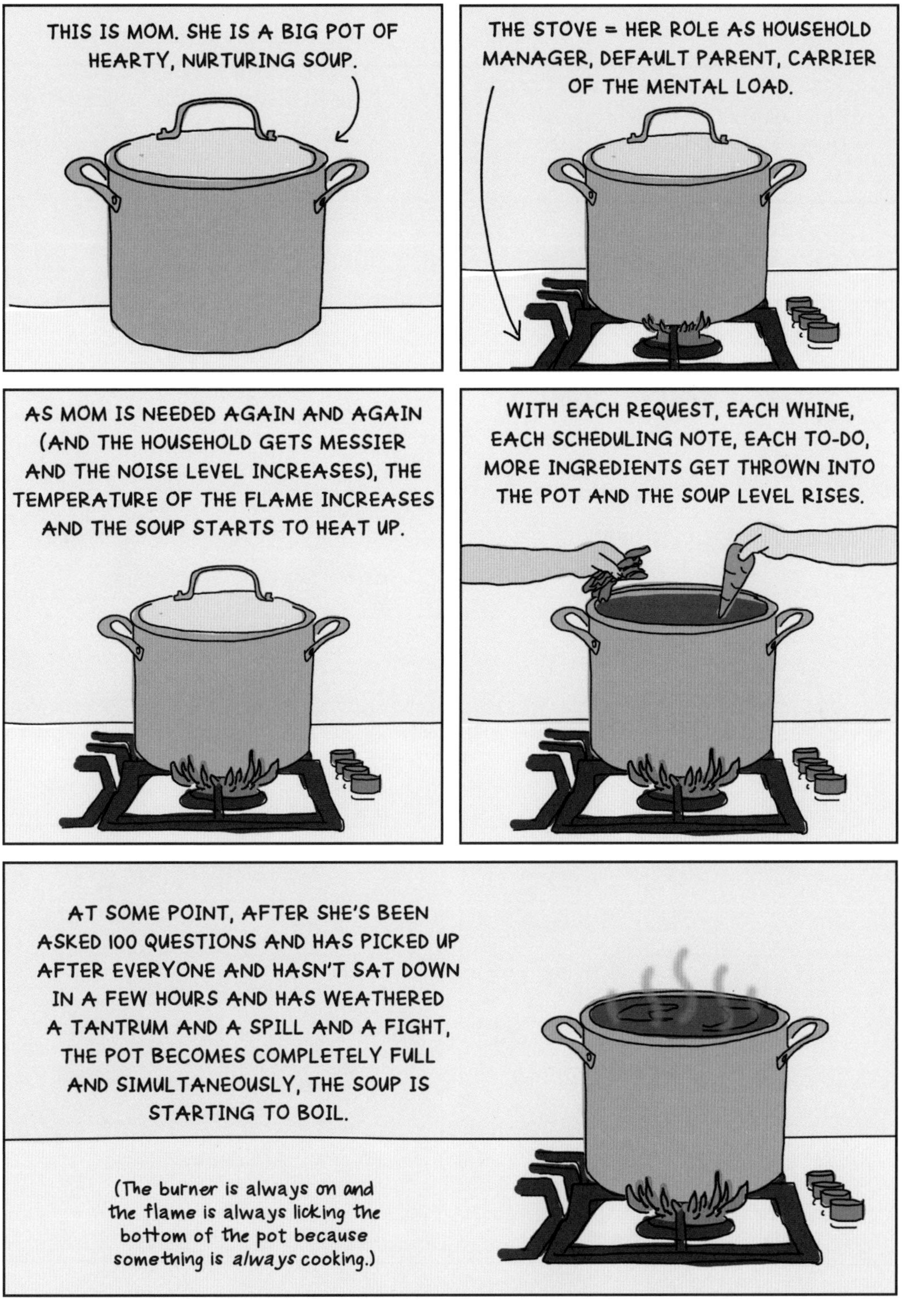
THIS IS MOM. SHE IS A BIG POT OF HEARTY, NURTURING SOUP.
THE STOVE = HER ROLE AS HOUSEHOLD MANAGER, DEFAULT PARENT, CARRIER OF THE MENTAL LOAD.
AS MOM IS NEEDED AGAIN AND AGAIN (AND THE HOUSEHOLD GETS MESSIER AND THE NOISE LEVEL INCREASES), THE TEMPERATURE OF THE FLAME INCREASES AND THE SOUP STARTS TO HEAT UP.
WITH EACH REQUEST, EACH WHINE, EACH SCHEDULING NOTE, EACH TO-DO, MORE INGREDIENTS GET THROWN INTO THE POT AND THE SOUP LEVEL RISES.
AT SOME POINT, AFTER SHE'S BEEN ASKED 100 QUESTIONS AND HAS PICKED UP AFTER EVERYONE AND HASN'T SAT DOWN IN A FEW HOURS AND HAS WEATHERED A TANTRUM AND A SPILL AND A FIGHT, THE POT BECOMES COMPLETELY FULL AND SIMULTANEOUSLY, THE SOUP IS STARTING TO BOIL.
(The burner is always on and the flame is always licking the bottom of the pot because something is *always* cooking.)

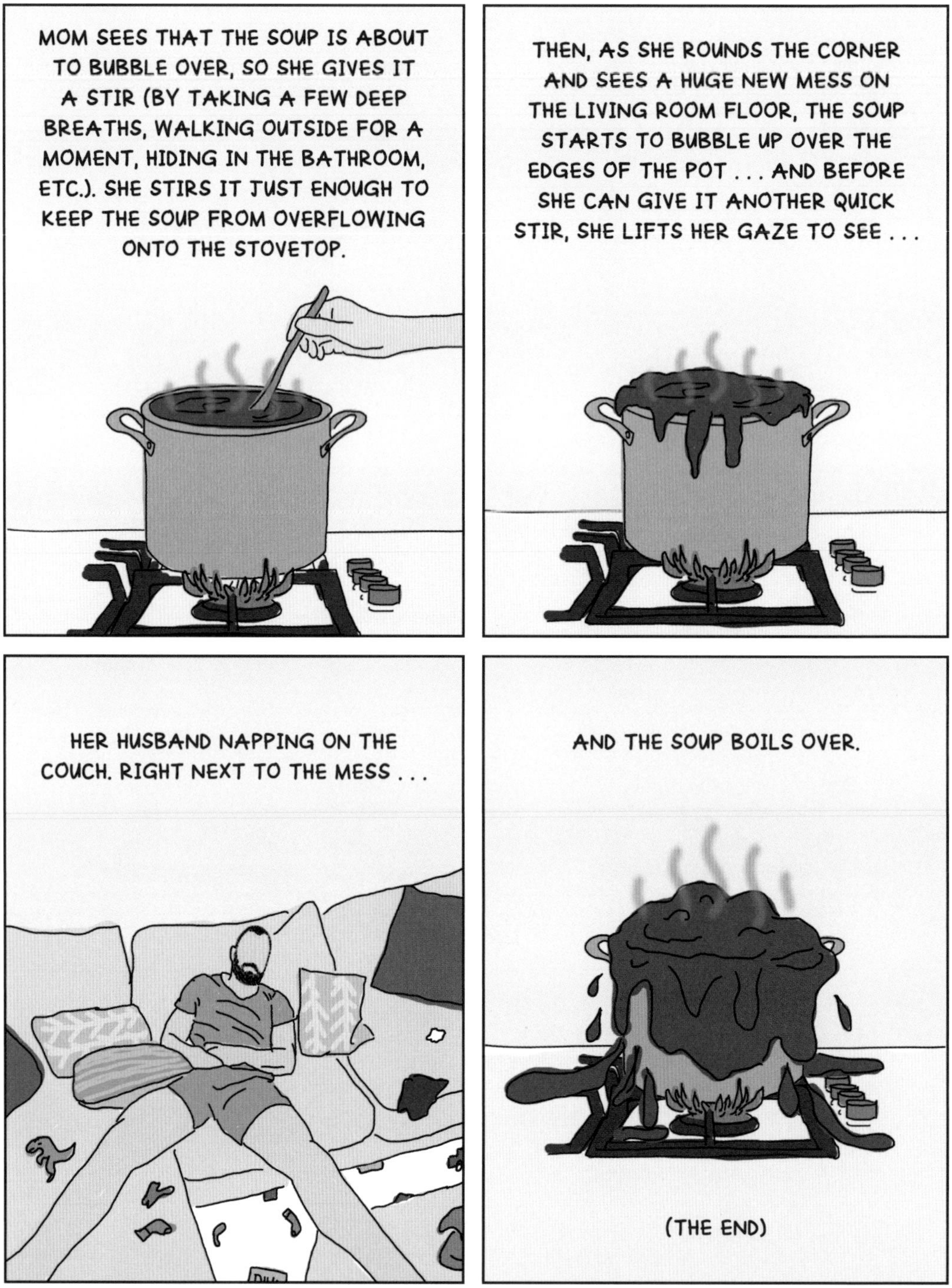
MOM SEES THAT THE SOUP IS ABOUT TO BUBBLE OVER, SO SHE GIVES IT A STIR (BY TAKING A FEW DEEP BREATHS, WALKING OUTSIDE FOR A MOMENT, HIDING IN THE BATHROOM, ETC.). SHE STIRS IT JUST ENOUGH TO KEEP THE SOUP FROM OVERFLOWING ONTO THE STOVETOP.
THEN, AS SHE ROUNDS THE CORNER AND SEES A HUGE NEW MESS ON THE LIVING ROOM FLOOR, THE SOUP STARTS TO BUBBLE UP OVER THE EDGES OF THE POT . . . AND BEFORE SHE CAN GIVE IT ANOTHER QUICK STIR, SHE LIFTS HER GAZE TO SEE . . .
HER HUSBAND NAPPING ON THE COUCH. RIGHT NEXT TO THE MESS . . .
AND THE SOUP BOILS OVER.
(THE END)

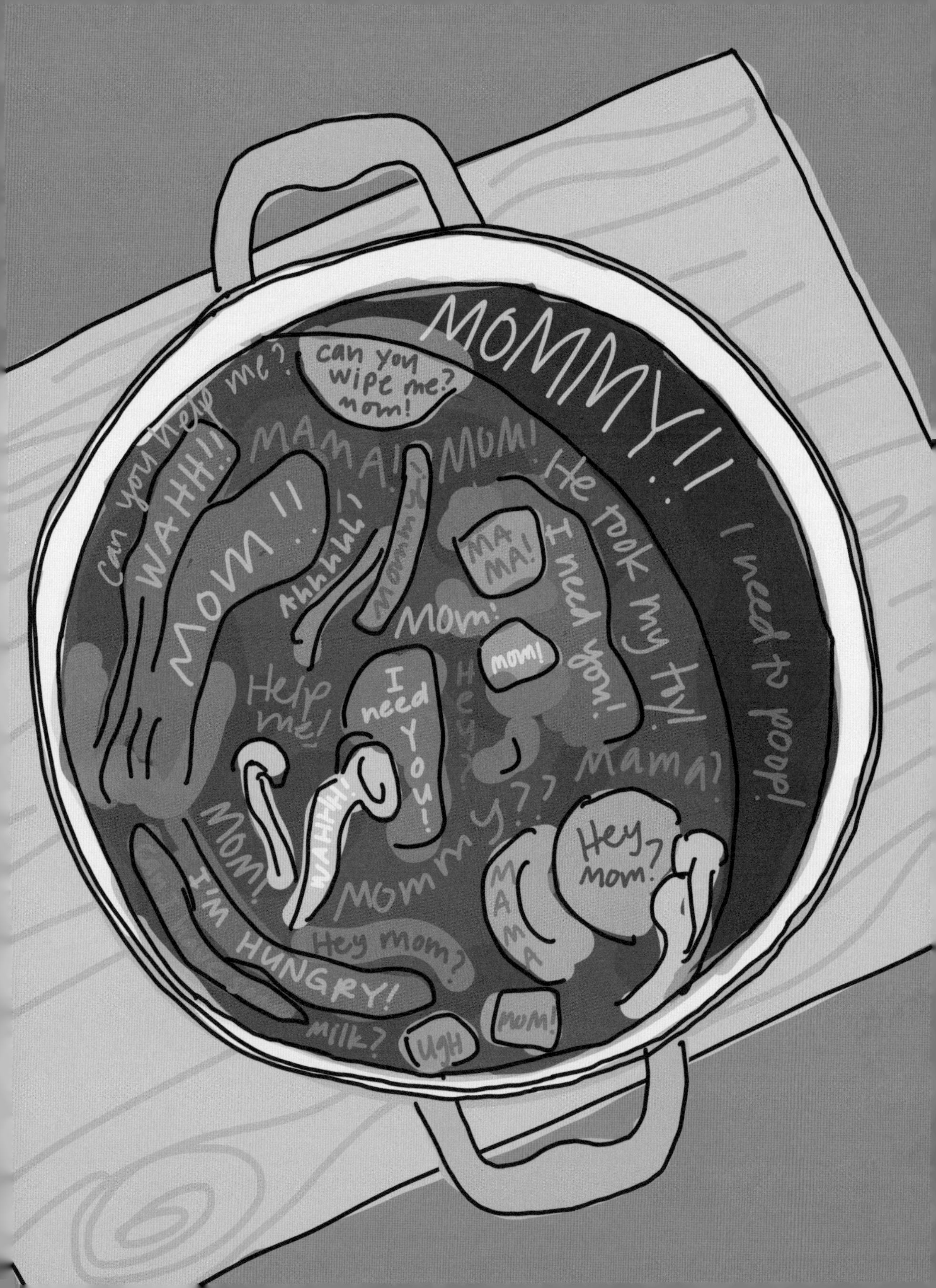
MOMMY!!
can you wipe me? mom!
Can you help me?
WAHH!!
MAMA!
MOM!
He took my toy!
I need to poop!
MOM!!
Ahhhhh!!
MA MA!
I need you!
Mom!
mom!
Help me!
I need YOU!
Mama?
Mommy??
MOM!
WAHH!
I'M HUNGRY!
MOM
Hey mom?
Hey? mom?
MAMA
milk?
UGH
mom!

# Default Parent and Preferred Parent Dynamics

For the entirety of our parenting journey, I have been the default and/or preferred parent for both of our children. This is an intense role no matter what, but also, in my experience, being the default parent can increase the intensity of postpartum anxiety and postpartum rage. And although I know that mom as the preferred parent is a common dynamic, in our household, this dynamic has always been VERY extreme. And when I say extreme, I mean bold, all caps,

I'll get to how this dynamic comes to be, but in case you don't know what it looks like, here are a few thrilling examples of how this dynamic plays out in our household on a daily basis.

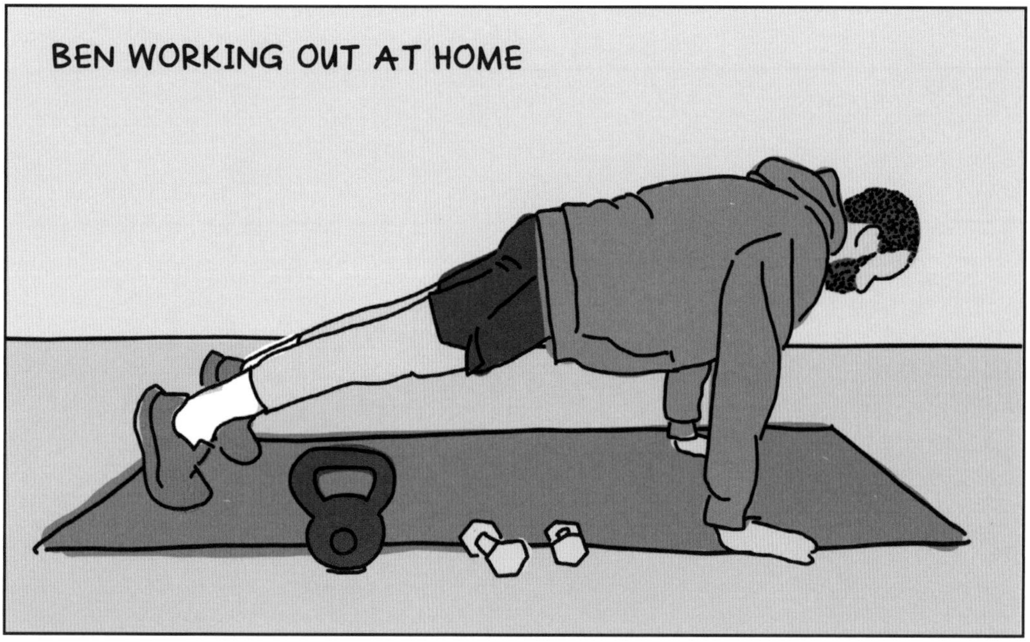
BEN WORKING OUT AT HOME

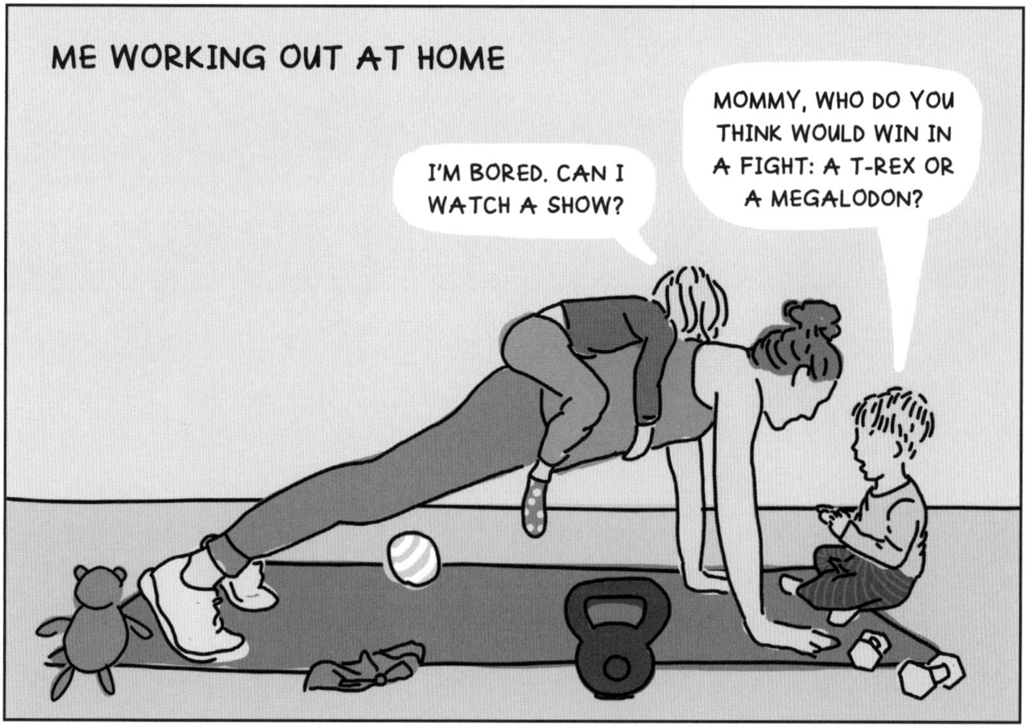
ME WORKING OUT AT HOME
I'M BORED. CAN I WATCH A SHOW?
MOMMY, WHO DO YOU THINK WOULD WIN IN A FIGHT: A T-REX OR A MEGALODON?

## BEN'S MORNINGS

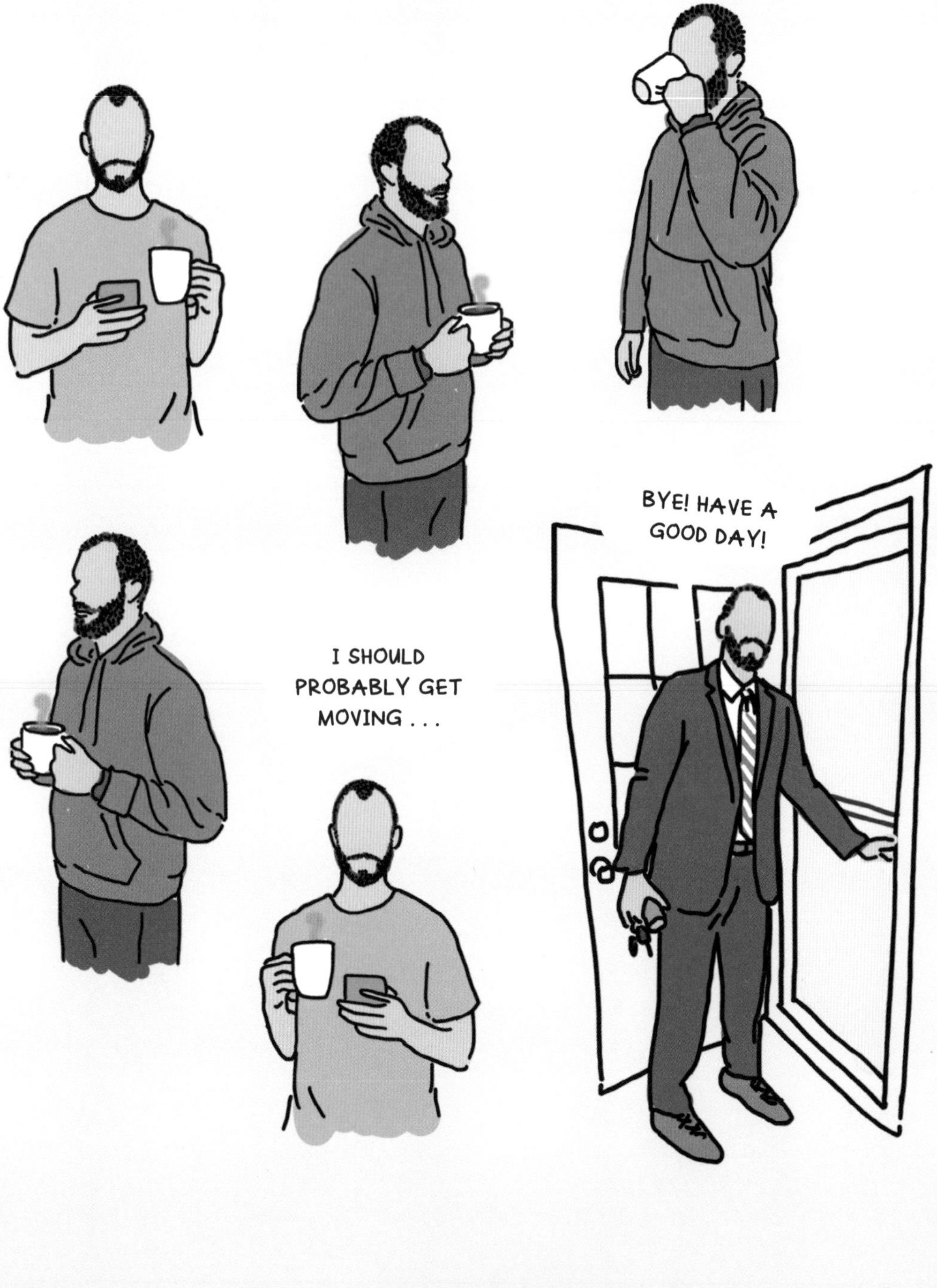
I SHOULD PROBABLY GET MOVING . . .
BYE! HAVE A GOOD DAY!

# MY MORNINGS

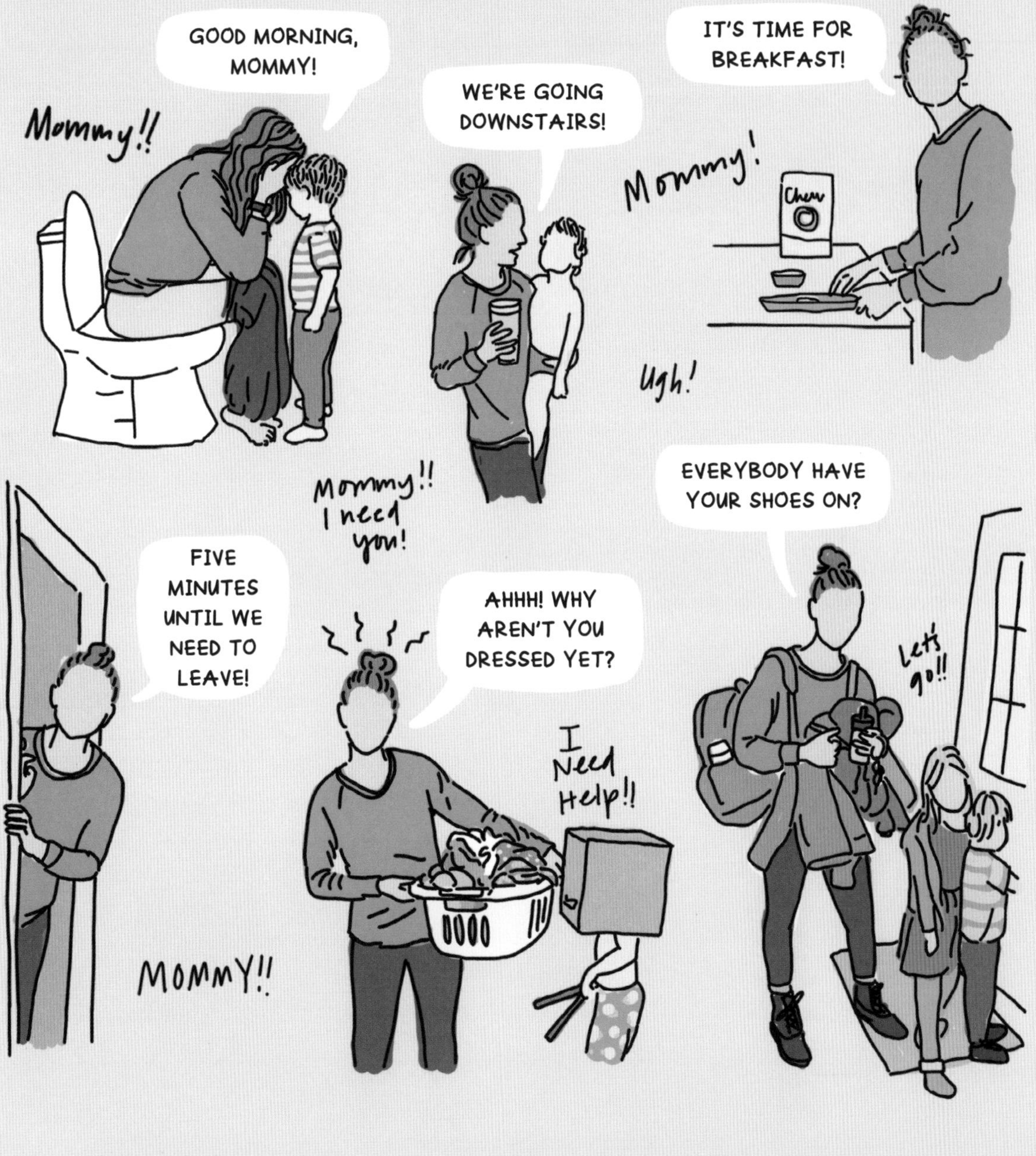
Mommy!!
GOOD MORNING, MOMMY!
WE'RE GOING DOWNSTAIRS!
Mommy!
IT'S TIME FOR BREAKFAST!
Ugh!
Mommy!! I need you!
FIVE MINUTES UNTIL WE NEED TO LEAVE!
MOMMY!!
AHHH! WHY AREN'T YOU DRESSED YET?
I Need Help!!
EVERYBODY HAVE YOUR SHOES ON?
Let's go!!

ME GOING TO A DIFFERENT PART OF THE HOUSE

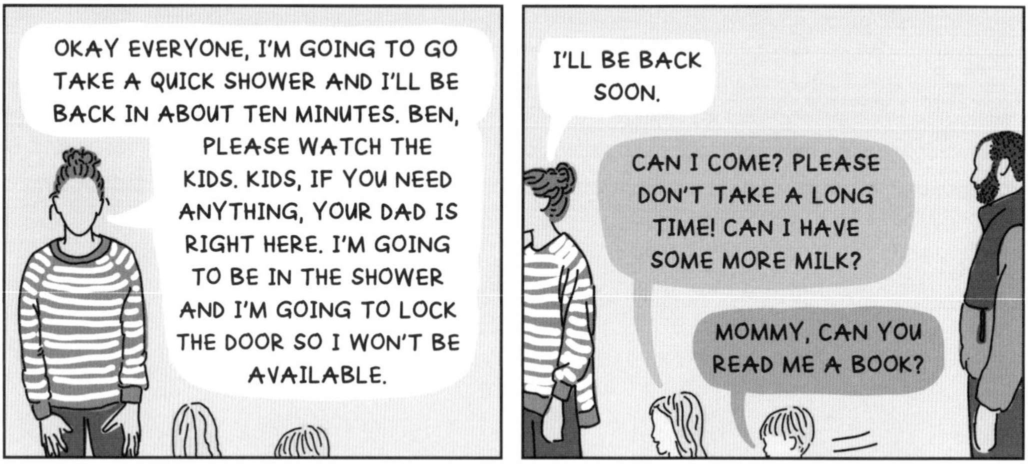
OKAY EVERYONE, I'M GOING TO GO TAKE A QUICK SHOWER AND I'LL BE BACK IN ABOUT TEN MINUTES. BEN, PLEASE WATCH THE KIDS. KIDS, IF YOU NEED ANYTHING, YOUR DAD IS RIGHT HERE. I'M GOING TO BE IN THE SHOWER AND I'M GOING TO LOCK THE DOOR SO I WON'T BE AVAILABLE.
I'LL BE BACK SOON.
CAN I COME? PLEASE DON'T TAKE A LONG TIME! CAN I HAVE SOME MORE MILK?
MOMMY, CAN YOU READ ME A BOOK?

BEN GOING TO A DIFFERENT PART OF THE HOUSE

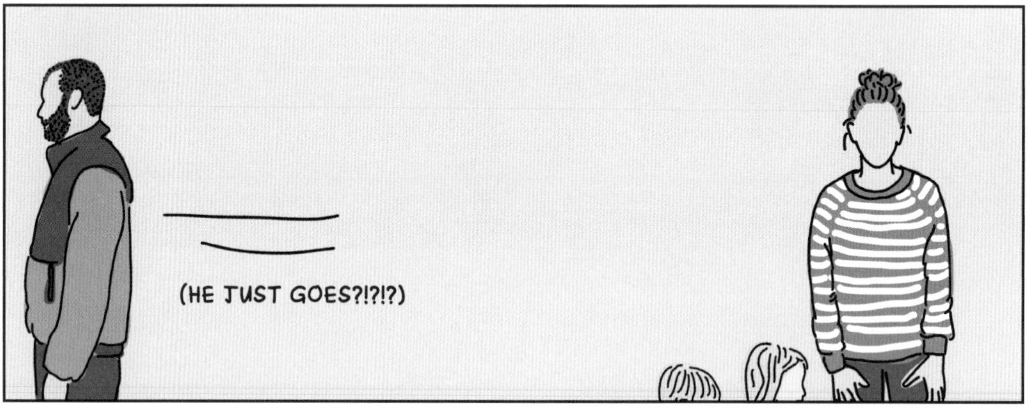
(HE JUST GOES?!?!?)

BEN NAPPING ON THE COUCH

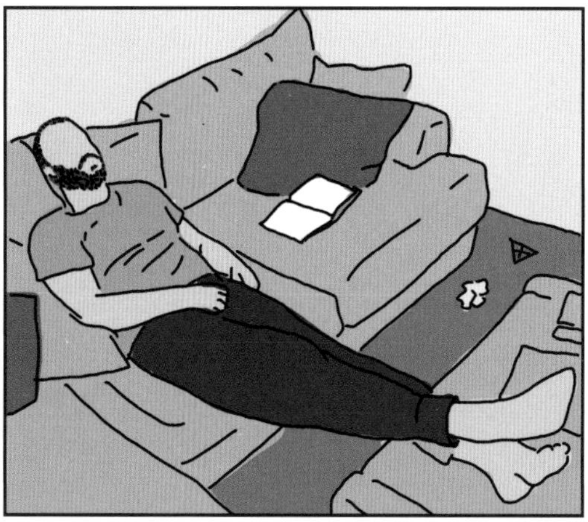

ME TRYING TO RELAX FOR JUST ONE FREAKING MINUTE ON THE COUCH

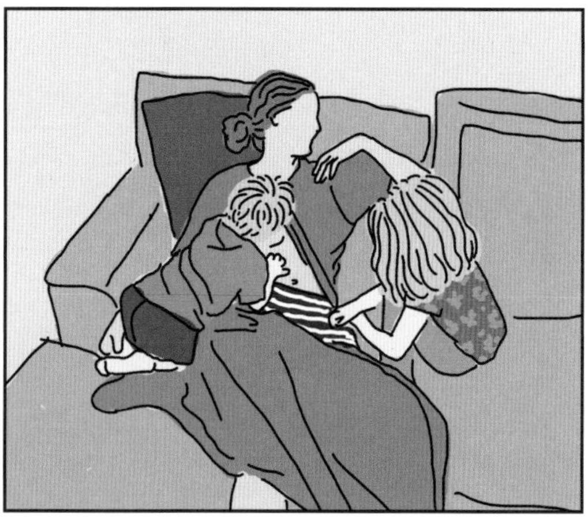

## LEAVING THE HOUSE WITH THE KIDS

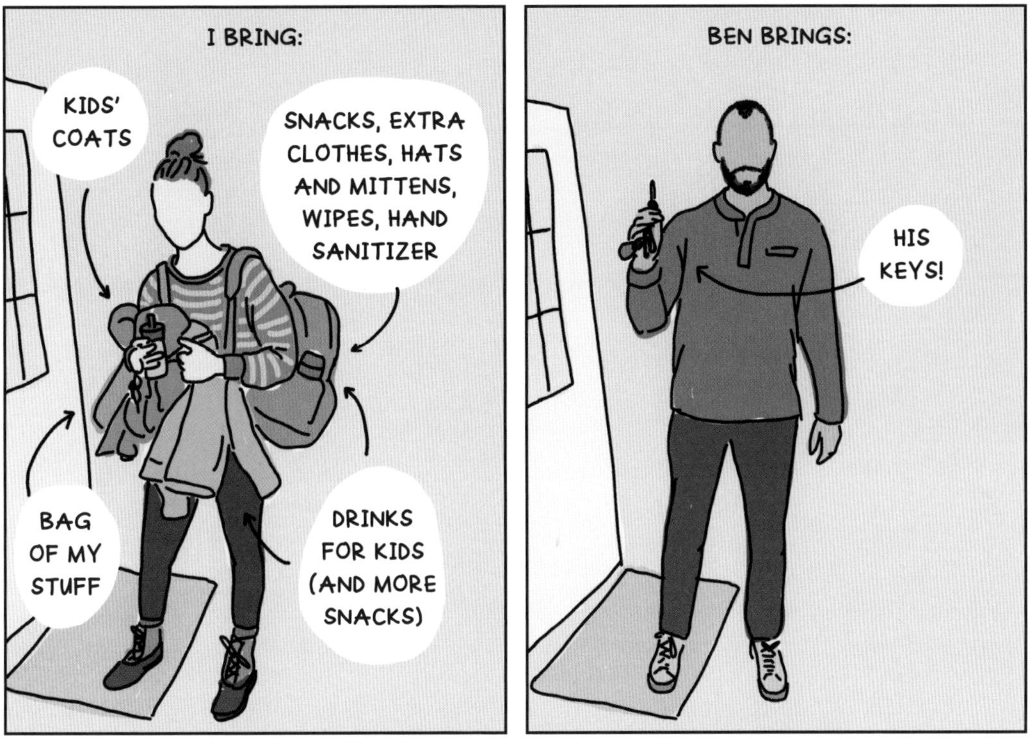
I BRING:
KIDS' COATS
SNACKS, EXTRA CLOTHES, HATS AND MITTENS, WIPES, HAND SANITIZER
BAG OF MY STUFF
DRINKS FOR KIDS (AND MORE SNACKS)
BEN BRINGS:
HIS KEYS!

## LEAVING THE HOUSE WITHOUT THE KIDS

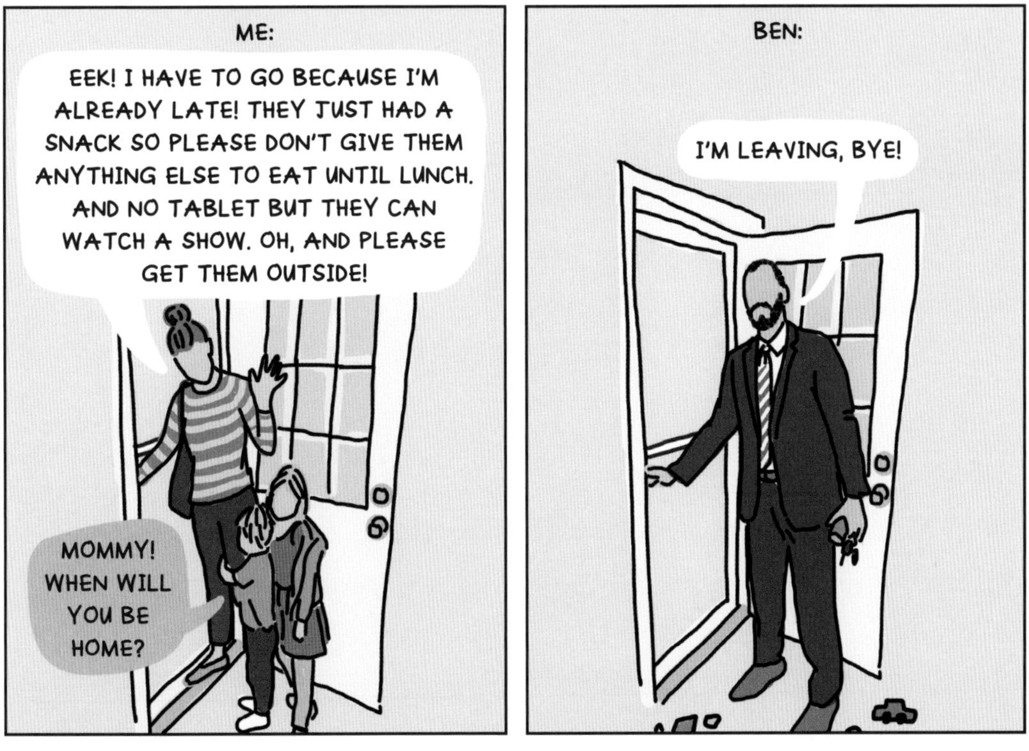
ME:
EEK! I HAVE TO GO BECAUSE I'M ALREADY LATE! THEY JUST HAD A SNACK SO PLEASE DON'T GIVE THEM ANYTHING ELSE TO EAT UNTIL LUNCH. AND NO TABLET BUT THEY CAN WATCH A SHOW. OH, AND PLEASE GET THEM OUTSIDE!
MOMMY! WHEN WILL YOU BE HOME?
BEN:
I'M LEAVING, BYE!

As you can imagine (if you haven't been through this kind of parenting imbalance), this dynamic is EXHAUSTING for the default or preferred parent, and frustrating for the non-preferred parent. Especially when it starts from birth and continues well into (or even past!) the toddler years, as it has for us.

To this day, I am the preferred parent for EVERYTHING. Well, everything except screen time and sweets—the kids would always rather Ben decide how much TV and how many cookies they'll get on any given day.

HA AND ALSO UGHHHHHH OF COURSE.

# The Parental Preference Cycle

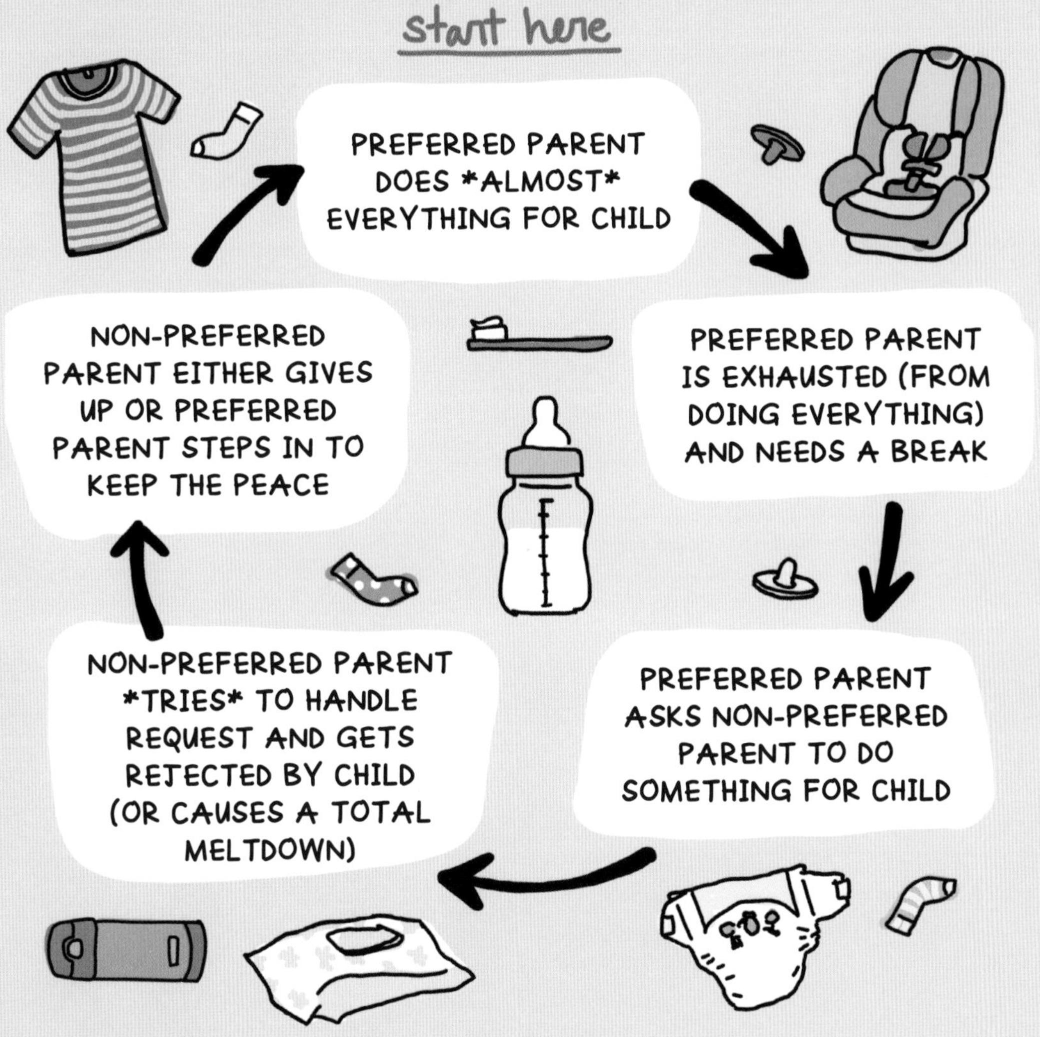

start here

**PREFERRED PARENT DOES \*ALMOST\* EVERYTHING FOR CHILD**

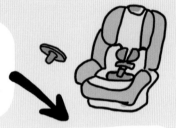

**PREFERRED PARENT IS EXHAUSTED (FROM DOING EVERYTHING) AND NEEDS A BREAK**

**NON-PREFERRED PARENT EITHER GIVES UP OR PREFERRED PARENT STEPS IN TO KEEP THE PEACE**

**PREFERRED PARENT ASKS NON-PREFERRED PARENT TO DO SOMETHING FOR CHILD**

**NON-PREFERRED PARENT \*TRIES\* TO HANDLE REQUEST AND GETS REJECTED BY CHILD (OR CAUSES A TOTAL MELTDOWN)**

What you can do about parental preference (I've tried most of these):

- Read tons of articles written by experts and then try to follow their advice and probably fail because it's really hard to have the non-preferred parent handle things when you're in a hurry or trying to get somewhere or it's bedtime and you just want to be DONE.

- Start doing everything really poorly until your child no longer wants you to handle anything. (Weaponized incompetence toward your child? Seems like a super healthy option . . . )

- Give up and handle everything for your child until he or she grows out of this phase (hopefully before they're twenty?).

- Lose it and yell at either your partner or the child (or both!) when your partner's attempt at handling something goes awry because he/she/they won't just persevere through the tantrum and do it anyway.

- Leave the house as often as possible so the child has no choice but to deal with the non-preferred parent.

THIS IS ONE OF THE ONLY THINGS THAT'S WORKED FOR US!

Something else to keep in mind if you're dealing with this dynamic in your home:

- Strong parental preference is REALLY hard on both parents.

- The preferred parent feels exhausted, touched-out, smothered, angry, frustrated, and jealous. Often he/she/they take that frustration out on their partner because it's "better" to take your anger out on an adult than on a baby or child.

- The non-preferred parent often feels rejected, left out, left behind, sad, lonely, and incompetent.

- Lashing out at each other doesn't help the situation (trust me on this one).

Parental preference is one of those things that no one warns you about when you're a new parent, but being the preferred parent can wreak havoc on your ability to take breaks when you need them and/or ask for help.

It also creates more inequality among parents, which leads to resentment and jealousy.

From one preferred parent to another, please know that:

YOU ARE NOT ALONE, AND THIS IS NOT EASY.

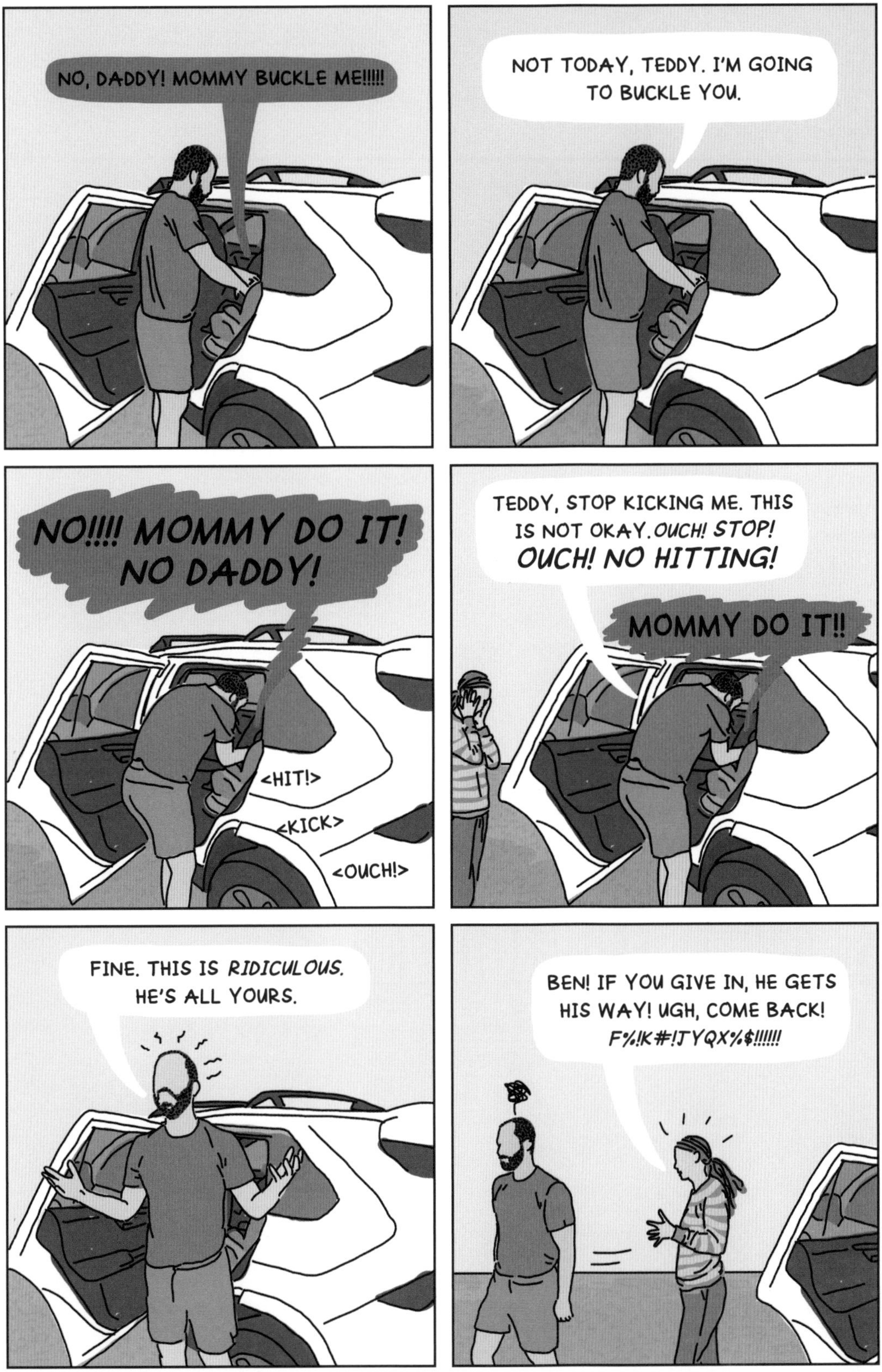
NO, DADDY! MOMMY BUCKLE ME!!!!!
NOT TODAY, TEDDY. I'M GOING TO BUCKLE YOU.
NO!!!! MOMMY DO IT! NO DADDY!
<HIT!>
<KICK>
<OUCH!>
TEDDY, STOP KICKING ME. THIS IS NOT OKAY. *OUCH! STOP!* *OUCH! NO HITTING!*
MOMMY DO IT!!
FINE. THIS IS *RIDICULOUS.* HE'S ALL YOURS.
BEN! IF YOU GIVE IN, HE GETS HIS WAY! UGH, COME BACK! *F%!K#!JTYQX%$!!!!!!*

# Maternal Gatekeeping

I am not looking to assign blame for the patterns that Ben and I have gotten stuck in over the years. It's no one person's fault—it's a combination of all of the previously discussed dynamics plus our personalities, our socialization, our role models, our cultural expectations, and our coping mechanisms (learned in childhood).

But there is one aspect of this that is primarily my "fault" (if we're trying to assign blame, which we're not), and it has an official name: "maternal gatekeeping."

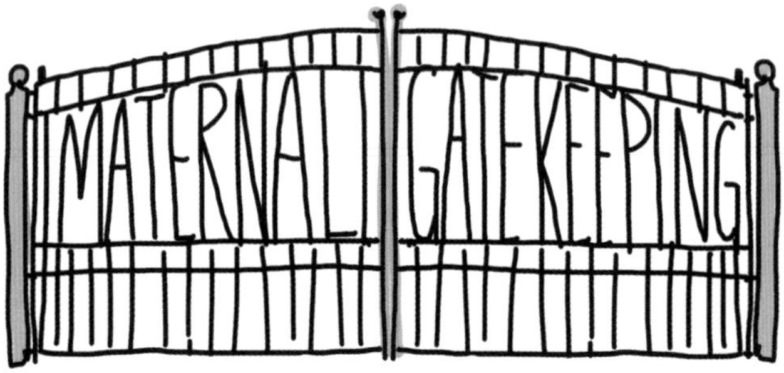
MATERNAL GATEKEEPING

Yes, this sounds fancy, but it's a pretty basic concept: It's when a mom, as the primary caregiver, acts as a gatekeeper for anything baby/kid-related and gets in the way of letting other caregivers take care of that baby in his/her/their own way.

For example . . .

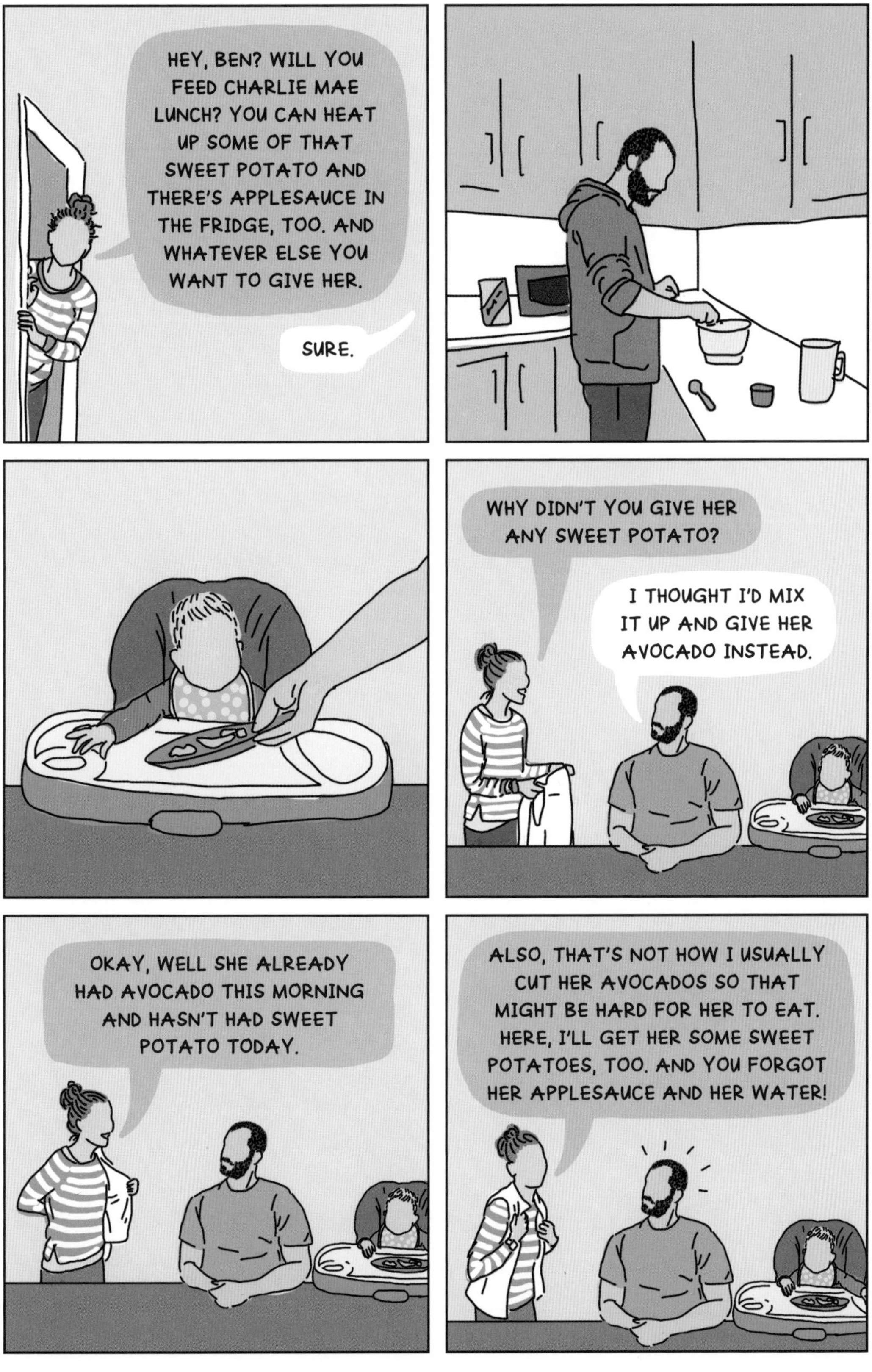
HEY, BEN? WILL YOU FEED CHARLIE MAE LUNCH? YOU CAN HEAT UP SOME OF THAT SWEET POTATO AND THERE'S APPLESAUCE IN THE FRIDGE, TOO. AND WHATEVER ELSE YOU WANT TO GIVE HER.
SURE.
WHY DIDN'T YOU GIVE HER ANY SWEET POTATO?
I THOUGHT I'D MIX IT UP AND GIVE HER AVOCADO INSTEAD.
OKAY, WELL SHE ALREADY HAD AVOCADO THIS MORNING AND HASN'T HAD SWEET POTATO TODAY.
ALSO, THAT'S NOT HOW I USUALLY CUT HER AVOCADOS SO THAT MIGHT BE HARD FOR HER TO EAT. HERE, I'LL GET HER SOME SWEET POTATOES, TOO. AND YOU FORGOT HER APPLESAUCE AND HER WATER!

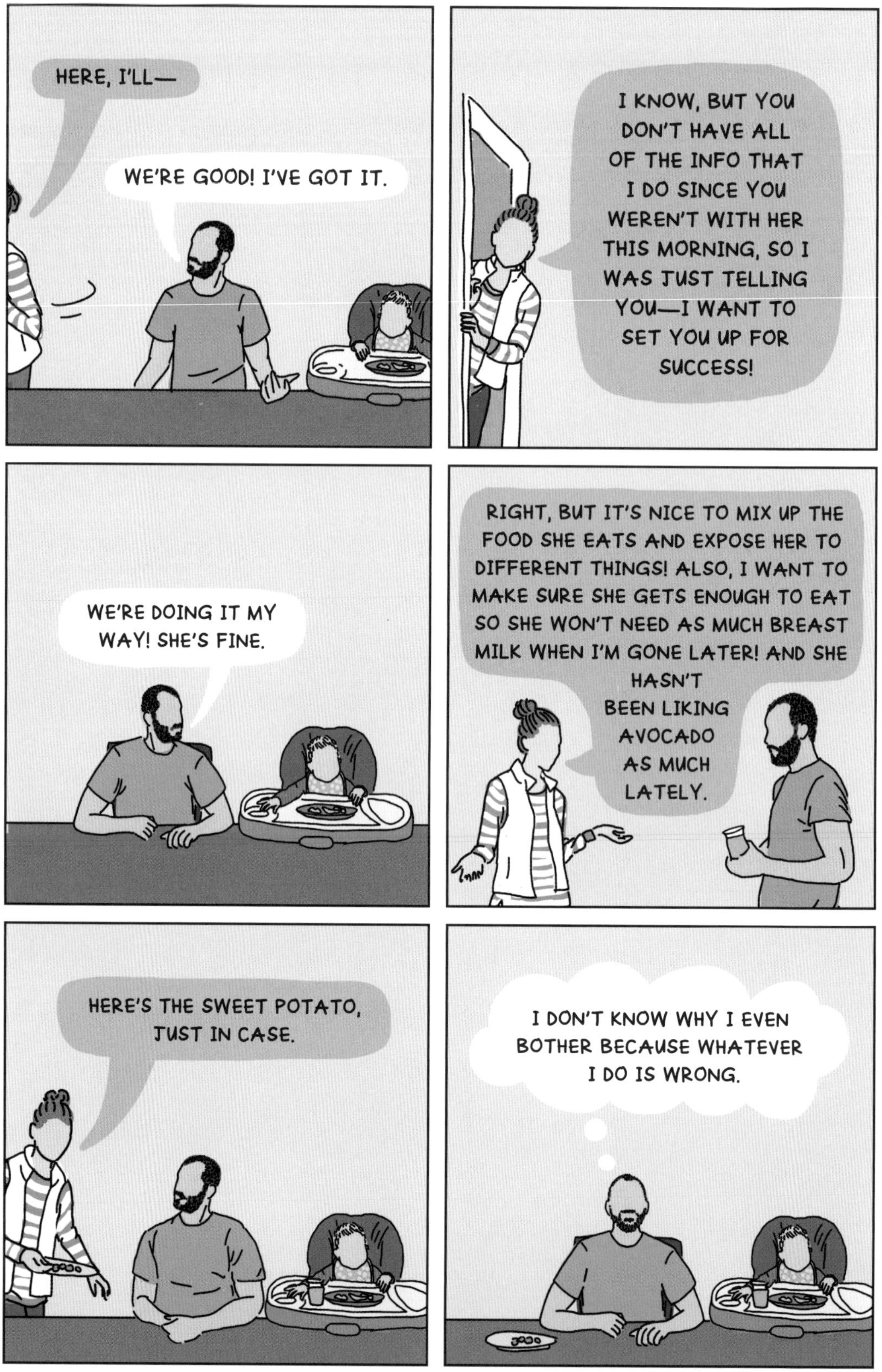
HERE, I'LL—
WE'RE GOOD! I'VE GOT IT.
I KNOW, BUT YOU DON'T HAVE ALL OF THE INFO THAT I DO SINCE YOU WEREN'T WITH HER THIS MORNING, SO I WAS JUST TELLING YOU—I WANT TO SET YOU UP FOR SUCCESS!
WE'RE DOING IT MY WAY! SHE'S FINE.
RIGHT, BUT IT'S NICE TO MIX UP THE FOOD SHE EATS AND EXPOSE HER TO DIFFERENT THINGS! ALSO, I WANT TO MAKE SURE SHE GETS ENOUGH TO EAT SO SHE WON'T NEED AS MUCH BREAST MILK WHEN I'M GONE LATER! AND SHE HASN'T BEEN LIKING AVOCADO AS MUCH LATELY.
HERE'S THE SWEET POTATO, JUST IN CASE.
I DON'T KNOW WHY I EVEN BOTHER BECAUSE WHATEVER I DO IS WRONG.

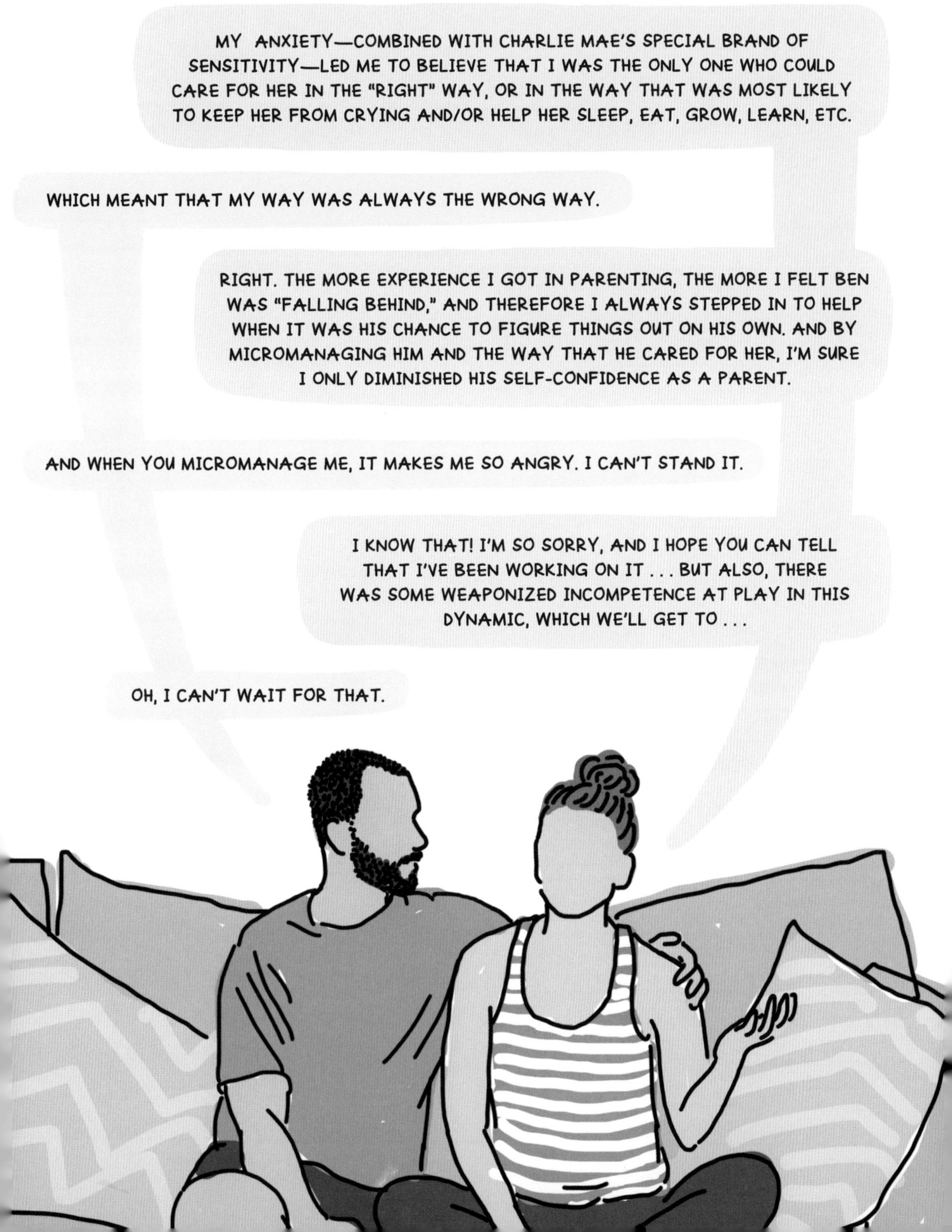

MY ANXIETY—COMBINED WITH CHARLIE MAE'S SPECIAL BRAND OF SENSITIVITY—LED ME TO BELIEVE THAT I WAS THE ONLY ONE WHO COULD CARE FOR HER IN THE "RIGHT" WAY, OR IN THE WAY THAT WAS MOST LIKELY TO KEEP HER FROM CRYING AND/OR HELP HER SLEEP, EAT, GROW, LEARN, ETC.
WHICH MEANT THAT MY WAY WAS ALWAYS THE WRONG WAY.
RIGHT. THE MORE EXPERIENCE I GOT IN PARENTING, THE MORE I FELT BEN WAS "FALLING BEHIND," AND THEREFORE I ALWAYS STEPPED IN TO HELP WHEN IT WAS HIS CHANCE TO FIGURE THINGS OUT ON HIS OWN. AND BY MICROMANAGING HIM AND THE WAY THAT HE CARED FOR HER, I'M SURE I ONLY DIMINISHED HIS SELF-CONFIDENCE AS A PARENT.
AND WHEN YOU MICROMANAGE ME, IT MAKES ME SO ANGRY. I CAN'T STAND IT.
I KNOW THAT! I'M SO SORRY, AND I HOPE YOU CAN TELL THAT I'VE BEEN WORKING ON IT . . . BUT ALSO, THERE WAS SOME WEAPONIZED INCOMPETENCE AT PLAY IN THIS DYNAMIC, WHICH WE'LL GET TO . . .
OH, I CAN'T WAIT FOR THAT.

Similarly, as our kids grew older, they picked up on this dynamic, which has only made it tougher to break the cycle. Maternal gatekeeping is a great way to enhance negative preferred and default parent patterns!

And here's the other thing about maternal gatekeeping: It hasn't just made my life (and Ben's life!) harder, but it's also made our children less flexible because they're so used to the way that I do things (which they've decided is the "right" way, of course).

When we expose our kids to different adults, caretakers, and/or family members who do things differently than we do, that helps our children build resilience; it helps them become more comfortable navigating the world—a world in which I will not always be there to cut off the crusts in the "right way" or remove the brown parts from the outside of my daughter's hamburger patty (which she likes plain, no bun, no toppings, and no, not cut like that, but like this . . . ).

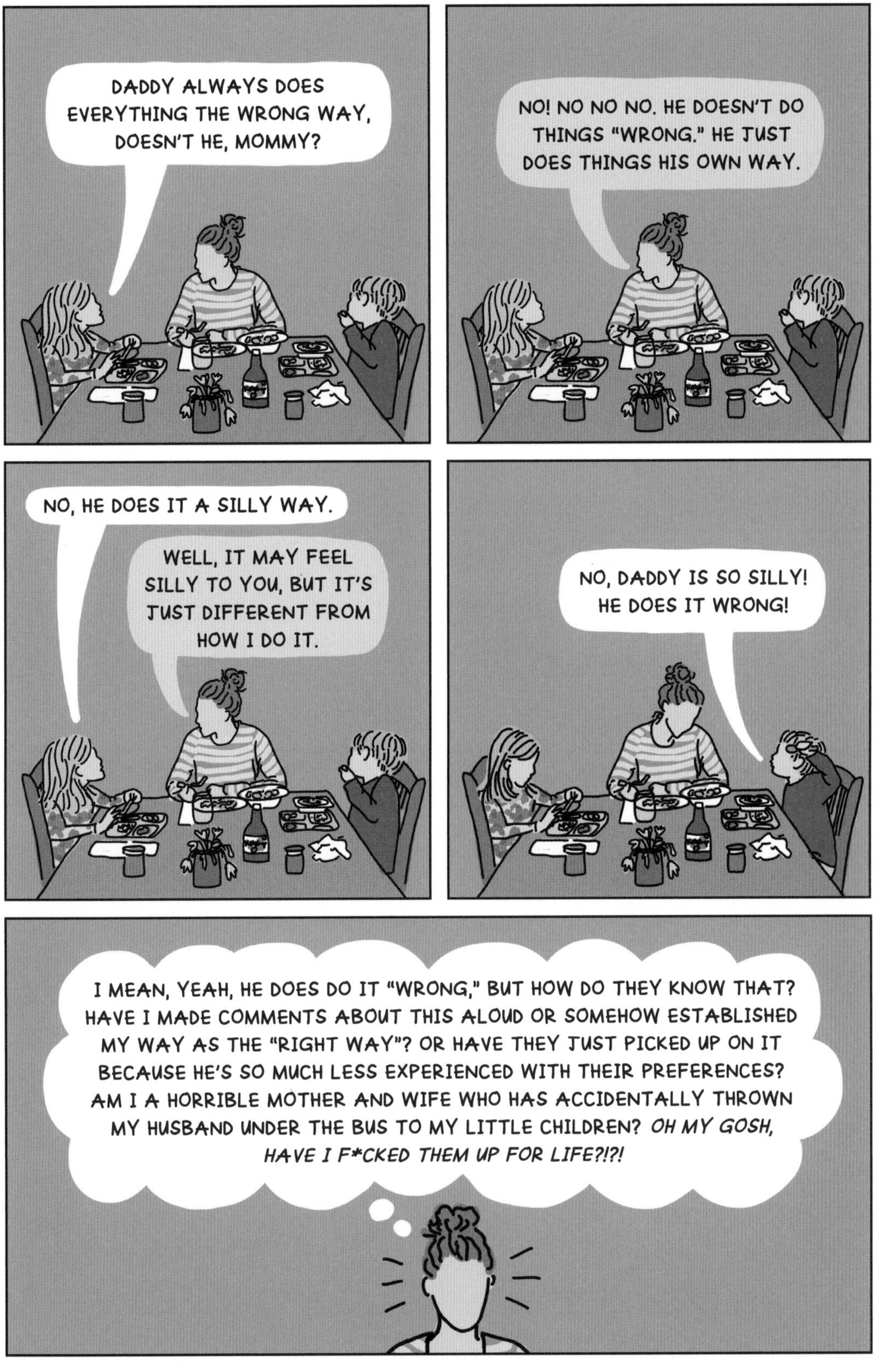
DADDY ALWAYS DOES EVERYTHING THE WRONG WAY, DOESN'T HE, MOMMY?
NO! NO NO NO. HE DOESN'T DO THINGS "WRONG." HE JUST DOES THINGS HIS OWN WAY.
NO, HE DOES IT A SILLY WAY.
WELL, IT MAY FEEL SILLY TO YOU, BUT IT'S JUST DIFFERENT FROM HOW I DO IT.
NO, DADDY IS SO SILLY! HE DOES IT WRONG!
I MEAN, YEAH, HE DOES DO IT "WRONG," BUT HOW DO THEY KNOW THAT? HAVE I MADE COMMENTS ABOUT THIS ALOUD OR SOMEHOW ESTABLISHED MY WAY AS THE "RIGHT WAY"? OR HAVE THEY JUST PICKED UP ON IT BECAUSE HE'S SO MUCH LESS EXPERIENCED WITH THEIR PREFERENCES? AM I A HORRIBLE MOTHER AND WIFE WHO HAS ACCIDENTALLY THROWN MY HUSBAND UNDER THE BUS TO MY LITTLE CHILDREN? *OH MY GOSH, HAVE I F*CKED THEM UP FOR LIFE?!?!*

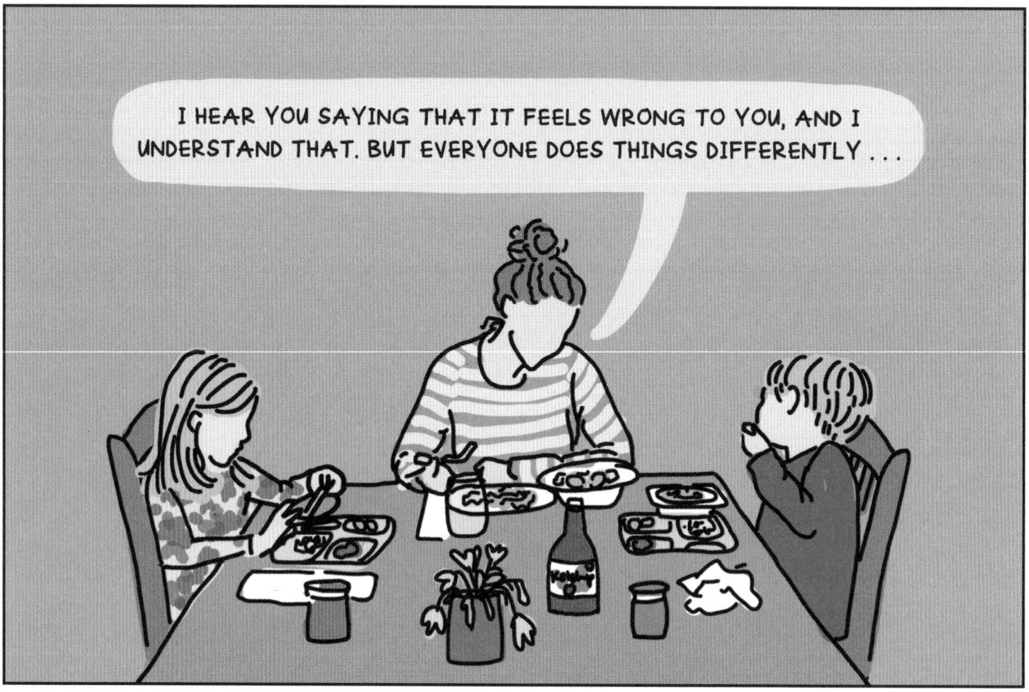
I HEAR YOU SAYING THAT IT FEELS WRONG TO YOU, AND I UNDERSTAND THAT. BUT EVERYONE DOES THINGS DIFFERENTLY . . .

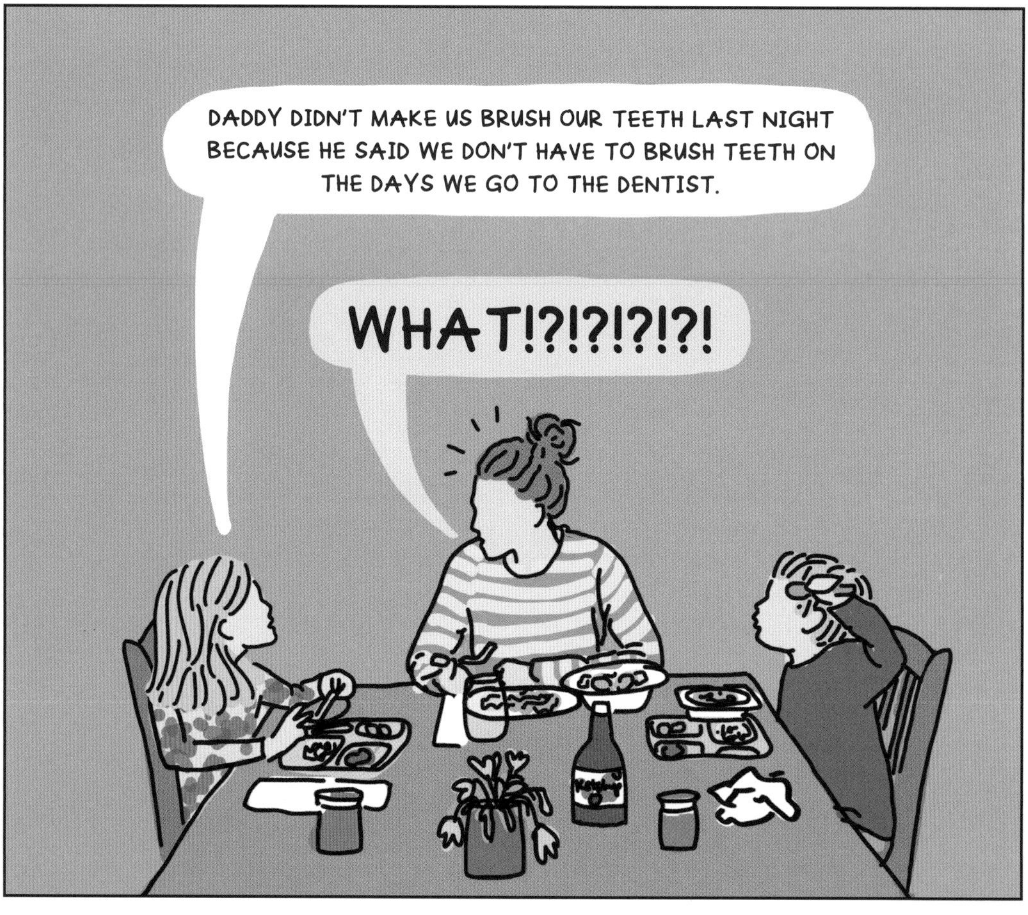
DADDY DIDN'T MAKE US BRUSH OUR TEETH LAST NIGHT BECAUSE HE SAID WE DON'T HAVE TO BRUSH TEETH ON THE DAYS WE GO TO THE DENTIST.
WHAT!?!?!?!?!

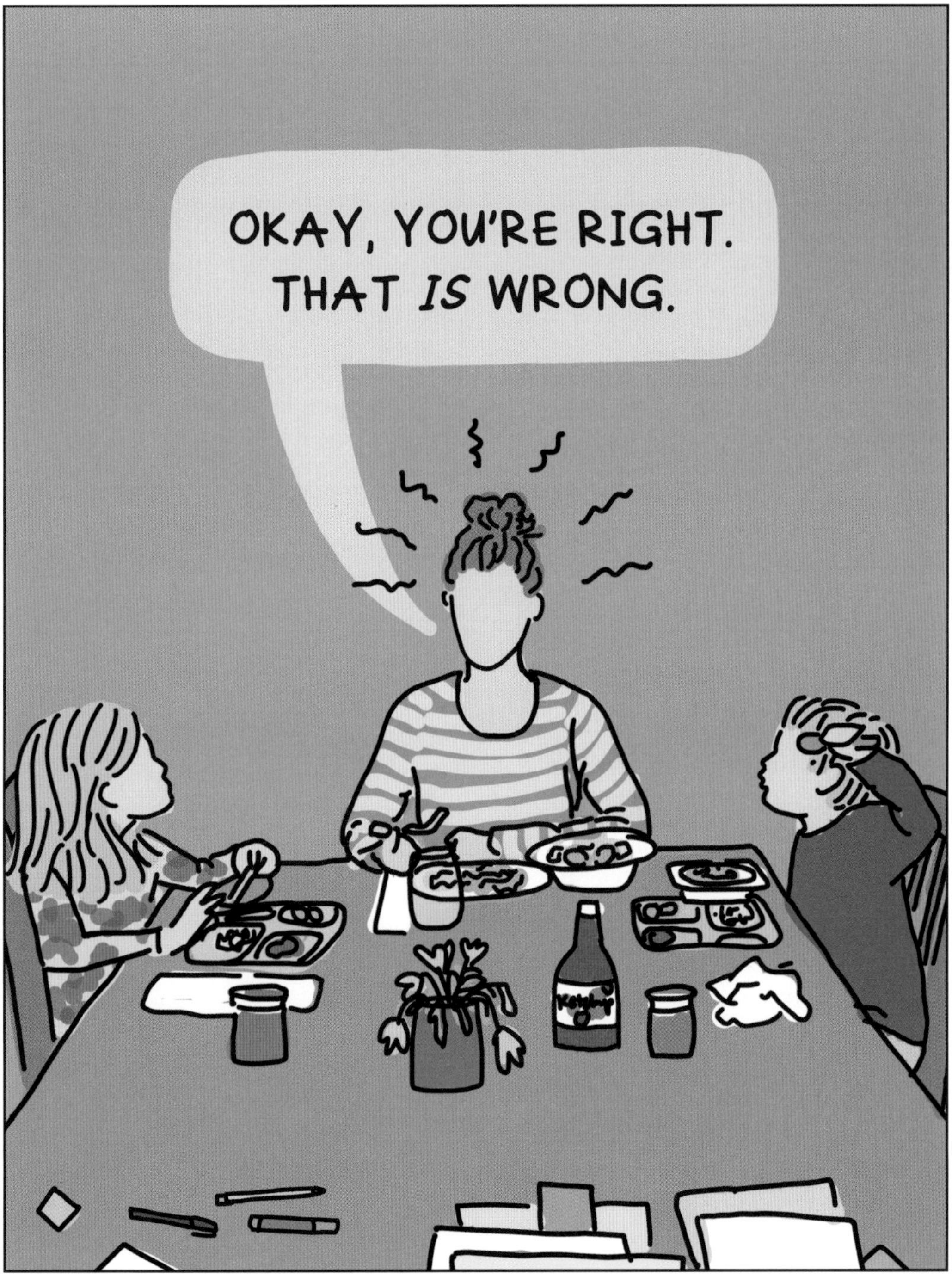
OKAY, YOU'RE RIGHT.
THAT *IS* WRONG.

# Hindsight

Hindsight is 20/20; we all know this by now. As I started to get distance from Charlie Mae's first year of life, I began to realize how all of these challenging dynamics had come together to create the perfect storm of imbalance and overwhelm in our household.

But now that I knew what could happen (and what had happened!), I swore to myself that I would do things differently the next time around:

- I decided that our next baby—if we were lucky enough to have one—was going to take a bottle and a Binky come hell or high water!

- Ben would wake up with our next baby in the night, and he'd be just as preferred as I was!

- I would back off and give him space!

- I would sleep-train our baby at 6 months so we could all sleep and I could avoid postpartum anxiety and rage!

I had learned how NOT to do things so I wouldn't make any of those mistakes again!

I was going to right my wrongs. I was still so, so, SO tired, but I had hope. Isn't that all it takes to do it all over again?

# Mantras and Affirmations for Modern Moms

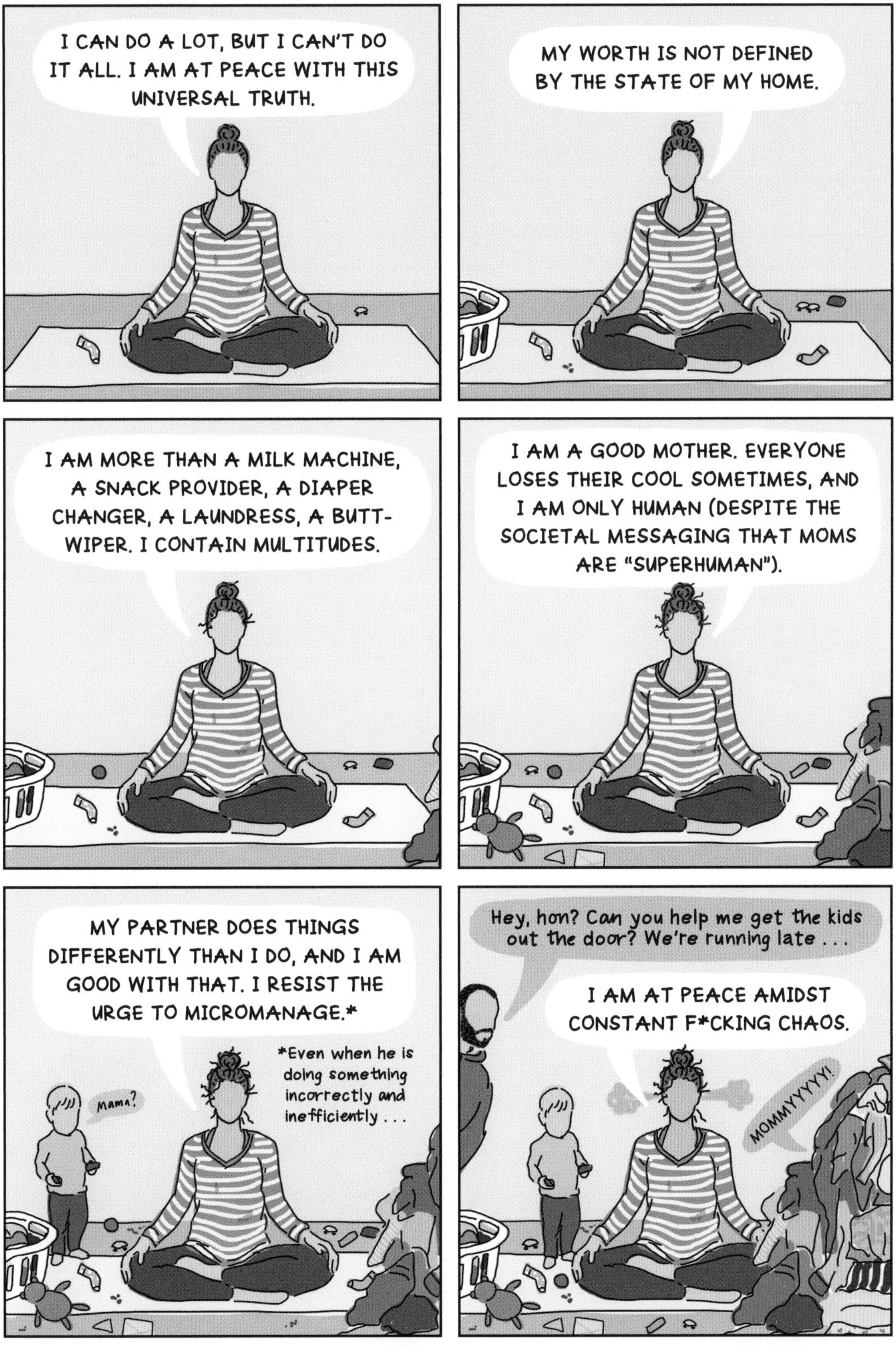
I CAN DO A LOT, BUT I CAN'T DO IT ALL. I AM AT PEACE WITH THIS UNIVERSAL TRUTH.
MY WORTH IS NOT DEFINED BY THE STATE OF MY HOME.
I AM MORE THAN A MILK MACHINE, A SNACK PROVIDER, A DIAPER CHANGER, A LAUNDRESS, A BUTT-WIPER. I CONTAIN MULTITUDES.
I AM A GOOD MOTHER. EVERYONE LOSES THEIR COOL SOMETIMES, AND I AM ONLY HUMAN (DESPITE THE SOCIETAL MESSAGING THAT MOMS ARE "SUPERHUMAN").
MY PARTNER DOES THINGS DIFFERENTLY THAN I DO, AND I AM GOOD WITH THAT. I RESIST THE URGE TO MICROMANAGE.*
*Even when he is doing something incorrectly and inefficiently . . .
MAMA?
Hey, hon? Can you help me get the kids out the door? We're running late . . .
I AM AT PEACE AMIDST CONSTANT F*CKING CHAOS.
MOMMYYYYY!

# Different Strokes for Different Folks.

BEN MAKES OUR CHILDREN'S LUNCHES. WE BUY BULK BOXES OF INDIVIDUALLY WRAPPED PIRATE'S BOOTY FOR THEIR SNACKS AND KEEP A SMALL CONTAINER OF SOME OF THESE BAGS IN THE PANTRY. WE STORE THE EXTRAS IN THE BASEMENT.

WHENEVER WE RUN OUT IN THE PANTRY, INSTEAD OF GOING DOWNSTAIRS AND FILLING UP THE PANTRY CONTAINER, BEN WILL JUST START WORKING OUT OF THE BASEMENT BOX.

EVERY MORNING, I WATCH HIM GO DOWN TO THE BASEMENT AND GRAB JUST TWO INDIVIDUAL BAGS OF PIRATE'S BOOTY FOR THE KIDS' LUNCHES.

HE DOESN'T BRING UP A NEW BOX. HE DOESN'T EVEN BRING UP A HANDFUL TO PUT IN THE OLD CONTAINER TO SAVE HIMSELF A FEW DAY'S WORTH OF WORK.

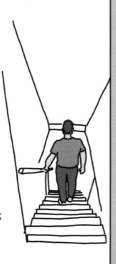

WHY DON'T YOU BRING UP A NEW BOX? OR JUST GRAB MORE THAN TWO BAGS WHEN YOU GO DOWN TO GET THOSE!?

MY METHOD WORKS JUST FINE.

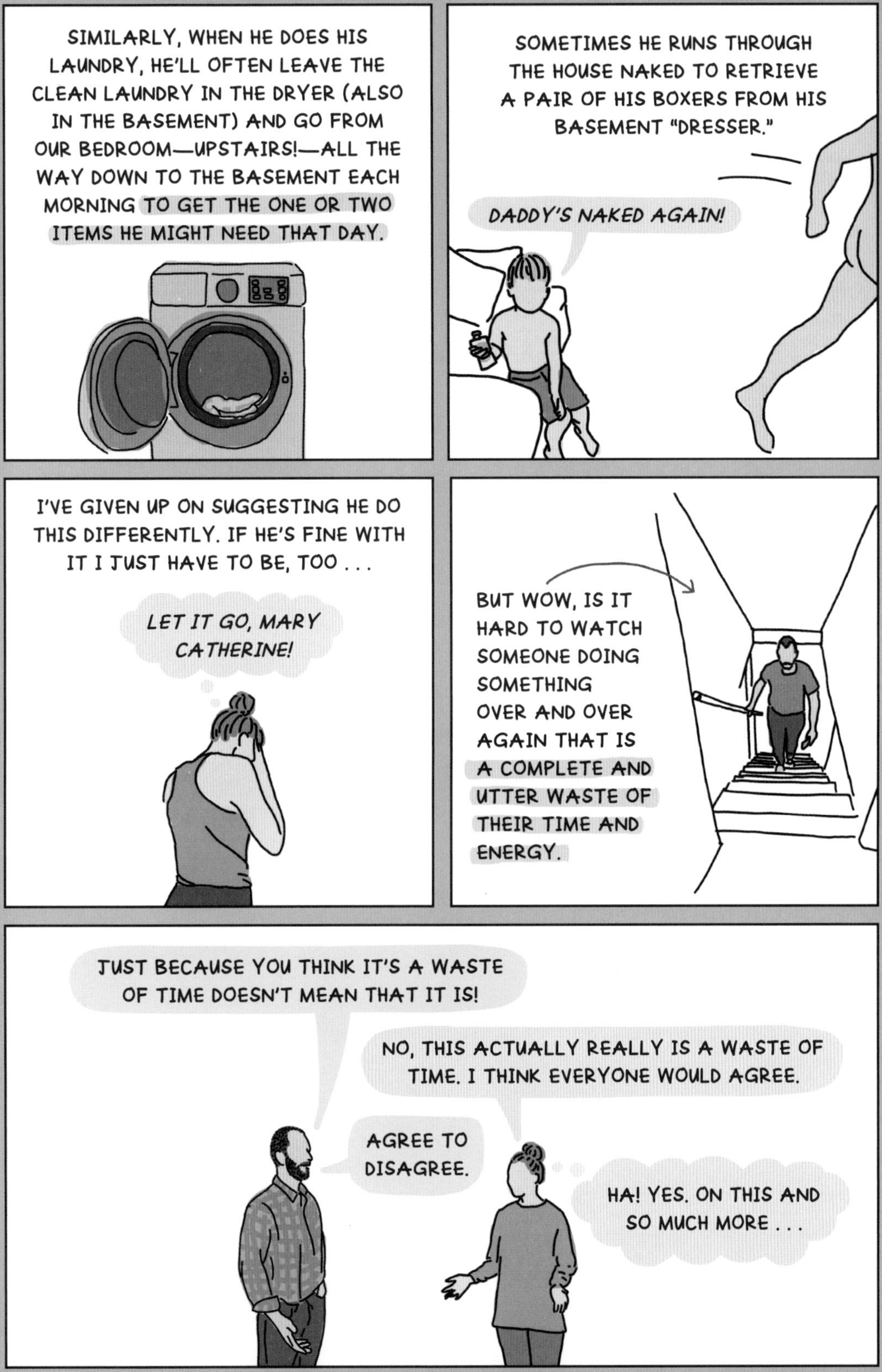
SIMILARLY, WHEN HE DOES HIS LAUNDRY, HE'LL OFTEN LEAVE THE CLEAN LAUNDRY IN THE DRYER (ALSO IN THE BASEMENT) AND GO FROM OUR BEDROOM—UPSTAIRS!—ALL THE WAY DOWN TO THE BASEMENT EACH MORNING TO GET THE ONE OR TWO ITEMS HE MIGHT NEED THAT DAY.
SOMETIMES HE RUNS THROUGH THE HOUSE NAKED TO RETRIEVE A PAIR OF HIS BOXERS FROM HIS BASEMENT "DRESSER."
DADDY'S NAKED AGAIN!
I'VE GIVEN UP ON SUGGESTING HE DO THIS DIFFERENTLY. IF HE'S FINE WITH IT I JUST HAVE TO BE, TOO . . .
LET IT GO, MARY CATHERINE!
BUT WOW, IS IT HARD TO WATCH SOMEONE DOING SOMETHING OVER AND OVER AGAIN THAT IS A COMPLETE AND UTTER WASTE OF THEIR TIME AND ENERGY.
JUST BECAUSE YOU THINK IT'S A WASTE OF TIME DOESN'T MEAN THAT IT IS!
NO, THIS ACTUALLY REALLY IS A WASTE OF TIME. I THINK EVERYONE WOULD AGREE.
AGREE TO DISAGREE.
HA! YES. ON THIS AND SO MUCH MORE . . .

# NEW!
# PREGNANCY TESTS FOR ANXIOUS PEOPLE

Box contains 50 tests, all of which can (and should be!) taken within one week—*because you can never be too sure.*

## NOW FEATURING

Test results written in a way that *just makes sense* to anxious people!

PREGNANCY TESTS *for* ANXIOUS PEOPLE

Digital
**15 DAYS SOONER**
THAN MEDICALLY POSSIBLE BUT STILL SOMEHOW

100% Accurate

NO OTHER BRAND INCLUDES THIS MANY TESTS!

**50** TESTS

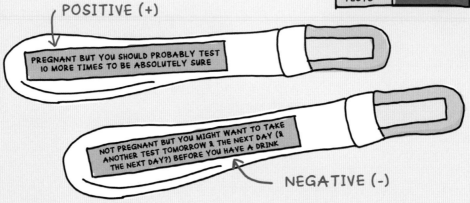

POSITIVE (+)

PREGNANT BUT YOU SHOULD PROBABLY TEST 10 MORE TIMES TO BE ABSOLUTELY SURE

NOT PREGNANT BUT YOU MIGHT WANT TO TAKE ANOTHER TEST TOMORROW & THE NEXT DAY (& THE NEXT DAY?) BEFORE YOU HAVE A DRINK

NEGATIVE (-)

# CHAPTER 5

# Postpartum Period No. 2: Our Family Is Growing (And So Is Mom's Anxiety!)

# I'm Not a Normal Mom,
# I'm ~~a Cool~~ an Anxious Mom!

Anxiety is tricky. Especially when you're a mom. It often disguises itself as a necessary part of the role. It convinces you that it's helping you keep everyone safe and everything handled. It can go dormant for a little while, and just when you think you're getting the hang of things, it rears its ugly head to remind you that you can't relax too much or everything will fall apart.

Throughout my second postpartum period, my anxiety was up and down. It definitely wasn't as bad as it was after I had Charlie Mae, but I think my baseline had become so high that even my "good days" were still very anxiety-filled.

And my anxiety, as we've already established, leads to perfectionism, micromanaging, obsessing about schedules and the "right" way to do everything, and constant productivity. The more anxious I am, the more productive I think I need to be! It's not great. So this is the backdrop against which we evolved into a family of four.

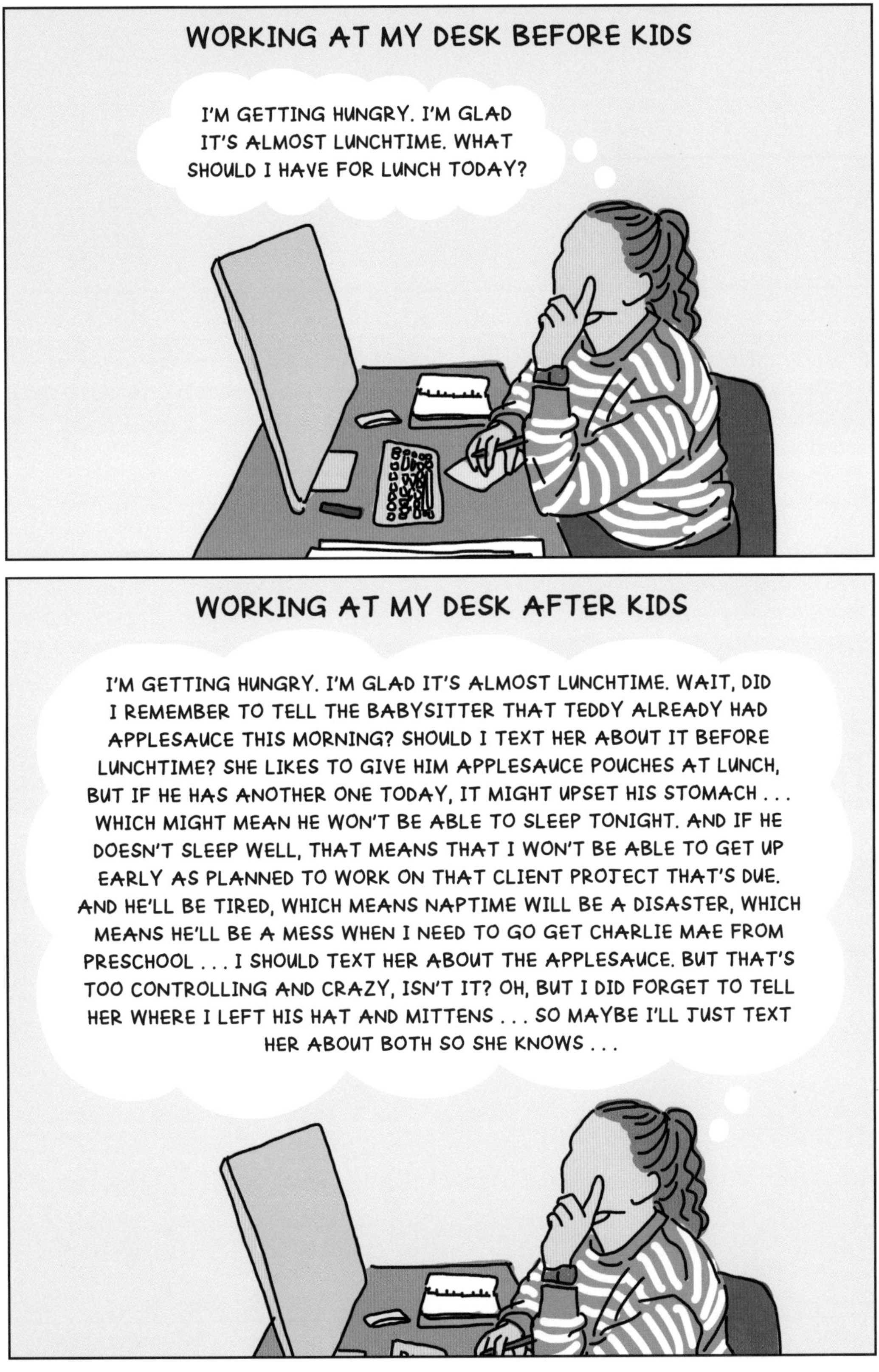
WORKING AT MY DESK BEFORE KIDS
I'M GETTING HUNGRY. I'M GLAD IT'S ALMOST LUNCHTIME. WHAT SHOULD I HAVE FOR LUNCH TODAY?
WORKING AT MY DESK AFTER KIDS
I'M GETTING HUNGRY. I'M GLAD IT'S ALMOST LUNCHTIME. WAIT, DID I REMEMBER TO TELL THE BABYSITTER THAT TEDDY ALREADY HAD APPLESAUCE THIS MORNING? SHOULD I TEXT HER ABOUT IT BEFORE LUNCHTIME? SHE LIKES TO GIVE HIM APPLESAUCE POUCHES AT LUNCH, BUT IF HE HAS ANOTHER ONE TODAY, IT MIGHT UPSET HIS STOMACH . . . WHICH MIGHT MEAN HE WON'T BE ABLE TO SLEEP TONIGHT. AND IF HE DOESN'T SLEEP WELL, THAT MEANS THAT I WON'T BE ABLE TO GET UP EARLY AS PLANNED TO WORK ON THAT CLIENT PROJECT THAT'S DUE. AND HE'LL BE TIRED, WHICH MEANS NAPTIME WILL BE A DISASTER, WHICH MEANS HE'LL BE A MESS WHEN I NEED TO GO GET CHARLIE MAE FROM PRESCHOOL . . . I SHOULD TEXT HER ABOUT THE APPLESAUCE. BUT THAT'S TOO CONTROLLING AND CRAZY, ISN'T IT? OH, BUT I DID FORGET TO TELL HER WHERE I LEFT HIS HAT AND MITTENS . . . SO MAYBE I'LL JUST TEXT HER ABOUT BOTH SO SHE KNOWS . . .

# Oh, How I Wish I Were the Kind of Gal Who Journals

I've always wanted to be the kind of person who journals every day, but I'm just not. Every therapist I've ever had (quite a few!) has encouraged me to do so. I've had to keep journals for classes I've taken, and I know all of the benefits of journaling and how much it can help with anxiety.

But at the end of the day, no matter how many times I start a journaling routine, I just don't do it. Is that because it's not outwardly "productive" and is only for me? Probably, and that's definitely something to look into and process (some other time because I'm too busy right now, OBVIOUSLY), but no matter the reason, I just am not a journaler even though I love to write.

That being said, I did have a daily blog for many years, which was the closest I've ever gotten to journaling regularly (it was outward-facing, which held me accountable!), and I kept that blog going up until my second child was a few years old.

I love looking back at old blog posts from when my kids were young because they're such a great time capsule and record of what happened and when.

So let's pretend that I am an avid journaler and kept a personal journal during the time between when we started trying for our second child (Teddy) and a few months after his birth. If I had, here's how some of those journal entries might have read, which I think will give you a picture of what was happening with my anxiety during this time . . .

(FYI: Ben doesn't journal either, but I've snuck a few of his imaginary journal pages in here, too. Because that's how married couples usually journal, right? They share a journal in which they confess their deepest, darkest frustrations with each other? Yeah, that's what I thought. Classic couples journaling shenanigans.)

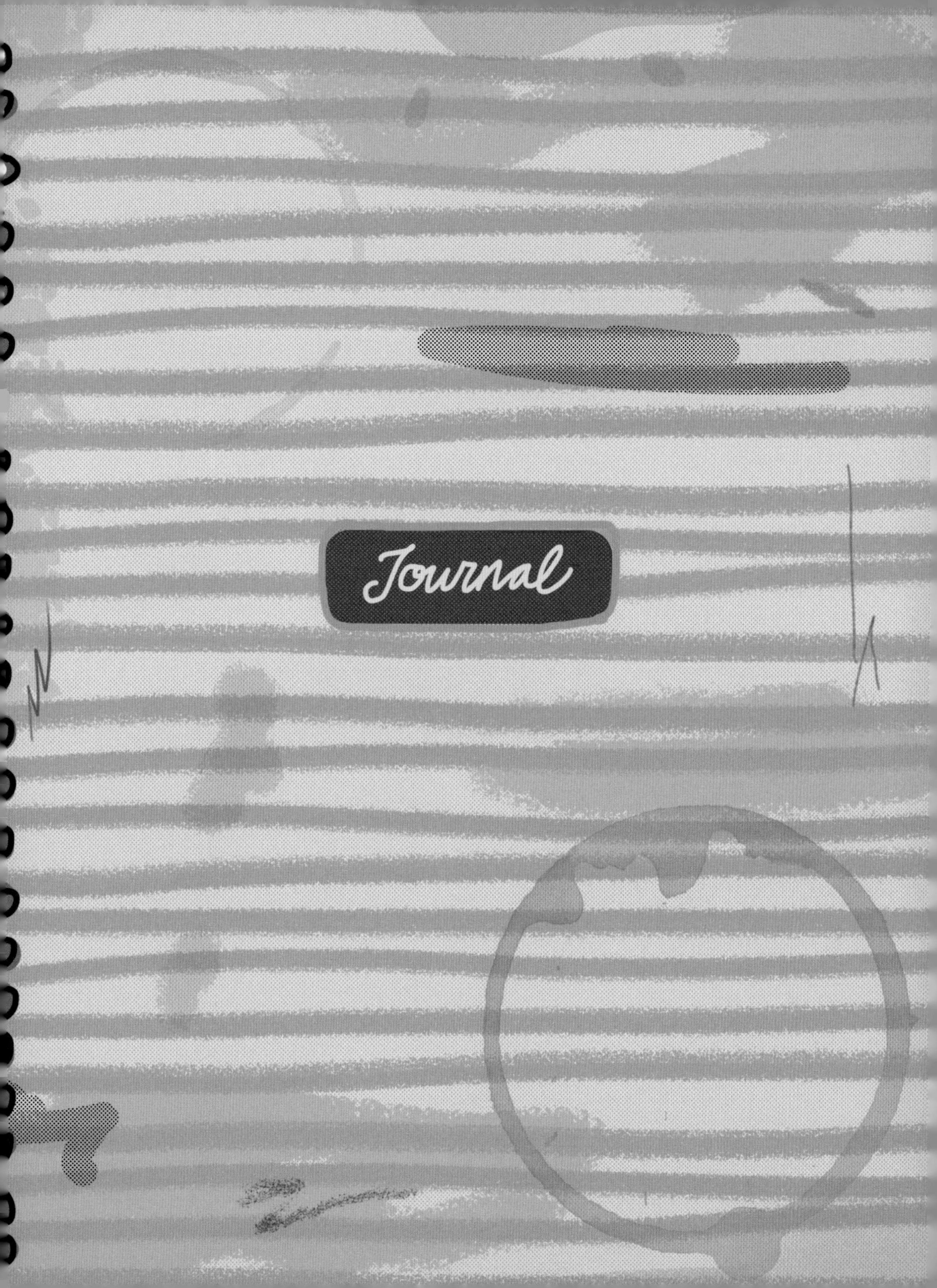
Journal

MAY 21, 2018

It's taken me almost 2 years to
summon the courage to try and
get pregnant again (and thus,
go through labor again), but today,
after many months of feeling
TOTALLY not ready, I woke up
feeling ready to start trying for
a second. And now that I'm feeling
ready, I'm READY.* I want to
be pregnant again, and I want
to be pregnant NOW.

CHARLIE MAE, 1.5 YEARS OLD

You'd think that my first experience with childbirth and having a baby
would have taught me that I'm totally not in control—and while I like
to say that I learned this lesson, I still don't think I've accepted it as
much as I need to in order to do it again.

I'm still the same me who wants to apply my type A, perfectionistic
tendencies to everything I do . . . so here we go, Ben! I'm using my
period tracking app, I'm planning our lives around when I'm ovulating,
I'm ready for another baby, so BUCKLE UP. Your driven wife is ready
to attempt to micromanage the un-micromanageable yet again!

*And by "ready" I mean that I'm as ready as I'll ever be. Yes, of
course there's a low rumbling of worry about another postpartum
period from HELL filled with anxiety and sleepless nights, but in order
to be "ready" I've had to push that feeling down as far as it will go
and just ignore it.

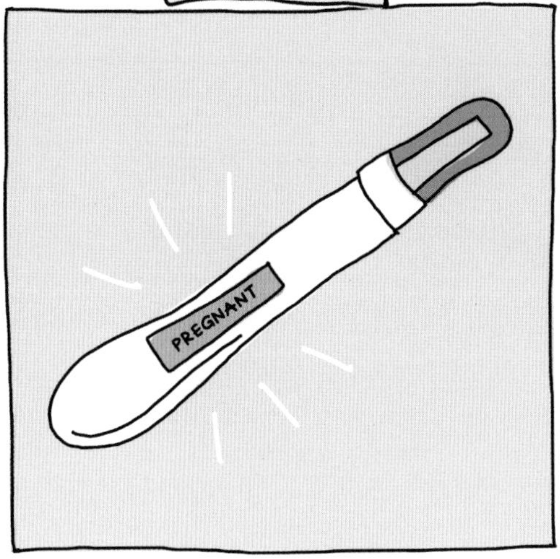
PREGNANT

EEEEEKKKKKK!!!!
IT'S HAPPENING!

JULY 3, 2018

OMG, I'm pregnant! It happened quickly, just like I'd hoped it would! Our baby will be due in March 2019, so Charlie Mae will be just over 2.5 years old when he or she is born. It's perfect timing! I feel so good about this pregnancy—unlike my first birth and postpartum period, I'm going to be a seasoned pro this time around so everything will have to be better and easier . . . right?

I'm going to keep telling myself lies like this because it's the only way I know how to do this, and it's much easier than feeling anxious about all of the challenges that are inevitably headed my way. My mantra: This baby will be my "easy" baby. I mean, it can't possibly be as hard as it was last time, right?! *RIGHT!?!??!?!*

AUGUST 14, 2018

We lost the baby. I'm heartbroken. Devastated. Can't stop crying.
I know it's not my fault, but it feels like it's definitely my fault—
I've failed again.

All of the clichés about the emotions associated with pregnancy loss
are clichés for a reason: I feel all of those things. I'm not ready to
write about it yet.

My body feels so empty.

I feel so empty.

OCTOBER 18, 2018

Ben took this snapshot just over
2 months ago. I was 10 weeks
along and felt like my belly had
just started to pop; this being my
2nd pregnancy, my uterus knew
what was up and had started to
expand immediately. I was over the
moon, feeling great, and excited
to hear our baby's heartbeat at
my 10-week appointment in just a
few days.

AUGUST 12, 2018

What I didn't know when this picture was taken was that our baby's
heart had already stopped beating. Our baby had stopped growing at
8 weeks, but was still nestled inside of my uterus while I—oblivious to
this fact—snapped pictures meant to capture what I thought was
my growing belly.

Within a few days of this picture being taken, after the appointment
where my midwife couldn't find the heartbeat with the doppler,
after the excruciating 24 hours in which I waited for the ultrasound
that would tell us what was happening inside my body, after the
heartbreaking 10 minutes lying on a table in the dark, watching the
ultrasound tech move her wand around my belly without saying a word
and knowing what her silence meant, we scheduled a D&C, a surgical
procedure that would remove our deceased baby from my womb.

While some women say that it wasn't helpful for them to hear how common pregnancy loss is, I found it very helpful. I took comfort in the statistics that 1 in 4 pregnancies end in loss. Not because I wanted this for other people, but because if it was extremely common, then maybe that didn't make it my fault. Maybe my baby really wasn't going to be able to survive in this world and that's why it stopped growing, not because I took an ibuprofen long before I knew I was pregnant, or demonstrated a deep twist in one of my yoga classes.

And I took comfort in all of the female family members who called to tell me that this had happened to them in the past, too, in between child 1 and 2, or child 2 and 3. It gave me hope that I would be able to go on and have another healthy baby someday, too.

The thing about pregnancy loss is that you're not just mourning the loss of this child that you were growing in your belly and are no longer going to get to meet, but you're also mourning the life plans that you had made based on this baby's impending arrival. Ben and I had started planning what our parental leaves would look like. We knew the rough age difference between our two kids and imagined Charlie Mae having a playmate sooner rather than later. We had a hazy outline of how the beginning of 2019 would go; after all, if we were having a baby in March, that would change the year in a big way.

But then in just 24 hours, we'd lost all of that "stability." We knew our plans weren't really stable in the first place, but we'd hoped that they could be and had talked things out because that's what you do. We'd done this before, and it had gone smoothly (the pregnancy part)

so we had just gone ahead with our life, planning around this big event as if it would happen for us again. And then out of nowhere, it ended. And we've been having to deal with that.

I've also been trying to focus on all of the good in our lives: The loss feels a little easier because we already have Charlie Mae. I've been able to look at her and hug her and not only feel enormous gratitude that I already have a healthy, wonderful child, but also be reminded that my body has done this before and that hopefully, that means it can do it again.

During all of this, I've been acutely aware of just how difficult it must be to suffer multiple losses, one after another, while hoping for a child. Or to be someone who can't get pregnant at all and wants to. It's all so devastating and complicated and just plain sad. So much sadness.

But what's so strange is that when you suffer a loss like this, you still have to wake up and go on with your day: you get up early and get your child ready, you take her to the park, you respond to emails, you eat lunch, you teach a yoga class, you scroll through your phone, you go to the grocery store.

No one knows that you've just been dealt a big blow, and you don't tell them because you don't want to talk about it, but you carry it around, feeling empty inside when you felt so full only one week ago. And then you keep waking up and going through your days and dealing with life, and the sadness starts to fade.

At one point you think, "I won't be able to talk about this publicly for a long time," and then only a little while later, you're surprised to find that you're ready to talk about your loss. If nothing else than to tell another woman who is recovering from a miscarriage or another loss that she is not alone, that you understand, and that you're sorry.

You're so, so sorry.

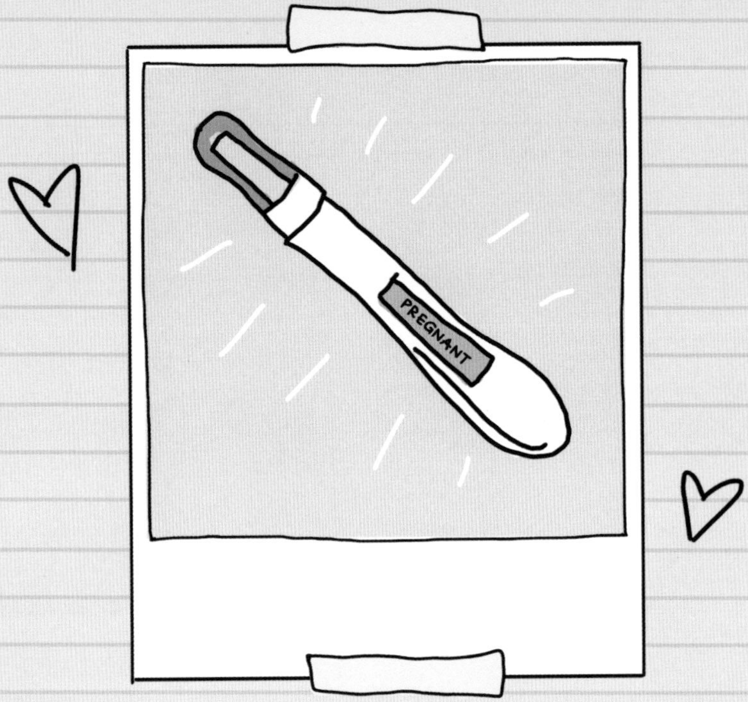
PREGNANT

NOVEMBER 7, 2018

I'm pregnant again!

I'm feeling cautiously optimistic about it. I'm not going to let myself get really excited until we hit 12 weeks (or maybe 24 weeks?), but I am excited. I can't help myself. But also I'm preparing for the worst. But trying to think positively. But not too positively or I'll jinx myself. I need to be realistic and I know the stats. And yes, my body has done this before, and I know it can do it again. But I might not be able to—I know that now. But I really hope everything is okay.

Come on, body! Come on, baby! Come on, Universe! We can do this!!!

At least I hope we can.

APRIL 10, 2019

Dear Second Child of Mine,

As I lay in bed last night, I felt
you kicking in my belly and started
writing this letter to you in
my head . . .

While it appears from the outside
that we're not ready for you at
all, that we haven't thought about
your impending arrival and are
unprepared, this is not the case.
We've been waiting for you all of
our lives.

BABY #2

What I didn't know the first time around, I made up for by obsessing
and perfecting all of the small, controllable details; but with you,
I know how little these details actually matter once you're holding a
new baby in your arms. Your sister taught me that all of the planning
and painting and buying and folding will not make it easier to adjust
to a new baby's presence in our lives but instead will just add to my
to-do list before you arrive, which is long and overwhelming enough
already. (Although I do promise to wash and fold the clothes that are
currently sitting in grocery sacks . . . )

In many ways, you're lucky, because you won't have the pressure of 10 months of anxious uncertainty rush in on you the second you enter the world. You'll have the love and the excitement, but not the same amount of figure-it-out-as-you-gos and nervous unknowns (although everything about you is an unknown, from your eye color to your personality to your sleep habits; *oh please be the laid-back baby I've only heard about in parenting fairy tales!*).

Your sister likes to press her ear against my belly and tell me about the noises that she hears "you" making. She fed you popcorn and milk from her sippy cup onto my belly the other night, and she's already started planning the games that you'll play together and which toys she'll share with you.

I know your experience of our family will be so different than hers has been thus far; you'll have her as your guide, your companion, your distraction, and in many ways, your competition, but she's just as excited as we are to meet you.

You should also know, Dear Babe, that there was another baby between you and your sister, but that he or she didn't make it this far. I have to think that this is because you were the baby that we were supposed to have, supposed to meet, and supposed to love, and for that reason I'm even more confident that we're ready for you to be a part of our little family unit (in another 14-ish weeks, of course!).

We're not perfect; we've all got a lot of growing to do, but we're your family, and we feel so lucky that you're going to be ours.

Thanks for picking us. And thanks in advance for your understanding about your lack of exciting new clothing and hand-me-down everything . . .

See you in July!

Love,

Your Bedraggled and Tired Yet Loving Mom

Here's a message from your sister!

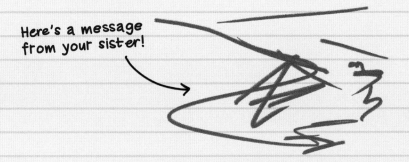

JULY 13, 2019

WOW. Just wow. Teddy was
born yesterday, and now I know
what an empowering, healing birth
feels like. I still can't believe it
happened the way that it did.
I had the unmedicated birth that
I wanted! My labor was short
and sweet! I'm too tired to write
the entire story, but here are the
highlights:

I started having contractions around 11:30 a.m. on Thursday. I was
at Whole Foods with Charlie Mae when I realized they were coming
somewhat regularly. Around 5 p.m. they were starting to get
stronger—I called my doula (I got one this time!) and my midwife
and gave them a heads-up. I was having back labor again but
tried not to freak out about it.

We left for the hospital a little after midnight, and on the 25-minute
drive we had the windows down and I was howling like a wild animal.
The theme of Teddy's entire labor and birth experience could be
summed up as raw, primal, and animalistic. I was a Wild Mother Beast.

I was checked for the first time around 1 a.m. and I was told I was
at 6 cm. One hour later I was at 9 cm (!!!) and finally got into the tub,
where I labored for the next 30 minutes.

When it was time to push, I got out so that I could get in a position that would hopefully lead to less tearing. I knew it was time to push because my body was pushing automatically—I had no control over it! And then in 5-7 pushes, he was out. Besides one scary moment right when he came out (he wasn't crying, so they sucked fluid out of his nose and mouth and then he did), everything was amazing. He was placed on my belly, and I was flooded with relief (his cord was too short to reach to my chest!).

Teddy was born at 3:17 a.m.—just 2 hours after arriving at the hospital—and by 4:15 a.m. everyone was out of our room. I was wide-awake, running on adrenaline and pure LOVE, the lights were low, my relaxing playlist was playing, and Ben was doing this:

My doula snapped this pic because she just couldn't believe how quickly Ben fell asleep after Teddy was born. It makes me laugh every time I look at it.

July 13, 2019

It's Ben—I can't believe I just passed out like
that, but it had been an intense few hours!

Mary Catherine was an amazing wild woman!
And Teddy was so beautiful and perfect, and
he was breastfeeding on Mary Catherine's chest
while she rested . . . the light was low, the yoga
music was on, and I just drifted off. The energy
was really different than it had been after
Charlie Mae's birth, and I was so glad about that.

This experience was so wonderful.

JULY 24, 2019

Oh my goodness, it's so much easier to recover from having a baby when you aren't horribly injured and depleted from the labor and delivery! And when you can actually walk and sit down without an inflatable donut! And when you kind of know what you're doing with breastfeeding and sleep! And when you have another child to take care of so you simply don't have as much time and energy to obsess about every single little decision and poop and noise! And when you already have all of the stuff and know how to use it!

This entire experience with Teddy has been so much easier than the first time around.* And so healing and empowering. I am full.

*Yes, there is still that low rumbling of worry about hitting the 4-month sleep regression and what will happen to our lives if Teddy stops sleeping like Charlie Mae did. Once again, I've decided not to focus on this because there's simply nothing I can do about it right now.

AUGUST 1, 2019

I just have to write this
down because I never want
to forget it—it made me
laugh so hard! Today, I asked
Ben to get Teddy dressed.
He took him upstairs and a
little while later, brought him
down dressed like this:

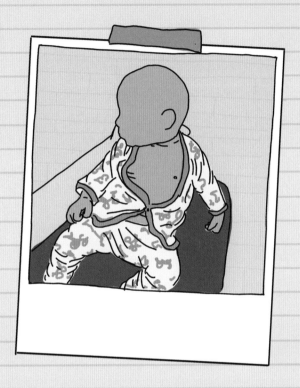

When he handed him to me in this outfit, I died. He actually thought
this is how you put this shirt on a baby.* HOW IS THIS REAL!? Oh Ben.
It's like he's never dressed a baby before! I can't stop laughing
about it.

*Even though this is funny, it's also pretty annoying. Is he doing
this on purpose in some sort of protest because I asked him to do
something that I often do? Or so that I won't ask him to do it again
in the future? Argh. I'm choosing to just laugh about it this time.

NOV. 5TH, 2019

Before we had Teddy, I knew
that life with two kids would
be bananas. In a general sense,
I understood that taking care
of a baby and a toddler at
the same time would be hard;
there would be another person
to keep happy and healthy and
therefore, mothering would
take more time and energy,
which would leave less time and
energy for everything else.

But what I didn't understand is that in practice, having two
kids means that there is absolutely NO time left for anything else—
unless I am paying someone (or multiple people) to take care of my
children.

And during the days and times in which both children are home with me
(which is a lot of the time right now), it means that I'm responding to
one child's needs while also anticipating the other child's needs EVERY
SINGLE SECOND OF THE DAY.

It means that when I sit down to nurse Teddy, Charlie Mae has either
an "urgent" need that only I can fulfill or wants to drape her body
over my opposite boob so that she can look into her brother's eyes
while he eats [and distract him, which makes feeding way harder].

It means *finally* getting both kids to bed around 8pm and then having zero (literally ZERO!!) left to give to anyone or anything else—not Ben ("Ugh, don't touch me!"), not myself, or my work, or my friends/family, or my unanswered text messages and emails from the day . . . the list goes on and on.

In fact, I'm so drained that I'm going to stop writing right now and rest.

Good night—

---

DECEMBER 19, 2019

Life has gotten HARD. Really, really hard.

Having a baby and a toddler is so much harder than I expected. Especially when you're the preferred parent and the default parent for both.

Teddy hasn't been sleeping very well for the past two-ish months, and on the nights he isn't keeping me up, Charlie Mae is. There are lots of nights when they're both up at different times and I'm handling it all.

I'm drowning in work. I feel anxious and overwhelmed all the time. It's the holidays—which means I've been spending all of my free time trying to make the holidays magical for everyone else while

Ben watches basketball on the couch because he's "so tired" (and I know he is, but COME ON).

Also, it seems that the in-home daycare where we send Charlie Mae isn't a good fit for Teddy, which means I'll probably have to find a new child care situation for the kids. And yes, I will have to be the one to find it because God forbid Ben ever handles any of the kid-related admin or scheduling.

I am just SO exhausted and frustrated. I'm sure the kids are picking up on my frustration, and I know it can't be good for them to see me so overwhelmed and angry at Ben—but I am and it's very hard to hide it. Am I just an angry person? Is there something wrong with me?

I need to get back in therapy, and Ben and I should really be in couples therapy LIKE I'VE BEEN SAYING FOR YEARS.

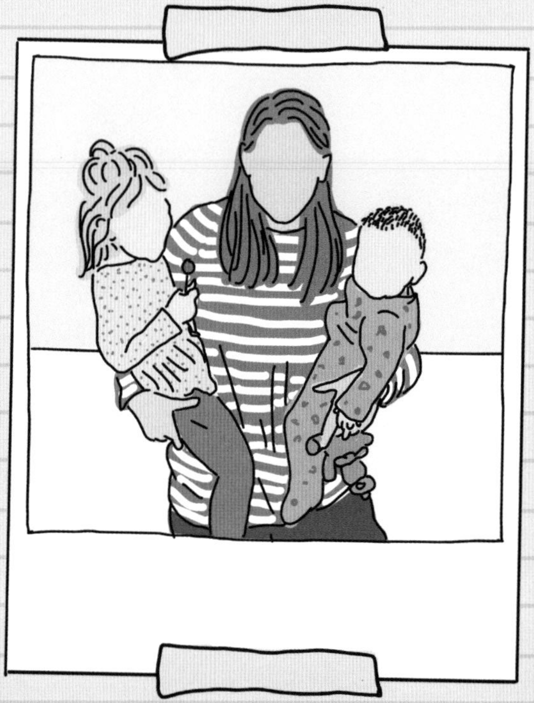

But who will have to research and book the therapist and then schedule all of our sessions and make sure we're both there? ME. Obviously. And that makes me angry, too. Why do I have to do everything!?!?

Happy 35th birthday to me.

Woo-freaking-hoo.

January 10, 2020

Mary Catherine has been so frustrated with me lately, and I'm not sure why.

I mean, I know she handles all of the nighttime wake-ups with the kids and that's super hard, but I've tried helping and it just doesn't work. I don't have breastmilk so I can't soothe Teddy, and if I try to help Charlie Mae in the night, she freaks out and just wants Mary Catherine.

Even when I do try to help, Mary Catherine just lies in bed awake, listening to us on the monitor and critiquing everything I do "wrong." So why should I even try?

On the days when I can swing it, I've been coming home early to give Mary Catherine breaks, but it's hard because everyone always wants her for everything, and the evenings are so tough with the kids. I know she has tons of work to do, but my work has been really crazy, too, and I'm in court handling criminal cases! I can't just leave because my family needs me! People are waiting in jail cells for their bail hearings! I wish she'd understand how important my work is and how hard all of this is for me, too.

Parenting young kids doesn't come naturally
to me. Loving them does, but caring for them
doesn't. I get so overwhelmed by all of the
sensory stimulation but really am doing my best,
and I think I'm a good dad! I mean, I know I am.
I love our kids SO, so much. It's just that not all
of us can be robot parents and keep pushing and
pushing past the point of exhaustion like Mary
Catherine can.

She's been talking about going to couples therapy,
and while I'm all for it, I just don't know when we'll
have the time . . . we hardly have time to talk to
each other or hang out as it is!

I hope the kids start sleeping better soon; that
would help everything, I think.

FEBRUARY 20, 2020

Before having Teddy, I felt like this would be our chance for a do-over. We'd handle nighttime wake-ups differently. I'd get Ben more involved in feeding and being the default parent at night. He'd be more competent since we've done all of this before, which means I'd get more breaks and thus feel less overwhelmed and lost in motherhood. I'd be on the lookout for PPA and postpartum rage. I'd give him more chances to do things his own way.

This was our chance to change the unhealthy dynamics that we established during Charlie Mae's first few years of life!

So why didn't that happen? How, at 7 months in, have we ended up in the same place—yet again? Sure, Teddy takes a bottle and a

Binky, so Ben has been able to soothe him better than he could with Charlie Mae, but I am still the nighttime parent, the default parent, and the preferred parent for Teddy (and Charlie Mae, of course). Ben still hasn't stepped up in the way I'd hoped he would. I know it's more complicated than that, but I'm just still so angry and frustrated so much of the time.

Are our roles in the family SO ingrained that even when trying to do things differently, we get the same outcome? Or did we not do things differently at all? HOW CAN WE CHANGE THIS DYNAMIC? What is wrong with us? What is wrong with Ben? What is wrong with me? Is it my anxiety? Have I unwittingly done this to us?

Ughhhhhh. HOW DID WE GET HERE AGAIN!?!?

# Welp, We're Screwed.

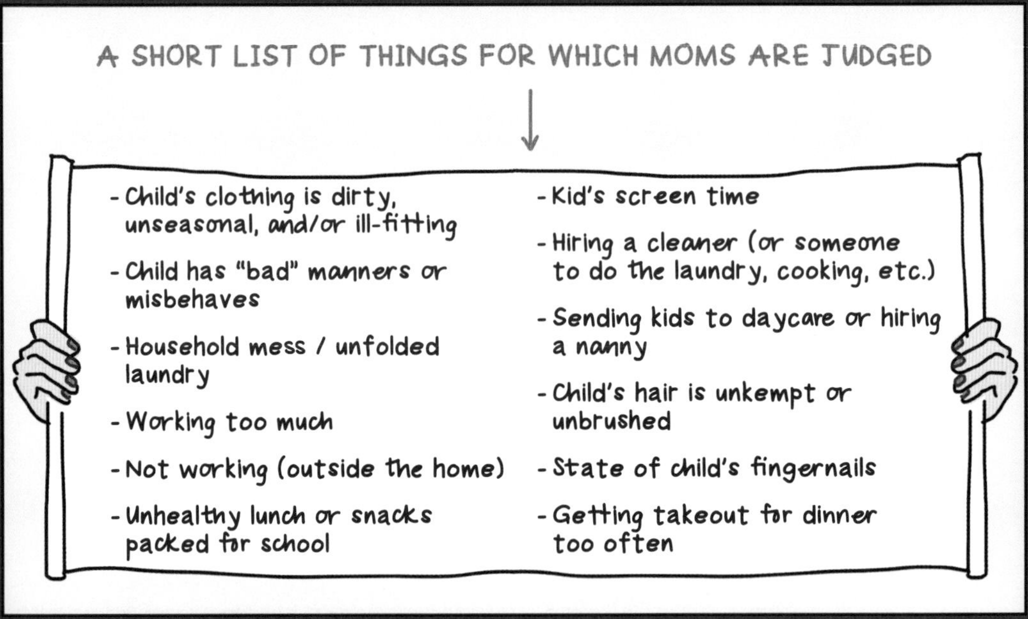
A SHORT LIST OF THINGS FOR WHICH MOMS ARE JUDGED
- Child's clothing is dirty, unseasonal, and/or ill-fitting
- Child has "bad" manners or misbehaves
- Household mess / unfolded laundry
- Working too much
- Not working (outside the home)
- Unhealthy lunch or snacks packed for school
- Kid's screen time
- Hiring a cleaner (or someone to do the laundry, cooking, etc.)
- Sending kids to daycare or hiring a nanny
- Child's hair is unkempt or unbrushed
- State of child's fingernails
- Getting takeout for dinner too often

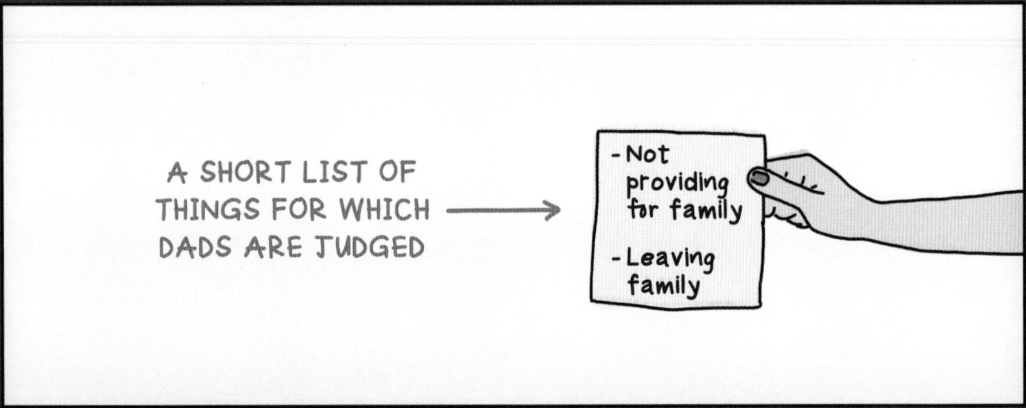
A SHORT LIST OF THINGS FOR WHICH DADS ARE JUDGED
- Not providing for family
- Leaving family

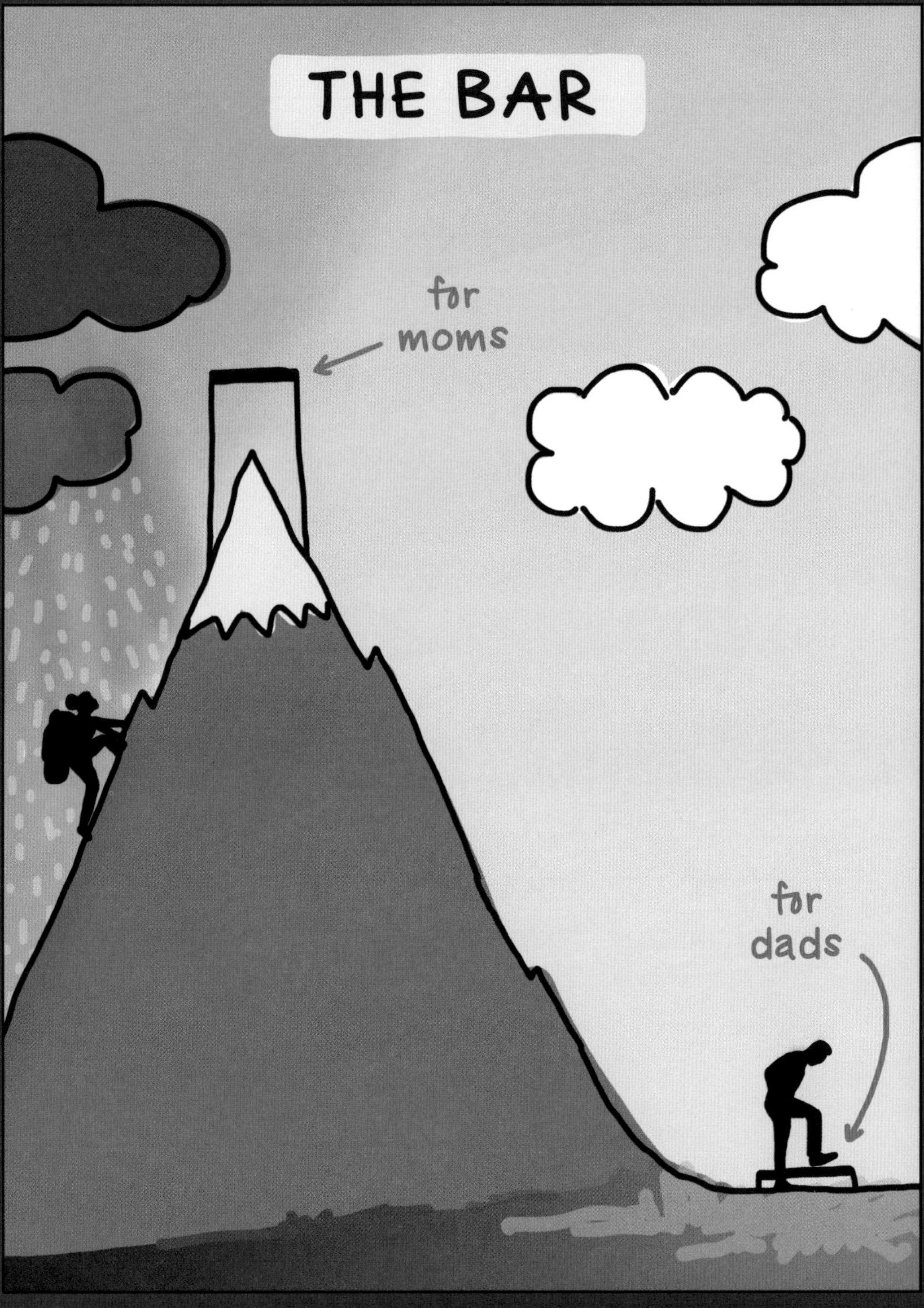
THE BAR
for moms
for dads

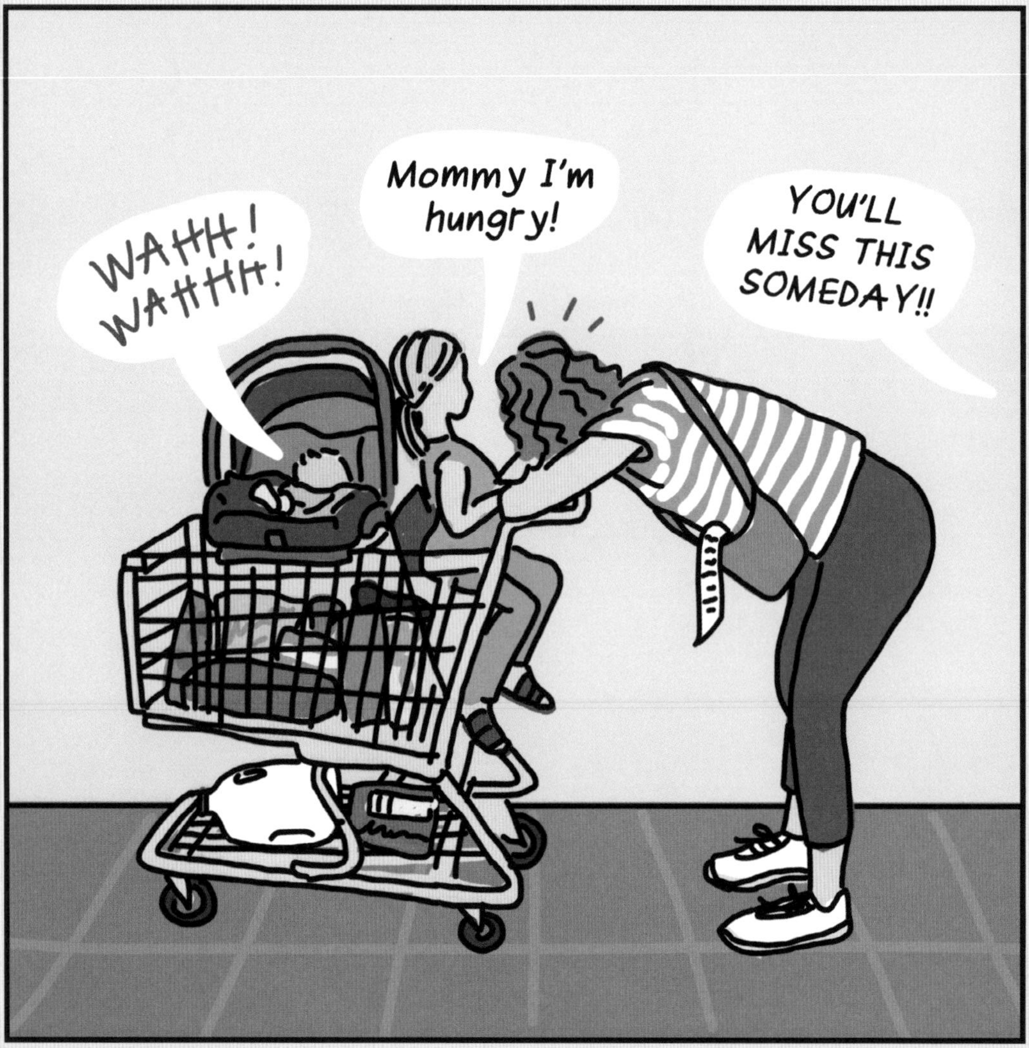
WAHH!
WAHHH!
Mommy I'm hungry!
YOU'LL MISS THIS SOMEDAY!!

# CHAPTER 6

# The Infamous, Relentless Mental Load of Motherhood

# Ugh, the Mental Load of Motherhood

**F**uck the mental load of motherhood. There, I said it.

EEK! IT MAKES ME NERVOUS TO WRITE THIS WORD IN MY BOOK, BUT I WANT TO MAKE IT CLEAR HOW MUCH I HATE THIS PART OF MOTHERHOOD!

I am so thankful for the term "the mental load of motherhood"—it's great to have a label for the invisible labor, the emotional labor, the brain power and energy that go into managing the household and the family and raising children in a loving, present way. I'm glad we have a name for the work we mothers are doing that takes up every extra moment of our days and yet goes mostly unseen by our partners and by society-at-large.

But I wish there was a more descriptive term for the mental load of motherhood. To me, this name doesn't fully capture the heavy, soul-sucking aspects of the most fulfilling job I've ever had; "the mental load" doesn't capture the thankless parts, the parts in which you feel completely alone and lost and overwhelmed, the way in which, once you become a mom, your brain learns that it can't ever turn off again OR THE WHOLE HOUSE OF CARDS WILL COLLAPSE AND EVERYONE WILL DIE, the way in which you're always thinking three steps ahead of your partner while simultaneously feeling like you're drowning and and and . . . you get it.

But because we can't call it what it is, "The Soul-Crushing, Invisible, Thankless, Never-Ending, Exhausting, Enraging, Mental Labor of Motherhood," I guess we'll stick with "the mental load" for now. But just know that every time I write "mental load," I am also thinking about all of those other adjectives.

I've come up with a metaphor for the mental load of motherhood that has been helpful for me in understanding how we got here, despite being in a fairly egalitarian relationship before kids; it's also helped me explain the slow creep of the mental load over time and begin to comprehend how I could have possibly let this happen.

The metaphor is laundry related, of course, because isn't everything once you're a mom?

## A Tangible Example of the Mental Load of Motherhood and How It Grows Over Time

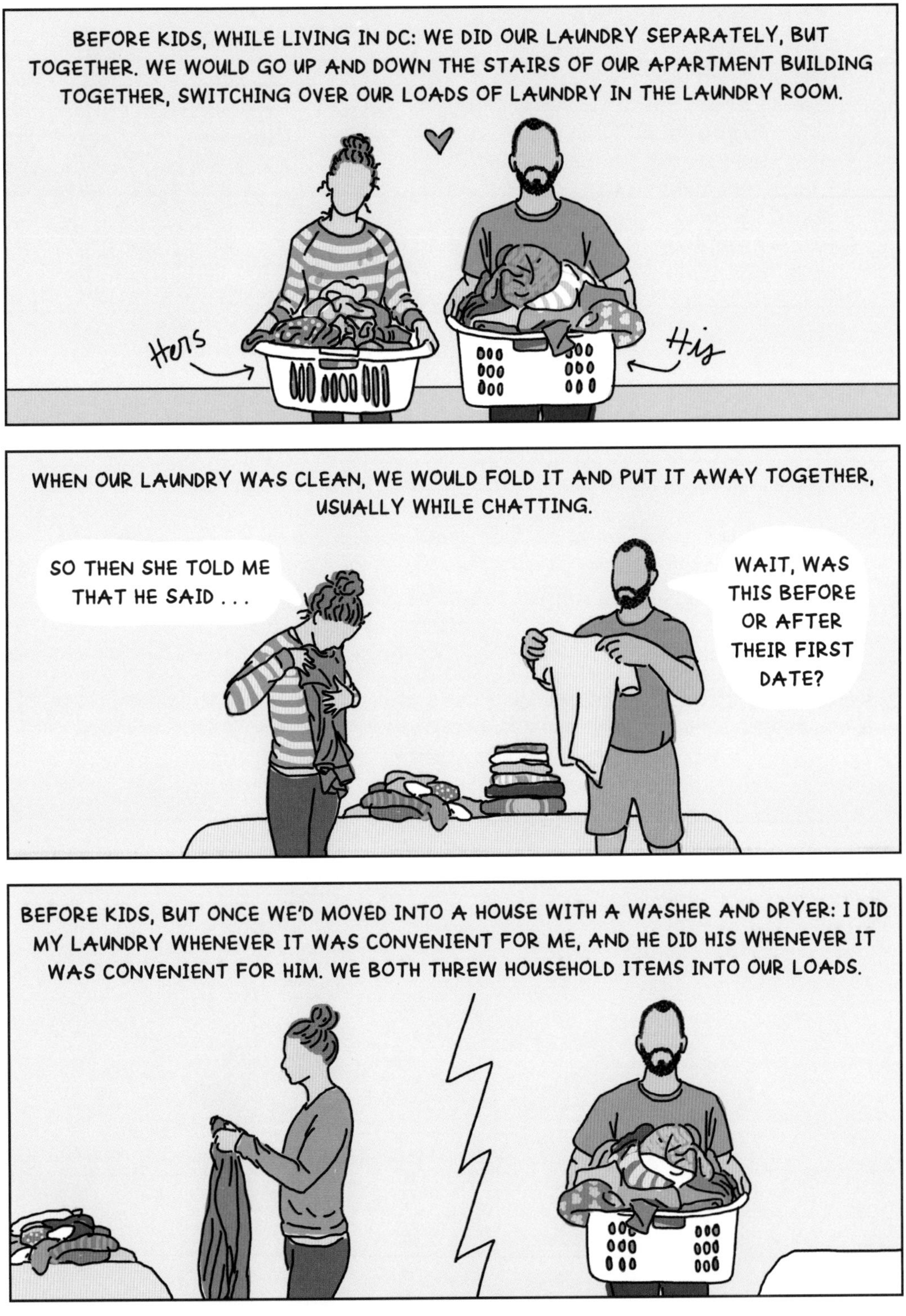
BEFORE KIDS, WHILE LIVING IN DC: WE DID OUR LAUNDRY SEPARATELY, BUT TOGETHER. WE WOULD GO UP AND DOWN THE STAIRS OF OUR APARTMENT BUILDING TOGETHER, SWITCHING OVER OUR LOADS OF LAUNDRY IN THE LAUNDRY ROOM.
Hers
His
WHEN OUR LAUNDRY WAS CLEAN, WE WOULD FOLD IT AND PUT IT AWAY TOGETHER, USUALLY WHILE CHATTING.
SO THEN SHE TOLD ME THAT HE SAID . . .
WAIT, WAS THIS BEFORE OR AFTER THEIR FIRST DATE?
BEFORE KIDS, BUT ONCE WE'D MOVED INTO A HOUSE WITH A WASHER AND DRYER: I DID MY LAUNDRY WHENEVER IT WAS CONVENIENT FOR ME, AND HE DID HIS WHENEVER IT WAS CONVENIENT FOR HIM. WE BOTH THREW HOUSEHOLD ITEMS INTO OUR LOADS.

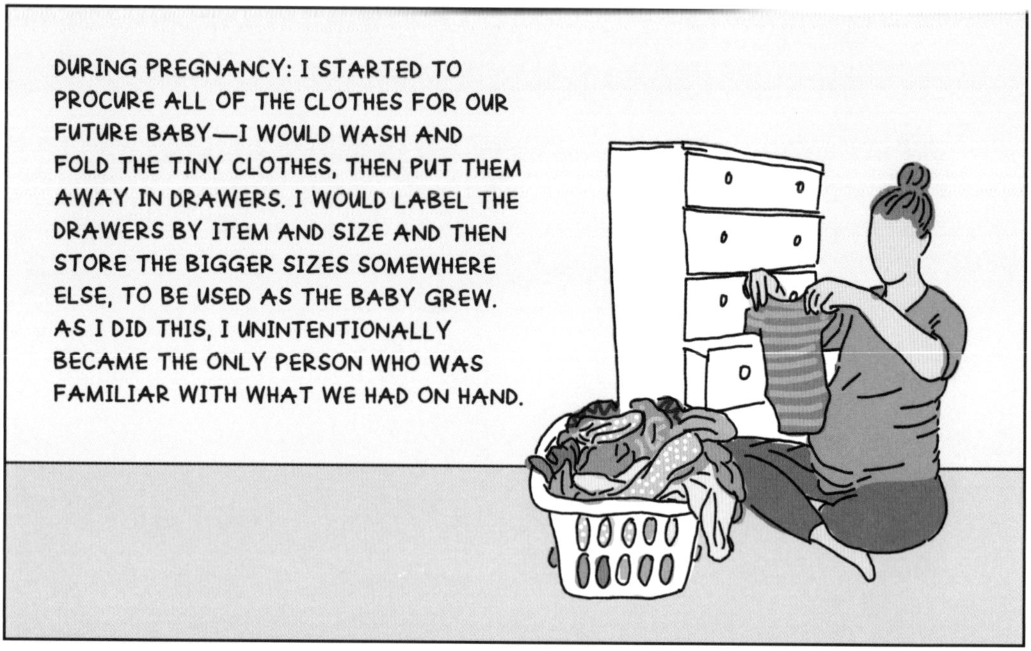
DURING PREGNANCY: I STARTED TO PROCURE ALL OF THE CLOTHES FOR OUR FUTURE BABY—I WOULD WASH AND FOLD THE TINY CLOTHES, THEN PUT THEM AWAY IN DRAWERS. I WOULD LABEL THE DRAWERS BY ITEM AND SIZE AND THEN STORE THE BIGGER SIZES SOMEWHERE ELSE, TO BE USED AS THE BABY GREW. AS I DID THIS, I UNINTENTIONALLY BECAME THE ONLY PERSON WHO WAS FAMILIAR WITH WHAT WE HAD ON HAND.

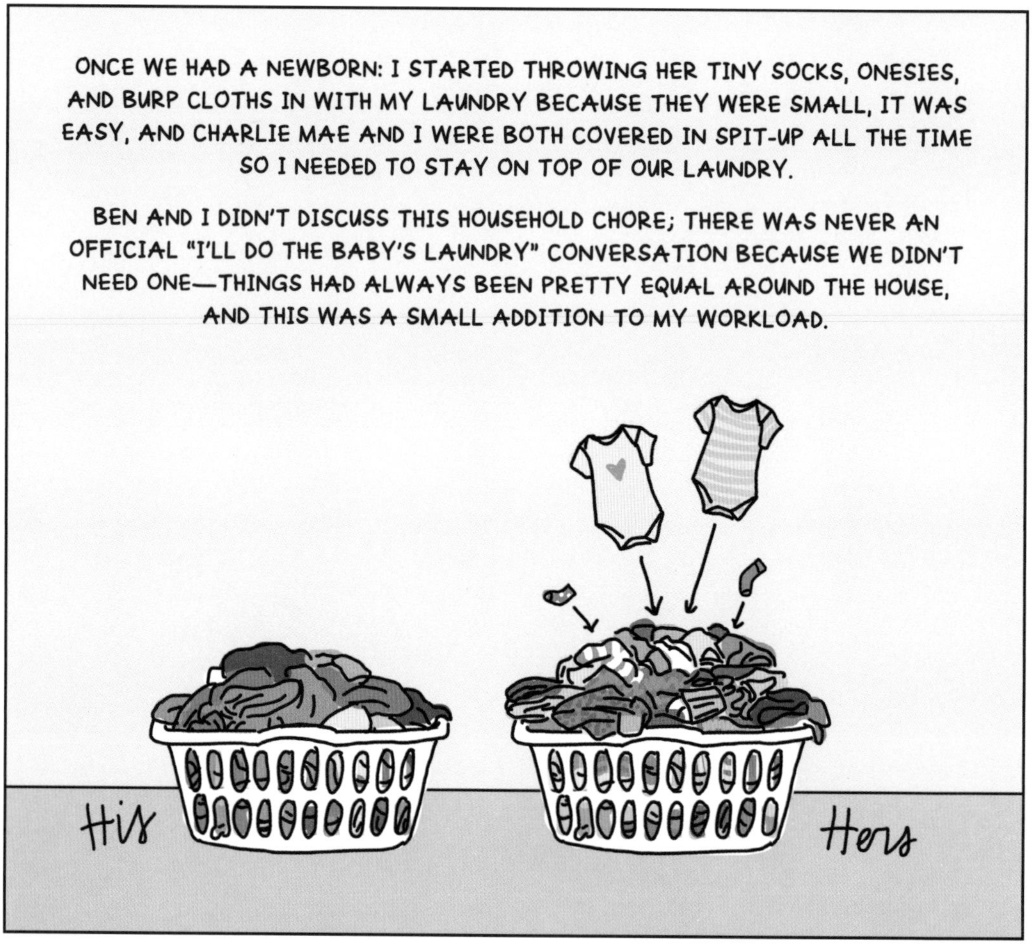
ONCE WE HAD A NEWBORN: I STARTED THROWING HER TINY SOCKS, ONESIES, AND BURP CLOTHS IN WITH MY LAUNDRY BECAUSE THEY WERE SMALL, IT WAS EASY, AND CHARLIE MAE AND I WERE BOTH COVERED IN SPIT-UP ALL THE TIME SO I NEEDED TO STAY ON TOP OF OUR LAUNDRY.
BEN AND I DIDN'T DISCUSS THIS HOUSEHOLD CHORE; THERE WAS NEVER AN OFFICIAL "I'LL DO THE BABY'S LAUNDRY" CONVERSATION BECAUSE WE DIDN'T NEED ONE—THINGS HAD ALWAYS BEEN PRETTY EQUAL AROUND THE HOUSE, AND THIS WAS A SMALL ADDITION TO MY WORKLOAD.
His
Hers

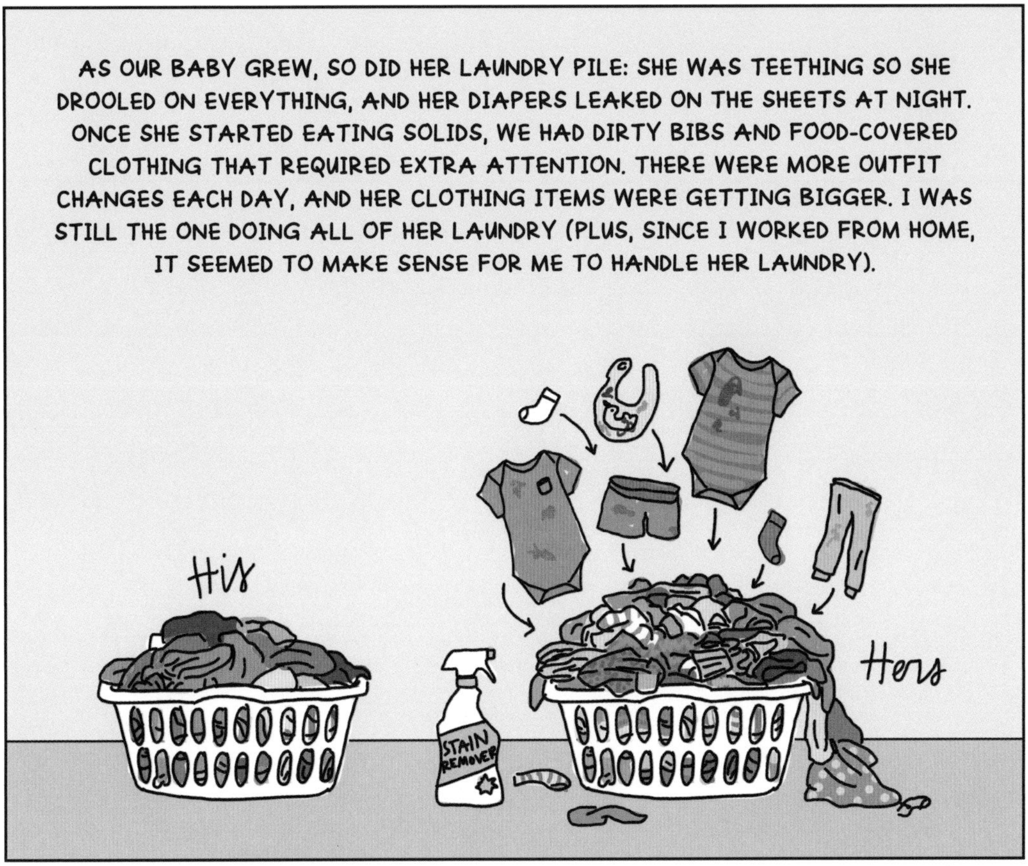
AS OUR BABY GREW, SO DID HER LAUNDRY PILE: SHE WAS TEETHING SO SHE DROOLED ON EVERYTHING, AND HER DIAPERS LEAKED ON THE SHEETS AT NIGHT. ONCE SHE STARTED EATING SOLIDS, WE HAD DIRTY BIBS AND FOOD-COVERED CLOTHING THAT REQUIRED EXTRA ATTENTION. THERE WERE MORE OUTFIT CHANGES EACH DAY, AND HER CLOTHING ITEMS WERE GETTING BIGGER. I WAS STILL THE ONE DOING ALL OF HER LAUNDRY (PLUS, SINCE I WORKED FROM HOME, IT SEEMED TO MAKE SENSE FOR ME TO HANDLE HER LAUNDRY).
His
STAIN REMOVER
Hers

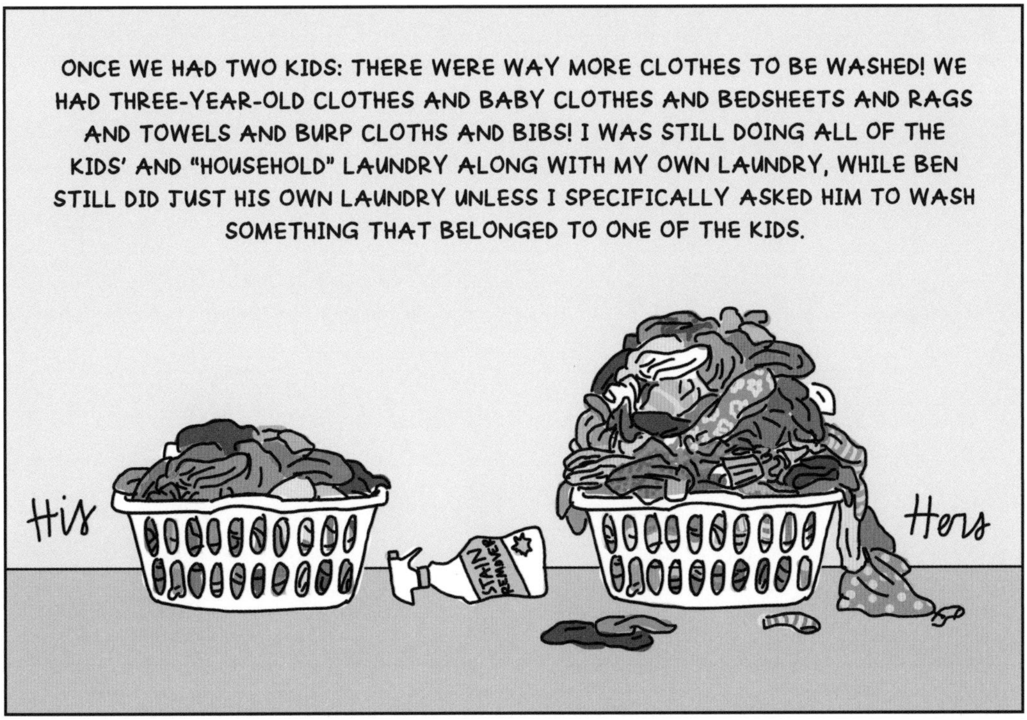
ONCE WE HAD TWO KIDS: THERE WERE WAY MORE CLOTHES TO BE WASHED! WE HAD THREE-YEAR-OLD CLOTHES AND BABY CLOTHES AND BEDSHEETS AND RAGS AND TOWELS AND BURP CLOTHS AND BIBS! I WAS STILL DOING ALL OF THE KIDS' AND "HOUSEHOLD" LAUNDRY ALONG WITH MY OWN LAUNDRY, WHILE BEN STILL DID JUST HIS OWN LAUNDRY UNLESS I SPECIFICALLY ASKED HIM TO WASH SOMETHING THAT BELONGED TO ONE OF THE KIDS.
His
STAIN REMOVER
Hers

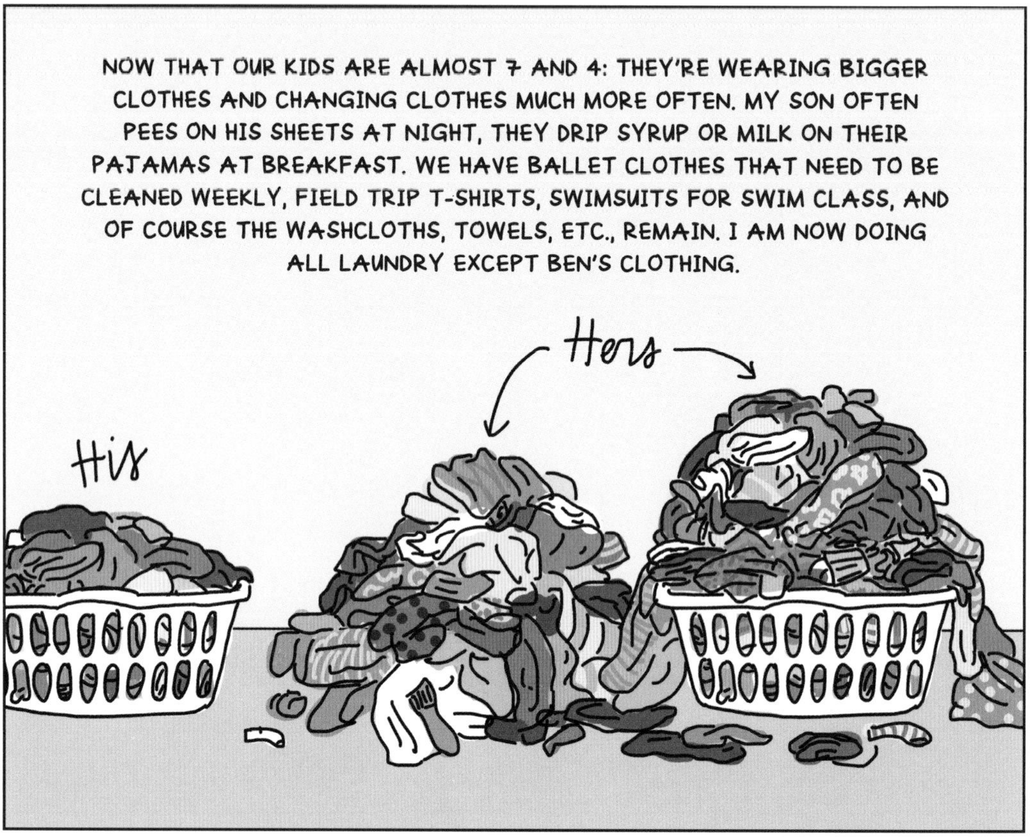
NOW THAT OUR KIDS ARE ALMOST 7 AND 4: THEY'RE WEARING BIGGER CLOTHES AND CHANGING CLOTHES MUCH MORE OFTEN. MY SON OFTEN PEES ON HIS SHEETS AT NIGHT, THEY DRIP SYRUP OR MILK ON THEIR PAJAMAS AT BREAKFAST. WE HAVE BALLET CLOTHES THAT NEED TO BE CLEANED WEEKLY, FIELD TRIP T-SHIRTS, SWIMSUITS FOR SWIM CLASS, AND OF COURSE THE WASHCLOTHS, TOWELS, ETC., REMAIN. I AM NOW DOING ALL LAUNDRY EXCEPT BEN'S CLOTHING.
Hers
His

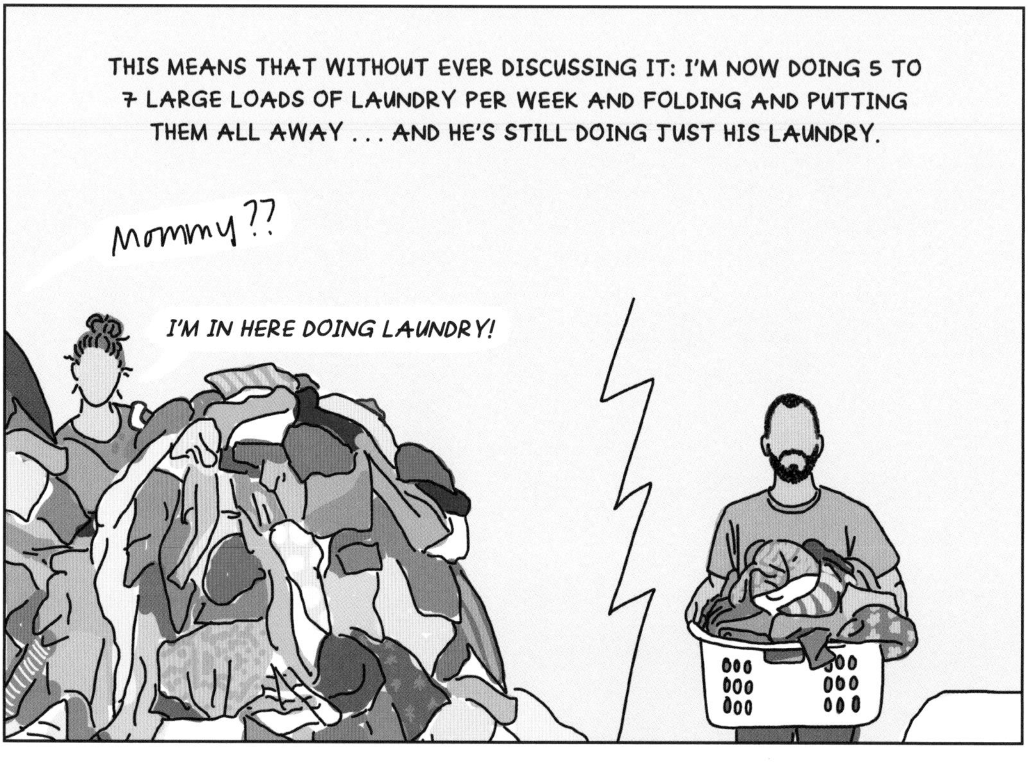
THIS MEANS THAT WITHOUT EVER DISCUSSING IT: I'M NOW DOING 5 TO 7 LARGE LOADS OF LAUNDRY PER WEEK AND FOLDING AND PUTTING THEM ALL AWAY . . . AND HE'S STILL DOING JUST HIS LAUNDRY.
Mommy??
I'M IN HERE DOING LAUNDRY!

## THE RESULT

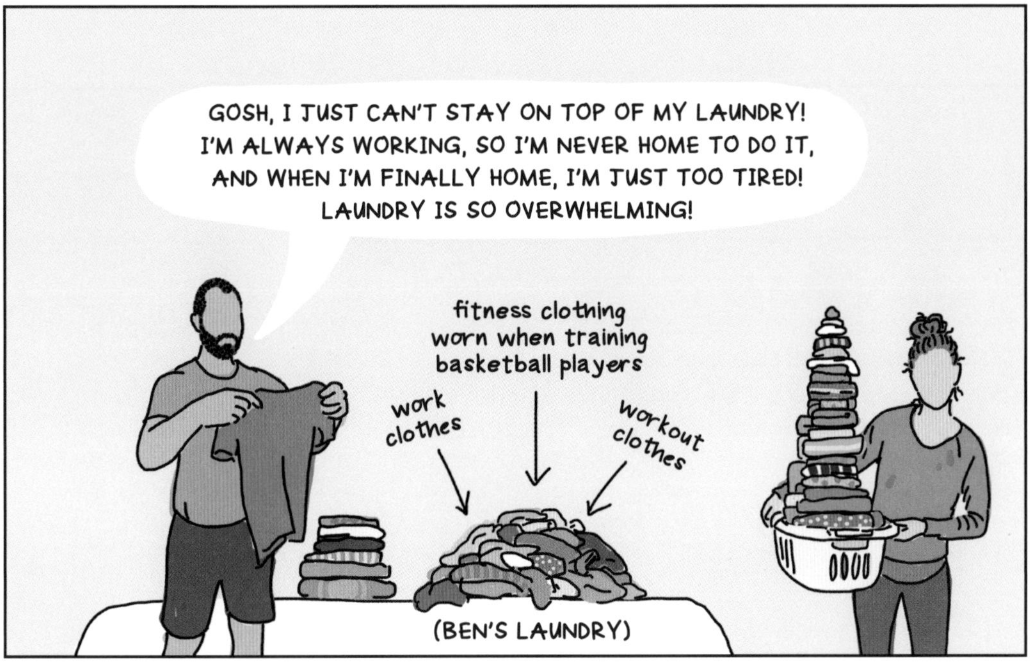
GOSH, I JUST CAN'T STAY ON TOP OF MY LAUNDRY! I'M ALWAYS WORKING, SO I'M NEVER HOME TO DO IT, AND WHEN I'M FINALLY HOME, I'M JUST TOO TIRED! LAUNDRY IS SO OVERWHELMING!
fitness clothing worn when training basketball players
work clothes
workout clothes
(BEN'S LAUNDRY)

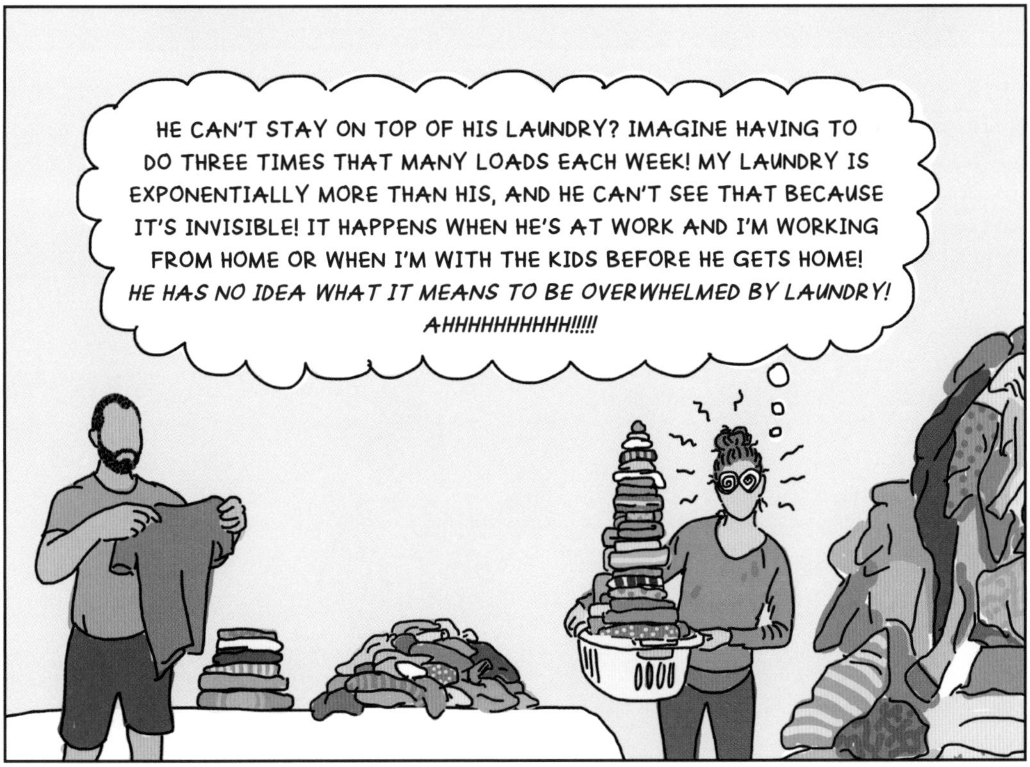
HE CAN'T STAY ON TOP OF HIS LAUNDRY? IMAGINE HAVING TO DO THREE TIMES THAT MANY LOADS EACH WEEK! MY LAUNDRY IS EXPONENTIALLY MORE THAN HIS, AND HE CAN'T SEE THAT BECAUSE IT'S INVISIBLE! IT HAPPENS WHEN HE'S AT WORK AND I'M WORKING FROM HOME OR WHEN I'M WITH THE KIDS BEFORE HE GETS HOME! *HE HAS NO IDEA WHAT IT MEANS TO BE OVERWHELMED BY LAUNDRY!* *AHHHHHHHHHH!!!!!*

Of course, once I realized that I was in charge of all of the laundry forever and ever (or until our kids are old enough to do their own), and it started feeling crippling to me, I could have asked Ben to help, but as is often the case in relationships, it isn't this simple.

For one, if he is supposed to do it but doesn't get to the kids' laundry, guess who it affects? Not him!

I'm the one who gets them dressed for school every day and puts them to bed most nights. I'm the one who will be changing the pee-soaked sheets.

So if he doesn't get to it—which he most likely won't since he can't even stay on top of his own laundry—it will screw up my life, not his. Plus, we've been dividing the laundry this way for almost seven years now, and patterns like this are hard to break! Whenever I thought about asking him to take it on, I felt sure that he'd resist because he doesn't want another task (who does?), and then I'd end up being the "nagging" wife.

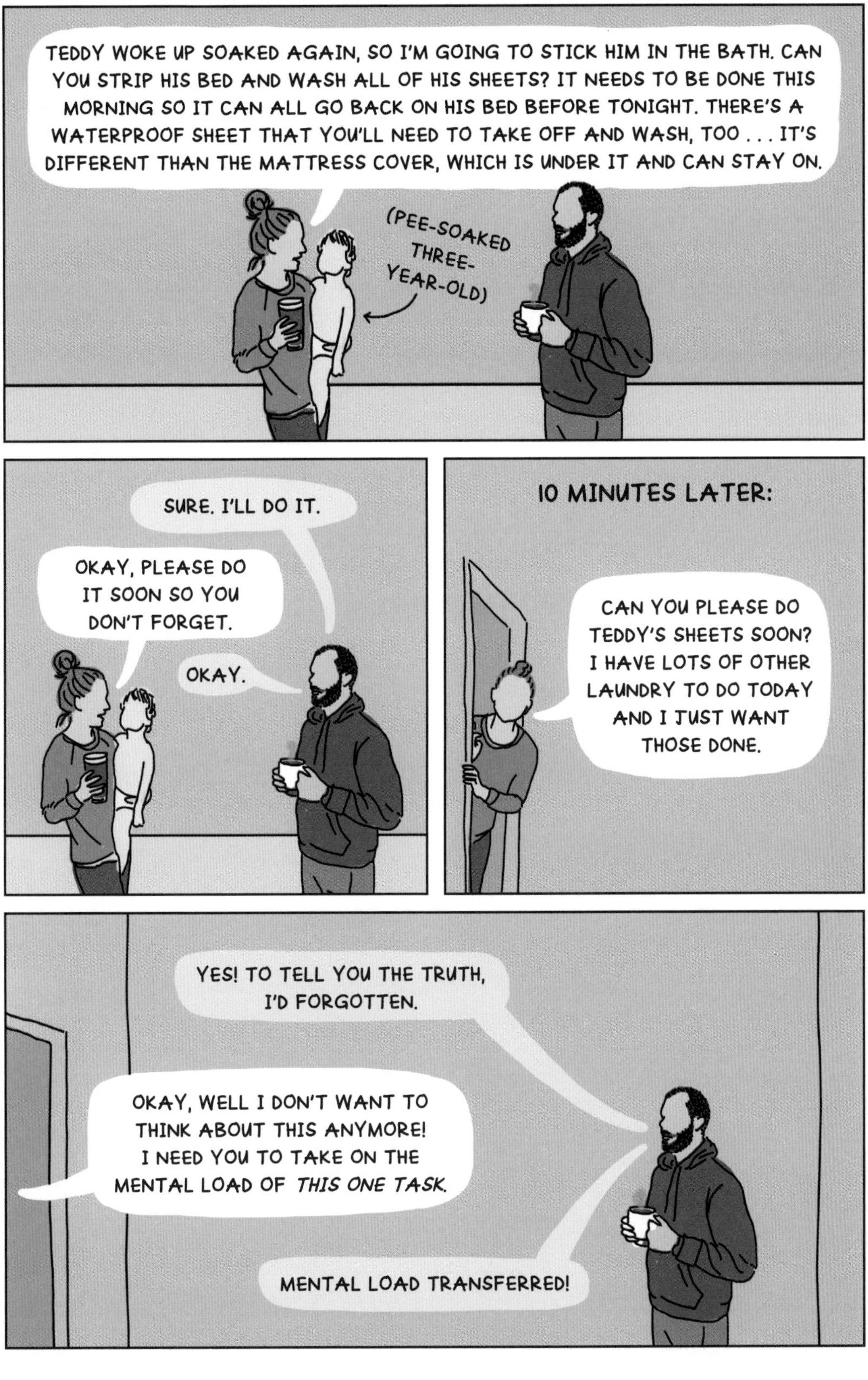
TEDDY WOKE UP SOAKED AGAIN, SO I'M GOING TO STICK HIM IN THE BATH. CAN YOU STRIP HIS BED AND WASH ALL OF HIS SHEETS? IT NEEDS TO BE DONE THIS MORNING SO IT CAN ALL GO BACK ON HIS BED BEFORE TONIGHT. THERE'S A WATERPROOF SHEET THAT YOU'LL NEED TO TAKE OFF AND WASH, TOO . . . IT'S DIFFERENT THAN THE MATTRESS COVER, WHICH IS UNDER IT AND CAN STAY ON.
(PEE-SOAKED THREE-YEAR-OLD)
SURE. I'LL DO IT.
OKAY, PLEASE DO IT SOON SO YOU DON'T FORGET.
OKAY.
10 MINUTES LATER:
CAN YOU PLEASE DO TEDDY'S SHEETS SOON? I HAVE LOTS OF OTHER LAUNDRY TO DO TODAY AND I JUST WANT THOSE DONE.
YES! TO TELL YOU THE TRUTH, I'D FORGOTTEN.
OKAY, WELL I DON'T WANT TO THINK ABOUT THIS ANYMORE! I NEED YOU TO TAKE ON THE MENTAL LOAD OF *THIS ONE TASK.*
MENTAL LOAD TRANSFERRED!

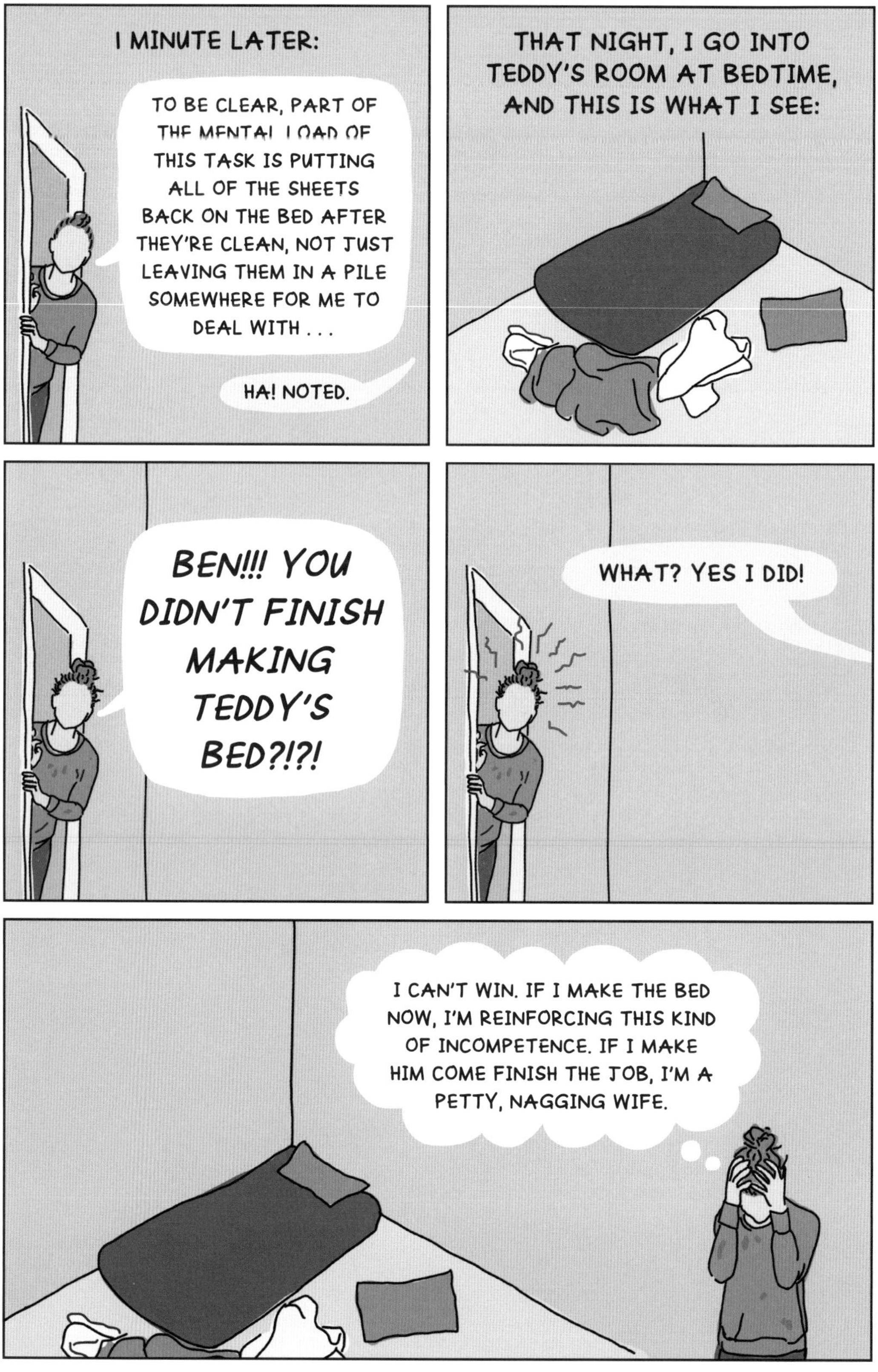
1 MINUTE LATER:
TO BE CLEAR, PART OF THE MENTAL LOAD OF THIS TASK IS PUTTING ALL OF THE SHEETS BACK ON THE BED AFTER THEY'RE CLEAN, NOT JUST LEAVING THEM IN A PILE SOMEWHERE FOR ME TO DEAL WITH . . .
HA! NOTED.
THAT NIGHT, I GO INTO TEDDY'S ROOM AT BEDTIME, AND THIS IS WHAT I SEE:
BEN!!! YOU DIDN'T FINISH MAKING TEDDY'S BED?!?!
WHAT? YES I DID!
I CAN'T WIN. IF I MAKE THE BED NOW, I'M REINFORCING THIS KIND OF INCOMPETENCE. IF I MAKE HIM COME FINISH THE JOB, I'M A PETTY, NAGGING WIFE.

This slow slide toward laundry inequality happened gradually, over time, and it happened so slowly that by the time I realized I was drowning in laundry and he wasn't, it had become a very hard pattern to change. (And he still thinks he's drowning in laundry because he personally has so much and has so little time to tackle it since he works so much! *Hmm . . . sounds like it might be hard to find time to do your work and handle household tasks, huh?*)

This laundry imbalance illuminates the workload that so many moms take on when it comes to raising kids. Again and again, I hear from moms who say some version of the following: "My husband is very involved in our household and kids' lives compared to many fathers and compared to his father and the generation before them. HOWEVER, we both work full-time, and yet I am still handling exponentially more of the household and child-rearing logistics." This observation is not anecdotal: It has been proven to be true in study after study.

And while laundry may seem like physical labor, not mental, it's a perfect example of how the physical labor of running a household goes hand-in-hand with the mental labor: You have to remember to put the dirty laundry in the washer, to move it to the dryer, to take it out and put it away. In order to run the washer and dryer, you need to ensure you have enough detergent and stain remover and dryer sheets. If a laundry basket breaks, you need to remember to replace it. You have to be sure that the clothing needed for certain events are ready for that event when it comes around, which involves thinking ahead, being proactive, and staying on top of the family's schedule. You need to know who is running out of clean underwear or socks and ensure they have clean ones when they need them . . . the list goes on and on.

# Why Is It SO Hard to Transfer the Mental Load?

Unfortunately, reversing this dynamic is so, SO hard. It's not that it can't be reversed (the book *Fair Play* by Eve Rodsky offers a great step-by-step way to make real change!), but for a lot of moms, when they're in the thick of it, the work it would take to make these changes can feel too overwhelming.

The longer a mom has been drowning in the household tasks, the harder it can be for her to get the energy to do the hard work it would take to make real change in her relationship . . .

## Treading Water:

### An Attempt to Explain Why It Can Feel Hard to Put in the Effort Needed to Achieve Household Equality

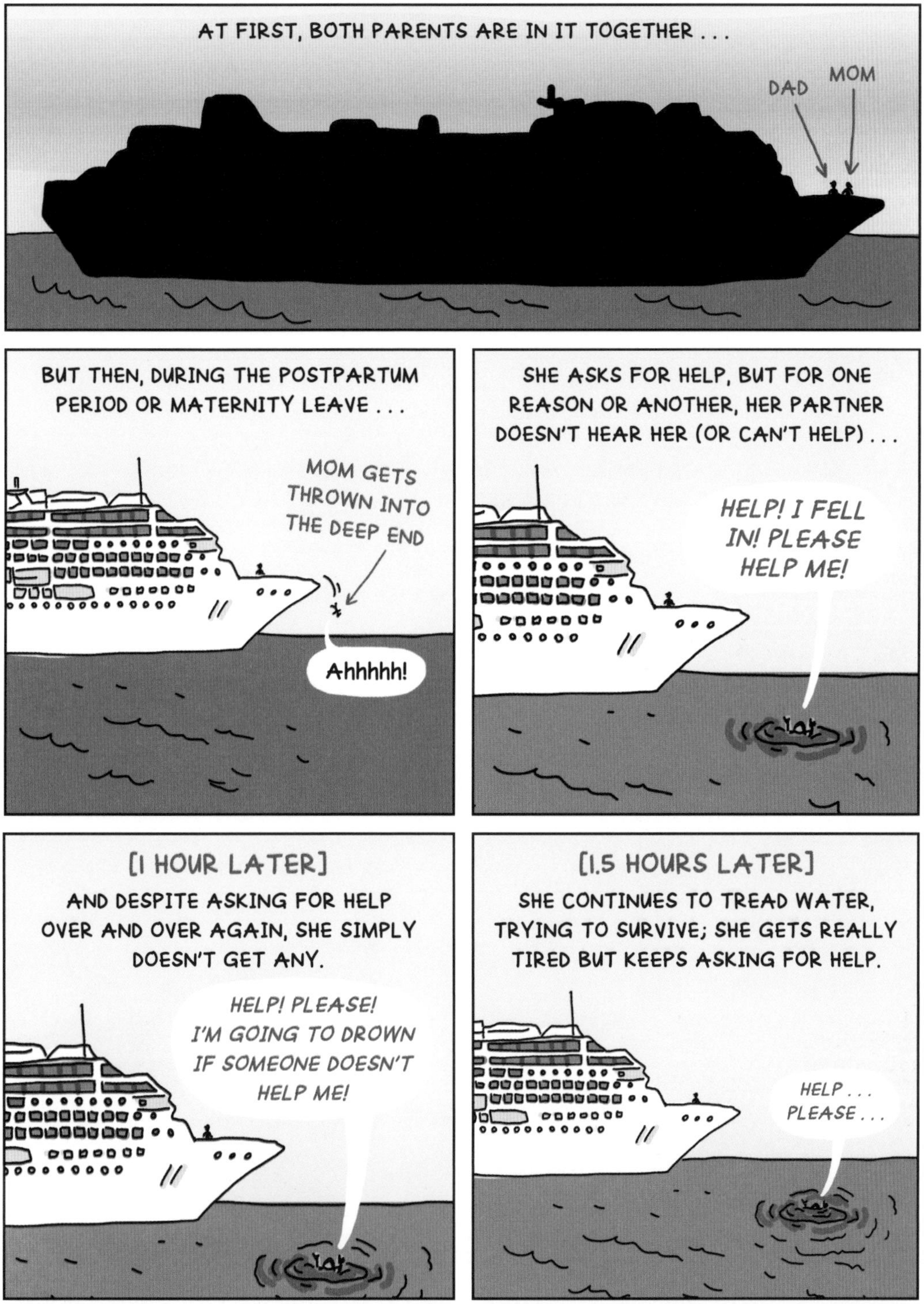
AT FIRST, BOTH PARENTS ARE IN IT TOGETHER . . .
DAD
MOM
BUT THEN, DURING THE POSTPARTUM PERIOD OR MATERNITY LEAVE . . .
MOM GETS THROWN INTO THE DEEP END
Ahhhhh!
SHE ASKS FOR HELP, BUT FOR ONE REASON OR ANOTHER, HER PARTNER DOESN'T HEAR HER (OR CAN'T HELP) . . .
HELP! I FELL IN! PLEASE HELP ME!
[1 HOUR LATER]
AND DESPITE ASKING FOR HELP OVER AND OVER AGAIN, SHE SIMPLY DOESN'T GET ANY.
HELP! PLEASE! I'M GOING TO DROWN IF SOMEONE DOESN'T HELP ME!
[1.5 HOURS LATER]
SHE CONTINUES TO TREAD WATER, TRYING TO SURVIVE; SHE GETS REALLY TIRED BUT KEEPS ASKING FOR HELP.
HELP . . . PLEASE . . .

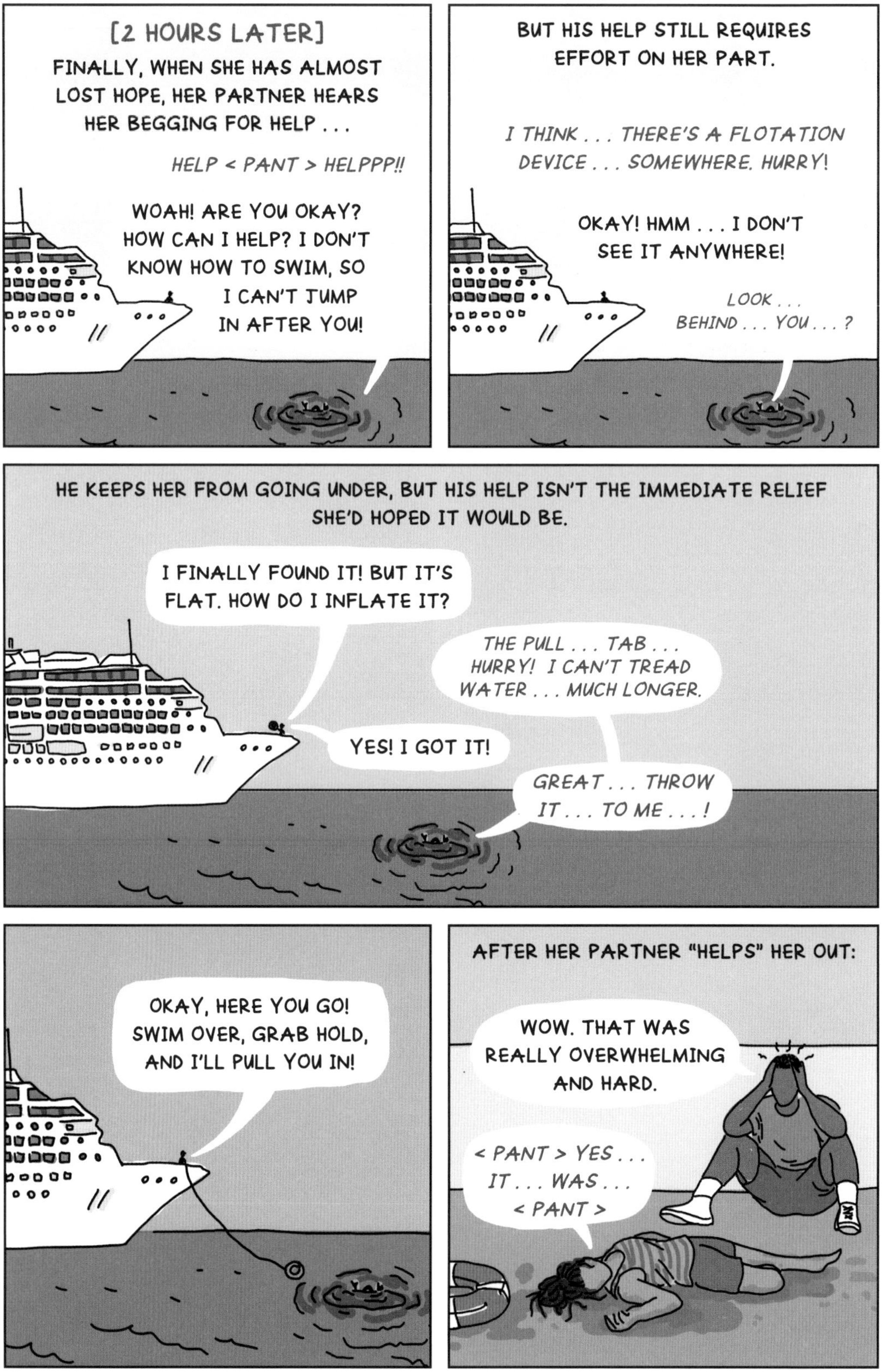
[2 HOURS LATER]
FINALLY, WHEN SHE HAS ALMOST LOST HOPE, HER PARTNER HEARS HER BEGGING FOR HELP . . .
HELP < PANT > HELPPP!!
WOAH! ARE YOU OKAY? HOW CAN I HELP? I DON'T KNOW HOW TO SWIM, SO I CAN'T JUMP IN AFTER YOU!
BUT HIS HELP STILL REQUIRES EFFORT ON HER PART.
I THINK . . . THERE'S A FLOTATION DEVICE . . . SOMEWHERE. HURRY!
OKAY! HMM . . . I DON'T SEE IT ANYWHERE!
LOOK . . . BEHIND . . . YOU . . . ?
HE KEEPS HER FROM GOING UNDER, BUT HIS HELP ISN'T THE IMMEDIATE RELIEF SHE'D HOPED IT WOULD BE.
I FINALLY FOUND IT! BUT IT'S FLAT. HOW DO I INFLATE IT?
THE PULL . . . TAB . . . HURRY! I CAN'T TREAD WATER . . . MUCH LONGER.
YES! I GOT IT!
GREAT . . . THROW IT . . . TO ME . . . !
OKAY, HERE YOU GO! SWIM OVER, GRAB HOLD, AND I'LL PULL YOU IN!
AFTER HER PARTNER "HELPS" HER OUT:
WOW. THAT WAS REALLY OVERWHELMING AND HARD.
< PANT > YES . . . IT . . . WAS . . . < PANT >

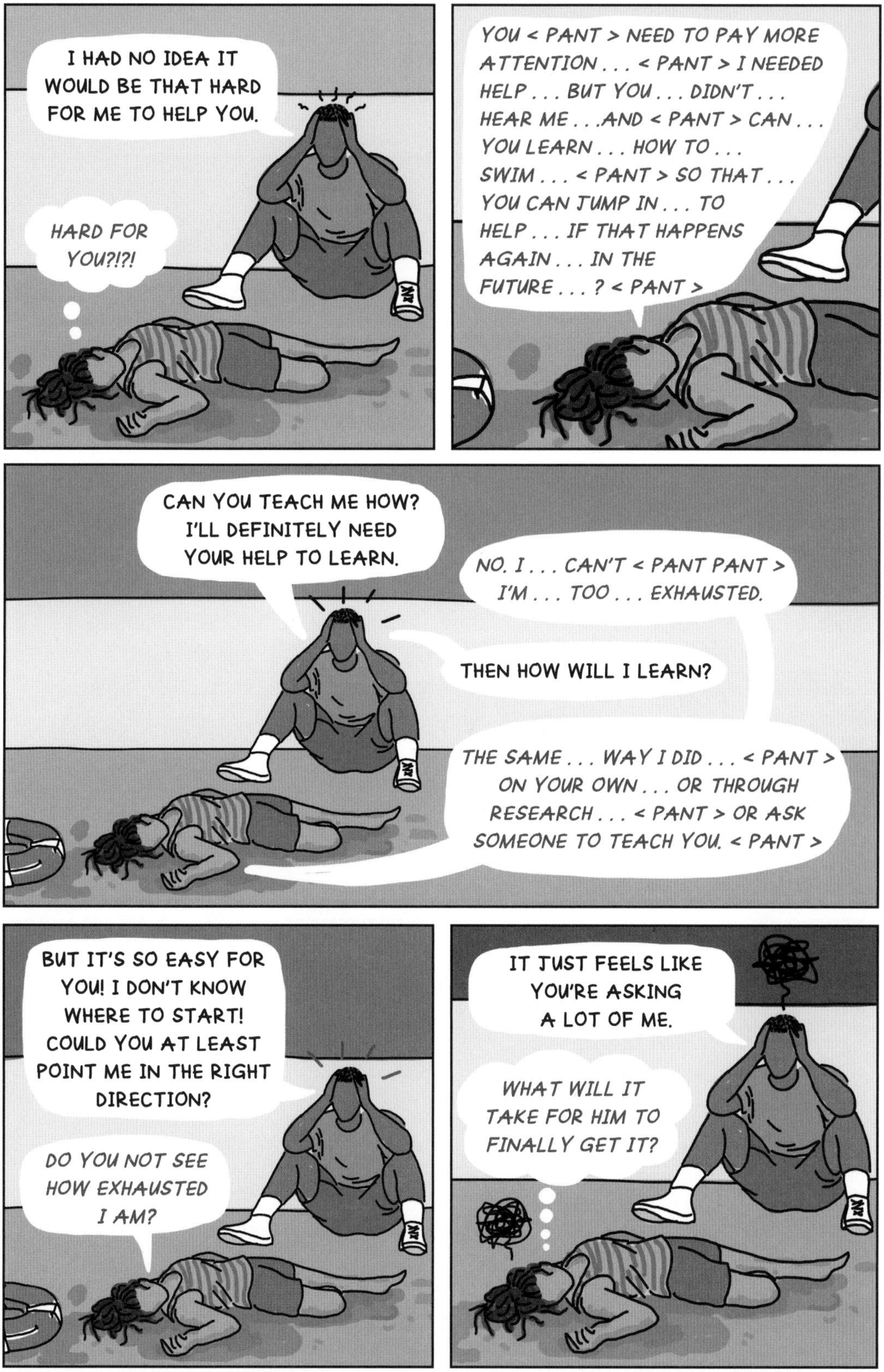
I HAD NO IDEA IT WOULD BE THAT HARD FOR ME TO HELP YOU.
HARD FOR YOU?!?!
YOU < PANT > NEED TO PAY MORE ATTENTION . . . < PANT > I NEEDED HELP . . . BUT YOU . . . DIDN'T . . . HEAR ME . . .AND < PANT > CAN . . . YOU LEARN . . . HOW TO . . . SWIM . . . < PANT > SO THAT . . . YOU CAN JUMP IN . . . TO HELP . . . IF THAT HAPPENS AGAIN . . . IN THE FUTURE . . . ? < PANT >
CAN YOU TEACH ME HOW? I'LL DEFINITELY NEED YOUR HELP TO LEARN.
NO. I . . . CAN'T < PANT PANT > I'M . . . TOO . . . EXHAUSTED.
THEN HOW WILL I LEARN?
THE SAME . . . WAY I DID . . . < PANT > ON YOUR OWN . . . OR THROUGH RESEARCH . . . < PANT > OR ASK SOMEONE TO TEACH YOU. < PANT >
BUT IT'S SO EASY FOR YOU! I DON'T KNOW WHERE TO START! COULD YOU AT LEAST POINT ME IN THE RIGHT DIRECTION?
DO YOU NOT SEE HOW EXHAUSTED I AM?
IT JUST FEELS LIKE YOU'RE ASKING A LOT OF ME.
WHAT WILL IT TAKE FOR HIM TO FINALLY GET IT?

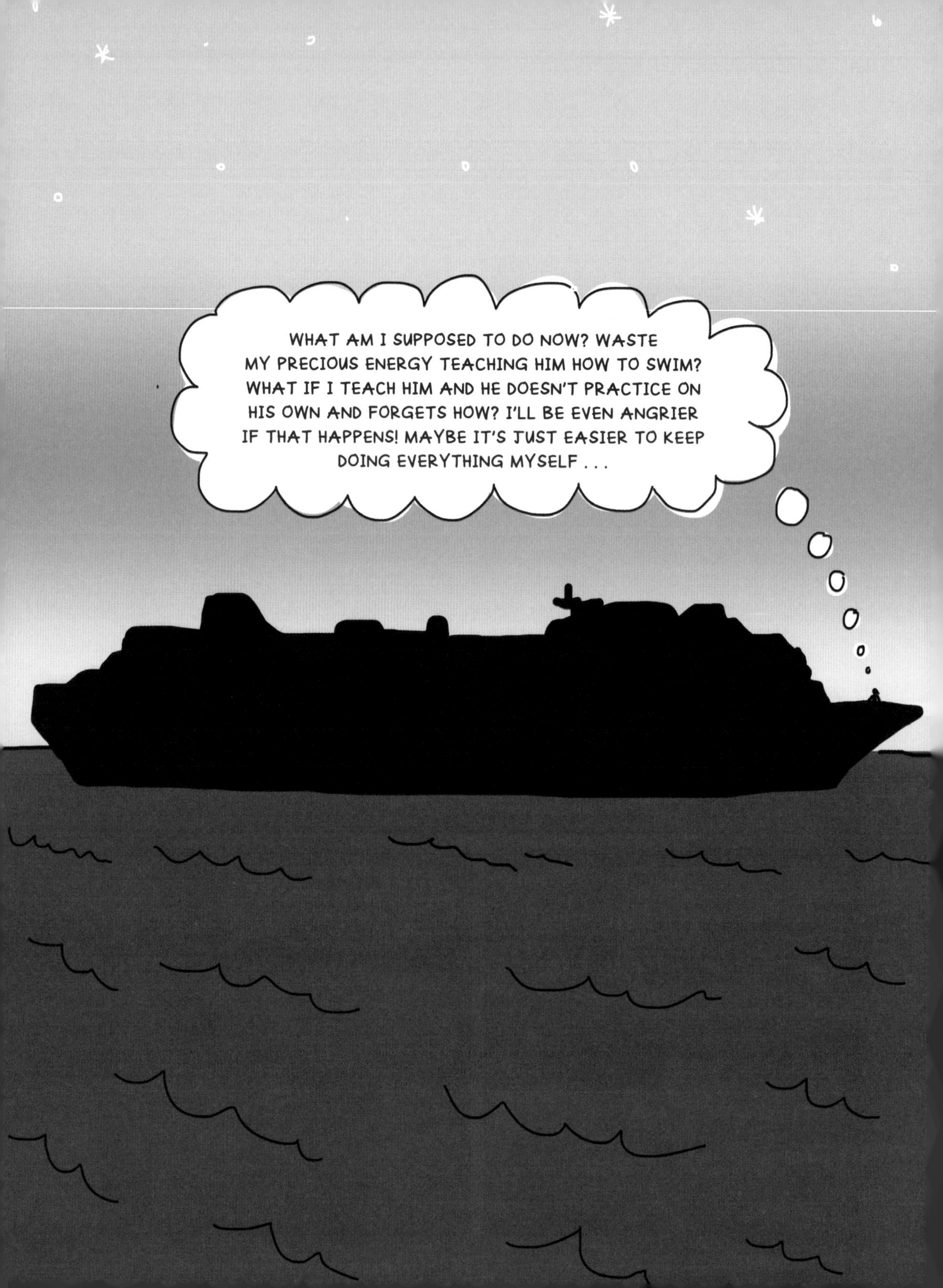
WHAT AM I SUPPOSED TO DO NOW? WASTE MY PRECIOUS ENERGY TEACHING HIM HOW TO SWIM? WHAT IF I TEACH HIM AND HE DOESN'T PRACTICE ON HIS OWN AND FORGETS HOW? I'LL BE EVEN ANGRIER IF THAT HAPPENS! MAYBE IT'S JUST EASIER TO KEEP DOING EVERYTHING MYSELF . . .

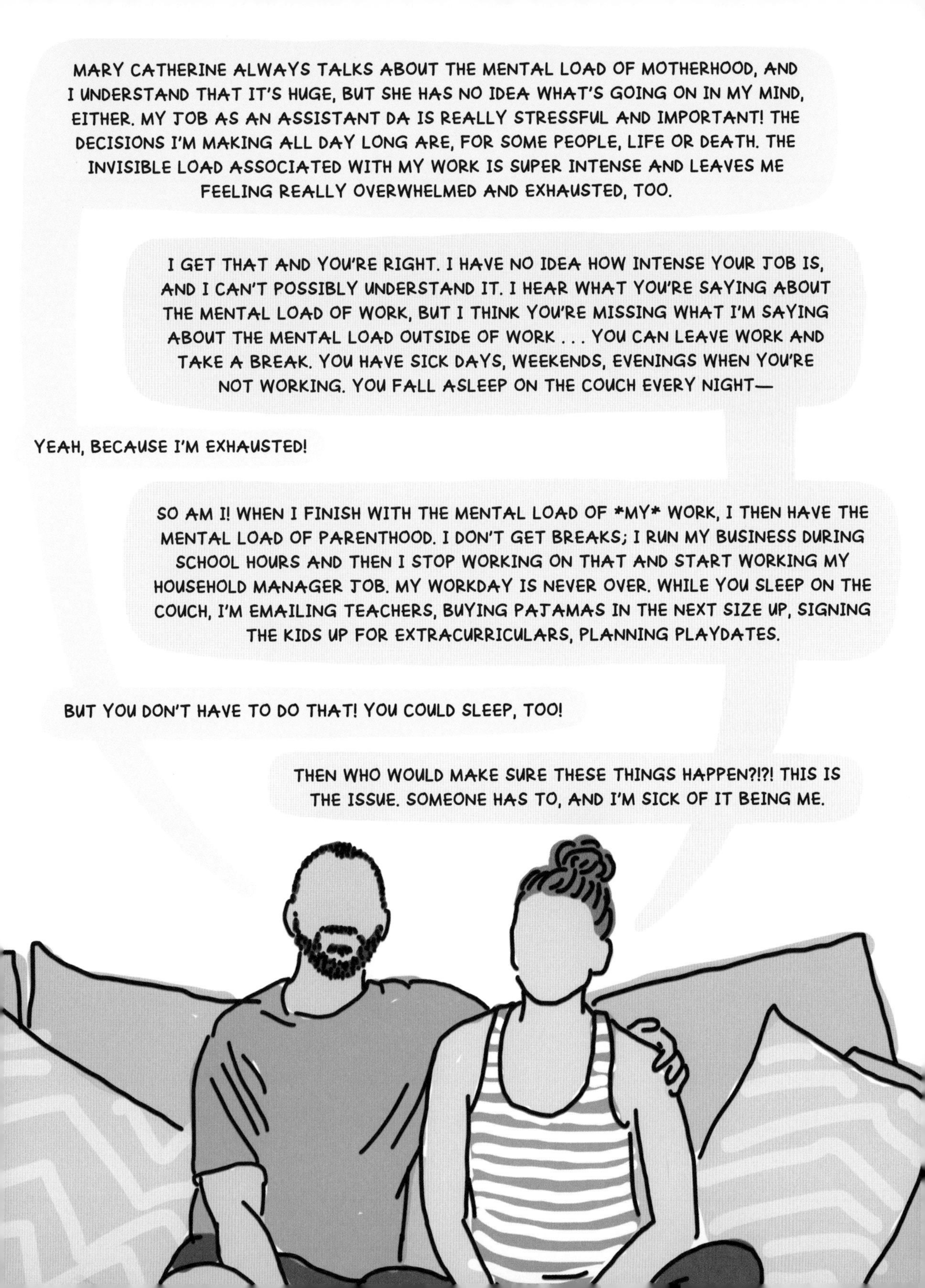
MARY CATHERINE ALWAYS TALKS ABOUT THE MENTAL LOAD OF MOTHERHOOD, AND I UNDERSTAND THAT IT'S HUGE, BUT SHE HAS NO IDEA WHAT'S GOING ON IN MY MIND, EITHER. MY JOB AS AN ASSISTANT DA IS REALLY STRESSFUL AND IMPORTANT! THE DECISIONS I'M MAKING ALL DAY LONG ARE, FOR SOME PEOPLE, LIFE OR DEATH. THE INVISIBLE LOAD ASSOCIATED WITH MY WORK IS SUPER INTENSE AND LEAVES ME FEELING REALLY OVERWHELMED AND EXHAUSTED, TOO.
I GET THAT AND YOU'RE RIGHT. I HAVE NO IDEA HOW INTENSE YOUR JOB IS, AND I CAN'T POSSIBLY UNDERSTAND IT. I HEAR WHAT YOU'RE SAYING ABOUT THE MENTAL LOAD OF WORK, BUT I THINK YOU'RE MISSING WHAT I'M SAYING ABOUT THE MENTAL LOAD OUTSIDE OF WORK . . . YOU CAN LEAVE WORK AND TAKE A BREAK. YOU HAVE SICK DAYS, WEEKENDS, EVENINGS WHEN YOU'RE NOT WORKING. YOU FALL ASLEEP ON THE COUCH EVERY NIGHT—
YEAH, BECAUSE I'M EXHAUSTED!
SO AM I! WHEN I FINISH WITH THE MENTAL LOAD OF *MY* WORK, I THEN HAVE THE MENTAL LOAD OF PARENTHOOD. I DON'T GET BREAKS; I RUN MY BUSINESS DURING SCHOOL HOURS AND THEN I STOP WORKING ON THAT AND START WORKING MY HOUSEHOLD MANAGER JOB. MY WORKDAY IS NEVER OVER. WHILE YOU SLEEP ON THE COUCH, I'M EMAILING TEACHERS, BUYING PAJAMAS IN THE NEXT SIZE UP, SIGNING THE KIDS UP FOR EXTRACURRICULARS, PLANNING PLAYDATES.
BUT YOU DON'T HAVE TO DO THAT! YOU COULD SLEEP, TOO!
THEN WHO WOULD MAKE SURE THESE THINGS HAPPEN?!?! THIS IS THE ISSUE. SOMEONE HAS TO, AND I'M SICK OF IT BEING ME.

# Incompetence: Weaponized and Learned

I can't talk about the mental load of motherhood without talking about a newish term, "weaponized incompetence." Weaponized incompetence is when someone does something badly on purpose—or claims they don't know how to do something—so that the burden falls on someone else. Weaponized incompetence runs rampant in many families and workplaces, and it's something that primarily affects women.

Here's an example of what we're talking about when we talk about weaponized incompetence . . .

Note: Before you read this comic, I want to remind you that Ben is a successful criminal prosecutor who runs a thriving basketball training business on the side. He is a competent, smart, adult man. He has been a functioning human being on this earth for forty years.

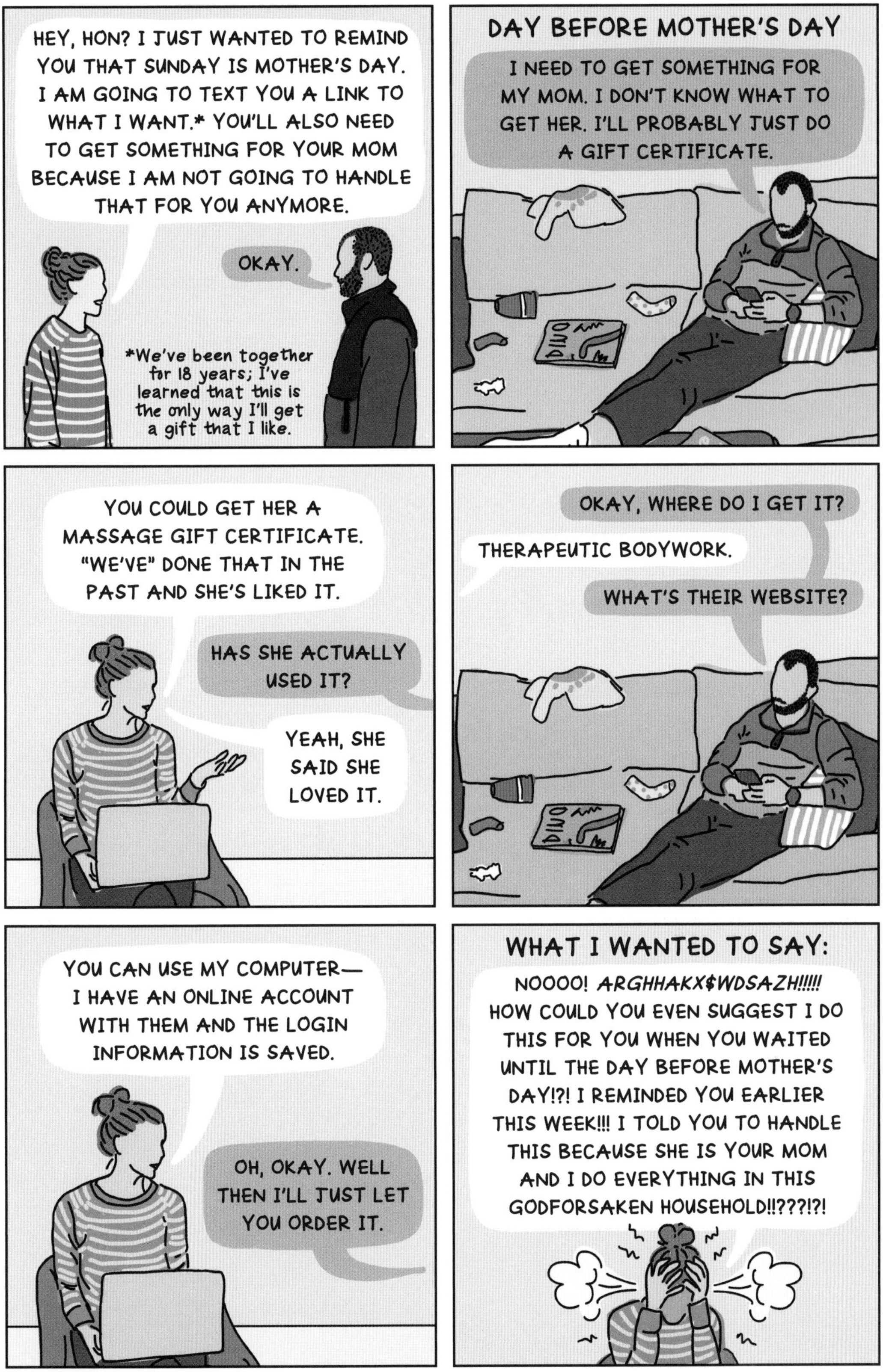
HEY, HON? I JUST WANTED TO REMIND YOU THAT SUNDAY IS MOTHER'S DAY. I AM GOING TO TEXT YOU A LINK TO WHAT I WANT.* YOU'LL ALSO NEED TO GET SOMETHING FOR YOUR MOM BECAUSE I AM NOT GOING TO HANDLE THAT FOR YOU ANYMORE.
OKAY.
*We've been together for 18 years; I've learned that this is the only way I'll get a gift that I like.
DAY BEFORE MOTHER'S DAY
I NEED TO GET SOMETHING FOR MY MOM. I DON'T KNOW WHAT TO GET HER. I'LL PROBABLY JUST DO A GIFT CERTIFICATE.
YOU COULD GET HER A MASSAGE GIFT CERTIFICATE. "WE'VE" DONE THAT IN THE PAST AND SHE'S LIKED IT.
HAS SHE ACTUALLY USED IT?
YEAH, SHE SAID SHE LOVED IT.
OKAY, WHERE DO I GET IT?
THERAPEUTIC BODYWORK.
WHAT'S THEIR WEBSITE?
YOU CAN USE MY COMPUTER— I HAVE AN ONLINE ACCOUNT WITH THEM AND THE LOGIN INFORMATION IS SAVED.
OH, OKAY. WELL THEN I'LL JUST LET YOU ORDER IT.
WHAT I WANTED TO SAY:
NOOOO! ARGHHAKX$WDSAZH!!!!! HOW COULD YOU EVEN SUGGEST I DO THIS FOR YOU WHEN YOU WAITED UNTIL THE DAY BEFORE MOTHER'S DAY!?! I REMINDED YOU EARLIER THIS WEEK!!! I TOLD YOU TO HANDLE THIS BECAUSE SHE IS YOUR MOM AND I DO EVERYTHING IN THIS GODFORSAKEN HOUSEHOLD!!???!?!

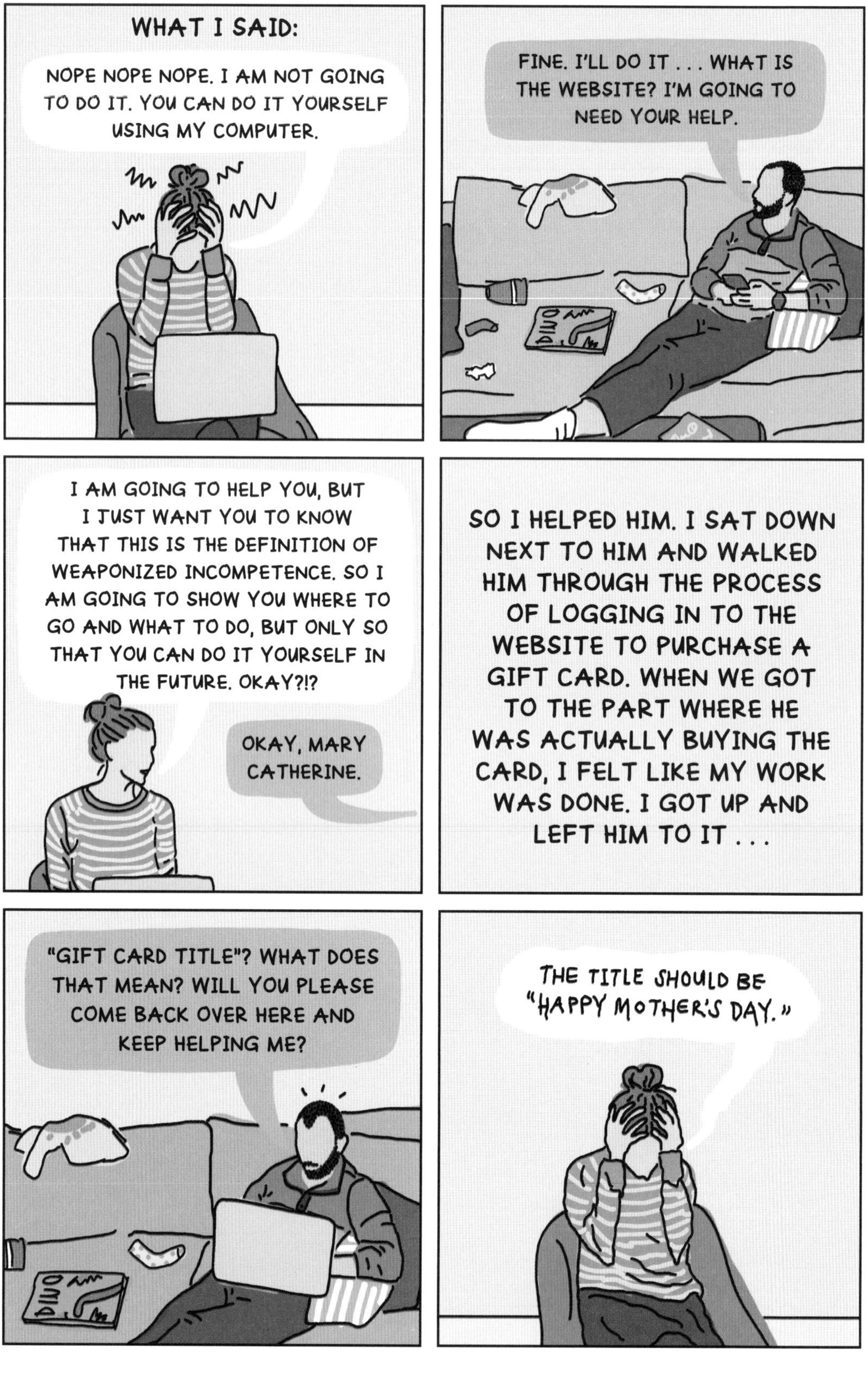
WHAT I SAID:
NOPE NOPE NOPE. I AM NOT GOING TO DO IT. YOU CAN DO IT YOURSELF USING MY COMPUTER.
FINE. I'LL DO IT . . . WHAT IS THE WEBSITE? I'M GOING TO NEED YOUR HELP.
I AM GOING TO HELP YOU, BUT I JUST WANT YOU TO KNOW THAT THIS IS THE DEFINITION OF WEAPONIZED INCOMPETENCE. SO I AM GOING TO SHOW YOU WHERE TO GO AND WHAT TO DO, BUT ONLY SO THAT YOU CAN DO IT YOURSELF IN THE FUTURE. OKAY?!?
OKAY, MARY CATHERINE.
SO I HELPED HIM. I SAT DOWN NEXT TO HIM AND WALKED HIM THROUGH THE PROCESS OF LOGGING IN TO THE WEBSITE TO PURCHASE A GIFT CARD. WHEN WE GOT TO THE PART WHERE HE WAS ACTUALLY BUYING THE CARD, I FELT LIKE MY WORK WAS DONE. I GOT UP AND LEFT HIM TO IT . . .
"GIFT CARD TITLE"? WHAT DOES THAT MEAN? WILL YOU PLEASE COME BACK OVER HERE AND KEEP HELPING ME?
THE TITLE SHOULD BE "HAPPY MOTHER'S DAY."

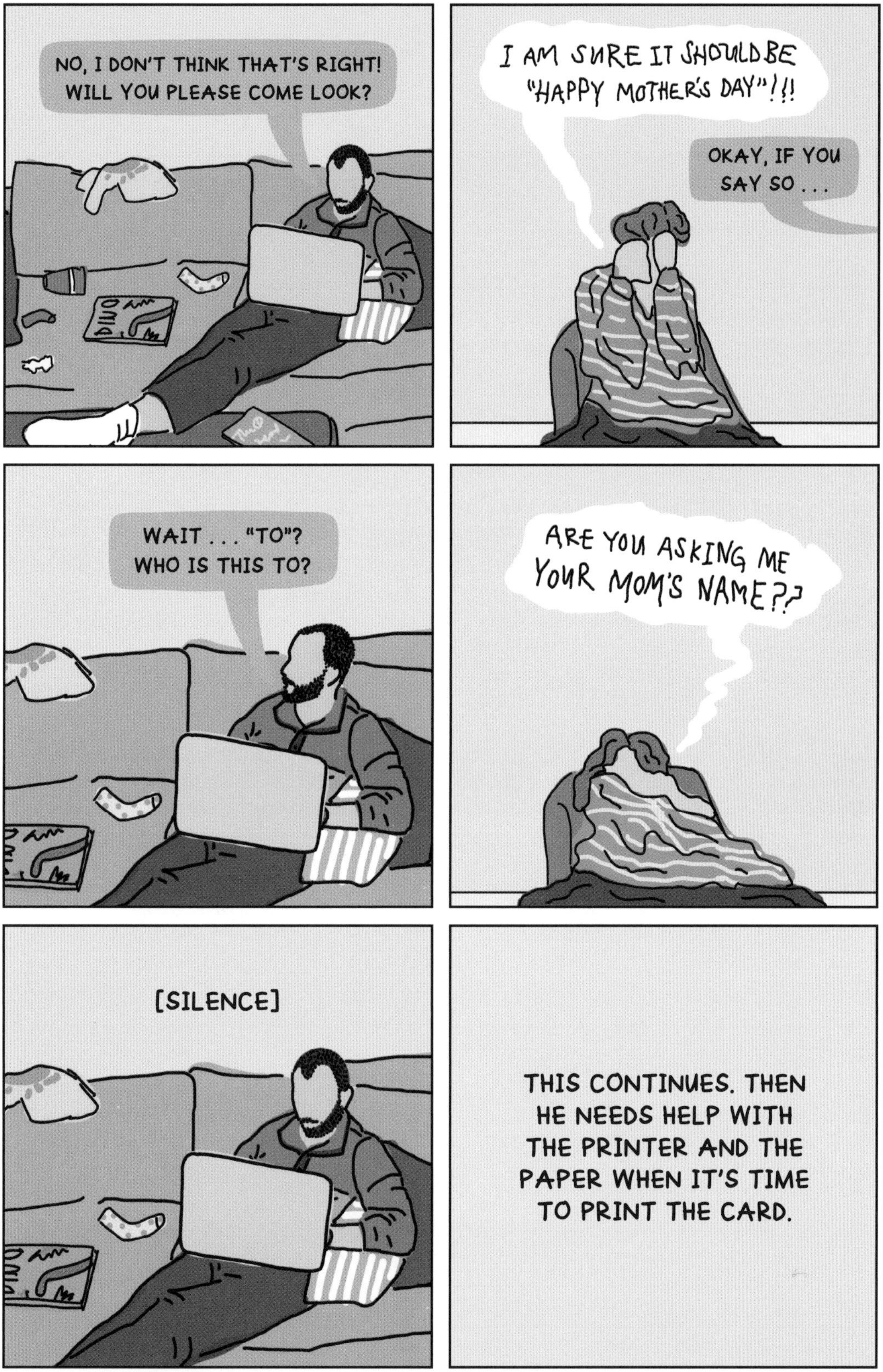

NO, I DON'T THINK THAT'S RIGHT! WILL YOU PLEASE COME LOOK?
I AM SURE IT SHOULD BE "HAPPY MOTHER'S DAY"!!!
OKAY, IF YOU SAY SO . . .
WAIT . . . "TO"? WHO IS THIS TO?
ARE YOU ASKING ME YOUR MOM'S NAME??
[SILENCE]
THIS CONTINUES. THEN HE NEEDS HELP WITH THE PRINTER AND THE PAPER WHEN IT'S TIME TO PRINT THE CARD.

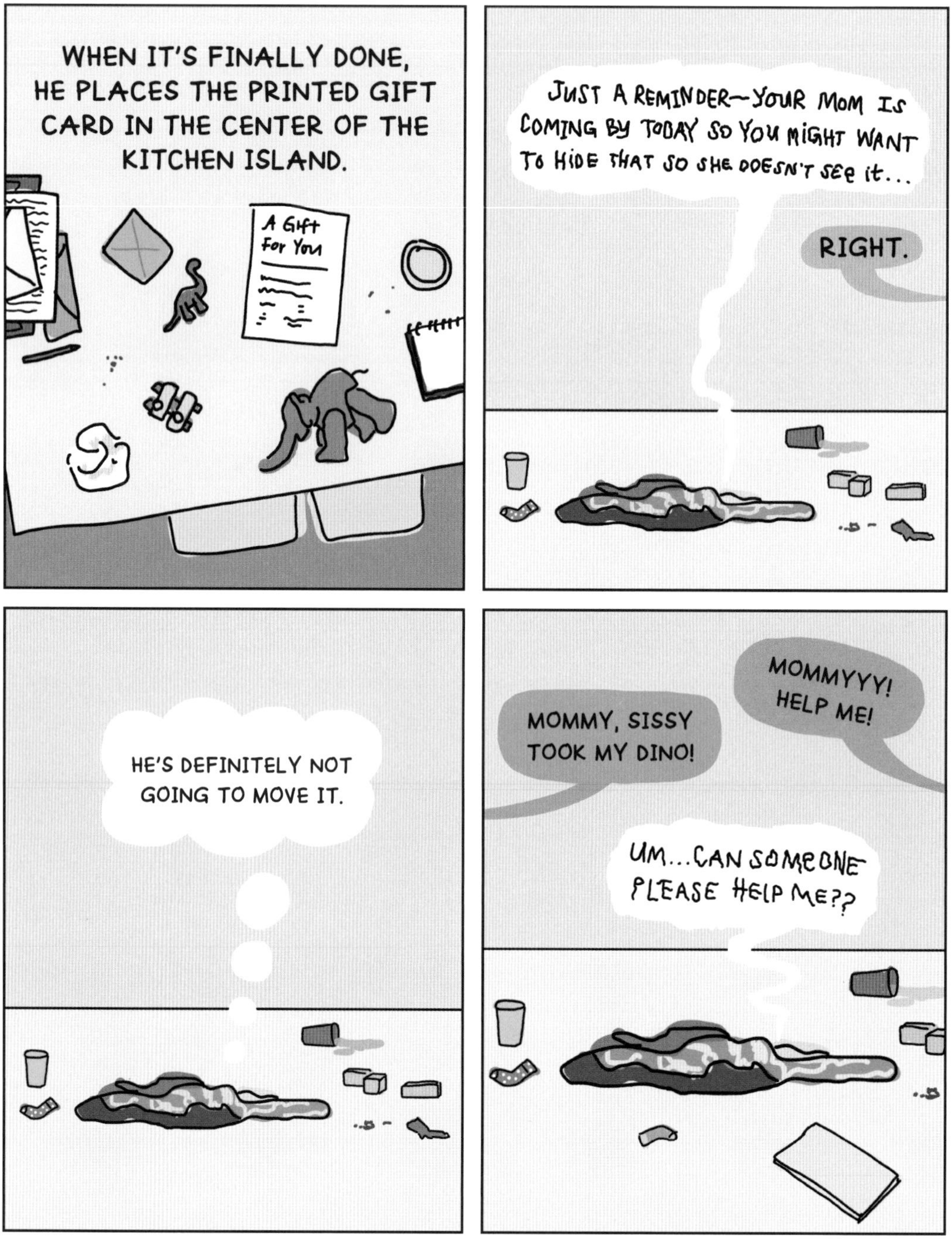

WHEN IT'S FINALLY DONE, HE PLACES THE PRINTED GIFT CARD IN THE CENTER OF THE KITCHEN ISLAND.
A Gift For You
JUST A REMINDER—YOUR MOM IS COMING BY TODAY SO YOU MIGHT WANT TO HIDE THAT SO SHE DOESN'T SEE IT...
RIGHT.
HE'S DEFINITELY NOT GOING TO MOVE IT.
MOMMYYY! HELP ME!
MOMMY, SISSY TOOK MY DINO!
UM...CAN SOMEONE PLEASE HELP ME??

# The Varying Degrees of Incompetence

I believe that there are degrees of weaponized incompetence. I know that there are men out there who PURPOSEFULLY slack on household tasks to avoid having to do them—there are many videos on social media made by these men sharing their "methods" with other men. This is horrible, sexist, and misogynistic. I hate it.

But in my own life, and in the stories that I hear from the feminist, equality-minded women who write to me, weaponized incompetence is not this intentional, malicious, and mocking pursuit.

In the case of many of the husbands who people write to me about, their incompetence isn't necessarily mean-spirited or purposeful; they're not being incompetent in a strategic way, but rather because they've been taught, over many years, that if they're incompetent at something, it doesn't really matter because eventually someone else (usually a woman) will swoop in and handle whatever it is that needs handling.

These men have been taught that in some arenas (i.e., work), they need to be focused, pay attention, and do tasks correctly. But in other arenas (i.e., home), they can check out, turn off their brains, do a half-assed or partial job, and everything will "just work itself out" (because of their partner's invisible labor).

This kind of incompetence is definitely not okay, but in my opinion it's more of a "learned incompetence" (based on following the path of least resistance) than a weaponized one (done strategically to get out of doing work).

Here's one way I like to think about it . . .

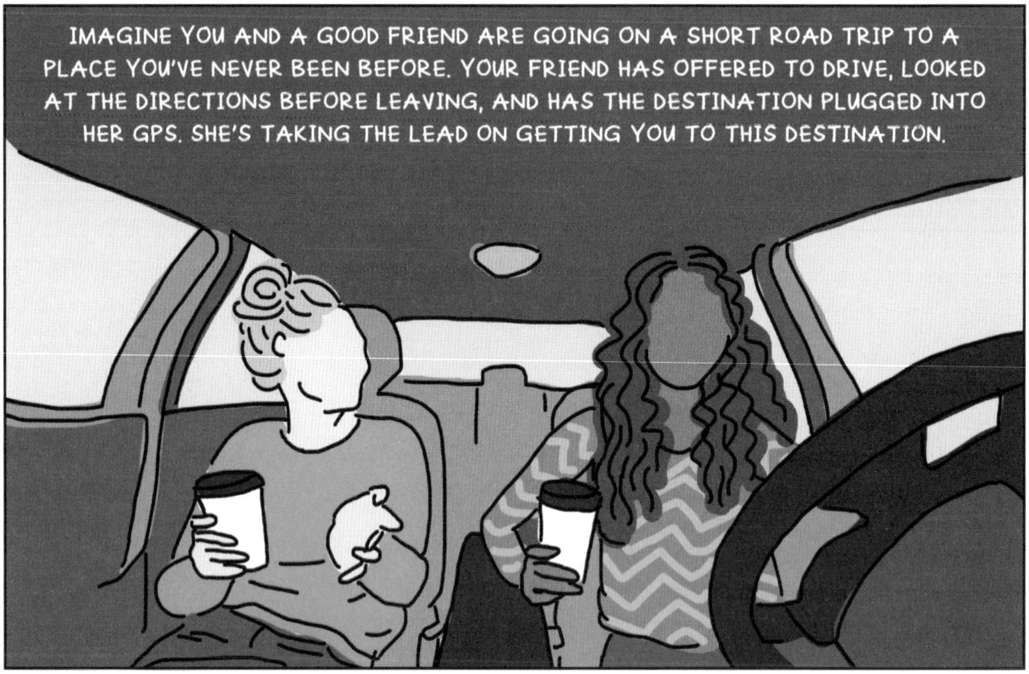
IMAGINE YOU AND A GOOD FRIEND ARE GOING ON A SHORT ROAD TRIP TO A PLACE YOU'VE NEVER BEEN BEFORE. YOUR FRIEND HAS OFFERED TO DRIVE, LOOKED AT THE DIRECTIONS BEFORE LEAVING, AND HAS THE DESTINATION PLUGGED INTO HER GPS. SHE'S TAKING THE LEAD ON GETTING YOU TO THIS DESTINATION.

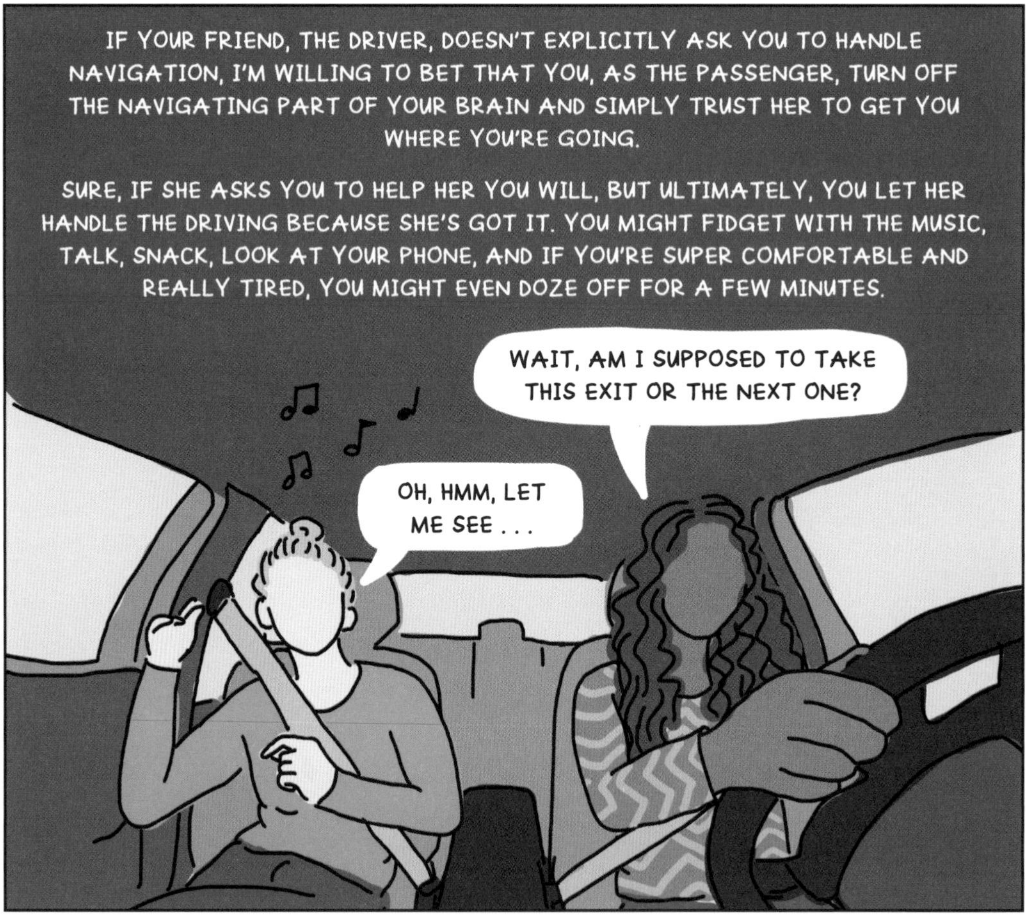
IF YOUR FRIEND, THE DRIVER, DOESN'T EXPLICITLY ASK YOU TO HANDLE NAVIGATION, I'M WILLING TO BET THAT YOU, AS THE PASSENGER, TURN OFF THE NAVIGATING PART OF YOUR BRAIN AND SIMPLY TRUST HER TO GET YOU WHERE YOU'RE GOING.
SURE, IF SHE ASKS YOU TO HELP HER YOU WILL, BUT ULTIMATELY, YOU LET HER HANDLE THE DRIVING BECAUSE SHE'S GOT IT. YOU MIGHT FIDGET WITH THE MUSIC, TALK, SNACK, LOOK AT YOUR PHONE, AND IF YOU'RE SUPER COMFORTABLE AND REALLY TIRED, YOU MIGHT EVEN DOZE OFF FOR A FEW MINUTES.
WAIT, AM I SUPPOSED TO TAKE THIS EXIT OR THE NEXT ONE?
OH, HMM, LET ME SEE . . .

I think this is what a lot of male partners are doing in the home because they have always been the passenger. (Even if they have been asked to help navigate MANY, MANY times, they have never been the driver and don't understand how much energy it takes). Here's how I think this happens:

## How Many Men Learn to Become Passengers

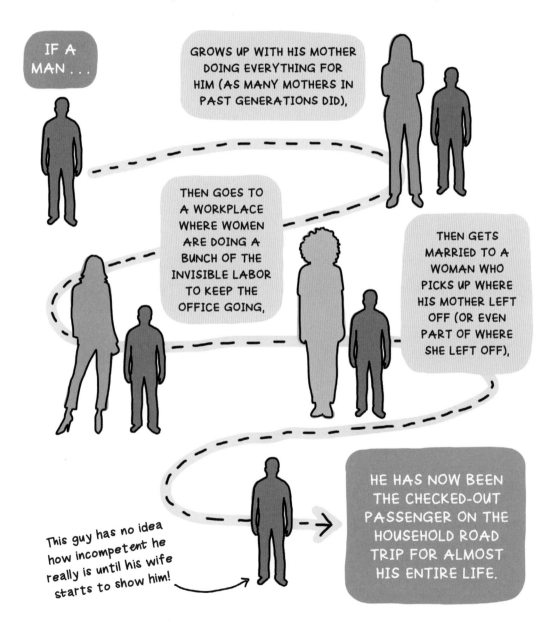

IF A MAN . . .

GROWS UP WITH HIS MOTHER DOING EVERYTHING FOR HIM (AS MANY MOTHERS IN PAST GENERATIONS DID),

THEN GOES TO A WORKPLACE WHERE WOMEN ARE DOING A BUNCH OF THE INVISIBLE LABOR TO KEEP THE OFFICE GOING,

THEN GETS MARRIED TO A WOMAN WHO PICKS UP WHERE HIS MOTHER LEFT OFF (OR EVEN PART OF WHERE SHE LEFT OFF),

This guy has no idea how incompetent he really is until his wife starts to show him!

HE HAS NOW BEEN THE CHECKED-OUT PASSENGER ON THE HOUSEHOLD ROAD TRIP FOR ALMOST HIS ENTIRE LIFE.

Does the fact that many men have been able to be checked-out passengers their entire lives make it okay that they're incompetent?

NO, OF COURSE NOT!

Does this excuse their behavior when they leave a mess for their wives to clean up?

ABSOLUTELY NOT!

Does it excuse them from not taking a step back and seeing themselves clearly and growing the F up by doing their fair share in the home?

NO WAY! THEY ARE ADULTS AND SHOULD KNOW BETTER!

But it does add some nuance to the situation.

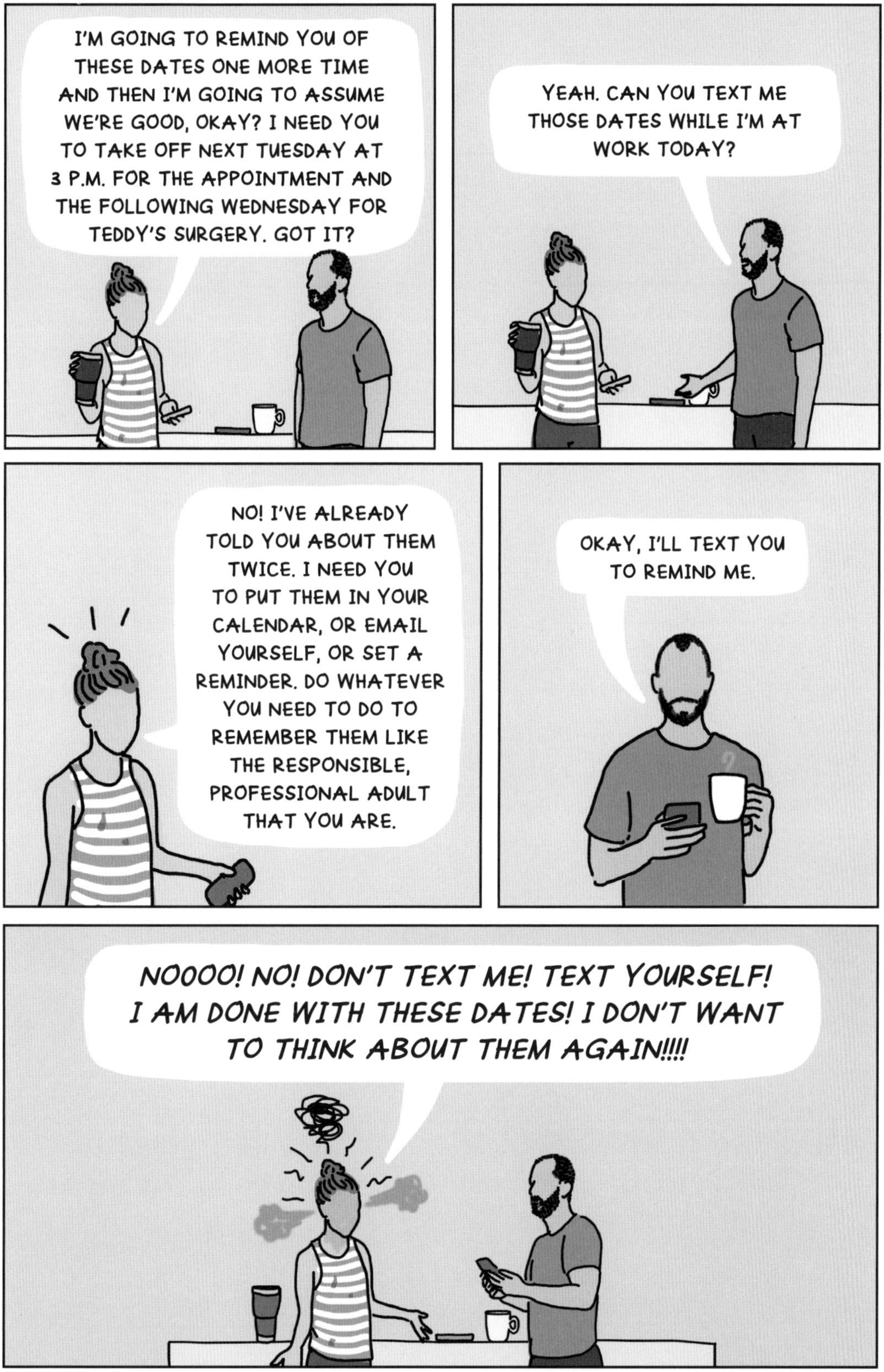
I'M GOING TO REMIND YOU OF THESE DATES ONE MORE TIME AND THEN I'M GOING TO ASSUME WE'RE GOOD, OKAY? I NEED YOU TO TAKE OFF NEXT TUESDAY AT 3 P.M. FOR THE APPOINTMENT AND THE FOLLOWING WEDNESDAY FOR TEDDY'S SURGERY. GOT IT?
YEAH. CAN YOU TEXT ME THOSE DATES WHILE I'M AT WORK TODAY?
NO! I'VE ALREADY TOLD YOU ABOUT THEM TWICE. I NEED YOU TO PUT THEM IN YOUR CALENDAR, OR EMAIL YOURSELF, OR SET A REMINDER. DO WHATEVER YOU NEED TO DO TO REMEMBER THEM LIKE THE RESPONSIBLE, PROFESSIONAL ADULT THAT YOU ARE.
OKAY, I'LL TEXT YOU TO REMIND ME.
NOOOO! NO! DON'T TEXT ME! TEXT YOURSELF! I AM DONE WITH THESE DATES! I DON'T WANT TO THINK ABOUT THEM AGAIN!!!!

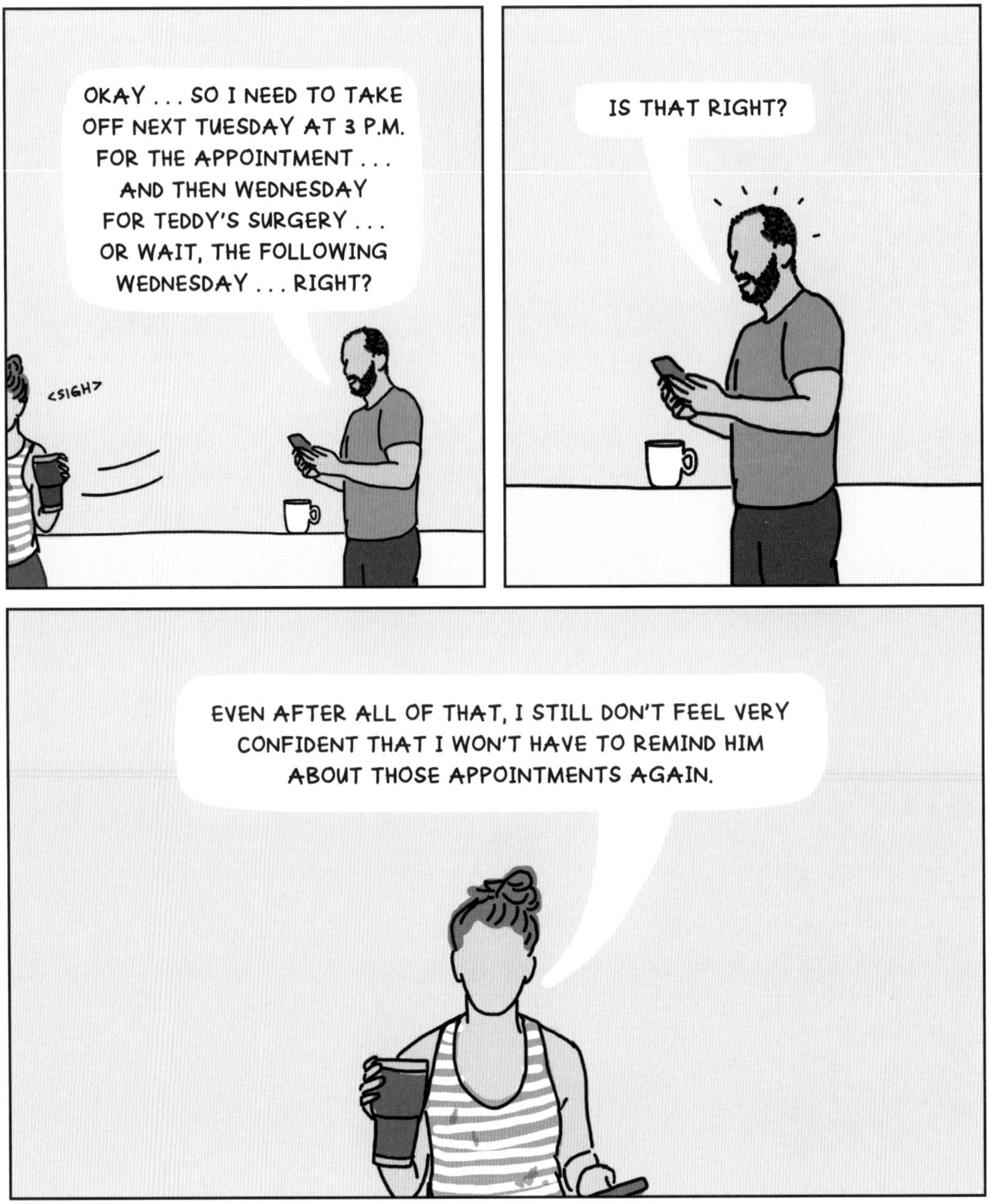
OKAY . . . SO I NEED TO TAKE OFF NEXT TUESDAY AT 3 P.M. FOR THE APPOINTMENT . . . AND THEN WEDNESDAY FOR TEDDY'S SURGERY . . . OR WAIT, THE FOLLOWING WEDNESDAY . . . RIGHT?
<SIGH>
IS THAT RIGHT?
EVEN AFTER ALL OF THAT, I STILL DON'T FEEL VERY CONFIDENT THAT I WON'T HAVE TO REMIND HIM ABOUT THOSE APPOINTMENTS AGAIN.

Sometimes we women play a part in all of this, too, even if we're trying our hardest not to. Most of us have been socially conditioned to believe that the realm of the household and children is our domain and reflects on us EVEN IF, INTELLECTUALLY, WE KNOW THIS IS BS.

Many of us have internalized these societal expectations, so we unknowingly enable our husbands, because at the end of the day, on some deep level, we feel like we're failing if we don't do everything.

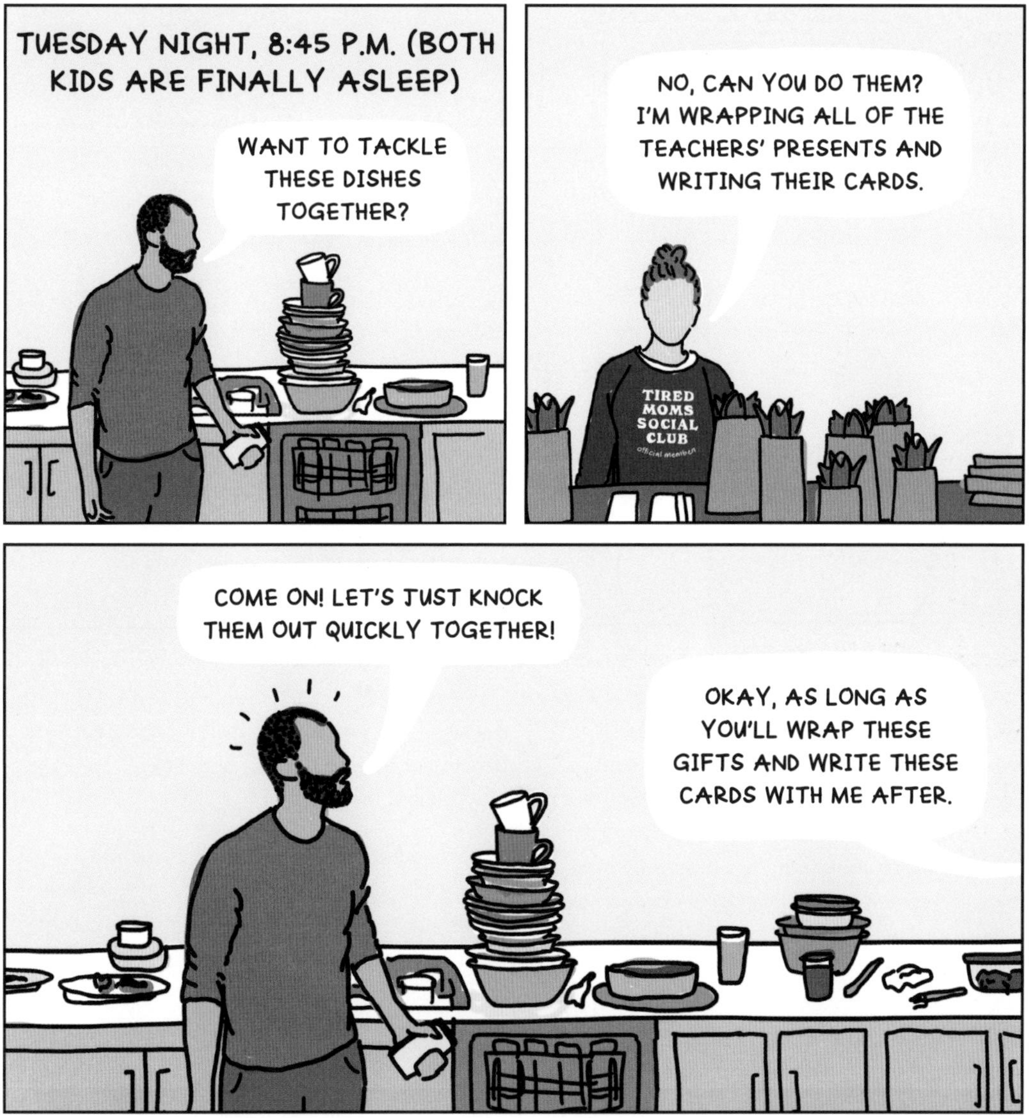
TUESDAY NIGHT, 8:45 P.M. (BOTH KIDS ARE FINALLY ASLEEP)
WANT TO TACKLE THESE DISHES TOGETHER?
NO, CAN YOU DO THEM? I'M WRAPPING ALL OF THE TEACHERS' PRESENTS AND WRITING THEIR CARDS.
TIRED MOMS SOCIAL CLUB
COME ON! LET'S JUST KNOCK THEM OUT QUICKLY TOGETHER!
OKAY, AS LONG AS YOU'LL WRAP THESE GIFTS AND WRITE THESE CARDS WITH ME AFTER.

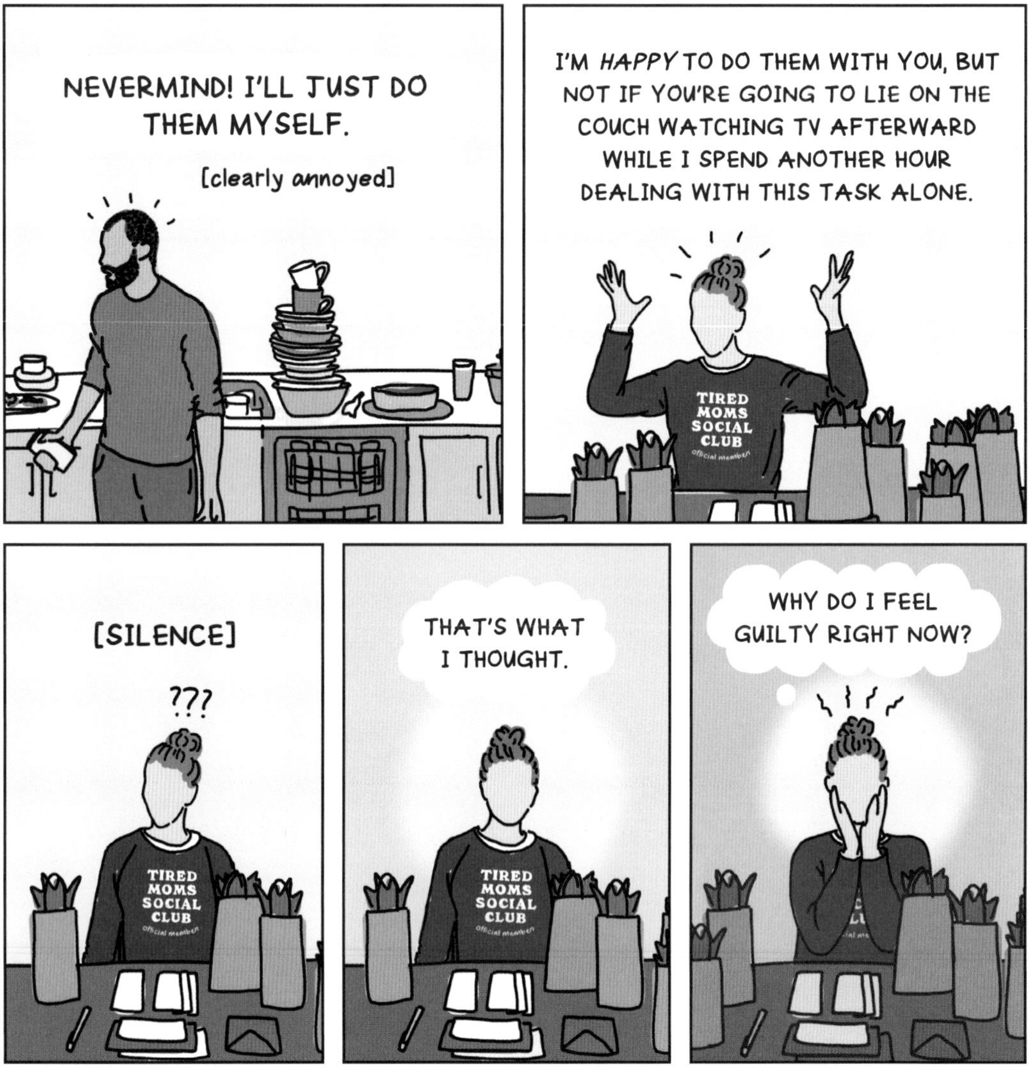
NEVERMIND! I'LL JUST DO THEM MYSELF.
[clearly annoyed]
I'M HAPPY TO DO THEM WITH YOU, BUT NOT IF YOU'RE GOING TO LIE ON THE COUCH WATCHING TV AFTERWARD WHILE I SPEND ANOTHER HOUR DEALING WITH THIS TASK ALONE.
TIRED MOMS SOCIAL CLUB
[SILENCE]
???
THAT'S WHAT I THOUGHT.
WHY DO I FEEL GUILTY RIGHT NOW?

Men aren't the only ones who practice weaponized incompetence. Plenty of women have told me that they purposefully won't learn how to do certain tasks that traditionally fall to men—like change a flat tire or operate the lawn mower—because they don't want to have to perform these tasks. We all do it in certain instances, but I'd argue that it only becomes a real problem when the person on the receiving end of that incompetence is less privileged, less valued, and less seen and appreciated by our society (as is the case for the woman in most heterosexual couples). Or when the person on the receiving end is desperately asking for help and their capable partner chooses not to learn how to help them.

Once you become aware of learned incompetence, it's easy to point out. I call Ben out when he's doing it now, and the more that I call him out, the more he's started to notice when he's doing it.

But noticing it isn't enough. I need him to WANT to change, and that's where things get tricky.

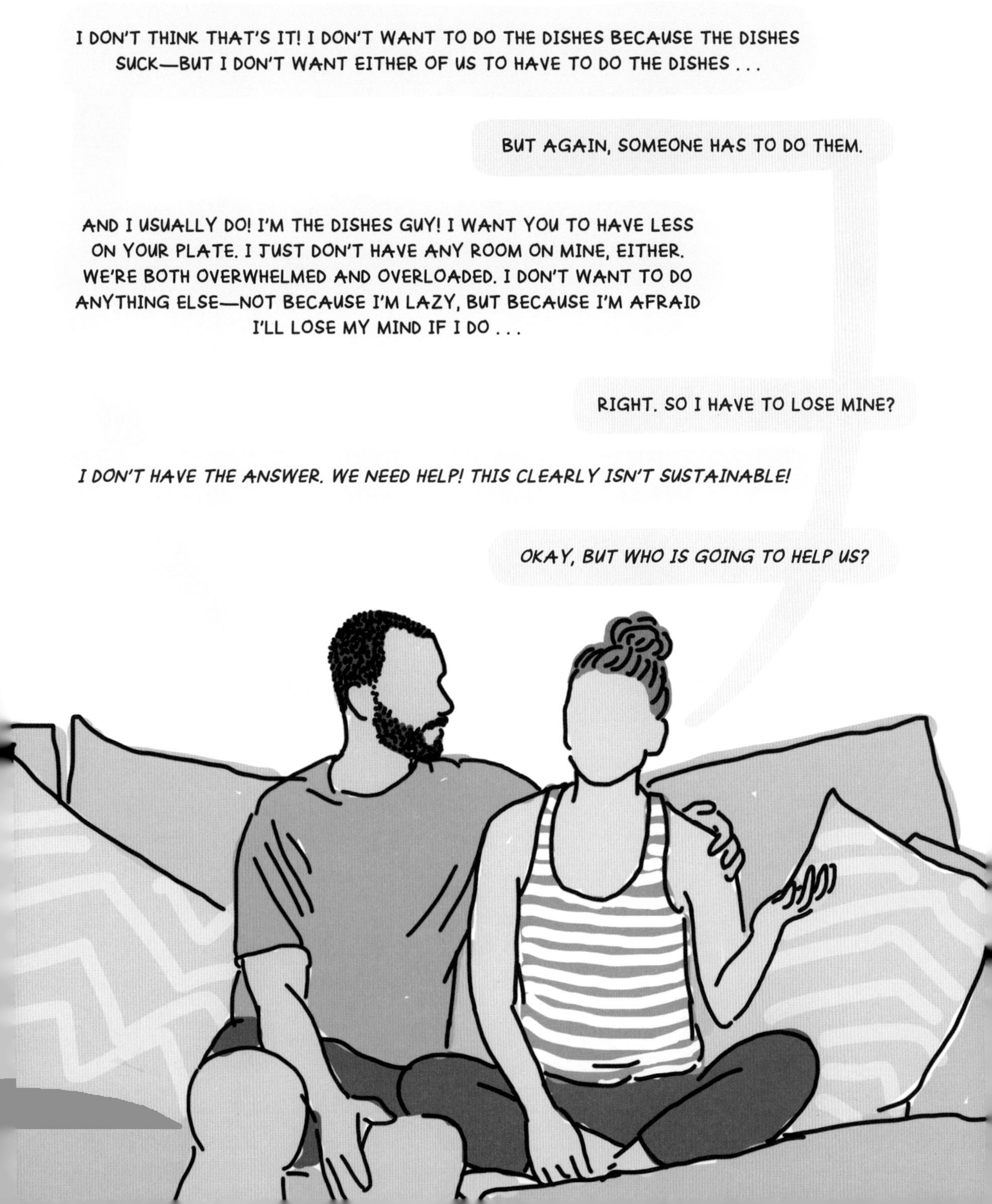
I DON'T THINK THAT'S IT! I DON'T WANT TO DO THE DISHES BECAUSE THE DISHES SUCK—BUT I DON'T WANT EITHER OF US TO HAVE TO DO THE DISHES . . .
BUT AGAIN, SOMEONE HAS TO DO THEM.
AND I USUALLY DO! I'M THE DISHES GUY! I WANT YOU TO HAVE LESS ON YOUR PLATE. I JUST DON'T HAVE ANY ROOM ON MINE, EITHER. WE'RE BOTH OVERWHELMED AND OVERLOADED. I DON'T WANT TO DO ANYTHING ELSE—NOT BECAUSE I'M LAZY, BUT BECAUSE I'M AFRAID I'LL LOSE MY MIND IF I DO . . .
RIGHT. SO I HAVE TO LOSE MINE?
*I DON'T HAVE THE ANSWER. WE NEED HELP! THIS CLEARLY ISN'T SUSTAINABLE!*
*OKAY, BUT WHO IS GOING TO HELP US?*

## What I Wish I'd Done Differently from the Beginning:
### The Laundry Metaphor Continues

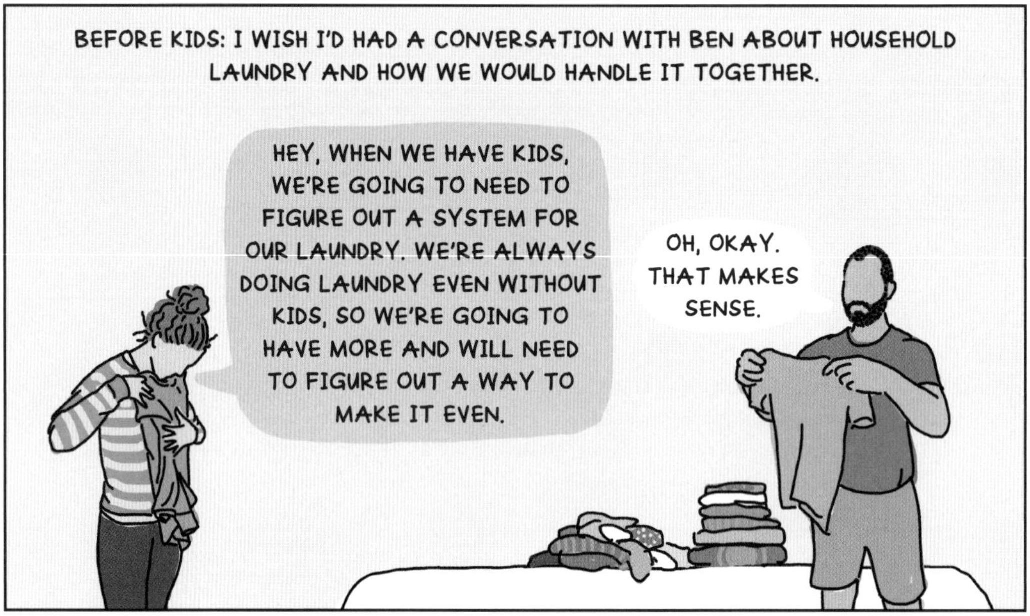
BEFORE KIDS: I WISH I'D HAD A CONVERSATION WITH BEN ABOUT HOUSEHOLD LAUNDRY AND HOW WE WOULD HANDLE IT TOGETHER.
HEY, WHEN WE HAVE KIDS, WE'RE GOING TO NEED TO FIGURE OUT A SYSTEM FOR OUR LAUNDRY. WE'RE ALWAYS DOING LAUNDRY EVEN WITHOUT KIDS, SO WE'RE GOING TO HAVE MORE AND WILL NEED TO FIGURE OUT A WAY TO MAKE IT EVEN.
OH, OKAY. THAT MAKES SENSE.

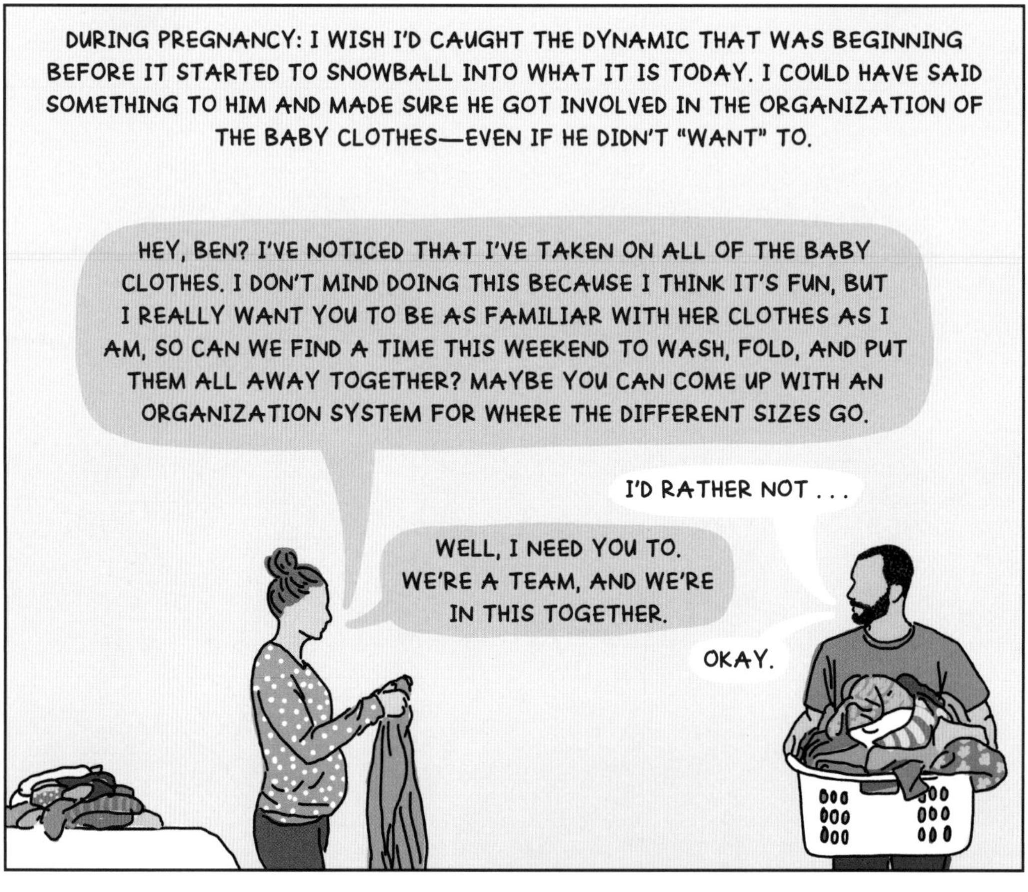
DURING PREGNANCY: I WISH I'D CAUGHT THE DYNAMIC THAT WAS BEGINNING BEFORE IT STARTED TO SNOWBALL INTO WHAT IT IS TODAY. I COULD HAVE SAID SOMETHING TO HIM AND MADE SURE HE GOT INVOLVED IN THE ORGANIZATION OF THE BABY CLOTHES—EVEN IF HE DIDN'T "WANT" TO.
HEY, BEN? I'VE NOTICED THAT I'VE TAKEN ON ALL OF THE BABY CLOTHES. I DON'T MIND DOING THIS BECAUSE I THINK IT'S FUN, BUT I REALLY WANT YOU TO BE AS FAMILIAR WITH HER CLOTHES AS I AM, SO CAN WE FIND A TIME THIS WEEKEND TO WASH, FOLD, AND PUT THEM ALL AWAY TOGETHER? MAYBE YOU CAN COME UP WITH AN ORGANIZATION SYSTEM FOR WHERE THE DIFFERENT SIZES GO.
I'D RATHER NOT . . .
WELL, I NEED YOU TO. WE'RE A TEAM, AND WE'RE IN THIS TOGETHER.
OKAY.

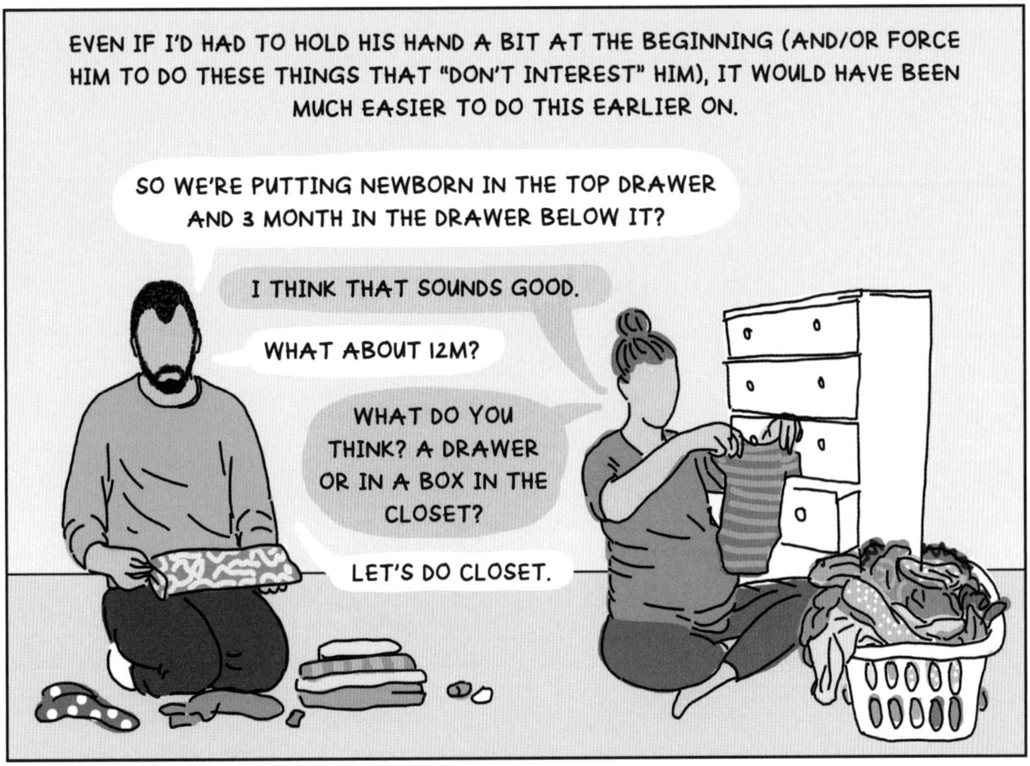
EVEN IF I'D HAD TO HOLD HIS HAND A BIT AT THE BEGINNING (AND/OR FORCE HIM TO DO THESE THINGS THAT "DON'T INTEREST" HIM), IT WOULD HAVE BEEN MUCH EASIER TO DO THIS EARLIER ON.
SO WE'RE PUTTING NEWBORN IN THE TOP DRAWER AND 3 MONTH IN THE DRAWER BELOW IT?
I THINK THAT SOUNDS GOOD.
WHAT ABOUT 12M?
WHAT DO YOU THINK? A DRAWER OR IN A BOX IN THE CLOSET?
LET'S DO CLOSET.

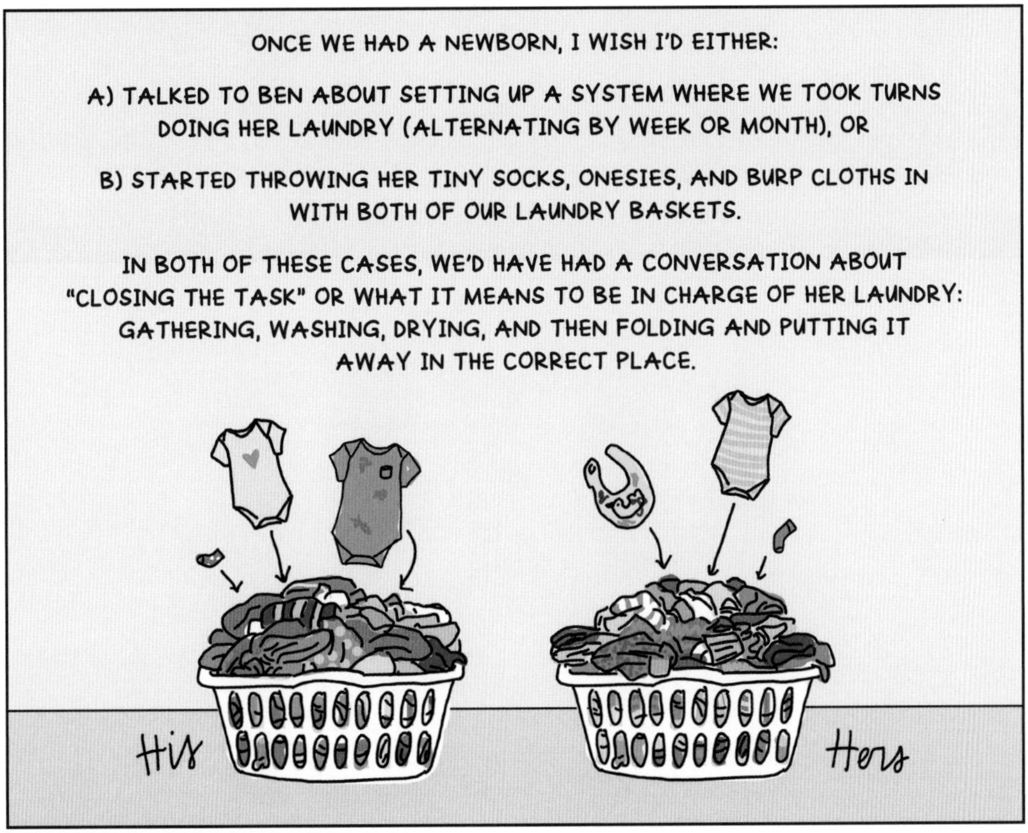
ONCE WE HAD A NEWBORN, I WISH I'D EITHER:
A) TALKED TO BEN ABOUT SETTING UP A SYSTEM WHERE WE TOOK TURNS DOING HER LAUNDRY (ALTERNATING BY WEEK OR MONTH), OR
B) STARTED THROWING HER TINY SOCKS, ONESIES, AND BURP CLOTHS IN WITH BOTH OF OUR LAUNDRY BASKETS.
IN BOTH OF THESE CASES, WE'D HAVE HAD A CONVERSATION ABOUT "CLOSING THE TASK" OR WHAT IT MEANS TO BE IN CHARGE OF HER LAUNDRY: GATHERING, WASHING, DRYING, AND THEN FOLDING AND PUTTING IT AWAY IN THE CORRECT PLACE.
His
Hers

ANOTHER OPTION WOULD HAVE BEEN TO HAVE A CONVERSATION WHERE I AGREED TO BE THE PERSON WHO WASHES THE KIDS' LAUNDRY AND HE AGREED TO BE THE PERSON WHO FOLDS AND PUTS IT AWAY, OR WHERE ONE OF US AGREED TO TAKE ON THE KIDS' LAUNDRY AND THE OTHER AGREED TO TAKE ON A DIFFERENT BUT EQUALLY TIME-CONSUMING HOUSEHOLD TASK.

IF I'D HAD THE FORESIGHT TO HAVE ANY OF THESE KINDS OF CONVERSATIONS WITH BEN EARLY ON, THEN AS CHARLIE MAE'S LAUNDRY PILE (AND LATER, THE KID-RELATED LAUNDRY PILE) GREW, BOTH OF OUR LAUNDRY PILES (OR HOUSEHOLD TASKS MENTAL LOAD) WOULD HAVE GROWN.

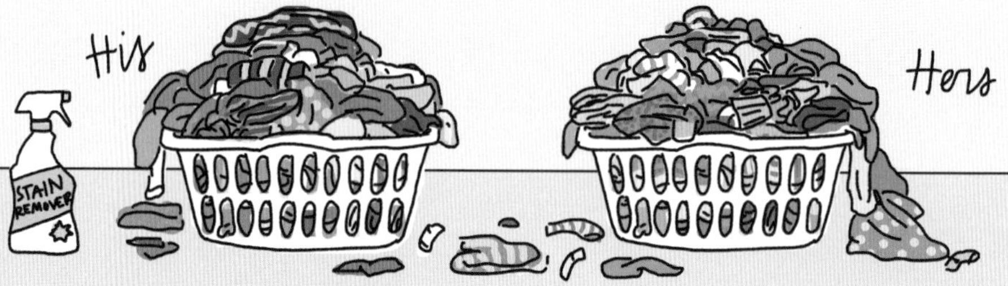
His
Hers
STAIN REMOVER

I'M NOT DELUSIONAL. I KNOW THAT THIS KIND OF SYSTEM MIGHT HAVE HAD ITS OWN SET OF ISSUES. BUT I WOULD HOPE THAT IF IT HAD BEEN AN ACTUAL CONVERSATION, WE WOULD HAVE BEEN ABLE TO REVISIT THE SUBJECT AND TWEAK AS NEEDED OVER THE YEARS.

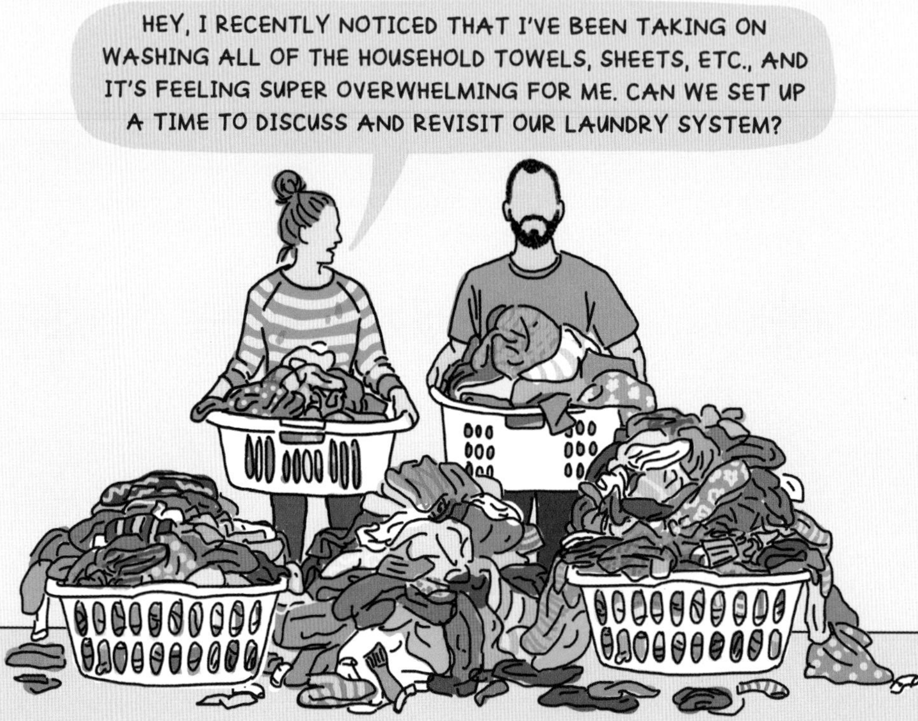
HEY, I RECENTLY NOTICED THAT I'VE BEEN TAKING ON WASHING ALL OF THE HOUSEHOLD TOWELS, SHEETS, ETC., AND IT'S FEELING SUPER OVERWHELMING FOR ME. CAN WE SET UP A TIME TO DISCUSS AND REVISIT OUR LAUNDRY SYSTEM?

## THE RESULT

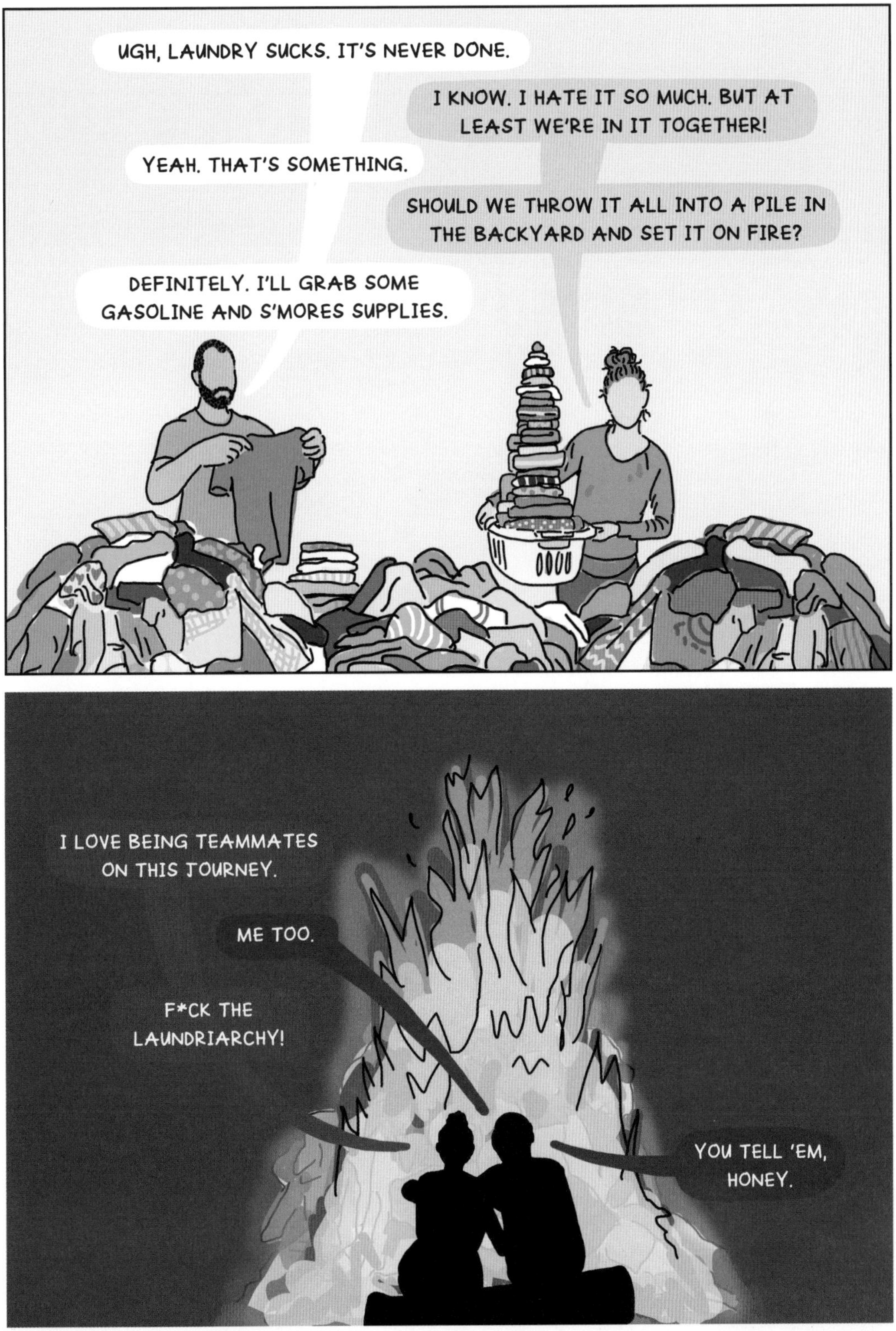

UGH, LAUNDRY SUCKS. IT'S NEVER DONE.
I KNOW. I HATE IT SO MUCH. BUT AT LEAST WE'RE IN IT TOGETHER!
YEAH. THAT'S SOMETHING.
SHOULD WE THROW IT ALL INTO A PILE IN THE BACKYARD AND SET IT ON FIRE?
DEFINITELY. I'LL GRAB SOME GASOLINE AND S'MORES SUPPLIES.
I LOVE BEING TEAMMATES ON THIS JOURNEY.
ME TOO.
F*CK THE LAUNDRIARCHY!
YOU TELL 'EM, HONEY.

# You're Going to Be the Death of Me.

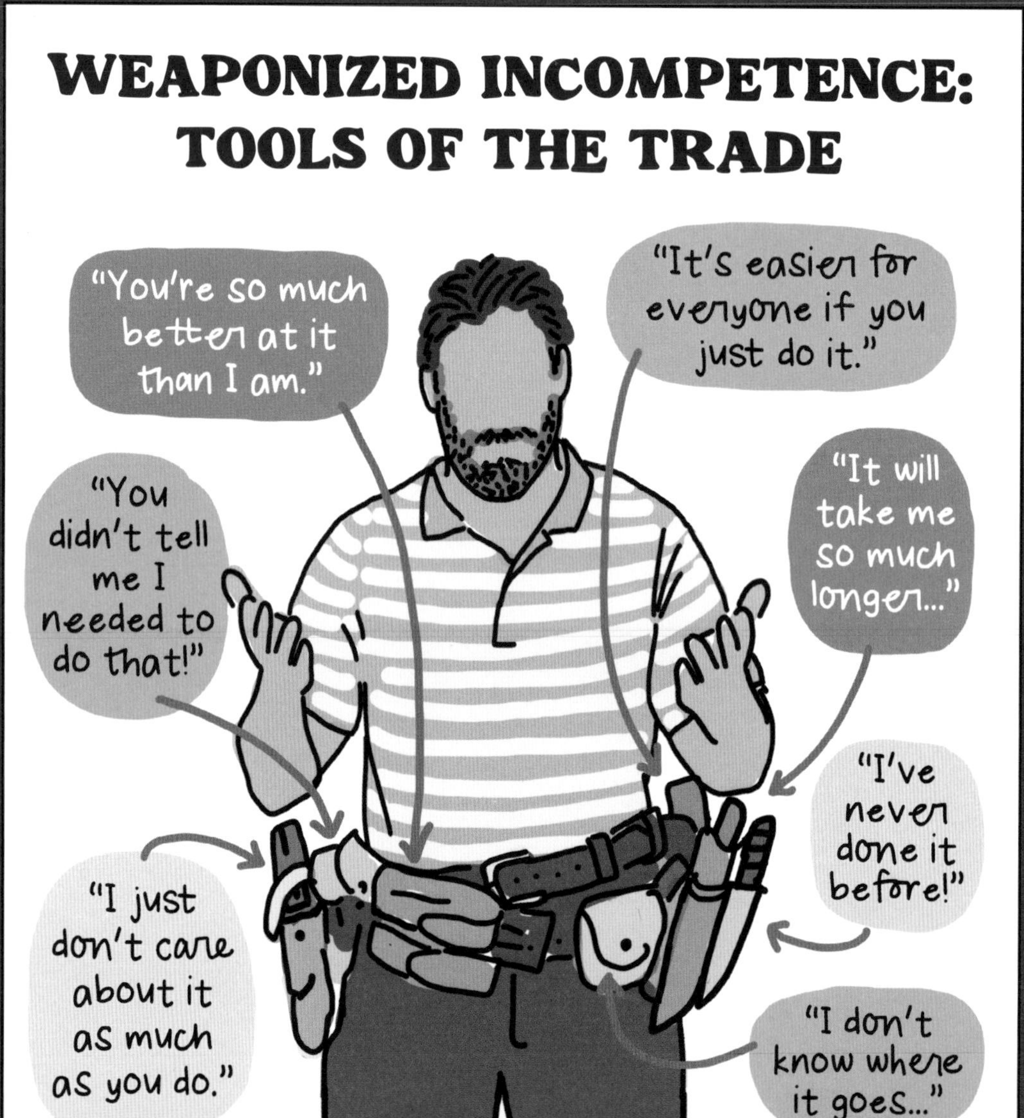
WEAPONIZED INCOMPETENCE: TOOLS OF THE TRADE
"You're so much better at it than I am."
"It's easier for everyone if you just do it."
"You didn't tell me I needed to do that!"
"It will take me so much longer..."
"I've never done it before!"
"I just don't care about it as much as you do."
"I don't know where it goes..."

# Tombstone Templates for Mothers

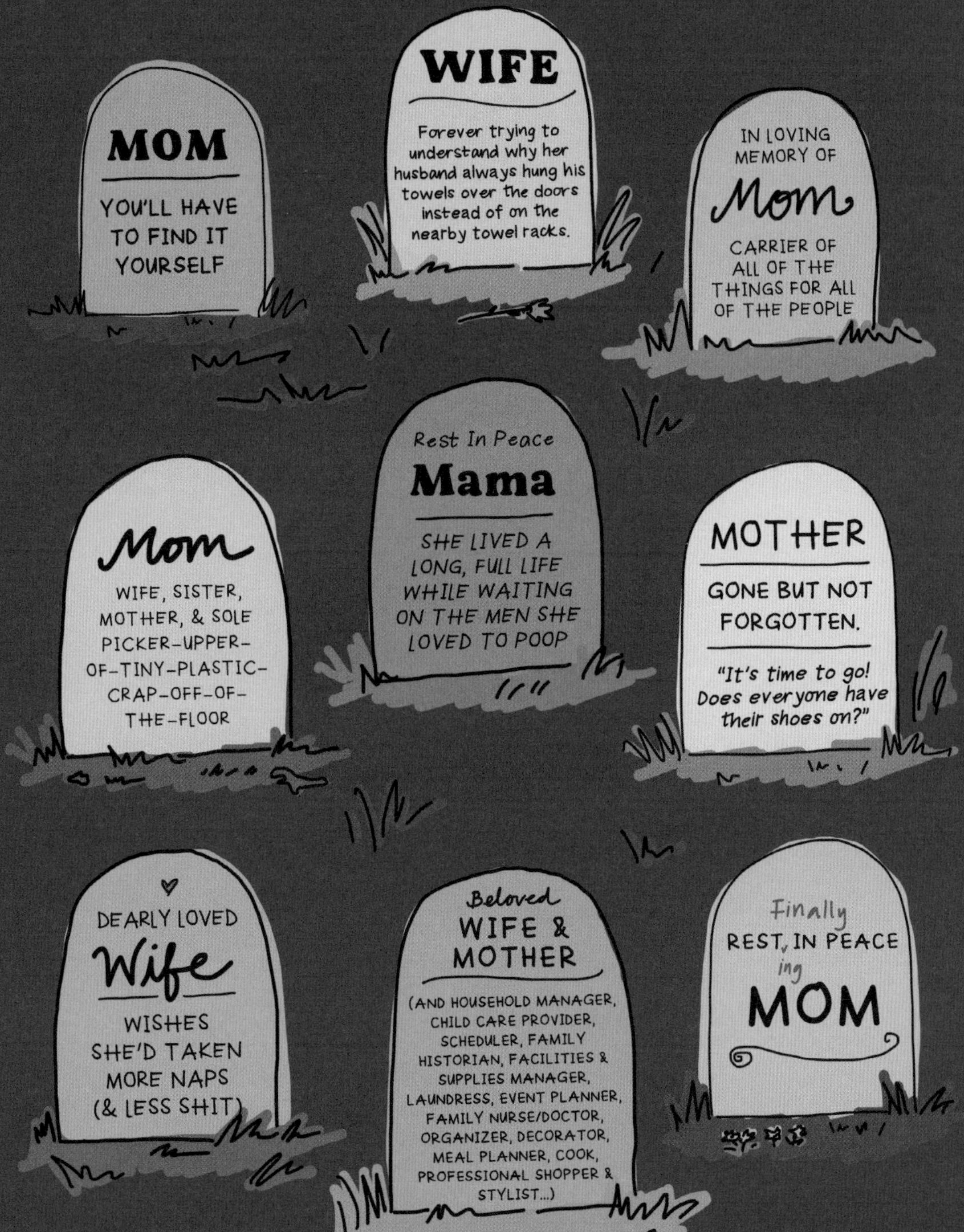
MOM
YOU'LL HAVE TO FIND IT YOURSELF
WIFE
Forever trying to understand why her husband always hung his towels over the doors instead of on the nearby towel racks.
IN LOVING MEMORY OF
Mom
CARRIER OF ALL OF THE THINGS FOR ALL OF THE PEOPLE
Mom
WIFE, SISTER, MOTHER, & SOLE PICKER-UPPER-OF-TINY-PLASTIC-CRAP-OFF-OF-THE-FLOOR
Rest In Peace
Mama
SHE LIVED A LONG, FULL LIFE WHILE WAITING ON THE MEN SHE LOVED TO POOP
MOTHER
GONE BUT NOT FORGOTTEN.
"It's time to go! Does everyone have their shoes on?"
DEARLY LOVED
Wife
WISHES SHE'D TAKEN MORE NAPS (& LESS SHIT)
Beloved
WIFE & MOTHER
(AND HOUSEHOLD MANAGER, CHILD CARE PROVIDER, SCHEDULER, FAMILY HISTORIAN, FACILITIES & SUPPLIES MANAGER, LAUNDRESS, EVENT PLANNER, FAMILY NURSE/DOCTOR, ORGANIZER, DECORATOR, MEAL PLANNER, COOK, PROFESSIONAL SHOPPER & STYLIST...)
Finally
REST IN PEACE
ing
MOM

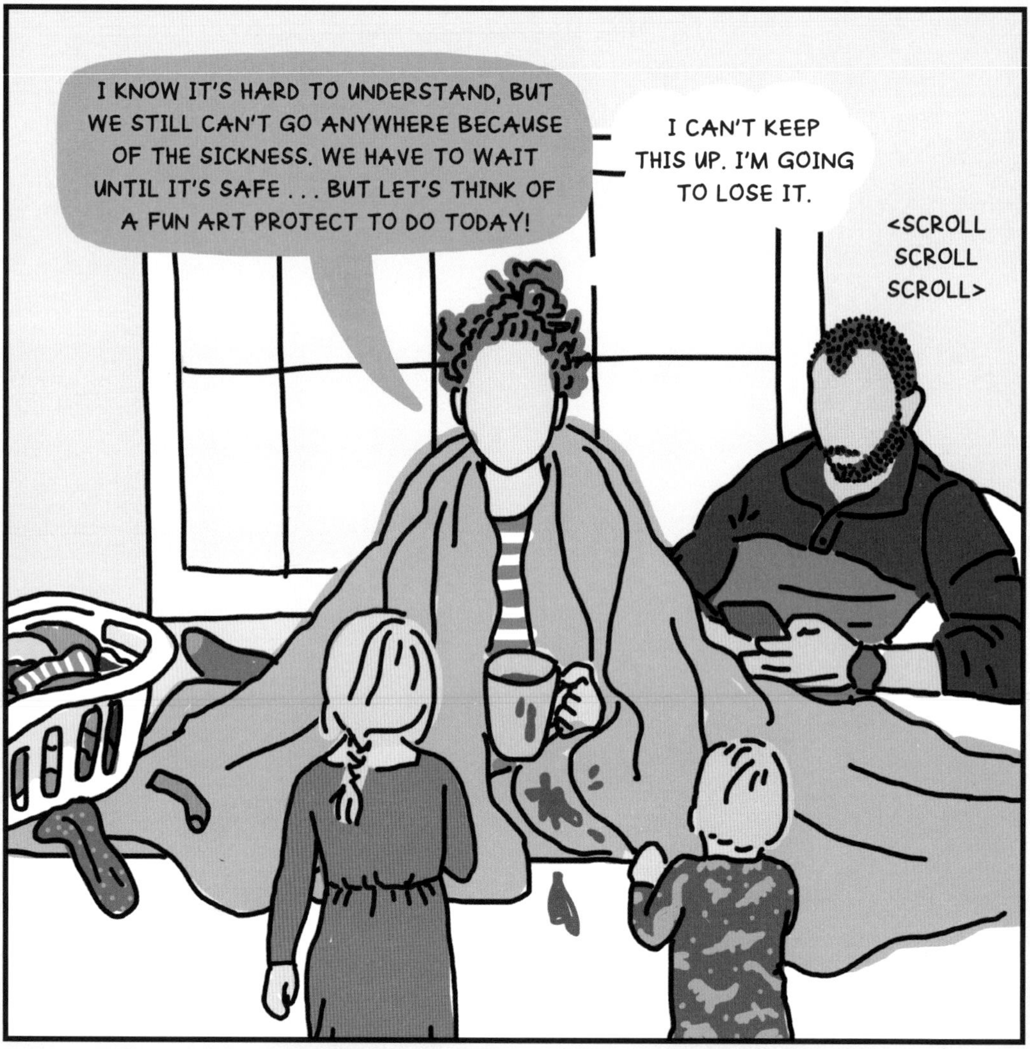
I KNOW IT'S HARD TO UNDERSTAND, BUT WE STILL CAN'T GO ANYWHERE BECAUSE OF THE SICKNESS. WE HAVE TO WAIT UNTIL IT'S SAFE . . . BUT LET'S THINK OF A FUN ART PROJECT TO DO TODAY!
I CAN'T KEEP THIS UP. I'M GOING TO LOSE IT.
<SCROLL SCROLL SCROLL>

# CHAPTER 7

# The Straw(s) That Broke the ~~Camel's~~ Mom's Back

# Trapped by the Pandemic

With two kids under four and two time-consuming careers, Ben and I were already at the end of our ropes. And then the pandemic hit, and things got SO MUCH WORSE.

During the pandemic, the challenges of being the default parent were amplified a thousandfold, and several things about motherhood became obvious to me that I'd never understood as clearly before. Being forced under the same roof at all times made certain truths about our relationship and household dynamic impossible to ignore or work around anymore; it became very clear to me that something had to change.

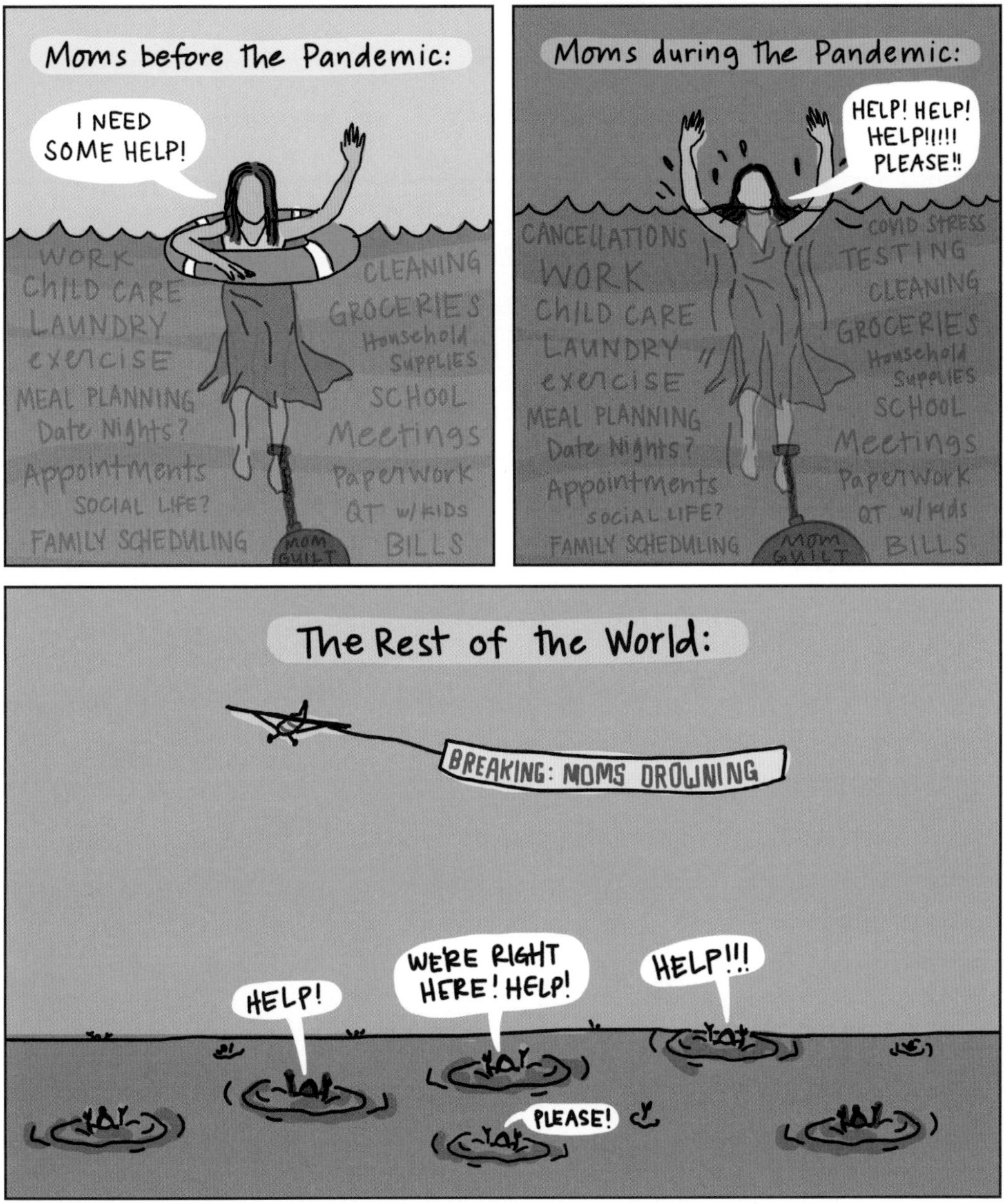
Moms before the Pandemic:
I NEED SOME HELP!
WORK
CHILD CARE
LAUNDRY
exercise
MEAL PLANNING
Date Nights?
Appointments
SOCIAL LIFE?
FAMILY SCHEDULING
MOM GUILT
CLEANING
GROCERIES
Household Supplies
SCHOOL
Meetings
Paperwork
QT w/KIDS
BILLS
Moms during the Pandemic:
HELP! HELP! HELP!!!!! PLEASE!!
CANCELLATIONS
WORK
CHILD CARE
LAUNDRY
exercise
MEAL PLANNING
Date Nights?
Appointments
SOCIAL LIFE?
FAMILY SCHEDULING
MOM GUILT
COVID STRESS
TESTING
CLEANING
GROCERIES
Household Supplies
SCHOOL
Meetings
Paperwork
QT w/kids
BILLS
The Rest of the World:
BREAKING: MOMS DROWNING
HELP!
WE'RE RIGHT HERE! HELP!
HELP!!!
PLEASE!

When you're the default/preferred parent of young children, having "help" from your partner isn't actually helpful if you're all stuck at home—because if you, the preferred parent, are anywhere in the house, your kids only want you. And if your partner doesn't put forth the HUGE effort it takes to keep them occupied and entertained when you're nearby but unavailable, it's miserable for everyone.

Since I couldn't leave the house to go work elsewhere and Ben couldn't take the kids anywhere to get them away from me (besides a walk, the yard, or a car ride), working during the pandemic was a recipe for resentment and frustration.

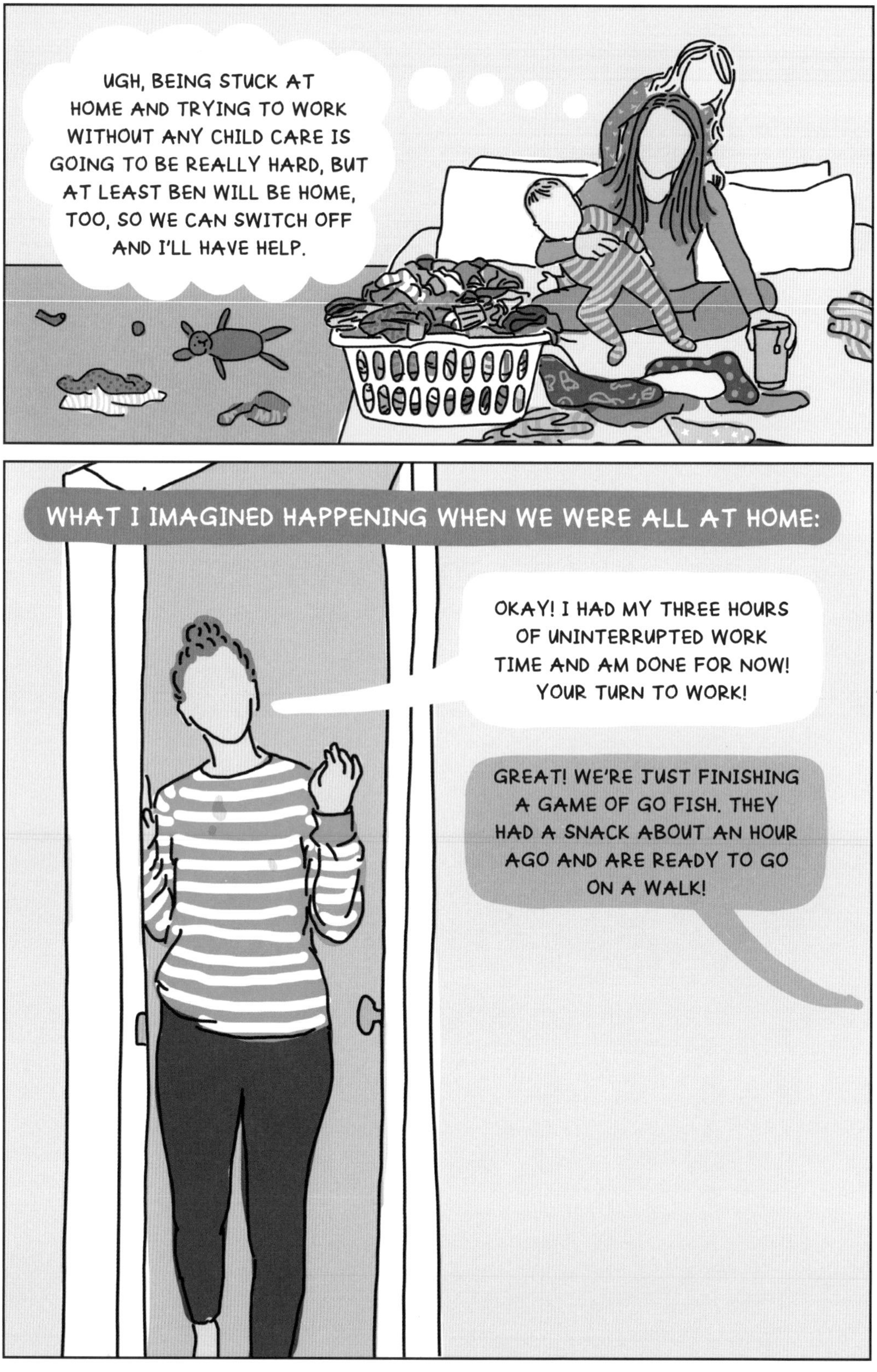
UGH, BEING STUCK AT HOME AND TRYING TO WORK WITHOUT ANY CHILD CARE IS GOING TO BE REALLY HARD, BUT AT LEAST BEN WILL BE HOME, TOO, SO WE CAN SWITCH OFF AND I'LL HAVE HELP.
WHAT I IMAGINED HAPPENING WHEN WE WERE ALL AT HOME:
OKAY! I HAD MY THREE HOURS OF UNINTERRUPTED WORK TIME AND AM DONE FOR NOW! YOUR TURN TO WORK!
GREAT! WE'RE JUST FINISHING A GAME OF GO FISH. THEY HAD A SNACK ABOUT AN HOUR AGO AND ARE READY TO GO ON A WALK!

WHAT ACTUALLY HAPPENED WHEN WE WERE ALL AT HOME:
THIS ISN'T WORKING! I NEED YOU TO KEEP THEM OCCUPIED! I CAN'T WORK WITH THEM SCREAMING AND CRYING FOR ME, SLIDING THINGS UNDER MY OFFICE DOOR, AND BANGING ON IT WHILE YELLING MY NAME!
I CAN'T GET THEM TO STOP! YOU NEED TO GO SOMEWHERE ELSE TO WORK! THEY CAN'T HANDLE YOU BEING IN THE HOUSE!
I CAN'T GO ANYWHERE! IT'S A PANDEMIC! CAN YOU PLEASE JUST TRY TO ENTERTAIN THEM? DO SOMETHING FUN WITH THEM? PLAY A GAME? TAKE THEM OUTSIDE? ANYTHING BUT MORE TV?
THAT DOESN'T WORK WHEN YOU'RE AROUND!
YES, IT DOES, IF YOU MAKE IT FUN AND ENGAGING FOR THEM! IF YOU ACTUALLY PLAY WITH THEM AND COME UP WITH EXCITING ACTIVITIES!!!
NO, IT DOESN'T. YOU JUST DON'T UNDERSTAND. CAN YOU GO WORK IN YOUR CAR?
NO! I NEED MORE SPACE THAN THAT! AND A BETTER WIFI SIGNAL! PLEASE, BEN.
YOU'VE CREATED THIS DYNAMIC BY BEING TOO AVAILABLE TO THEM. IF YOU WEREN'T SUCH A SUPERMOM, THEY WOULDN'T NEED YOU EVERY SECOND!
NO, I HAVEN'T! YOU'VE CREATED IT BY BEING TOO UNAVAILABLE! THEY ONLY WANT ME BECAUSE I ACTUALLY PAY ATTENTION TO THEM WHEN I'M WITH THEM! YOU'RE ALWAYS ON YOUR PHONE!
OH YEAH, I'M SUCH A DEADBEAT DAD.
THAT'S NOT WHAT I'M SAYING!

Another challenging aspect of motherhood that was heightened during the pandemic is the way in which the household care tasks associated with illness always fall on mom. Here's what happened during the pandemic:

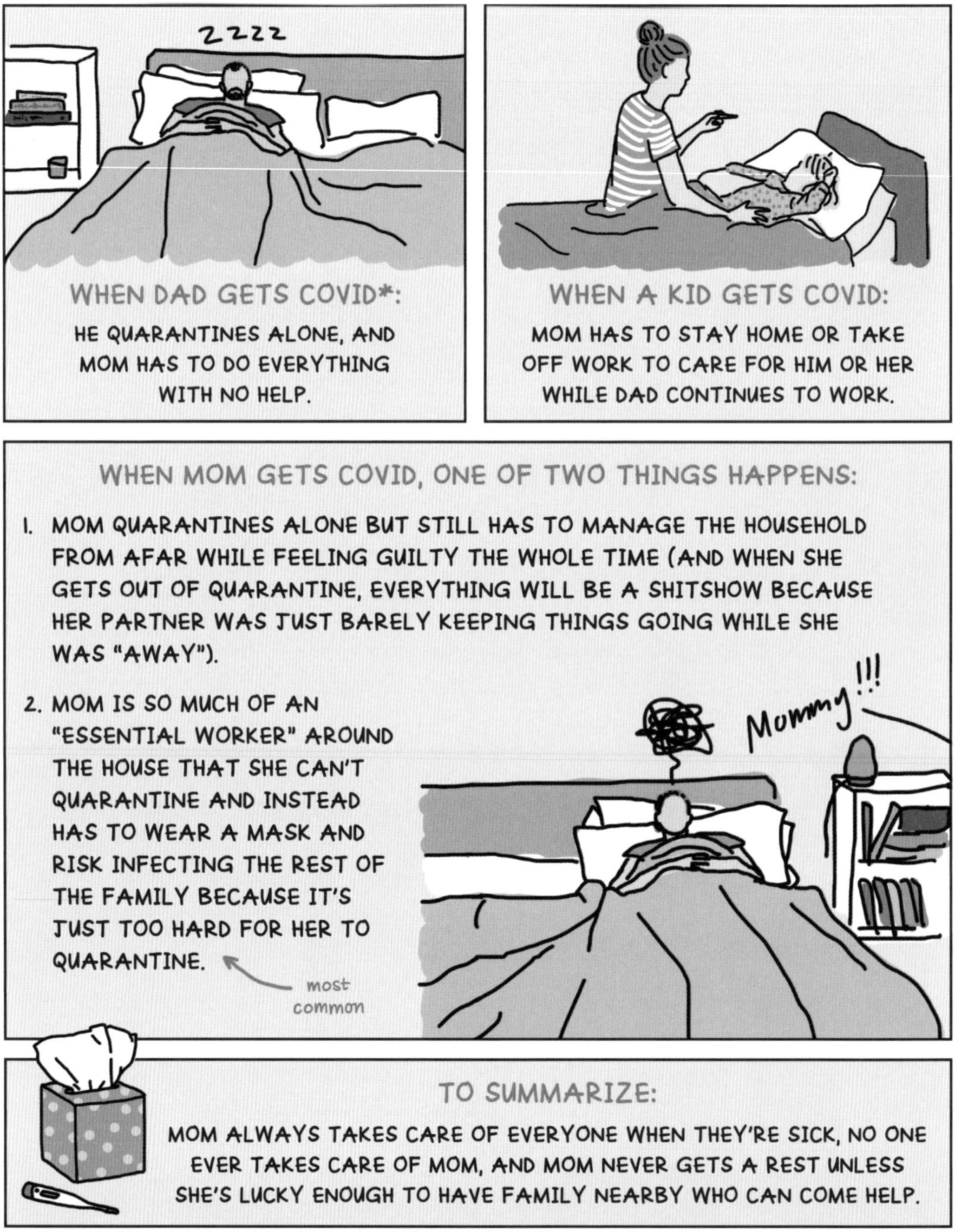
ZZZZ
WHEN DAD GETS COVID*:
HE QUARANTINES ALONE, AND MOM HAS TO DO EVERYTHING WITH NO HELP.
WHEN A KID GETS COVID:
MOM HAS TO STAY HOME OR TAKE OFF WORK TO CARE FOR HIM OR HER WHILE DAD CONTINUES TO WORK.
WHEN MOM GETS COVID, ONE OF TWO THINGS HAPPENS:
1. MOM QUARANTINES ALONE BUT STILL HAS TO MANAGE THE HOUSEHOLD FROM AFAR WHILE FEELING GUILTY THE WHOLE TIME (AND WHEN SHE GETS OUT OF QUARANTINE, EVERYTHING WILL BE A SHITSHOW BECAUSE HER PARTNER WAS JUST BARELY KEEPING THINGS GOING WHILE SHE WAS "AWAY").
2. MOM IS SO MUCH OF AN "ESSENTIAL WORKER" AROUND THE HOUSE THAT SHE CAN'T QUARANTINE AND INSTEAD HAS TO WEAR A MASK AND RISK INFECTING THE REST OF THE FAMILY BECAUSE IT'S JUST TOO HARD FOR HER TO QUARANTINE.
most common
Mommy!!!
TO SUMMARIZE:
MOM ALWAYS TAKES CARE OF EVERYONE WHEN THEY'RE SICK, NO ONE EVER TAKES CARE OF MOM, AND MOM NEVER GETS A REST UNLESS SHE'S LUCKY ENOUGH TO HAVE FAMILY NEARBY WHO CAN COME HELP.

*NOTE: THE WORD "COVID" COULD BE REPLACED WITH ANY ILLNESS, AND THE WORD "QUARANTINES" COULD BE REPLACED WITH "RESTS IN BED."

Speaking of sickness, here are some other common illness-related scenarios that play out in families all over the world (again, I know this because I get messages from women all over the world about it):

| MOM | DAD |
| --- | --- |
| -ALWAYS SICK BECAUSE SHE'S ALWAYS TAKING CARE OF THE KIDS AND THUS AROUND THEIR GERMS | -RARELY SICK BECAUSE HE'S NOT WITH THE KIDS AS MUCH (OR THEY'RE NOT ALL OVER HIM IN THE SAME WAY) |
| -WHEN SHE GETS SICK, SHE HAS TO POWER THROUGH AND KEEP DOING EVERYTHING FOR THE HOUSEHOLD | -WHEN HE GETS SICK, HE GETS TO SLEEP IT OFF/STAY IN BED UNTIL HE'S BETTER, AND NO ONE BOTHERS HIM |
| -IF SHE WORKS OUTSIDE THE HOME: USES SICK DAYS FOR HERSELF AND THE KIDS<br><br>-IF SHE DOESN'T WORK OUTSIDE THE HOME: SHE HAS NO SICK DAYS EVER | -USES SICK DAYS WHEN HE IS SICK |
| -IF SHE'S BEDRIDDEN, SHE KNOWS ALL OF THE HOUSEHOLD TASKS ARE PILING UP AROUND HER WHILE SHE LIES IN BED | -IF HE'S BEDRIDDEN, HE KNOWS THE HOUSE WILL KEEP FUNCTIONING WITHOUT HIM AND HE WON'T HAVE A BIG MESS WAITING FOR HIM |
| -IS OFTEN SICK FOR A MUCH LONGER TIME BECAUSE SHE CAN'T ADEQUATELY REST | -ILLNESS CLEARS UP MORE QUICKLY BECAUSE HE CAN REST AND GET SLEEP |

To me, nothing captures the inequality surrounding illness more than a message I received from a mom a few years ago, which said something like this:

## When the Household Has a Stomach Bug That Makes People Throw Up

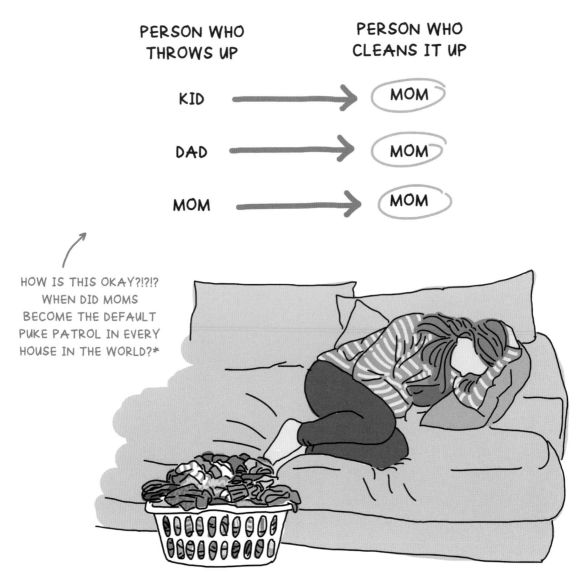

| PERSON WHO THROWS UP | | PERSON WHO CLEANS IT UP |
|---|---|---|
| KID | ⟶ | MOM |
| DAD | ⟶ | MOM |
| MOM | ⟶ | MOM |

HOW IS THIS OKAY?!?!? WHEN DID MOMS BECOME THE DEFAULT PUKE PATROL IN EVERY HOUSE IN THE WORLD?*

*EXCEPT MY FRIEND MEGAN'S HOUSE BECAUSE SHE HAS A PUKE PHOBIA. LUCKY HER!

# Finding My People during a Global Pandemic

The combination of being the default parent trapped at home, the default parent for illness-related phenomena, and all the other pandemic-related issues (virtual schooling, trying to work while caring for kids, the anxiety surrounding COVID, etc.) brought moms to a breaking point during the pandemic.

In my case, reaching this breaking point was a big catalyst toward starting to take back my life and fight for the alone time, help, equality, and community that I needed.

One of the first steps was sharing my experiences of motherhood online. In the thick of the pandemic, I started posting short, autobiographical comics about motherhood to my personal Instagram account.

The comics started out simple and silly but quickly became a very important creative and therapeutic outlet for me. They gave me a way to vent and connect with other moms, which was something I was really lacking at that point in my motherhood journey.

Each time that I posted a comic and other moms commented,

ME TOO! I THOUGHT I WAS THE ONLY ONE!

I felt encouraged to keep going. This was something for me that I could do while stuck at home. This was something that fed me: being honest about my struggles with strangers on the internet. I'd been blogging for around ten years at this point, so transitioning from writing about my feelings and my life to drawing about them was fairly simple.

Then, a little over a year after I'd been making comics, my "Double Standards of Parenting" comic (pages 14–15) went viral. In a matter of weeks, I went from 15,000 to 150,000 followers.

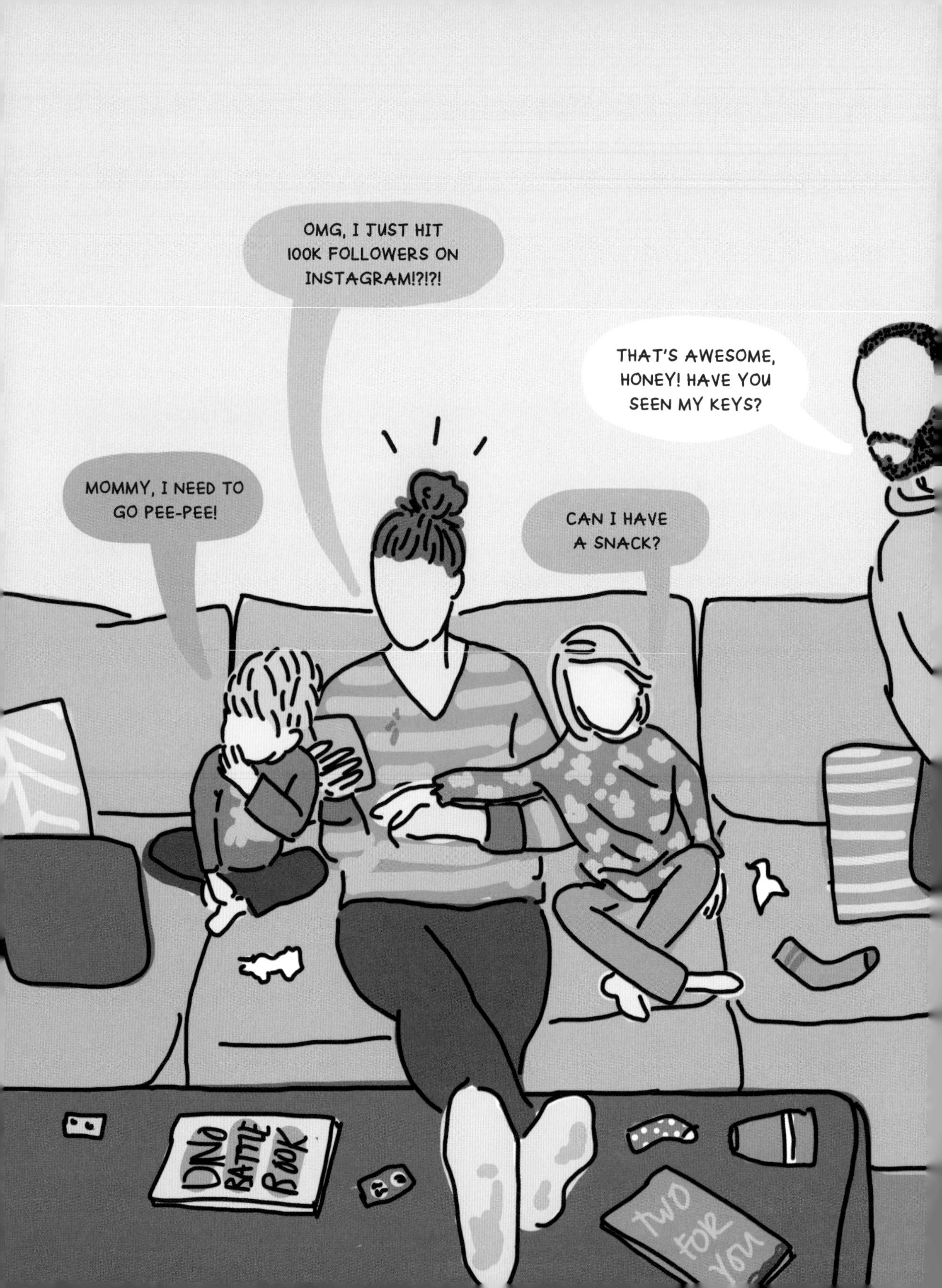
OMG, I JUST HIT 100K FOLLOWERS ON INSTAGRAM!?!?!
THAT'S AWESOME, HONEY! HAVE YOU SEEN MY KEYS?
MOMMY, I NEED TO GO PEE-PEE!
CAN I HAVE A SNACK?
DINO BATTLE BOOK
TWO FOR YOU

My comic was translated into other languages and went viral around the world. I received messages from moms in more than forty countries telling me how much my work meant to them and how sick they were of the double standards.

> I'M A MOM OF TWO FROM MEXICO, AND I WANTED TO TELL YOU WHAT A BIG INSPIRATION YOU'VE BEEN TO ME. YOU KNOW HOW TO PUT ALL MY THOUGHTS ON PAPER IN SUCH A SIMPLE AND TRUE WAY. I LOVE SENDING MY HUSBAND YOUR COMICS BECAUSE HE REALLY GETS THEM THAT WAY, BETTER THAN ANYTHING I CAN SAY TO HIM.

> I AM A MOM FROM CHILE AND I LOVE SEEING YOUR COMICS. THEY MAKE ME LAUGH, THEY MAKE ME FEEL LIKE WE WOMEN ARE NOT ALONE, AND THEY MAKE ME REALIZE HOW AMAZING AND STRONG WE ARE. EVEN THOUGH I'M SO TIRED AND SO FRUSTRATED SO MUCH OF THE TIME . . .

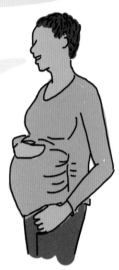

> EVERYTHING YOU POST IS SO ACCURATE! I'M IN LOVE WITH YOUR PAGE AND AM SUPPORTING YOU ALL THE WAY FROM LEBANON! EVEN WITH DIFFERENT CULTURES, THIS PAGE REPRESENTS 100% OF MY DAILY LIFE.

> THANK YOU FOR CREATING A SAFE SPACE TO VENT AND SHARE ABOUT ALL THINGS MOM LIFE. YOUR ACCOUNT IS SUCH A BALM TO MY SOUL IN THIS WORLD THAT SEEMS TO HATE WOMEN AND MOTHERS. LOVE FROM THE UK.

Something about receiving all of these messages changed me. I had known that how I was feeling was not okay. I had known that the mental load of motherhood was crushing me, but now that I knew how common that was—how women all over the world felt the same way that I did—I didn't want to just sit around complaining about it. I was energized and galvanized to keep connecting with this community of like-minded moms.

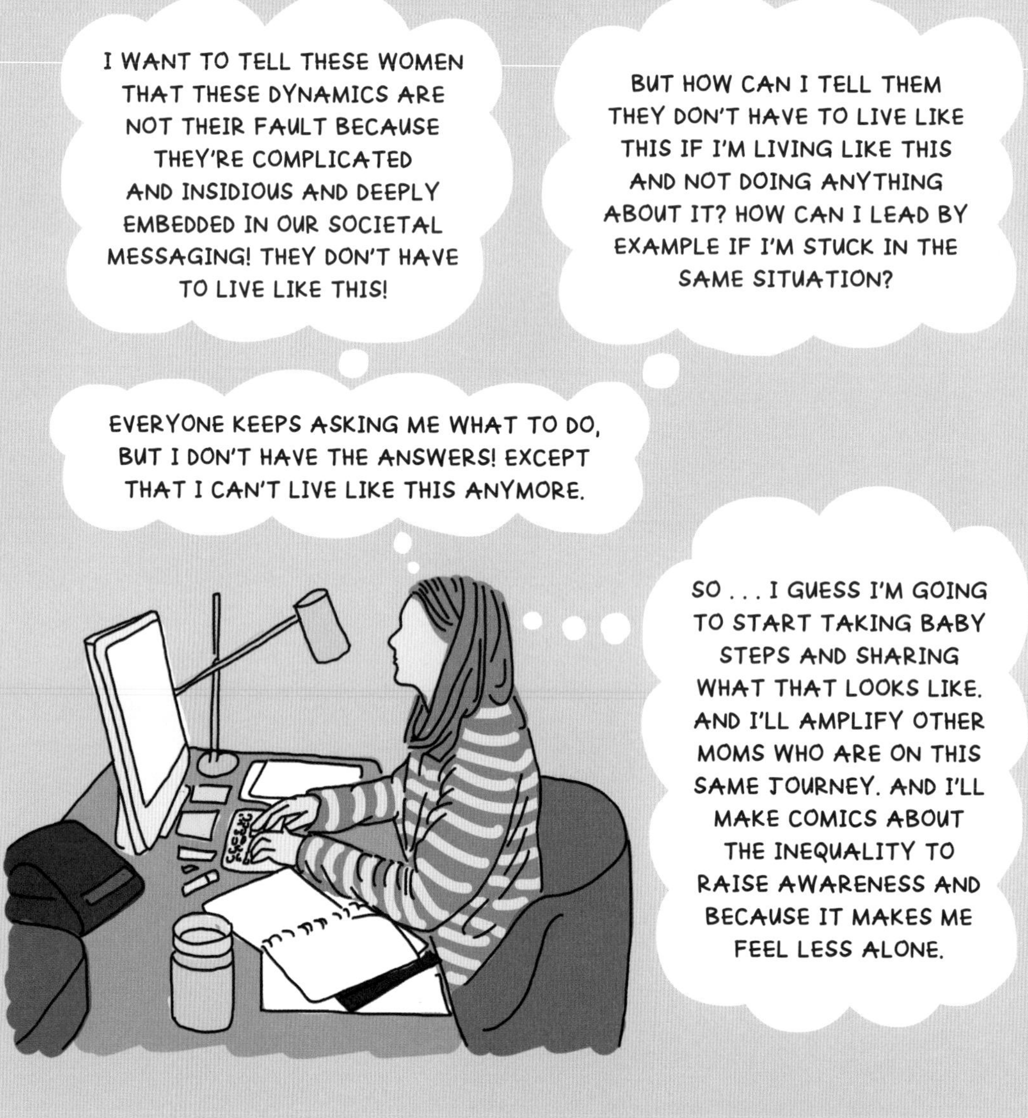
I WANT TO TELL THESE WOMEN THAT THESE DYNAMICS ARE NOT THEIR FAULT BECAUSE THEY'RE COMPLICATED AND INSIDIOUS AND DEEPLY EMBEDDED IN OUR SOCIETAL MESSAGING! THEY DON'T HAVE TO LIVE LIKE THIS!
BUT HOW CAN I TELL THEM THEY DON'T HAVE TO LIVE LIKE THIS IF I'M LIVING LIKE THIS AND NOT DOING ANYTHING ABOUT IT? HOW CAN I LEAD BY EXAMPLE IF I'M STUCK IN THE SAME SITUATION?
EVERYONE KEEPS ASKING ME WHAT TO DO, BUT I DON'T HAVE THE ANSWERS! EXCEPT THAT I CAN'T LIVE LIKE THIS ANYMORE.
SO . . . I GUESS I'M GOING TO START TAKING BABY STEPS AND SHARING WHAT THAT LOOKS LIKE. AND I'LL AMPLIFY OTHER MOMS WHO ARE ON THIS SAME JOURNEY. AND I'LL MAKE COMICS ABOUT THE INEQUALITY TO RAISE AWARENESS AND BECAUSE IT MAKES ME FEEL LESS ALONE.

Let me be clear: Gaining a large audience in less than a year was not all sunshine and rainbows. It came with A LOT of trolls. A lot of men who hate women. A lot of women who are uncomfortable with the messages I'm sharing. A lot of people who think I'm a "sad, angry, pathetic woman" who should just "get a divorce already."

People called me abusive. They called Ben a loser and a dud. And a divorce lawyer reached out to Ben via email because he assumed Ben was looking for a way out. Did all of this affect me? Of course it did. I second-guessed myself. I cried. I was anxious and scared.

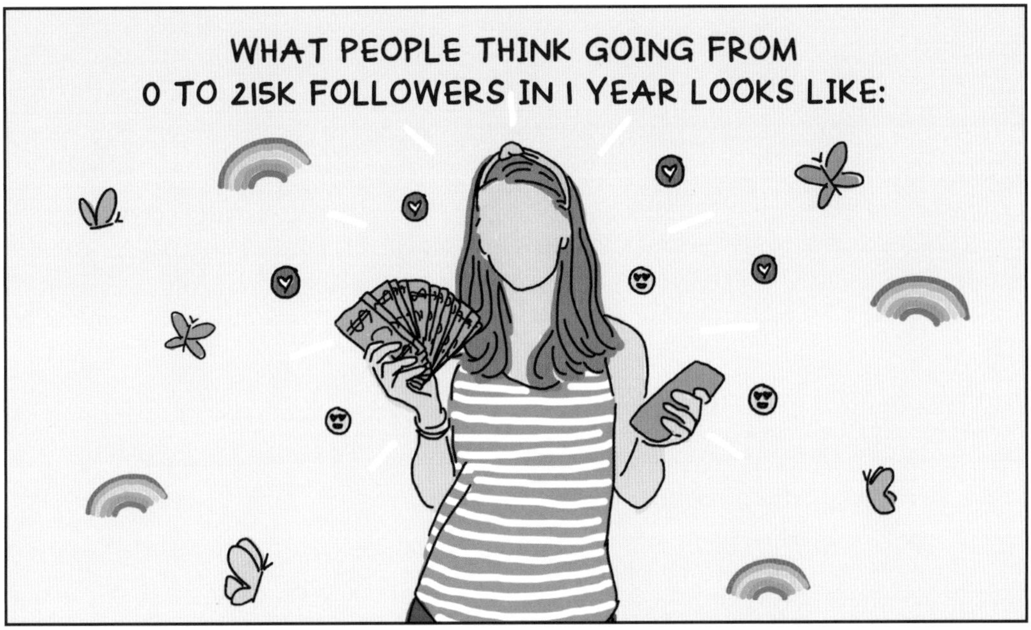
WHAT PEOPLE THINK GOING FROM
0 TO 215K FOLLOWERS IN 1 YEAR LOOKS LIKE:

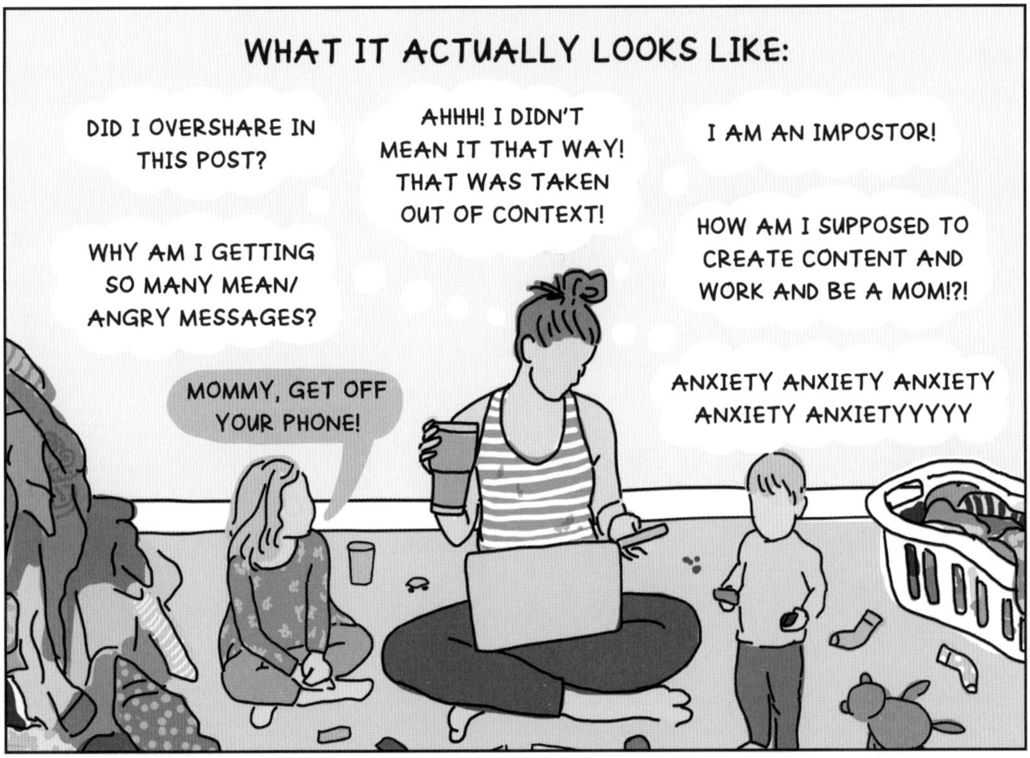
WHAT IT ACTUALLY LOOKS LIKE:
DID I OVERSHARE IN THIS POST?
AHHH! I DIDN'T MEAN IT THAT WAY! THAT WAS TAKEN OUT OF CONTEXT!
I AM AN IMPOSTOR!
WHY AM I GETTING SO MANY MEAN/ ANGRY MESSAGES?
HOW AM I SUPPOSED TO CREATE CONTENT AND WORK AND BE A MOM!?!
MOMMY, GET OFF YOUR PHONE!
ANXIETY ANXIETY ANXIETY ANXIETY ANXIETYYYYY

But more than anything, all of this made me want to keep going. It made me want to keep making comics, keep speaking up for moms (and women). And most importantly, all of this made me want to get help, make a change, and work on my marriage and the inequality in our household. I wanted to find a new path and a way out of this messed-up dynamic.

So that's what I started to do.

MUCH, MUCH, MUCH HARDER
THAN IT SOUNDS.

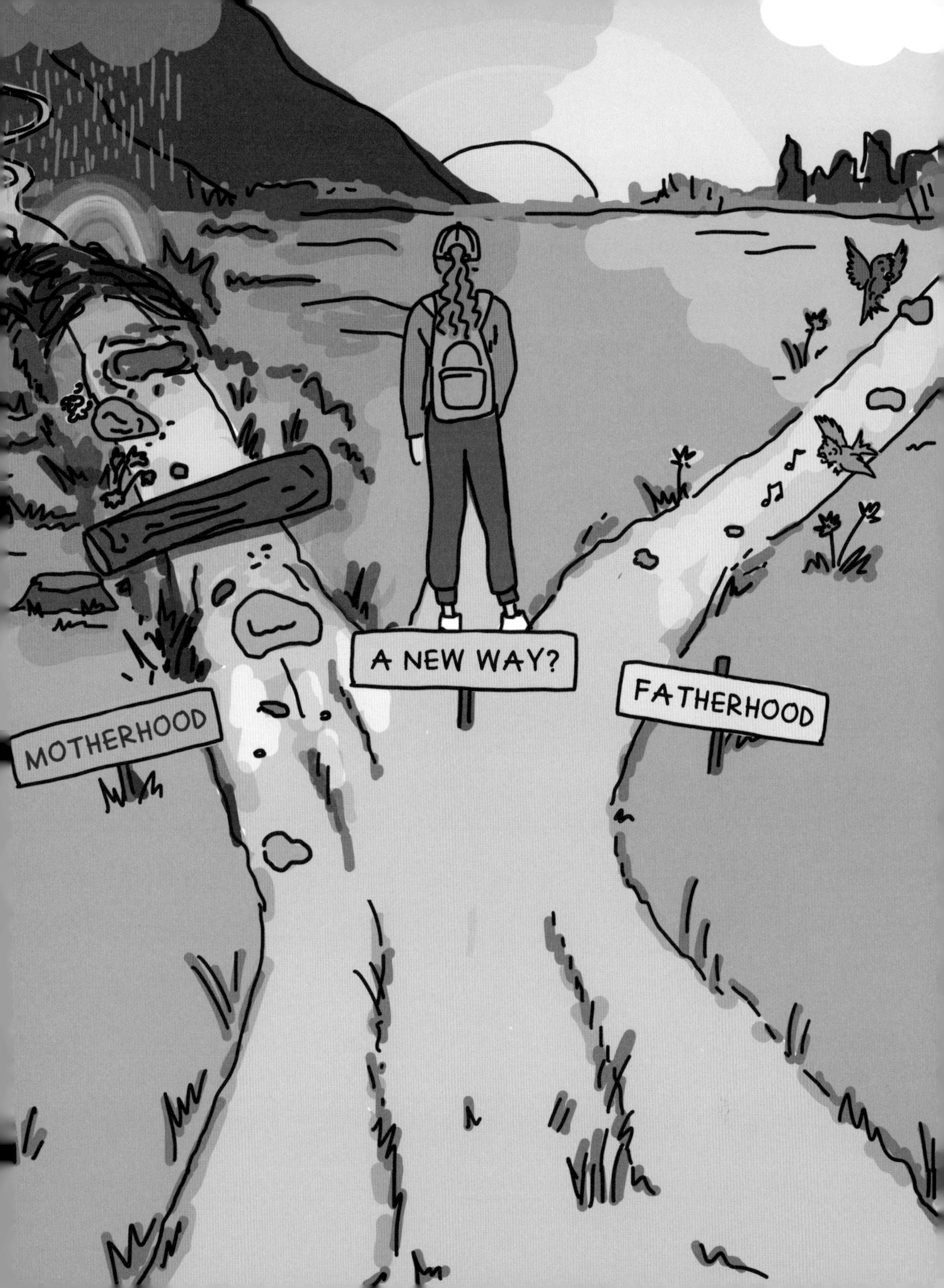
A NEW WAY?
MOTHERHOOD
FATHERHOOD

# Please Go to Bed.

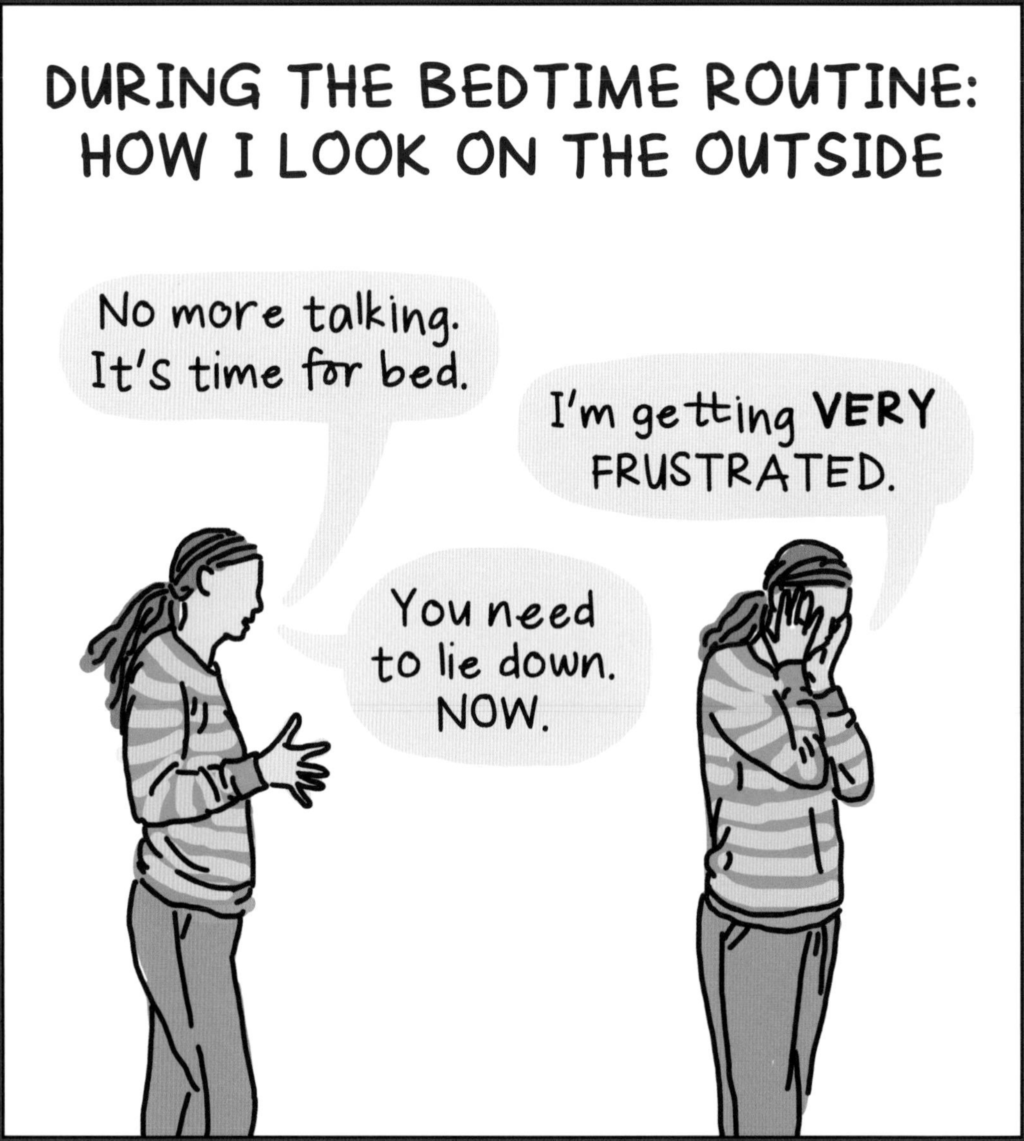
DURING THE BEDTIME ROUTINE: HOW I LOOK ON THE OUTSIDE
No more talking. It's time for bed.
You need to lie down. NOW.
I'm getting VERY FRUSTRATED.

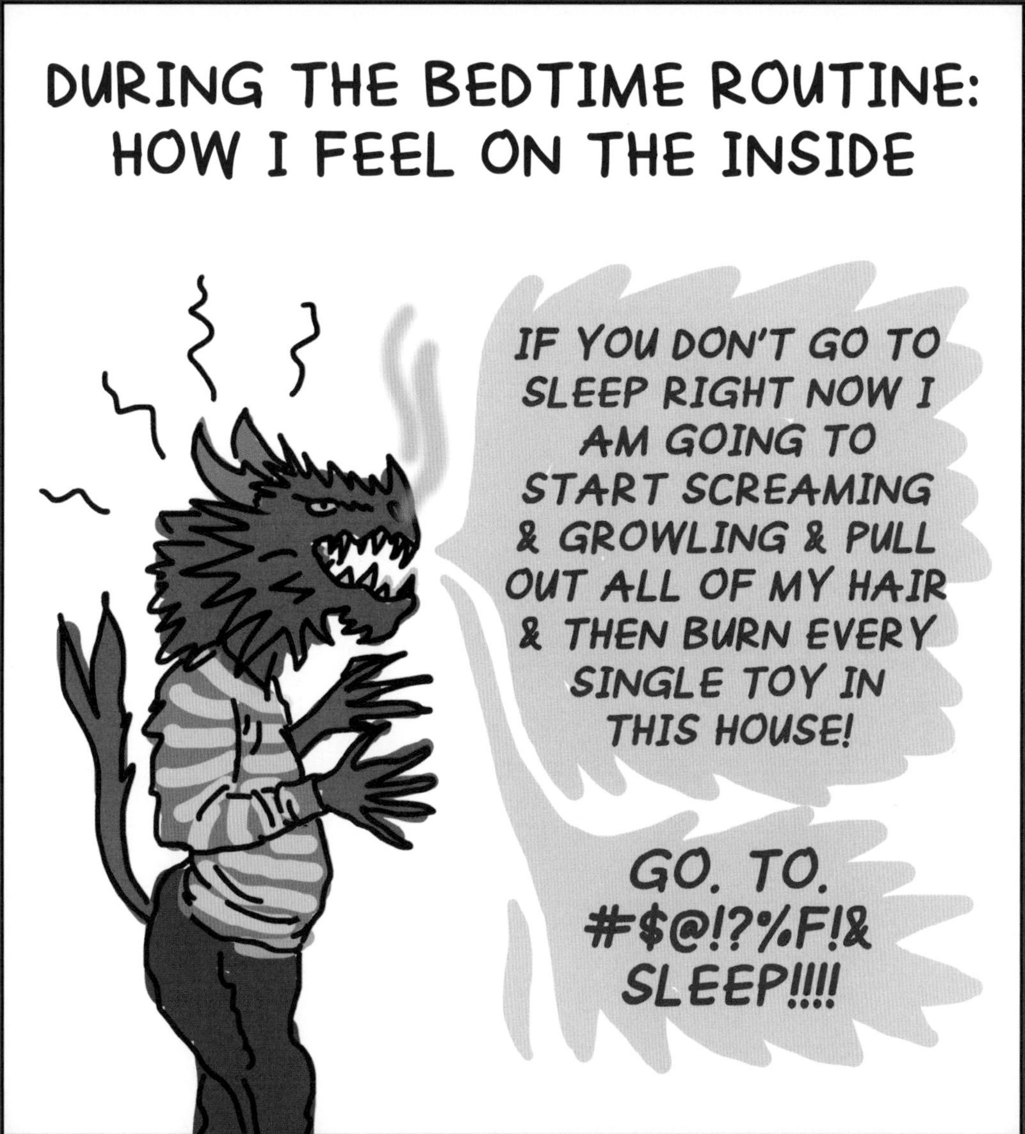
DURING THE BEDTIME ROUTINE: HOW I FEEL ON THE INSIDE
IF YOU DON'T GO TO SLEEP RIGHT NOW I AM GOING TO START SCREAMING & GROWLING & PULL OUT ALL OF MY HAIR & THEN BURN EVERY SINGLE TOY IN THIS HOUSE!
GO. TO. #$@!?%F!& SLEEP!!!!

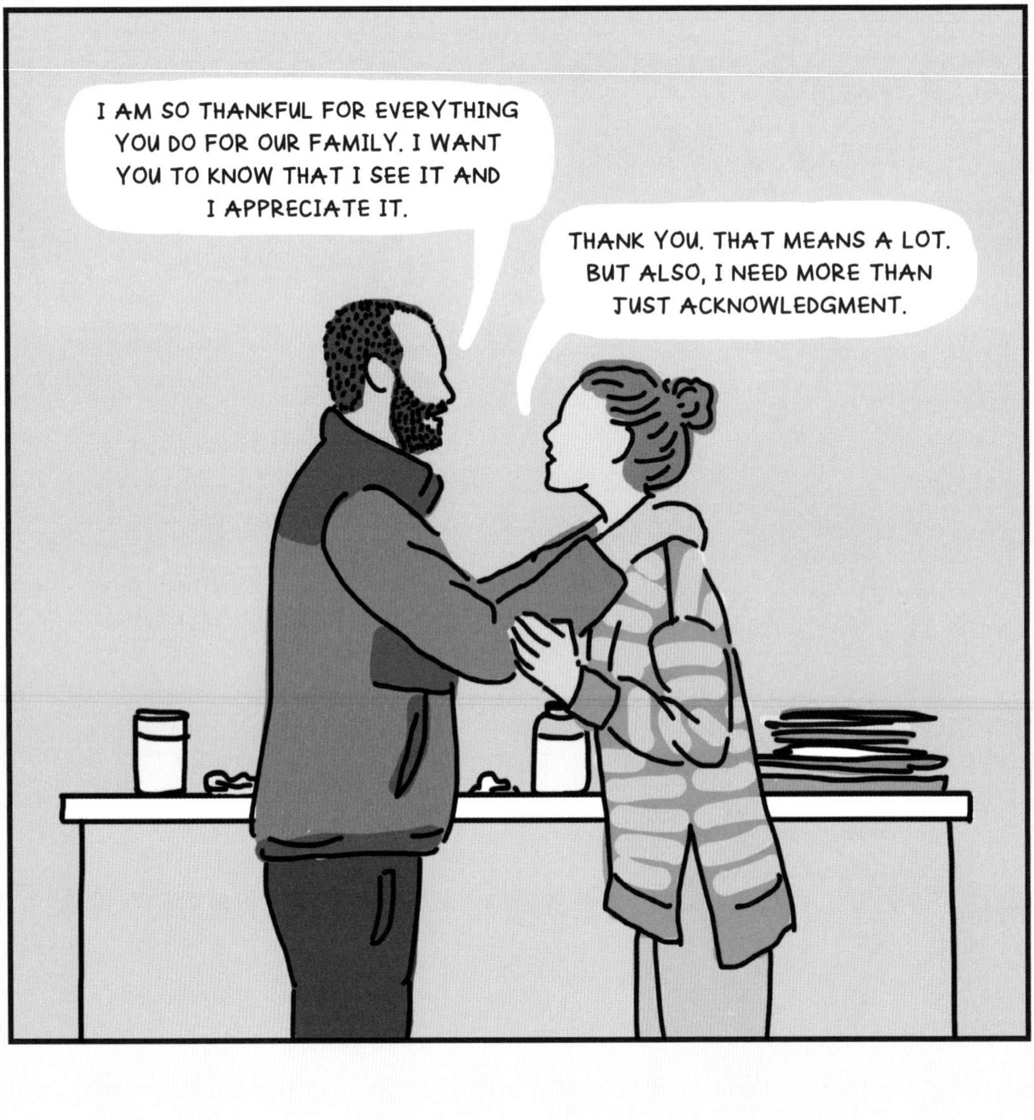
I AM SO THANKFUL FOR EVERYTHING YOU DO FOR OUR FAMILY. I WANT YOU TO KNOW THAT I SEE IT AND I APPRECIATE IT.
THANK YOU. THAT MEANS A LOT. BUT ALSO, I NEED MORE THAN JUST ACKNOWLEDGMENT.

# CHAPTER 8

# It's Time to Get Help. But Where Do We Even Begin?

As I hope you know by now, this is not a how-to or self-help book that will leave you with a tidy step-by-step approach to fixing all of the inequalities, dynamics, and challenges that I've introduced in these pages (and personally experienced).

I do not have the answers. I am not on the other side, living in an egalitarian relationship with a husband who shares 50 percent of the household labor and mental load of parenting. I lost it on Ben just this morning for leaving the clean, washed Tupperware ON THE COUNTER RIGHT ABOVE THE CABINET WHERE IT GOES.

TUPPERWARE
CABINET

But I have experienced some big successes in changing some of these dynamics over the past few years, and I think these successes are worth sharing, because even though they might look small on the outside, they've been pretty big (on the inside) for me.

The other thing I must note here is that in addition to being very conscientious about making changes in my life and relationship, time has passed and our kids are getting older (as they do). When I started writing this book, they had just turned three and six, and now they're four and seven, which means that parenting them is getting easier—and that at least some of the challenges we experienced in those intense early years (the ones that created so many of our longer-term imbalances) are slowly becoming less intense or disappearing altogether.

That being said, here are some of the changes I've made in the years since reaching my "breaking point" that have seriously affected my quality of life . . .

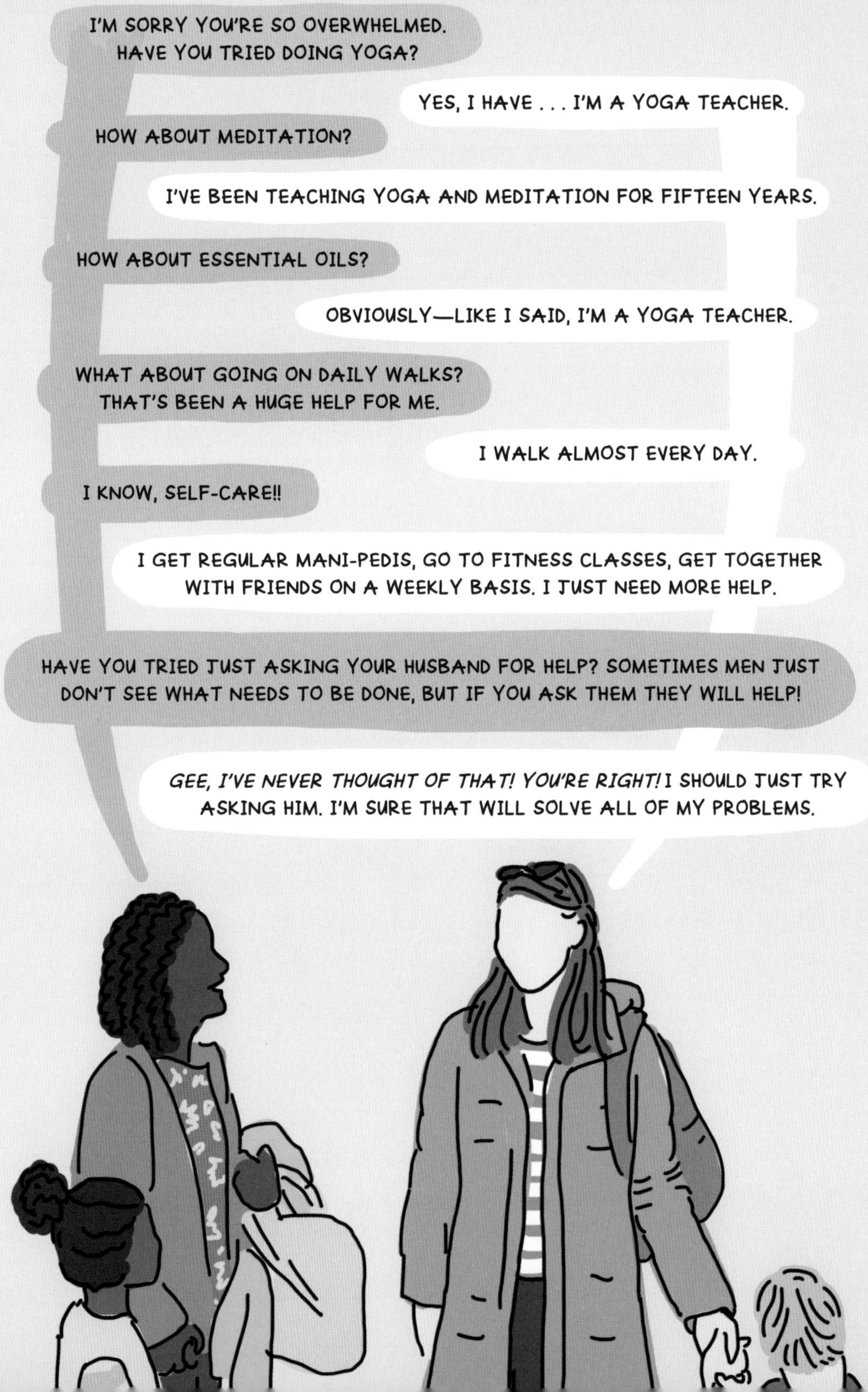
I'M SORRY YOU'RE SO OVERWHELMED. HAVE YOU TRIED DOING YOGA?
YES, I HAVE . . . I'M A YOGA TEACHER.
HOW ABOUT MEDITATION?
I'VE BEEN TEACHING YOGA AND MEDITATION FOR FIFTEEN YEARS.
HOW ABOUT ESSENTIAL OILS?
OBVIOUSLY—LIKE I SAID, I'M A YOGA TEACHER.
WHAT ABOUT GOING ON DAILY WALKS? THAT'S BEEN A HUGE HELP FOR ME.
I WALK ALMOST EVERY DAY.
I KNOW, SELF-CARE!!
I GET REGULAR MANI-PEDIS, GO TO FITNESS CLASSES, GET TOGETHER WITH FRIENDS ON A WEEKLY BASIS. I JUST NEED MORE HELP.
HAVE YOU TRIED JUST ASKING YOUR HUSBAND FOR HELP? SOMETIMES MEN JUST DON'T SEE WHAT NEEDS TO BE DONE, BUT IF YOU ASK THEM THEY WILL HELP!
*GEE, I'VE NEVER THOUGHT OF THAT! YOU'RE RIGHT!* I SHOULD JUST TRY ASKING HIM. I'M SURE THAT WILL SOLVE ALL OF MY PROBLEMS.

# All of the Therapy (With a Side of Meds)

During the pandemic, I finally got back into individual therapy, which I hadn't done since before Teddy's birth. I started seeing a new therapist online, and right away, she identified something she thought might help . . .

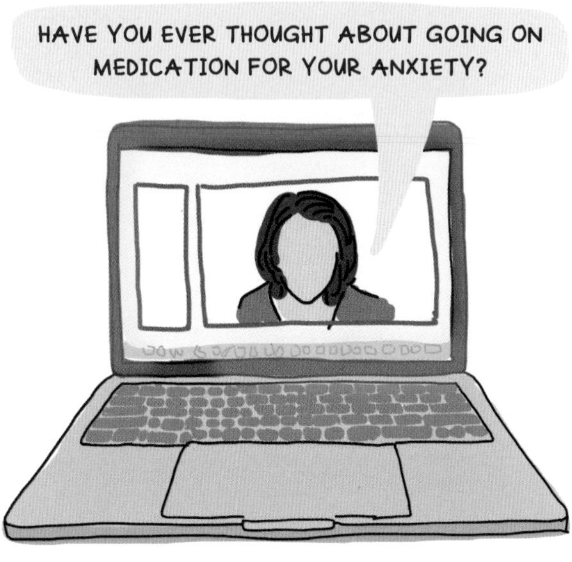
HAVE YOU EVER THOUGHT ABOUT GOING ON MEDICATION FOR YOUR ANXIETY?

(MY THERAPIST)

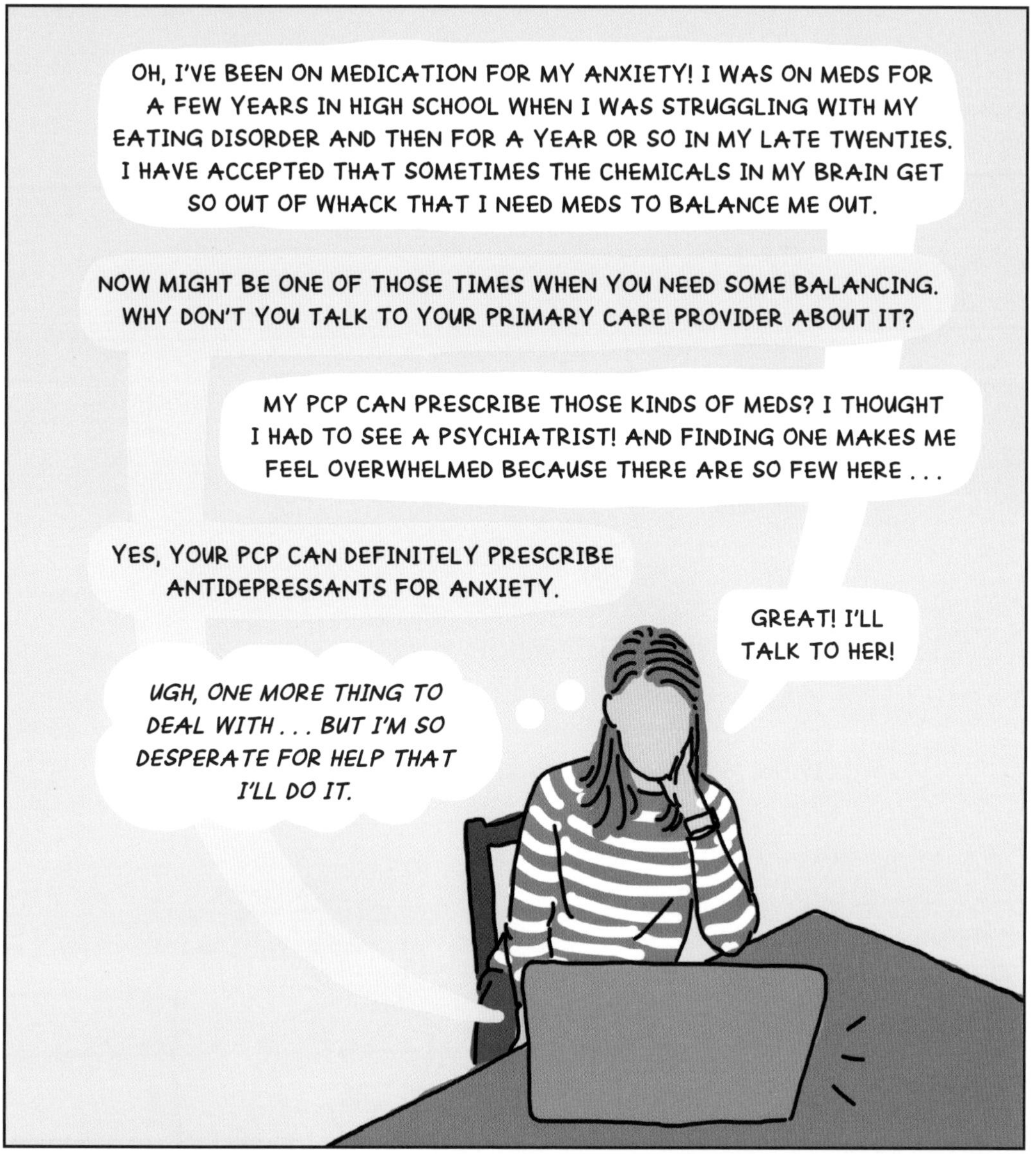
OH, I'VE BEEN ON MEDICATION FOR MY ANXIETY! I WAS ON MEDS FOR A FEW YEARS IN HIGH SCHOOL WHEN I WAS STRUGGLING WITH MY EATING DISORDER AND THEN FOR A YEAR OR SO IN MY LATE TWENTIES. I HAVE ACCEPTED THAT SOMETIMES THE CHEMICALS IN MY BRAIN GET SO OUT OF WHACK THAT I NEED MEDS TO BALANCE ME OUT.
NOW MIGHT BE ONE OF THOSE TIMES WHEN YOU NEED SOME BALANCING. WHY DON'T YOU TALK TO YOUR PRIMARY CARE PROVIDER ABOUT IT?
MY PCP CAN PRESCRIBE THOSE KINDS OF MEDS? I THOUGHT I HAD TO SEE A PSYCHIATRIST! AND FINDING ONE MAKES ME FEEL OVERWHELMED BECAUSE THERE ARE SO FEW HERE . . .
YES, YOUR PCP CAN DEFINITELY PRESCRIBE ANTIDEPRESSANTS FOR ANXIETY.
GREAT! I'LL TALK TO HER!
*UGH, ONE MORE THING TO DEAL WITH . . . BUT I'M SO DESPERATE FOR HELP THAT I'LL DO IT.*

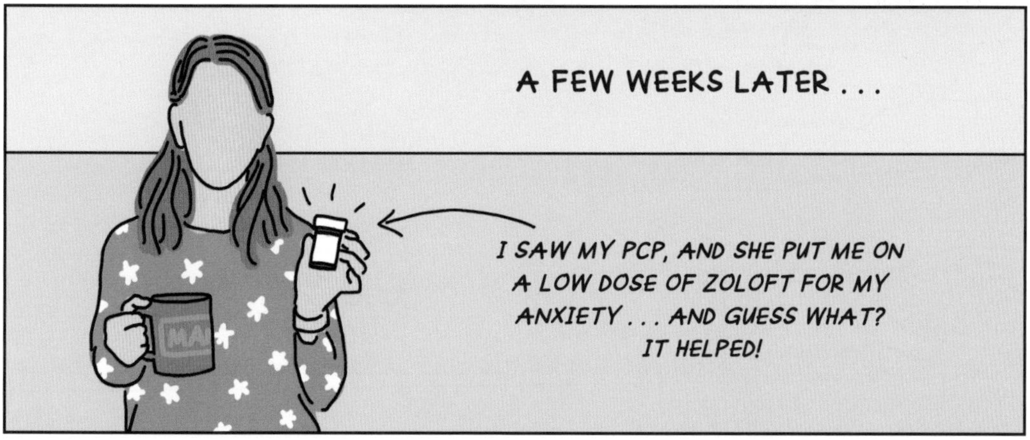
A FEW WEEKS LATER . . .
*I SAW MY PCP, AND SHE PUT ME ON A LOW DOSE OF ZOLOFT FOR MY ANXIETY . . . AND GUESS WHAT? IT HELPED!*

I am a huge believer in therapy. My dad is a therapist. My late stepmom was a therapist. My mom has gone to therapy my entire life, and I have gone to therapy on and off since I was fourteen. Ben, however, has only gone to individual therapy a handful of times in his entire life—and it was at my urging.

But about a year and a half into the pandemic—at my insistence because I was losing it—we started couples therapy.

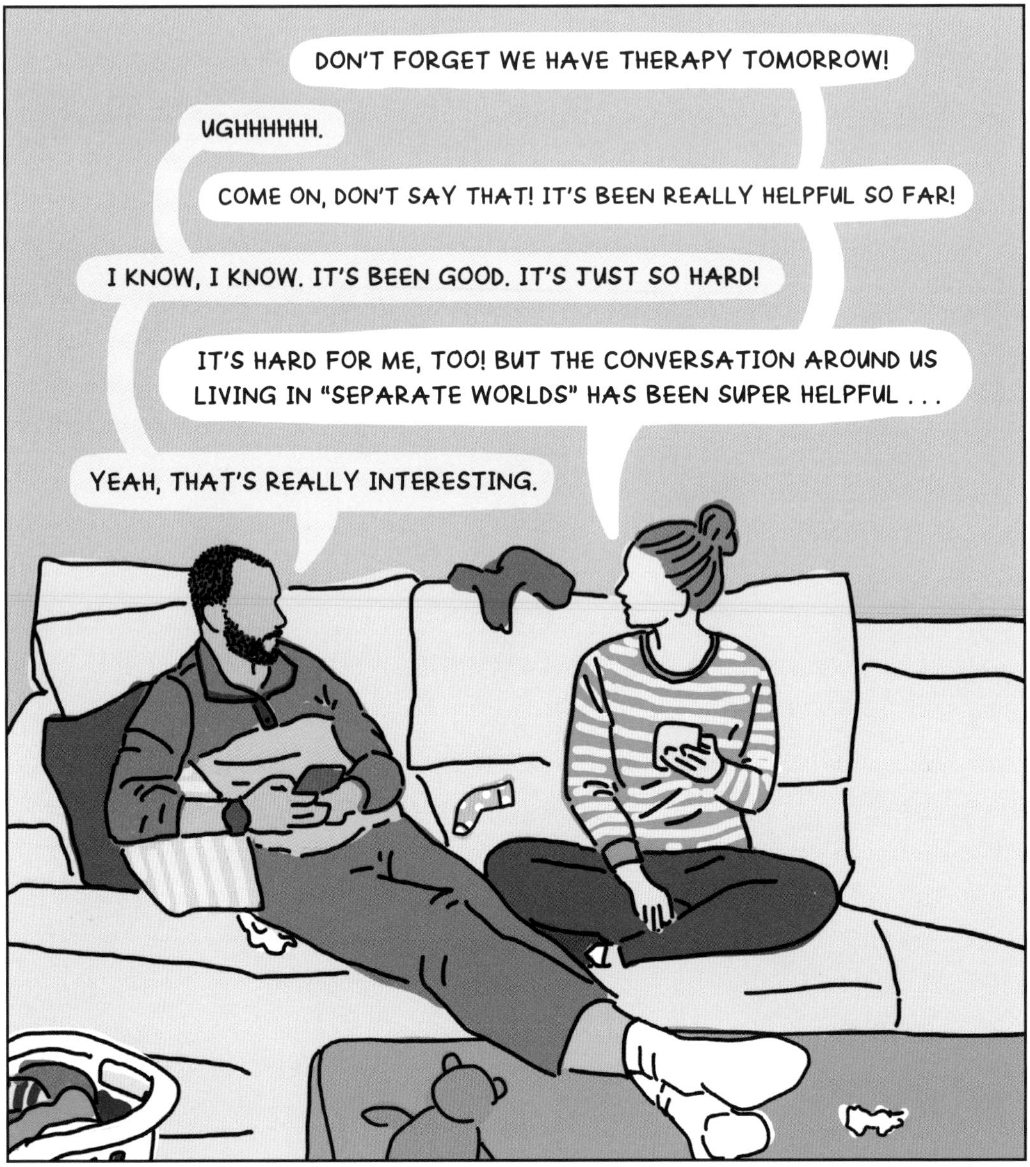
DON'T FORGET WE HAVE THERAPY TOMORROW!
UGHHHHHH.
COME ON, DON'T SAY THAT! IT'S BEEN REALLY HELPFUL SO FAR!
I KNOW, I KNOW. IT'S BEEN GOOD. IT'S JUST SO HARD!
IT'S HARD FOR ME, TOO! BUT THE CONVERSATION AROUND US LIVING IN "SEPARATE WORLDS" HAS BEEN SUPER HELPFUL . . .
YEAH, THAT'S REALLY INTERESTING.

# What We've Learned in Therapy about Our Separate Worlds

BEN LIVES IN THIS WORLD. HIS WORLD IS MADE UP OF HIS THOUGHTS, HIS LIFE HISTORY, HIS CHILDHOOD, HIS EXPERIENCES, AND HIS WORLDVIEW. IT HAS BEEN MOLDED BY THE STORIES HE TELLS HIMSELF ABOUT HIS LIFE AND HIS BRAIN AND HIS PERSPECTIVE.

I LIVE IN THIS WORLD. I'VE CREATED THIS WORLD BASED ON MY HISTORY, MY LIFE EXPERIENCES, AND MY WORLDVIEW. IT'S COLORED BY THE STORIES I TELL MYSELF ABOUT MY LIFE AND BY MY BRAIN AND MY PERSPECTIVE.

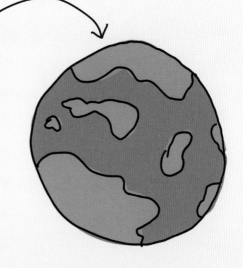

THIS IS OUR MARRIAGE/RELATIONSHIP. IT IS ANOTHER SEPARATE WORLD THAT WE HAVE CREATED TOGETHER—IT HAS BEEN WOVEN TOGETHER FROM PARTS OF EACH OF OUR WORLDS, THE THINGS WE HAVE GONE THROUGH TOGETHER, THE WAYS IN WHICH WE HAVE LEARNED TO RELY ON EACH OTHER OR NOT RELY ON EACH OTHER, AND THE DYNAMICS AND PATTERNS WE HAVE CREATED TOGETHER. IN ORDER TO MAKE OUR WORLD HEALTHIER AND HAPPIER, WE NEED TO UNDERSTAND EACH OTHER'S WORLD.

The "Two Distinct Worlds" concept comes from Imago Relationship Therapy, created by Dr. Harville Hendrix and Dr. Helen LaKelly Hunt in 1980.

BEN'S WORLD
MY WORLD
(I'm on this plane!
Or should be!)

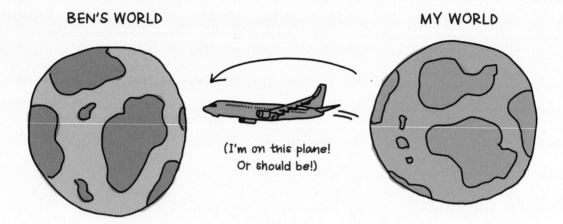

IF I WANT TO UNDERSTAND BEN'S WORLD, I NEED TO GO THERE AND BE CURIOUS ABOUT WHAT IT'S LIKE. I CAN'T GO INTO HIS WORLD AND CHANGE IT—I DID NOT CREATE IT! BUT IF I LOOK, LISTEN, OBSERVE, AND TRY TO UNDERSTAND THE CULTURE OF HIS WORLD, I CAN BETTER UNDERSTAND HIM AS A PERSON WHEN HE'S IN OUR NEW WORLD TOGETHER.

BEN'S WORLD
MY WORLD
(Ben is on this plane!
I may have forced him
to go, but he's going!)

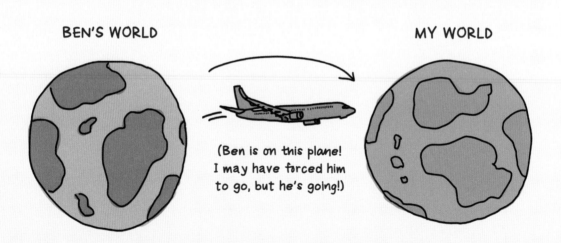

IN ORDER TO UNDERSTAND ME AND WHY I AM THE WAY THAT I AM WHEN I'M IN OUR WORLD TOGETHER, BEN HAS TO COME VISIT MY WORLD AND GET TO KNOW ME AND MY CULTURE, TOO.

I have never been to Indonesia. If I met someone from Indonesia and they told me what Indonesia is like, I could listen and get a general understanding of their country, but I wouldn't really know what it was like to go there. If this person acted a certain way, I might assume it was just a part of their personality when in reality, it could be a cultural behavior—it could be something this person learned when growing up in a country very different from mine.

Visiting Indonesia can at least help me begin to understand the reason that the Indonesian person acts the way she does—and it will help me connect with her in a deeper way, now that I know what she is referring to when she speaks of Indonesian culture.

So now, through therapy, Ben and I take turns visiting each other's worlds and learning about our different cultures and histories. Then we return to our world together, a little more informed and with a little more understanding and compassion, which helps us communicate more lovingly and ask for what we need (and appreciate it when our partner gives it to us!).

The world we share isn't all sunshine, good communication, and equality. We've been known to snap at each other about household annoyances right after a deep therapy session. We haven't solved our laundry issues, and Ben is still leaving the empty TP roll out for someone else to deal with (AGHHH!), but we're working on it.

And we love each other. Right now, that's enough for me.

*One more therapy note that I just have to share here: A well-known relationship expert and couples therapist, psychologist Terry Real, has coined a therapy term that I think about all the time: "normal marital hatred." Real says that anyone who is married knows exactly what he's talking about when he uses this phrase. He also says that "the hardest thing in the world is another person." I wholeheartedly agree on both counts.

# Getting the Hell Out of Dodge

Another small change I've made is to leave the house without my family a lot more. Before I started making a conscious effort to do this, I hardly left except to teach yoga, work out, or run an errand (remember, I work from home!).

When we had only Charlie Mae, leaving the house was hard: *She didn't take a bottle! She wanted me! It was so tough for Ben! I felt guilty!* So I just didn't leave much.

Then we had Teddy, and it got more intense. Then the pandemic hit, and to top it all off, we didn't have any non-family babysitters and we only called on our family babysitters when absolutely necessary (usually for work or a once-in-a-blue-moon day date).

But you know what? You won't be surprised to learn that never leaving—never getting a break from being a mom and wife—was making me a "worser" (to quote my son) mom and wife.

So I started slowly and began leaving the house more—or rather, forcing myself to leave the house more. When I was invited somewhere, instead of going with my usual, knee-jerk "Oh, I can't," I started saying:

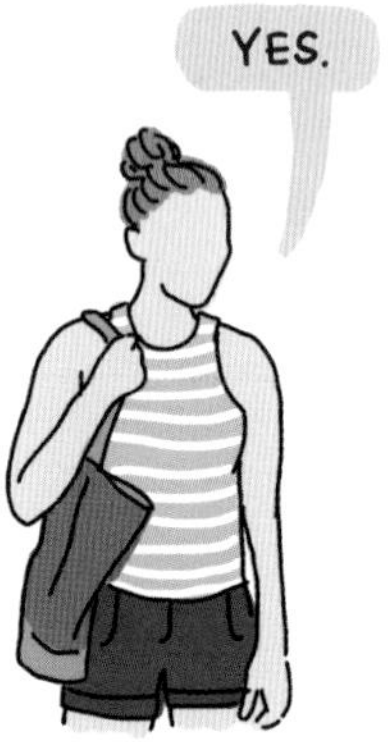
YES.

Saying yes changed everything.

Now, on a regular basis, I go out on walks alone, I do things with my friends, I lead yoga retreats, I go on trips, and I go to fitness classes.

Not only does leaving give me a break, but also it's a great chance for Ben to experience being the default parent and for the kids to get more used to having him do things for them.

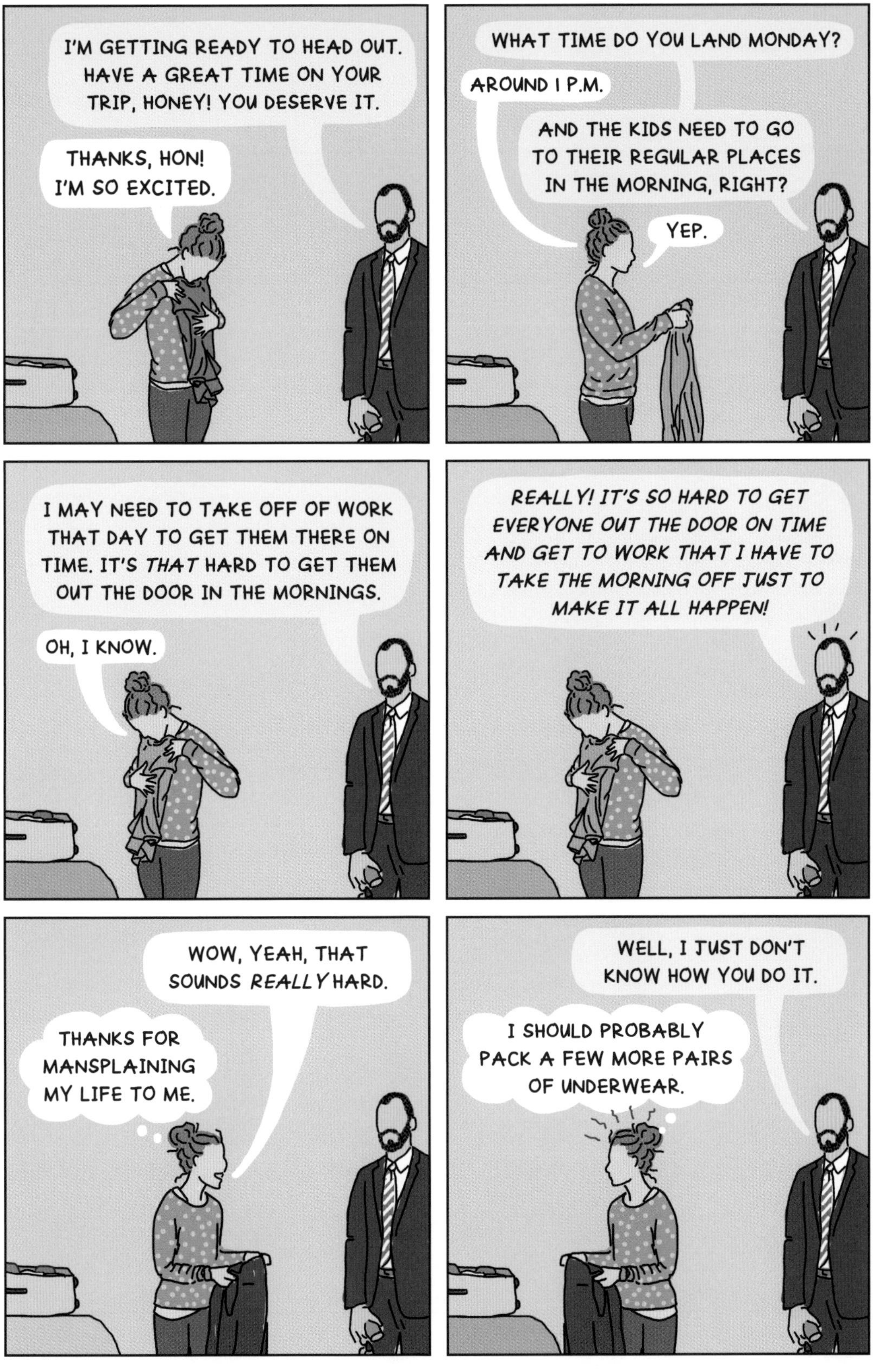
I'M GETTING READY TO HEAD OUT. HAVE A GREAT TIME ON YOUR TRIP, HONEY! YOU DESERVE IT.
THANKS, HON! I'M SO EXCITED.
WHAT TIME DO YOU LAND MONDAY?
AROUND 1 P.M.
AND THE KIDS NEED TO GO TO THEIR REGULAR PLACES IN THE MORNING, RIGHT?
YEP.
I MAY NEED TO TAKE OFF OF WORK THAT DAY TO GET THEM THERE ON TIME. IT'S *THAT* HARD TO GET THEM OUT THE DOOR IN THE MORNINGS.
OH, I KNOW.
*REALLY! IT'S SO HARD TO GET EVERYONE OUT THE DOOR ON TIME AND GET TO WORK THAT I HAVE TO TAKE THE MORNING OFF JUST TO MAKE IT ALL HAPPEN!*
WOW, YEAH, THAT SOUNDS *REALLY* HARD.
THANKS FOR MANSPLAINING MY LIFE TO ME.
WELL, I JUST DON'T KNOW HOW YOU DO IT.
I SHOULD PROBABLY PACK A FEW MORE PAIRS OF UNDERWEAR.

# Hello, Would You Like to Be a Part of My Village?

Despite living near Ben's side of the family (who are all very wonderful and very helpful), we didn't have much of a village in our early days of parenting. There are many reasons for this, but a big part of this goes back to the fact that Charlie Mae struggled with anyone but me for such a long time that it created a situation where I was nervous about leaving her with others. Now, though? Seven years later? We've got the makings of a very small village.

How did we find babysitters? The way that everyone said we would: through word of mouth. By asking around. Through sheer luck. But again, it took seven years. And that's not okay.

If you're a newer parent, or a mom who finds yourself feeling village-less, I know how hard it can be to find a few babysitters you can trust, but I pinky promise you will be SO glad you put in the effort once you're comfortable with them.

Babysitters have changed my life in so many ways (shout-out to the INCREDIBLE babysitter-turned-friend, Courtney, who enabled me to keep working during the pandemic).

I am saying this as someone who thought I could never leave my children with a babysitter because it was just too hard and my kids couldn't handle it . . . But they can handle it, and now that they're older, they love babysitters.

SPEAKING OF BABYSITTERS, I MUST MAKE A VERY IMPORTANT DISTINCTION HERE: DADS ARE NOT BABYSITTERS.

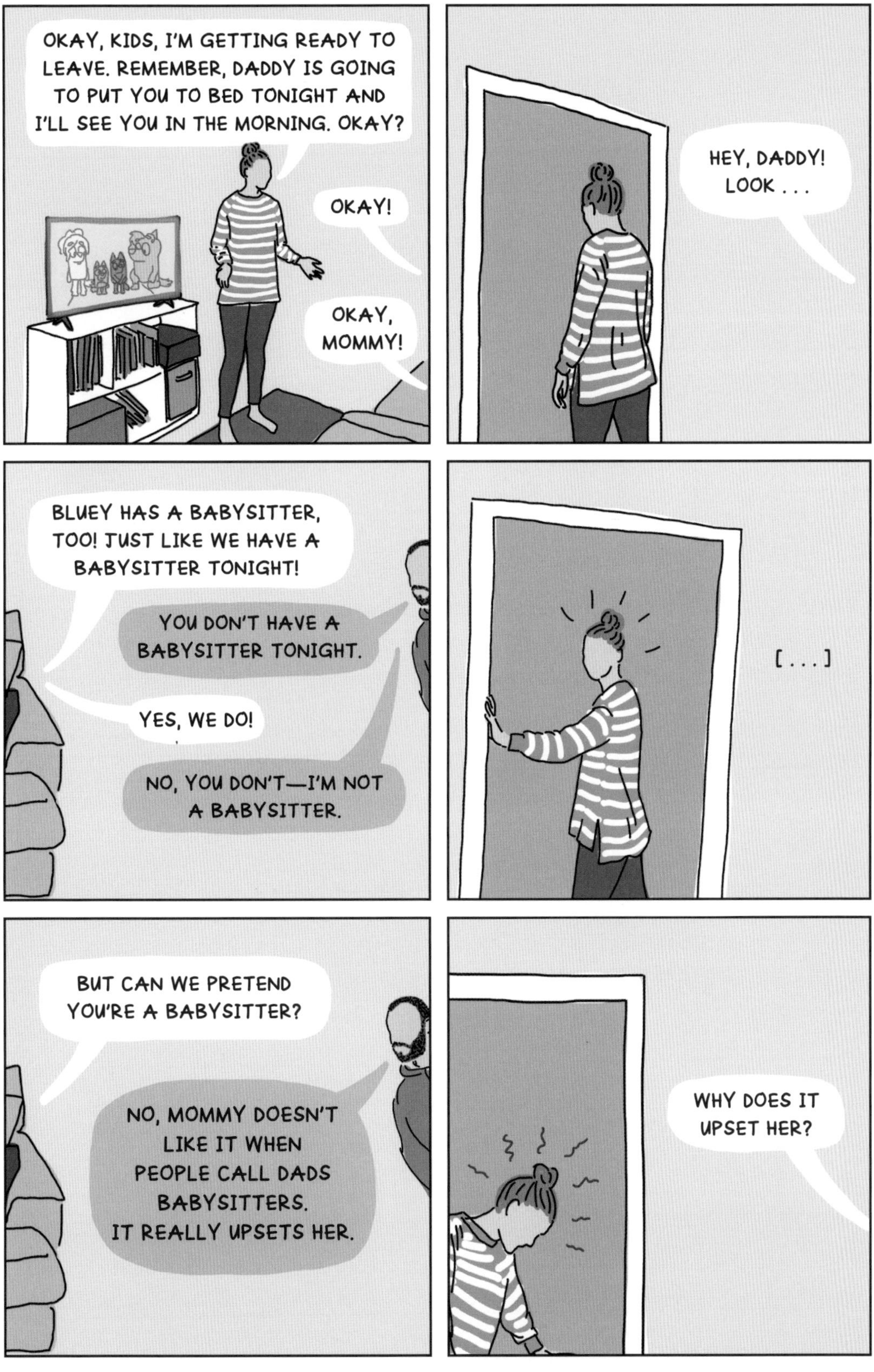
OKAY, KIDS, I'M GETTING READY TO LEAVE. REMEMBER, DADDY IS GOING TO PUT YOU TO BED TONIGHT AND I'LL SEE YOU IN THE MORNING. OKAY?
OKAY!
OKAY, MOMMY!
HEY, DADDY! LOOK . . .
BLUEY HAS A BABYSITTER, TOO! JUST LIKE WE HAVE A BABYSITTER TONIGHT!
YOU DON'T HAVE A BABYSITTER TONIGHT.
YES, WE DO!
NO, YOU DON'T—I'M NOT A BABYSITTER.
[. . .]
BUT CAN WE PRETEND YOU'RE A BABYSITTER?
NO, MOMMY DOESN'T LIKE IT WHEN PEOPLE CALL DADS BABYSITTERS.
IT REALLY UPSETS HER.
WHY DOES IT UPSET HER?

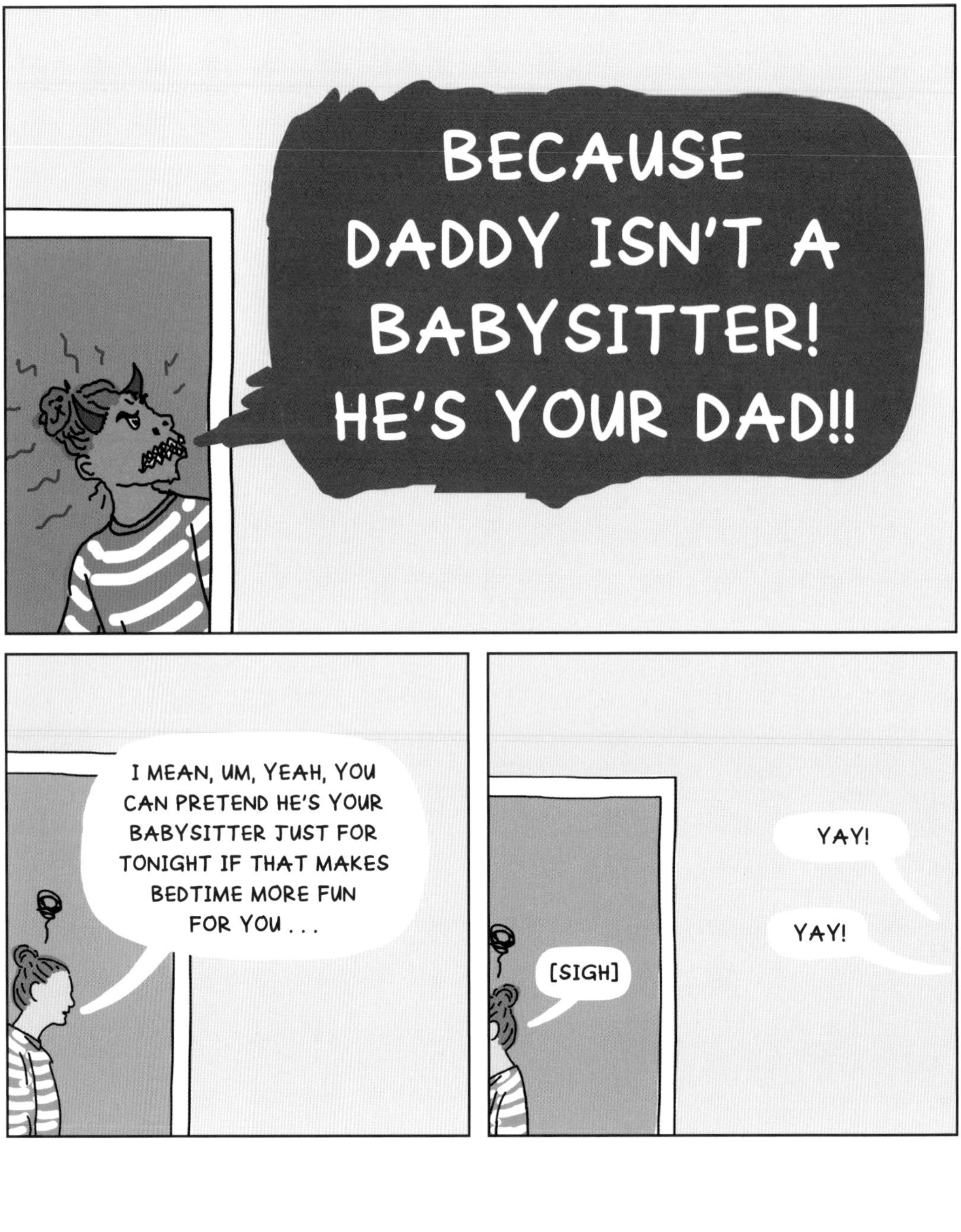

BECAUSE DADDY ISN'T A BABYSITTER! HE'S YOUR DAD!!
I MEAN, UM, YEAH, YOU CAN PRETEND HE'S YOUR BABYSITTER JUST FOR TONIGHT IF THAT MAKES BEDTIME MORE FUN FOR YOU . . .
YAY!
YAY!
[SIGH]

# Mom Friends

Local mom friends have been another game-changer for me, but it took me a long time to make them.

In all honesty, I always thought I would make them easily once I became a mom. But I didn't! My perfect storm of anxiety, overwhelm, exhaustion, and desperation made me scared to put myself out there in any way.

My need to have Charlie Mae at home during naptime—sleeping (or trying to get her to sleep) in her own bed—made me stay home from a lot of baby groups that might have helped me make friends.

My slight social anxiety made me nervous to talk to "strangers" at the playground. In fact, it wasn't until Charlie Mae's second year of preschool that I really started to find and connect with my people—and that connection took WORK.

But now, I feel like a total social butterfly (inasmuch as an extroverted introvert can be a social butterfly). I have a few tight-knit groups of mom friends that I see regularly. We do dinner, wine and chocolate after bedtime, walks, and fitness classes together. We meet for playdates and to take our kids to the beach, to dinner (it's CHAOS), and to the movies (also chaos, *but with popcorn!*).

My mom friends—more than anything else—have made me feel less alone in parenting. If I could give any mother reading this only one piece of advice, it *might* be this: Do whatever you can to make at least one good, local mom friend with a child your child's age. It will save you.

(THIS MIGHT SOUND LIKE AN EXAGGERATION, BUT I AM DEAD SERIOUS.)

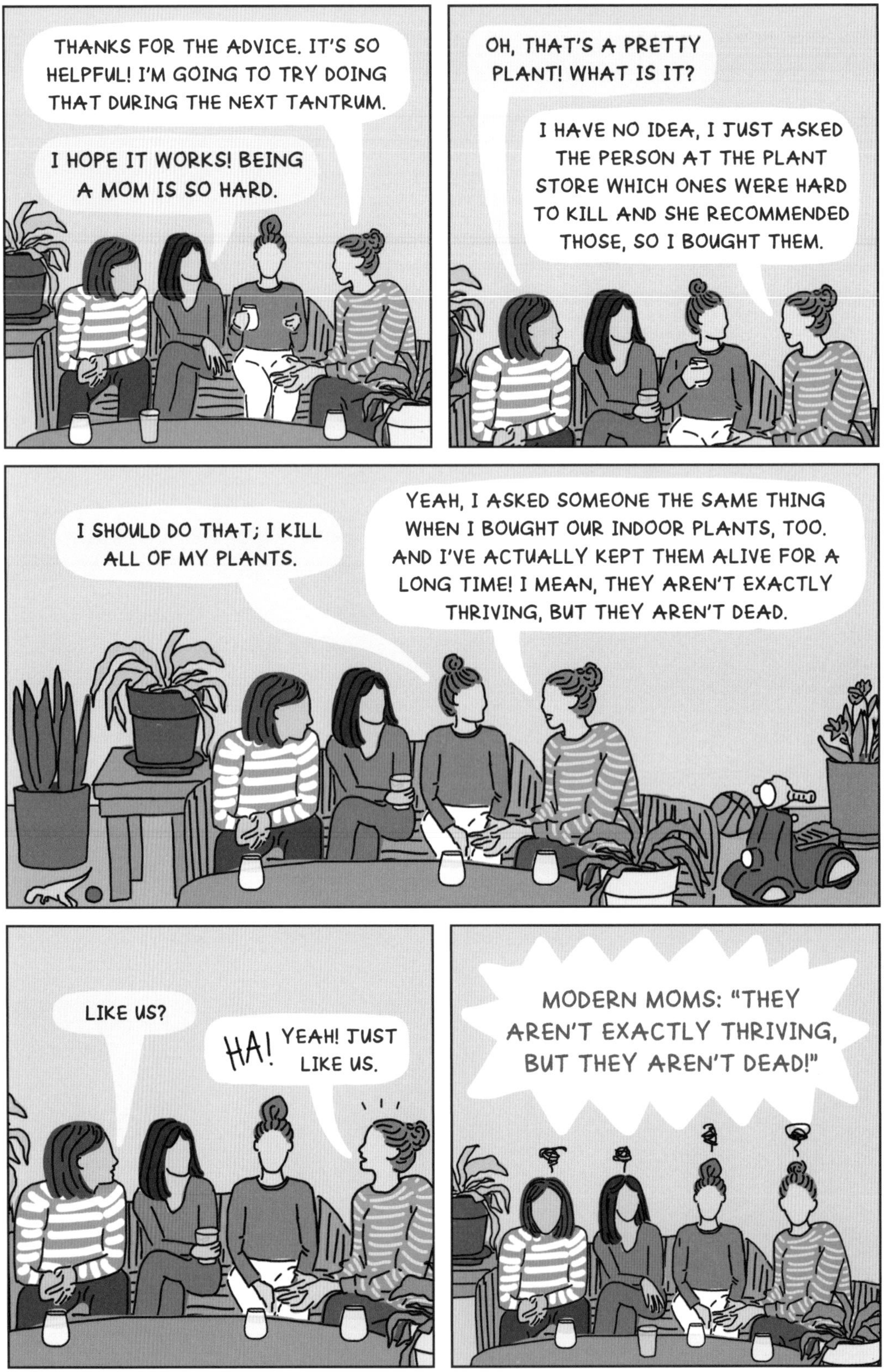
THANKS FOR THE ADVICE. IT'S SO HELPFUL! I'M GOING TO TRY DOING THAT DURING THE NEXT TANTRUM.
I HOPE IT WORKS! BEING A MOM IS SO HARD.
OH, THAT'S A PRETTY PLANT! WHAT IS IT?
I HAVE NO IDEA, I JUST ASKED THE PERSON AT THE PLANT STORE WHICH ONES WERE HARD TO KILL AND SHE RECOMMENDED THOSE, SO I BOUGHT THEM.
I SHOULD DO THAT; I KILL ALL OF MY PLANTS.
YEAH, I ASKED SOMEONE THE SAME THING WHEN I BOUGHT OUR INDOOR PLANTS, TOO. AND I'VE ACTUALLY KEPT THEM ALIVE FOR A LONG TIME! I MEAN, THEY AREN'T EXACTLY THRIVING, BUT THEY AREN'T DEAD.
LIKE US?
HA! YEAH! JUST LIKE US.
MODERN MOMS: "THEY AREN'T EXACTLY THRIVING, BUT THEY AREN'T DEAD!"

Here's the thing about mom friends: They get you in a way that other friends don't and can't. The more time that you spend with mom friends, the more they get to know your kids and your motherhood struggles and the more you get to know theirs. You can talk to mom friends about your kids without feeling like that boring friend who "only talks about her kids now that she's a mom."

Mom friends get it when you have to stop talking midsentence or interrupt them to talk to your kid or run after a toddler who is about to wander into oncoming traffic to retrieve a piece of trash. Every time that I spend time with a mom friend, I leave the interaction feeling much less alone in motherhood—even if that time together was mostly spent managing the chaos that is young children playing together (or next to each other, or fighting . . . ).

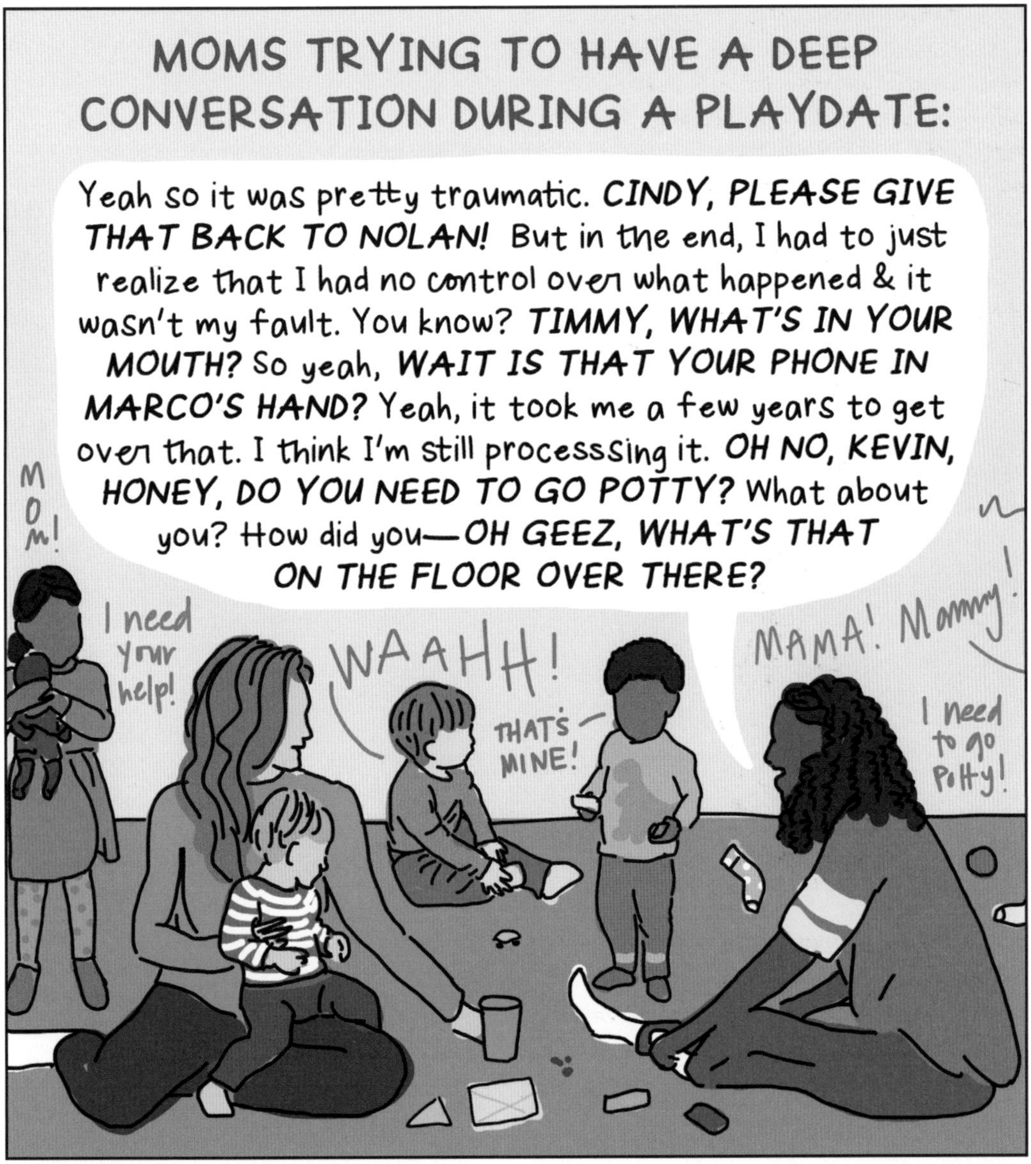
MOMS TRYING TO HAVE A DEEP CONVERSATION DURING A PLAYDATE:
Yeah so it was pretty traumatic. CINDY, PLEASE GIVE THAT BACK TO NOLAN! But in the end, I had to just realize that I had no control over what happened & it wasn't my fault. You know? TIMMY, WHAT'S IN YOUR MOUTH? So yeah, WAIT IS THAT YOUR PHONE IN MARCO'S HAND? Yeah, it took me a few years to get over that. I think I'm still processsing it. OH NO, KEVIN, HONEY, DO YOU NEED TO GO POTTY? What about you? How did you—OH GEEZ, WHAT'S THAT ON THE FLOOR OVER THERE?
MOM!
I need your help!
WAAHH!
THAT'S MINE!
MAMA! Mommy!
I need to go Potty!

# Outsource That Sh*t

Being able to outsource anything is a privilege and one that shouldn't be taken lightly. I am well aware of this. However, for many moms who might be able to outsource (from a financial standpoint), what's stopping them from actually hiring someone to clean the house or do their laundry is just plain guilt, a feeling of failure, or a sense of embarrassment about outsourcing a household task that they feel they "should" be doing.

But you know who doesn't seem to have this kind of guilt about outsourcing household tasks?

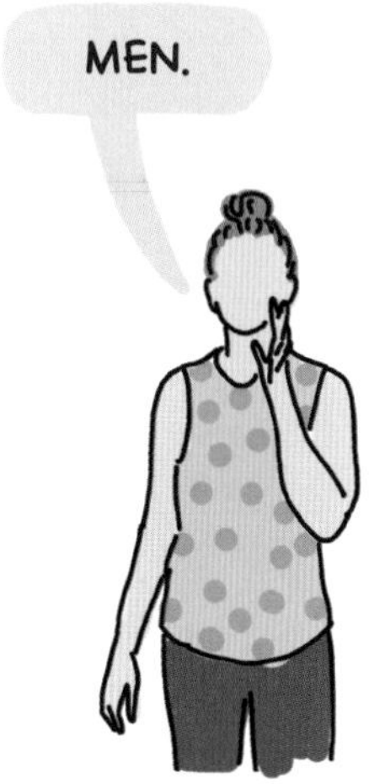
MEN.

And you know why? Because they don't see household tasks as theirs. Those tasks don't belong to them in the first place. So why would they feel guilty about outsourcing them?

# IF DADS SPOKE ABOUT OUTSOURCING THE WAY MOMS DO:

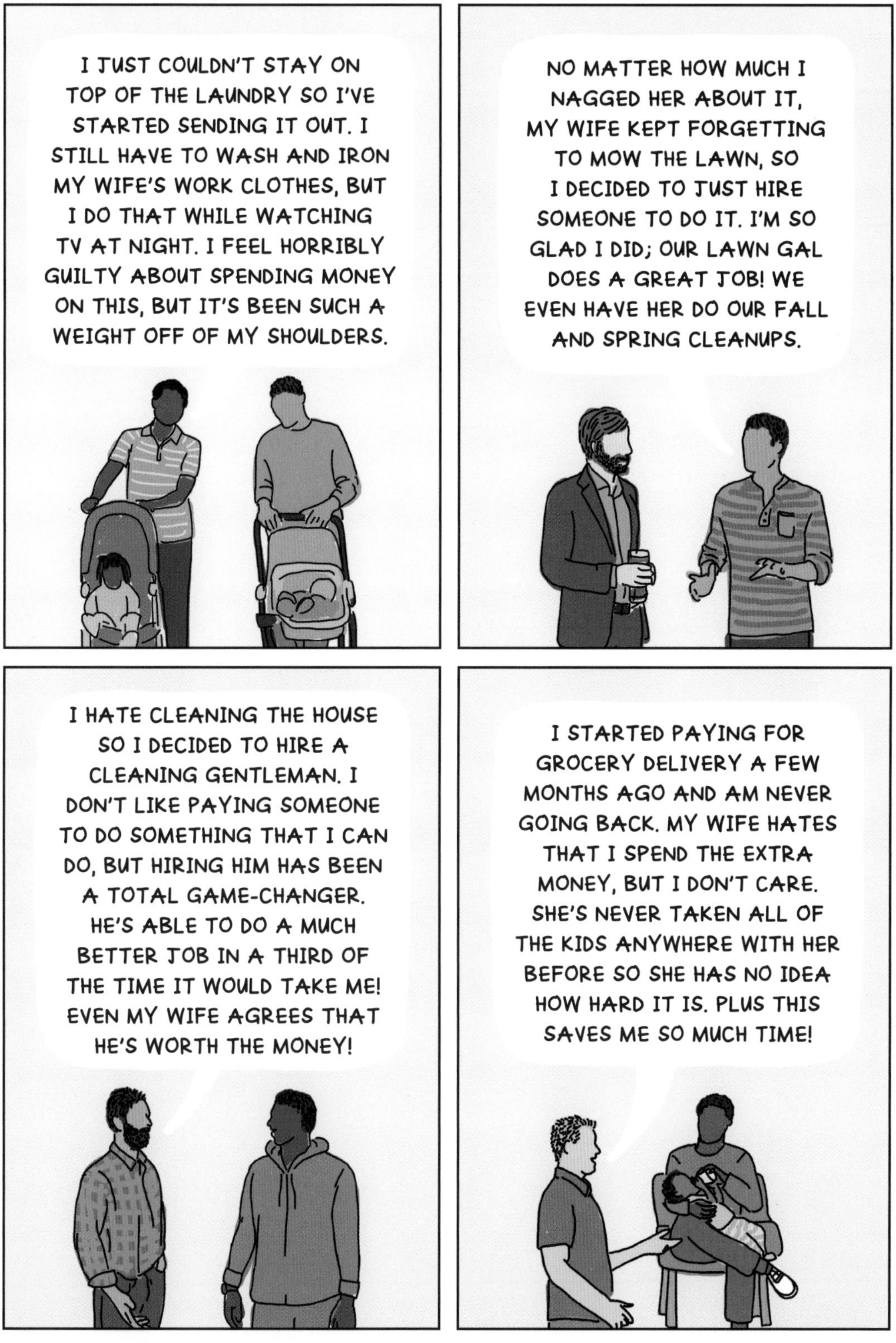
I JUST COULDN'T STAY ON TOP OF THE LAUNDRY SO I'VE STARTED SENDING IT OUT. I STILL HAVE TO WASH AND IRON MY WIFE'S WORK CLOTHES, BUT I DO THAT WHILE WATCHING TV AT NIGHT. I FEEL HORRIBLY GUILTY ABOUT SPENDING MONEY ON THIS, BUT IT'S BEEN SUCH A WEIGHT OFF OF MY SHOULDERS.
NO MATTER HOW MUCH I NAGGED HER ABOUT IT, MY WIFE KEPT FORGETTING TO MOW THE LAWN, SO I DECIDED TO JUST HIRE SOMEONE TO DO IT. I'M SO GLAD I DID; OUR LAWN GAL DOES A GREAT JOB! WE EVEN HAVE HER DO OUR FALL AND SPRING CLEANUPS.
I HATE CLEANING THE HOUSE SO I DECIDED TO HIRE A CLEANING GENTLEMAN. I DON'T LIKE PAYING SOMEONE TO DO SOMETHING THAT I CAN DO, BUT HIRING HIM HAS BEEN A TOTAL GAME-CHANGER. HE'S ABLE TO DO A MUCH BETTER JOB IN A THIRD OF THE TIME IT WOULD TAKE ME! EVEN MY WIFE AGREES THAT HE'S WORTH THE MONEY!
I STARTED PAYING FOR GROCERY DELIVERY A FEW MONTHS AGO AND AM NEVER GOING BACK. MY WIFE HATES THAT I SPEND THE EXTRA MONEY, BUT I DON'T CARE. SHE'S NEVER TAKEN ALL OF THE KIDS ANYWHERE WITH HER BEFORE SO SHE HAS NO IDEA HOW HARD IT IS. PLUS THIS SAVES ME SO MUCH TIME!

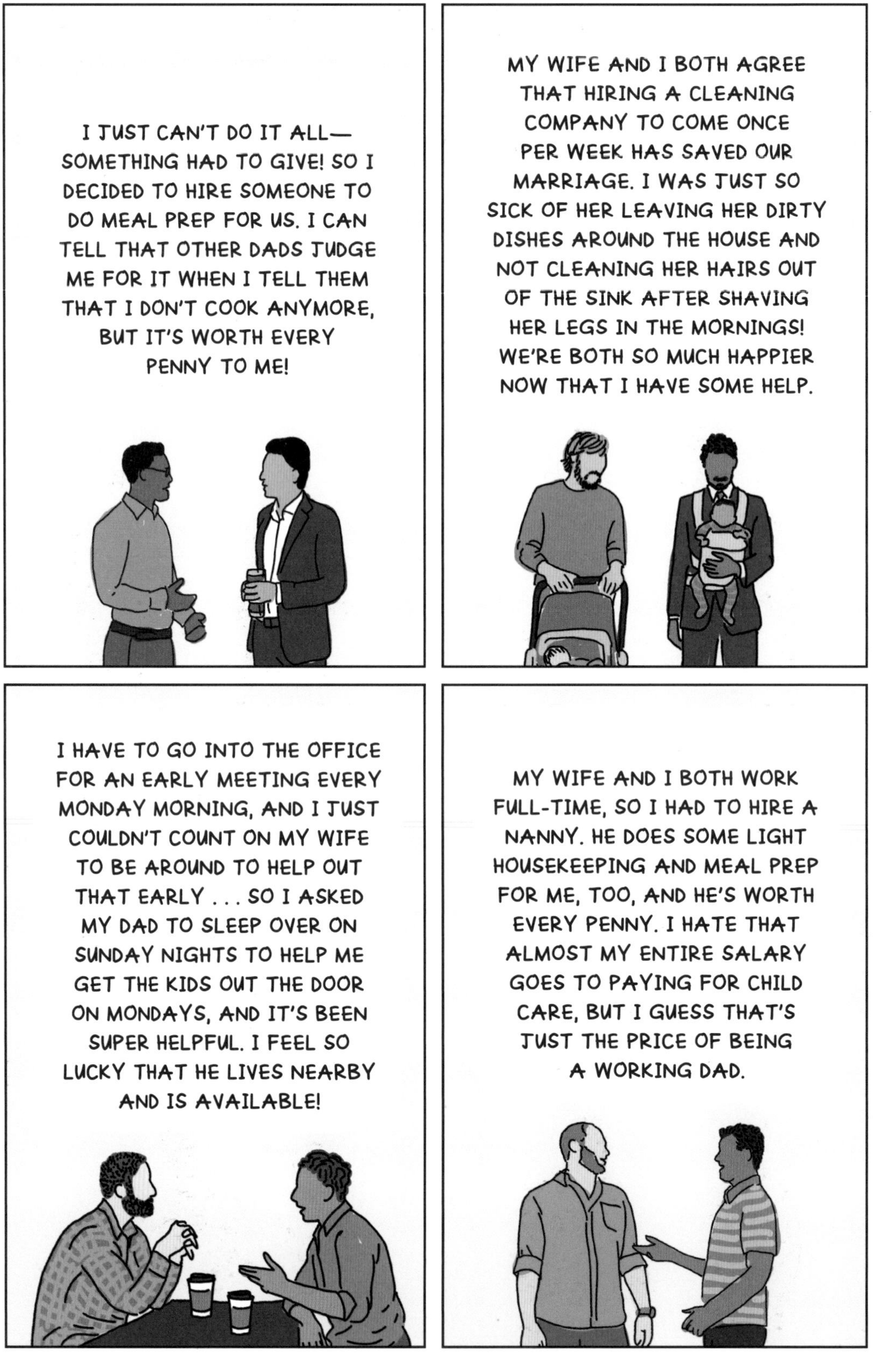
I JUST CAN'T DO IT ALL—SOMETHING HAD TO GIVE! SO I DECIDED TO HIRE SOMEONE TO DO MEAL PREP FOR US. I CAN TELL THAT OTHER DADS JUDGE ME FOR IT WHEN I TELL THEM THAT I DON'T COOK ANYMORE, BUT IT'S WORTH EVERY PENNY TO ME!
MY WIFE AND I BOTH AGREE THAT HIRING A CLEANING COMPANY TO COME ONCE PER WEEK HAS SAVED OUR MARRIAGE. I WAS JUST SO SICK OF HER LEAVING HER DIRTY DISHES AROUND THE HOUSE AND NOT CLEANING HER HAIRS OUT OF THE SINK AFTER SHAVING HER LEGS IN THE MORNINGS! WE'RE BOTH SO MUCH HAPPIER NOW THAT I HAVE SOME HELP.
I HAVE TO GO INTO THE OFFICE FOR AN EARLY MEETING EVERY MONDAY MORNING, AND I JUST COULDN'T COUNT ON MY WIFE TO BE AROUND TO HELP OUT THAT EARLY . . . SO I ASKED MY DAD TO SLEEP OVER ON SUNDAY NIGHTS TO HELP ME GET THE KIDS OUT THE DOOR ON MONDAYS, AND IT'S BEEN SUPER HELPFUL. I FEEL SO LUCKY THAT HE LIVES NEARBY AND IS AVAILABLE!
MY WIFE AND I BOTH WORK FULL-TIME, SO I HAD TO HIRE A NANNY. HE DOES SOME LIGHT HOUSEKEEPING AND MEAL PREP FOR ME, TOO, AND HE'S WORTH EVERY PENNY. I HATE THAT ALMOST MY ENTIRE SALARY GOES TO PAYING FOR CHILD CARE, BUT I GUESS THAT'S JUST THE PRICE OF BEING A WORKING DAD.

A few years ago, on Instagram, I did a call for pictures of "laundry piles." My community sent in hundreds of images of their household laundry piles that I shared to my Instagram story. The direct messages that I received in respond to these images said things like:

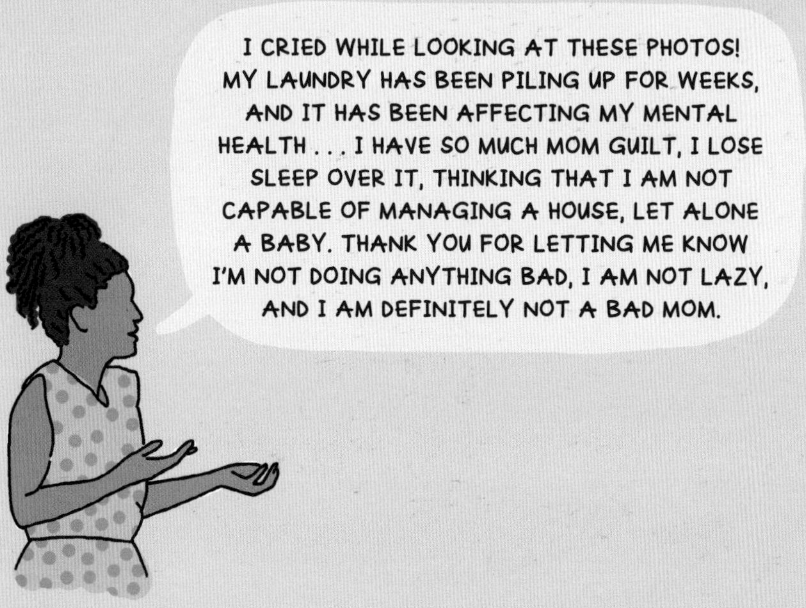
I CRIED WHILE LOOKING AT THESE PHOTOS! MY LAUNDRY HAS BEEN PILING UP FOR WEEKS, AND IT HAS BEEN AFFECTING MY MENTAL HEALTH . . . I HAVE SO MUCH MOM GUILT, I LOSE SLEEP OVER IT, THINKING THAT I AM NOT CAPABLE OF MANAGING A HOUSE, LET ALONE A BABY. THANK YOU FOR LETTING ME KNOW I'M NOT DOING ANYTHING BAD, I AM NOT LAZY, AND I AM DEFINITELY NOT A BAD MOM.

As I waded through responses like this and thought about my own experience with the crippling, never-ending nature of laundry, I started to realize why laundry piles are so triggering for so many of us women . . .

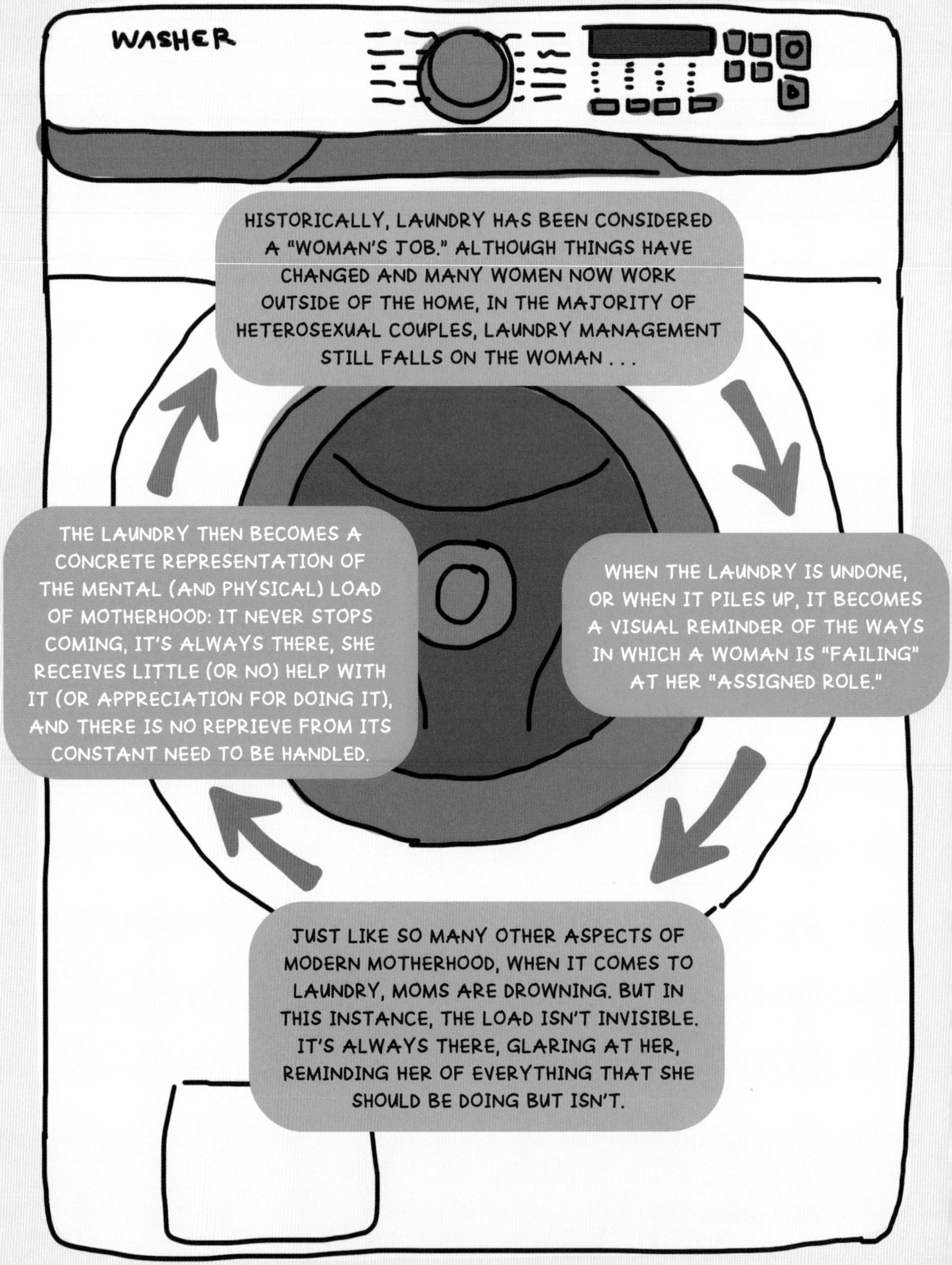
WASHER
HISTORICALLY, LAUNDRY HAS BEEN CONSIDERED A "WOMAN'S JOB." ALTHOUGH THINGS HAVE CHANGED AND MANY WOMEN NOW WORK OUTSIDE OF THE HOME, IN THE MAJORITY OF HETEROSEXUAL COUPLES, LAUNDRY MANAGEMENT STILL FALLS ON THE WOMAN . . .
WHEN THE LAUNDRY IS UNDONE, OR WHEN IT PILES UP, IT BECOMES A VISUAL REMINDER OF THE WAYS IN WHICH A WOMAN IS "FAILING" AT HER "ASSIGNED ROLE."
JUST LIKE SO MANY OTHER ASPECTS OF MODERN MOTHERHOOD, WHEN IT COMES TO LAUNDRY, MOMS ARE DROWNING. BUT IN THIS INSTANCE, THE LOAD ISN'T INVISIBLE. IT'S ALWAYS THERE, GLARING AT HER, REMINDING HER OF EVERYTHING THAT SHE SHOULD BE DOING BUT ISN'T.
THE LAUNDRY THEN BECOMES A CONCRETE REPRESENTATION OF THE MENTAL (AND PHYSICAL) LOAD OF MOTHERHOOD: IT NEVER STOPS COMING, IT'S ALWAYS THERE, SHE RECEIVES LITTLE (OR NO) HELP WITH IT (OR APPRECIATION FOR DOING IT), AND THERE IS NO REPRIEVE FROM ITS CONSTANT NEED TO BE HANDLED.

Over the past year or so, I have come to understand a few things about laundry (that apply to any/all household tasks):

1. Laundry piles are normal. Everyone has them.

2. Laundry is NOT a woman's job.

3. You are NOT a "bad mom" or "bad wife" if you can't stay on top of the laundry because laundry is morally neutral (credit goes to KC Davis for this idea).

4. If you choose to outsource your laundry, you are not a failure.

And so, despite my guilt about spending money on things that we could do ourselves, I decided to outsource folding and putting away our laundry.

And yes, taking this off of my plate and out of my sight line has been life-changing.

Here are a few other household tasks I've decided to outsource over the past few years:

1. Yard maintenance: spring and fall clean-ups, mowing the lawn

2. Organization projects

3. House cleaning (we have a team come once per month for a deep clean)

4. General handyman tasks that we have the skills to do (or figure out) but not the time or energy to tackle

In all of these cases, I am SO happy to have the help, and the people we have hired are happy to have the work. It's a win-win, and despite my initial stress about outsourcing each of these tasks (have I mentioned that I hate spending money on things that we could do ourselves?), I have made peace with outsourcing these items and am so, so grateful to have these helpers in our life.

# Eat the Damn Peach

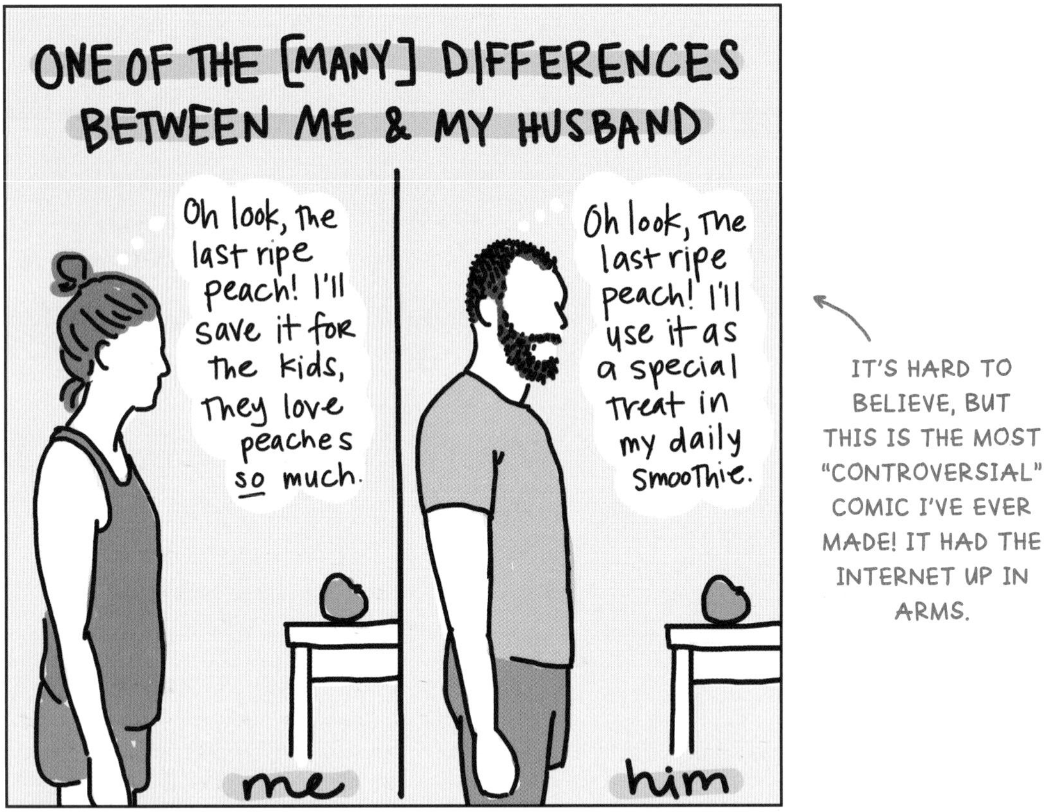
ONE OF THE [MANY] DIFFERENCES BETWEEN ME & MY HUSBAND
Oh look, the last ripe peach! I'll save it for the kids, they love peaches so much.
Oh look, the last ripe peach! I'll use it as a special treat in my daily smoothie.
me
him
IT'S HARD TO BELIEVE, BUT THIS IS THE MOST "CONTROVERSIAL" COMIC I'VE EVER MADE! IT HAD THE INTERNET UP IN ARMS.

When I shared this comic with my followers, they immediately understood my message: Moms often think about their kids before they think about themselves, and many dads think about themselves before they think about their kids. Yes, this is a generalization, but it's also a very real issue.

Prior to posting this comic, I always saved all of the ripe peaches for my kids because I loved how much they loved them.

Ben, on the other hand, loves adding peaches to his smoothie and has often taken the last peach to use in this way. He sees no issue with doing so, and therein lies the issue.

The number of moms I've spoken to whose husbands will make themselves lunch and then sit down to eat it without even thinking about what anyone else in the house is eating for lunch is staggering. Meanwhile, moms are making everyone else lunch before they even think about making something for themselves.

After sharing this comic (and reading all of the comments from moms who could relate), I decided to reframe my thinking. And from there, a (small) movement was born in my little corner of the internet.

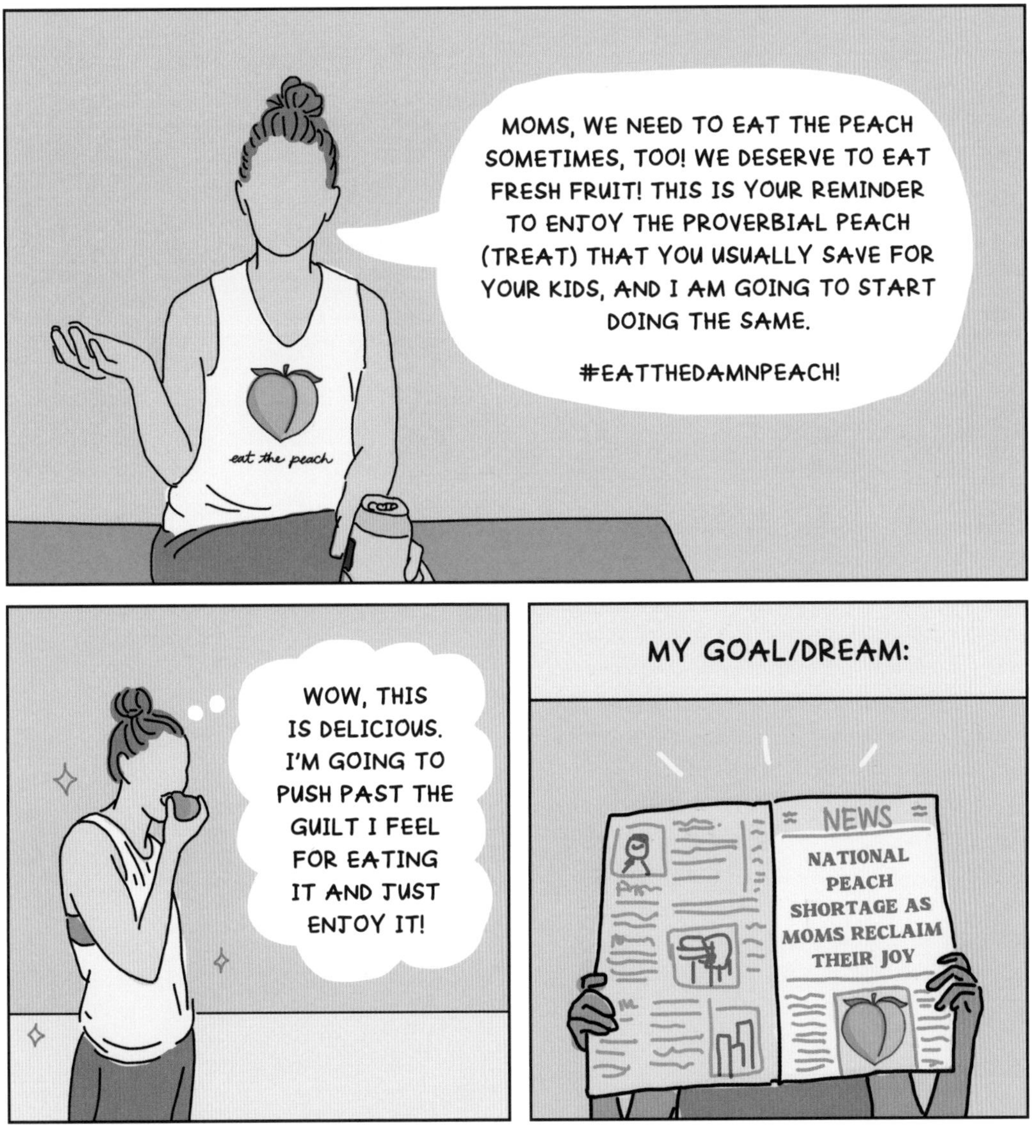
MOMS, WE NEED TO EAT THE PEACH SOMETIMES, TOO! WE DESERVE TO EAT FRESH FRUIT! THIS IS YOUR REMINDER TO ENJOY THE PROVERBIAL PEACH (TREAT) THAT YOU USUALLY SAVE FOR YOUR KIDS, AND I AM GOING TO START DOING THE SAME.
#EATTHEDAMNPEACH!
eat the peach
WOW, THIS IS DELICIOUS. I'M GOING TO PUSH PAST THE GUILT I FEEL FOR EATING IT AND JUST ENJOY IT!
MY GOAL/DREAM:
NEWS
NATIONAL PEACH SHORTAGE AS MOMS RECLAIM THEIR JOY

I started eating some of the delicious fresh fruit that I would have normally saved for the kids and then snapped a pic and shared it. Soon, other moms were doing the same and sending me proof.

Moms deserve to experience simple joys, too. We deserve more than just our childrens' scraps. The age of mom as the sacrificial lamb is over (at least in my life).

With each fresh strawberry, peach, plum, or handful of blueberries that I eat, I am reminded that I am more than just a caretaker . . . and as silly as this may seem, it's been a real shift for me in how I think about myself.

# "But Have You Tried Having Regular Date Nights?"

I f one more therapist, friend, or random person tells me that getting a babysitter and scheduling a regular date night is a great way to reconnect with my husband, I'm going to . . . well, tell them that they're right because yeah, I know that works.

How do I know this? Not because we've had a regularly scheduled date night since becoming parents (because we haven't!), but because we've started going on dates *just a little more regularly* in the past year and it has been really helpful. And by "a little more regularly" I mean we've gone from two or three dates per year to about six or seven. But hey, that means we've almost tripled our alone time! That's big! It beats our usual attempts at spending time together at home, which always start with the best of intentions and end with Ben sleeping on the couch.

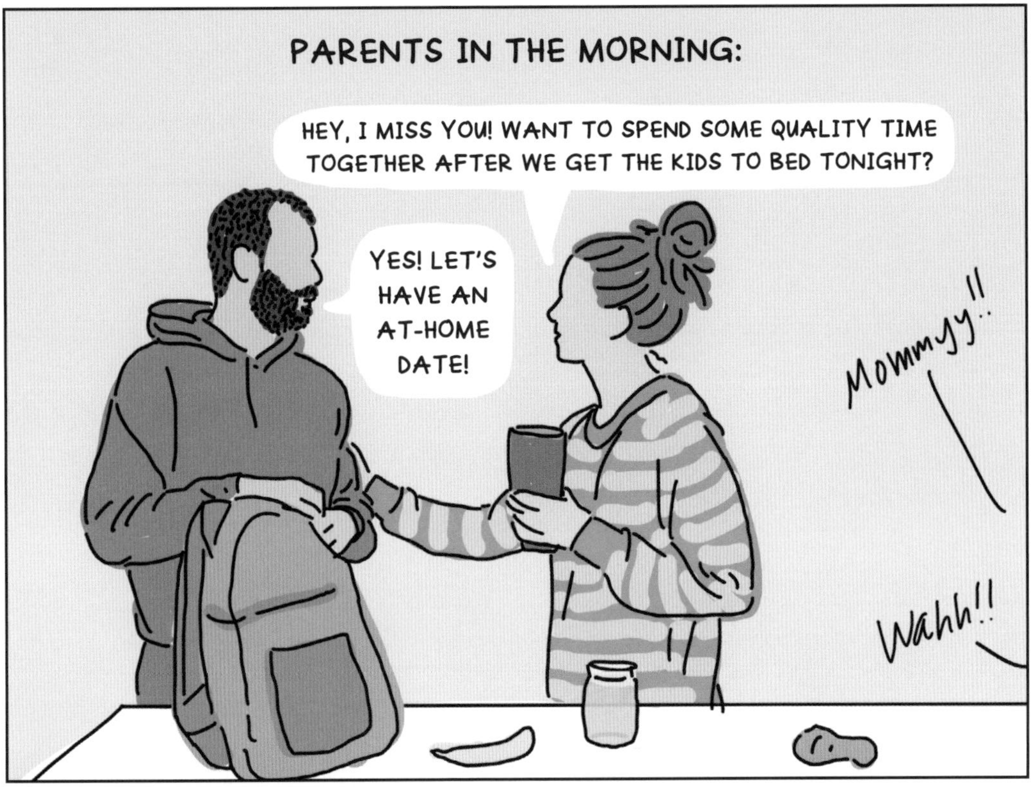
PARENTS IN THE MORNING:
HEY, I MISS YOU! WANT TO SPEND SOME QUALITY TIME TOGETHER AFTER WE GET THE KIDS TO BED TONIGHT?
YES! LET'S HAVE AN AT-HOME DATE!
Mommyy!!
Wahh!!

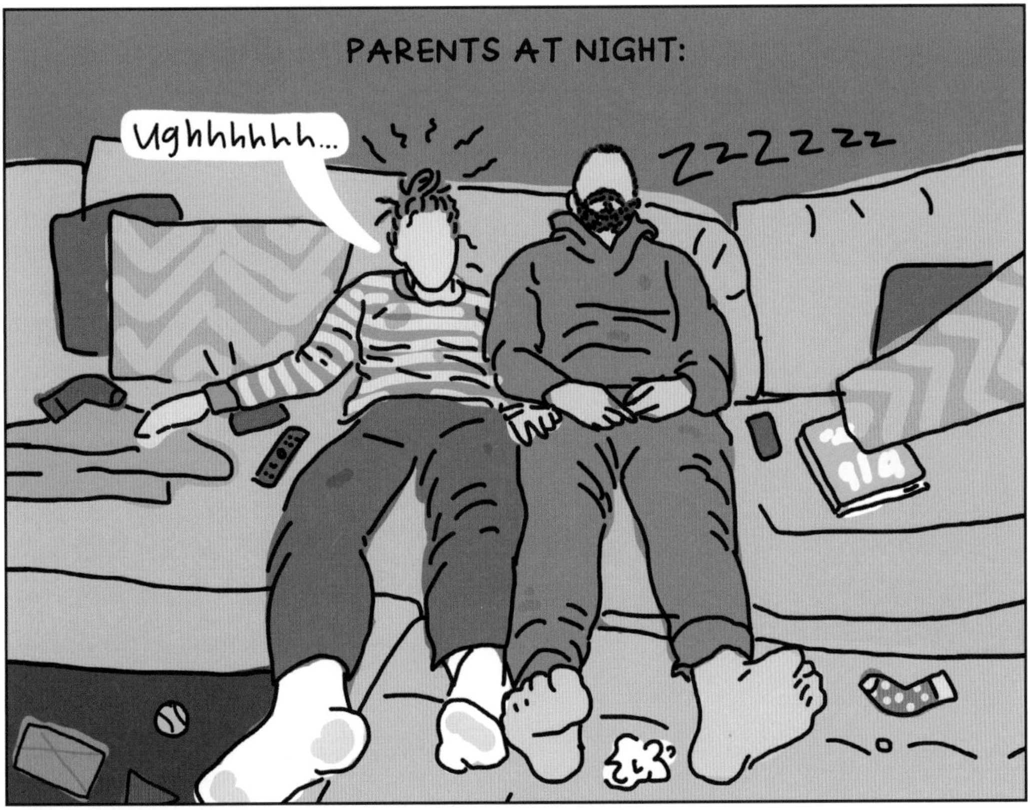
PARENTS AT NIGHT:
Ughhhhhh...
ZZZZZZZ

Here's the thing about date nights: They're not good for your relationship if going on a date is super stressful for the mom or the default parent. In order for a date night to be relaxing, it can't be too much more work for one parent. If one parent is scheduling the date and preparing the food for the kids ahead of time and cleaning the house for the babysitter and making a list and setting out all of the bedtime stuff, then the date just becomes another thing on that parent's list. And a couples therapist telling a couple that they need to schedule date nights IS NOT helpful if said therapist is just adding more to the overwhelmed parent's plate (ahem . . . not that I know this from experience . . . ).

But what has been working for us when it comes to date night is not always having a date "night" at all, but instead, having a day date or even a morning date. Our kids are happier and easier in the mornings and tougher at bedtime, so we've been trying to do dates that don't require someone else to put the kids to bed. We go out to brunch or go for a walk on the beach. If we go to dinner, we go at 5 p.m. (ha!). If at all possible, we drop the kids at a family member's house so we don't even have to clean up first. Getting a babysitter used to really stress me out, but the more we've prioritized it, the easier it's gotten. We're learning. And again, our kids are getting older and easier, which is another important piece of the date night puzzle (for us).

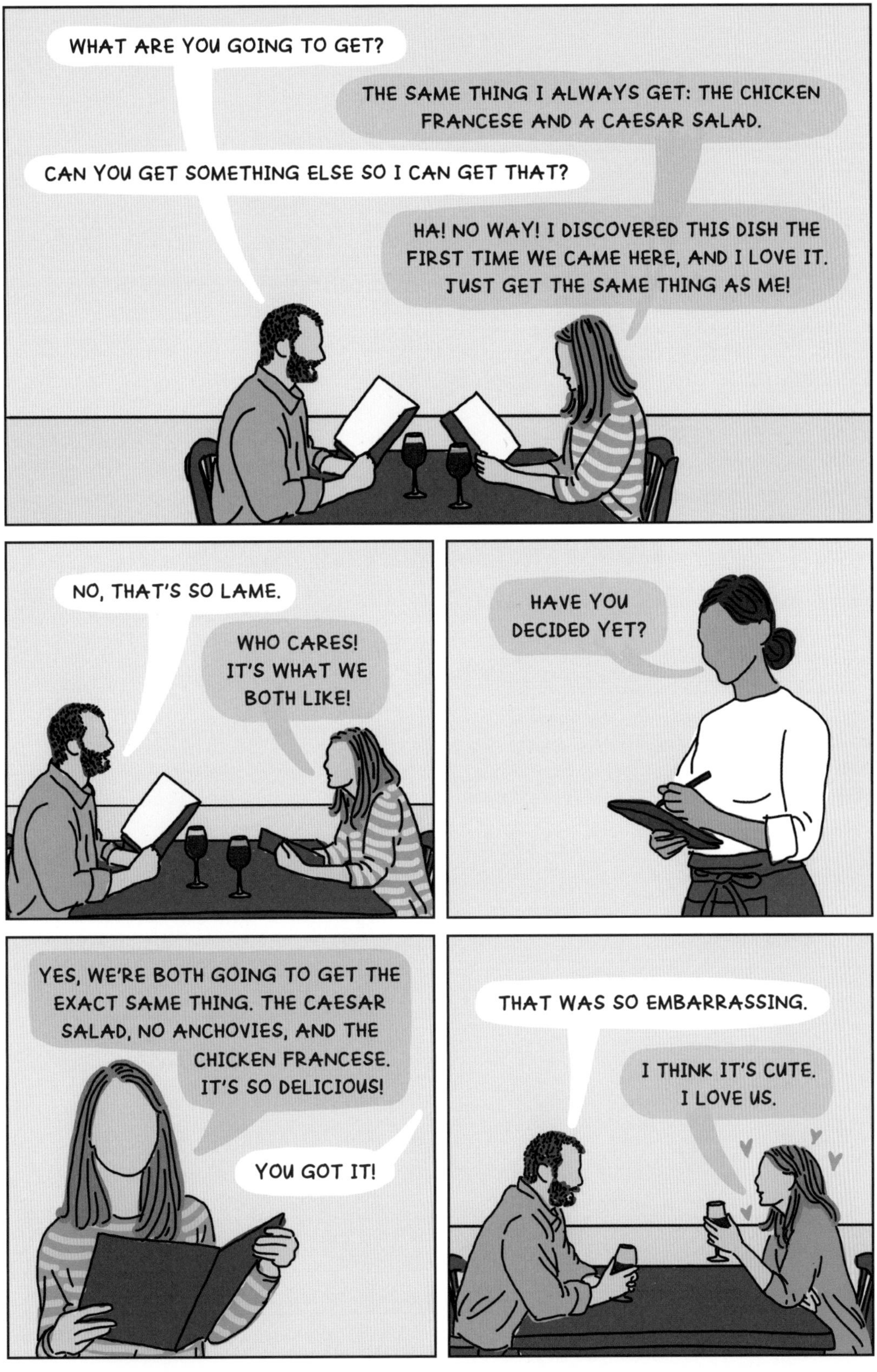
WHAT ARE YOU GOING TO GET?
THE SAME THING I ALWAYS GET: THE CHICKEN FRANCESE AND A CAESAR SALAD.
CAN YOU GET SOMETHING ELSE SO I CAN GET THAT?
HA! NO WAY! I DISCOVERED THIS DISH THE FIRST TIME WE CAME HERE, AND I LOVE IT. JUST GET THE SAME THING AS ME!
NO, THAT'S SO LAME.
WHO CARES! IT'S WHAT WE BOTH LIKE!
HAVE YOU DECIDED YET?
YES, WE'RE BOTH GOING TO GET THE EXACT SAME THING. THE CAESAR SALAD, NO ANCHOVIES, AND THE CHICKEN FRANCESE. IT'S SO DELICIOUS!
YOU GOT IT!
THAT WAS SO EMBARRASSING.
I THINK IT'S CUTE. I LOVE US.

# Stop (It), Drop (It), and Challenge the Status Quo

One of the very hardest changes that I've made has involved learning how to let go of household and child-related tasks that I've always been the one to handle.

For instance, asking Ben to take one of our kids to their annual pediatrician's appointment, to stay home with one of our kids on a sick day, or to handle the preschool paperwork.

Asking him to handle these items isn't always the hardest part—sometimes the hardest part is letting go of my own need for control and trusting him to handle things in his own way (and if he doesn't, letting him deal with the consequences of his actions or inactions).

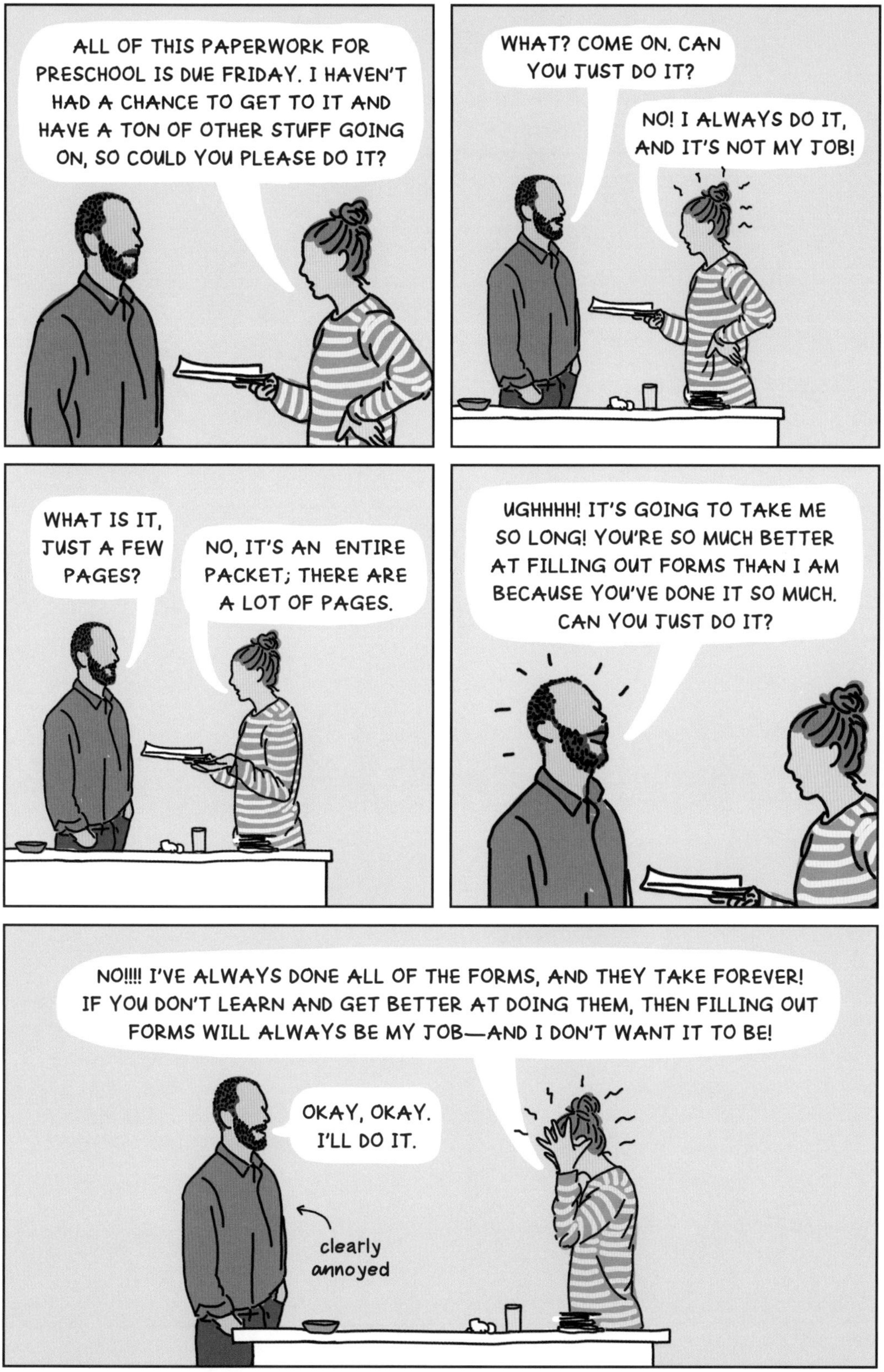
ALL OF THIS PAPERWORK FOR PRESCHOOL IS DUE FRIDAY. I HAVEN'T HAD A CHANCE TO GET TO IT AND HAVE A TON OF OTHER STUFF GOING ON, SO COULD YOU PLEASE DO IT?
WHAT? COME ON. CAN YOU JUST DO IT?
NO! I ALWAYS DO IT, AND IT'S NOT MY JOB!
WHAT IS IT, JUST A FEW PAGES?
NO, IT'S AN ENTIRE PACKET; THERE ARE A LOT OF PAGES.
UGHHHH! IT'S GOING TO TAKE ME SO LONG! YOU'RE SO MUCH BETTER AT FILLING OUT FORMS THAN I AM BECAUSE YOU'VE DONE IT SO MUCH. CAN YOU JUST DO IT?
NO!!!! I'VE ALWAYS DONE ALL OF THE FORMS, AND THEY TAKE FOREVER! IF YOU DON'T LEARN AND GET BETTER AT DOING THEM, THEN FILLING OUT FORMS WILL ALWAYS BE MY JOB—AND I DON'T WANT IT TO BE!
OKAY, OKAY. I'LL DO IT.
clearly annoyed

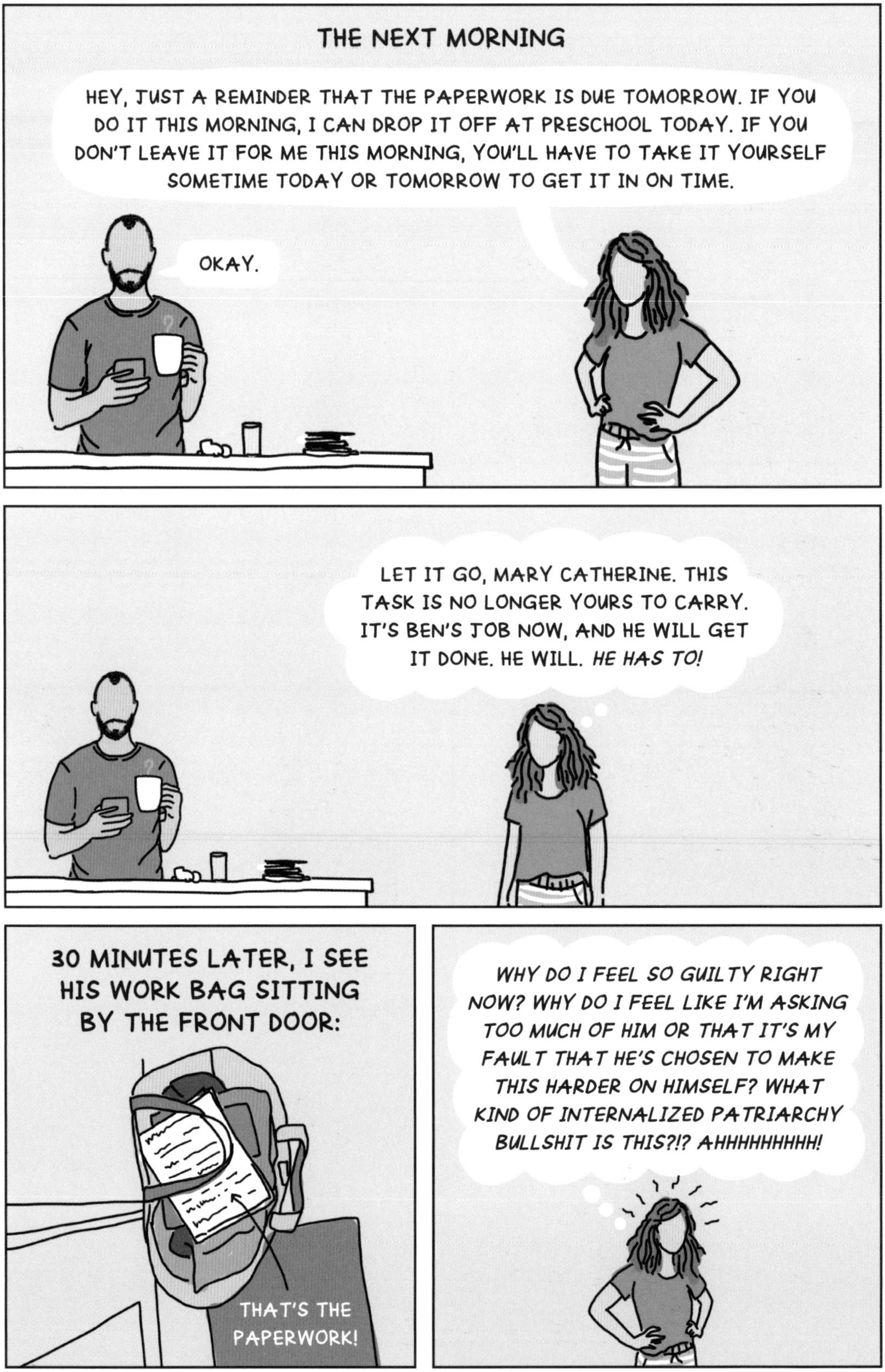
THE NEXT MORNING
HEY, JUST A REMINDER THAT THE PAPERWORK IS DUE TOMORROW. IF YOU DO IT THIS MORNING, I CAN DROP IT OFF AT PRESCHOOL TODAY. IF YOU DON'T LEAVE IT FOR ME THIS MORNING, YOU'LL HAVE TO TAKE IT YOURSELF SOMETIME TODAY OR TOMORROW TO GET IT IN ON TIME.
OKAY.
LET IT GO, MARY CATHERINE. THIS TASK IS NO LONGER YOURS TO CARRY. IT'S BEN'S JOB NOW, AND HE WILL GET IT DONE. HE WILL. *HE HAS TO!*
30 MINUTES LATER, I SEE HIS WORK BAG SITTING BY THE FRONT DOOR:
THAT'S THE PAPERWORK!
*WHY DO I FEEL SO GUILTY RIGHT NOW? WHY DO I FEEL LIKE I'M ASKING TOO MUCH OF HIM OR THAT IT'S MY FAULT THAT HE'S CHOSEN TO MAKE THIS HARDER ON HIMSELF? WHAT KIND OF INTERNALIZED PATRIARCHY BULLSHIT IS THIS?!? AHHHHHHHHH!*

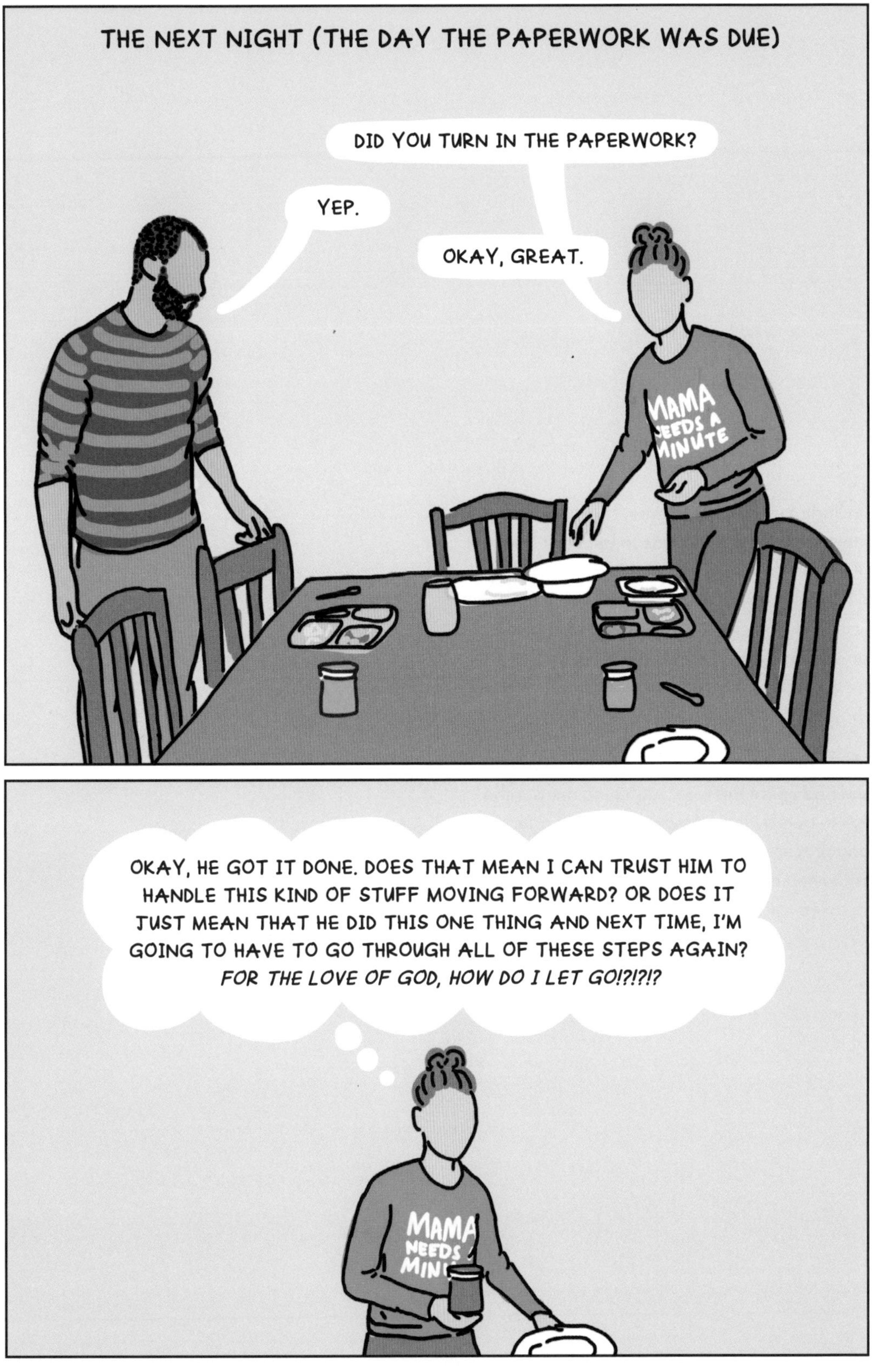
THE NEXT NIGHT (THE DAY THE PAPERWORK WAS DUE)
DID YOU TURN IN THE PAPERWORK?
YEP.
OKAY, GREAT.
MAMA NEEDS A MINUTE
OKAY, HE GOT IT DONE. DOES THAT MEAN I CAN TRUST HIM TO HANDLE THIS KIND OF STUFF MOVING FORWARD? OR DOES IT JUST MEAN THAT HE DID THIS ONE THING AND NEXT TIME, I'M GOING TO HAVE TO GO THROUGH ALL OF THESE STEPS AGAIN? *FOR THE LOVE OF GOD, HOW DO I LET GO!?!?!?*

Similarly for the longest time, I was the only one who could put our kids to bed. Not Ben, not other family, not babysitters. Eventually, we got to the point where Ben could put them to bed if I wasn't home, but if I was around, it was just too hard because they wanted me. So I was the bedtime parent almost every night unless I physically left the house.

Earlier this year, when my dad was visiting and had spent the week watching me put the kids to bed by myself every night—an hour-long process that left me feeling spent and exhausted at the end of an already tiring day—he asked me about it . . .

REMEMBER HOW MY DAD IS A THERAPIST? I GET LOTS OF FREE THERAPIZING, AND IT'S *MOSTLY* SUPER HELPFUL . . .

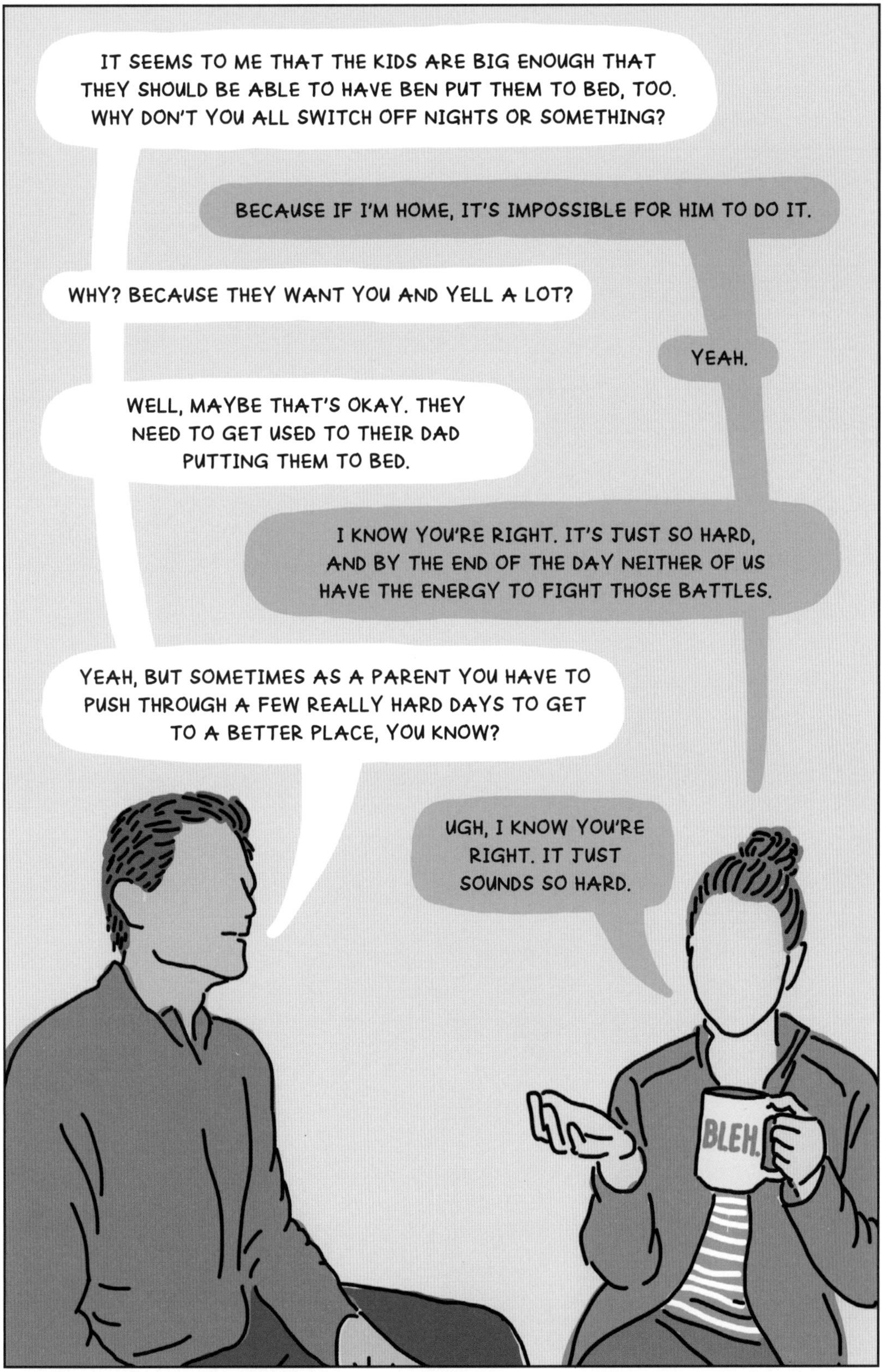
IT SEEMS TO ME THAT THE KIDS ARE BIG ENOUGH THAT THEY SHOULD BE ABLE TO HAVE BEN PUT THEM TO BED, TOO. WHY DON'T YOU ALL SWITCH OFF NIGHTS OR SOMETHING?
BECAUSE IF I'M HOME, IT'S IMPOSSIBLE FOR HIM TO DO IT.
WHY? BECAUSE THEY WANT YOU AND YELL A LOT?
YEAH.
WELL, MAYBE THAT'S OKAY. THEY NEED TO GET USED TO THEIR DAD PUTTING THEM TO BED.
I KNOW YOU'RE RIGHT. IT'S JUST SO HARD, AND BY THE END OF THE DAY NEITHER OF US HAVE THE ENERGY TO FIGHT THOSE BATTLES.
YEAH, BUT SOMETIMES AS A PARENT YOU HAVE TO PUSH THROUGH A FEW REALLY HARD DAYS TO GET TO A BETTER PLACE, YOU KNOW?
UGH, I KNOW YOU'RE RIGHT. IT JUST SOUNDS SO HARD.
BLEH.

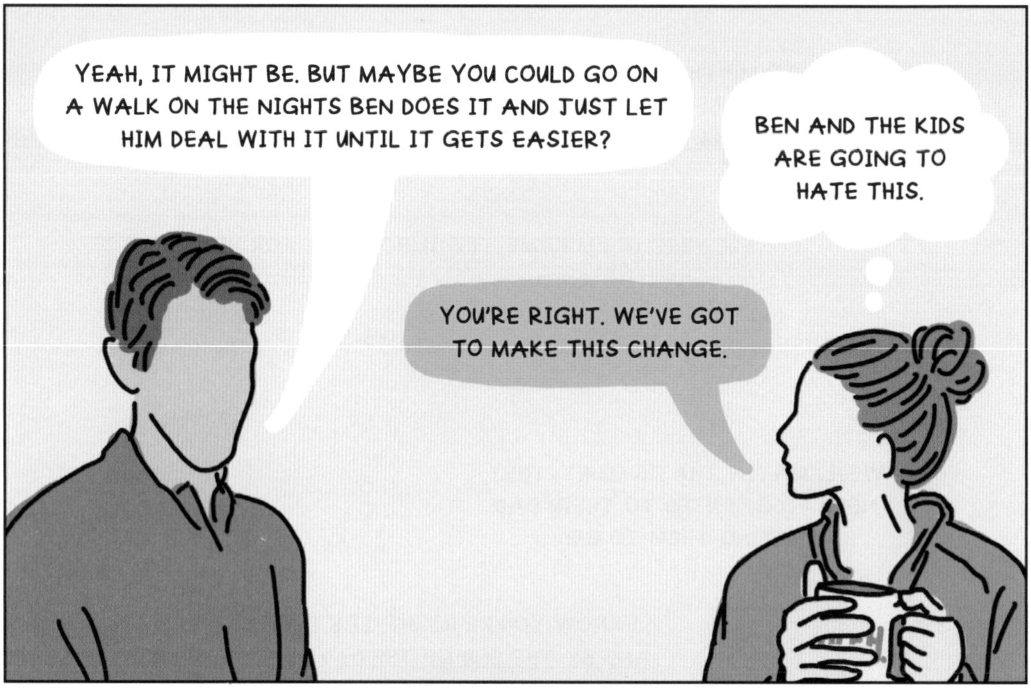
YEAH, IT MIGHT BE. BUT MAYBE YOU COULD GO ON A WALK ON THE NIGHTS BEN DOES IT AND JUST LET HIM DEAL WITH IT UNTIL IT GETS EASIER?
BEN AND THE KIDS ARE GOING TO HATE THIS.
YOU'RE RIGHT. WE'VE GOT TO MAKE THIS CHANGE.

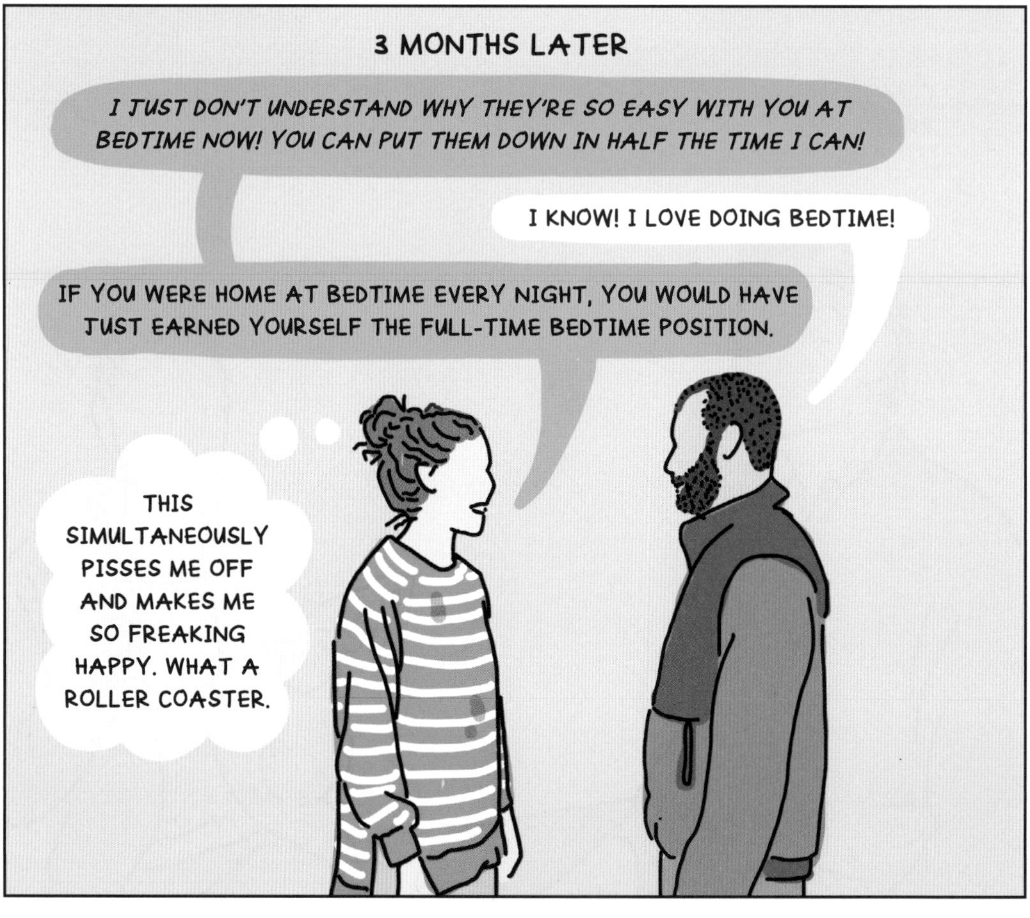
3 MONTHS LATER
I JUST DON'T UNDERSTAND WHY THEY'RE SO EASY WITH YOU AT BEDTIME NOW! YOU CAN PUT THEM DOWN IN HALF THE TIME I CAN!
I KNOW! I LOVE DOING BEDTIME!
IF YOU WERE HOME AT BEDTIME EVERY NIGHT, YOU WOULD HAVE JUST EARNED YOURSELF THE FULL-TIME BEDTIME POSITION.
THIS SIMULTANEOUSLY PISSES ME OFF AND MAKES ME SO FREAKING HAPPY. WHAT A ROLLER COASTER.

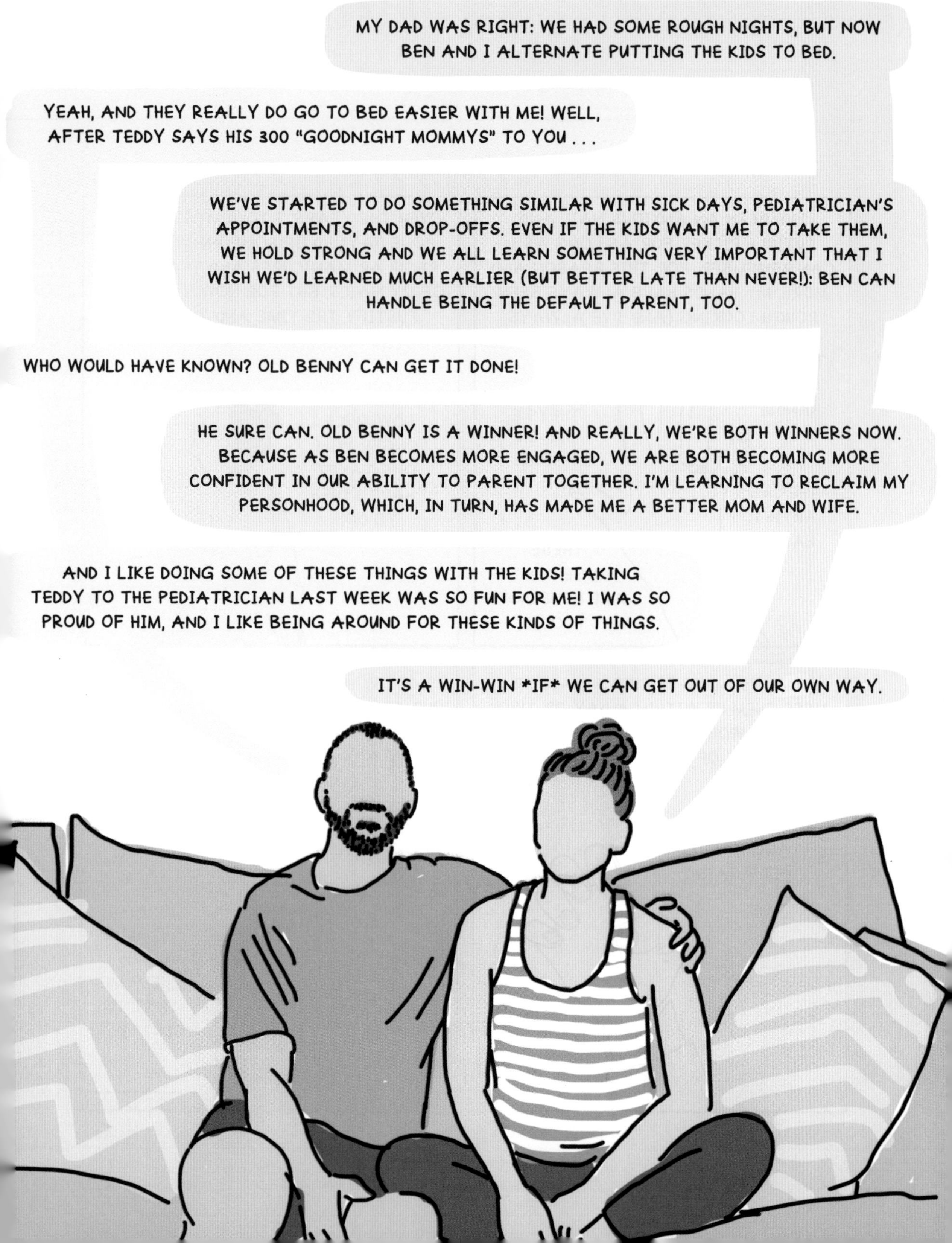
MY DAD WAS RIGHT: WE HAD SOME ROUGH NIGHTS, BUT NOW BEN AND I ALTERNATE PUTTING THE KIDS TO BED.
YEAH, AND THEY REALLY DO GO TO BED EASIER WITH ME! WELL, AFTER TEDDY SAYS HIS 300 "GOODNIGHT MOMMYS" TO YOU . . .
WE'VE STARTED TO DO SOMETHING SIMILAR WITH SICK DAYS, PEDIATRICIAN'S APPOINTMENTS, AND DROP-OFFS. EVEN IF THE KIDS WANT ME TO TAKE THEM, WE HOLD STRONG AND WE ALL LEARN SOMETHING VERY IMPORTANT THAT I WISH WE'D LEARNED MUCH EARLIER (BUT BETTER LATE THAN NEVER!): BEN CAN HANDLE BEING THE DEFAULT PARENT, TOO.
WHO WOULD HAVE KNOWN? OLD BENNY CAN GET IT DONE!
HE SURE CAN. OLD BENNY IS A WINNER! AND REALLY, WE'RE BOTH WINNERS NOW. BECAUSE AS BEN BECOMES MORE ENGAGED, WE ARE BOTH BECOMING MORE CONFIDENT IN OUR ABILITY TO PARENT TOGETHER. I'M LEARNING TO RECLAIM MY PERSONHOOD, WHICH, IN TURN, HAS MADE ME A BETTER MOM AND WIFE.
AND I LIKE DOING SOME OF THESE THINGS WITH THE KIDS! TAKING TEDDY TO THE PEDIATRICIAN LAST WEEK WAS SO FUN FOR ME! I WAS SO PROUD OF HIM, AND I LIKE BEING AROUND FOR THESE KINDS OF THINGS.
IT'S A WIN-WIN *IF* WE CAN GET OUT OF OUR OWN WAY.

# Treat Yo Self.

I'VE BEEN AN ANXIOUS NAIL AND CUTICLE PICKER FOR AS LONG AS I CAN REMEMBER. FOR THIS REASON AND MORE, MY HANDS HAVE ALWAYS BEEN ROUGH-LOOKING (AND I'VE ALWAYS HATED THEM).

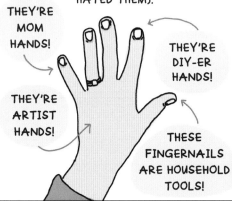

THEY'RE MOM HANDS!

THEY'RE DIY-ER HANDS!

THEY'RE ARTIST HANDS!

THESE FINGERNAILS ARE HOUSEHOLD TOOLS!

OVER THE YEARS, I TOLD MYSELF THAT "ONE DAY" I'D BE SOMEONE WHO GOT REGULAR MANICURES AND TOOK CARE OF MY NAILS, BUT FOR NOW, I COULDN'T JUSTIFY THE TIME AND THE COST.

HOW MUCH LONGER WILL THIS TAKE? I HAVE STUFF TO DO!

PLUS, I'D ALWAYS CHIP A NAIL OR MESS THEM UP WITHIN A DAY OR TWO, AND IT WOULD FEEL LIKE A TOTAL WASTE OF TIME AND MONEY.

ARGHH! I DID IT AGAIN!

LAST WINTER, I SAID SOMETHING TO OUR CHILDRENS' LIBRARIAN ABOUT HOW PRETTY HER NAILS LOOKED. HER REPLY WAS A LIGHTBULB MOMENT FOR ME:

I GET GEL MANICURES BECAUSE IF I DON'T, I PICK AT MY NAILS. IT'S THE ONLY WAY I CAN KEEP FROM DOING THAT.

MAYBE GEL MANICURES WOULD HELP ME LEARN NOT TO PICK?

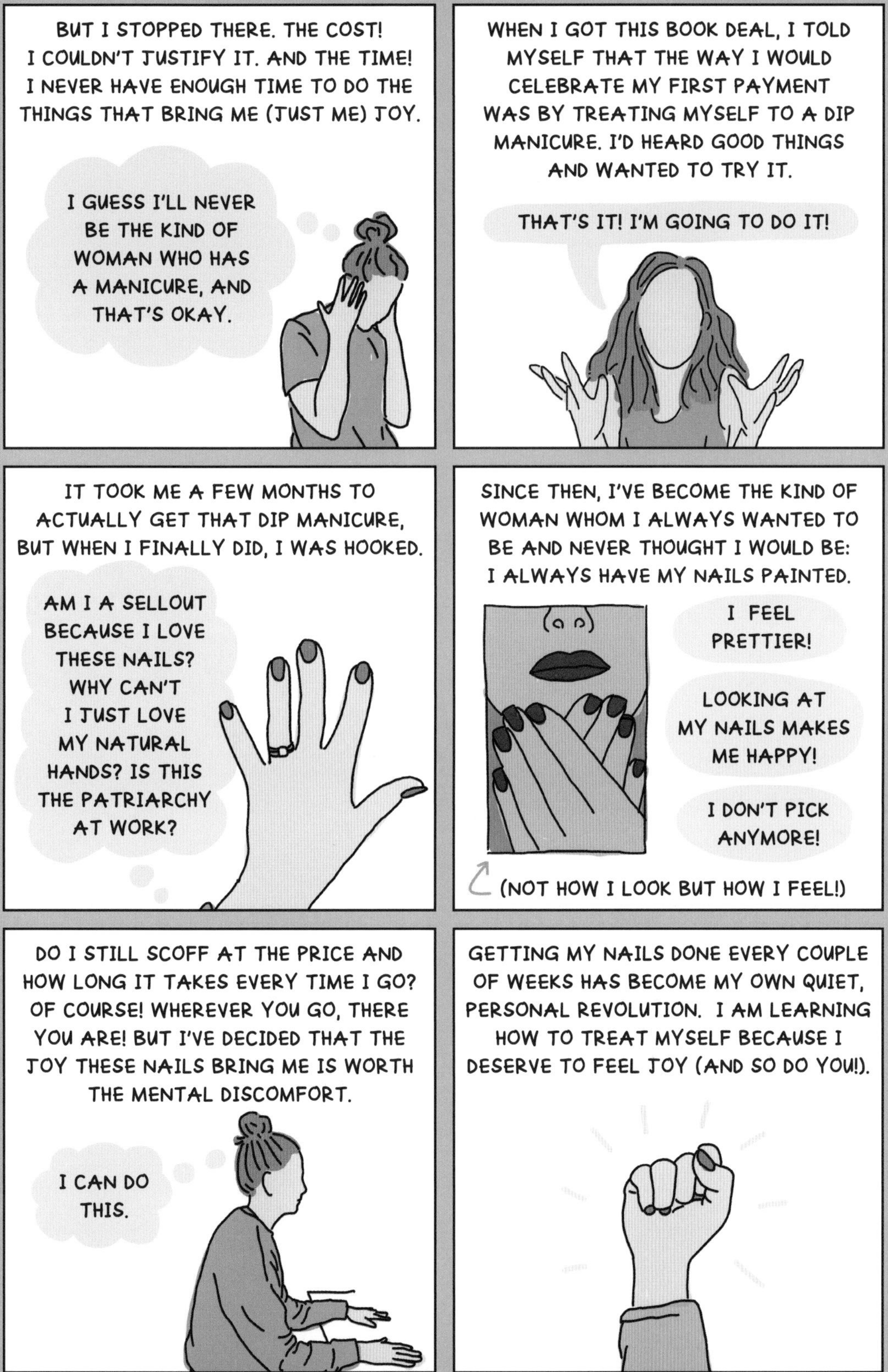
BUT I STOPPED THERE. THE COST! I COULDN'T JUSTIFY IT. AND THE TIME! I NEVER HAVE ENOUGH TIME TO DO THE THINGS THAT BRING ME (JUST ME) JOY.
I GUESS I'LL NEVER BE THE KIND OF WOMAN WHO HAS A MANICURE, AND THAT'S OKAY.
WHEN I GOT THIS BOOK DEAL, I TOLD MYSELF THAT THE WAY I WOULD CELEBRATE MY FIRST PAYMENT WAS BY TREATING MYSELF TO A DIP MANICURE. I'D HEARD GOOD THINGS AND WANTED TO TRY IT.
THAT'S IT! I'M GOING TO DO IT!
IT TOOK ME A FEW MONTHS TO ACTUALLY GET THAT DIP MANICURE, BUT WHEN I FINALLY DID, I WAS HOOKED.
AM I A SELLOUT BECAUSE I LOVE THESE NAILS? WHY CAN'T I JUST LOVE MY NATURAL HANDS? IS THIS THE PATRIARCHY AT WORK?
SINCE THEN, I'VE BECOME THE KIND OF WOMAN WHOM I ALWAYS WANTED TO BE AND NEVER THOUGHT I WOULD BE: I ALWAYS HAVE MY NAILS PAINTED.
I FEEL PRETTIER!
LOOKING AT MY NAILS MAKES ME HAPPY!
I DON'T PICK ANYMORE!
(NOT HOW I LOOK BUT HOW I FEEL!)
DO I STILL SCOFF AT THE PRICE AND HOW LONG IT TAKES EVERY TIME I GO? OF COURSE! WHEREVER YOU GO, THERE YOU ARE! BUT I'VE DECIDED THAT THE JOY THESE NAILS BRING ME IS WORTH THE MENTAL DISCOMFORT.
I CAN DO THIS.
GETTING MY NAILS DONE EVERY COUPLE OF WEEKS HAS BECOME MY OWN QUIET, PERSONAL REVOLUTION. I AM LEARNING HOW TO TREAT MYSELF BECAUSE I DESERVE TO FEEL JOY (AND SO DO YOU!).

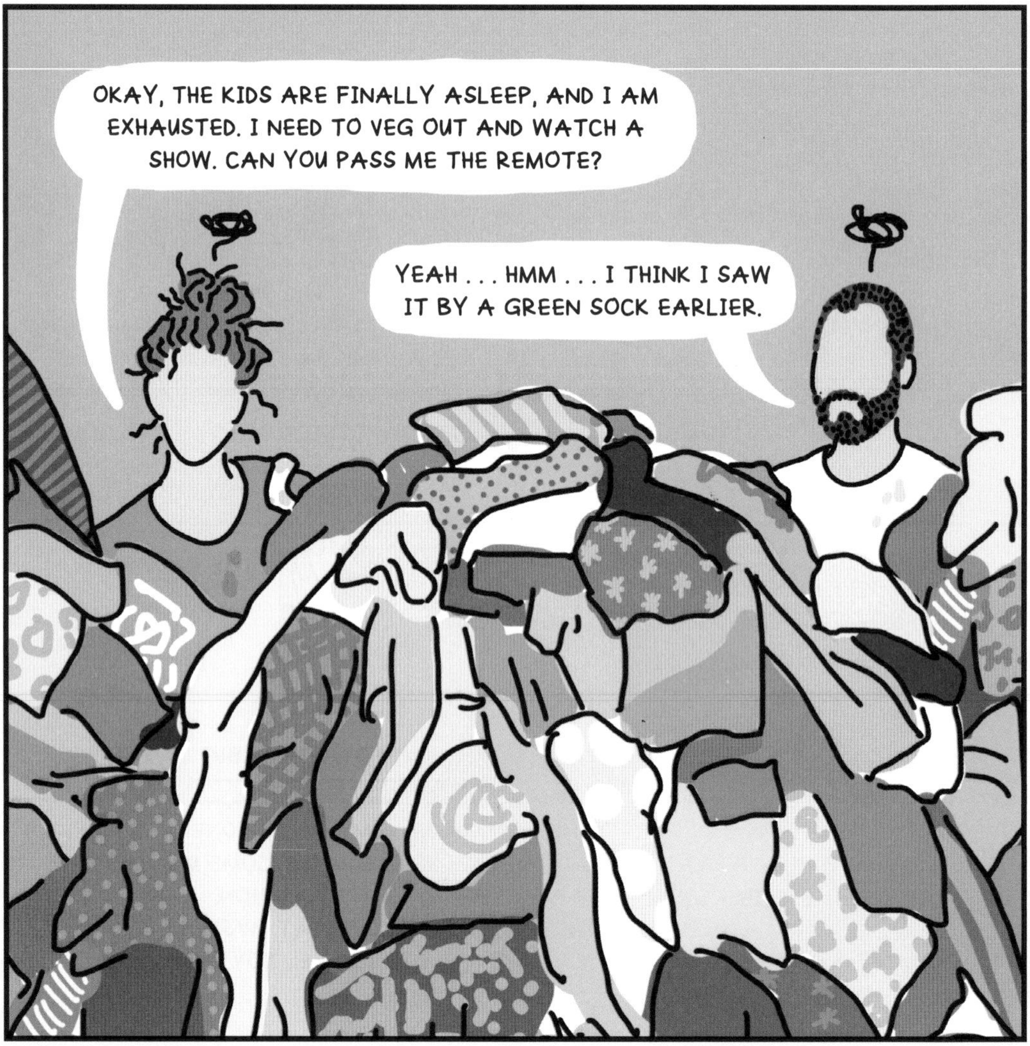
OKAY, THE KIDS ARE FINALLY ASLEEP, AND I AM EXHAUSTED. I NEED TO VEG OUT AND WATCH A SHOW. CAN YOU PASS ME THE REMOTE?
YEAH . . . HMM . . . I THINK I SAW IT BY A GREEN SOCK EARLIER.

# Wait, What? There's No Happily Ever After?

Nope, there's no happily ever after. I know that doesn't come as a surprise. And there's not even a "We've figured out most of these issues!"

I hope things continue to get easier, and I think they will; but for now, they're still hard. We have ups and downs.

Bucking internalized cultural norms and societal expectations is hard. Changing deep-seated relationship dynamics is even harder. Learning how to live with and parent with another person—no matter how much you love them—is a lifelong journey.

This is why so many couples eventually decide to go their separate ways after becoming parents: because none of this is easy or enjoyable. It's hard work. And it becomes even harder when you have no time or energy and aren't getting any sleep or alone time together (and have no village and a child who only wants one parent, etc., etc., etc., etc., ETC.). It's just plain hard. I wish it wasn't, but the reality of modern motherhood is that it just IS.

But when it comes to equality between moms and dads, I'm hopeful for the next generation. The fact that so many teens find my comics "cringe" (HA!) makes me think that they're living in a less binary, less stereotypical world where the current status quo feels old-fashioned. I am hopeful for my children, if they choose to become parents, because I believe that we are raising them both to be equally involved in the household and in caring for others. I will not raise a son who has never done his own laundry—and some of the household laundry, too! And I will not raise a daughter who believes that her worth lies in the state of her home.

Just this morning, in fact, I had a conversation with my kids in the car that gave me hope . . .

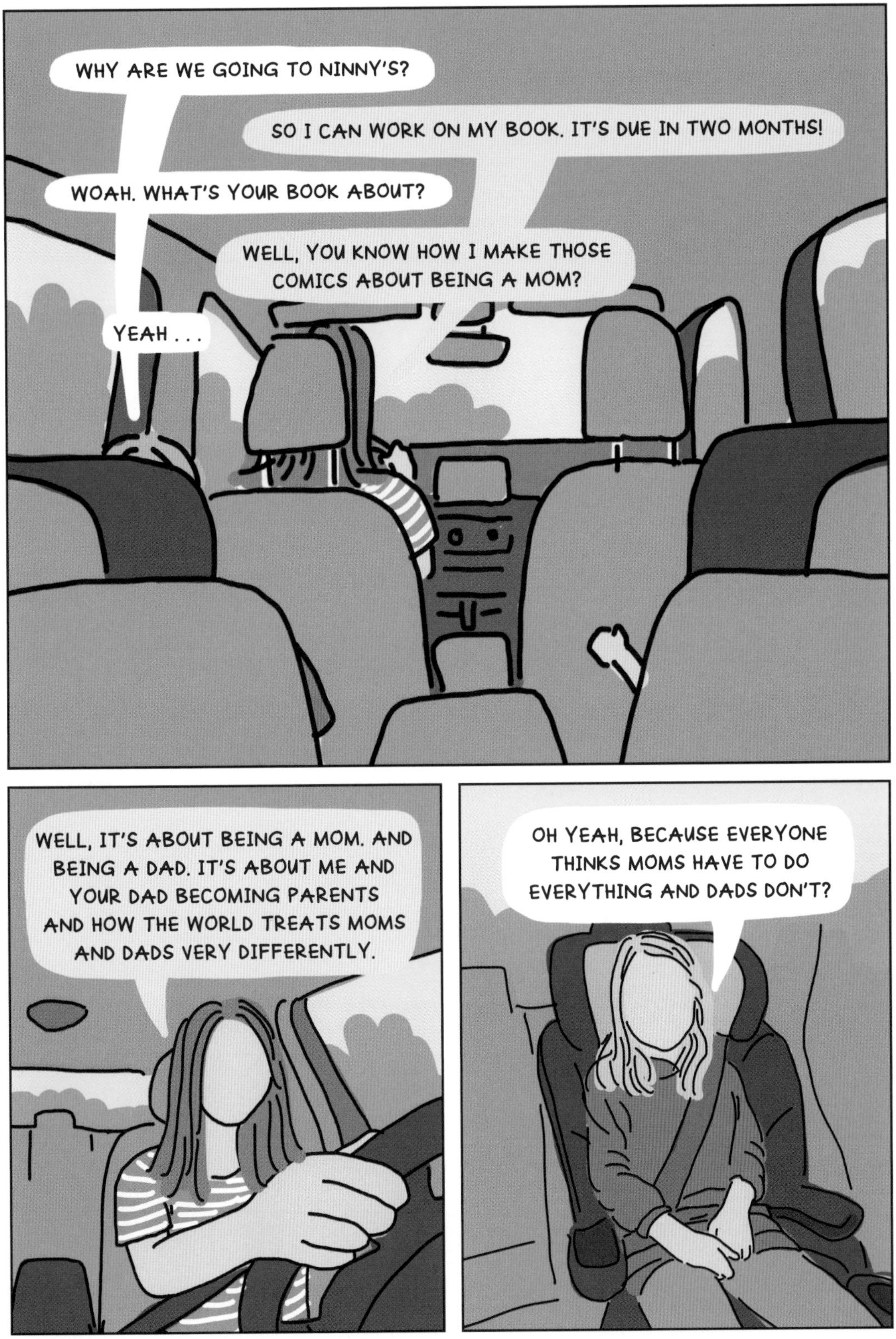
WHY ARE WE GOING TO NINNY'S?
SO I CAN WORK ON MY BOOK. IT'S DUE IN TWO MONTHS!
WOAH. WHAT'S YOUR BOOK ABOUT?
WELL, YOU KNOW HOW I MAKE THOSE COMICS ABOUT BEING A MOM?
YEAH . . .
WELL, IT'S ABOUT BEING A MOM. AND BEING A DAD. IT'S ABOUT ME AND YOUR DAD BECOMING PARENTS AND HOW THE WORLD TREATS MOMS AND DADS VERY DIFFERENTLY.
OH YEAH, BECAUSE EVERYONE THINKS MOMS HAVE TO DO EVERYTHING AND DADS DON'T?

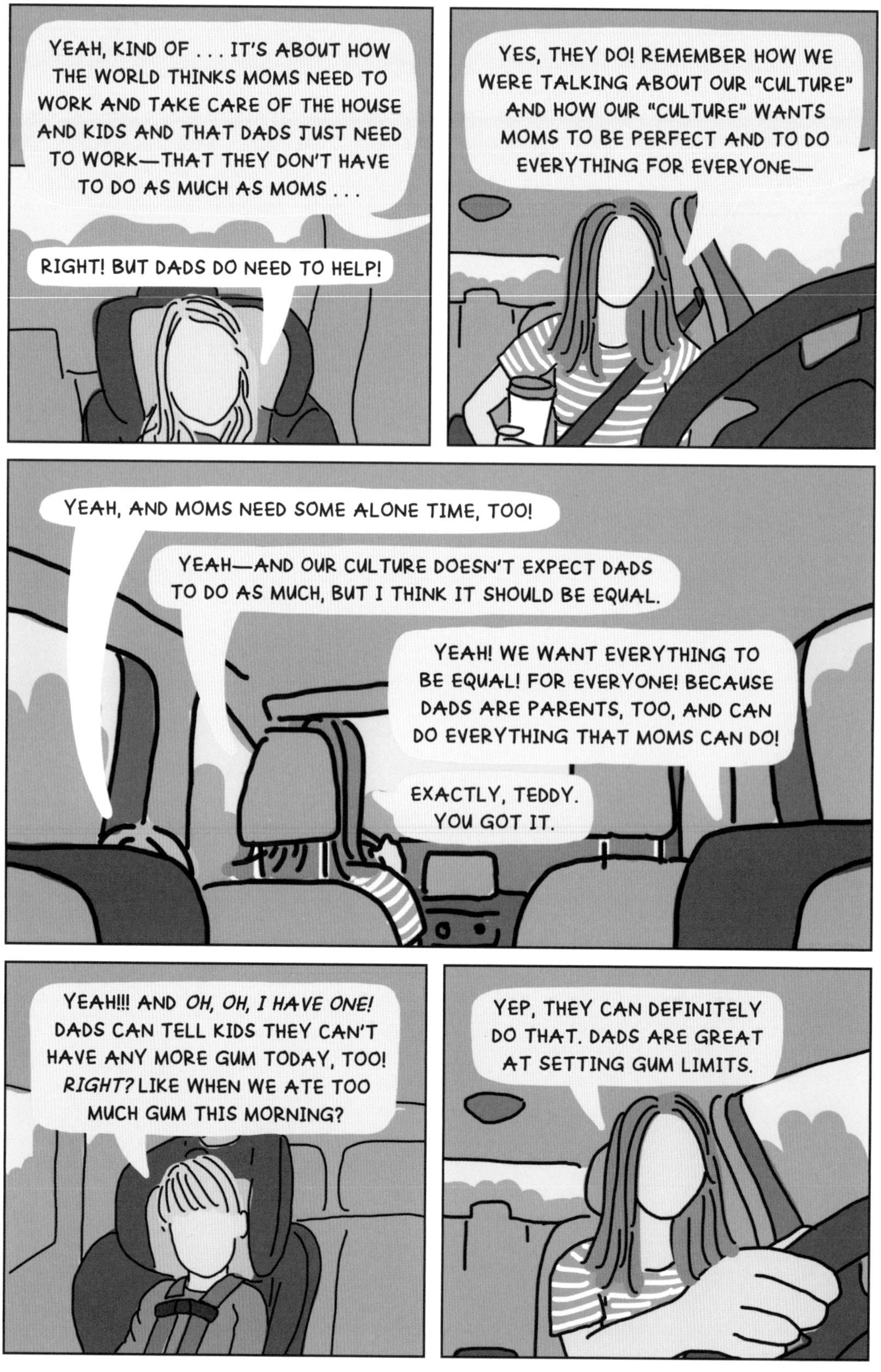
YEAH, KIND OF . . . IT'S ABOUT HOW THE WORLD THINKS MOMS NEED TO WORK AND TAKE CARE OF THE HOUSE AND KIDS AND THAT DADS JUST NEED TO WORK—THAT THEY DON'T HAVE TO DO AS MUCH AS MOMS . . .
RIGHT! BUT DADS DO NEED TO HELP!
YES, THEY DO! REMEMBER HOW WE WERE TALKING ABOUT OUR "CULTURE" AND HOW OUR "CULTURE" WANTS MOMS TO BE PERFECT AND TO DO EVERYTHING FOR EVERYONE—
YEAH, AND MOMS NEED SOME ALONE TIME, TOO!
YEAH—AND OUR CULTURE DOESN'T EXPECT DADS TO DO AS MUCH, BUT I THINK IT SHOULD BE EQUAL.
YEAH! WE WANT EVERYTHING TO BE EQUAL! FOR EVERYONE! BECAUSE DADS ARE PARENTS, TOO, AND CAN DO EVERYTHING THAT MOMS CAN DO!
EXACTLY, TEDDY. YOU GOT IT.
YEAH!!! AND *OH, OH, I HAVE ONE!* DADS CAN TELL KIDS THEY CAN'T HAVE ANY MORE GUM TODAY, TOO! *RIGHT?* LIKE WHEN WE ATE TOO MUCH GUM THIS MORNING?
YEP, THEY CAN DEFINITELY DO THAT. DADS ARE GREAT AT SETTING GUM LIMITS.

Conversations like this make me hopeful. They also make me worried that I'm screwing up my kids, of course, but mostly they make me happy that this topic is one that we're talking about in our house. We're trying our best to raise two feminist children.

(But to be fair, we also have lots of conversations that I think are deep but later find out were not deep for my children, at all . . . so who the heck knows?!?)

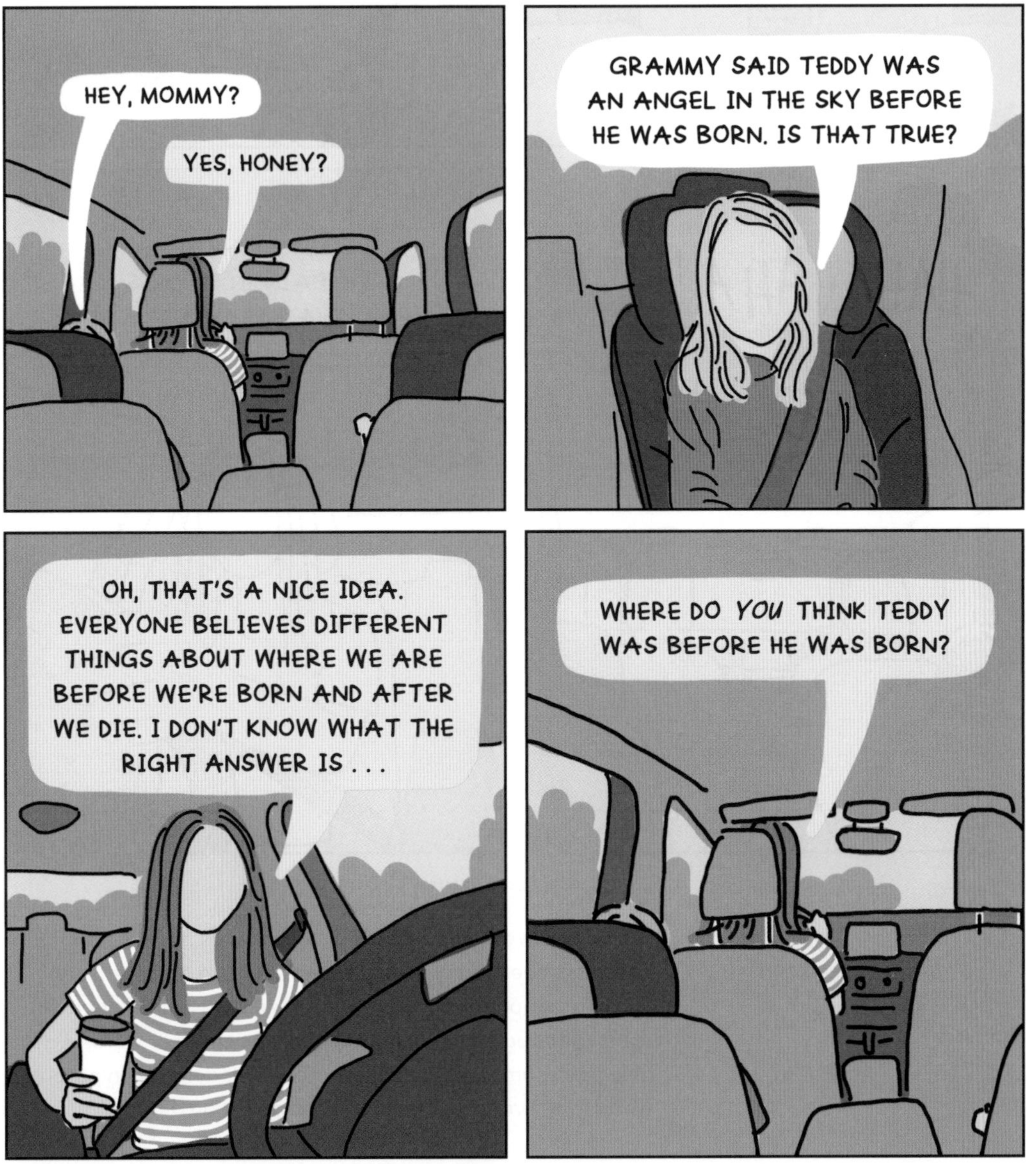
HEY, MOMMY?
YES, HONEY?
GRAMMY SAID TEDDY WAS AN ANGEL IN THE SKY BEFORE HE WAS BORN. IS THAT TRUE?
OH, THAT'S A NICE IDEA. EVERYONE BELIEVES DIFFERENT THINGS ABOUT WHERE WE ARE BEFORE WE'RE BORN AND AFTER WE DIE. I DON'T KNOW WHAT THE RIGHT ANSWER IS . . .
WHERE DO *YOU* THINK TEDDY WAS BEFORE HE WAS BORN?

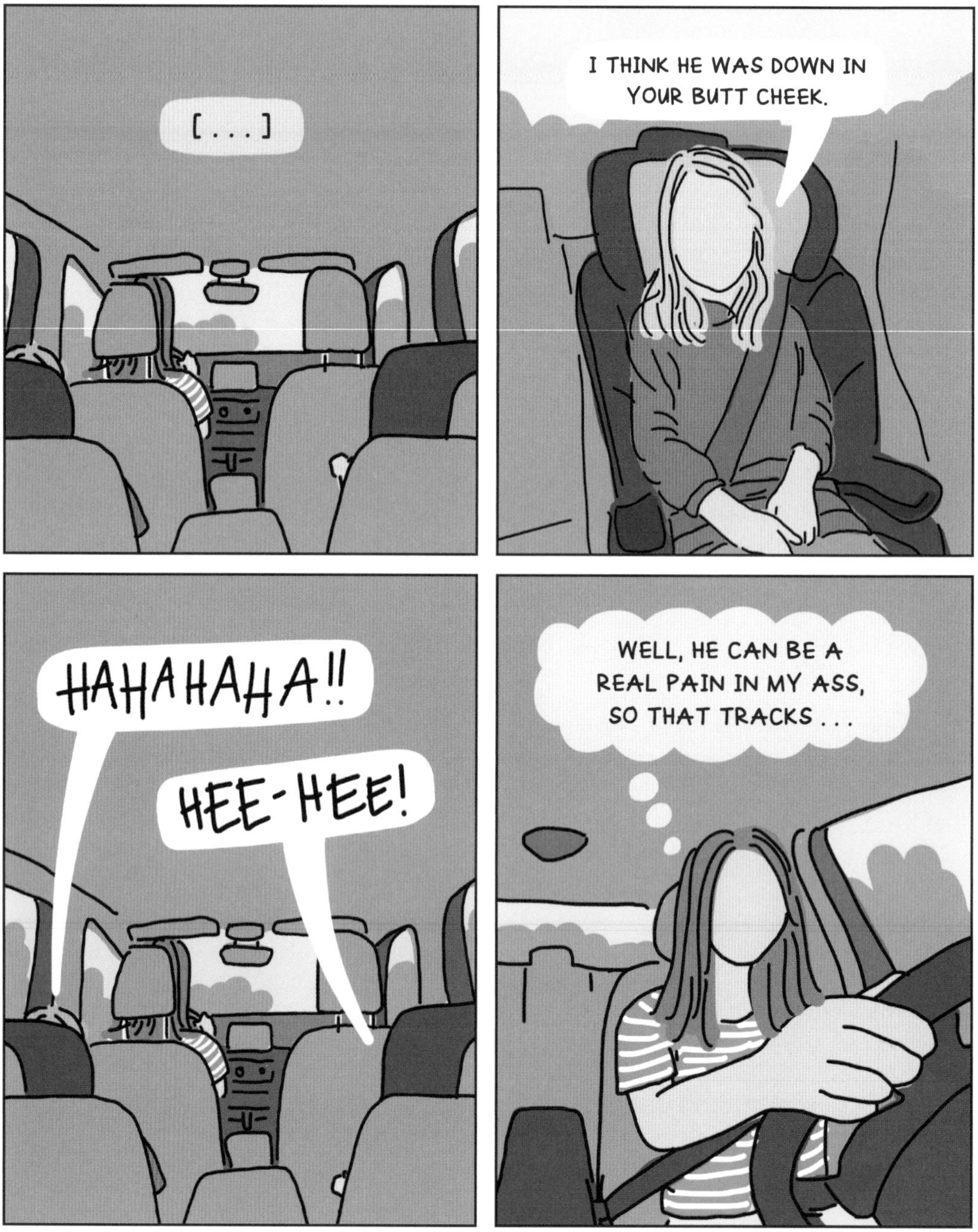
[ . . . ]
I THINK HE WAS DOWN IN YOUR BUTT CHEEK.
HAHAHAHA!!
HEE-HEE!
WELL, HE CAN BE A REAL PAIN IN MY ASS, SO THAT TRACKS . . .

I know that we've made a ton of mistakes as parents, but there have also been many wins; whenever I get a glimpse of my "feminist propaganda" (thanks for that phrase, internet troll!) coming through in one of my children's actions or words, I get a little thrill. I am so excited to see how their generation parents, works, and lives more equally. Like I said, I am hopeful.

# A Final Word from Me to You

So where do we go from here? What do I say to all of the moms who message me on a daily basis asking me what we can do about all of this inequality? What advice can I give to the moms asking me how to handle the "weaponized incompetence," the mental load, and husbands who take naps on the toy-covered couch while their wives clean up around their sleeping bodies, silently raging?

My response to them, unfortunately, is the same thing I've said to you in this book: that I can't offer you an easy solution. There are a lot of smart people who have ideas for us on what can help (and I recommend reading books written by the many experts in this field—or following them on social media!), but ultimately, I haven't figured it out yet.

I certainly wish I had.

But what I have figured out is that I can't will Ben to change overnight. I can't will myself to change overnight, either (oh, how I wish I could!). I can't will our children to change overnight. I can't erase our patriarchal societal structure and all of the ways in which it harms women (and men!). I can't single-handedly explain away Ben's entire life of social and societal conditioning, just as he can't explain away mine.

All I can do is work on myself and hope that the changes I make in my own life make a difference in my childrens' lives, in Ben's life, and in the lives of the moms whom I connect with in real life or on the internet.

Oh, and I can go on strike or leave town if I need a break. That's always an option, too.

# 5 Ways to Take a Much-Needed Break When You're a Tired Mom

## 1. WALK OUT THE FRONT DOOR AND JUST KEEP WALKING.

KEEP WALKING IF YOU'RE IN THE MOOD FOR A WALK, OR FIND SOMEWHERE TO SIT AND HIDE FROM YOUR FAMILY WHILE YOU STARE INTO THE ABYSS.

## 2. GET INTO A VEHICLE AND DRIVE AWAY.

SCREEECH!!!

GO SOMEWHERE ELSE! ANYWHERE ELSE! AN ABANDONED PARKING LOT IS FINE! AS LONG AS IT'S NOWHERE NEAR YOUR FAMILY.

## 3. GET THE HELL OUT OF DODGE.

CATCH YOU LATER, BITCHES!

GO OUT OF TOWN! TAKE A VACATION! BOOK A HOTEL ROOM IN ANOTHER TOWN! IT DOESN'T MATTER WHERE YOU GO— ANYWHERE WILL FEEL LIKE A BREAK.

## 4. MOVE TO ANOTHER COUNTRY, DYE YOUR HAIR, AND CHANGE YOUR NAME.

THIS SHOULD BUY YOU AT LEAST A WEEK OR SO UNTIL THEY HUNT YOU DOWN AND BRING YOU HOME BECAUSE SOMEONE NEEDS HELP FINDING THEIR SNEAKERS.

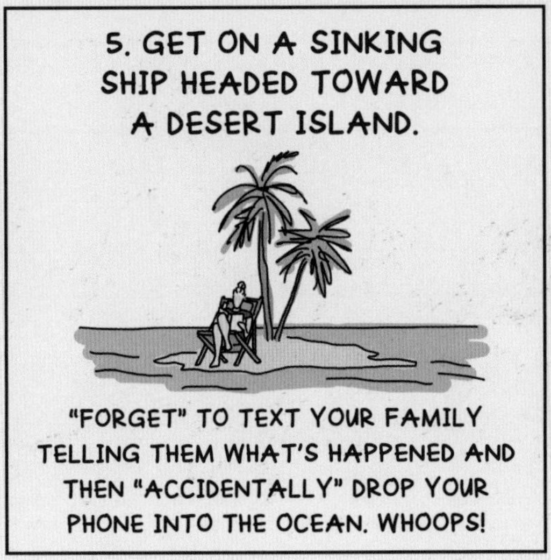
5. GET ON A SINKING SHIP HEADED TOWARD A DESERT ISLAND.
"FORGET" TO TEXT YOUR FAMILY TELLING THEM WHAT'S HAPPENED AND THEN "ACCIDENTALLY" DROP YOUR PHONE INTO THE OCEAN. WHOOPS!

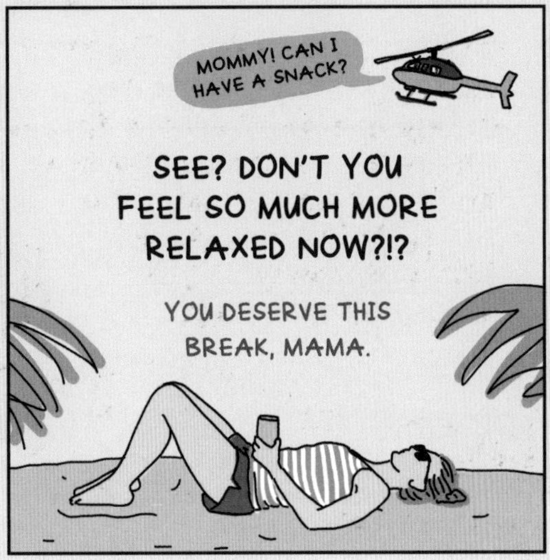
MOMMY! CAN I HAVE A SNACK?
SEE? DON'T YOU FEEL SO MUCH MORE RELAXED NOW?!?
YOU DESERVE THIS BREAK, MAMA.

***BONUS!***

**NONE OF THOSE IDEAS WORK FOR YOU?**
**HERE'S ONE MORE IDEA:**

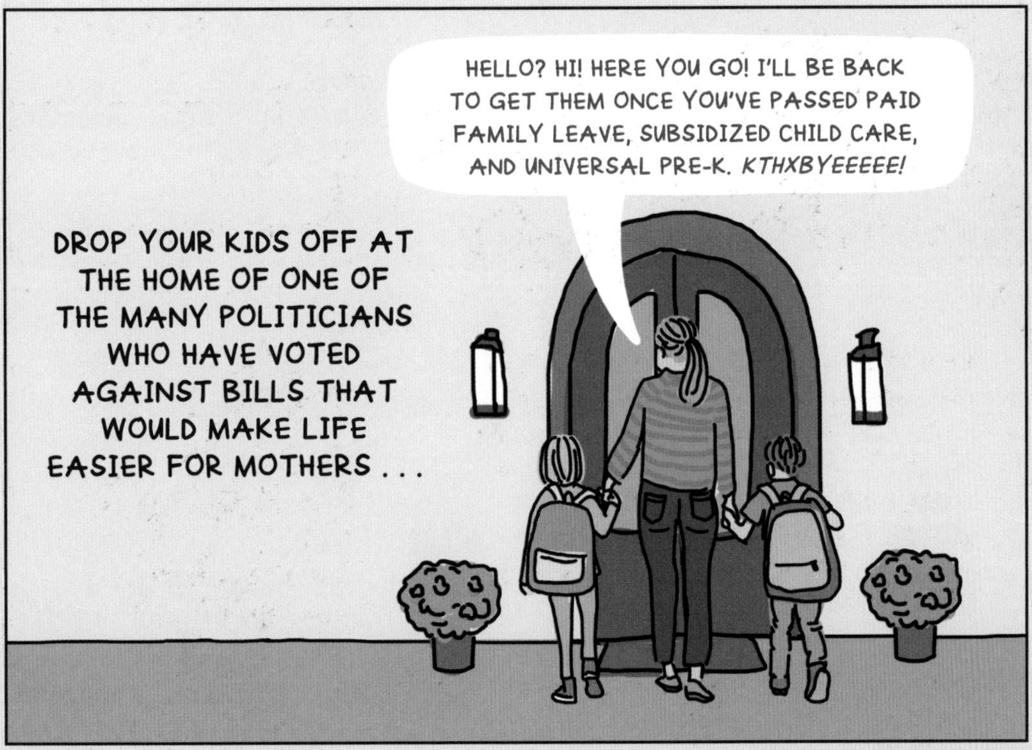
DROP YOUR KIDS OFF AT THE HOME OF ONE OF THE MANY POLITICIANS WHO HAVE VOTED AGAINST BILLS THAT WOULD MAKE LIFE EASIER FOR MOTHERS . . .
HELLO? HI! HERE YOU GO! I'LL BE BACK TO GET THEM ONCE YOU'VE PASSED PAID FAMILY LEAVE, SUBSIDIZED CHILD CARE, AND UNIVERSAL PRE-K. *KTHXBYEEEEE!*

## My Wish for Moms Everywhere:
### A Fairy Tale

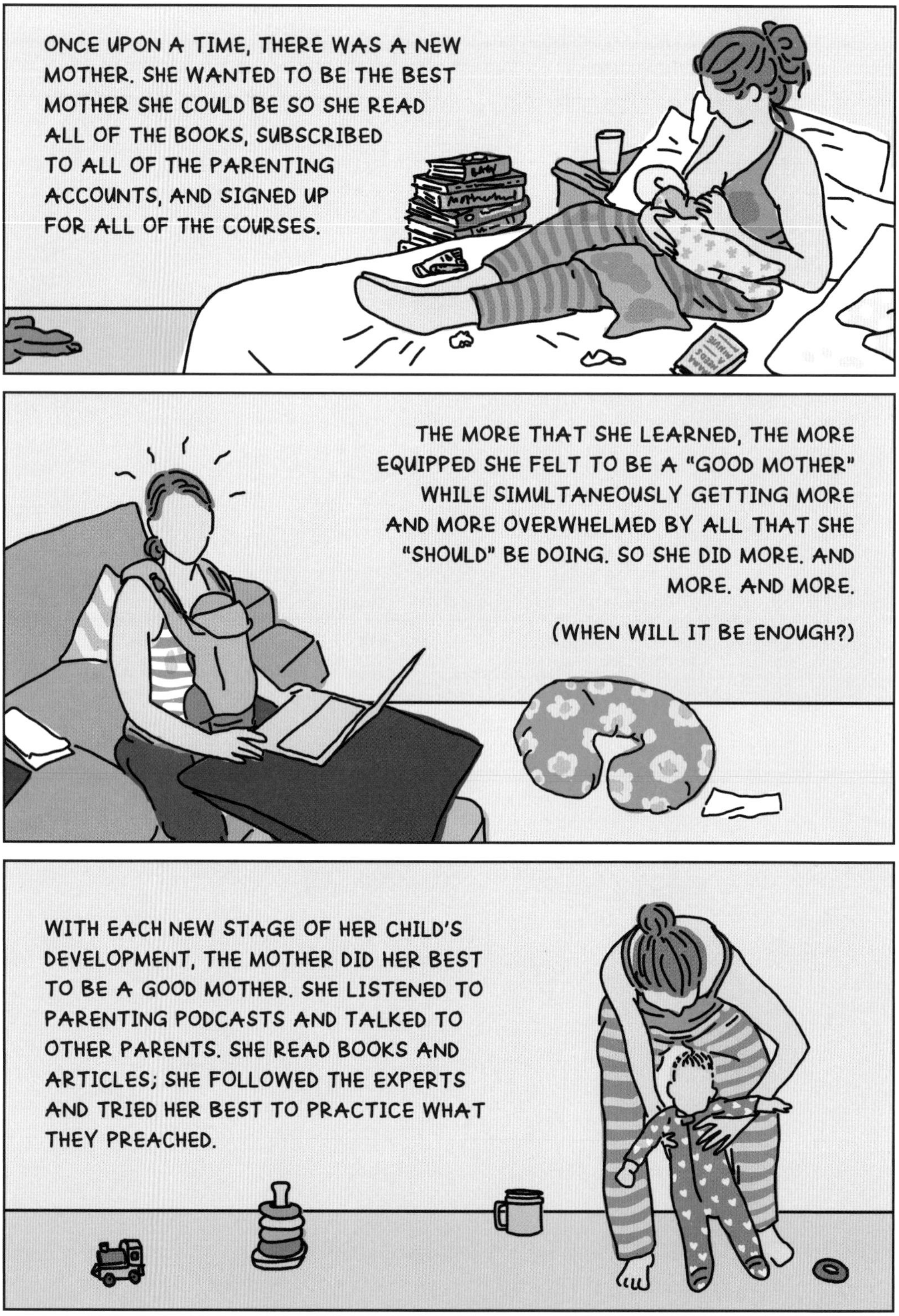
ONCE UPON A TIME, THERE WAS A NEW MOTHER. SHE WANTED TO BE THE BEST MOTHER SHE COULD BE SO SHE READ ALL OF THE BOOKS, SUBSCRIBED TO ALL OF THE PARENTING ACCOUNTS, AND SIGNED UP FOR ALL OF THE COURSES.
THE MORE THAT SHE LEARNED, THE MORE EQUIPPED SHE FELT TO BE A "GOOD MOTHER" WHILE SIMULTANEOUSLY GETTING MORE AND MORE OVERWHELMED BY ALL THAT SHE "SHOULD" BE DOING. SO SHE DID MORE. AND MORE. AND MORE.
(WHEN WILL IT BE ENOUGH?)
WITH EACH NEW STAGE OF HER CHILD'S DEVELOPMENT, THE MOTHER DID HER BEST TO BE A GOOD MOTHER. SHE LISTENED TO PARENTING PODCASTS AND TALKED TO OTHER PARENTS. SHE READ BOOKS AND ARTICLES; SHE FOLLOWED THE EXPERTS AND TRIED HER BEST TO PRACTICE WHAT THEY PREACHED.

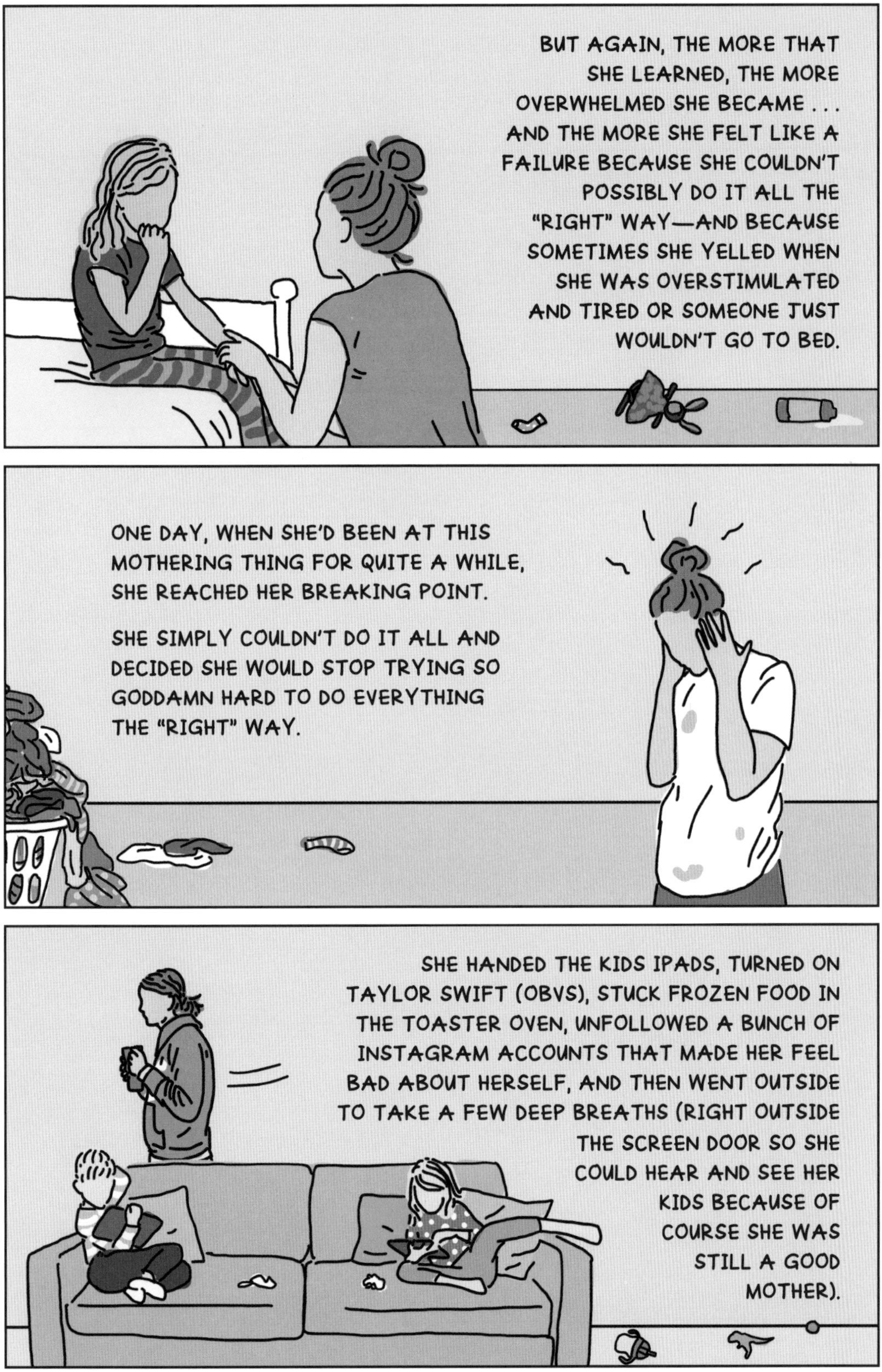
BUT AGAIN, THE MORE THAT SHE LEARNED, THE MORE OVERWHELMED SHE BECAME . . . AND THE MORE SHE FELT LIKE A FAILURE BECAUSE SHE COULDN'T POSSIBLY DO IT ALL THE "RIGHT" WAY—AND BECAUSE SOMETIMES SHE YELLED WHEN SHE WAS OVERSTIMULATED AND TIRED OR SOMEONE JUST WOULDN'T GO TO BED.
ONE DAY, WHEN SHE'D BEEN AT THIS MOTHERING THING FOR QUITE A WHILE, SHE REACHED HER BREAKING POINT.
SHE SIMPLY COULDN'T DO IT ALL AND DECIDED SHE WOULD STOP TRYING SO GODDAMN HARD TO DO EVERYTHING THE "RIGHT" WAY.
SHE HANDED THE KIDS IPADS, TURNED ON TAYLOR SWIFT (OBVS), STUCK FROZEN FOOD IN THE TOASTER OVEN, UNFOLLOWED A BUNCH OF INSTAGRAM ACCOUNTS THAT MADE HER FEEL BAD ABOUT HERSELF, AND THEN WENT OUTSIDE TO TAKE A FEW DEEP BREATHS (RIGHT OUTSIDE THE SCREEN DOOR SO SHE COULD HEAR AND SEE HER KIDS BECAUSE OF COURSE SHE WAS STILL A GOOD MOTHER).

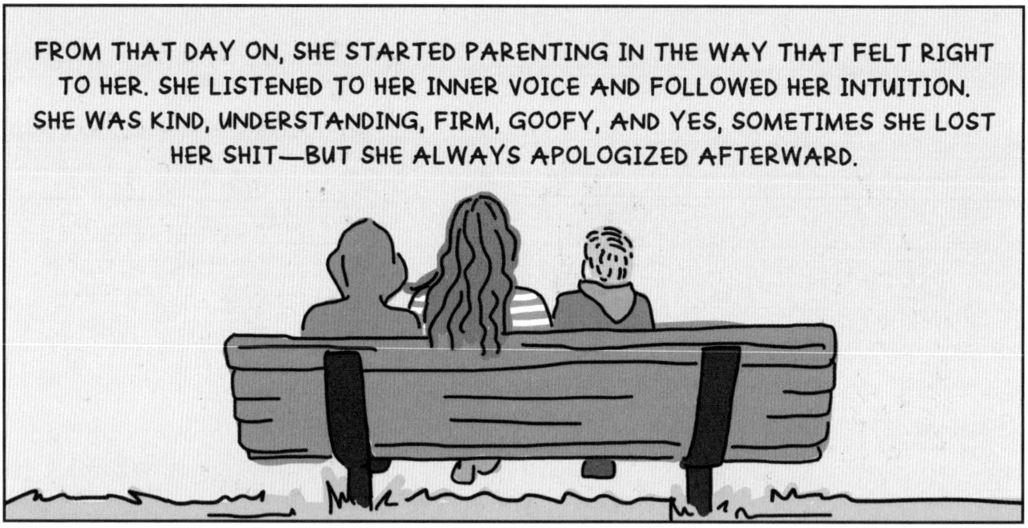
FROM THAT DAY ON, SHE STARTED PARENTING IN THE WAY THAT FELT RIGHT TO HER. SHE LISTENED TO HER INNER VOICE AND FOLLOWED HER INTUITION. SHE WAS KIND, UNDERSTANDING, FIRM, GOOFY, AND YES, SOMETIMES SHE LOST HER SHIT—BUT SHE ALWAYS APOLOGIZED AFTERWARD.

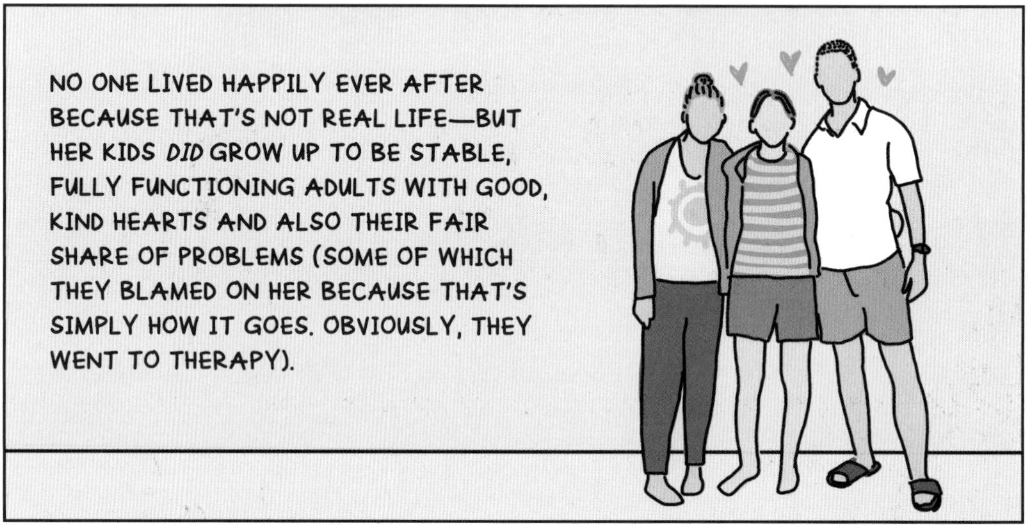
NO ONE LIVED HAPPILY EVER AFTER BECAUSE THAT'S NOT REAL LIFE—BUT HER KIDS *DID* GROW UP TO BE STABLE, FULLY FUNCTIONING ADULTS WITH GOOD, KIND HEARTS AND ALSO THEIR FAIR SHARE OF PROBLEMS (SOME OF WHICH THEY BLAMED ON HER BECAUSE THAT'S SIMPLY HOW IT GOES. OBVIOUSLY, THEY WENT TO THERAPY).

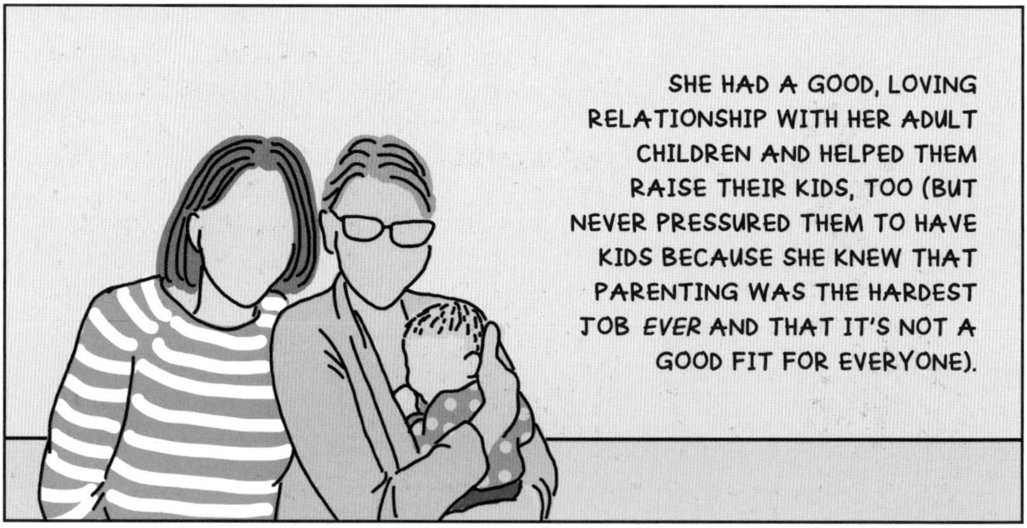
SHE HAD A GOOD, LOVING RELATIONSHIP WITH HER ADULT CHILDREN AND HELPED THEM RAISE THEIR KIDS, TOO (BUT NEVER PRESSURED THEM TO HAVE KIDS BECAUSE SHE KNEW THAT PARENTING WAS THE HARDEST JOB *EVER* AND THAT IT'S NOT A GOOD FIT FOR EVERYONE).

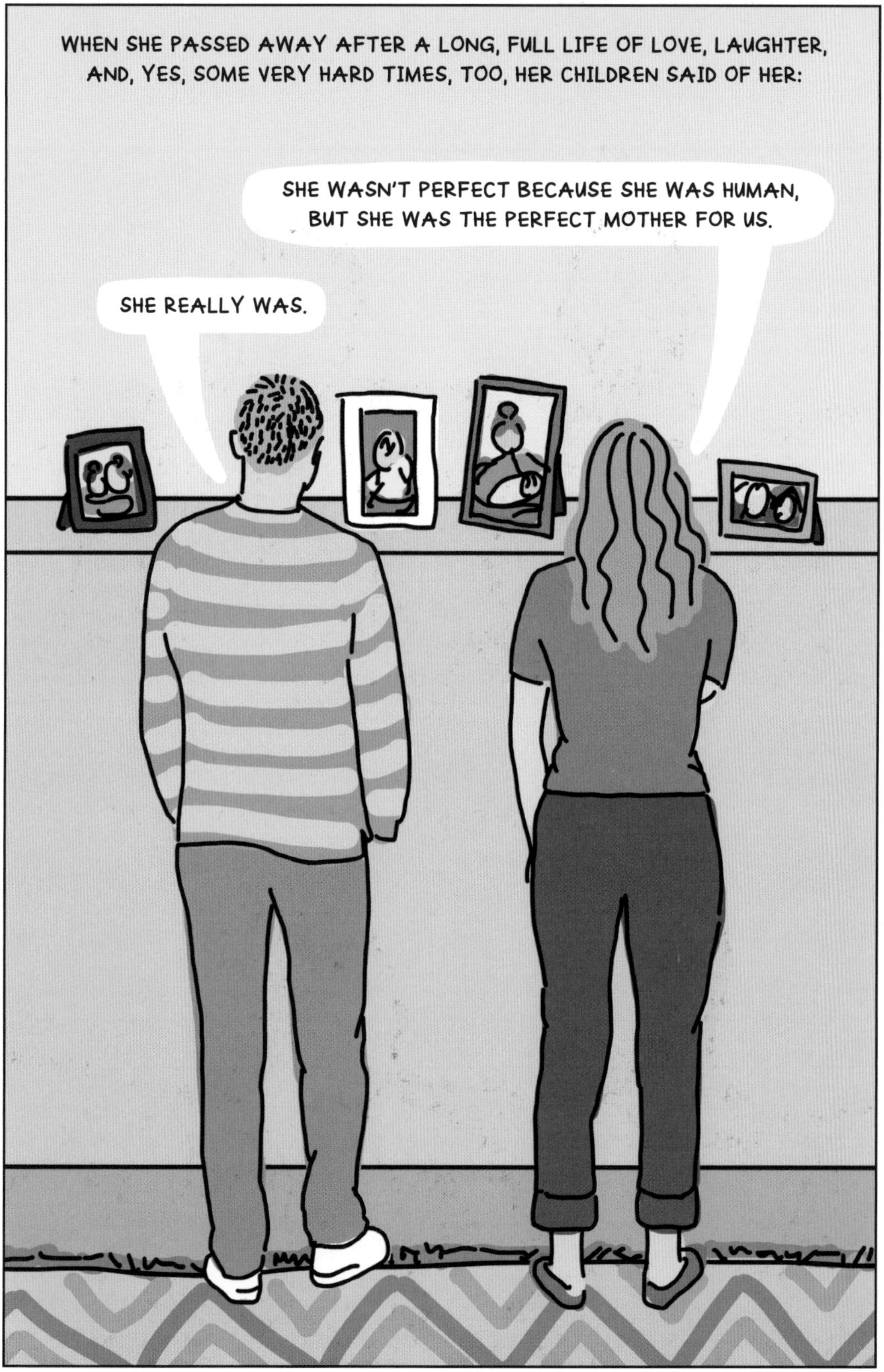
WHEN SHE PASSED AWAY AFTER A LONG, FULL LIFE OF LOVE, LAUGHTER, AND, YES, SOME VERY HARD TIMES, TOO, HER CHILDREN SAID OF HER:
SHE WASN'T PERFECT BECAUSE SHE WAS HUMAN, BUT SHE WAS THE PERFECT MOTHER FOR US.
SHE REALLY WAS.

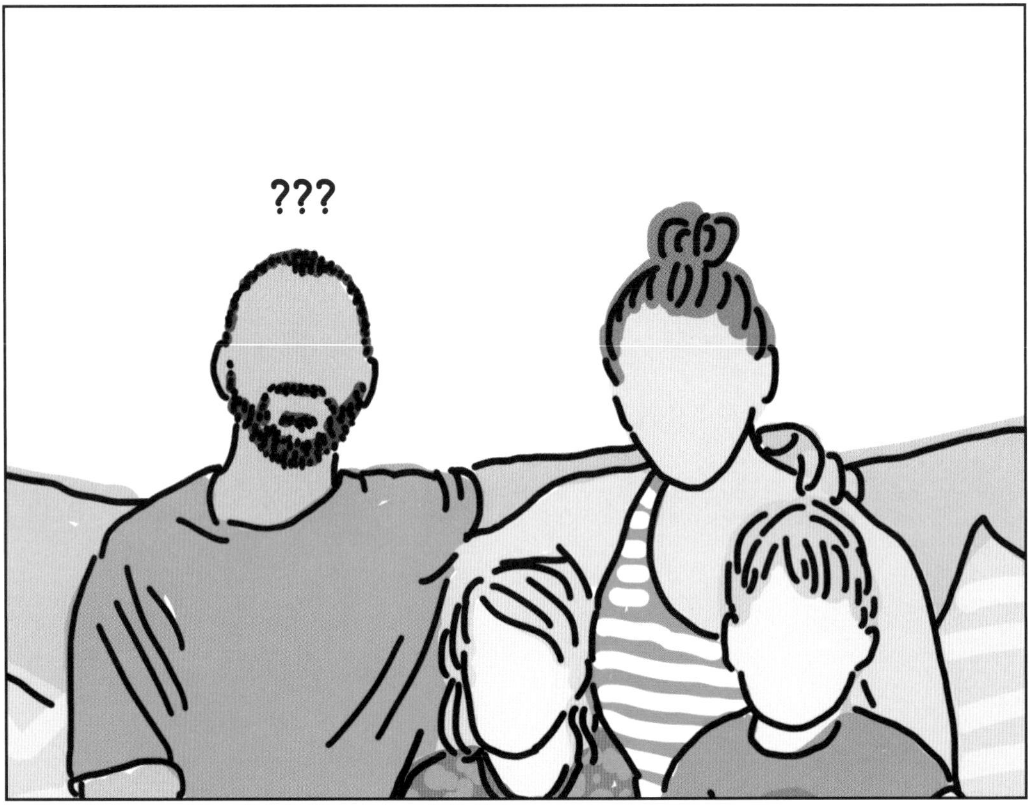
???

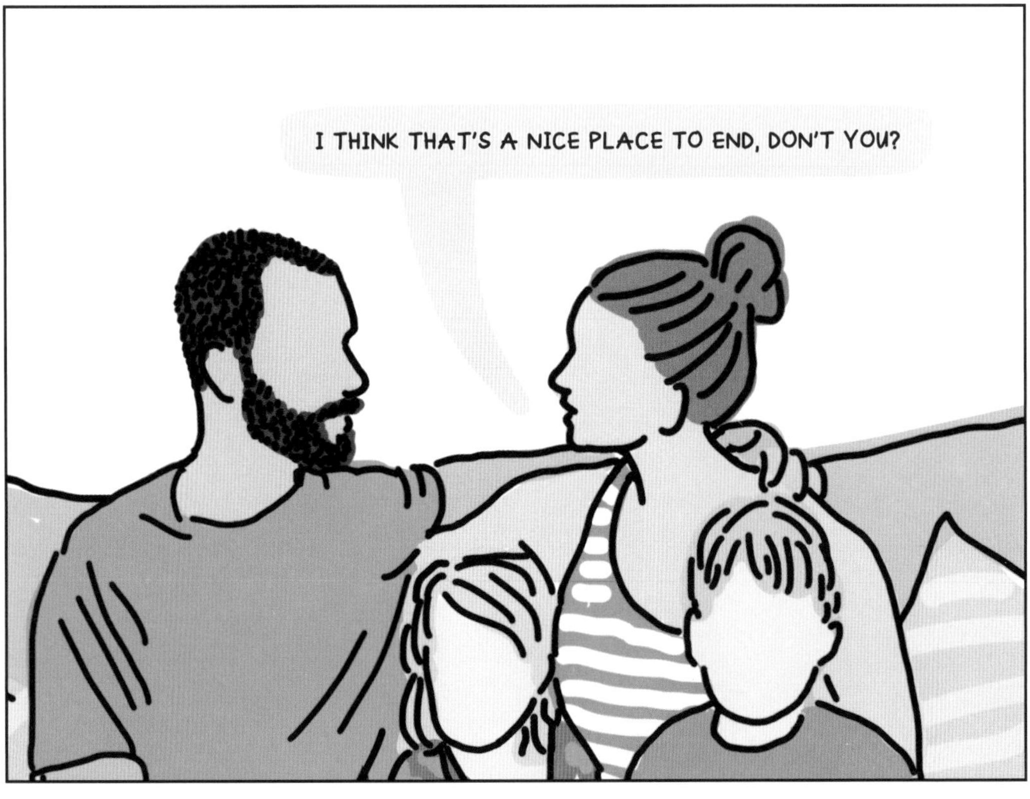
I THINK THAT'S A NICE PLACE TO END, DON'T YOU?

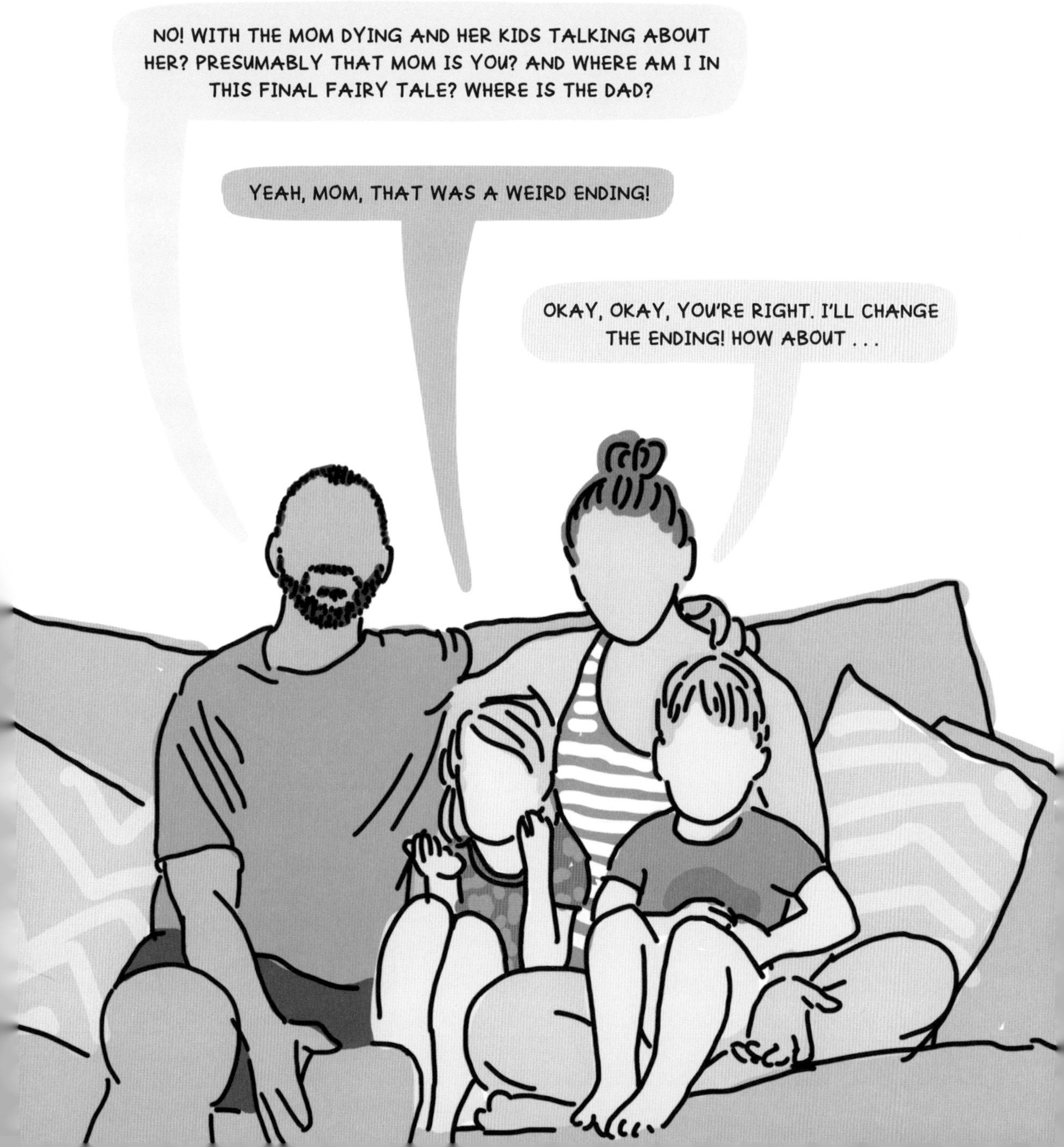
NO! WITH THE MOM DYING AND HER KIDS TALKING ABOUT HER? PRESUMABLY THAT MOM IS YOU? AND WHERE AM I IN THIS FINAL FAIRY TALE? WHERE IS THE DAD?
YEAH, MOM, THAT WAS A WEIRD ENDING!
OKAY, OKAY, YOU'RE RIGHT. I'LL CHANGE THE ENDING! HOW ABOUT . . .

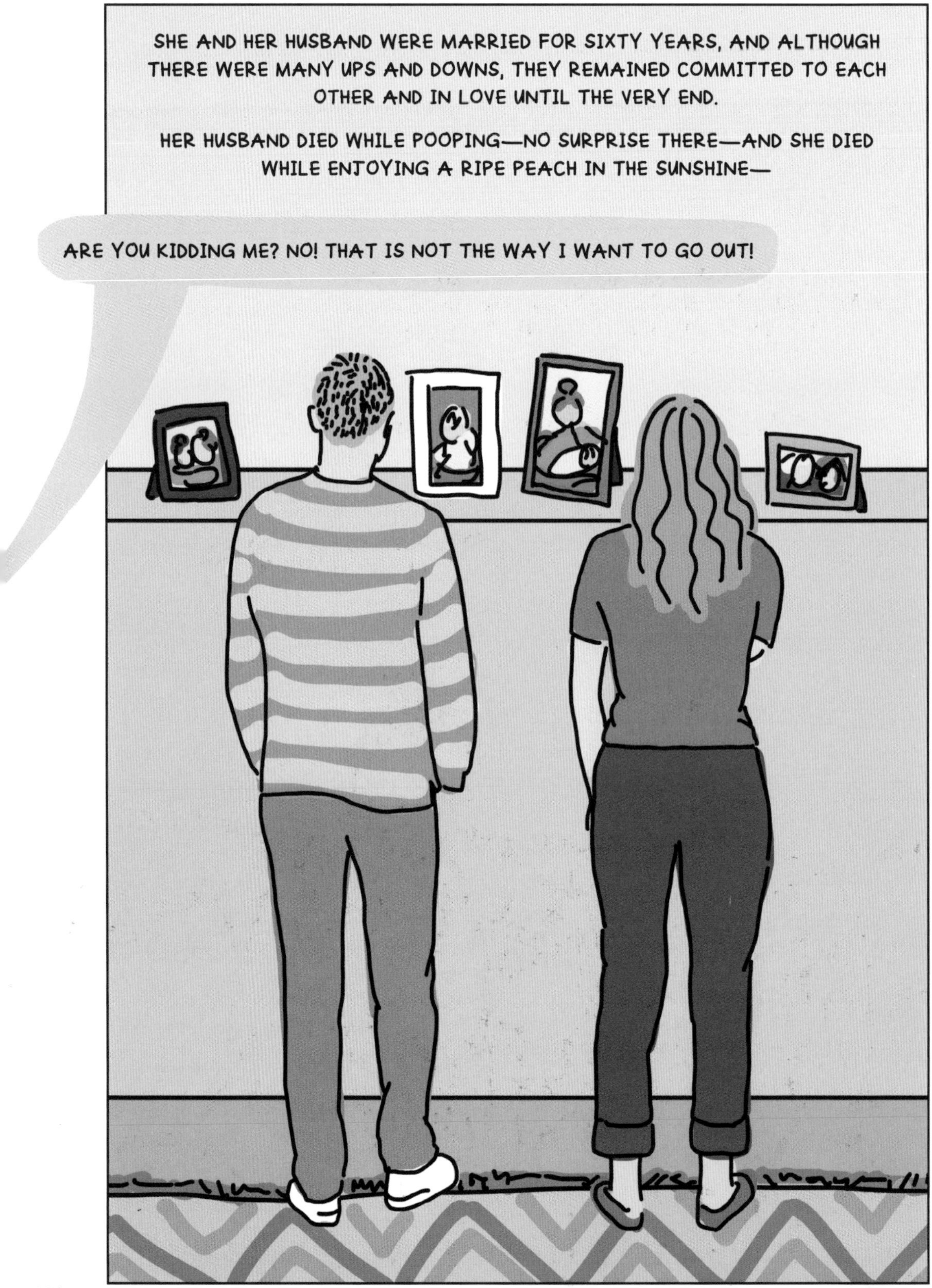
SHE AND HER HUSBAND WERE MARRIED FOR SIXTY YEARS, AND ALTHOUGH THERE WERE MANY UPS AND DOWNS, THEY REMAINED COMMITTED TO EACH OTHER AND IN LOVE UNTIL THE VERY END.
HER HUSBAND DIED WHILE POOPING—NO SURPRISE THERE—AND SHE DIED WHILE ENJOYING A RIPE PEACH IN THE SUNSHINE—
ARE YOU KIDDING ME? NO! THAT IS NOT THE WAY I WANT TO GO OUT!

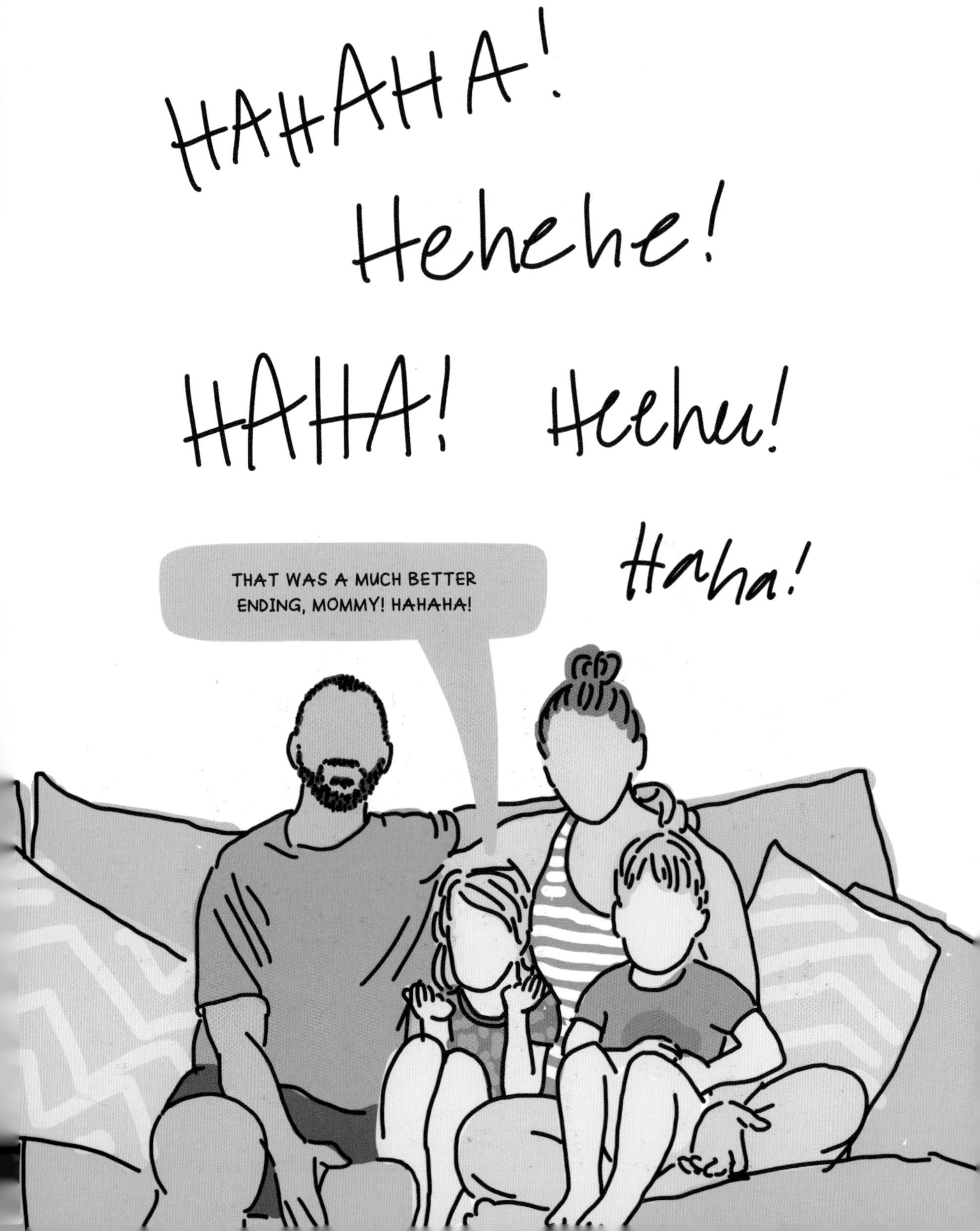
HAHAHA!
Hehehe!
HAHA!
Heehee!
Haha!
THAT WAS A MUCH BETTER ENDING, MOMMY! HAHAHA!

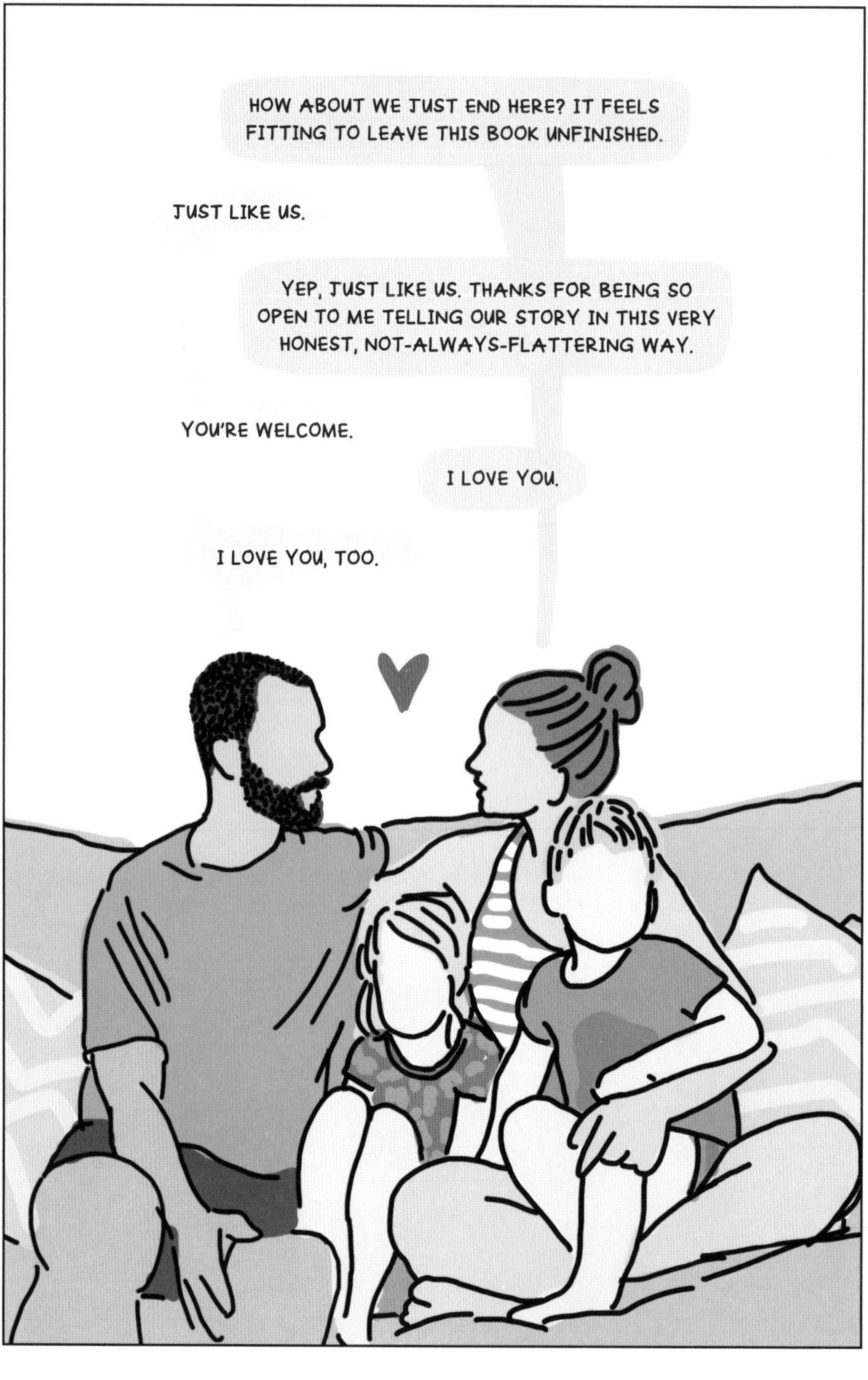
HOW ABOUT WE JUST END HERE? IT FEELS FITTING TO LEAVE THIS BOOK UNFINISHED.
JUST LIKE US.
YEP, JUST LIKE US. THANKS FOR BEING SO OPEN TO ME TELLING OUR STORY IN THIS VERY HONEST, NOT-ALWAYS-FLATTERING WAY.
YOU'RE WELCOME.
I LOVE YOU.
I LOVE YOU, TOO.

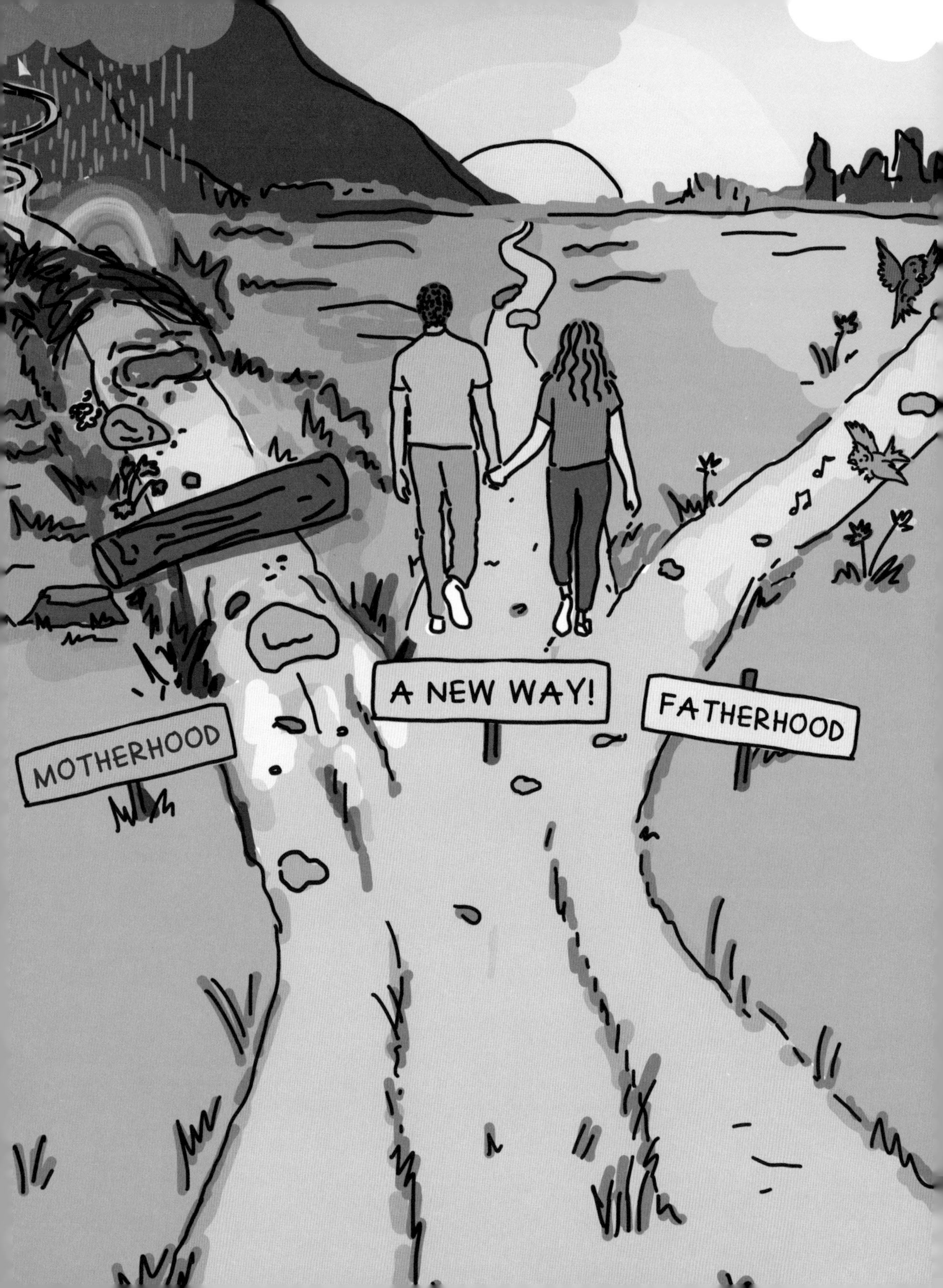
A NEW WAY!
FATHERHOOD
MOTHERHOOD

# Acknowledgments

IT TAKES A VILLAGE
(PAID AND UNPAID!)

This book simply *would not exist* if it wasn't for SO MANY people. Here are \*just some\* of them . . .

First and foremost, thank you to Ben, Charlie Mae, and Teddy. Our little family is the greatest joy of my life and this book wouldn't exist without you all—on so many levels (ha!). Thank you for posing for inspiration pictures and for being a constant source of inspiration for my comics. Thank you for challenging me, making me laugh, annoying me, snuggling with me, and loving me despite all of my (many) imperfections.

Ben, you are such a good sport! It takes a very strong person to be okay with—nay, supportive of!—someone writing a book that includes unflattering stories about them. Thank you for being strong enough to withstand scrutiny and for being okay with me telling our story in such a public way. I am so glad that you IM-ed me asking for a bar of soap way back in 2004.

Charlie Mae and Teddy, becoming your mother is the best thing that has ever happened to me. I would go through all of the challenges covered in this book 100,000 more times if it meant I could be your mom. I am so lucky.

Without the help of the following people (who make up our local village), mama never would have gotten a minute to work on this book:

- My mother-in-law, Susanne, and my aunts-in-law, Nancy (Ninny!) and Marcia, who always answer our desperate texts for child care help and who show up with smiles and goodies.

- Our child care provider, Holly, who has enabled me and Ben to be working parents. You and your family have been total saviors over the past few years, and we are so lucky to have you in our lives.

- Our many reliable babysitters—especially Courtney F., who was my lifeline during the pandemic.

- All of my Cape Cod mom friends—Anna, Megan, Mandy, Shea, Carolina, Michelle, Erin: for changing everything for me and for showing me that I am not alone in motherhood. I appreciate your honesty, support, late-night texts, sense of humor, play-date invites, and carpool help. I am so grateful to have you all in my life.

- Our laundry goddess, Courtney A., who has singlehandedly solved so many of our laundry problems, and our cleaning company, Cleangreen, who I wish we could afford to have come every week but whose monthly cleanings help keep me sane.

And now for my thank yous to our non-local village:

- **To my mom (Deema):** WOW. You did all of this with three kids? And with very little money? And at times, as a single mom? I don't know how you did it (seriously: HOW THE HELL DID YOU DO IT?), but thank you for teaching me what it means to be a nurturing, involved, thoughtful, creative mother. Also, I never would have had the courage to go down such an unconventional career path if I hadn't had your unending support and belief that I could do anything (and your help hauling my crazy high school art projects all over the state of Georgia). Now that I'm a mom I know how much you did for us, and I am so, so grateful.

- **To my dad (Baba):** Thank you for showing me (and Ben) what it means to be a present, loving, emotionally available father (and now, grandfather). Thank you for being the rare kind of dad who was never afraid to talk to me about "feminine issues" (like—gasp—periods!) and for always being up for editing my comics about the patriarchy from which you, as a middle-class white man, have clearly benefited. Lastly, as detailed in this book, thank you for sharing your wise observational insights about how our little family unit functions (or dysfunctions?) and in doing so, encouraging me to step back so that Ben can step forward.

- **To my brothers, Peter and Patrick:** There is nothing like growing up alongside someone else—as I watch Charlie Mae and Teddy love each other (and fight with each other), I am constantly reminded of how lucky I am to have had you two as my siblings as we figured out how to be

humans in this crazy world. Thanks for being such weirdos and for getting me on so many levels. Love you both so much.

- **To Kelly,** thank you for being my oldest friend and for appreciating my very first attempts at "comics" (although I didn't call them that at the time): the notes that I wrote you/drew you in high school (and middle school?). I don't think I would have made it through adolescence without you. Or I would have, but it would have sucked.

- **To Laura and Jessica,** my soulmate friends of twenty-plus years: I can't possibly say enough about what our friendship (Pookieship?) has meant to me so I will say this: Thank you for always supporting my artistic endeavors—from my college paintings, to my blog, to proofreading my comics (from the very beginning!), and of course, for being some of my first readers of this book. I hope that the art within these pages lives up to your artistic expectations for me—I know I set the bar high when I drew that Cookie Monster for that poster we made to hang in Cowan.

- **To Sara,** who is so much more than a business partner (wink!). I am so grateful that you applied for that job at Tranquil Space so many years ago. Your constant support as a friend, a fellow mom, and a colleague (in many different forms over the years!) has added heaps of joy and laughter to my life. You are the person I call to vent because you always get it and never try to FIX things when I just want to bitch about how hard all of this is . . . and everyone needs a friend like that—especially when navigating early motherhood.

- **To all of my Instagram followers and long-ago blog readers:** Um, this book is here because of you. Because you made me feel less alone and showed me that there are like-minded women out there who are navigating the same challenges that I am. I hope this book speaks to you. Thank you for your support.

- **To my yoga students and yoga friends:** Thank you for reminding me that I am more than just a mom. Thank you for being the adults whom I interact with IN PERSON after spending my days working from home and/or wrangling children.

- **To the Centerville Public Library, the Osterville Public Library, and the Panera in Hyannis:** Thank you for being the places I went to escape my family and work on this book. We all need a third place with Wi-Fi, and you were my third place(s).

- **To my agent, Danielle Svetcov (at Levine Greenberg Rostan Literary Agency),** a fellow mother, thank you for understanding my vision and helping me navigate the unknown book publishing world. I am so grateful for your guidance and your warm, supportive, calming energy.

- **To my editor, Rachel Hiles (at Chronicle Books),** thank you for getting me and my work. Your thoughtfulness, deep understanding of this subject matter, and ability to cut fluff *to get to the heart of the matter* made this book so much better than I imagined it could be. I LOVED having a fellow mom-in-the-trenches creating this book with me.

- **To Lizzie and Wynne,** the designer extraordinaires at Chronicle Books who took my raw, rough InDesign file and transformed it into an elevated work of art, thank you for being design geniuses! I am so grateful for your talent and expertise.

And lastly, thank you to technology, for entertaining our kids when MAMA NEEDED A BREAK.

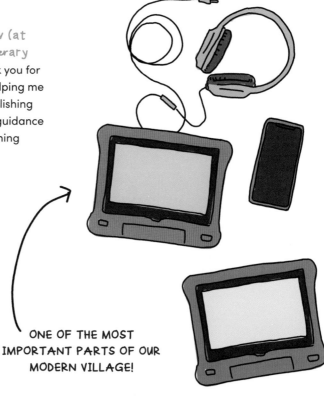

ONE OF THE MOST
IMPORTANT PARTS OF OUR
MODERN VILLAGE!

# About the Author

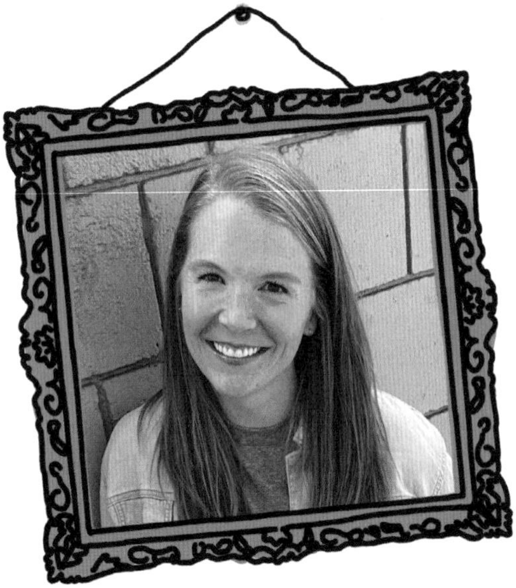

Mary Catherine Starr is an artist and graphic designer. Her popular Instagram account @momlife_comics explores motherhood, marriage, and the double standards of parenting through funny, relatable, and sometimes maddening comics. She lives on Cape Cod, Massachusetts, with her husband, their two children, a fish named Moonlight, and her son's large collection of plastic dinosaurs.

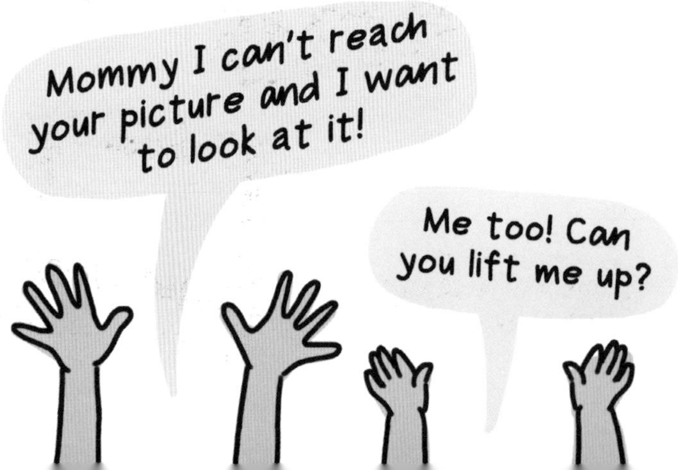
Mommy I can't reach your picture and I want to look at it!
Me too! Can you lift me up?